GW00367517

Guide to Housing Benefit and Council Tax Benefit 2006-07

JOHN ZEBEDEE, MARTIN WARD AND SAM LISTER

Shelter

CHARTERED INSTITUTE OF HOUSING

The Chartered Institute of Housing (CIH) is the only professional body for individuals working in housing. Its primary aim is to maximise the contribution that housing professionals make to the well-being of communities. Membership status is dependent on completion of a professional qualification and a track record of professional achievement. The CIH is a registered charity and a non-profit making organisation.

CIH has more than 19,000 members working for local authorities, housing associations, government bodies, educational establishments and the private sector in the UK and Asian Pacific. For further information, please write to:

Chartered Institute of Housing
Octavia House
Westwood Way
Coventry CV4 8JP

Telephone: 024 7685 1700
Fax: 024 7669 5110
E-mail: *customer.services@cih.org*
Web site: *www.cih.org*

SHELTER

We are the fourth richest country in the world, and yet millions of people in Britain wake up every day in housing that is run-down, overcrowded, or dangerous. Many others have lost their home altogether. Bad housing robs us of security, health, and a fair chance in life.

Shelter believes everyone should have a home.

We help more than 170,000 people a year fight for their rights, get back on their feet, and find and keep a home. We also tackle the root causes of bad housing by campaigning for new laws, policies, and solutions.

Our website gets more than 100,000 visits a month; visit www.shelter.org.uk to join our campaign, find housing advice, or give us a donation.

We need your help to continue our work. Please support us.

For more information about Shelter, please contact:

88 Old Street
London EC1V 9HU

Telephone: 0845 458 4590

For help with your housing problems, phone Shelter's free housing advice helpline on 0808 800 4444 from 8am to midnight, seven days a week.

Guide to Housing Benefit, Peter McGurk and Nick Raynsford, 1982-88 (1st to 9th editions); Martin Ward and John Zebedee, 1988-90 (10th to 12th editions).

Guide to Housing Benefit and Community Charge Benefit, Martin Ward and John Zebedee, 1990-93 (13th to 15th editions).

Guide to Housing Benefit and Council Tax Benefit, John Zebedee and Martin Ward, 1993-2003 (16th to 25th editions: 1st to 10th of this title).

Guide to Housing Benefit and Council Tax Benefit, John Zebedee, Martin Ward and Sam Lister with additional material by Colin Hull, 2003-07 (26th to 29th editions: 11th to 14th of this title).

John Zebedee is an independent benefits trainer and writer (email: *johnzebedee@hotmail.com*). He has taught over 1,800 courses for local authorities, housing associations, advice and law centres and others.

Martin Ward is an independent benefits consultant and trainer (e-mail: *mward@info-training.co.uk*). He maintains a web-site which gives convenient access to relevant legislation and other useful sources – *www.info-training.co.uk*

Sam Lister is policy officer at the Chartered Institute of Housing (email: *sam.lister@cih.org*) and chair of the management board of the Worcester Housing and Benefits Advice Centre.

John Zebedee and Martin Ward have specialised in housing benefit since the introduction of the 1982-83 scheme and in council tax benefit since it was introduced in 1993.

ISBN 1-905018-16-9
978-1-905018-16-1

Production by Davies Communications (020 7482 8844)

Printed by Antony Rowe Ltd

Cover design: Jeremy Spencer

Preface

This is the twenty-ninth in our series of guides. This edition covers the rules about housing benefit and council tax benefit as they apply from April 2006, using the information available on 1st April 2006.

We welcome comments and criticisms on the contents of our guide and make every effort to ensure it is accurate. However, the only statement of the law is found in the relevant Acts, regulations, orders and rules (chapter 1).

Colin Hull wrote chapter 11 (Help with rates in Northern Ireland), and we are very grateful for his work.

This guide has been written with the help and encouragement of many other people. This year we thank the following in particular:

Kully Bains, John Booty, Mary Connolly, Chris Harrington, Michael Iyekekpolor, Ryan James, Penny Matthews, Phillip J. Miall, Nick Price, Jim Read, Jonathan Reid, Jan Roxby, Maureen Sharp, Mark Tindley, Gordon Walker, Linda Davies and Peter Singer (editing and production) as well as staff from the Department for Work and Pensions and the Rent Service. Their help has been essential to the production of this guide.

John Zebedee, Martin Ward and Sam Lister

April 2006

Contents

Abbreviations

The principal abbreviations used in the guide are given below. A key to the marginal references can be found at the end of chapter 1 in table 1.3.

CTB	Council tax benefit
CTC	Child tax credit
DSD	The Department for Social Development in Northern Ireland
DWP	The Department for Work and Pensions in Great Britain
EP	Extended payment
GB	England, Scotland and Wales
GLHA	The DWP Guidance Local Housing Allowance
GM	The DWP Housing Benefit and Council Tax Benefit Guidance Manual
HB	Housing benefit
HRA	Housing revenue account
IB	Incapacity benefit
IS	Income support
JSA	Jobseeker's allowance (including JSA (Cont) & JSA(IB))
JSA(Cont)	Contribution-based jobseeker's allowance
JSA(IB)	Income-based jobseeker's allowance
NI	Northern Ireland
NIHE	The Northern Ireland Housing Executive
OG	The DWP HB/CTB Overpayments Guide
RCA	The Rate Collection Agency in Northern Ireland
SDA	Severe disablement allowance
SI	Statutory instrument
SPC	State pension credit (including guarantee credit and/or savings credit)
SR	Statutory rules (Northern Ireland)
UK	England, Scotland, Wales and Northern Ireland
WTC	Working tax credit

1 Introduction

1.1 Welcome to this guide, which comes in the 23rd year of the housing benefit (HB) scheme and the 12th of the council tax benefit (CTB) scheme. HB and CTB are important schemes providing people with help towards paying their rent and council tax and, in Northern Ireland, rates. Our guide is for use by anyone who is interested in the schemes, including administrators, advisers, claimants and landlords.

1.2 The guide describes the HB and CTB schemes administered throughout the United Kingdom from April 2006 and, where there are variations in the scheme between England, Scotland, Wales and Northern Ireland, these are explained. This chapter summarises the HB and CTB schemes and explains:

- the schemes in overview (paras. 1.3-18);
- which authorities are responsible for administering the schemes (paras. 1.19-32);
- how they should go about making their decisions on claims, etc (para. 1.33 onwards);
- the legal and other sources of information (para. 1.33 onwards); and
- the guide terminology, references and marginal references (paras. 1.62-67).

Overview of the HB and CTB schemes

WHO GETS HB AND CTB?

1.3 Except for certain categories of claimant (para. 1.9) nearly everyone with low enough income and capital (as described in paragraphs 1.11-13) can get CTB and, if they pay rent for the place where they live, HB. HB and CTB are a significant source of help to many households. Table 1.1 sets out some basic statistics about the numbers of claimants, the average amount of payment and expenditure on the scheme.

Table 1.1: Key HB and CTB statistics

HB CLAIMS IN GREAT BRITAIN AS AT MAY 2005*	
Number of claimants	3.957 million
Average weekly payment	£63.30
Claimants on IS/JSA(IB)/SPC	2.871 million (73%)
MAIN CTB CLAIMS IN GREAT BRITAIN AS AT MAY 2005*	
Number of claimants	4.96 million
Average weekly payment	£13.58
Claimants on IS/JSA(IB)/SPC	3.503 million (71%)
TAKE UP OF HB/CTB IN GREAT BRITAIN 2003-04*	
HB by caseload	between 84 and 90%
HB by expenditure	between 88 and 93%
CTB by caseload (local authority tenants)	between 87 and 92%
CTB by caseload (owner occupiers)	between 35 and 40%
ANNUAL EXPENDITURE IN GREAT BRITAIN IN 2003-04*	
HB claims	£12.356 billion
CTB claims	£3.274 billion
HB CLAIMS IN NORTHERN IRELAND PAID BY NIHE AS AT AUGUST 2005**	
Number of claimants	129,733
Average weekly payment	£55.58

* Source: DWP, Information and Analysis Directorate

** Source: DSD Statistics and Research Agency

POLICY OBJECTIVES AND PRINCIPLES OF THE SCHEMES

1.4 The purpose of the HB scheme is to ensure that people have a sufficient income to afford to pay the rent (in Northern Ireland, rent and rates) of reasonably priced accommodation which is suitable for their needs. In Great Britain the CTB scheme provides assistance with council tax and takes two forms. Claimants eligible for both forms are aw arded whichever is the most valuable. 'Main CTB' is by far the more common. It helps people on low incomes pay their council tax.

1.5 The other form of CTB is 'alternative maximum CTB' – more commonly known as 'second adult rebate' – and is described in chapter 8. It is not based on the claimant's needs or resources but on the income of certain adults in the claimant's household. Its purpose is to compensate the head of household for the loss of a council tax discount caused by other adults who live with them. It is payable where the income of those adults is too low to contribute towards increased council tax caused by their presence.

1.6 HB and main CTB are part of the wider state 'safety net' designed to ensure that citizens have sufficient means to sustain a minimum reasonable standard of living. One half of that safety net is provided by IS/JSA(IB)/guarantee credit which ensures that a person has sufficient income to meet reasonable living expenses but, crucially, does not include any allowance for rent/council tax payments and so claimants in receipt of these benefit are assumed to be entitled to the maximum help (para. 1.11). Note that certain other types of housing costs are included in IS/JSA(IB)/guarantee credit – see paragraph 1.9 and chapter 2.

1.7 As a safety net, HB/CTB is only available with respect to the accommodation that the claimant occupies as their home. Where it is unclear which dwelling the claimant is living in as their home, for example, where they are temporarily absent or have more than one home, there are special rules for determining which dwelling they are assumed to be occupying – see chapter 3. Further, since the safety net is only intended to support the minimum standard of living considered necessary, the level of help available is limited by criteria which restrict the amount of HB to what is judged to be reasonable and appropriate.

1.8 These criteria are translated into rules designed to ensure that the system cannot be exploited either by landlords charging excessive rents or by claimants living in accommodation that is unnecessarily lavish or expensive. What is reasonable is judged by comparison with local rent levels. What is appropriate is judged by reference to the claimant's household size and the range of the market it is considered reasonable for the state to cover for the person claiming benefit. In addition the appropriate level of benefit is also judged by reference to what it is considered that the claimant can afford to contribute towards the rent.

EXCLUSIONS FROM BENEFIT

1.9 For reasons of policy the Government has legislated to exclude some groups from benefit altogether; for example, many full-time students and people who have only come to live in the UK recently cannot get HB or CTB. For details of these rules, see chapters 20 and 21 respectively. Chapter 2 describes other categories of claimant who are excluded (notably young people who have recently left care) and certain types of housing cost which are ineligible for help with HB. These restrictions are usually designed to

- prevent abuse (such as a contrived rent liability); or
- avoid the possibility of double subsidy where help is provided through an alternative scheme (such as help with mortgage costs through IS/JSA(IB)/guarantee credit) or is the responsibility of another agency.

CALCULATION OF BENEFIT

1.10 Generally rents charged by local authorities and (in most cases) housing associations are assumed to be both reasonable and appropriate. In the private sector the judgment about whether a particular rent is reasonable or appropriate is made by the authority with reference to rental valuations determined by the rent officer (or in Northern Ireland the NIHE) – as described in chapters 6 and 10. Except in the pathfinder authority areas, where the authority decides that the rent is reasonable and appropriate the maximum amount of HB is based on 100 per cent of the rent. In the pathfinder authority areas (chapter 22) the appropriate (and maximum) amount of HB for private sector tenants is based on a flat rate allowance which varies according to the household's size regardless of whether this is more or less than the actual rent. In both pathfinder and non-pathfinder areas the maximum HB is reduced by any assumed contribution payable by the claimant or other members of their household, as described in chapter 7. In contrast to help with rent there are generally no limits to what is judged appropriate for help with the council tax or rates. Benefit is therefore based on 100 per cent of the council tax/rates, less any assumed contribution by the claimant or their household members (chapter 7). Chapters 9 and 11 describe how the maximum amount of help with council tax/rates is calculated.

1.11 The amount that the claimant and their family is considered to be able to contribute towards their rent/council tax/rates is judged by reference to their own resources and by any assumed contribution made by other adults living in the same household who are not dependent on them (known as 'non-dependants'). Chapter 4 describes which people are considered to be members of the claimant's family and their wider household. Where the claimant is on IS/JSA/guarantee credit it is assumed that they have insufficient resources to afford to make a contribution towards their rent/council tax/rates and so are entitled to maximum help.

The maximum help with HB is the amount of rent judged to be appropriate less any assumed contribution from non-dependants. The help with main CTB/HB for rates is the full council tax/rates less any assumed non-dependant contribution.

1.12 Where the claimant is not on IS/JSA(IB)/guarantee credit the calculation of benefit involves comparing the claimant's family assessed income against their notional minimum needs to determine their appropriate contribution. Chapters 13-15 describe how household income is assessed. In Great Britain some minor variations in the calculation of income in each local authority area are permitted, as described in chapter 22. The household's notional minimum needs are calculated by adding together standard allowances whose rates are set annually (para. 1.14). The allowances which apply in each case depend on the claimant's circumstances, such as their family size and any disability or care needs (chapter 12). The aggregate allowance is known as the 'applicable amount'.

1.13 If the claimant's income is less than or equal to their applicable amount they will receive the maximum benefit (para. 1.11). As their income increases above their applicable amount, HB and main CTB are withdrawn by a percentage of that excess income – this percentage of excess income is judged to be the appropriate contribution for the claimant to make towards their rent/council tax. The percentage or taper for HB (in Northern Ireland HB for rent) is 65% and for main CTB (in Northern Ireland HB for rates) is 20%.

1.14 The rate of the benefit allowances which comprise the applicable amount are up-rated annually in April (together with other social security benefits and tax credits), usually in line with inflation. Paragraph 1.62 gives details of when the rates benefit quoted in this guide takes effect. Chapter 12 and appendices 4 and 5 set out the benefit rates from April 2006. Occasionally, as part of government reforms, selected allowances are restructured and new rates set in addition to the annual up-rating. Such one-off changes are usually introduced in October.

CLAIMS AND AWARDS

AA 1,5 NIAA 1,5 **1.15** Even where a person would be entitled to it HB/CTB cannot be awarded unless a claim is made, and there are numerous procedural rules involved in claiming (chapter 5). Once an award has been made it will continue to be paid indefinitely until the claimant's circumstances change so that either: they are no longer entitled at all (paras. 2.3-4) or the amount of benefit they are entitled to is different and the authority replaces it with a new award (chapter 17). With the exception of claimants in receipt of the pension credit, claimants are expected to keep the council informed about changes in their circumstances (chapter 17). Failure to do so is one of the principal causes of underpayments (paras. 17.37-39) and overpayments (chapter 18) – though councils do themselves make mistakes too. Disagreements about the correct award often result in appeals (chapter 19).

NOTICE OF AWARDS AND PAYMENT OF BENEFIT

1.16 Once an authority has received all the necessary information to complete a claim it must decide it within certain time limits and notify the claimant of the outcome. There are rules about what claimants must be told and when and how benefit is awarded (chapter 16). An award of HB will take the form of a rent rebate or rent allowance. A rent rebate is an award of HB to a tenant of the authority administering the HB scheme (which takes the form of a reduced liability for rent). A rent allowance is a cash payment which can be used by the claimant towards their full rental liability. The rent allowance is paid directly to the claimant or, in certain circumstances, to his or her landlord (chapter 16).

AA 134, 139, 191
NIAA 126, 167

ADMINISTRATION, EXPENDITURE AND SUBSIDY

1.17 HB and CTB are national welfare benefits administered by local councils in Great Britain and in Northern Ireland by executive agencies of the NI government (paras 1.19-24). Responsibility for running the HB and CTB schemes gives administering authorities a prime role in maintaining the incomes of disadvantaged groups. In Great Britain authorities are reimbursed for their expenditure through central government subsidy payments. Chapter 23 gives more detail about subsidy payments to councils in Great Britain. In Northern Ireland HB is financed directly as part of overall government expenditure.

AA 134(1),(1A),(1B), (2), 139(1),(2), 191
NIAA 126(2),(3)

CHANGE AND REFORM

1.18 HB was first introduced throughout the UK in 1982-83 and was replaced with a new HB scheme in 1988. CTB came in because of the introduction of council tax in Great Britain in 1993. Since the introduction of the HB scheme in 1982, and CTB from 1993, both schemes have been subject to almost constant change and reform (hence the need for an annual guide). Most, but not all, major changes in the rules are introduced in April or October each year. Table 1.2 summarises changes to the HB and CTB scheme over the past year. Earlier editions of this guide give similar lists (in table 2.1 in most editions).

Table 1.2 Summary of changes since April 2005

SI 2005/2032 21st July 2005	Eight authorities' council taxes are capped for 2005-06.
SI 2005/236 SI 2005/238 25th July 2005	Salford becomes the last of 18 authorities experimenting with local housing allowances.
SI 2005/1719 NISR 2005/331 1st August 2005	Correction of rules about rent free periods.
SI 2005/2183 NISR 2005/374 5th August 2005	Disregard of payments from the London Bombings Charitable Relief Fund.
SI 2005/1807 NISR 2005/332 August/September 2005	Up-rating of figures used in assessing student cases.
SI 2005/1983 NISR 2005/383 1st September 2005	'Age-related payments' (to help with council tax or other costs) are disregarded in full for HB/CTB purposes.
NISR 2005/221 NISR 2005/319 1st September 2005	Certain young care leavers in Northern Ireland excluded from HB.
SI 2005/2465 NIST 2005/424 1st/3rd October 2005	Clarification of rules about payments to third partiesand payments in kind.
SI 2005/2502 NISR 2005/444 3rd October 2005	Corrections to rules about 60+s and rules about underpayments.
SI 2005/273 NISR 2005/148 3rd October 2005	Amendments relating to charitable and voluntary payments and personal injury payments.
SI 2005/2687 24th October 2005 NISR 2005/458 14th November 2005	HB/CTB law is amended to bring it up to date in relation to law about care homes and independent hospitals.

SI 2005/2984 NISR 2005/493 10th November 2005	Date of claim can be date of first contact or date of bereavement or separation. Clarification of rules about offices at which claims are made, and about incomplete claims. All claims limits which were 'four weeks' are now 'one month'. The so-called 'cooling-off' period definitely no longer applies when terminating HB/CTB. Improved disregards relating to charitable and voluntary payments and personal injury payments, which are now disregarded wholly as income. Rules about payments on account and payments to landlords improved. Clarification of child care disregard. Various rules about income and how it is estimated brought up to date.
The Civil Partnership Act SI 2005/2877 SI 2005/2878 SI 2005/3137 NISR 2005/536 NISR 2005/539 5th December 2005	HB/CTB law (and most other law) amended to treat civil partners in the same way as married couples, and so that a same-sex couple are treated in the same way as an opposite-sex couple if they live together as though they were married/civil partners. This applies to all HB/CTB rules ranging from the rent officer's size criteria, to non-dependant deductions for couples, to war pensions, to the definitions of 'relative' and 'close relative'.
SI 2005/3391 NISR 2005/550 12th December 2005	Improved disregard of payments from the London Bombings Charitable Relief Fund, which are now disregarded wholly as income and capital.
SI 2005/3205 NISR 2005/513 18th December 2005	'Pension Protection Fund' payments (for those who lose their pensions in certain circumstances) count in full as income.
SI 2005/2465 NISR 2005/424 SI 2005/3294 30th December 2005	HB/CTB law is amended to bring it up to date in relation to adoption law.
SI 2003/1589 NISR 2003/367 28th January 2006	'Back to work bonus' (since it no longer exists) is no longer disregarded as capital.

SI 2006/54 9th February 2006	Subsidy order for 2004-05 becomes law.
SI 2006/213 SI 2006/214 SI 2006/215 SI 2006/216 SI 2006/217 6th March 2006	Consolidation of HB and CTB regulations (revoking over 200 sets of regulations in force since 1987). Various transitional rules preserved. Continuity of the law not affected though most regulation numbers change.
SI 2005/2465 NISR 2005/424 1st April 2005	The lower capital limit increases from £3,000 to £6,000 for under 60s, bringing them into line with 60+s.
SI 2005/2865 SI 2005/2866 1st April 2006	Changes to council tax rules about exemption, discounts and enforcement, to bring civil partners into line with married couples.
SI 2006/559 1st April 2006	New figures apply for subsidy for housing revenue account rent rebates.
SI 2006/645 NISR 2006/109 1st/3rd April 2006	Main annual up-rating of HB/CTB figures.
SI 2005/2502 NISR 2005/444 1st/3rd April 2006	Changes and improvements to the HB rules about first day of entitlement (including in the case of retrospective awards), date of implementation of changes (e.g. when moving home), eligible rent when entitlement starts, changes and ends (including further rules about part-weeks), and converting eligible rent from monthly to weekly amounts. No time limit any longer applies in the case of claims from a hostel with daily liability for rent. Abolition of hospital down-rating in assessing someone's applicable amount. All arrears of working tax credit and child tax credit are now disregarded as income and, for at least 52 weeks, as capital. Other clarifications and corrections to the law.

SI 2006/588 NISR 2006/97 1st/6th April 2006	(1st April) New form of second adult rebate introduced for student households with non-dependants on JSA(IB), IS or guarantee credit. (6th April) Payments from the 'Pension Protection Fund' now count as income for 60+s.
SI 2006/644 3rd April 2006	Where the landlord is a housing authority but the dwelling is subject to certain types of housing management order made under the Housing Acts payment must take the form of a rent allowance rather than a rent rebate.
SI 2006/718 NISR 2003/128 1st/3rd/10th April 2006	Amendments to the rules about applicable amounts and non-dependants to reflect the fact that child benefit can in some circumstances be awarded until the person reaches 20.
SI 2005/2465 NISR 2005/424 6th April 2005	Deferred income from a personal pension scheme ceases to count as notional income for under 60s.
SI 2005/2677 NISR 2006/104 6th April 2006	HB/CTB rules amended to take effect of the introduction of new rules about deferred state retirement pension. Lump sum payments are disregarded as capital and the notional income rule does not apply when increased payments are not requested. (This amendment was done only to the pre-consolidation regulations but it is expected that it will be carried forward to the consolidating regulations.)
SI 2000/2239 NISR 2000/260 10th April 2006	Bereavement premium ceases to apply.
SI 2005/2904 NISR 2005/459 10th April 2005	Rules about recovery of HB overpayments re-written, making it clear that recovery from the payee is always an option but that there is nearly always an alternative person from whom an overpayment may be recovered. Overpayment and underlying entitlement rules clarified for when someone moves home. Clarification of

	definition of 'official error'. New power to recover from Swiss benefits.
SI 2005/3360 NISR 2005/580 10th April 2006	HB/CTB law is amended to bring it up to date in relation to law about hospital in-patients.
SI 2006/1003 SI 2006/1926 NISR 2006/178 30th April 2006	Further amendments to rules about the eligibility of recent migrants.
July 2006	HB consolidation regulations for Northern Ireland expected
2007	It is likely that from around 2007 it will be made easier to claim HB/CTB by internet (DWP circulars HB/CTB G11/2005, G12/2005, G1/2006, G2/2006).
2008	This remains the likely year in which the DWP will introduce local housing allowances nationally for private sector tenants (but not housing association or most social sector tenants) – and probably for new claims only (DWP magazine Housing Benefit Direct, February 2006, March 2006).

Administration

1.19 Different arrangements apply in England and Wales, in Scotland, and in Northern Ireland. In any individual authority in Great Britain HB/CTB may be administered by one or more departments, usually the housing or treasurer's/ finance department or by an external contractor acting on behalf of the council. For Northern Ireland, see paragraphs 1.22-24.

ENGLAND AND WALES

1.20 In some areas of England there are two tiers of local government. The authority responsible for administering the scheme is the 'housing authority'. The 'housing authority' means the council of a district, London borough or unitary authority or the Common Council of the City of London, but not a county council (unless it is a unitary authority). Tenants of a housing authority claim housing benefit from their landlord and are paid by rent rebate. All other tenants, including tenants of county councils, claim both HB and CTB from their local council which is also their housing authority and will be paid their HB by rent allowance. Throughout Wales there is only one tier of local government so claimants should apply to their county or county borough council for both HB and CTB. Therefore all local authority tenants in Wales will be paid HB by rent rebate. In both England and Wales agency arrangements may exist for the administration of HB but not CTB (para. 1.25).

SCOTLAND

1.21 In Scotland, there is only one tier of local government so all local authority (council) tenants claim HB and CTB from their landlord and will be paid HB in the form of a rent rebate. All other tenants of housing associations or other landlords (whether public or private) receive rent allowances and CTB from the local council. Since April 2002 this includes all former tenants of Scottish Homes who previously received their HB from their landlord as a rent rebate (see Housing (Scotland) Act 2001, schedule 10 paragraph 17). As in England and Wales agency arrangements may exist for the administration of HB but not CTB (para. 1.25).

NORTHERN IRELAND

1.22 Northern Ireland has a social security system which is separate from, but generally mirrors, that in the rest of the United Kingdom. As described in the next two paragraphs, there are two main areas of housing benefit policy which are unique to Northern Ireland. Further details of variations between the legal systems may be found in paragraphs 1.40 and 1.43.

1.23 There is no council tax in Northern Ireland. Occupiers of domestic property are liable for rates instead (explained fully in chapter 11 of this guide). Help with domestic rates is provided through HB. As a general rule tenants (as opposed to owner occupiers) make their claim from the Northern Ireland Housing Executive (NIHE) although there are some exceptions: see chapter 11 for details. Owner occupiers make their claim for HB from the Rate Collection Agency (RCA), but again see chapter 11 for exceptions. The RCA is an Executive Agency of the Department of Finance and Personnel and is responsible for the collection of rates due to the 26 district councils and the regional rate. It receives payment from the Northern Ireland Housing Executive for properties in the public sector.

1.24 Decisions about the appropriate level of rent for rent allowance claimants are made by the Northern Ireland Housing Executive which is also responsible for administering housing benefit for tenants. In effect, the Executive carries out the same function as rent officers in England, Wales and Scotland.

AGENCY ARRANGEMENTS AND OUT OF BOROUGH PLACEMENTS

1.25 Authorities in Great Britain (but not Northern Ireland) may make arrangements for housing benefit (but not council tax benefit) by which: AA 134 (1A),(5), 191

- one carries out the functions of the other; or
- functions are carried out jointly or by a joint committee.

Agency arrangements sometimes apply to local authority tenants living in property situated outside the landlord authority's boundaries, for example properties for which the local authority has secured nomination agreements with the landlord to house its homeless applicants. In such a case, they may receive a rent rebate from their landlord authority as opposed to the authority in which they live if agency arrangements have been agreed. However, note that where the local authority is the landlord of the claimant (such as properties it has leased for homeless households) it is obliged to administer HB itself by way of a rent rebate even if the property is outside its boundary (see also para. 16.14) – but any CTB will have to be claimed from the authority in which the property is located.

CONTRACTING OUT ADMINISTRATION

SI 2002 No. 1888

1.26 Authorities can contract out the administration of HB and CTB to private companies and a number have done so. Prior to July 2002 an authority which contracted out its administration remained responsible for all decisions on each claim, resulting in a considerable duplication of work. From 25th July 2002 contractors are authorised to make decisions subject to the requirement that they provide the authority with a daily 10% random sample of claims on which decisions have been made for checking.

1.27 The Deregulation and Contracting Out Act 1994 permits contractors to communicate directly with the DWP. The contracting out of HB/CTB administration does not affect an individual's entitlement or their right of appeal to an independent appeal tribunal.

BEST VALUE IN ENGLAND AND WALES

SI 2005 No. 598 sch 7
SI 2005 No. 665 sch 8

1.28 The Local Government Act 1999 places the duty of 'Best Value' upon authorities in England and Wales. The Act requires authorities to secure continuous improvement in their services. Authorities must conduct performance reviews and publish annual performance plans. Section 4(1) of the Act allows the Secretary of State to set by order performance indicators and standards. The indicators reflect policy priorities such as speed, accuracy and value for money. The indicators for 2006-07 are as follows:

- claim security judged in relation to the number of claimants visited, fraud investigators in post, investigations undertaken, and convictions or benefit penalties imposed (in Wales only, judged by per 1000 caseload);
- average time for processing new claims;
- average time for processing notifications of changes of circumstance;

- percentage of cases for which amount of benefit was correct on the information available from a sample of cases checked post-decision;
- for HB only, the percentage of recoverable overpayments that were recovered in the year (in England only, there are separate indicators for: percentage identified within that year that are recovered; the percentage of all debt recovered in that year; and the percentage of all debt written off as unrecoverable).

INSPECTION AND AUDIT

1.29 The Audit Commission Act 1998 allows the Commission at the request of the Secretary of State to conduct studies designed to improve economy, efficiency, effectiveness and performance by authorities in their administration of HB/CTB. In Wales these functions are carried out by the Wales Audit Office under the Public Audit (Wales) Act 2004.

BENEFIT INSPECTIONS AND PERFORMANCE STANDARDS

1.30 The Administration Act provides the Secretary of State with wide powers to inspect and report on authorities' administration of HB/CTB and in particular their performance in the prevention and detection of fraud. These functions are carried out by the Benefit Fraud Inspectorate (BFI) and are known as benefit inspections. Following a benefit inspection the BFI will publish a report which, apart from any findings which may compromise claim security, can be viewed on-line *(www.bfi.gov.uk)*. Because of the BFI's wide powers these reports can sometimes be a useful tool for advisers to persuade an authority to modify its practices where particular mistakes are repeated. AA 139A-139C

1.31 The role of the BFI is to improve standards of administration generally and promote good practice. During an inspection, authorities are scored against performance standards for four key aspects of HB/CTB administration: claims administration; security, user focus and resource management. There are 19 different performance measures (PM1-19) defining standards against which authorities' performance is judged. For example, PM1 sets a standard of 36 days as the average speed for processing new claims, and PM3 a standard of 90% for the percentage of new claims decided within 14 days of all the information being received. Details can be found in circulars A6/2005 and A10/2005. The standards are available on-line and can be viewed at *www.dwp.gov.uk/housingbenefit/publications/perf-stands/*. Reference to the standards may be useful for advisers where particular problems persist.

DWP POWERS TO INTERVENE FOR POOR ADMINISTRATION

1.32 The Secretary of State has wide powers to ensure that an authority takes action on any failings identified in a benefit inspection report. The Secretary AA 139D-139H of State can invite the authority to consider the report and give directions as to standards to be achieved. A failure to comply with a direction is a serious matter which ultimately could result in the authority being forced to put all or part of its administration to tender.

Proper decision-making

1.33 The authority's primary duty is one of proper decision-making. It has to apply the rules of the HB/CTB schemes to the facts of the individual case with the aim of arriving at sound decisions regarding benefit entitlement. The necessary steps in the decision-making process are:

- identifying the relevant facts in the case;
- proper consideration of the available evidence where the facts are in doubt or in dispute;
- establishing facts 'on the balance of probability' where necessary;
- correct interpretation of the law and its application to the facts of the case; and
- arriving at decisions that can be understood in terms of the relevant law and facts.

DISPUTED FACTS

1.34 The only facts which are relevant to the authority are those which have a bearing in relation to the application of the specific rules of the HB/CTB schemes. Where there is a disagreement about the facts between the authority and the claimant or other person affected, the authority must consider the available evidence to decide what the true position is. A factual dispute may also be the trigger for a request for revision, supersession or an appeal to an independent appeal tribunal (chapters 17 and 19).

1.35 The requirement of proof means that a disputed fact must be established to the satisfaction of the authority and, on appeal, the appeal tribunal. This does not, however, mean that the fact must be established with absolute certainty. In civil cases, such as matters involving HB/CTB, the appropriate test is 'on the balance of probability'. In other words, if the greater weight of evidence supports for example the claimant's view of the disputed fact then the claimant has proved the matter on the balance of probability.

AA 5(1) NIAA 5(1) HB 86 HB60+ 67 NIHB 81 NIHB60+ 64 CTB 72 CTB60+ 57

1.36 In the first instance the burden of proof is on the claimant to support his or her claim by supplying the authority with all the evidence it reasonably requires (para. 5.17). The DWP's Verification Framework seeks to set out the minimum standards for collecting evidence when a claim is made (para. 5.22). However, where the authority asserts a particular proposition, for example, that a recoverable overpayment has occurred, the authority must have evidence to support its assertion.

1.37 The burden of proof is only decisive, however, where:

- there is no evidence – consequently where the authority asserts a disputed fact it must have evidence to support that assertion; or
- the evidence is exactly balanced – in which case the party on whom the burden of proof lies should not succeed.

ISSUES OF LAW

1.38 The rules of the HB/CTB schemes in Great Britain are set out in legislation passed by the UK parliament. (For Northern Ireland variations see paragraphs 1.22-24, 1.40 and 1.43.) Issues of law involve the application and interpretation of that legislation. For example, the question of whether or not the claimant's son counts as a non-dependant for HB/CTB purposes could only be answered by consideration of the definition of 'non-dependant' in the regulations as well as the relevant facts of the case. A dispute over the correct interpretation and application of the legislation may be the trigger for a request for revision or supersession or an appeal to an independent appeal tribunal (chapters 17 and 19). While legal disputes do not fall within the Local Government Ombudsman's remit, negligent reading of the benefit regulations by the authority may constitute maladministration. Guidance on how to complain, what constitutes maladministration and recent Ombudsman's reports on HB complaints can be viewed on-line at *www.lgo.org.uk*

THE ACTS

1.39 In England, Wales and Scotland, the Acts of Parliament are as follows. The outline rules relating to HB and CTB entitlement are contained in the Social Security Contributions and Benefits Act 1992 (as amended), and the Social Security Administration Act 1992 (as amended) which sets the conditions for a valid claim. Together these two Acts are sometimes referred to as the 'Benefit Acts'. Section 115 of the Immigration and Asylum Act 1999 (which applies to GB and NI) provides the outline framework excluding certain persons subject to immigration control from HB and CTB entitlement. The outline rules on the administration of the HB/CTB schemes are contained in the Social Security Administration Act 1992 (as amended). The Child Support, Pensions and Social Security Act 2000 contains the outline framework for decision-making and appeal arrangements as well as the separate discretionary housing payments scheme.

1.40 Although the social security system in Northern Ireland is separate from that in England, Wales and Scotland, the legislation generally mirrors Great Britain's so as to maintain a UK-wide social security system. For each GB Act there is a Northern Ireland equivalent which is (as far as possible) laid out in a similar manner. Thus there are the Social Security Contributions and Benefits (Northern Ireland) Act 1992 and the Social Security Administration (Northern Ireland) Act 1992. The form of primary legislation in Northern Ireland depends on the system of governance in place at the time it was made. During periods of direct rule from Westminster, primary legislation is mainly made by orders in council or, occasionally, (usually in the case of consolidating legislation) an Act of the UK parliament. During periods of devolved government primary legislation is made by the Northern Ireland Assembly. However, the Assembly's powers are heavily circumscribed because it is under a duty to mirror the legislation in Great Britain so as to maintain a UK-wide social security system (s87 Northern Ireland Act 1998).

REGULATIONS, ORDERS AND RULES

1.41 The Acts enable the government, normally following consultation with the local authority associations, to formulate delegated legislation – 'regulations', 'orders' and 'rules'– which contain and amend the details of the schemes (appendix 1, which lists both those relating to England, Wales and Scotland and those relating to Northern Ireland).

1.42 In England, Wales and Scotland, the main detailed rules for HB and CTB are set out in regulations. However, for each scheme there is a separate set of regulations for claimants aged under 60 and those aged 60 or over – making four sets of regulations, two for HB and two for CTB. In effect there are two HB and two CTB schemes running in parallel and while there are rules which are identical, there are also differences (mainly in the way that income is calculated). The main regulations for each scheme are as follows:

- for HB, claimants aged under 60: the Housing Benefit Regulations 2006 (SI 2006 No. 213);
- for HB, claimants aged 60+: the Housing Benefit (Persons who have attained the qualifying age for state pension credit) Regulations 2006 (SI 2006 No. 214);
- for CTB claimants aged under 60: the Council Tax Benefit Regulations 2006 (SI 2006 No.215);
- for CTB claimants aged 60+: the Council Tax Benefit (persons who have attained the qualifying age for state pension credit) Regulations 2006 (SI 2006 No. 216).

All four sets of regulations consolidate the previous regulations which had been the subject of over 200 sets of amendment regulations since 1987. Consolidation does not affect the continuity of the law. Claimants who benefited from any form of transitional protection under the pre-consolidation regulations have these rights preserved by the Housing Benefit and Council Tax Benefit (Consequential Provisions) Regulations 2006 (SI 2006 No. 217). The details of the HB/CTB decision-making and appeal arrangements are contained in SI 2001 No. 1002, The Housing Benefit and Council Tax Benefit (Decisions and Appeals) Regulations.

1.43 In Northern Ireland, the legislation generally mirrors that in Great Britain and is in the form of 'statutory rules' (SR). For each GB statutory instrument there is a Northern Ireland equivalent which is (as far as possible) laid out in a similar manner. At the time of writing (April 2006) the DSD is working on the consolidation of the HB regulations for Northern Ireland. The new regulations are expected to be published and come into force in July 2006. As in Great Britain there will be two sets of HB regulations (one each for claimants aged under and over 60). References in this Guide are taken from the draft consolidation regulations. The regulations when published will be known as:

- for claimants aged under 60: the Housing Benefit Regulations (Northern Ireland) 2006;
- for HB, claimants aged 60+: the Housing Benefit (Persons who have attained the qualifying age for state pension credit) Regulations (Northern Ireland) 2006.

As in Great Britain, claimants who benefit from any form of transitional protection have these rights preserved by the Housing Benefit and Council Tax Benefit (Consequential Provisions) Regulations (Northern Ireland) 2006.

OBTAINING THE LEGISLATION

1.44 Members of the public have a right to see copies of the relevant legal material together with the details of any local scheme (para. 22.10) at an authority's principal office. For information on Commissioners' decisions, see paragraphs 1.51-52.

1.45 The many and frequent amendments to the relevant legislation mean that it can be quite difficult to keep track of the current rules of the schemes. However, this has been improved by the publication of the new consolidating regulations which came into force in March 2006 (para. 1.42). The 2006 regulations can be accessed on-line at: *www.opsi.gov.uk/si/si200602.htm* (scroll down to numbers 213-217). For the time being, at least until further amendments accumulate, these will provide a pretty up to date statement of the law. Recent amendment regulations can also be tracked on-line at *www.opsi.gov.uk/stat.htm* or for Northern Ireland at *www.opsi.gov.uk/legislation/northernireland/ni-srni.htm*. The DWP publishes a loose-leaf work entitled *The Law Relating to Social Security* which is kept up to date with regular supplements. Volume 8 (Parts 1 and 2) contains relevant sections of the Acts and statutory instruments relating to HB/CTB. A parallel series is available for Northern Ireland. The advantage of this work is that, with the exception of the most recent changes, it shows the law as amended. However, at the time of writing (April 2006) the last supplement (No. 72) was issued in September 2005, prior to the consolidating regulations. Further supplements are expected during 2006. This work is now available on-line at *www.dwp.gov.uk/advisers/docs/lawvols/bluevol/index.asp* for Great Britain and *www.dsdni.gov.uk/law_relating_to_social_security* for Northern Ireland. Many public reference libraries hold paper copies of *The Law Relating to Social Security* and also provide free on-line access.

1.46 The Child Poverty Action Group's *Housing Benefit and Council Tax Benefit Legislation* (18th edition 2005-06 ISBN 1 901698 82 3) also contains all the law relevant in Great Britain at the point of publication. It provides a detailed commentary on the legislation together with any relevant case law and highlights any contentious legal opinions. Readers may find it particularly useful where they require expansion on a particular point raised in the guide.

OTHER RELEVANT LEGISLATION

1.47 In addition to the Benefit Acts and regulations (paras. 1.39-43), other legislation circumscribes authorities in the way in which they administer HB/CTB. The Human Rights Act (para. 1.53) sets limits on how legislation is to be interpreted for all public authorities. The Local Government Acts define the limits of local authority powers and duties. Various other Acts provide rules of conduct in relation to public administration generally such as anti-discrimination legislation (e.g. Race Relations Act 1976). The Local Government Finance Act 1982 and Audit Commission Act 1998 cover the auditing of, and public rights of access to, local authority accounts. They also place upon local authorities a duty to secure economy, efficiency and effectiveness in their administration of HB/CTB. Various other Acts regulate the conduct and performance of local authority administration (paras. 1.19-32).

1.48 The Data Protection Act 1998 controls the use of, and access to, information about an individual held on a computer or any other retrievable filing system. However, contrary to popular belief, it does not apply to prevent disclosure to the extent that other legislation requires it for a particular purpose. Further guidance for authorities on the protection of personal information can be found in the guidance manual (GM, chapter C8).

STATUTORY INTERPRETATION AND CASE LAW

1.49 In the first instance, where there is no ambiguity, legislation should be taken to mean exactly what it says. The general rule is that the authority may not look beyond the relevant legislation itself to determine its meaning. However, certain forms of assistance are permissible, or must be considered, such as the precedents contained within case law on the meaning of a word or phrase. For example, where in the past a matter in dispute has been considered in the High Court (Court of Session in Scotland) the interpretation made by a judge in the course of deciding such a case will in particular instances be binding upon all authorities. Relevant cases are identified in the appropriate paragraphs of this guide and are fully referenced, together with any published report, in appendix 2.

1.50 Decisions in HB cases are often highly persuasive though not binding with regard to CTB and *vice versa* (and a similar principle applies as between English and Welsh, Scottish, and Northern Ireland cases – see also para.1.52). Equally, many of the words and phrases which were brought forward into the HB/CTB schemes from the old supplementary benefit (SB) scheme, or other parts of social security law, have a body of case law attached. Again, as an aid to interpretation such decisions are of persuasive value though not binding upon authorities.

COMMISSIONERS' DECISIONS

1.51 Social Security Commissioners are appointed to decide appeals brought by individuals, the Secretary of State for Work and Pensions and authorities on questions of law from the decision of appeal tribunals.

1.52 Commissioners' decisions on HB or CTB, as appropriate, constitute a body of case law. However, the Commissioners themselves may decide that a certain body of case law, although not strictly HB/CTB decisions, is binding – for example decisions relating to good cause and backdating (para. 5.53). In Northern Ireland the Commissioners have decided that the authorities are obliged to take account of HB decisions of the Commissioners and the Courts in Great Britain *(C001/03-04(HB))*. Commissioners' decisions are binding on authorities, and in effect have the same status as High Court decisions (para. 1.49). The most significant Commissioners' decisions are available on-line at *www.osscsc.gov.uk* for Great Britain. Northern Ireland decisions can also be accessed on-line at *www.dsdni.gov.uk/index/law_and_legislation/nidoc_database.htm*. Further details about the status of Commissioners' decisions and how to access them can be found in appendix 2 and paras. 19.65-68 and 19.95.

THE HUMAN RIGHTS ACT 1998

1.53 The Human Rights Act 1998 came into force on 2nd October 2000. It gives effect in the UK to the rights and freedoms guaranteed under the European Convention for the Protection of Human Rights and Fundamental Freedoms ('the Convention'). Authorities and appeal tribunals are under a duty to act compatibly with the Convention rights and all legislation must be read compatibly with the Convention rights as far as it is possible to do so. Also, courts and tribunals must have regard to the jurisprudence of the European Court of Human Rights and decisions and opinions of the Commission and Committee of Ministers. It is unlawful for the authority to act (or fail to act) in a way which is incompatible with a Convention right.

1.54 An authority does not act unlawfully if it could not have acted differently as a result of a provision of primary legislation. Nor does the authority act unlawfully where:

- it acts under a provision of secondary legislation;
- that primary legislation under which the secondary legislation is made cannot be interpreted in a way that is compatible with the Convention rights; and
- the authority is acting so as to enforce or give effect to that provision.

However, secondary legislation can be declared invalid by the courts where the primary legislation under which it is made is not directly in conflict with the Convention (thus allowing for the possibility of alternative secondary legislation that is compatible).

JUDGMENT

1.55 There are numerous occasions in the regulations where a decision must be made on the basis of what is 'reasonable' or 'appropriate'. For example, where the claimant has left the home through fear of violence then in specific instances the authority must treat the claimant as occupying two dwelling and consequently potentially entitled to HB on both dwellings 'if it is reasonable' that housing benefit should be paid in respect of both dwellings. There is no single right or wrong answer. In such cases the authority must exercise judgment in the light of the facts of the individual case. For example, if the claimant had brought the threats of violence upon him or herself by engaging in criminal activities it might be considered inappropriate to use public funds to meet the cost of two homes.

DISCRETION

1.56 Where an authority has a choice under the regulations to do or not do something, e.g. to make payments of a rent allowance to the claimant's landlord where there is no mandatory requirement to do so, this is a discretionary power. Such powers make the application of the regulations flexible and adaptable to the individual circumstances of the case.

CONTROLS ON EXERCISE OF JUDGMENT OR DISCRETION

1.57 In exercising judgment or discretion, authorities are bound by the established principles of administrative law that the courts have steadily evolved. If they are not in accordance with these principles, decisions may be open to legal challenge by way of judicial review (see *Judicial Review Proceedings,* Jonathan Manning, 2nd edition (2004), the Legal Action Group, ISBN 1903307171; or for Scotland see *Judicial Review in Scotland,* Tom Mullen and Tony Prosser, Wiley, ISBN 0471966142). For example, an authority must consider its discretionary powers in individual cases. It must not fetter its discretion by applying predetermined rules rigidly without giving genuine consideration to the merits of the individual case. The authority cannot decide, for example, that it will never use its power to make direct payments to landlords where it has the discretionary power to do so.

1.58 A power must be exercised reasonably. An authority will be considered to have acted unreasonably if, having regard to the nature of the subject matter:

- it takes into account matters which it ought not to consider; or
- it refuses or neglects to consider matters which it ought to take into account.

An authority will also have acted unreasonably if it comes to a conclusion that no reasonable authority could have come to.

DWP GUIDANCE MANUAL

1.59 The Department for Work and Pensions (DWP) is the central government department responsible for housing benefit and council tax benefit policy. It produces the *Housing Benefit and Council Tax Benefit Guidance Manual* (GM). The manual advises authorities on how to interpret the regulations and on administrative arrangements. Interesting or contentious parts of the manual are identified in this guide. The DWP also issues guidance on: the subsidy arrangements *(Subsidy Guidance Manual);* DWP policy on overpayments, *(HB/CTB Overpayments Guide)*(OG); Discretionary Housing Payments; and other aspects of HB/CTB administration which together with the Guidance Manuals are now available on-line at *www.dwp.gov.uk/housingbenefit/manuals/*. Print versions of most of these manuals can also be obtained from Corporate Document Services, 7 Eastgate, Leeds LS2 7LY (tel: 0113 399 4040).

DWP CIRCULARS

1.60 In addition to the GM, the DWP also issues regular circulars to authorities advising them of recent or forthcoming changes and other important matters. There are now three main types of circular distinguished by a prefix – A for adjudication and operations, F for fraud and S for statistics and subsidy. There are two further occasional series denoted G for general and U for urgent. In general the circulars are intended to supplement the Guidance Manual (GM) and in most cases provide authorities with guidance on recent changes to the HB/CTB schemes, or occasionally aspects of the scheme which authorities' find difficult. New circulars will contain advice as to whether it should be annotated against the guidance manual. Past 'A' circulars are eventually incorporated and superceded by amendments to the guidance manual. For a list of circulars in current use see A21/2005 paragraph 49 (the earliest A circular now in use is A27(Revised)/2003). 'A' and 'S' circulars are available on-line at: *www.dwp.gov.uk/hbctb/*. 'U' and 'G' circulars can be viewed on-line at *www.dwp.gov.uk/housingbenefit/news/newsletter/bulletins/*. Strictly speaking DWP circulars do not apply to Northern Ireland although the authorities there generally accept the validity of 'A' circulars (unless the law in Northern Ireland is different) and are happy to be referred to them where relevant. No separate series of circulars have been issued by the DSD for Northern Ireland. In practice the authorities copy and adapt the DWP circulars for their own use.

STATUS OF DWP ADVICE

1.61 While the Acts and regulations are binding upon authorities and appeal tribunals, the GM and DWP circulars are for information and guidance only and do not have the force of law (see the introduction to the GM), and this has been confirmed by the Commissioners *(CH/3853/2001)*. Authorities do, however, often cite DWP advice in support of their decisions. The courts sometimes rehearse the advice contained within the GM with approval while recognising that it is not an aid to legal interpretation (see for example *R v Maidstone BC ex parte Bunce*).

Using this guide

BENEFITS AND TAX CREDITS RATES

1.62 The benefit rates quoted in this guide are: in the case of HB claims for rent where the rent is paid weekly or in weekly multiples those which apply from 3rd April 2006, and from 1st April 2006 for HB for rent in all other cases, and in all cases for CTB or, in Northern Ireland, for HB for rates. Other benefit rates are increased during the week commencing 10th April 2006 but must be taken into account for HB and CTB purposes from 1st/3rd April 2006. This includes the working tax credit (WTC) and child tax credit (CTC) which increase from 6th April in line with the tax year but which can be ignored for HB/CTB purposes for up to 30 weeks (para. 13.44). Student figures (chapter 21) apply from September 2005. A summary of other benefit rates for 2006-07 is printed at the back of the guide (appendix 5). The tax and national insurance rates quoted are those which apply from 6th April 2006 to 5th April 2007.

TERMS USED IN THIS GUIDE

1.63 A number of different public authorities are involved in the administration of HB/CTB (paras. 1.20-21 and 1.23). The term 'authority' is used in this guide to cover them all, including the equivalent institutions in Northern Ireland. The term 'tenant' is used to describe any kind of rent-payer including, for example, licensees. The term 'housing benefit' (HB) is used to cover the two types of help with rent payments – rent rebates and rent allowances – and in Northern Ireland only, also includes help with rates in the form of rate rebates. This guide uses housing benefit as the general term, and rent rebate or rent allowance or rate rebate when this is more appropriate. The term 'CTB' is used to refer to both forms of CTB. One of these – 'alternative maximum council tax benefit' – is referred to in this guide, as in DWP guidance and most local authority forms, as 'second adult rebate'. Where it is more appropriate, the specific term 'main CTB' or 'second adult rebate' is used. The term 'state pension credit' is used to refer to either type of pension credit – the 'guarantee credit' and 'savings credit'. The term guarantee credit is used to refer to any award of pension credit which includes an amount of guarantee credit – whether it is paid with or without the savings credit. The term savings credit is used to refer to awards of pension credit which consist solely of an award of the savings credit.

REFERENCES AND ABBREVIATIONS

1.64 A list of abbreviations used in the text is given at the front of this guide following the contents page. Paragraphs 1.65-66 and table 1.3 explain how to use the references in the margins throughout the guide.

HOW TO USE THE MARGINAL REFERENCES

1.65 The following paragraphs illustrate how to use the commonest references found in the inside margins of this guide. The sections, regulations, paragraphs, etc, shown in marginal references have in many cases been amended by subsequent law. The sources mentioned in paragraphs 1.39-43 and quoted in the marginal references set out the law as so amended.

1.66 The following are examples of how the marginal references apply. Table 1.3 at the end of this chapter provides a key to the marginal references used in this guide.

CBA 130(1)(a)
NICBA 129(1)(a)

This means, in Great Britain section 131(1)(a) of the Social Security Contributions and Benefits Act 1992 – in other words, sub-section 1, paragraph 'a' of section 131. In Northern Ireland the equivalent reference is section 129(1)(a) the Social Security Contributions and Benefits (Northern Ireland) Act 1992. (This gives the law about the basic conditions of entitlement to housing benefit: para. 2.12.)

HB 74(9)
HB60+ 55(9)
NIHB 71(9)
NIHB60+ 53(9)
CTB 58(9)
CTB60+ 42(9)

These mean regulation 74(9) of the Housing Benefit Regulations 2006; regulation 55(9) of the Housing Benefit (Persons who have attained the qualifying age for state pension credit) Regulations 2006; regulation 71(9) of the Housing Benefit Regulations (Northern Ireland); regulation 53(9) of the Housing Benefit (Persons who have attained the qualifying age for state pension credit) Regulations (Northern Ireland) 2006; regulation 58(9) of the Council Tax Benefits Regulations 1992; and regulation 42(9) of the Council Tax Benefit (Persons who have attained the qualifying age for state pension credit) Regulations 2006 – in other words, paragraph 9 of each of those regulations. (These give the law about assessing the income of non-dependants: para. 7.25.)

HB sch 6 para 11(a) NIHB sch 7 para 11(a) CTB sch 5 para 11(a)

These mean schedule 7 paragraph 11a of the Housing Benefit Regulations 2006; schedule 6 paragraph 11a of the Housing Benefit Regulations (Northern Ireland); and schedule 5 paragraph 11(a) of the Council Tax Benefits Regulations 2006 – in other words, paragraph 11(a) of the appropriate schedule in each of those regulations. (These give the law about money deposited with a housing association: para. 13.79. Note that in this case there is no specific rule to take account of claimants aged 60+ in either HB or CTB)

Table 1.3: Key to marginal references

Each reference applies to Great Britain only unless otherwise stated or prefixed by 'NI' (e.g. NIAA) in which case it applies to Northern Ireland only.

AA	The Social Security Administration Act 1992, followed by section number.
Art	Article number (See EC/38/2004).
CBA	The Social Security Contributions and Benefits Act 1992, followed by section number.
CPR	The Housing Benefit and Council Tax Benefit (Consequential Provisions) Regulations 2006, SI No. 217, followed by the regulation number.
CTB	The Council Tax Benefit Regulations 2006 (as amended), SI No. 215 followed by regulation number.
CTB60+	The Council Tax Benefit (Persons who have attained the age for state pension credit) Regulations 2006 (as amended), SI No. 216, followed by regulation number.
CPSA	The Child Support, Pensions and Social Security Act, followed by the section number.
DAR	The Housing Benefit and Council Tax Benefit (Decisions and Appeals) Regulations 2001, SI No. 1002, (as amended), followed by the regulation number.
DAR99	The Social Security and Child Support (Decisions and Appeals) Regulations 1999, SI No. 991, (as amended), followed by the regulation number.
EC/38/2004	European Community Directive 2004/38/EC, followed by article number.
HB	The Housing Benefit Regulations 2006, SI No. 214, (as amended), followed by the regulation number.
HB60+	The Housing Benefit (Persons who have attained the age for state pension credit) Regulations 2006, SI No. 214 (as amended), followed by regulation number.
IAA99	The Immigration and Asylum Act 1999, followed by the section number.

NIAA	The Social Security Administration (Northern Ireland) Act 1992, followed by the section number.
NICBA	The Social Security Contributions and Benefits (Northern Ireland) Act 1992, followed by the section number.
NICPR	The Housing Benefit and Council Tax Benefit (Consequential Provisions) Regulations (Northern Ireland) 2006, followed by the regulation number.
NICPSA	The Child Support, Pensions and Social Security Act (Northern Ireland) 2000, followed by the section number.
NIDAR	The Housing Benefit (Decisions and Appeals) Regulations (Northern Ireland) 2001 SR No. 213 (as amended), followed by regulation number.
NIDAR99	The Social Security and Child Support (Decisions and Appeals) Regulations (Northern Ireland) 1999 SR No. 162 (as amended), followed by regulation number.
NIHB	The Housing Benefit Regulations (Northern Ireland) 2006, followed by regulation number.
NIHB60+	The Housing Benefit (Persons who have attained the age for state pension credit) Regulations (Northern Ireland) 2006, followed by the regulation number.
NISR	Statutory Rules of Northern Ireland (equivalent to Statutory Instruments in GB).
NISSCPR	The Social Security Commissioners (Procedure) Regulations (Northern Ireland) 1999, SR No. 225 (as amended), followed by the regulation number.
Reg	Regulation, followed by regulation number.
ROO	In England and Wales, The Rent Officers (Housing Benefit Functions) Order 1997, SI 1984; in Scotland, The Rent Officers (Housing Benefit Functions) (Scotland) Order 1997, SI 1985; in both cases followed by article number or schedule and paragraph number.
sch	schedule.
SI	statutory instrument, followed by year and reference number (where no separate reference is given for Northern Ireland (i.e. NISR) the reference applies to the whole of the UK, in any other case GB only).

SR	statutory rules, followed by year and reference number (apply to NI only).
SSCPR	The Social Security Commissioners (Procedure) Regulations 1999, SI No. 1495 (as amended); followed by the regulation number.

2 Who is eligible for HB/CTB?

2.1 This chapter explains the basic rules about who can get HB and/or CTB. It describes:

- the basic conditions of benefit for HB/CTB claims;
- who is eligible for CTB;
- who is eligible for HB;
- what payments HB can meet; and
- 'contrived' and other lettings where HB cannot be paid.

2.2 The conditions in this chapter usually come first in the order of things an authority is likely to consider when deciding a claim. But there are other conditions – for example, the claimant must occupy the dwelling as his or her home (chapter 3), and not have too much income or capital (chapter 7).

Basic conditions for benefit

AA 1(1),(1A),(1B)
CBA 130(1),(4),
1(1),(3),(4),(5),(6),
134(1)(4)
IAA 1(1),(1A),(1B)
NICBA 129(1),
130(1),(3)

2.3 The Social Security Acts (paras 1.39-40) set out the basic conditions of entitlement to HB/CTB. To be entitled to HB/CTB the claimant must satisfy all the basic conditions set out in paragraph 2.4 in every case. The circumstances in which a claimant satisfies or is deemed to satisfy these conditions are set out in detailed regulations which it is the purpose of this guide to describe. Once an award is made, benefit will continue until the claimant no longer satisfies all of the basic conditions, at which point benefit will end (para. 17.21).

2.4 The basic conditions for HB and CTB are:

(a) for HB the claimant must satisfy the additional conditions in paragraph 2.12 and for CTB the claimant must satisfy the additional conditions in paragraph 2.8; and

(b) a valid claim has been made which includes details of any national insurance number(s) (chapter 5); and

(c) they are not a member of an excluded group (paras. 1.9, 2.9 and 2.14); and

(d) except in the case of a claim for CTB second adult rebate (chapter 8), their capital does not exceed the maximum amount (para. 13.13); and

(e) the maximum amount of benefit appropriate in their case (para 7.4) is greater than zero (i.e. the eligible rent/council tax/rates is greater than any non-dependant charges); and

(f) either:

- their income is not too high as defined by the needs of their household (para. 2.6); or
- (in the case of CTB only) they are entitled to a second adult rebate on the basis of the income of other adults who live with them (chapter 8).

2.5 The conditions for CTB are similar to HB, but with some subtle differences. For example, liability for rent mainly depends on the landlord and tenant having agreed a genuine contract, whereas liability for council tax is imposed (paras. 2.33-68 and chapter 9). These are dealt with in the guide as they arise.

2.6 A claimant's income will be deemed low enough if either:

- ◆ they are in receipt of IS/JSA(IB)/guarantee credit or treated as being in receipt of those benefits (paras. 7.5-6); or
- ◆ they have no income (para. 7.9); or
- ◆ their income is less than their applicable amount (para. 7.9);
- ◆ their income is greater than their applicable amount but by an amount which is less than the standard deduction (known as the taper) which is applied as described in paragraphs 7.10-11.

In addition in the case of HB (in Northern Ireland HB for rent only) the calculated amount of HB must be greater than or equal to the minimum amount of benefit (para. 7.12) whether or not the taper applies.

2.7 Straightforward examples of who can get HB and CTB are in table 2.1. In the public sector, HB can be awarded (as a rent rebate (paras. 1.16 and 16.14) to people renting from a council, the Northern Ireland Housing Executive, and people placed by housing authorities in 'bed and breakfast' establishments and hostels. In the private sector, HB can be awarded (as a rent allowance) to people renting from a private landlord, housing association, co-op or hostel. CTB (and in Northern Ireland HB for rates) is not dependent on tenure. Typical examples of who can get CTB (which in all cases would be awarded as a rebate) would be home owners, leaseholders, tenants, and so on.

Table 2.1: Straightforward examples of who can get HB/CTB

People who own their home	Not eligible for HB (because not liable for rent) Eligible for CTB
People in shared ownership schemes	Eligible for HB (on their rent) Eligible for CTB
People renting self-contained accommodation	Eligible for HB Eligible for CTB
People renting non-self-contained accommodation	Eligible for HB Not eligible for CTB (because not liable for council tax)

Who is eligible for CTB?

CBA 131(3) **2.8** To be eligible for main CTB, or second adult rebate, the claimant must satisfy all of the conditions in items (b) to (f) of paragraph 2.4 as well as the additional conditions referred to in item (a) of that paragraph. The additional conditions are that to be eligible for CTB the claimant must be:

- liable to pay the council tax in respect of a dwelling (para. 9.7); and
- a resident of that dwelling (para. 9.7).

EXCLUSIONS FROM CTB

2.9 The following are the main categories of people who cannot get CTB:

- owners (and other landlords) of unoccupied dwellings (para. 9.8);
- owners (and other landlords) of houses in multiple occupation (para. 9.8);
- all under-18-year-olds (para. 9.11);
- people who are severely mentally impaired (unless they are liable for council tax, which is unusual: para. 9.10-11);
- full-time students who are not liable for council tax (para. 9.10-11);
- most other full-time students (para. 21.24 – and see para. 2.11 about second adult rebate);
- certain people who are recent migrants (chapter 20).

2.10 In the first case above, the exclusion is because they are not resident in the dwelling; in the next four cases it is because they are not liable for council tax on their dwelling; and in the last two it is because CTB law specifically excludes them from eligibility.

2.11 The rules for second adult rebate differ for students. In general, students are eligible for second adult rebate even if they are not eligible for main CTB.

Who is eligible for HB?

2.12 To be eligible for HB the claimant must satisfy all of the conditions in items (b) to (f) of paragraph 2.4 as well as the additional conditions referred to in item (a) of that paragraph. The additional conditions are that to be eligible for HB the claimant must be: CBA 130(1)(a) NICBA 129(1)(a)

- liable to make payments (of rent or certain other items) in respect of a dwelling in the UK (para. 2.33); and
- living in that dwelling as his or her normal home (chapter 3).

2.13 There are numerous further rules about which payments count or do not count for the purposes of the first rule above and which determine that, in certain circumstances, a person can be treated as liable to make payments even if he or she is not so liable and conversely can treated as not being liable even if they do have a legal liability. The remainder of this chapter describes these.

EXCLUSIONS FROM HB

2.14 The following groups of claimant cannot get HB – because HB law specifically excludes them from eligibility:

- certain people who are recent migrants (chapter 20);
- most full-time students (para. 21.24);
- many under-18-year-old care leavers (see below); and
- many members of religious orders (see below).

CARE LEAVERS AGED UNDER 18

2.15 The following rules apply, under section 6 of the Children (Leaving Care) Act 2000 (in Northern Ireland, section 6 of the Children (Leaving Care) Act (Northern Ireland) 2002), to 16-year-olds and 17-year-olds who have left local authority care (see para. 2.18 for differences in the four UK countries as to who is deemed to be a care leaver). In such cases the responsibility for maintenance and accommodation falls with the social services authority. There is no equivalent rule for CTB as persons aged under 18-years cannot be liable for council tax. SI 2001 No 2189 SI 2001 No 2874 SI 2004 No 747 SI 2004 No 1732 NISR 2005 No 221

2.16 Except where the circumstances in paragraph 2.18 apply, a person is not eligible for HB if he or she is aged 16 or 17 and:

- has been looked after (in Scotland only, looked after and 'accommodated') by the social services authority for a period or periods amounting to at least 13 weeks beginning after they reached the age of 14 and ending after they reached the age of 16; or
- in England, Wales and Northern Ireland only, was not subject to a care order at the time they became 16 because of being in hospital or being detained in a remand centre, a young offenders institution or a secure training centre or any other institution as the result of a court order; and immediately beforehand they had been looked after by a local authority for a period or periods amounting to at least 13 weeks which began after they reached the age of 14.

2.17 In calculating the 13 week periods (in all four countries), no account should be taken of any time during which the child was looked after by social services in certain pre-planned short-term placements (respite care). To qualify each such placement must not exceed four weeks and at the end of it the child must be returned to the care of his or her parent (or the person who has parental responsibility). In Scotland only, whether a person has been 'accommodated' includes instances where the person has been placed under a supervision requirement following a children's hearing.

2.18 The above exclusion from HB does not apply, however, if the following circumstances apply:

- in England, Wales and Northern Ireland to anyone who lived with someone under a family placement for a continuous period of six months or more unless the family placement broke down and the child ceased to live with the person concerned. This rule applies whether the period of six months commenced before or after the child ceased to be looked after by the local authority;
- in Scotland the authorities have placed the young person with their family. Family in this instance includes any person aged at least 18 or who was looking after them before they went into care; or
- SI 2004 No 747 Reg (2)(2)(c) — in Scotland to a care leaver who left care before 1st April 2004. These persons will still be entitled to benefit in the normal way.
- NISR 2005 No 324 Reg 2(2) — in Northern Ireland a care leaver who left care before 1st September 2005. These persons will still be entitled to benefit in the normal way.

MEMBERS OF CERTAIN RELIGIOUS ORDERS

2.19 Members of a religious order are not eligible for HB if they are maintained fully by that order. Monks and nuns in enclosed orders are excluded under this provision. The DWP (GM A3.42) points out that members of religious communities (as opposed to religious orders) are often eligible for HB since they frequently do paid work or retain their own possessions. The reason there is no similar exclusion from CTB is that the council tax bill goes to the owner in such cases.

HB 9(1)(j)
HB60+ 9(1)(j)
NIHB 9(1)(j)
NIHB60+ 9(1)(j)

Which housing costs can HB meet?

2.20 HB is available towards a claimant's 'eligible rent'. As explained in chapter 10, this typically includes all or part of a claimant's rent in the day-to-day sense of the word. This section describes the several special types of accommodation in relation to which there are extra rules.

CARE HOMES AND INDEPENDENT HOSPITALS

2.21 Except for claimants who are transitionally protected (para. 2.23) residents of 'care homes' and 'independent hospitals' are not eligible for HB. In Scotland the equivalent institutions are known as the 'care home service' and 'independent healthcare service' and in Northern Ireland 'residential care homes', 'nursing homes' and 'independent hospitals'. See paragraphs 3.21-22 and 3.32-34 where residence is unlikely to be permanent.

HB 2(1), 9(1)(k),(4)
HB60+ 9(1)(k),(4)
NIHB
2(1), 9(1)(k),(4)
NIHB60+ 9(1)(k),(4

LOCAL AUTHORITY 'PART III' RESIDENTIAL ACCOMMODATION

2.22 People provided with residential accommodation by social services provided under Part III of the National Assistance Act 1948 (in Scotland, section 59 of the Social Work (Scotland) Act 1968, in Northern Ireland article 15 of the Health and Personal Social Services (Northern Ireland) Order 1972), sometimes referred to as 'Part III' accommodation, are not eligible for HB as this type of accommodation falls within the definition of care home or independent hospital (para. 2.21). The same transitional protection applies as to other care home residents (para. 2.23).

TRANSITIONALLY PROTECTED CARE HOME RESIDENTS

2.23 The following claimants in 'care homes' and 'independent hospitals' (para. 2.21) or their equivalent Scottish or Northern Irish institutions are transitionally protected and remain entitled to HB:

CPR sch 3 para 9
NICPR sch 3 para 9

- People who were eligible for HB on 29th October 1990 remain eligible for HB while resident in any type of care home, including if they move between homes.

- People in remunerative work (paras. 7.29-34) who were eligible for HB on 31st March 1993 remain eligible for HB until they move (other than temporarily) or until HB ceases for any reason.
- People paying a commercial rent to a close relative (para. 2.40) who were eligible for HB in respect of a care home on 31st March 1993 remain eligible for HB until they move (other than temporarily) or until HB ceases for any reason.
- Except in Scotland, claimants are eligible for HB if they are in a small home not required to register under the Care Standards Act 2000 or that has been refused registration.
- Claimants are eligible for HB while resident in a care home which does not have to be registered because it is managed or provided by a body created by an Act of Parliament or incorporated by Royal Charter – such as the Salvation Army or Royal British Legion (GM A4.104).

HOUSING COSTS MET THROUGH IS/JSA(IB)

HB 11(2),(4)
NIHB 11(1),(4)

2.24 Claimants whose accommodation costs are included in their income IS/JSA(IB) are excluded from help through the HB scheme. The main examples are home owners (para. 2.25), Crown tenants (para. 2.30) and payments for a tent and its pitch. Where a person on HB becomes eligible for help with their housing costs through IS/JSA(IB) for the first time (e.g. if they buy their home) then HB can continue for a further four weeks following the IS/JSA(IB) award

OWNER-OCCUPIERS AND LONG LEASEHOLDERS

HB 2(1) 12(2)(a),(c)
HB60+
2(1) 12(2)(a),(c)
NIHB
2(1) 13(2)(a)
NIHB60+
2(1) 13(2)(a)

2.25 Owner occupiers and, except where para. 2.26 applies, long leaseholders (leaseholders whose lease was for more than 21 years) are not eligible for HB (though mortgage repayments, ground rent and service charges can be met through IS/JSA(IB)/guarantee credit). This also applies to those who have the right to sell the freehold only with the consent of other joint owners.

HOUSING ASSOCIATION SHARED OWNERSHIP AND CO-OWNERSHIP SCHEMES

HB 2(1)
12(2)(a),(b)
HB60+ 2(1)
12(2)(a),(b)

2.26 In Great Britain, the following rules apply in relation shared ownership and co-ownership schemes:

- Equity sharers buying part of their home from a housing association (or a housing authority) and renting the other part under a shared ownership scheme are eligible for HB on the rental element (and their mortgage interest payments can be met through IS/JSA(IB)/guarantee credit);
- payments under a co-ownership scheme are not eligible for HB. A co-ownership scheme is one in which the tenant is a member of the

association, who on ceasing to be a member of the association, will be entitled to a payment related to the value of the home. Note however, the position of tenants of housing co-operatives (para. 2.27).

CO-OP TENANTS

2.27 Co-operative tenants are eligible for HB for their rent provided they have no more than a nominal equity share in the property.

HB 12(1)
HB60+ 12(1)
NIHB 13(1)
NIHB60+ 13(1)

HIRE PURCHASE, CREDIT SALE AND CONDITIONAL SALE AGREEMENTS

2.28 The following payments are not eligible for help under the HB scheme:

HB 12(2)(d)
HB60+ 12(2)(d)
NIHB 13(2)(b)
NIHB60+ 13(2)(b)

- a hire purchase agreement (for example to buy a mobile home);
- a credit sale agreement; or
- a conditional sale agreement unless it is for land. Conditional sale agreements are agreements for the sales of goods or land under which the purchase price is payable by instalments and the goods or land remain the seller's until the instalments are paid.

RENTAL PURCHASE AGREEMENTS

2.29 Payments under a rental purchase scheme are eligible for HB. A rental purchase agreement is one in which the whole or part of the purchase price is paid in instalments over a specified period of time and completion of the sale is deferred until the final instalment of a specified amount of the purchase price has been paid (GM A4.41).

HB 12(1)(i)
HB60+ 12(1)(i)
NIHB 13(1)(h)
NIHB60+ 13(1)(h)

CROWN TENANTS

2.30 In Great Britain Crown tenants are excluded from HB. In Northern Ireland this applies only to tenants of Ministry of Defence property. A Crown tenant is a person whose home is occupied under a tenancy or licence agreement where the owner is the Crown or a government department. This exclusion applies even where the landlord employs a managing agent such as a housing association (GM A8.30). However, certain occupiers of Crown property do not count as Crown tenants (para. 2.33) and so are eligible for HB.

HB 2(1) 12(2)(e)
HB60+ 2(1) 12(2)(e)
NIHB 2(1) 13(2)(c)
NIHB60+ 2(1) 13(2)(c)

2.31 Crown tenants can get IS/JSA(IB)/guarantee credit towards their rent. If they do not qualify for IS/JSA(IB)/guarantee credit, they may qualify for rent rebates under voluntary schemes established by their landlords. Authorities often administer these schemes, but the schemes are quite separate from HB itself (GM A8.60-67).

OCCUPIERS OF CROWN PROPERTY WHO ARE ENTITLED

HB 2(1)
HB60+ 2(1)
NIHB 2(1)
NIHB60+ 2(1)

2.32 Despite the exclusion in paragraph 2.30, the following occupiers of Crown property are entitled to HB:

- tenants and licensees of the Duchies of Cornwall and Lancaster are eligible for HB (GM A8.95-96);
- tenants and licensees of properties managed by the Crown Estate Commissioners;
- former Crown tenants and licensees whose agreement to occupy a Crown property has been terminated but who are continuing to occupy against the wishes of their landlord are eligible for HB (because they are no longer a tenant). The occupier must be liable to pay mesne or violent profits – for further guidance see GM A8.90-94.

Liability to pay rent

CBA 130(1)(a)
NICBA 129(1)(a)
HB 8(1)(a)
NIHB 8(1)(a)
NIHB60+ 8(1)(a)

2.33 The general rule is that a claimant is eligible for HB only if he or she is liable (has a legal obligation or duty) to pay rent for the home.

THE NATURE OF LIABILITY FOR RENT

2.34 Liability for rent can arise whether or not there is a written agreement (GM A3.10): it can arise by word of mouth alone *(R v Poole Borough Council ex p Ross)*. The landlord must have the right to grant the tenancy in the first place, and must have the intention of repossessing the property if the claimant does not pay rent. It is not possible in law to grant a tenancy to oneself, nor can liability arise under a tenancy 'granted' to someone who already has the right to occupy the property in question. In the second case, for example, if a couple are joint owners of a property and one leaves, the other has the right to occupy all of it, so the absent one cannot 'grant' a tenancy to the present one. Several further points are mentioned in the following paragraphs.

2.35 Certain people, such as those with learning difficulties, may appear unable to enter into a liability. Nonetheless, someone formally appointed to act for them, such as a receiver appointed by the Court of Protection, can enter into a liability on that individual's behalf. According to the common law a person aged under 18 can enter into a legally binding contract for goods and services which are 'necessities' (e.g. food, clothing, shelter) so a young person can have a legal liability to pay rent. Determining liability may become complex when the person is assisted by a social services department.

HB 8(1)(b)-(e),(2)
HB60+ 8(1)(b)-(e),(2)
NIHB 8(1)(b)-(e),(2)
NIHB60+ 8(1)(b)-(e),(2)

TREATING A CLAIMANT AS LIABLE EVEN WHEN HE OR SHE IS NOT

2.36 Any of the following, even if not liable to pay rent, are treated by law as liable, and are therefore eligible for HB:

- the partner of the liable person (including the partner of a full-time student who is not eligible for HB: para. 21.26);
- a former partner of the liable person who has to make the payments in order to continue to live in the home because the liable person (whether a natural person or a corporation: CH/3013/2003) is not doing so;
- anyone who has to make the payments if he or she is to continue to live in the home because the liable person is not making the payments and the authority considers it reasonable to treat him or her as liable to make those payments;
- a person whose liability is waived by the landlord as reasonable compensation for repairs or redecoration work actually carried out by the tenant – but only up to a maximum of eight benefit weeks in respect of any one waiver;
- someone who has actually met his or her liability before claiming.

2.37 Where the rent is varied either during an award or retrospectively, the claimant is treated as liable for the revised amount due.

'CONTRIVED' LETTINGS AND OTHER EXCLUSIONS FROM HB

2.38 The remainder of this chapter describes the circumstances in which a claimant cannot get HB, even though he or she is in fact liable for rent. The law does this by saying the claimant is treated as not liable to make the payments.

Examples: Treated as liable to pay rent

A claimant has been deserted by her partner. Although she is not the tenant the landlord will allow her to remain in the property if she continues to pay the rent. She should be treated as liable if her former partner is not paying the rent.

A claimant is the son of a council tenant. He takes over responsibility for paying rent while his father is working abroad for two years. The son should be treated as liable if it is reasonable to do so.

LANDLORD A CLOSE RELATIVE RESIDING IN THE DWELLING

2.39 Where the claimant's landlord is a 'close relative' (para. 2.40) of the claimant, or of the claimant's partner, and the landlord also resides in the dwelling (para. 2.42), the claimant is not eligible for HB. HB 9(1)(b) HB60+ 9(1)(b) NIHB 9(1)(b) NIHB60+ 9(1)(b)

WHO COUNTS AS A CLOSE RELATIVE?

2.40 A 'close relative' is: HB 2(1) HB60+ 2(1) NIHB 2(1) NIHB60+ 2(1)

- a parent, step-parent or parent-in-law; or

- brother or sister; or
- son, son-in-law, daughter, daughter-in-law, step-son, step-daughter; or
- the partner of any of the above.

2.41 Arguably the term 'brother' and 'sister' should be taken to include 'half-brothers' and 'half-sisters' (GM A3.33-34) (following Commissioner's decision *R(SB) 22/87*). 'Step-brothers' and 'step-sisters' are not treated as close relatives for HB purposes (HB/CTB A27/97 para. 4).

WHAT DOES 'RESIDES IN' MEAN?

2.42 Before January 1999 (when the law changed) this rule referred to a claimant who 'resided with' the landlord, intentionally making this the same as the definition used in relation to non-dependants (para. 4.45). The rule now refers to the landlord 'residing in' the dwelling. The DWP did not intend this apparent drafting error (Circular A1/99, para. 13), and it seems safe to assume that the definition of 'resides with' (para. 4.45) also applies here.

NON-COMMERCIAL AGREEMENTS

HB 9(1)(a),(2)
HB60+ 9(1)(a),(2)
NIHB 9(1)(a),(2)
NIHB60+ 9(1)(a),(2)

2.43 A claimant is not eligible for HB if the agreement under which he or she occupies the dwelling is not on a commercial basis. What constitutes a 'commercial basis' is not defined in the regulations but the authority must have regard to whether the agreement contains terms which are not enforceable at law in determining whether or not it is a commercial one.

2.44 In *R v Sheffield CC HBRB ex parte Smith and others,* it was held that the authority must not only consider the amount payable for the accommodation but also the other terms of the agreement. The important factor is whether the arrangements are at 'arm's length' or more akin to the arrangements that would exist between close relatives who generally only make contributions to their keep or household running costs. Similarly, in *R v Sutton London Borough Council ex parte Partridge,* it was held that what is 'commercial' is not necessarily confined to the financial relationship. In *R v Poole Borough Council ex parte Ross,* it was held that absence of a written tenancy agreement does not itself mean there is no liability to make payments, and that an element of friendship between the parties does not itself make it non-commercial. And in *Campbell and Others v South Northamptonshire District Council and Another,* it was held that it was not an infringement of the right to freedom of religion to take into account claimants' manifestations of their religious belief when determining the factual question of whether their tenancy was on a commercial basis. Religious reasons could not turn that which was non-commercial into that which was. Similarly, friendliness between the parties cannot change a commercial agreement into a non-commercial one (*CH/4854/2003*).

FORMER FOSTER CHILDREN; DISABILITY-RELATED LETTINGS

2.45 More specifically, the DWP has advised that an arrangement that involves a former foster child remaining in his or her foster accommodation and paying rent once the fostering allowance ceases, for example where the foster child reaches the age of 18, should not normally be treated as a non-commercial arrangement (HB/CTB A30/95 para. 17 iv).

2.46 Similar considerations can apply to disability-related lettings. In *CH/296/2003,* the landlord was the father of the tenant who lived at the same address in a self-contained flat, and suffered from Asperger's syndrome and autism, and could live independently with support. The commissioner held that, while a family arrangement may be indicative that an arrangement is not commercial, it is one factor and is not decisive. The fact that the landlord might not evict but might accept a lower rent if HB was not awarded, was not evidence of non-commerciality. It might be bowing to the inevitable. The tribunal did not place enough weight on items such as these but overemphasised the care and support aspects of the arrangements. The Commissioner made his own finding of fact that the letting was not non-commercial.

CONTRIVED LIABILITIES

2.47 A claimant is not eligible for HB if the authority is satisfied that his or her liability was created to take advantage of the HB scheme. This is commonly referred to as a 'contrived' letting. General DWP guidance on this is in GM paragraphs A3.81-92.

HB 9(1)(l)
HB60+ 9(1)(l)
NIHB 9(1)(l)
NIHB60+ 9(1)(l)

2.48 In *R v Solihull MBC HBRB ex parte Simpson* the Court considered that while the ability to attract HB could never realistically be the sole purpose of a tenancy, equally, and importantly, anyone eligible for HB must, by definition, have entered into an agreement to pay a rent which he could not afford. The mere fact of having done so could not of itself, except perhaps in extreme cases, be evidence of an arrangement entered in order to take advantage of the scheme. A similar point was made in *R v Sutton LBC HBRB ex parte Keegan.* The judge quashed the review board's decision not to award HB because 'it had attached a wholly disproportionate weight to the fact that the claimant could not meet her liability to pay rent'.

2.49 In the Sutton case the judge considered that before an agreement could be said to be 'contrived' the means, circumstances and intentions of the claimant and the landlord must be considered. In particular, consideration should be given to the consequences if HB is not to be paid. If it seems likely that the landlord will have to ask the claimant to leave the dwelling so that it can be re-let or sold, this is evidence that the liability has not been created to take advantage of the scheme.

2.50 In the Solihull case it was held that 'an arrangement whereby persons, who would in any event be eligible for HB, were provided with accommodation by a parent or relation who was then to receive rent generated from HB was not of itself an arrangement created to take advantage of the HB scheme'.

2.51 *R v Manchester CC ex parte Baragrove Properties* provides an example of the sort of extreme case envisaged in the Solihull judgment. In this case the authority was found to have acted correctly in interpreting the rule as permitting exclusion from HB entitlement cases where landlords were specifically charging higher rents to vulnerable tenants and where the authority could not use its powers to restrict the eligible rent (para. 10.58).

2.52 In *CSHB/718/2002,* the Commissioner emphasised the need for clarity in deciding why someone is not eligible for HB. There is a difference between not being liable for rent at all (paras. 2.33-34) and being liable in a way that was created to take advantage of the scheme. The claimant rented from his mother who was for all or part of the time in a nursing home. He did not pay any of the HB he received to his mother. The council said his tenancy was created to take advantage of the scheme. The Commissioner quashed this decision and directed a rehearing because the authority had failed to consider whether the claimant was disentitled by not being liable in the first place, and also failed to look at whether the intention to abuse the scheme existed at the time the agreement was created (he did not claim HB for the first three years of the tenancy).

RENTING A FORMER JOINT HOME FROM AN EX-PARTNER

HB 9(1)(c)
HB60+ 9(1)(c)
NIHB 9(1)(c)
NIHB60+ 9(1)(c)

2.53 Where a married or unmarried couple separate and the one remaining in the home, or a new partner, makes payments to the one who has left, the person making the payments is not eligible for HB.

2.54 In *R (Painter) v Carmarthenshire County Council HBRB,* Mr Painter had originally been a lodger renting a bedroom and with the right to use the common parts. He subsequently formed a relationship with his landlady and moved into her room and jointly occupied the accommodation. The relationship ended and Mr Painter reverted back to a tenant and was liable to make payments of rent. The authority decided that Mr Painter was not eligible for HB because he was renting a former joint home from an ex-partner. It was argued that this rule only applied if the dwelling in respect of which the payments were due was the same dwelling which had been occupied during the relationship. Mr Painter submitted that the dwelling was in fact different. It no longer included the landlady's room. Additionally it was argued that if the regulation was applicable, it was incompatible with the Human Rights Act 1998. The Court held that the informal arrangements to occupy separate rooms did not affect the reality of the situation that the dwelling remained the same. It also held that there had been no breach of the Convention rights. Any discrimination was justifiable as a precaution against potential abuse of the housing benefit scheme.

RESPONSIBILITY FOR THE LANDLORD'S CHILD

2.55 A claimant is not eligible for HB if he or she is responsible, or a partner is responsible, for the landlord's child (i.e. someone under the age of 16). The DWP (GM A3.54) emphasises that 'responsibility for a child' means more than 'cares for'. HB 9(1)(d) HB60+9(1)(d) NIHB 9(1)(d) NIHB60+ 9(1)(d)

2.56 This is a difficult rule to interpret as it blurs certain established concepts so far as means-tested benefits are concerned. It would appear to apply where the 'landlord' is the biological mother or father of a child, or has adopted a child, but where the child is nevertheless considered to be part of the claimant's family for JSA(IB), IS or HB purposes. The legality of this rule and the argument that it offended the Human Rights Convention was argued in *R v Secretary of State for Social Security, ex parte Tucker.* The Court held that the rule was not *ultra vires* nor contrary to the European Convention on Human Rights.

TRUSTS

2.57 A trust is an arrangement under which property is transferred to one or more people known as trustees. Trustees are required to look after the property or deal with it for the benefit of someone else, 'the beneficiary', or for some other purpose such as that of a charity.

RENTING FROM A TRUST OF WHICH ONE IS A TRUSTEE OR BENEFICIARY

2.58 A claimant is not eligible for HB if his or her landlord is a trustee of a trust of which one of the following is a trustee or a beneficiary: HB 9(1)(e),(3) HB60+ 9(1)(e),(3) NIHB 9(1)(e),(3) NIHB60+ 9(1)(e),(3)

- the claimant or partner; or
- the claimant's or partner's close relative (para. 3.31) if the close relative 'resides with' (para. 4.45) the claimant; or
- the claimant's, or partner's, former partner,

unless in each case the claimant satisfies the authority that the liability was not intended to take advantage of the HB scheme.

RENTING FROM A TRUST OF WHICH ONE'S CHILD IS A BENEFICIARY

2.59 A claimant is not eligible for HB if his or her landlord is a trustee of a trust of which the claimant's or partner's child is a beneficiary. Unlike in the previous paragraph, this rule has no exception. HB 9(1)(f) HB60+ 9(1)(f) NIHB 9(1)(f) NIHB60+ 9(1)(f)

RENTING FROM A COMPANY OF WHICH ONE IS A DIRECTOR OR AN EMPLOYEE

HB 9(1)(e),(3)
HB60+ 9(1)(e),(3)
NIHB 9(1)(e),(3)
NIHB60+ 9(1)(e),(3)

2.60 A claimant is not eligible for HB if his or her landlord is a company of which one of the following is a director or an employee:

- the claimant or partner; or
- the claimant's or partner's close relative (para. 2.40) if the close relative 'resides with' (para. 2.42) the claimant; or
- the claimant's, or partner's, former partner;

unless in each case the claimant satisfies the authority that the liability was not intended to take advantage of the HB scheme. Note also that this rule does not apply if a claimant is employed by a company and rents from a director of the company (since a director is not the company itself).

2.61 The DWP advises (GM para. A3.56) that a 'company' means a registered company. This can be checked with Companies House and, if the company is registered in England, Scotland or Wales, this can be done on-line at *www.companies-house.gov.uk* – for a small fee (normally £1.00).

FORMER NON-DEPENDANTS

HB 9(1)(g),(3)
HB60+ 9(1)(g),(3)
NIHB 9(1)(g),(3)
NIHB60+ 9(1)(g),(3)

2.62 A claimant is not eligible for HB if:

- he or she was, at any time prior to the creation of the rent liability, a non-dependant of someone who resided in the dwelling; and
- that person continues to reside in the dwelling,

unless the claimant satisfies the authority that the liability was not intended to take advantage of the HB scheme.

FORMER OWNERS

HB 9(1)(h)
HB60+ 9(1)(h)
NIHB 9(1)(h)
NIHB60+ 9(1)(h)

2.63 A claimant is not eligible for HB if:

- he or she, or a partner, previously owned the dwelling; and
- owned it within the last five years,

unless the claimant is able to satisfy the authority that he or she or a partner could not have continued to live in the dwelling without letting go of ownership.

2.64 This could be the case, for example, if a claimant is able to provide evidence that a mortgage lender would have sought possession unless the liable person had agreed to the transfer of the property and the establishment of a rental agreement; or if a housing association agrees to take over ownership of a property and take on the ex-owner as a tenant (these arrangements are generally referred to as mortgage rescue schemes – see GM A3.67-71). However, authorities are entitled to examine what other options a claimant might have had, such as getting work to finance the mortgage, taking in a tenant, etc *(CH/1586/2004)*. In each case the authority will need to obtain from the former owner an explanation of his or her reasons for giving up ownership of the property (GM A3.67-71).

TIED ACCOMMODATION

2.65 A claimant is not eligible for HB if his or her, or a partner's, occupation of the dwelling is a condition of employment by the landlord.

HB 9(1)(i)
HB60+ 9(1)(i)
NIHB 9(1)(i)
NIHB60+ 9(1)(i)

2.66 The DWP advises (GM A3.76) that this test should not be taken to mean 'as a result of the employment'. A retired employee, for example, may continue to live in previously tied accommodation but this would no longer be as a condition of employment by the landlord, and so this rule would not prevent eligibility for HB.

ILLEGAL AND UNLAWFUL TENANCIES AND SUB TENANCIES

2.67 Sub-tenancies which are created in breach of a clause in the head lease not to sublet or assign the tenancy do not prevent the assignment or sub-letting from being valid between the head tenant and sub-tenant: *Governors of Peabody Donation Fund v Higgins* (not a HB case). Such lettings are unlawful rather than illegal and expose the head tenant to eviction for breach of the agreement. Given that there is a legal liability for rent it seems that these lettings are eligible for HB, unless it is also a letting to which paragraphs 2.38-66 above apply.

2.68 An illegal letting is one in which its creation would necessarily involve committing a criminal offence. An example would be where a landlord lets a dwelling which he or she knows is in contravention of a Housing Act prohibition order. In contrast to unlawful contracts, illegal contracts are generally not binding (see *A Casebook on Contract,* Ninth Edition, J.C. Smith) and so would not be eligible for HB. Where a letting was not illegal at the time it was created (e.g. prior to a closing order) it seems likely it would remain binding until the end of the next rental period, or if let on a fixed term at the end of the fixed term.

3 Occupying the home, absences and moves

3.1 One of the main conditions for getting HB is that the claimant must be treated as occupying the accommodation in question as his or her home. This chapter explains this, and covers

- what it means to occupy somewhere as a home for HB purposes;
- when HB can be awarded on two homes;
- when a claimant can get HB before moving in;
- when a claimant can get HB on an old home when they have no current liability on which they may claim HB;
- how HB and CTB work when the claimant is temporarily absent.

3.2 This chapter does not apply to CTB – except for the rules about temporary absence (para. 3.31). Instead, the equivalent condition for getting CTB is that the claimant must be resident in his or her dwelling (para. 2.8). In practice this usually means the same thing as the HB condition mentioned above. There are no rules about two homes and moving home in CTB. CTB can be awarded on only one home at a time.

HB: occupation as a home

CBA 130(1)(a)
NICBA 129(1)(a)
HB 7(1)
HB60+ 7(1)
NIHB 7(1)
NIHB60+ 7(1)

3.3 HB can only be awarded on accommodation that the claimant is treated as occupying as a home. Accommodation occupied only for a holiday or business purposes is not a home and therefore is not eligible. Except as described later in this chapter, HB is usually only payable on one home – the home the claimant 'normally occupies' or if a member of a family 'normally occupies' with their family (CH/2521/2002). In certain specific circumstances however, such as where statutory overcrowding would arise, the 'dwelling occupied as the home' might comprise more than one building (*Secretary of State for Work and Pensions v Miah R(JSA)9/03* see para 3.25). The rules in this section do not apply to CTB (para. 3.2).

3.4 The general rule is that 'occupying' a home means more than simply being liable for rent: it means being physically present. An exception was made in CH/2957/2004. In that case the claimant, aged 87, had terminated her former tenancy and her family had moved her furniture and possessions into her new home, but the claimant was unable to move in because she was taken ill at the last minute. The Commissioner held that in these circumstances the claimant should be treated as 'normally occupying' the new home.

Doubts about a claimant's occupation of the dwelling can often arise as a result of residency checks by an authority's visiting/fraud officers. If there is any doubt as to whether or not the claimant occupies the dwelling, the authority should consider all the relevant evidence before determining this matter.

3.5 In considering which home the claimant normally occupies, the authority must have regard to any other dwelling occupied by the claimant or family, no matter whether it is here or abroad. The DWP advises (GM para. A3.126) that this requirement is not intended to exclude from eligibility someone who has set up home in this country but whose family, no longer being part of his or her household, remain abroad. Further specific rules are given in the remainder of this chapter. HB 7(2) HB60+ 7(2) NIHB 7(2) HB60+ 7(2)

HB: moving home and having two homes

3.6 There are several different rules about what happens when someone moves home or has two homes; in only some of these cases is the claimant eligible for HB on two homes at a time. The rules are very specific. This section does not apply at all to CTB (para. 3.2). It is never possible to get CTB on more than one dwelling at a time.

CLAIMANTS WHO HAVE MOVED BUT REMAIN LIABLE FOR RENT AT THEIR OLD HOME

3.7 A claimant moving from one rented dwelling to another rented dwelling is eligible for HB on both of them – but only if all three of the following conditions are met: HB 7(6)(d) HB60+ 7(6)(d) NIHB 7(6)(d) NIHB60+ 7(6)(d)

- only for the period after he or she has moved into the new dwelling;
- only if his or her liability for rent on both dwellings could not reasonably have been avoided; and
- only for up to four weeks.

This is the 'two homes' version of the rule (for the 'one home' version, see para. 3.9). It is often called the overlapping HB rule. For how HB is calculated in such cases see paragraph 3.29. Note that the rule does not apply when a claimant moves out for repairs to be done (para. 3.23).

3.8 This 'two homes' version of the rule applies, for example, where a claimant in housing need is offered at short notice an appropriate new tenancy and is obliged to take up liability for the new tenancy before the period of notice required by the landlord of the old home has expired. HB is only payable on both properties during this period, however, if the claimant has a liability for and has actually moved into the new property whilst having a liability to make payments on the old home. If the claimant is still in fact occupying and liable to make payments on the old home then the fact that he or she has a liability on the new home and may have transferred some items of furniture does not mean that he or she has met the test of having 'moved into' the new home. In such instances HB is only payable on the old home, not the new home.

HB 7(7) HB60+ 7(7) NIHB 7(7) NIHB60+ 7(7)

3.9 Similarly, since 4th October 2004, a claimant moving from a rented dwelling to a non-rented dwelling is eligible for HB on the one he or she has left – but only if all three of the following conditions are met:

- only for the period after he or she has moved into the new dwelling;
- only if his or her liability for rent on that former dwelling could not reasonably have been avoided; and
- only for up to four weeks.

This is the 'one home' version of the rule (for the 'two homes' version, see para. 3.7). It could apply when the claimant moves from a rented home to one he or she owns, or to a care home, or to live with parents, or to a prison following sentencing, and so on. In particular, in the case of moving to a care home, this rule can apply following an award of HB during a trial period (para. 3.32 and the example nearby).

3.10 For many years, the DWP has suggested (in relation to the 'two homes' version of the rule) that it should only be used in 'exceptional circumstances' (GM A3.330). There is no such test in the law. The question of whether something is '(un)exceptional' is obviously different from the question of whether something is '(un)reasonable', and it is surprising to find such questionable guidance persisting for so long. Though in considering whether liability for rent could reasonably have been avoided the authority may look at what alternatives were open to the claimant *(CH/4546/2002),* that does not change the test of what is reasonable into what is exceptional.

3.11 For both versions of the rule, there is no legal requirement for a separate claim to be made for HB for the period in question. That said, the authority does, of course, need information and evidence that enable it to identify that the conditions of the rules are met (for example, that there remains a liability at the old address, and that it could not reasonably have been avoided).

CLAIMANTS WHO HAVE MOVED BECAUSE OF FEAR OF VIOLENCE

HB 7(6)(a) HB60+ 7(6)(a) NIHB 7(6)(a) NIHB60+ 7(6)(a)

3.12 A claimant is eligible for HB on two rented homes for up to 52 weeks if he or she:

- has left and remains absent from the former home through fear of violence
  - in the home, or

  - by a person who was formerly a member of the claimant's family; and
- has an intention to return to it; and
- is liable for rent on both that home and where he or she is now living; and
- it is reasonable to meet the rent on both homes.

3.13 For how HB is calculated in such cases see paragraph 3.29. If the claimant does not intend to return to the old dwelling, the previous rule applies instead (allowing HB to be paid on both for only four weeks: para. 3.7). If he or she is liable for rent on the old dwelling but not the new one, the rule about absences from home – described in paragraphs 3.32, 3.34 and table 3.1 – applies instead.

HB 7(10)
HB60+ 7(10)
NIHB 7(10)
NIHB60+ 7(10)

3.14 Actual violence need not have occurred for the rule to apply. The claimant has only to be afraid of violence occurring. If the authority considers, however, that the fear of violence is one that is not reasonably held (CH/1237/2004, para. 18) or that the claimant brought it upon himself or herself, it may consider it unreasonable that HB should be paid in respect of both homes.

3.15 The feared violence in the home need not be related to a family or former family member. It could be related to anyone, e.g. a neighbour, so long as it is feared that violence could occur in the home. Where the fear is of violence outside the home it must be a former member of the claimant's family who poses the threat of violence. This would include not only an ex-partner but also an adult child. On the other hand, it is of course the case that someone who is afraid of violence outside the home may well be afraid of it coming into the home.

3.16 Authorities are advised to check regularly that the claimant intends to return to the previous home (GM A3.301). If the claimant subsequently decides not to return, HB on the former home stops. The HB paid on the former home while the claimant had the intention to return will have been properly paid and is not an overpayment (GM A3.302).

CLAIMANTS WAITING FOR ADAPTATIONS FOR A DISABILITY

3.17 If a claimant becomes liable for rent on a new dwelling, but does not move into it straight away because they are necessarily waiting for it to be adapted to meet their disablement needs or those of a family member (para. 4.7), the claimant is eligible for HB for up to four weeks before moving in, so long as the delay in moving is reasonable.

HB 7(6)(e)
HB60+ 7(6)(e)
NIHB 7(6)(e)
NIHB60+ 7(6)(e)

3.18 In this case, if the claimant is also liable for rent on their old home, they are eligible for HB on both homes during those four weeks. For how HB is calculated in such cases, see paragraph 3.29. Whether in the case of HB for one home or two, HB can be awarded only after the claimant has moved in and the claim must be made promptly: paragraph 3.30.

HB 7(8)(c)(i)
HB60+ 7(8)(c)(i)
NIHB 7(8)(c)(i)
NIHB60+ 7(8)(c)(i)

CLAIMANTS WAITING FOR A SOCIAL FUND PAYMENT

HB 7(8)(c)(ii)
HB60+ 7(8)(c)(ii)
NIHB 7(8)(c)(ii)
NIHB60+ 7(8)(c)(ii)

3.19 If a claimant becomes liable for rent on a new dwelling, but does not move into it straight away because he or she:

- has applied for a social fund payment to help with the move or with setting up home; and
- is aged 60 or more, or has a child aged under 6, or someone in the family is disabled in one of the ways relevant to a disability premium or disabled child premium,

the claimant is eligible for HB for up to four weeks before moving in, so long as the delay in moving is reasonable.

3.20 In this case, the claimant is not eligible for HB on his or her old home as well – a feature of the rule that has been criticized frequently over the years as discriminating against someone moving from a furnished rented home to his or her first unfurnished rented home. HB can be awarded only after the claimant has moved in and the claim must be made promptly: paragraph 3.30.

CLAIMANTS WAITING TO LEAVE HOSPITAL OR A CARE HOME

HB 7(8)(c)(iii)
HB60+ 7(8)(c)(iii)
NIHB 7(8)(c)(iii)
NIHB60+ 7(8)(c)(iii)

3.21 If a claimant becomes liable for rent on a new dwelling, but does not move into it straight away because they are waiting to leave a hospital, care home or independent hospital (para. 2.21), they are eligible for HB for up to four weeks before moving in, so long as the delay in moving is reasonable.

3.22 This might well arise if someone's discharge from hospital is delayed, or someone cannot immediately manage to leave a care home. HB can be awarded only after the claimant has moved in and the claim must be made promptly: paragraph 3.30.

MOVING OUT FOR REPAIRS TO BE DONE

HB 7(4)
HB60+ 7(4)
NIHB 7(4)
NIHB60+ 7(4)

3.23 A claimant who has had to leave his or her normal home while it is having essential repairs, and who has to make payments (rent or mortgage payments) on one but not both the normal home and the temporary accommodation, is treated as occupying the home for which payments made. If the payments due on that home are mortgage payments, the claimant is not eligible for HB. The other rules about moving home (above) and absences from home (below) do not apply to such claimants.

LARGE FAMILIES

HB 7(6)(c)
HB60+ 7(6)(c)
NIHB 7(6)(c)
NIHB60+ 7(6)(c)

3.24 Where the claimant's family (para. 4.7) is so large they have been housed by a housing authority in two separate dwellings, the claimant is eligible for HB on both homes. The DWP (GM para. A3.320) advises that both homes should be provided, but not necessarily owned, by the local authority. There is no time limit in this case.

3.25 Independently of the above rule, however, the Court of Appeal has held that a claimant (in what were fairly uncommon circumstances) can occupy two nearby houses as 'one home' for JSA(IB) purposes and this is strongly persuasive for HB (but not CTB): *Secretary of State for Work and Pensions v Miah, R(JSA)9/03).*

SINGLE AND LONE PARENT STUDENTS AND TRAINEES

3.26 A single claimant or lone parent who is a student or on a government training course, and who has two homes but pays rent on only one, is treated as normally occupying that one (and is thus eligible for HB on it), even if he or she in fact normally lives in the other one. HB 7(3) HB60+ 7(3) NIHB 7(3) NIHB60+ 7(3)

3.27 The training courses referred to are those provided by, or under arrangements made with or approved by, a government department, the Secretary of State, Scottish Enterprise, or Highlands and Islands Enterprise. This definition includes training courses arranged by a local authority on behalf of one of these entities. The training course may be provided by the local authority itself or the local authority may contract with an external organisation to provide the course. HB 7(18) HB60+ 7(18) NIHB 7(18) NIHB60+ 7(18)

Example: Occupation as a home

The claimant normally lives with her parents but rents accommodation whilst on a government training course. In such circumstances she should be considered as normally occupying the rented accommodation during the period she is liable to pay housing costs.

STUDENT COUPLES

3.28 A couple (para. 4.9) are eligible for HB on two homes if one is a student who personally fulfils the criteria for student eligibility for HB and the other is not a student, or if both are students each of whom personally fulfils the criteria for student eligibility for HB (table 21.1). But occupying two homes must be unavoidable and it must be reasonable to pay HB on two homes (table 21.2). There is no time limit in this case. HB 7(6)(b) HB60+ 7(6)(b) NIHB 7(6)(b) NIHB60+ 7(6)(b)

CALCULATION OF BENEFIT ON TWO HOMES

3.29 In the cases above in which HB is awarded on two homes (paras. 3.17, 3.19 and 3.21), a question that is not addressed in the law is that of how HB should be assessed. It appears that in these cases there is one benefit calculation based on the aggregated eligible rent of the two properties (GM A5.280-281), but other interpretations seem possible. Where the dwellings are in different areas, authorities need to liaise and/or establish agency arrangements (para. 1.25).

ENTITLEMENT PRIOR TO MOVING IN: PROMPT CLAIMS

HB 7(9) HB60+ 7(9) NIHB 7(9) NIHB60+ 7(9)

3.30 In the cases above in which HB is awarded before someone moves in (paras. 3.17, 3.19 and 3.21), it is necessary to claim promptly (i.e. before or in the first week of the new liability for rent – unless the claimant requests and is awarded backdated benefit (paras. 5.53-54), or the claimant or any partner is aged 60+: paras. 5.51-52). If the claim is then refused (perhaps because at that time the authority is not sure that the claimant will in fact move in), and the claimant reapplies within four weeks, the reapplication should be treated as having been made at the same time as the refused claim. And the award of HB cannot start until the claimant actually does move in.

HB and CTB: temporary absence

3.31 Claimants can, in the circumstances described in the remainder of this chapter, get HB and/or CTB even while temporarily absent from their home. In practice, the rules for HB and CTB are the same. (For a period prior to 4th April 2005 they were temporarily more generous for CTB as a result of commissioner's decision *CH/2111/2003*. From 4th April 2005, the law was amended to bring CTB back into line with HB.)

HB 7(11)-(17) HB60+ 7(11)-(17) NIHB 7(11)-(17) NIHB60+ 7(11)-(17) CTB 8 CTB60+ 8

3.32 There are three specific rules about temporary absences. During an absence from their home, a claimant remains eligible:

- for up to 13 weeks during a trial period in a care home (or immediately following that: *Secretary of State for Work and Pensions v Selby District Council*) – so long as the claimant intends to return to their normal home if the care home is unsuitable (but if the claimant was absent from home for another reason before this, their total absence from home must not exceed 52 weeks); or
- for up to 52 weeks if they are absent (in the UK or abroad) for one of the reasons in table 3.1 – so long as the claimant intends to return to their normal home within 52 weeks or, in exceptional circumstances, not substantially later; or
- for up to 13 weeks during an absence (in the UK or abroad) for any other reason – so long as the claimant intends to return to their normal home within a strict 13 weeks.

HB 7(18) HB60+ 7(18) NIHB 7(18) NIHB60+ 7(18) CTB 8(7) CTB60+ 8(7)

3.33 Many of the reasons in table 3.1 refer to an absence being 'medically approved'. This means certified by a medical practitioner. The DWP advises (GM para. A3.240) that a medical practitioner could, for example, be a GP or nurse, and that the approval need not necessarily be in the form of a certificate.

Example: Trying out a care home and then deciding to stay there

A woman who rents her home has been on HB and CTB for a while. She then goes into a care home for a six-week trial period to see if it suits her.

- She remains eligible for HB and CTB.

In the fourth week of her trial period, she decides that this is the care home for her. She gives four weeks' notice to her former landlord, and informs the authority of these matters promptly. The authority is satisfied that she could not reasonably have avoided the liability at her old address.

- She remains eligible for HB and CTB for the additional four-week period.

ABSENCES: ADDITIONAL CONDITIONS

3.34 In each of the above three cases (para. 3.32), there are three further conditions which must be met in order for HB/CTB to be granted during the absence:

HB 7(11)-(17)
HB60+ 7(11)-(17)
NIHB 7(11)-(17)
NIHB60+ 7(11)-(17)
CTB 8(2)-(6)
CTB60+ 8(2)-(6)

- the claimant must still be liable for rent/council tax on their normal home; and
- the part of the home the claimant normally occupies must not be let or sub-let; and
- the claimant must provide the authority with the information and evidence needed for the claim to continue (para. 3.43 and chapter 17).

Table 3.1: People who can get HB/CTB during an absence of up to 52 weeks

HB 7(16)(c)
HB60+ 7(16)(c)
NIHB 7(16)(c)
NIHB60+ 7(16)(c)
CTB 8(4)
CTB60+ 8(4)

Claimants in prison etc, who have not yet been sentenced (e.g. on remand).

Claimants in a bail hostel or bailed to live away from their normal home.

Claimants in a care home or independent hospital (para. 2.21) who are not just trying it out (e.g. during periods of respite care).

Claimants in hospital, or receiving medically approved* care.

Claimants undergoing medical treatment or medically approved* convalescence or who are absent because their partner or child is undergoing this.

Claimants undertaking medically approved* care of someone else.

Claimants caring for a child whose parent or guardian is absent from home in order to receive medical treatment or medically approved* care.

Claimants following a government training course (as defined in para. 3.27).

Students who are eligible for HB/CTB (e.g. if they have to study abroad for part of their course).

Claimants absent because of fear of violence in their normal home (regardless of who it would be from) or fear of violence from a former member of their family (whether this would occur in the normal home or elsewhere). This would apply to people other than those mentioned in paragraph 3.12 because, for example, they are staying with relatives and are not liable to pay rent on two homes but intend to return to occupy their original homes.

* For 'medically approved' see paragraph 3.33.

COUNTING THE LENGTH OF THE ABSENCE

3.35 In *R v Penwith DC HBRB ex parte Burt* it was held that the 13-week and 52-week time limits refer to absences which are continuous. So if the claimant (with the exception of prisoners on temporary leave: para. 3.40) returns to, and occupies the dwelling as a home, even for a short time, the allowable period of temporary absence starts again. The DWP suggests (GM para. A3.170) that a stay at home lasting, for example, only a few hours may not break the absence but one that lasts at least 24 hours may do so.

3.36 Depending upon the facts of the case, however, the authority may decide that the claimant's normal home is elsewhere for HB purposes (paras. 3.3-5). If another person occupying the dwelling starts paying rent in the absence of the claimant, the authority should consider treating that other person as liable and therefore eligible for HB (para. 2.36).

3.37 The assessment of whether or not the period of temporary absence is likely to exceed 13/52 weeks has to be made by reference to the date at which the claimant left the house (CH/1237/2004, para. 12). Continued entitlement has to be judged on a week by week basis. If at any date it becomes likely that the 13/52 weeks will be exceeded, then that is a relevant change of circumstances, allowing a re-consideration of the entitlement (CH/1237/2004, para. 12). Once it becomes clear that the claimant is going to be away for more than 13 or 52 weeks, HB/CTB entitlement ends under the temporary absence rule (but see para. 3.9 for the circumstances in which the claimant may be entitled to up to four weeks additional entitlement). Also note that in the case of the absences in table 3.1 if the absence is unlikely to substantially exceed the 52-week period, and if there are exceptional circumstances, the authority must pay up to the end of the 52nd week of absence. DWP guidance (GM para. A3.232) suggests that the term 'substantially exceed' relates to periods of absence greater than 15 months. It is, however, for the individual authority to interpret the term. The GM illustrates the concept of exceptional circumstances with the examples of someone prevented from returning home by an unanticipated event, and a discharge from hospital being delayed by a relapse. Other circumstances may also be considered.

Example: Remand and conviction

A man has been receiving HB for a while. He is then arrested and detained on remand pending his trial.

- The authority should assume that he will be absent for no more than 52 weeks. He therefore remains eligible for HB.

Fifteen weeks later he is tried, found guilty, and sentenced to a term of one year's imprisonment.

- Although he may well serve only six months in prison (after remission), and although the 15 weeks he has been on remand will count towards this, his total absence from home will now exceed 13 weeks. So his eligibility for HB under the temporary absence rule ceases, because the fact that he has been sentenced is a change in his circumstances (chapter 17). (But the HB he was awarded for his 15 weeks on remand was nonetheless correctly paid.) If, however, the necessary conditions are met (para. 3.9) the claimant may be entitled to a further four weeks of HB.

ABSENCES IN PRISON, ETC

3.38 As indicated in table 3.1, until they are sentenced, a claimant in prison etc can get HB for up to 52 weeks. This means that (almost) all prisoners on remand can get HB.

3.39 If and when the claimant is sentenced to prison etc, this counts as a change of circumstances. The relevant question is then: 'Will they return home within 13 weeks of when they left home?' Only if the answer is 'yes' can the claimant continue to get HB under the temporary absence rule. However, in deciding this, account must be taken of any remission the prisoner may get for good behaviour, so prisoners with a sentence of up to six months (or up to ten months if they are on Home Detention Curfew) are likely to be entitled. For further guidance see GM A3.210-218.

PRISONERS ON TEMPORARY RELEASE

HB 7(14)-(15)
HB60+ 7(14)-(15)
NIHB 7(14)-(15)
CTB60+ 8(5)-(6)

3.40 Prisoners on temporary release (home leave) are counted as still being in prison, unless they were already eligible for this immediately beforehand under the above rules (paras. 3.38-39).

ABSENCES ON BAIL

HB 7(16)(c)
HB60+ 7(16)(c)
NIHB 7(16)(c)
NIHB60+ 7(16)(c)
CTB 8(4)(a)
CTB60+ 8(4)(a)

3.41 As indicated in table 3.1, a person on bail can get HB for up to 52 weeks. This applies whether the person is in a bail hostel or bailed to live anywhere other than his or her normal home (e.g. at a relative's).

DEATH OF CLAIMANT

3.42 There is no provision to award HB/CTB following the death of the claimant. HB must cease at the end of the benefit week containing the date of the death (paras. 2.4, 2.12 and 17.21) and CTB ceases on the day before the date of the death (because there is no liability for council tax from the date of death onwards). If the claimant has a surviving partner, he or she may make their own claim, but is not 'covered' by their deceased partner's claim. Also, the fact that the estate of the deceased may be required to pay for a notice period on the property does not mean that the deceased (or the estate) is somehow still entitled to HB.

NOTIFYING A TEMPORARY ABSENCE

HB60+ 69(6)(c)
NIHB60+ 66(4)(c)
CTB60+ 59(7)(b)

3.43 If the claimant or any partner is aged 60+ and on SPC, there is a specific duty to notify the authority of an absence exceeding or likely to exceed 13 weeks. Apart from that, it has been held that there is no requirement in law to notify the authority in advance of a temporary absence *(CH/996/2004)*. On the other hand, it makes sense for a claimant (of any age) to notify any absence that is longer than (say) a couple of weeks – to avoid any difficulties that might arise if they were visited during the absence.

4 The claimant's household

4.1 This chapter describes:

- the different categories of claimant and the people who may live in the claimant's household;
- the circumstances in which the claimant is considered to be responsible for a child or young person for HB and main CTB;
- the circumstances in which partners and children or young people are treated as members of the claimant's household; and
- other people who may reside with the claimant or live in the same accommodation.

4.2 Authorities need to identify and correctly categorise the people who live with the claimant to work out HB/CTB entitlement since:

- only one member of what counts as the claimant's family for benefit purposes can claim HB/CTB;
- in the case of second adult rebate, partners and/or jointly liable persons can affect entitlement;
- in the case of HB/main CTB fixed deductions are made in certain cases for other people who live in the claimant's household who are classified as 'non-dependants';
- second adult rebate is worked out on the basis of the gross income of certain people who reside with the claimant known as 'second adults';
- the amount of HB/main CTB received where the claimant is not in receipt of income support/income-based JSA or pension credit is worked out on the basis of the combined needs of the claimant's family (in the form of the applicable amount) and the income and capital of the claimant and any partner;
- money from (sub-) tenants and boarders is taken into account in the assessment of the claimant's income for HB/main CTB where the claimant is not in receipt of income support/income-based JSA or pension credit.

Household composition

4.3 The concept of the household is an important one for HB/CTB purposes but it is not defined in legislation. It should be given its common sense meaning of a domestic establishment involving two or more people living together as a unit *(R(IS)1/99)*. People living in one dwelling (for example a house or flat) do not necessarily live together in the same household if for example they have completely separate living arrangements *(R(SB)4/83)*.

4.4 The claimant's household may consist of:

- the claimant;
- the claimant's family;
- any other person who lives in the dwelling and who is classified as a 'non-dependant' for HB/main CTB.

4.5 In addition to the above, certain other people such as joint occupiers, (sub) tenants, boarders, carers and au pairs may live in the same accommodation as the claimant.

THE CLAIMANT

4.6 The claimant may be: HB 2(1) HB60+ 2(1) NIHB 2(1) NIHB60+ 2(1) CTB 2(1) CTB60+ 2(1)

- single – i.e. a claimant who does not have a partner and is not responsible for a child/young person; or
- a lone parent – i.e. someone who does not have a partner but who is responsible for and is a member of the same household as a child/young person; or
- a member of a couple or polygamous marriage.

THE FAMILY

4.7 The claimant's family for benefit purposes consists of: CBA 137(1) NICBA 133(1)

- the claimant's partner(s), if a member of the same household; and
- any child(ren) or young person(s) the claimant is responsible for (not just sons and daughters) and who are treated as members of the household.

PARTNERS

4.8 A partner means:

- where a claimant is a member of a couple, the other member of that couple; or CBA 137(1) NICBA 133(1) HB 2(1) HB60+ 2(1)
- where a claimant is polygamously married to two or more members of the household, any such member. NIHB 2(1) NIHB60+ 2(1) CTB 2(1)

4.9 The term 'couple' refers to: CTB60+ 2(1)

- a man and woman who are married to each other and are members of the same household;
- a man and woman who are not married to each other but are living together as husband and wife;

- two people of the same sex who are civil partners of each other and are members of the same household (from 5th December 2005 or later see para. 4.15.); or
- two people of the same sex who are not civil partners of each other but are living together as if they were civil partners (from 5th December 2005 or later see para. 4.15.).

4.10 The partner must be a member of the same household as the claimant. It is possible, for example for a married couple or civil partners to live in the same dwelling but live separate lives and thus not constitute a household (CIS/072/1994). In such a case one would not be the partner of the other for HB/CTB purposes.

4.11 The Gender Recognition Act 2004 (effective from 4th April 2005) enables transsexual people in possession of a full gender recognition certificate from a Gender Recognition Panel to be legally recognised in their acquired gender (DWP G9/2004 para. 12).

4.12 The Civil Partnership Act 2004 enables same-sex couples to obtain legal recognition of their relationship by forming a civil partnership. They may do so by registering as civil partners of each other provided:

- they are of the same sex;
- they are not already in a civil partnership or lawfully married;
- they are not within the prohibited degrees of relationship, (e.g. two sisters, etc – A16/2005 Appendix A)
- they are both aged sixteen or over (and, if either of them is under 18 and the registration is to take place in England and Wales or Northern Ireland, the consent of the appropriate people or bodies has been obtained).
- in Scotland (the law makes explicit) that they understand the nature of a civil partnership and validly consent to its formation.

4.13 The Act also provides that a person should be treated as having formed a civil partnership where they have entered into specified analogous arrangements in other countries such as a geregistreerd partnerschap in the Netherlands or a pacte civil de solidatité in France.

IMPLEMENTATION DATES FOR THE CIVIL PARTNERSHIP RELATED PROVISIONS IN THE HB/CTB SCHEMES

4.14 From 5 December 2005 civil partners and those living together as civil partners (para. 4.17) making new claims for HB/CTB should be treated as couples from the outset. Normal overpayment rules apply if the claimant fails to disclose that they are civil partners or living together as civil partners and this results in too much benefit being paid.

4.15 Transitional arrangements apply to claimants who are living with someone else as if they were civil partners on the 5th December 2005 or start to do so after that date. The DWP's policy intention is that couples affected should be given a reasonable period of time to become aware of the change in the law (DWP A16/2005 para. 6). There are three dates from which a decision implementing the rules for those who live together as civil partners could take effect. SI 2005 No 2877 Art 3

- For existing cases at 5th December 2005, in which HB/CTB is in payment in association with a 'passporting' benefit (IS, JSA(IB) or Pension Credit Guarantee) the authority should apply the civil partnership rules from the date that The Pension Service/Jobcentre Plus makes the decision in relation to the passporting benefit. This avoids HB/CTB overpayments being created.
- For existing cases at 5 December 2005, not associated with a 'passporting' benefit, the authority should apply the rules from the date it becomes aware of the relevant circumstances, either because the claimant reports the change; or as a result of an administrative intervention.
- The authority may use an earlier date if it considers that the claimant could reasonably have been expected to have reported the matter at an earlier date.

4.16 It is the earliest of those three dates which is to be used when the authority supersedes its relevant decisions. Where there would be an underpayment of HB/CTB, due to the existence of the civil partnership, the authority may reassess entitlement and pay any arrears. SI 2005 No 2877 Art 3 DAR 8(2),(10) NIDAR 8(2),(10)

LIVING TOGETHER AS HUSBAND AND WIFE OR AS CIVIL PARTNERS

4.17 A man and woman who are married to each other and same sex civil partners are treated as one unit as long as they are members of the same household. Either member of the couple but not both may claim. The same rules apply to a man and woman who are not married to each other but are 'living together as husband and wife' and to two people of the same sex who are not civil partners of each other but who are 'living together as if they were civil partners'. A same-sex couple are regarded as 'living together as if they were civil partners' if they would be regarded as 'living together as husband and wife' were they instead two people of the opposite sex. HB 2(1) HB60+ 2(1) NIHB 2(1) NIHB60+ 2(1) CTB 2(1) CTB60+ 2(1)

4.18 Neither the Act nor regulations define the phrase 'living together as husband and wife'. The latest DWP guidance on the matter notes that 'the nature of modern-day relationships and marriages has changed' and that 'there is no longer as clear a definition against which we can measure whether two people are 'living together as husband and wife' (LTAHAW) (DWP A16/2005).

4.19 The first consideration when a man and woman appear to be living together as husband and wife is that of the purpose of the parties in living together *(Crake and Butterworth v the Supplementary Benefit Commission)*. The HB/CTB schemes recognise many different ways in which a man and woman (or two individuals of the same sex) could live together in the same dwelling, e.g. joint occupiers, landlady/lodger, etc.

4.20 If the purpose of the parties is unclear, the question of whether a couple are living together as husband and wife can only be decided by looking at their relationship and living arrangements and asking whether they can reasonably be said to be that of a married couple. Whilst the phrase 'living together as husband and wife' existed in the former HB scheme, it attracted most attention within the former supplementary benefit scheme as the 'co-habitation rule'. A body of case law developed. This is considered in detail in vol. 3, chapter 11, paras. 11039-11069 of the DWP *Decision Maker's Guide (www.dwp.gov.uk/publications/dwp/dmg/index.asp)*. The case law (see Crake para. 4.19) suggests that the following factors need to be considered before deciding that a couple are 'living together as husband and wife':

- whether or not they share the same household;
- the stability of the relationship;
- the financial arrangements;
- the presence or absence of a sexual relationship;
- shared responsibility for a child;
- public acknowledgment that they are a couple.

4.21 While all the above factors should be considered, none individually is conclusive. What matters is the general relationship as a whole *(R(SB)17/81)*. Appendix A of DWP A16/2005 provides authorities with advice regarding the information they should gather and the questions they should ask when considering whether two people are living together as husband and wife or as civil partners.

4.22 Because the DWP has treated two people as a couple does not mean that the authority must do so. The case of *R v Penwith DC HBRB ex parte Menear* does not provide a basis for concluding that the DWP decision for IS/JSA or pension credit awards is conclusive for HB/CTB purposes *(R(H)9/04)*. Where parallel decisions have to be made the authority may regard the existence of a considered decision by the DWP as satisfactory evidence of a state of affairs, in the absence of anything to compel a contrary conclusion. Where the claimant asserts that the DWP's decision as to their family status is wrong, the authority has to reach its own conclusion (*R(H)9/04* para. 37).

POLYGAMOUS MARRIAGE

4.23 A polygamous marriage means a marriage in which a party to it is married to more than one person. The ceremony of marriage must have taken place under the law of a country which permits polygamy. No marriage that takes place in the UK is valid if one of the partners is already married.

HB 2(1)
HB60+ 2(1)
NIHB 2(1)
NIHB60+ 2(1)
CTB 2(1)
CTB60+ 2(1)

ABSENCE AND MEMBERSHIP OF THE SAME HOUSEHOLD

4.24 The claimant and/or any partner is normally treated as a member of the household even if temporarily living away from the other members of the family. Temporary absence is not defined for the purpose of CTB but for the purpose of HB the claimant or partner is no longer counted as a member of the household where they are living away from the other members of the family and:

HB 21(1),(2)
HB60+ 21(1),(2)
NIHB 19(1),(2)
NIHB60+ 19(1),(2)
CTB 11(1)
CTB60+ 11(1)

- do not intend to resume living with them; or
- the absence is likely to exceed 52 weeks, unless there are exceptional circumstances where the person has no control over the length of the absence such as hospitalisation and the absence is unlikely to be substantially more than 52 weeks.

4.25 Where someone is no longer counted as a member of the household their needs, income and capital should not be taken into account when calculating benefit. Any money actually received from an absent partner should be treated as maintenance (para. 13.111).

CHILDREN AND YOUNG PERSONS

4.26 A child is defined as someone under the age of 16. A new definition of a young person applies from 10th April 2006 with the coming into force of the Child Benefit Act 2005. A young person is defined as someone aged 16 or over who meets the definition of a qualifying young person for child benefit purposes and who is not on income support or income based job seeker's allowance nor a person aged 16 or 17 who would be excluded from HB if they made a claim as a result of the Children Leaving Care Act (paras. 2.15-18).

HB 2(1), 19
HB60+ 2(1), 19
NIHB 2(1), 17
NIHB60+ 2(1), 17
CTB 2(1), 9
CTB60+ 2(1), 9

4.27 A qualifying young person for child benefit purposes is:

- a person aged 16, from the date they attain that age up to and including the 31st August that next follows that date; or
- a person aged 16 years and over but under 20 who is undertaking a course of full-time, non-advanced education started before reaching the age of 19; or
- a person aged 16 years or over but under 20 who is undertaking approved training that is not provided through a contract of employment and that was started before reaching the age of 19.

4.28 Full-time education is education undertaken in pursuit of a course, where the average time spent during the term time in receiving tuition or engaging in practical work or supervised study, or taking examinations exceeds 12 hours per week. A person is treated as undertaking a course of FTE during the period between the end of one course and the start of another where they are enrolled on and start the latter course. Non-advanced education is education up to and including the following and equivalents: GCE (A Level), advanced GNVQ or equivalent, Scottish certificate of education (higher level) or Scottish certificate of sixth year studies.

4.29 Approved training means the training provided:

- in England – under 'Entry to Employment' or 'Programme Led Pathways';
- in Wales – under 'Skillbuild', 'Skillbuild Plus' or 'Foundation Modern Apprenticeships';
- in Scotland – under 'Get Ready for Work', 'Skillseekers' or 'Modern Apprenticeships'; or
- in Northern Ireland – under 'Access' or 'Jobskills Traineeships'.

4.30 A person remains a qualifying young person for child benefit purposes where they have left relevant education or approved training up to and including the week including the terminal date; or if they attain the age of 20 on or before that date, the week including the last Monday before they were 20. The terminal date is whichever of the following dates occurs first after they have ceased relevant education or approved training:

- the last day in February;
- the last day in May;
- the last day in August;
- the last day in November.

4.31 Child benefit is extended for 16 and 17 year olds where they:

- have ceased to be in relevant education or training;
- are registered for work, education or training with the Careers or Connexions Service;
- are not engaged in remunerative work; and
- an application for payment of child benefit during the extension period has been made within three months of the date relevant education or training ended.

The child benefit extension period begins on the first day of the week after the week in which relevant education or training stopped and ends 20 weeks later.

4.32 Once the young person is no longer counted for child benefit purposes they become a non-dependant for HB/main CTB purposes. HB and CTB claims should be re-assessed to exclude the young person's personal allowance and, where appropriate, the family premiums. In the case of HB/main CTB no non-dependant deduction is made for anyone under 18 (table 7.2). Non-dependants, aged 18 or over, who are not disregarded for the purpose of council tax discounts (appendix 6) count as second adults for second adult rebate.

RESPONSIBILITY FOR A CHILD OR YOUNG PERSON

4.33 The claimant is considered responsible for any child or young person they normally live with. Deciding responsibility is usually straightforward but where the child or young person spends equal amounts of time in different households (e.g. where the parents have separated), or where there is doubt over which household they are living in, the child or young person is treated as normally living with the person who gets the child benefit. If no-one gets child benefit, the child or young person is considered the responsibility of:

HB 20(1), 2
HB60+ 20(1), 2
NIHB 18(1), 2
NIHB60+ 18(1), 2
CTB 10(1), 2
CTB60+ 10(1), 2

- the person who has claimed child benefit; or
- the person the authority considers has 'primary responsibility' if more than one person has made a claim for the child benefit or no claim has been made.

4.34 A child or young person can only be the responsibility of one person in any one benefit week (GM C1.91). If the claimant has a child or young person who lives with them and that child or young person in turn has a child, for example, the claimant's daughter and the daughter's baby, the authority must decide whether the daughter is dependent on the claimant or forms a family of her own. If the daughter receives income support (or income-based JSA) for herself and her baby she should not be considered part of the claimant's family (GM C1.69).

HB 20(3)
HB60+ 20(3)
NIHB 18(3)
NIHB60+ 18(3)
CTB 10(3)
CTB60+ 10(3)

4.35 Where the claimant is treated as not responsible for a child or young person because for example a child spends more time in another household arguably they should be treated as not occupying the claimant's dwelling for rent officer referral purposes and thus not count for the purpose of the size criteria (*R v Swale BC HBRB ex p Marchant*) (para. 6.26). It is also arguable that in some circumstances a child should be included in more than one household, as a result of *Hockenjos v Secretary of State for Social Security (No. 2)*. This was a JSA case where both members of a separated couple were held to be entitled to a personal allowance for each of their children. This may have a bearing on HB and CTB in limited circumstances (subject to later developments in the law in CIS/1616/2004 and CJSA/2507/2002). The DWP has not issued guidance on this and authorities' approaches are likely to vary, but in at least one case in the UK this in known to have been done in HB/CTB.

CHILD/YOUNG PERSON'S MEMBERSHIP OF THE SAME HOUSEHOLD

HB 21(1),(2)
HB60+ 21(1),(2)
NIHB 19(1),(2)
NIHB60+ 19(1),(2)
CTB 11(1)
CTB60+ 11(1)

4.36 Where the claimant is treated as responsible for a child or young person, that child or young person is counted as a member of the claimant's household (with the exceptions identified in para. 4.38). This is the case even where the child or young person is temporarily living away from the other members of the family.

4.37 Temporary absence is not defined for the purposes of CTB, but for the purposes of HB the child or young person is no longer counted as a member of the household where they are living away from the other members of the family and:

- do not intend to resume living with them; or
- the absence is likely to exceed 52 weeks, unless there are exceptional circumstances where the child or young person has no control over the length of the absence such as hospitalisation and the absence is unlikely to be substantially more than 52 weeks.

HB 21(3)(4)
HB60+ 21(3)(4)
NIHB 19(3)(4)
NIHB60+ 19(3)(4)
CTB 11(2)(3)
CTB60+ 11(2)(3)

4.38 A child or young person is not counted as a member of the claimant's household where they are:

- absent from the claimant's home and being looked after by a local authority, or in Scotland or Northern Ireland are in the care of a local authority or the Department;
- a foster child placed with the claimant or partner by a local authority or voluntary organisation, or in Scotland and Northern Ireland boarded out with the claimant or partner; or
- placed for adoption or custodianship with the claimant or partner or elsewhere (though once adopted, they become a member of the household).

HB 21(5)
HB60+ 21(5)
NIHB 19(5)
NIHB60+ 19(5)
CTB 11(4)
CTB60+ 11(4)

4.39 A child or young person in local authority care who lives with the claimant under supervision must be treated as a member of the household. So must a child or young person in care who returns to live with the claimant for part or all of a benefit week if, given the nature and frequency of the visits, it is reasonable to do so.

4.40 A child or young person who is absent in any other circumstance, e.g. attending boarding school, should be regarded as temporarily absent and treated as a member of the family (GM C1.140).

Non-dependants

HB 3(1),(2)
HB60+ 3(1),(2)
NIHB 3(1),(2)
NIHB60+ 3(1),(2)
CTB 2(1)
CTB60+ 2(1)

4.41 A non-dependant is someone who normally resides with the claimant on a non-commercial basis such as an adult son or daughter, or other relative. Consequently someone who is staying with the claimant but normally resides elsewhere is not a non-dependant. Someone who normally resides with the claimant and has a legal liability to make payments in respect of the dwelling but who the authority treat as not liable to make such payments for HB (para. 2.38) (and related provisions for CTB also falls into the category of non-dependant.

4.42 The definition of a non-dependant specifically excludes:

- members of the claimant's benefit family (para. 4.7);
- a child or young person who lives with the claimant but who is not a member of the claimant's household, e.g. foster children (para. 4.38);
- the persons identified in paras. 4.46-4.49 and para 4.51.

4.43 Where the claimant resides with the landlord, neither the landlord nor a member of the landlord's family, e.g. a landlady's adult daughter, are treated as non-dependants of the claimant.

4.44 Non-dependants cannot claim HB/CTB for any payments they may make for their keep. If, however, a non-dependant has to make payments so that they can continue to live in the home because the liable person isn't doing so, then the authority may if it is reasonable to do so treat them as liable and thus potentially entitled to HB (para. 2.36). Payments made by the non-dependant to the claimant are disregarded from the claimant's income (table 13.2) – instead a fixed deduction may be made from the claimant's HB/main CTB where a non-dependant is present (para. 7.17).

RESIDING WITH

4.45 There is no definition of 'residing with' in the CTB rules. For HB purposes a person does not count as normally residing with the claimant and consequently is not a non-dependant if they only share a bathroom, lavatory and/or communal area (e.g. halls, passageways and rooms in common use in sheltered accommodation). Thus people in self-contained accommodation within the same building as the claimant, e.g. a granny annex, do not count as non-dependants even if they share a bathroom and lavatory with the claimant. But the finding that someone shares more of the accommodation than a bathroom, lavatory and/or communal area with the claimant is a necessary but not sufficient condition for deciding that they reside with the claimant (*Kadhim v Brent LBC*). They must also have the sort of relationship that could be described as residing with in an ordinary sense. This is more than simply sharing specific areas of the accommodation.

HB 3(4)
sch 1 para 8
HB60+ 3(4)
sch 1 para 8
NIHB 3(4)
sch 1 para 8
NIHB60+ 3(4)
sch 1 para 8

Other people who may live in the claimant's dwelling

BOARDERS

HB sch 5 para 42 HB60+ 2(1) sch 5 para 9 NIHB sch 6 para 45 NIHB60+ 2(1) sch 6 para 10 CTB sch 4 para 23 CTB60+ 2(1) sch 3 para 9

4.46 A boarder is someone who lives in board and lodging accommodation. This is accommodation that is provided for a charge which is inclusive of the provision of at least some cooked or prepared meals. To count as board and lodging accommodation the meals must be either cooked or prepared by someone other than the claimant or a member of their family. They must also be consumed in that accommodation or associated premises. A person whose payment does not include an element for some cooked or prepared meals should be treated as a tenant or sub-tenant (para. 4.48). The claimant's income from a boarder is taken into account in the assessment of HB/main CTB where the claimant is not in receipt of income support/income-based JSA or the pension credit. The treatment of income from a boarder is different from that of income from a tenant or sub-tenant (table 13.2). Boarders can claim HB but not CTB in their own right.

JOINT OCCUPIERS

HB 3(2)(d),(3) HB60+ 3(2)(d),(3) NIHB 3(2)(d),(3) CTB 3(2)(d),(e),(3) CTB60+ 3(2)(d),(e),(3)

4.47 For HB purposes a joint occupier is someone other than the claimant's partner who is jointly liable with the claimant to make payments in order to occupy the dwelling (paras. 2.33-68), e.g. joint tenants. For CTB purposes a joint occupier is someone other than the claimant's partner who is jointly and severally liable for the council tax or who is liable to make payments to the claimant on a commercial basis in order to live there, except where that liability is in question as defined by paragraphs 2.39, 2.43, 2.47 or 2.62. Joint occupiers may be eligible for the appropriate benefit in their own right. For the purpose of calculating benefit the total council tax/rates and/or rent is apportioned between them (paras. 9.26-29, 10.6, 11.27).

TENANTS AND SUB-TENANTS

HB sch 5 para 22 HB60+ sch 5 para 10 NIHB sch 6 para 23 NIHB60+ sch 6 para 11 CTB sch 4 para 22 CTB60+ sch 3 para 10

4.48 A tenant or sub-tenant is someone who is contractually liable to pay the claimant for the right to occupy part of the claimant's accommodation, but who is not:

- a member of the claimant's family;
- a non-dependant;
- a joint occupier;
- a boarder.

4.49 Where the payment includes something for meals, the person should be treated as a boarder (para. 4.46). A formal tenancy or sub-tenancy does not have to exist for someone to be treated as a tenant or sub-tenant for HB/CTB purposes, nor does this treatment create or imply the existence of a legal tenancy or sub-tenancy. In this respect the HB/CTB regulations and the landlord/tenant provisions of the Housing and Rent Acts do not accord precisely. A tenant or sub-tenant is able to claim HB in their own right. However, where the authority thinks the tenancy or sub-tenancy is contrived, HB is not awarded and instead the tenant or sub-tenant is treated as a non-dependant (para. 4.41). For the treatment of the claimant's income from a tenant or sub-tenant, see table 13.2.

AU PAIR

4.50 Au pairs are usually young people from abroad who are expected to do light housework such as cleaning, dusting, taking care of children and shopping in return for lodgings, board and pocket money. The correct treatment of an au pair in the claimant's household for HB/CTB purposes is ambiguous but the DWP advises that au pairs should not be treated as non-dependants (GM C1.185).

A CARER

4.51 A carer who lives with the claimant does not count as a non-dependant (or boarder) if they are looking after the claimant or partner and engaged by a charitable or voluntary organisation (not a public or local authority) which makes a charge to the claimant or partner for the services provided.

HB 3(2)(f)
HB60+ 3(2)(f)
NIHB 3(2)(f)
NIHB60+ 3(2)(f)
CTB 3(2)(f)
CTB60+ 3(2)(f)

SECOND ADULTS

4.52 Non-dependants, au pairs and carers, if they are aged 18 or over and not disregarded for the purpose of council tax discounts (para. 9.16-17), count as second adults for the purpose of second adult rebate (paras. 8.5-7).

5 Making a claim

5.1 This chapter describes how to claim HB and CTB and when awards start. Many of the rules about this have changed this year. The chapter explains:

- who makes the claim;
- how and where to claim;
- the information and evidence needed;
- how incomplete claims are dealt with;
- when awards start (date of claim and first day of entitlement);
- awards for past periods for 60+s; and
- backdating for 'good cause'.

5.2 This chapter does not apply when someone already on HB/CTB moves from one address to another within an authority's area, as this is a change in circumstances (para. 17.30) and does not require a claim for HB/CTB.

Who makes the claim

AA 1,5
NIAA 1,5

5.3 The general rule is that the claimant is responsible for making the claim. There are further rules for couples (and polygamous marriages) and people who are unable to act.

COUPLES

HB 82(1)
HB60+ 63(1)
NIHB 79(1)
NIHB60+ 62(1)
CTB 68(1)
CTB60+ 52(1)

5.4 In the case of a couple or polygamous marriage (paras. 4.9, 4.23) one partner makes the claim (though in practice both may be asked to sign the claim form). They may choose between them which partner this is to be. If they cannot agree, the authority must choose. In some cases a couple are better off if one partner rather than the other is the claimant. These are identified in this guide as they arise (e.g. paras. 12.15-16, 12.24).

HB 82(6)
HB60+ 63(6)
NIHB 79(6)
NIHB60+ 62(6)
CTB 68(6)
CTB60+ 52(6)

PEOPLE UNABLE TO ACT

5.5 A claim may be made by a third party if the claimant is unable, for the time being, to act. In such cases, that person takes over all rights and responsibilities in relation to the HB/CTB claim.

HB 82(2)
HB60+ 63(2)
NIHB 79(2)
NIHB60+ 62(2)
CTB 68(2)
CTB60+ 52(2)

5.6 Where one of the following has been appointed to act for the claimant, the authority must accept a claim from him or her:

- a receiver appointed by the Court of Protection;

- an attorney;
- in Scotland, a judicial factor or other guardian;
- in Northern Ireland, a controller appointed by the High Court; or
- a person appointed by the DWP to act on the claimant's behalf in connection with some other benefit.

5.7 In any other case, the authority may accept a written request from an individual over 18, or a firm or organisation, to be an appointee, for example, a friend or relative, a social worker or solicitor. In doing this the authority should take account of any conflict of interests between the claimant and appointee. Either the authority or the appointee can terminate the appointment by giving four weeks' written notice.

HB 82(3)-(5)
HB60+ 63(3)-(5)
NIHB 79(3)-(5)
NIHB60+ 62(3)-(5)
CTB 68(3)-(5)
CTB60+ 52(3)-(5)

How and where to claim

THE NEW RULES

5.8 Since 10th November 2005, a claim for HB/CTB can be started by any means of communication (e.g. telephone, internet, email, letter, visit) but must always be followed up in writing (usually on a form), and must always be accompanied or supplemented by appropriate information and evidence (para. 5.17). It may be made at one of various local authority or DWP offices, as described below.

OFFICES USED IN CONNECTION WITH CLAIMS

5.9 The law refers to three types of office which may be used in connection with a claim for HB/CTB:

HB 2(1),83(4)
HB60+ 2(1),64(5)
NIHB 2(1),80(4)
NIHB60+ 2(1),63(5)
CTB 2(1),69(4)
CTB60+ 2(1),53(4)

(a) A 'designated office' is somewhere chosen by the authority for the receipt of HB/CTB claims and notifications about changes of circumstances. The authority can have just one designated office (e.g. its benefit office or call centre) or many – including perhaps its homeless persons unit, the office of a housing association or hostel, or anywhere else. HB/CTB claim forms must include the postal address of any designated office(s) and may also include their email address(es).

(b) An 'appropriate DWP office' (also called an 'appropriate social security office') is any office of the DWP which is normally open to the public for claims for JSA(IB) or IS or pension credit. One example is a Jobcentre Plus office.

(c) An 'authorised office' means somewhere chosen by the DWP and authorised by the authority for the receipt of HB/CTB claims. This includes DWP call centres which take claims for HB/CTB in conjunction with a claim for another benefit.

HB/CTB CLAIMS MADE WITH A CLAIM FOR ANOTHER STATE BENEFIT

5.10 Someone also claiming JSA(IB), IS or pension credit (of either kind) is, as part of the process of claiming that benefit, also invited to claim HB/CTB (para. 5.9(b),(c)). During 2006 this is expected to apply equally to incapacity benefit.

5.11 The following description applies in most areas where the DWP's customer 'management' system (CMS) operates. The DWP takes the HB/CTB claim by telephone, and then sends the claimant forms to sign and take in to their local Jobcentre Plus office. The DWP sends the authority a 'Local Authority Input Document' which confirms what information and evidence the DWP has collected and verified. This does not always give the authority all the information it needs to decide the HB/CTB claim and its contents do not necessarily have to be accepted by the authority (para. 5.21).

HB 111 HB60+ 92 CTB 94 CTB60+ 79

5.12 The law does not always keep up with administrative developments, but the general principle is that the DWP should forward details relevant to HB/CTB to the authority within two working days of receipt (GM part D para. W.1.304). If the authority does not award HB/CTB it should advise the DWP to stop them sending further details relating to that claimant.

5.13 In areas with substantial delays caused by the DWP, it is highly advisable to also claim HB/CTB direct from the authority (para. 5.14). In such cases, the law is clear that a person with no income because of waiting for a decision from the DWP is entitled to maximum HB/CTB (para. 7.4). Claimants must not be told that they must 'wait for their DWP claim to be assessed' before they can claim HB/CTB.

HB/CTB CLAIMS MADE DIRECT TO THE AUTHORITY

HB 83(1),(2) HB60+ 64(2),(3) NIHB 80(1),(2) NIHB60+ 63(1),(2) CTB 69(1),(2) CTB60+ 53(1),(2)

5.14 Anyone may claim HB/CTB direct from the authority (para. 5.9(a)). The claim may be started by any means (paras. 5.8, 5.34) but nearly all claimants are required to complete the authority's application form – which must be supplied free of charge. Generally, authorities design their own application forms, though various organisations have made recommendations.

5.15 Although HB and CTB are legally two different benefits, authorities usually have one form for claiming both; and a claim for CTB always includes a claim for both main CTB and second adult rebate (GM para. B2.63). Many authorities have forms in different languages and some have forms for certain groups of claimants (e.g. those who wish to claim only second adult rebate).

AMENDING OR WITHDRAWING A CLAIM

5.16 Before a decision is made on a claim, the claimant may:

HB 87
HB60+ 68
NIHB 82
NIHB60+ 65
CTB 73
CTB60+ 58

- write withdrawing the claim: the authority is then under no duty to decide it;
- write amending the claim: the amendment is treated as having been made from the outset.

Information and evidence

5.17 The authority may ask the claimant to provide 'certificates, documents, information and evidence' if they are 'reasonably required... in order to determine... entitlement'. This applies in deciding whether a claim is complete (para. 5.25), and also during the course of an award (para. 17.66).

HB 83(1),86(1)
HB60+ 64(2),67(1)
NIHB 80(1),81(1)
NIHB60+ 63(1),64(1)
CTB 69(1),72(1)
CTB60+ 53(1),57(1)

5.18 The authority must write to the claimant to ask for these (para. 5.26). It may additionally request the claimant to attend an interview, but may not insist on this: *R v Liverpool CC ex parte Johnson No. 2*. Evidence should be obtained direct from a third party only with the claimant's written agreement (GM para. C8.230) – which in practice is usually given by signing the declaration on the application form.

5.19 An authority may not require any information or evidence whatsoever about the following types of payment, whether they are made to a claimant, partner, child, young person, non-dependant or second adult. These payments are in any case always disregarded in the assessment of HB and CTB:

HB 86(2),(4)
HB60+ 67(2),(4)
NIHB 81(2),(4)
NIHB60+ 64(2),(4)
CTB 72(2),(4)
CTB60+ 57(2),(4)

- payments from the Macfarlane Trusts, the Eileen Trust, the Skipton Fund, the Fund or the London Bombings Charitable Relief Fund, and in certain cases payments of money which originally derived from those sources (para. 13.60);
- payments in kind of capital from a charity or from the above sources;
- payments in kind of income from any source.

A 'payment in kind' is a payment made in goods (e.g. food, fuel) rather than in money (e.g. cash, cheques).

5.20 In HB only (except for claims for HB made in respect of a hostel: para. 6.10) the claimant must either provide their National Insurance (NI) number and the NI number of their partner, along with information or evidence establishing these; or provide information or evidence enabling it to be ascertained; or make an application for an NI number and give information or evidence to assist with this.

AA1(1A)
NIAA 1(1A)
HB 4
HB60+ 4
NIHB 4
NIHB 60+
CTB 4
CTB 60+ 4

INFORMATION AND EVIDENCE FROM THE DWP

5.21 For claimants who have been (lawfully) awarded JSA(IB), IS or guarantee credit, this award is binding as proof that (at the relevant date) the claimant therefore fulfils the income-related conditions for receiving maximum HB/CTB (para. 7.5): *R v Penwith District Council ex parte Menear* and *R v South Ribble Council Housing Benefit Review Board*. For claimants who have been (lawfully) awarded savings credit, then certain figures are binding on the authority (para. 13.151). In other respects (such as household details, non-dependants, liability for rent, and so on) the authority must make its own decision about all aspects of HB/CTB.

PROOF AND THE VERIFICATION FRAMEWORK

5.22 The law does not specify what proof the authority should require about any particular matter (though a forged document does not prove anything, even if its contents are true: *R v Winston*). Most authorities follow the DWP's Verification Framework ('VF'), contained in the DWP's HB/CTB Security Manual (2004) as amended by various circulars. This gives general advice about proof, and advises that claimants should provide the original of a document rather than a copy.

5.23 The VF is guidance, not law. It does not apply if it conflicts with the legal test of what the authority can lawfully require (para 5.17): CH/2323/2002; and does not apply to tribunals: CH/5088/2002. The VF itself specifies that it does not apply to hostel claimants (para. 6.10) for the first 13 weeks of their claim.

Incomplete claims

5.24 If a claim is incomplete in some way, the authority must give the claimant the chance to complete it – as described in this section. (In the law, an incomplete claim is also described as being 'defective'.)

WHAT IS A COMPLETE CLAIM

AA 1,5,6
NIAA 1,5
HB 83(1),(9)
HB60+ 64(2),(10)
NIHB 80(1),(9)
NIHB60+ 63(1),(10)
CTB 69(1),(9)
CTB60+ 53(1),(9)

5.25 A claim is complete if it is made in writing and is:

- on a 'properly completed' form approved by the authority. 'Properly completed' means completed in accordance with its instructions, including any instructions to provide information and evidence in connection with the claim; or
- in some other written form which the authority accepts as sufficient in the circumstances of a particular case or a class of cases, having regard to the sufficiency of the written information and evidence supplied with it.

DEALING WITH INCOMPLETE CLAIMS

5.26 If the above two conditions are not met, the authority has the following duties. HB 83(6)-(8) 86(1)(2) HB60+ 64(3)-(9) 67(1),(2) NIHB 80(6-(8) NIHB60+ 63(7)-(9) CTB 69(2)-(8) 72(1),(2) CTB60+ 53(2)-(8) 57(1),(2)

- If the claim is not on an approved form (and the authority does not accept the form it is in as sufficient), the authority must send the claimant an approved form for completion, or request further information and evidence, as appropriate.
- If the claim is on an approved form but is not properly completed (including claims which are not supported by sufficient information or evidence), the authority must request the claimant to complete the claim – for example, return the form to the claimant for completion (keeping a copy or record of the returned form), or request further information and evidence, as appropriate.

The authority must also inform the claimant of the duty to notify relevant changes of circumstances which occur, and say what these are likely to be.

5.27 The claimant must be allowed at least one month to provide what is required, and must be allowed longer if it is reasonable to do so. Some authorities send a reminder, allowing a further period for the reply. If the claimant does what is required within the time limit, the claim is treated as having been complete from the outset.

DECIDING INCOMPLETE CLAIMS

5.28 A claim must be decided even if the claimant does not complete it (para. 5.27). In such a case, the authority might (as appropriate): HB 89 HB60+ 70 NIHB 84 NIHB60+ 67 CTB 75 CTB60+ 60

- decide that the claimant is not entitled to HB/CTB because they do not satisfy the conditions of entitlement, as they have not provided the necessary information or evidence; or
- draw a negative inference in order to make its decision. For example, if a claimant's bank statement shows that he withdrew £20,000 three weeks ago, and the claimant refuses to explain this, it might be reasonable to decide that he does not qualify for HB/CTB because his capital remains £20,000.

In each of the above cases, the claimant may appeal against the decision to a tribunal (chapter 19).

When HB/CTB starts

5.29 HB and CTB start on the Monday following the claimant's 'date of claim', unless the 'week-one-yes rule' applies, in which case they start on a date up to one week earlier. The details are in the remainder of this chapter. The main rules are:

- the 'date of claim' usually means the date the claimant first notified their intention (to one of the relevant offices) to claim HB/CTB – but it can be earlier (para. 5.33);
- the 'week-one-yes rule' applies if the claimant becomes liable for rent/council tax, and moves in, and claims HB/CTB, all in the same benefit week (para. 5.49).

DURATION OF AWARD

5.30 There is no fixed limit to an award of HB/CTB. Entitlement may change if there is a change in circumstances (chapter 17). Otherwise it simply continues until the claimant:

- stops being entitled – for example, gains too much capital or income, dies or becomes an ineligible student (para. 17.21);
- gets an extended payment (para. 17.82); or
- fails to respond to a request for information or evidence and then the award of HB/CTB is terminated (para. 17.79).

DEFINITION OF 'MONTH'

5.31 Many of the rules in this Guide refer to allowing someone a 'month' to do something in connection with a claim, an appeal, etc. This means a calendar month, and the month is counted as follows *(R(IB) 4/02)*:

- if the authority issues a letter on 26th June inviting the claimant to provide something, the claimant has provided it within a month if he or she gets it to the authority by the end of 26th July;
- if the authority issues a letter on 31st January inviting a claimant to provide something, the claimant has provided it within a month if he or she gets it to the authority by the end of 28th or 29th February (depending on whether it is a leap year).

DEFINITION OF 'BENEFIT WEEK'

HB 2(1)
HB60+ 2(1)
NIHB 2(1)
NIHB60+ 2(1)
CTB 2(1)
CTB60+ 2(1)

5.32 Many of the rules in this Guide refer to a 'benefit week'. A benefit week (for HB/CTB) is defined as beginning on a Monday and ending on the following Sunday.

Date of claim

HB 83(5)
HB60+ 64(6)
NIHB 80(5)
NIHB60+ 63(6)
CTB 69(5)
CTB60+ 53(5)

5.33 The rules about what counts as the claimant's 'date of claim' are summarised in table 5.1. Further details follow.

Table 5.1 Date of claim for HB/CTB: summary

Situation	Date of claim
The claimant asked for a form (or notified an intention to claim) and returns it, properly completed within one month of when it was sent out (or longer if reasonable)	The day the claimant asked for it (or notified the intention to claim)
The claim is made within one month of the claimant's partner's death or the claimant's and partner's separation, and the partner was on HB/CTB at the time	The day of the death or separation
The claimant or a partner was awarded JSA(IB), IS or guarantee credit, and the claim for HB/CTB is received within one month of when the claim for that benefit was received	The first day of their entitlement to JSA(IB), IS or guarantee credit
The claimant or a partner is on JSA(IB), IS or guarantee credit, and the claim for HB/CTB is received within a month of them first becoming liable for rent/council tax	The first day of their liability for rent/council tax
In any other case	The day the HB/CTB claim is received
But if the claimant or any partner is aged 60+ (regardless of whether they have 'good cause')	Up to 12 months before the day the claim was received
And if the claimant and any partner are under 60 and have 'good cause'	Up to 52 weeks before the day the claimant requested backdating

◆ *Detailed rules are in para. 5.34 onwards.*

NOTIFYING AN INTENTION TO CLAIM

HB 83(5)(d)
HB60+ 64(6)(d)
NIHB 80(5)(d)
NIHB60+ 63(6)(d)
CTB 69(5)(d)
CTB60+ 53(5)(d)

5.34 This rule applies if:

- the claimant notified their intention to claim HB/CTB to the authority's designated office, or an appropriate DWP office, or an authorised office (para. 5.9);
- that office sent the claimant an application form; and
- the claimant returned the form to one of those offices within one month of when it was sent out, or longer if reasonable.

5.35 In this case, the date of claim is the day the claimant notified their intention to claim to the office in question. For this rule the notification can be done 'by any means' (which includes telephoning, emailing, texting, visiting or sending a friend, as well as writing a letter).

Example: Date of claim following notification of an intention to claim

On Thursday 25th May 2006, a claimant realises she might qualify for HB/CTB and telephones the authority to ask to claim. The authority sends an application form out that very day. She posts it back and it reaches the authority on Wednesday 14th June 2006.

Her date of claim is Thursday 25th May 2006 and (unless the week-one-yes rule applies: para. 5.49) the first day of her entitlement to HB/CTB is the following Monday, 29th May 2006.

CLAIMS FOLLOWING DEATH OR SEPARATION

HB 83(5)(c)
HB60+ 64(6)(c)
NIHB 80(5)(c)
NIHB60+ 63(6)(c)
CTB 69(5)(c)
CTB60+ 53(5)(c)

5.36 This rule applies if:

- the claimant claims HB/CTB within one month of their partner's death or of their separation from their partner; and
- that partner was on HB/CTB at the time of the death or separation.

5.37 In this case, the date of claim is the date of the separation or death in question, the intention being that there should be no gap in entitlement to HB/CTB. This is the only rule which does not specify where the claim has to be made, so presumably any of the offices mentioned in paragraph 5.9 is acceptable. The one month time limit cannot be extended, but if the claimant is aged 60+ another rule applies instead (para. 5.51) and if they are under 60 they may have good cause for backdating (para. 5.53).

PASSPORT BENEFIT CLAIMANTS WHO CLAIM HB/CTB WITHIN ONE MONTH

5.38 This rule applies if:

- the claimant or a partner claims and is awarded a passport benefit (JSA(IB), IS or guarantee credit); and
- the claimant's HB/CTB claim is received by the authority's designated office or an appropriate DWP office (para. 5.9) no more than one month after the passport benefit claim was received by the DWP.

HB 83(5)(a)
HB60+ 64(6)(a)
NIHB 80(5)(a)
NIHB60+ 63(6)(c)
CTB 69(5)(a)
CTB60+ 53(5)(a)

5.39 In this case, the date of claim for HB/CTB is the date of first entitlement to the passport benefit (and in the case of JSA(IB) this means the first 'waiting day'). The one month time limit cannot be extended.

PASSPORT BENEFIT CLAIMANTS WHO BECOME LIABLE FOR RENT OR COUNCIL TAX

5.40 This rule applies if:

- the claimant or a partner is receiving a passport benefit (JSA(IB), IS or guarantee credit); and
- the claimant becomes liable for rent or council tax for the first time; and
- the claimant's HB/CTB claim is received by the authority's designated office or an appropriate DWP office (para. 5.9) no more than one month after the new liability begins.

HB 83(5)(b)
HB60+ 64(6)(b)
NIHB 80(5)(b)
NIHB60+ 63(6)(b)
CTB 69(5)(b)
CTB60+ 53(5)(b)

5.41 In this case, the date of claim for HB is the first day of their new liability for rent; the date of claim for CTB is the first day of their new liability for council tax. The one month time limit cannot be extended.

OTHER CLAIMS

5.42 This rule applies if none of the earlier rules applies (but see also paras 5.51 and 5.53 for past periods).

5.43 In this case, the date of claim is the day the claim is received at the authority's designated office, an appropriate DWP officer, or an authorised office (para. 5.9).

HB 83(5)(e)
HB60+ 64(6)(e)
NIHB 80(5)(e)
NIHB 63(6)(e)
CTB 69(5)(e)
CTB60+ 53(5)(e)

ADVANCE CLAIMS

5.44 This rule applies if a claimant claims:

- HB/CTB up to 17 weeks before their 60th birthday; or
- if aged 60+, HB/CTB up to 17 weeks before an event which makes them entitled to HB/CTB; or
- If under 60, HB/CTB up to 13 weeks before an event which makes them entitled to HB/CTB; or

HB 7(7),83(10),(11)
HB60+ 7(7)
64(11),(12)
NIHB 7(9)
80(10),(11)
NIHB60+ 7(9)
63(11),(12)
CTB 69(10)
(12),(13)
CTB60+ 53(10),(12

- CTB, or HB for rates in Northern Ireland, up to eight weeks before they become liable for council tax/rates;
- HB for a period of up to four weeks before moving into their home if they meet the conditions in paragraph 3.30.

5.45 In these cases, the date of claim is:

- in the first three cases above, any date in the week before the benefit week (para. 5.32) containing the birthday or event in question;
- in the fourth case above, the date of first liability for council tax/rates;
- in the fifth case above, the day the claim was received (para. 5.43), or if later, the date the claimant actually moves in.

DELAYS IN SETTING COUNCIL TAXES

CTB 69(11)
CTB60+ 53(11)

5.46 This rule applies if:

- an authority delays setting its council taxes until after 31st March in any year; and
- a CTB claim is received within four weeks after the setting of the council taxes.

5.47 In this case, the date of claim is set so that the claimant's entitlement begins on 1st April in that year (or the benefit week in which the person's entitlement begins if this falls between 1st April and the date the claim is received).

First day of entitlement

THE GENERAL RULE

HB 76(1)
HB60+ 57(1)
NIHB 73(1)
NIHB60+ 55(1)
CTB 64(1)
CTB60+ 48(1)

5.48 The general rule is the claimant's first day of entitlement to HB/CTB is the Monday following their 'date of claim' (as described earlier). Even if their date of claim is a Monday, their first day of entitlement is the following Monday. The exceptions follow.

THE WEEK-ONE-YES RULE

HB 76(2),80(4)(a)
HB60+ 57(2)
61(4)(a)
NIHB 73(2),77(4)(a)
NIHB60+ 55(2)
60(4)(a)
CTB 64(2),(5),57(1)
CTB60+
48(2)(5),40(1)

5.49 The week-one-yes rule applies only if the claimant or partner becomes liable for rent/council tax, and moves in, in the benefit week (para. 5.32) containing their 'date of claim'. In such cases, their first day of entitlement to HB/CTB is the day their liability for rent or council tax begins. In Northern Ireland the week-one-yes rule also applies to HB for rates if the rates are included in the rent.

If the result of the above is that the first day of entitlement is not a Monday, in the first benefit week the claimant's HB/CTB is calculated and awarded on a daily basis (the daily amount of HB/CTB being one-seventh of the weekly rent.)

Examples: First day of entitlement

THE GENERAL RULE

A man claims HB/CTB because his income has reduced. His date of claim is Wednesday 26th July 2006.

His first day of entitlement to HB/CTB is the Monday following his date of claim, which is Monday 31st July 2006.

THE WEEK-ONE-YES RULE: WHOLE WEEKS

A woman moves into her flat on Monday 1st May 2006, and is liable for rent and council tax from that very day. Her date of claim is Thursday 4th May 2006.

Her first day of entitlement to HB/CTB is the day her liability for rent/council tax begins, which is Monday 1st May 2006. (The answer is the same whether the rent is due weekly, monthly or on any other basis.)

THE WEEK-ONE-YES RULE: PART WEEKS

A woman moves into her flat on Saturday 1st June 2006, and is liable for rent and council tax from that very day. Her date of claim is Friday 31st May 2006.

Her first day of entitlement to HB/CTB is the day her liability for rent/council tax begins, which is Saturday 1st June 2006. In her first week she gets two-sevenths of a week's HB and CTB (for the Saturday and the Sunday). (The answer is the same whether the rent is due weekly, monthly or on any other basis.)

THE RULE FOR HOSTELS WITH DAILY RENTS

5.50 Since 1st April 2006, there is a new rule which applies only to residents of hostels (para. 6.10) who are liable to pay their rent on a daily basis. In their case, there is no time limit on when they may claim, and their HB is always awarded back to when they moved into the hostel: in other words, their first day of entitlement to HB is always the day they moved in. In practice this rule is likely to be used only for quite short periods (as leaving it any longer may mean the claimant is no longer available to provide the information and evidence necessary for their claim).

Awards for past periods for 60+s

5.51 In the case of a person aged 60 or more, or whose partner is, a claim covers any period in the 12 months before the day the claim is actually received – but only back to their 60th birthday, or the day they became liable for rent or council tax, if these would be later. HB60+ 64(1) NIHB60+ 63(1) CTB60+ 56

5.52 The claimant does not have to ask for this rule to apply: it applies automatically in all cases. In it not the same as 'backdating', and entitlement in the past need not have been continuous or even at the same address.

Example: Awards for past periods for 60+s

A claimant aged 70 sends in his first ever claim for HB/CTB. It reaches the authority on Thursday 21st September 2006. He would have qualified for several years for a small amount of HB/CTB had he applied.

His date of claim is Wednesday 21st September 2005 and (unless the week-one-yes rule applies: para. 5.49) the first day of his entitlement to HB/CTB is the following Monday, 26th September 2005.

Backdating for 'good cause'

BACKDATING HB/CTB

HB 83(12)
HB60+ 64(13)
NIHB 80(12)
NIHB60+ 63(13)
CTB 69(14)
CTB60+ 53(13)

5.53 The rules about backdating HB/CTB are as follows:

- HB/CTB must be backdated if the claimant requests this in writing, and 'had continuous good cause for [his or her] failure to make a claim'.
- HB/CTB cannot be backdated more than 52 weeks before the date on which the authority received the claimant's written request for backdating (even if this is later than when the claimant made his or her claim for HB/CTB).
- It is the date of claim which is backdated. So even if the claimant is not currently entitled to any HB/CTB, a claim can be backdated (if the above conditions are met) to a period when they were entitled;
- HB/CTB during any backdated period is calculated using the figures and calculation rules which applied at that time.

5.54 Backdating does not apply if the claimant or any partner is aged 60+, because for them there is an automatic equivalent to backdating (para. 5.51). The only exception is that if the claimant is aged 60+ but under 61, that rule only applies for periods back to their 60th birthday, and backdating applies for the remainder of the 52 weeks before that.

WHAT IS AND IS NOT 'BACKDATING'?

5.55 The question of backdating only arises when HB/CTB is requested for a past period for which the claimant has not already claimed HB/CTB. Basing a claim on an application form which was (on the balance of probability) received at the authority's designated office or an appropriate DWP office, but was then mislaid, does not count as backdating.

HOW TO CLAIM BACKDATED HB/CTB

5.56 Most authorities include a question on their HB/CTB application forms about whether the claimant wishes to claim backdating, but it is also possible to write a letter (at the time of claiming or later) to request backdating.

BACKDATING IS OBLIGATORY IF THERE IS 'GOOD CAUSE'

5.57 Backdating is obligatory once the authority determines that the claimant had good cause for failure to make the claim earlier and that his or her good cause lasted throughout the period in question (whether for the same reason throughout, or for a combination of successive reasons).

'GOOD CAUSE'

5.58 Good cause has been explained (in relation to various social security benefits) by commissioners and courts right back to the late 1940s, and this case law is binding in HB/CTB: CH/5221/2001. DWP guidance (GM chapter A2, annex A) gives a good summary of the case law up to April 2002, but there have been a number of further cases since then. The following is a brief summary of the main principles.

5.59 Good cause includes 'any fact that would probably have caused a reasonable person to act as the claimant did', but it is for the claimant to establish they have good cause. A claimant is expected to take reasonable steps to ascertain what his or her rights may be, but 'claimants cannot always be assumed to have an understanding of public administration' (this paragraph: CS/371/1949, quoted with approval in CH/450/2004).

5.60 The case law shows that the circumstances in which a claimant has good cause usually fall into four broad categories:

- the claimant was so ill (physically or mentally) or otherwise unable to act that they could not claim and could not ask someone to claim for them;
- someone the claimant should have been able to rely on (such as the authority, the DWP, an advice agency and possibly others) advised them they could not get HB/CTB when in fact they could;
- there were good reasons for the claimant not believing they could claim, amounting to more than just not thinking or not caring;
- some external factor prevented the claimant from making a claim (e.g. failure of the postal services, imprisonment).

Example: Backdating for good cause

A single claimant under 60 sends in his first ever claim for HB/CTB. It reaches the authority on Thursday 21st September 2006. He would have qualified for several years for a small amount of HB/CTB had he applied. With his claim he writes requesting his HB/CTB to be backdated to Sunday 4th June 2006 when he was admitted to hospital in an emergency. He was so ill that it was impossible for him to communicate throughout his time in hospital. He came home from hospital on Wednesday 13th September 2006, but took a few days to start thinking about his finances. He has a grown-up daughter living with him (and who remained in his house throughout).

Although his daughter could perhaps have decided to claim for him, this has no effect on his backdating request: CH/3817/2004. Whilst in hospital and unable to communicate he could not claim and could not ask someone to claim for him, so he had good cause. Taking eight days to claim, after such a bad illness, is how a reasonable person would act, so during those eight days he also had good cause.

Because he had continuous good cause, his HB/CTB must be backdated to Sunday 4th June 2006, the day he went into hospital. His HB/CTB therefore start on Monday 5th June 2006.

Note that in any backdating case, it is often possible to think of some other fact that might alter the answer. In this case for example, was he so ill before he went into hospital that his HB/CTB should be backdated to an earlier date? We do not know.

6 Referrals to the rent officer, etc

6.1 In Great Britain, authorities must refer details of many HB cases to the rent officer following a claim for HB and then at certain times during an award of HB. This does not apply to certain claims in the pathfinder areas with local housing allowances (para. 22.22 and table 22.1), but for all other areas this chapter explains the rules and covers:

- which cases must be referred to the rent officer, and when and how they are referred;
- the rent officer's determinations and how they are made;
- how errors and appeals are dealt with; and
- the rules about pre-tenancy determinations.

Rent officers are independent of the authority. In England, they are employed by the Rent Service, an executive agency of the DWP; in Wales, by the Rent Officer Service, an executive agency of the Welsh Assembly; and in Scotland by the Rent Registration Service, an executive agency of the Scottish Executive.

6.2 In Northern Ireland, there is no requirement to refer to the rent officer (and no rent officer). Instead, the Northern Ireland Housing Executive (NIHE) makes all decisions on HB claims including rent restriction. However, such decisions are required in exactly the same circumstances as referrals are required to be made to the rent officer in Great Britain, and the NIHE makes its decisions on the same basis that the rent officer makes his or her determinations in Great Britain (paras. 6.23-34) – with some exceptions mentioned in the chapter as they arise.

6.3 Rent officer referrals can be required in many kinds of rent allowance cases (including claims from private tenants or licensees, hostel residents, people renting a houseboat, mooring, mobile home or caravan site, people with a rental purchase agreement, and – in certain circumstances – housing association tenants). They are never required in rent rebate cases (claims from tenants of the authority administering HB). They relate only to HB for rent (not CTB or HB for rates in Northern Ireland).

WHY ARE REFERRALS MADE TO THE RENT OFFICER?

6.4 As described in this chapter, in Great Britain the rent officer provides the authority with various figures in respect of the cases referred to him or her – and in Northern Ireland similar rental valuations are made by the NIHE. In both cases, these figures are used in different ways depending on whether the HB case in question is an 'Old Scheme' or 'New Scheme' case (as defined in para. 10.7).

- In Old Scheme cases in Great Britain, the rent officer's figures are used to establish whether the authority might receive reduced HB subsidy on any part of the claimant's HB (chapter 23). In such cases in Northern Ireland, those subsidy implications do not apply. However, in either case, in assessing the HB claim, the authority must make its own determination of eligible rent based on the HB regulations (paras. 10.51 onwards).
- In New Scheme cases, the authority uses the rent officer's figures in calculating the claimant's 'eligible rent' (paras. 10.33 onwards): they are binding on the authority for this purpose.

6.5 The rent officer does not distinguish (in making his or her determinations) between the above types of case: it is the authority that decides which cases fall within which scheme. This is an important duty for the authority, since it can make a substantial difference to the amount of HB a claimant qualifies for.

Which cases are referred and when?

GENERAL RULES AND EXCEPTIONS

6.6 The authority must refer all HB cases to the rent officer, and the Executive in Northern Ireland must make a rent decision in all HB cases, except those falling in the list of exceptions in table 6.1. The referral or decision must be made at the following times:

HB 14(1)-(3),(8)
sch 2 para 2
HB60+ (1)-(3),(9)
sch 2 para 2
NIHB 15(1)
sch 3 para 2
NIHB60+ 15(3)
sch 3 para 2

(a) whenever it receives a new HB claim – unless less than 52 weeks have passed since it last made a referral for the dwelling and there has been no 'relevant change of circumstances'; and

(b) whenever it receives notification of a 'relevant change of circumstances' relating to an award of HB – even if less than 52 weeks have passed since it last made a referral for the dwelling; and

(c) whenever 52 weeks have passed since it last made a referral for the dwelling.

6.7 What counts as a 'relevant change of circumstances' is defined in paragraph 6.11 (and see also para. 6.8). Table 6.2 shows what date the rent officer's figures are implemented from.

6.8 The effect of point (a) in paragraph 6.6 is that if, say, a couple with no children claim HB and the case is referred to the rent officer, and six months later the couple move out and a claim for the dwelling is received from another couple with no children, then there is no referral because less than 52 weeks have passed

Table 6.1: Cases which are never referred to the rent officer

HB 14(1)
sch 2 paras 3-11
HB60 14(1)
sch 2 paras 3-11
NIHB 15(3)
sch 3 paras 3-6
NIHB60+ 15(3)
sch 3 paras 3-6

- Rent rebate cases (i.e. council tenants renting from the authority administering their HB, or in Northern Ireland tenants of the NI Housing Executive).
- Tenancies in England and Wales entered into before 15th January 1989 and tenancies in Scotland entered into before 2nd January 1989 (in other words, 'regulated tenancies': the dates just mentioned are those when the 1988 Housing Acts came into force).
- In Northern Ireland any controlled letting subject to the Rent (Northern Ireland) Order 1978, SI 1978 No. 1050.
- Any other 'regulated tenancies' which continue to fall within the Rent Act 1977 or the Rent (Agriculture) Act 1976 (these applied before the 1988 Housing Acts came into force). For example, a tenant whose tenancy began in 1988, but who was later transferred by the landlord to alternative accommodation, may still have a 'regulated tenancy'.
- Housing Action Trust lettings.
- Bail hostels.
- Lettings of former local authority or new towns housing stock which has been transferred to a new owner (for example, a housing association) under the Housing Act 1985 (or equivalent new towns provisions) or the tenants choice provisions of the Housing Act 1988 – unless there has been a rent increase since the date of the transfer and the authority states in the referral that the rent is unreasonably expensive or (for transfers which took place before 7th October 2002 only) that the accommodation is unreasonably large.
- Lettings where the landlord is a registered housing association or other registered social landlord – unless the authority considers that the accommodation is unreasonably large or the rent is unreasonably expensive, in which case the authority must make a referral and must state in making the referral that the rent is unreasonably expensive or that the accommodation is unreasonably large. In such cases, the authority should take into account all relevant factors: for example, in considering whether the accommodation is unreasonably large, the authority must not simply adopt the rent officer's size criteria (paras. 6.24-26).

and there has been no 'relevant change of circumstances' (since a change in identity is not sufficient: table 6.3). More detail is given in the example below.

Table 6.2: When rent office figures are implemented

DAR 7(2ZA),8(6A),(6B)
NIDAR 7(2ZA),8(6A),(6B)

REASON TRIGGERING THE REFERRAL	DATE RENT OFFICER FIGURE IS IMPLEMENTED FROM
A claim	The start of the award of HB
A 'relevant change of circumstances'	The date the change itself takes effect (typically the following Monday: chapter 17)
52 weeks have passed	If the rent officer's new determination means that the claimant qualifies for: *more HB or the same amount, and the claimant's rent is payable weekly or in multiples of weeks:* the day the referral was due, unless that is not a Monday, in which case from the Monday immediately before that day *more HB or the same amount, and the claimant's rent is payable otherwise than above:* the day the referral was due (which could be any day of the week) *less HB (regardless of when rent is payable):* the Monday following the date the rent officer determination 'was received' by the authority.

Example: Rent officer referrals, time limits and implementation dates

The claimant's first ever claim for HB is received by the authority on Tuesday 9th May 2006 and the authority refers the details to the rent officer that very day. The authority awards HB from Monday 15th May 2006.

- The rent officer's figures apply from Monday 15th May 2006.

There are no changes in the claimant's circumstances, so the next referral to the rent officer is due 52 weeks after the last one, which is Tuesday 8th May 2007. The referral is made. The rent officer's reply is received by the authority on Thursday 17th May 2007.

- If the rent officer's new figures mean the claimant is entitled to more HB (or the same amount) and the claimant's rent is due weekly or in multiples of weeks, then they apply to her case from Monday 7th May 2007.
- If the rent officer's new figures mean the claimant is entitled to more HB (or the same amount) and the claimant's rent is due calendar monthly or daily, then they apply to her case from Tuesday 8th May 2007 (i.e. on a daily basis).
- If the rent officer's new figures mean the claimant is entitled to less HB, then they apply to her case from Monday 21st May 2007 (the Monday after the authority received them).

The claimant's non-dependant (who has been there all along so far) moves out on Saturday 10th June 2007. Because this is a relevant change of circumstances, a further referral is required on Saturday 10th June 2007 and can be made up to three days after that date. It is in fact made on Monday 12th June 2007.

- The resulting new figures (whether higher, lower or the same) apply to the claimant's case from the Monday after the change of circumstances, namely Monday 12th June 2007.

REPRESENTATIVE REFERRALS FOR HOSTEL CASES

6.9 For hostel cases in Great Britain (para. 6.10), no referral is required if a rent officer determination has been made for similar accommodation within the hostel during the previous 12 months, unless there is a 'relevant change of circumstances' (para. 6.11). For these purposes, accommodation must be treated as similar if it provides the same number of bed spaces. It may also be treated as similar in other appropriate cases. The earlier referral applies to any such similar accommodation within the hostel. In Northern Ireland the NIHE decides whether a fresh decision is required in hostel cases on the same basis.

WHAT IS A 'HOSTEL'?

6.10 A 'hostel' is defined for HB purposes as any building (other than a care home or independent hospital: paras. 2.21-22) to which both the following apply:

HB 2(1)
HB60+ 2(1)
NIHB 2(1)
NIHB60+ 2(1)

- it provides domestic accommodation which is not self-contained together with meals or adequate facilities for preparing food; and
- it is:
  - managed or run by a registered housing association or registered social landlord, or
  - run on a non-commercial basis, and wholly or partly funded by a government department or agency or local authority, or
  - managed by a registered charity or non-profit-making voluntary organisation which provides care, support or supervision with a view to assisting the rehabilitation of the residents or their resettlement into the community.

WHAT IS A 'RELEVANT CHANGE OF CIRCUMSTANCES'?

6.11 Table 6.3 lists all the changes which count as a 'relevant change of circumstances' for the purposes of the rules described earlier. If there has been a 'relevant change of circumstances' since an HB case was last referred to the rent officer, a further referral must be made to the rent officer as a result of that change. If the authority does not become aware of such a change straightaway, a referral must be made when it does become aware of it.

HB 14(1)
sch 2 para 2
HB60+ 14(1)
sch 2 para 2
NIHB 15(3)
sch 3 para 2
NIHB60+ 15(3)
sch 3 para 3

Table 6.3: 'Relevant changes of circumstances'

- Except in hostel cases (para. 6.10), there has been a change in the number of occupiers.
- Any child or young person in the household has reached the age of 10 or 16 – but only if, at the last referral, the rent officer gave a size-related rent determination (para. 6.24).
- There has been a change in the composition of the household – but only if, at the last referral, the rent officer gave a size-related rent determination (para. 6.24). (One example is when two people have ceased to be a couple.)
- There has been a substantial change or improvement in the condition of the dwelling – regardless of whether there has been an associated change in the rent. (For example, central heating has been installed.)
- The claimant has moved to a new dwelling.
- There has been a substantial change in the terms of the letting agreement (excluding a change in a term relating to rent alone) – regardless of whether there has been an associated change in the rent. (For example, the landlord has taken over the responsibility for internal decorations from the tenant or *vice versa.*)
- There has been a rent increase and:
  - the rent increase was made under a term of the letting agreement (which need not be in writing) and that term is the same (or substantially the same) as at the previous referral to the rent officer; and
  - at the previous referral, the rent officer did not make any of the following determinations: a 'significantly high rent determination', a 'size-related rent determination' or an 'exceptionally high rent determination' (paras. 6.23-27).
- At the previous referral to the rent officer, the claimant was not a 'young individual' (para. 6.12), but the claimant in the current case is a 'young individual'.

DEFINITION OF 'YOUNG INDIVIDUAL'

6.12 Every claimant who is a 'single claimant' (para. 4.6) and is under the age of 25 is a 'young individual' (see also table 6.4) unless he or she:

HB 2(1),13(4)
HB60+ 2(1),13(4)
ROO 6(2)
NIHB 2(1),14(5)
NIHB60+ 2(1),14(5)

(a) rents his or her home from the authority, or in Northern Ireland the Housing Executive, itself;

(b) rents his or her home from a registered housing association or registered social landlord;

(c) is under the age of 22 and was formerly in social services care under a court order (under section 31(1)(a) of the Children Act 1989 in England and Wales, or equivalent provisions in Scotland and Northern Ireland) which applied (or continued to apply) after his or her 16th birthday;

(d) is under the age of 22 and was formerly provided with accommodation by social services (under section 20 of the Children Act 1989 in England and Wales, or equivalent provisions in Scotland and Northern Ireland) but is no longer in that accommodation or remains in it but the accommodation is no longer provided by social services;

(e) has one or more non-dependant(s);

(f) qualifies for a severe disability premium in the assessment of his or her HB (para. 12.23), income support or JSA(IB);

(g) lives in a care home or independent hospital (paras. 2.21-22);

(h) lives in certain types of hostel (as defined in para. 6.10).

6.13 As described in chapter 10, the rules applying to young individuals take account of the rent officer's 'single room rent determination'. It is the authority (not the rent officer) which decides whether someone is a 'young individual'. Note that (e) above applies only to non-dependants: having a sub-tenant, boarder or joint occupier does not stop someone being a 'young individual'. Technically, it is also worth noting that the law works in a peculiar way in the following cases:

- for claimants who fall in case (a) above, the law defines them as 'young individuals' but then says that no referral may be made to the rent officer in their case: this is the same as saying that they are not 'young individuals';
- for claimants who fall in cases (e) or (f) above, the law defines them as 'young individuals' but then says that the authority must ignore any single room rent determination made by the rent officer in their cases: this is the same as saying that they are not 'young individuals';
- for claimants who fall in cases (g) or (h) above, the law defines them as 'young individuals' but then says that the rent officer may not make a

single room rent determination in their cases: this is the same as saying that they are not 'young individuals' (except that it is the rent officer who determines whether they live in the accommodation described in those cases, not the authority).

Making the referral

TIME LIMITS AND METHOD OF REFERRAL

HB 14(6),(7)
HB60+ 14(6),(7)

6.14 The referral must be made within three working days of the event triggering it (table 6.3) or as soon as practicable thereafter. Days when the authority's offices are closed for receiving or determining claims do not count as 'working days' for this purpose. The DWP recommends authorities use a standard form (HBR1). Authorities and rent officers may agree to communicate electronically rather than in writing.

INFORMATION REQUIRED BY THE RENT OFFICER

HB 14(2),(3),114
HB60+ 14(2),(3),95

6.15 Table 6.4 lists the information the authority should give when making a referral to the rent officer. The law specifically requires certain information to be included (this is indicated in the table) and also generally requires the authority to provide any other information required by the rent officer. This other information can sometimes vary from rent officer to rent officer: the table shows what information is normally required.

Table 6.4: Information required by the rent officer

IDENTIFICATION AND GENERAL INFORMATION

- A case reference number.
- The claimant's name.
- The address of the property.
- The number of occupiers there.
- The age and sex of those occupiers and their relationship to the claimant (e.g. 'son', 'sub-tenant').
- The date the claimant commenced occupation (which may be approximate if necessary).
- Whether the landlord is a registered housing association or other registered social landlord.

- The details of the letting agreement, including the period of the letting.
- The type of accommodation (e.g. house, bedsit, room).
- In the case of a room, its location within the property (e.g. 'first floor, front').
- Details of all the rooms in the property, the ones the claimant has sole use of, and the ones the claimant has shared use of.

RENT, SERVICES, ETC

- Whether the claimant is a 'young individual' (para. 6.12)*.
- If the rent includes a charge for cleaning of rooms or windows (except so far as this is eligible for HB: para. 10.98); emergency alarms; medical, nursing or personal care; or general counselling or support:
    - the fact that it does*; and
    - the authority's valuation of the total value of these ineligible items*.
- The gross actual rent on the property after deducting the above valuation (if applicable)*.
- Whether the rent includes any amount for water charges, fuel or meals (but no valuation of any of these is required)*.
- Details of all other eligible and ineligible services included in the rent, and details of any variable service charges.
- Whether central heating is provided.
- Whether a garage is provided.
- Whether the accommodation is furnished fully, partly or minimally, or is unfurnished.
- Who is responsible for internal decorations (landlord or claimant).
- If the claimant is a joint occupier (para. 6.35) the figures for rent and services mentioned above should be those for the whole property*.
- In the case of combined domestic and business premises, the figures for rent and services mentioned above should relate only to the domestic part.
- The figures for rent and services mentioned above should be given for the period for which rent is due. For example, if the claimant's rent is due calendar monthly, they should be given as calendar monthly figures.

* **Note**
Items marked with an asterisk are those specifically mentioned in the law (para. 6.15).

The rent officer's determinations

ROO sch 1 paras 1-7 NIHB sch 2 paras 1-6 NIHB60+ sch 2 paras 1-6

6.16 The rent officer (in Northern Ireland the Housing Executive) may provide one or more of the following determinations. More information on each is given in the next few paragraphs:

- a claim-related rent determination;
- a local reference rent determination;
- a single room rent determination;
- certain determinations relating to service charges.

The rent officer does not make any determinations if the referral is withdrawn by the authority. The rent officer is not required to visit the dwelling but does so in some cases.

GENERAL RULES AND ASSUMPTIONS ABOUT DETERMINATIONS

ROO sch 1 paras 1-5,7,8 NIHB sch 2 paras 1-5,7,8 NIHB60+ sch 2 paras 1-5,7,8

6.17 In making the determinations described below (paras. 6.22-34), the rent officer (in Northern Ireland the Housing Executive):

- must base these on the facts as they stood on the date on which the authority made the referral, unless the claimant had left the accommodation by that date, in which case they are based on the facts as they stood at the end of the claimant's letting;
- provides these for the same period (e.g. weekly, calendar monthly) as that for which the authority supplied the information to the rent officer (table 6.4);
- must 'assume that no one who would have been entitled to housing benefit had sought or is seeking the tenancy';
- must ignore all rents payable to housing associations, other registered social landlords and registered charities;
- must include the value of any meals provided to the claimant (except that, in the case of the exceptionally high rent determination, the rent officer may choose whether to include meals or not);
- must exclude the value of all other service charges which are ineligible for HB (para. 10.75 onwards).

'LOCALITY', 'NEIGHBOURHOOD' AND 'VICINITY'

ROO sch 1 paras 1-4 NIHB sch 2 paras 1-5 NIHB sch 2 paras 1-5

6.18 In the past, the rent officer made all his or her determinations by reference to the 'locality', a concept which was not defined, but which was held in the Court of Appeal *(R (Saadat and Others) v the Rent Service)* to mean a relatively limited area. The law was amended as a result on 6th November 2001, eleven days after the judgment. Since then, the rent officer makes his or her determinations by reference to the 'locality', the 'neighbourhood' or the 'vicinity', as defined below. (In all the following, 'area' is not defined in the law and takes its ordinary English meaning.) No amending rules have yet been introduced for Northern Ireland and so the term 'locality' is still in use for all Northern Ireland rent decisions and so the *Saadat* decision may be relevant.

6.19 In Great Britain, 'locality' (used in determining local reference rents: para. 6.28; and single room rents: para. 6.31) means an area: ROO sch 1 para 4(6)

- which comprises two or more neighbourhoods (as defined below), one of which must be the neighbourhood where the dwelling is, and each of which must adjoin at least one other; AND
- where a tenant of the dwelling 'could reasonably be expected to live having regard to facilities and services for the purposes of health, education, recreation, personal banking and shopping which are in or accessible from the neighbourhood of the dwelling, taking account of the distance of travel, by public and private transport, to and from facilities of the same type and similar standard'; AND
- which contains 'residential premises of a variety of types' including ones held on a 'variety of tenancies'.

6.20 'Neighbourhood' (used in determining exceptionally high rents: para. 6.27; and in part of the definition of locality: para. 6.19) means: ROO sch 1 para 3(5)

- in the case of dwelling in a town or city, 'that part of that town or city where the dwelling is located which is a distinct area of residential accommodation';
- in the case of a dwelling not in a town or city, 'the area surrounding the dwelling which is a distinct area of residential accommodation' and where there are dwellings satisfying the size criteria (table 6.5).

6.21 'Vicinity' (used in determining significantly high rents: para. 6.23; and size-related rents: para. 6.24) means: ROO sch 1 para 1(4)

- 'the area immediately surrounding the dwelling';
- however, for size-related rents only (not significantly high rents), if 'the area immediately surrounding the dwelling' contains no dwellings matching the size criteria (table 6.5), 'vicinity' instead means 'the area nearest to the [claimant's] dwelling where there is such a dwelling'.

CLAIM-RELATED RENT DETERMINATIONS

6.22 In all cases, the rent officer must make a 'claim-related rent determination.' This is the only, lower or lowest of the following (the latter three are described in the following paragraphs): ROO sch 1 para 6 NIHB sch 2 para 6 NIHB60+ sch 2 para 6

- the referred rent, adjusted (as regards service charges) in accordance with the general rules and assumptions (para. 6.17);
- the significantly high rent;
- the size-related rent;
- the exceptionally high rent.

SIGNIFICANTLY HIGH RENT DETERMINATIONS

ROO sch 1 para 1
NIHB sch 2 para 1
NIHB60+ sch 2 para 1

6.23 The rent officer determines whether the referred rent for the dwelling is 'significantly higher than the rent which the landlord might reasonably have been expected to obtain'. If it is, he or she makes a significantly high rent determination: this is the amount 'the landlord might reasonably have been expected to obtain' for the dwelling, having regard to 'the level of rent under similar tenancies [or licences] of similar dwellings in the vicinity (or as similar as regards tenancy [or licence], dwelling and vicinity as reasonably practicable'. 'Vicinity' is defined in para. 6.21. Also, the general rules and assumptions apply (para. 6.17). In Northern Ireland 'locality' is still used instead of 'vicinity'.

SIZE-RELATED RENT DETERMINATIONS

ROO sch 1 para 2
NIHB sch 2 para 2
NIHB60+ sch 2 para 2

6.24 Except in the case of site rents for caravans or mobile homes and mooring charges for houseboats, the rent officer also determines whether the dwelling exceeds the size criteria given in paragraph 6.25 and table 6.5. If it does, he or she makes a size-related rent determination: this is the amount 'the landlord might reasonably have been expected to obtain' on a dwelling which:

- is in 'the same vicinity' (in Northern Ireland 'locality'); and
- is let under a similar tenancy under the same terms as the tenancy of the dwelling in question; and
- matches those size criteria; and
- is in a reasonable state of repair; and
- in other respects, matches the claimant's dwelling 'as closely as reasonably practicable'.

'Vicinity' is defined in para. 6.21. Also, the general rules and assumptions apply (para. 6.17).

6.25 The size criteria (para. 6.24 and table 6.5) allow for every 'occupier' – which is defined for this purpose as 'a person (whether or not identified by name) who is stated [by the authority], in the application [to the rent officer] for the determination, to occupy the dwelling'. There is no further definition, but the term appears intended to have a degree of flexibility. Note that (as circular HB/CTB A18/97 points out), the authority (not the rent officer) determines whether or not someone is an 'occupier'; and the term is not expressly limited to those

Table 6.5: The rent officer's size criteria

These are relevant for size-related rent determinations (para. 6.24), exceptionally high rent determinations (para. 6.27) and local reference rent determinations (para. 6.28). For who counts as an occupier for these purposes, see paragraphs 6.25-26.

- ◆ One room is allowed as a bedroom for each of the following occupiers, each occupier coming only within the first category which applies to him or her:
  - a couple (para. 4.9);
  - a single person aged 16 or more;
  - two children of the same sex under the age of 16;
  - two children (of the same or opposite sexes) under the age of 10;
  - a child under the age of 16.
- ◆ One, two or three living rooms ('rooms suitable for living in') are allowed as follows:
  - one if there are one to three occupiers;
  - two if there are four to six occupiers;
  - three if there are seven or more occupiers.
- ◆ The size criteria relate to the total number of rooms allowed (under either of the above headings). It is irrelevant whether the claimant actually uses those rooms as bedrooms or living rooms.

Example: The rent officer's size criteria

A couple have two children aged 6 and 8. No-one else lives with them. Their dwelling has three bedrooms, one living room, a kitchen, a bathroom, a toilet and several uninhabitable cupboards.

The rent officer's size criteria ignore the kitchen, bathroom and toilet. The criteria allow them four bedrooms/living rooms in all, as follows:

- ◆ one room as a bedroom for the couple;
- ◆ one room as a bedroom for the two children;
- ◆ two rooms as living rooms – because there are four occupiers.

Their four rooms (three bedrooms and one living room) do not exceed the size criteria because bedrooms and living rooms are interchangeable for these purposes.

whose circumstances are taken into account in the calculation of the claimant's entitlement to HB (though see below). It is clear that all the following should be included as 'occupiers' for this purpose:

- the claimant and members of his or her family (paras. 4.7-40); and
- everyone else who normally lives in the dwelling, such as non-dependants, (sub-)tenants, boarders, joint occupiers, certain carers (para. 4.51) and certain other children and young persons who do not count as a member of the family (para. 4.6).

6.26 The Court of Appeal in *R v Swale BC HBRB ex p Marchant* held in 1999 that a child who spends time in the homes of each of his or her parents (who live apart) counts as an 'occupier' only in the home of the parent who is 'responsible' for him or her (para. 4.33 – typically the one who receives child benefit). However, the more recent *Hockenjos* case (para. 4.35) may over-ride this in appropriate circumstances. *Marchant* does not apply in other difficult situations. One example is that of a grown-up child who lives away from home for part(s) of the year (perhaps as a student) but returns home from time to time (perhaps in the holidays). It is clear that he or she counts as an 'occupier' in weeks in which he or she is treated as a non-dependant. In other weeks (if any), it can be argued that he or she counts as an 'occupier' (since the definition of 'occupier' appears flexible and is unaffected in this situation by the Marchant case), but it is unlikely that all local authorities will agree with this. Matters such as this are open to appeal.

EXCEPTIONALLY HIGH RENT DETERMINATIONS

ROO 6(2) sch 1 para 3 NIHB sch 2 para 3 NIHB60+ sch 2 para 3

6.27 Except in the case of hostels (para. 6.10) or care homes and independent hospitals (para. 2.21-22), the rent officer also determines whether either of the figures described above (paras. 6.23-26), or (if he or she has not made a determination in either of those cases) the referred rent for the dwelling, is 'exceptionally high'. If it is, he or she makes an exceptionally high rent determination: this is 'the highest rent, which is not an exceptionally high rent and which a landlord might reasonably have been expected to obtain' on a dwelling which:

- is in 'the same neighbourhood'(in Northern Ireland 'locality'); and
- matches the size criteria (table 6.5); and
- is in a reasonable state of repair.

'Neighbourhood' is defined in para. 6.20. Also the general rules and assumptions apply (para. 6.17).

LOCAL REFERENCE RENT DETERMINATIONS

ROO 6(2) sch 1 para 4 NIHB sch 2 para 4 NIHB60+ sch 2 para 4

6.28 Except in the case of hostels (para. 6.10) or care homes and independent hospitals (para. 2.21-22), the rent officer also determines whether any of the figures described above (paras. 6.23-27), or (if he or she has not made a determination in any of those cases) the referred rent for the dwelling, is greater than the 'local reference rent' described below. If it is, he or she makes a local reference rent determination (in other words, notifies the authority of the local reference rent). If it is not, he or she notifies the authority that it is not.

6.29 In determining the 'local reference rent', the rent officer takes account of the range of rents 'which a landlord might reasonably have been expected to obtain' on dwellings which:

- are in 'the same locality'; and
- match the size criteria (table 6.5) or have the same number of rooms as the claimant's dwelling, if less; and
- in the case of one-room dwellings, are in the same category as the claimant's dwelling (see below); and
- are let on an assured tenancy (or a similar tenancy or licence, including a student letting when appropriate); and
- are in a reasonable state of repair.

'Locality' is defined in para. 6.19 (except for Northern Ireland: para. 6.18). Also the general rules and assumptions apply (para. 6.17).

The categories (mentioned above) of one-room dwellings are:

- one-room dwellings where a 'substantial' part of the rent is 'fairly attributable' to 'board and attendance' included within the rent;
- other one-room dwellings where the tenant shares a kitchen, toilet, bathroom and living room ('room suitable for living in') with someone who is not a member of his or her household (paras. 4.3-5 and 6.26); and
- other one-room dwellings.

For the purposes of deciding whether it is a one-room dwelling in the first place, the definition of a 'room' is the same as in the note to table 6.6.

6.30 The 'local reference rent' is then the figure which is half-way between:

- the lowest such rent which is not an 'exceptionally low rent'; and
- the highest such rent which is not an 'exceptionally high rent'.

SINGLE ROOM RENT DETERMINATIONS

6.31 Except in the case of hostels (para. 6.10) or care homes and independent hospitals (paras. 2.21-22), and only if the authority states in the referral that the claimant is a 'young individual' (para. 6.12), the rent officer also determines whether the claimant's rent is greater than the 'single room rent' described below. If it is, he or she makes a single room rent determination (in other words, notifies the authority of the single room rent). If it is not, he or she notifies the authority that it is not.

ROO 6(2)
sch 1 para 5
NIHB 15(3)(c)
sch 2 para 5
NIHB60+ 15(3)(c)
sch 2 para 5

6.32 In determining the 'single room rent', the rent officer takes account of the range of rents 'which a landlord might reasonably have been expected to obtain' on dwellings which:

- provide exclusive use of one bedroom;
- provide no other bedroom;
- provide shared use of a living room ('room suitable for living in');
- provide shared use of a toilet and bathroom;
- provide shared use of a kitchen (and no exclusive use of facilities for cooking food);
- do not provide board and attendance;
- are in 'the same locality';
- are let on an assured tenancy (or a similar tenancy or licence, including a student letting when appropriate);
- are in a reasonable state of repair.

'Locality' is defined in para. 6.19 (para. 6.18 for Northern Ireland). Also the general rules and assumptions apply (para. 6.17).

6.33 The 'single room rent' is then the figure which is half-way between:

- the lowest such rent which is not an 'exceptionally low rent'; and
- the highest such rent which is not an 'exceptionally high rent'.

SERVICE CHARGES DETERMINATIONS

ROO sch 1 paras 6(3),7 NIHB sch 2 paras 6(3),(7) NIHB60+ sch 2 paras 6(3),(7)

6.34 Except in the case of a hostel (para. 6.10); the rent officer must determine the value of the ineligible service charges (apart from meals) he or she excluded in making the claim-related rent determination (unless the amount is negligible).

JOINT OCCUPIERS

ROO 2(1)(a) NIHB 2(1)(a) NIHB60+ 2(1)(a)

6.35 In the case of accommodation occupied by joint occupiers, the rent officer's determinations (apart from the single room rent determination) relate to the dwelling as a whole. It is for the authority to make any necessary apportionment (para. 10.6).

NOTIFICATION AND TIME LIMITS

ROO sch 1 para 9

6.36 In Great Britain only, the rent officer has a duty to notify the authority of the following:

- the claim-related rent (all cases);
- the local reference rent (if any);
- the single room rent (if any);

- except in the case of a hostel (para. 6.10), the value of the ineligible service charges (apart from meals and support charges) he or she has excluded in making his or her claim-related rent determination;
- whether the claim-related rent includes an amount for ineligible meals (as can be the case if it is an exceptionally high rent determination).

6.37 The rent officer should notify the authority of the above determinations within five working days or, if the rent officer intends to inspect the dwelling, within 25 working days (or, in either case, as soon as reasonably practicable after that). The period begins on the day the rent officer receives the referral from the authority or (if he or she has requested this) on the day he or she receives further information needed from the authority. ROO 2(1)(a),3(1)(a)

Table 6.6: Indicative rent levels: the rent officer's categories of dwelling

(a) One-room dwellings where a 'substantial' part of the rent is 'fairly attributable' to 'board and attendance' included within the rent.

(b) Other one-room dwellings where the tenant shares a kitchen or toilet with someone who is not a member of his or her household (paras. 4.3-5 and 6.26).

(c) Other one-room dwellings.

(d) Two-room dwellings.

(e) Three-room dwellings.

(f) Four-room dwellings.

(g) Five-room dwellings.

(h) Six-room dwellings.

Note: Definition of 'room'

For these purposes, a 'room' is defined as a 'bedroom or room suitable for living in':

- including a room the claimant shares with any member of his or her household, including a non-dependant (paras. 3.5-8), or with a boarder or (sub-)tenant (paras. 4.46, 4.48-49);
- but (in the case of one-room dwellings: categories (a) to (c)) excluding a room he or she shares with anyone else.

INDICATIVE RENT LEVELS

ROO sch 1 para 11 NIHB sch 2 para 9 NIHB60+ sch 2 para 9

6.38 Separate from the provisions described above, the rent officer provides each authority, on the first working day of each month, with 'indicative rent levels' for its area. The law allows the authority to take these into account in estimating payments on account (para. 16.16), and the subsidy rules encourage this. Indicative rent levels do not apply to site rents for caravans or mobile homes, houseboat moorings or rental purchase agreements. (They also do not take account of the rent officer's size criteria: table 6.5.)

6.39 One 'indicative rent level' is provided for each category of dwelling shown in table 6.6. In determining the indicative rent level for each category, the rent officer takes account of the range of rents 'which a landlord might reasonably have been expected to obtain' on dwellings which:

- are in that category;
- are in the area of the authority (not 'the locality' of the dwelling);
- are let on an assured tenancy (or a similar tenancy or licence); and
- are in a reasonable state of repair;
- adjusted – as regards service charges only – in accordance with the general rules and assumptions (para. 6.17).

The 'indicative rent level' for each category is then:

- the lowest such rent which is not an 'exceptionally low rent'; plus
- one-quarter of the difference between that and the highest such rent which is not an 'exceptionally high rent'.

Appeals and errors

6.40 There is no right of appeal to a social security appeal tribunal against the rent determinations made by the rent officer (or in Northern Ireland against rent decisions made by the NIHE). Instead, the following procedures apply (paras. 6.41-50 for Great Britain; para. 6.51 for Northern Ireland). In England the courts have considered that these procedures are sufficiently independent to comply with the Human Rights Act: *R (on the application of Cumpsty) v The Rent Service.* This case is at least very strongly persuasive in Wales and Scotland.

APPEALS BY THE CLAIMANT

HB 16 HB60+ 16

6.41 This section applies only in Great Britain. For Northern Ireland, see para. 6.51. If a claimant makes written representations to the authority relating wholly or partly to any determination by the rent officer (and does so within six weeks of notification of the HB decision based on that rent officer determination), the authority must, within seven days of receipt apply to the rent officer for a re-determination for the case in question. The authority must forward the claimant's representations at the same time. This must be done even if the representations are made by a later claimant at the same address. There are however limitations (in the next paragraph).

6.42 For any particular claimant and any particular dwelling, only one application to the rent officer may be made in respect of any particular determination (plus one in respect of any particular substitute determination: para. 6.49). This is the case regardless of whether the authority itself has previously chosen to make an application for a re-determination. HB 16 HB60+ 16

6.43 However, a claimant who considers that a referral should or should not have been made in the first place (e.g. a claimant who disputes whether he or she falls within one of the exceptions described earlier in this chapter) has the right to use the ordinary HB appeals procedure (chapter 19) to challenge this. This is because the determination whether or not to refer a case to the rent officer is made by the authority.

APPEALS BY THE AUTHORITY

6.44 The authority (in Great Britain only) may itself choose to apply to the rent officer for a re-determination. For any particular claimant and any particular dwelling, it may do this only once in respect of any particular determination (plus once in respect of any particular substitute determination: para. 6.49); unless a re-determination is subsequently made as a result of an appeal by the claimant (para. 6.41), in which case the authority may do this once more.

RENT OFFICER RE-DETERMINATIONS

6.45 In each of the cases described above (paras. 6.41-44), the rent officer must make a complete re-determination. Even if the application for a re-determination relates only to one figure, the rent officer has to reconsider all matters pertaining to the case in question. All the assumptions, etc, applying to determinations (para. 6.17 onwards) apply equally to re-determinations. Re-determinations should be made within 20 working days or as soon as practicable after that. The period begins on the day the rent officer receives the application from the authority or (if he or she has requested this) on the day he or she receives further information needed from the authority. HB 15 HB60+ 15 ROO 4, sch 3

6.46 The rent officer making the re-determination (called a 're-determination officer') must seek and have regard to the advice of one or two other rent officers. In England, the Rent Service (formerly the rent officer service) has set up independent re-determination units and advises that reasons for their re-determinations are always supplied to the claimant and the authority. Similar arrangements are in place in Wales and Scotland. It would certainly be open to challenge if reasons were not given (as happened fairly frequently in the past).

HOW THE RE-DETERMINATION AFFECTS HB

6.47 In broad terms, re-determinations affect HB in the same way as determinations (para. 6.4). However, in 'New Scheme' cases (para. 10.7), the following further rules apply:

- If the effect of the re-determination is that the 'maximum rent' increases, this applies from the date of the rent officer's original determination. So the claimant is awarded any resulting arrears of HB (but this applies only to the claimant in question, not to a previous claimant at the same address).
- If the effect of the re-determination is that the 'maximum rent' reduces, this applies from the date of the rent officer's re-determination following the appeal: the reduction is not applied retrospectively. So it does not mean (unless the authority delays applying it) that the claimant has been overpaid HB.

DEALING WITH ERRORS

ROO 4A(1),(7) **6.48** The rent officer has a duty to notify the authority, as soon as is practicable, upon discovering that he or she has made an error, other than one of professional judgment, in a determination or re-determination (including a substitute determination or substitute re-determination). This applies in Great Britain only. The authority must then apply to the rent officer for a substitute determination (or substitute re-determination), and the DWP advises (circular HB/CTB G5/2005) that only one such application need be made covering all future cases (rather than the authority applying on a case by case basis).

ROO 4A(1) **6.49** The authority must apply, on a case by case basis, to the rent officer for a substitute determination (or substitute re-determination) if it discovers that it made an error in its application to the rent officer as regards the size of the dwelling, the number of occupiers, the composition of the household or the terms of the tenancy. In all such cases, the authority must state the nature of the error and withdraw any outstanding applications for rent officer determinations in that case.

ROO 4A(2) **6.50** All the assumptions, etc, applying to determinations (para. 6.17 onwards) also apply to substitute determinations/re-determinations. In broad terms, substitute determinations and substitute re-determinations affect HB in the same way as re-determinations (para. 6.47).

APPEALS IN NORTHERN IRELAND

NIDAR 4(1) sch para 1 **6.51** In Northern Ireland a decision to restrict the rent is made by the Executive so the decision can be revised or superseded in the normal way (para. 17.43). Application for a revision must be made wihin one month. However, a decision which restricts the rent cannot be appealed.

Pre-tenancy determinations

HOW TO GET A PRE-TENANCY DETERMINATION

6.52 People can find out whether their HB would be likely to be restricted if they claimed HB, by asking for a 'pre-tenancy determination' ('PTD'). Any 'prospective occupier' of any dwelling (other than a council letting) may apply to the authority requesting it to refer the rent to the rent officer. So may any current occupier of a dwelling whose current agreement commenced at least 11 months previously and who is contemplating entering a new agreement there (but see para. 6.55). Authorities have standard forms for people who require a PTD.

HB 14(5)
HB60+ 14(5)
ROO 3(1)
NIHB 16(5)
NIHB60+ 16(5)

6.53 The main conditions for getting a PTD are that the person must:

HB 14(1)
HB60+ 14(1)
NIHB 16(1)
NIHB60+ 16(1)

- indicate on the form that he or she would be likely to claim HB if he or she took up the letting (or took up the new agreement);
- sign the form; and
- obtain a signature on the form from the landlord consenting to a referral. The landlord will be expected to provide the rent officer with necessary information and allow access to the dwelling.

THE AUTHORITY'S DUTIES

6.54 With two exceptions (para. 6.55), whenever an authority receives a request for a PTD, it must refer the details to the rent officer within two working days of the date of the request for the PTD. The rent officer's duties in such cases are described in paragraph 6.56.

HB 14(6)
HB60+ 14(6)

6.55 First, if the request for the PTD is invalid (e.g. if the landlord has not consented), the authority must return it to the person along with a notification of why it is invalid. Secondly, if:

HB 14(5)
HB60+ 14(5)

- the authority already has a rent officer determination which was made for the dwelling in question; and
- the conditions for making a further referral to the rent officer are not met (table 6.3),

the authority must, within four working days of the request for the PTD, supply details of that determination to the person along with a notification of why a current PTD referral cannot be made.

RENT OFFICER AND NIHE TIME LIMITS

6.56 When the rent officer receives a referral requesting a PTD, he or she makes the same determinations as in any other case referred to him or her. The rent officer notifies the result to the authority within five working days. In Northern Ireland where the Executive receives a PTD it should make a decision within seven days.

ROO 2(1)(a),3(1)(a)
NIHB 16(3)
NIHB60+ 16(3)

CLAIMS FOR HB FOLLOWING A PRE-TENANCY DETERMINATION

HB 12(3),13(1),14 HB60+ 12(3),13(1),14

6.57 With two exceptions (para. 6.58), when the authority receives an HB claim on a dwelling to which a PTD applies, the authority uses the PTD in the same way as if it had been a rent officer determination made following the claim (i.e. no additional referral is required).

6.58 The PTD does not apply, and a referral must be made to the rent officer, if:

- the PTD was made more than 12 months ago; or
- the circumstances indicated in the claim for HB are different from those indicated in the request for the PTD (i.e. there are differences between them which constitute a 'relevant change of circumstances': para. 6.11).

CALCULATING 'MAXIMUM RENTS' FROM PRE-TENANCY DETERMINATIONS

HB 13(7),(8) HB60+ 13(7),(8) NIHB 14(9),(10) NIHB60+ 14(9),(10)

6.59 With the exceptions described in the previous and following paragraphs, whenever the authority is required to calculate a 'maximum rent' in assessing a claimant's eligible rent (chapter 10), it uses the rent officer figures provided in the PTD.

6.60 If the claimant's actual rent at the date of his or her claim for HB is lower than the 'maximum rent' calculated from the rent officer figures provided in the PTD, similar points arise as in paragraph 10.45.

APPEALS

DAR 1(2),3(1)(a) NIDAR 1(2),3(1)(a)

6.61 There is no right of appeal relating to a pre-tenancy determination until and unless it is used in connection with the determination of a claim for HB (in which case the ordinary rules about appeals about rent officer determinations apply: paras. 6.4 onwards).

7 Calculating HB and main CTB

7.1 This chapter explains:

- how to calculate HB and main CTB;
- who counts as a non-dependant, and how non-dependant deductions affect HB and main CTB; and
- how figures are converted to weekly amounts and when they are rounded.

Different rules apply to second adult rebate (chapter 8), 'extended payments' (para. 17.81) and 'continuing payments' (para. 17.94).

7.2 In broad terms, claimants with no income or low income (including all claimants on JSA(IB), IS or guarantee credit) qualify for maximum benefit – which may be reduced if there are non-dependants in their home. The more income claimants have, the less benefit they get, but there is no general upper limit. The level of income at which benefit entitlement runs out varies from claimant to claimant depending on a wide range of factors.

How much HB/CTB

7.3 The next few paragraphs explain with examples how to calculate entitlement to HB and main CTB on a weekly basis. Table 7.1 summarises the rules.

MAXIMUM BENEFIT

CBA 130(1),(4) 131(1),(3) HB 70 HB60+ 50 NIHB 67 NIHB 60+ 50 CTB 57 CTB60+ 40

7.4 The starting point for all calculations of HB and main CTB is the claimant's 'maximum benefit'. On a weekly basis, this is:

- in calculating HB:
  - the whole of the claimant's weekly eligible rent (chapter 10) and/or rates in Northern Ireland (chapter 11),
  - minus any non-dependant deductions which apply;
- in calculating main CTB:
  - the whole of the claimant's weekly eligible council tax (chapter 9),
  - minus any non-dependant deductions which apply.

CLAIMANTS ON JSA(IB), IS OR GUARANTEE CREDIT

CBA 130(1),(3) 131(5),(6) HB 2(3), sch 5 paras 4,5, sch 6 paras 5,6 HB60+ 2(3) NIHB 2(3) sch 6 paras 4,5, sch 7 paras 5,6 NIHB60+ 2(3),24 CTB 2(4) sch 4 paras 4,5, sch 5 paras 5,6 CTB60+ 2(4)

7.5 A claimant qualifies for maximum benefit (para. 7.4) whilst he or she (or any partner) is:

- on income-based jobseeker's allowance (JSA(IB)); or
- on income support (IS); or
- on guarantee credit; or
- treated as receiving JSA(IB) or IS (para. 7.6).

CLAIMANTS TREATED AS BEING ON JSA(IB) OR IS

HB 2(1),(3) NIHB 2(1),(3) NIHB60+ 2(1),(3) CTB 2(1),(4)

7.6 A claimant also qualifies for maximum benefit (para. 7.4) whilst he or she (or any partner) is:

- entitled to JSA(IB) but not receiving it because of a sanction; or
- in the 'waiting days' before his or her JSA(IB) starts – or would start apart from a sanction; or
- subject to a restriction in his or her JSA(IB) or IS as a result of breaching a community order; or
- disqualified from getting JSA(IB) following certain convictions (para. 7.16).

7.7 In these cases, the law works by treating the claimant as though he or she was actually on JSA(IB) or IS.

CLAIMANTS NOT ON JSA(IB), IS OR GUARANTEE CREDIT

7.8 In any case other than those described above (paras. 7.5-7), if the claimant's capital (assessed as in chapters 13 to 15) is over £16,000, then he or she does not qualify for any HB or main CTB at all, and so the remainder of this chapter does not apply. Otherwise, the claimant's weekly income (chapters 13 to 15) is compared with his or her applicable amount (chapter 12).

7.9 If the claimant has no income, or has income which is less than (or equal to) his or her applicable amount, the claimant qualifies for maximum benefit (para. 7.4). CBA 130(1),(3) NICBA 129(1),(3)

7.10 If the claimant's weekly income is more than his or her applicable amount, the difference between the two is known as 'excess income'. The claimant qualifies for: CBA 130(1),(3), 131(5),(8) NICBA 129(1),(3)

- maximum benefit (para. 7.4);
- minus a percentage of this excess income (para. 7.11).

HB 71
HB60+ 51
NIHB 68
NIHB60+ 49
CTB 59
CTB60+ 43

7.11 The percentage, also known as a 'taper', is as follows:

- 65 per cent in calculating HB (for rent);
- 20 per cent in calculating main CTB;
- 20 per cent in calculating HB for rates in Northern Ireland.

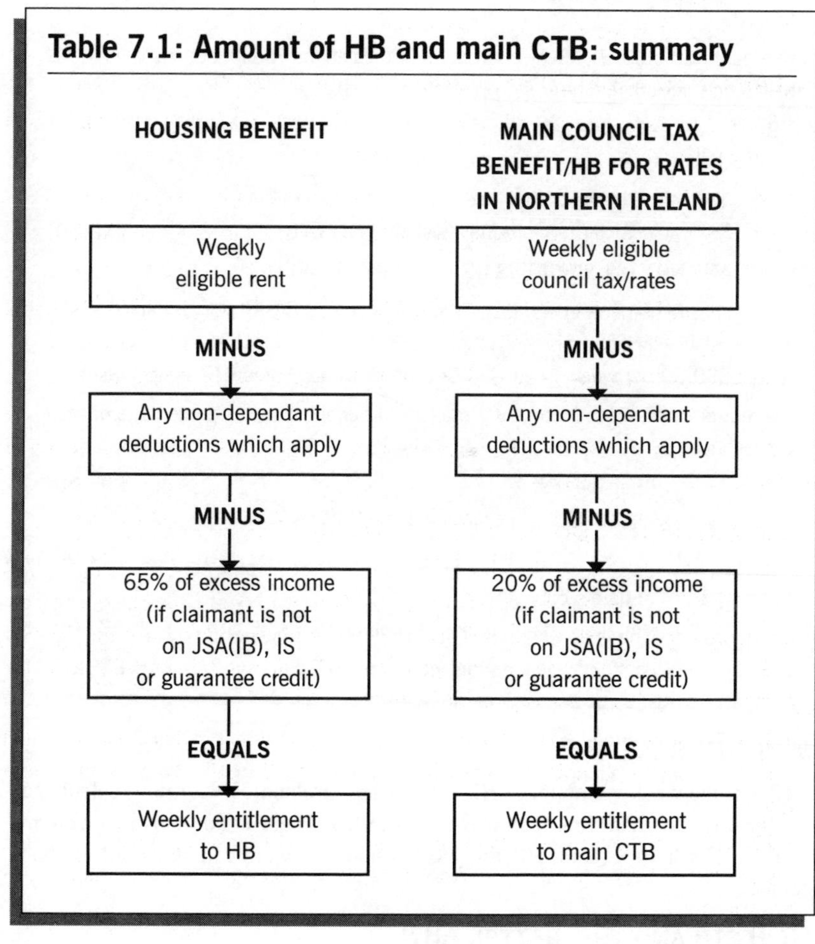

Table 7.1: Amount of HB and main CTB: summary
HOUSING BENEFIT
MAIN COUNCIL TAX BENEFIT/HB FOR RATES IN NORTHERN IRELAND
Weekly eligible rent
Weekly eligible council tax/rates
MINUS
Any non-dependant deductions which apply
MINUS
65% of excess income (if claimant is not on JSA(IB), IS or guarantee credit)
20% of excess income (if claimant is not on JSA(IB), IS or guarantee credit)
EQUALS
Weekly entitlement to HB
Weekly entitlement to main CTB

Examples: Calculating HB and main CTB

CLAIMANT ON JSA(IB), IS OR GUARANTEE CREDIT

A claimant has no non-dependants: she lives alone. Her eligible rent is £85.00 per week. The council tax on her home would be £16.00 per week apart from the fact that she qualifies for a 25% council tax discount, which reduces her liability to £12.00 per week.

Claimants on JSA(IB), IS or guarantee credit get maximum benefit – which is based on their eligible rent and eligible council tax.

HB:	Eligible rent	
	equals weekly HB	£85.00
Main CTB:	Eligible council tax	
	equals weekly main CTB	£12.00

CLAIMANT NOT ON JSA(IB), IS OR GUARANTEE CREDIT

A couple have no non-dependants. They are not on JSA(IB), IS or guarantee credit. Their joint weekly income exceeds their applicable amount by £20.00. Their eligible rent is £90.00 per week. Their eligible council tax liability is £17.56 per week.

Claimants with excess income get maximum benefit minus a percentage of their excess income.

HB:	Eligible rent	£90.00
	minus 65% of excess income (65% x £20.00)	£13.00
	equals weekly HB	£77.00
Main CTB:	Eligible council tax	£17.56
	minus 20% of excess income (20% x £20.00)	£4.00
	equals weekly main CTB	£13.56

MINIMUM BENEFIT

7.12 If the weekly amount of HB (in Northern Ireland, HB for rent) calculated as above is less than 50p, then it is not awarded. There is no equivalent rule in CTB (in Northern Ireland, HB for rates), where an award can be as little as one penny.

HB 75
HB60+ 56
NIHB 72
NIHB60+ 54

MAIN CTB AND THE 'BETTER BUY'

7.13 If the amount of a claimant's main CTB calculated as above is lower than his or her entitlement to second adult rebate, he or she will not get main CTB, but will get second adult rebate instead. This is because of the 'better buy' comparison, described in paragraphs 8.29 onwards. Examples are given at the end of chapter 8.

CBA 131(9)

HB AND RENT-FREE PERIODS

HB 81(1),(2)
HB60+ 62(1),(2)
NIHB 78(1),(2)
NIHB60+ 61(1),(2)

7.14 The following additional rules apply if a claimant has rent-free weeks or other rent-free periods. They do not apply in cases where a landlord has waived the rent in return for works carried out by the tenant (para. 2.36). No HB is awarded during rent-free periods, including in Northern Ireland rate-free periods where rates are paid with the rent. HB is awarded only for periods in which rent is due (and in the unlikely event that a rent-free period begins or ends part way through a benefit week, the eligible rent that week is calculated on a daily basis: para. 7.41).

HB 81(3)
HB60+ 62(3)
NIHB 78(3)
NIHB60+ 61(3)

7.15 During the periods in which rent is due, the calculation factors (i.e. applicable amount, income and any non-dependant deductions) are adjusted as follows:

- if rent is expressed on a weekly basis: multiply the calculation factors by 52 or 53, then divide by the number of weeks when rent is due in that year;
- if rent is not expressed on a weekly basis: multiply the calculation factors by 365 or 366, then divide by the number of days when rent is due in that year.

OTHER REASONS HB/CTB MAY BE LOWER

7.16 It is also worth bearing in mind that the claimant's actual entitlement can be reduced for the following reasons:

- to recover a recoverable overpayment (para. 18.10);
- to recover an administrative penalty (para. 18.75); or
- to punish him or her for two or more convictions relating to fraud in the space of three years (vulgarly known as the 'two strikes' provisions). This can only be done on the instructions of the DWP and in practice it rarely if ever occurs. The details are in the 2003-04 edition of this guide (and in GM A6.190-241).

Non-dependant deductions

7.17 HB and main CTB are normally reduced for each non-dependant living in the claimant's home. The next paragraphs explain when a deduction is or is not made, and the additional rules involved. There are some differences between HB (for rent), main CTB, and HB for rates in Northern Ireland. These are mentioned whenever they arise. There are also differences if the claimant or any partner is aged 65 or over. In their case the deductions are delayed, as described in paragraphs 7.37-38.

7.18 Non-dependants are usually adult sons, daughters, other relatives or friends who live in the claimant's household on a non-commercial basis (paras.

4.41-43). Some claimants receive money from their non-dependants to pay for their keep. This may include a contribution towards rent, council tax, food or household expenses. This money is not treated as the claimants' income (table 13.2). Instead deductions are made from the claimant's HB and main CTB. However, these deductions are not related to what the non-dependant actually pays. They are fixed sums which apply even if the non-dependant pays the claimant nothing at all. The level of deductions (table 7.3) is high in some cases, and may cause claimants hardship.

HB 3
HB60+ 3
NIHB 3
NIHB60+ 3
CTB 3
CTB60+ 3

The question of who counts as a non-dependant is not always straightforward. In a recent case *(CH/4004/2004)* the claimant's cousin came to stay with her for ten weeks in early 2003, having been deported from the USA. She took him in rather than see him live on the streets as he had no source of income while waiting for applications for an NI number and JSA. He slept on the sofa. The tribunal failed to consider whether he was 'normally' residing with the claimant (and, incidentally, failed to take account of information included with the claim that she may be entitled to disability living allowance). The commissioner decided that he was not 'normally' residing with her and so no non-dependant deduction was to be applied.

CASES IN WHICH NO DEDUCTION IS MADE

7.19 As described in paragraphs 7.20-22 and table 7.2, there are three types of case in which no non-dependant deduction is made.

7.20 No deduction applies in respect of any of the following, because they are defined in the law as not being non-dependants (para. 4.42):

HB 3(2)
HB60+ 3(2)
NIHB 3(2)
NIHB60+ 3(2)
CTB 3(2)
CTB60+ 3(2)

- children aged under 16 and young persons aged 16 to 18 inclusive (whether or not they are counted as a member of the family for HB/CTB purposes);
- boarders, (sub-)tenants and joint occupiers;
- carers provided by a charity or voluntary organisation for whom the claimant or partner are charged;
- the claimant's landlord and members of the landlord's household.

7.21 There are no non-dependant deductions in either HB or main CTB if the claimant or any partner:

HB 2(1),74(6)
HB60+ 2(1),55(6)
NIHB 2(1),71(6)
NIHB60+ 2(1),53(6
CTB 2(1),58(6)
CTB60+ 2(1),42(6)

- is registered blind or has ceased to be registered blind within the past 28 weeks because of regaining sight (para. 12.13); or
- receives the care component of disability living allowance payable at any rate; or
- receives attendance allowance payable at any rate or any of the related benefits in paragraph 12.35.

In such cases, if the claimant has more than one non-dependant, no deduction applies for any of them. (Note that the second and third cases cease to apply when disability living allowance or attendance allowance themselves cease – for example, when the claimant or partner have been in hospital for four weeks.)

HB 74(7),(8),(10) HB60+ 55(7)-(9) NIHB 71(7),(8),(1) NIHB60+ 53(7)/(8),(10) CTB 58(7),(8) CTB60+ (7),(8)

7.22 No deduction applies in respect of any non-dependant who falls within certain groups. The main groups are summarised in table 7.2. As indicated there, there are some differences between the groups applying for HB purposes and those applying for main CTB purposes. Appendix 6 defines all the relevant categories of people and gives the detailed rules about whether a non-dependant deduction applies in HB and main CTB.

Table 7.2: Non-dependants for whom no deduction applies

HB 2(1),74(7) (8),(10) HB60+ 2(1) 55(7)-(9) NIHB 2(1) 71(6),(8),(10) NIHB60+ 2(1) 53(6),(7),(10) CTB 2(1) 58(7),(8) CTB60+ 2(1) 42(7),(8)

- Non-dependants aged under 18.
- Non-dependants aged under 25 who are on JSA(IB) or IS.
- Non-dependants on either kind of SPC.
- In CTB (or in Northern Ireland, HB for rates only), non-dependants aged 25+ who are on JSA(IB) or IS. (In HB for rent there is a deduction in such cases.)
- Non-dependants who are students (but in HB only, and only if the claimant and any partner are under 65, there is a deduction in the summer vacation if they take up remunerative work).
- Non-dependants receiving a Work Based Training Allowance.
- Non-dependants in prison or similar forms of detention.
- Non-dependants who have been in hospital for 52 weeks or more.
- Non-dependants whose normal home is elsewhere.
- In CTB only, non-dependants who fall within any of the groups who are 'disregarded persons' for council tax purposes. (In HB there is a deduction in such cases unless they fall within any of the earlier entries in this table.)

Note:
Appendix 6 gives full information about all the above categories of people. It includes all the 'disregarded persons' mentioned above – such as (in various circumstances) education leavers, students, student nurses, apprentices, people who are severely mentally impaired, and carers.

CASES IN WHICH A DEDUCTION IS MADE

7.23 In cases other than those described above, a non-dependant deduction is made. The amount depends upon whether the non-dependant is in 'remunerative work' (paras. 7.29-34) and, if so, on the level of his or her gross income. The amounts for HB and main CTB are different, and are listed in table 7.3. Additional rules for claimants who are joint occupiers and for non-dependant couples are in paragraphs 7.35-36.

HB 74(1),(2)
HB60+ 55(1),(2)
NIHB 71(1),(2)
NIHB60+ 53(1),(2)
CTB 58(1),(2)
CTB60+ 42(1),(2)

Table 7.3: Summary of weekly non-dependant deductions

	Deduction in HB (for rent)	Deduction in main CTB (and HB for rates in Northern Ireland)
Non-dependants in remunerative work with gross income of:		
£338.00 per week or more	£47.75	£6.95
between £271.00 and £337.99 per week	£43.50	£5.80
between £204.00 and £270.99 per week	£38.20	£4.60
between £157.00 and £203.99 per week	£23.35	£4.60
between £106.00 and £156.99 per week	£17.00	£2.30
under £106.00 per week	£7.40	£2.30
Non-dependants not in remunerative work (regardless of income level)	£7.40	£2.30

Notes:

'Remunerative work' is defined in paras. 7.29 onwards.

Don't forget that there is no deduction at all in the cases in table 7.2.

NON-DEPENDANTS IN REMUNERATIVE WORK

7.24 For non-dependants in remunerative work, there are six possible levels of deduction in HB and four in main CTB (table 7.3), depending in either case on the level of the non-dependant's gross income (unless no deduction is appropriate at all: paras. 7.20-22).

HB 74(1),(2)
HB60+ 55(1),(2)
NIHB 71(1),(2)
NIHB60+ 53(1),(2)
CTB 58(1),(2)
CTB60+ 42(1),(2)

HB 74(9) HB60+ 55(10) NIHB 71(9) NIHB60+ 53(9) CTB 58(9) CTB60+ 42(9)

7.25 It is the non-dependant's gross income, not net income, which is relevant. So long as the non-dependant is in remunerative work, the rule relates to his or her income from all sources. The only exception is that the following types of income are always disregarded:

- disability living allowance (either or both components);
- attendance allowance and the related benefits in entries (e) to (g) of paragraph 12.35;
- payments from the Macfarlane Trusts, the Eileen Trust, the Skipton Fund, the Fund or the Independent Living Funds, including payments in kind from these sources and payments of money which originally derived from them (para. 13.60);
- payments from the London Bombings Charitable Relief Fund (para. 13.117).

7.26 As regards any other source of income, there are no rules saying how the gross amount is to be assessed, though none of the disregards in chapter 14 applies. The DWP advises correctly that for non-dependants with savings, the actual interest received should be included here (GM para. A5.178). However the DWP also advises (GM para. A5.177) that if a non-dependant is self-employed, 'gross income' means before the deduction of tax, national insurance or expenses. This seems obviously wrong, since it must be plain in this context that 'gross income' means before the deduction of tax and national insurance (but after the deduction of expenses), and DWP's advice seems to contradict *R(IS)16/93* (para. 14.14).

7.27 It is up to individual authorities to decide what level of evidence is required about the income of a non-dependant in remunerative work. If there is no evidence (and only if the claimant is in remunerative work), the highest deduction is made (table 7.3). In such cases, if the evidence is later provided, and reveals that a lower deduction should have been made, this means that the claimant has been awarded too little benefit: the claimant must be awarded the arrears – if he or she provides the evidence within one month of the notification of the decision on his or her claim (though the time limit can be extended in certain circumstances: para. 17.40).

NON-DEPENDANTS NOT IN REMUNERATIVE WORK

HB 74(1) HB60+ 55(1) NIHB 71(1) NIHB60+ 53(1) CTB 58(1) CTB60+ 42(1)

7.28 For non-dependants not in remunerative work, the lowest level of deduction applies in both HB and main CTB (table 7.3) regardless of the amount – if any – of the non-dependant's income (unless no deduction is appropriate at all: paras. 7.19-22).

'REMUNERATIVE WORK'

7.29 Remunerative work is work: HB 6(1) HB60+ 6(1) NIHB 6(1) NIHB60+ 6(1) CTB 6(1) CTB 60+ 6(1)

- for which payment is made, or expected to be made; and
- which averages 16 hours or more per week.

Examples: Calculating HB and main CTB

CLAIMANT ON INCOME SUPPORT WITH WORKING NON-DEPENDANT

A lone parent is on income support. Her eligible rent is £65.00 per week. Her eligible council tax liability is £15.00 per week. Her 26-year-old son lives with her. He earns £325 per week gross for a 35-hour week.

Claimants on income support get maximum benefit, which in this case involves a non-dependant deduction. The son is in remunerative work with gross income of at least £322 per week, so the highest level of deduction applies in both HB and main CTB (table 7.3).

HB:	Eligible rent	£65.00
	minus non-dependant deduction, which in this case is	£47.75
	equals weekly HB	£17.25
Main CTB:	Eligible council tax	£15.00
	minus non-dependant deduction, which in this case is	£6.95
	equals weekly main CTB	£8.05

CLAIMANT ON INCOME SUPPORT WITH NON-DEPENDANT ON INCOME SUPPORT

The son in the previous example loses his job and starts receiving income support.

The calculation is as above, except that now there is no non-dependant deduction in main CTB and the lowest deduction applies in HB (table 7.3).

HB:	Eligible rent	£65.00
	minus non-dependant deduction, which in this case is	£7.40
	equals weekly HB	£57.60
Main CTB:	Eligible council tax	£15.00
	no non-dependant deduction applies	
	equals weekly main CTB	£15.00

HB 6(2)-(5) HB60+ 6(2)-(5) NIHB 6(2),(4)-(6) NIHB60+ 6(2),(4),(5) CTB 6(2)-(5) CTB 60+ 6(2)-(5)

7.30 In calculating a weekly average of income, authorities should take into account any recognisable cycle. If there is no such cycle, they should take into account the expected hours of work per week and also (except where the non-dependant is just starting work) the average during the period immediately prior to the claim. This period should be five weeks unless some other period would result in a more accurate estimation in an individual case.

HB 6(5) HB60+ 6(5) NIHB 6(5) NIHB60+ 6(5) CTB 6(5) CTB 60+ 6(5)

7.31 Once it is established that a person is in remunerative work, he or she continues to count as being in remunerative work during any recognised, customary or other holiday, and also during any period of absence without good cause (but not during sick leave, maternity leave, paternity leave or adoption leave: para. 7.33).

HB 6(3) HB60+ 6(3) NIHB 6(3) NIHB60+ 6(3) CTB 6(3) CTB 60+ 6(3)

7.32 A further rule applies to people employed in schools, other educational establishments, or anywhere else where their recognisable cycle of work is one year. Their average weekly hours are found by considering only the periods when they work (e.g. school term-times). The result applies both during those periods and during the periods when they do not work (e.g. school holidays). (Note however that changes in income – e.g. between term-time and holidays – are taken into account.)

2(1),HB 6(6)-(8) HB60+ 2(1),6(6)-(8) NIHB 2(1),6(6)-(8) NIHB60+ 2(1) 6(6)-(8) CTB 2(1),6(3)-(8) CTB 60+ 2(1) 6(3)-(3)

7.33 A non-dependant is treated as not being in remunerative work in any of the following cases:

- in any benefit week during which he or she receives JSA(IB), IS or pension credit for four days or more (regardless of his or her other circumstances);
- on any day on which he or she is on maternity, paternity or adoption leave, i.e. is absent from work for one of those reasons, and has a right to return to work under his or her contract or under employment law;
- on any day on which he or she is absent from work because he or she is ill (whether or not receiving statutory sick pay and regardless of whether the employer is making up his or her wages). However, an absence due to illness which falls wholly within a benefit week (Monday to Sunday) will not be taken into account, because of the rules on changes of circumstances (para. 17.18);
- on any day for which he or she has been or will be paid a Sports Council sports award, so long as he or she is not expected to receive any other payment for that day.

7.34 The following are also not remunerative work:

- education (since this is not 'work');
- training (since this is not 'work') including attendance on government training schemes and the New Deal (para. 13.64) (but those paid by their employer do not count as trainees);

- voluntary or other work for which the person is paid expenses only (since it is not 'remunerative');
- periods of lay-off (since this is absence with good cause).

NON-DEPENDANT COUPLES

7.35 In the case of a non-dependant couple (or a polygamous marriage), only one deduction applies, being the higher (or highest) of any that would have applied to the individuals if they were single claimants. In appropriate cases, there is no deduction (e.g. if they are both under 18). For the purpose of the various gross income limits in table 7.3, each non-dependant partner is treated as possessing the gross income of both of them.

HB 74(3),(4)
HB60+ 55(3),(4)
NIHB 71(4)
NIHB60+ 53(4)
CTB 58(3),(4)
CTB60+ 42(3),(4)

NON-DEPENDANTS OF JOINT OCCUPIERS

7.36 The following rules apply when a claimant is jointly liable for the rent or council tax on his or her home with one or more other persons who are not his or her partner, and there is also a non-dependant living there. They would arise, for example, if a brother and sister are joint occupiers and have a non-dependant living with them. The law is slightly unclear in some of these cases but the key question is 'whose household is the non-dependant part of?' Having decided that, the rules work as follows:

HB 74(5)
HB60+ 55(5)
NIHB 71(5)
NIHB60+ 53(5)
CTB 58(5)
CTB60+ 42(5)

- If the non-dependant is part of the household of only one of them, then the whole non-dependant deduction is made in any claim for benefit made by that one, and no deduction is made in any claim for benefit made by the others.
- If the non-dependant is part of the household of more than one of them, the amount of the non-dependant deduction is shared between them. Any of them claiming benefit gets his or her resulting share of the non-dependant deduction. In main CTB, the share must be equal between the joint occupiers (but only between the ones who are jointly liable for the council tax on the home: para. 9.27). In HB, the share need not be equal: the authority should take into account the number of joint occupiers concerned and the proportion of rent each pays (para. 10.6).

DELAYED EFFECT OF NON-DEPENDANT CHANGES FOR PEOPLE AGED 65 OR MORE

7.37 This rule applies when:

HB60+ 59(10)-(13)
NIHB60+ 53(10)-(1
CTB60+ 50(10)-(13

- the claimant or any partner is aged 65 or more; and
- a non-dependant moves in, or there is any change in a non-dependant's circumstances which causes an increase in the amount of the deduction.

Examples: Non-dependant changes for people aged 65+

A non-dependant moves in on Wednesday 4th October 2006.

This takes effect 26 weeks and 5 days later – on Monday 9th April 2007.

A non-dependant moves in on Wednesday 4th October 2006, then her income increases on 1st January 2007.

Both things take effect on Monday 9th April 2007.

A non-dependant moves in on Wednesday 4th October 2006, then he moves out on Sunday 8th April 2007.

No deduction is ever made for him.

7.38 In such cases the change in entitlement to HB or main CTB is not implemented until the day 26 weeks after the change actually occurred or, if that is not a Monday, the following Monday. At that point, the claimant's current circumstances are taken into account (not the ones applying 26 weeks or more ago, nor any applying in the intervening period): this is illustrated in the examples.

Conversion to weekly amounts and rounding

7.39 HB and CTB are assessed on a weekly basis (though for technical reasons to do with the council tax itself some of the CTB regulations are expressed on a daily basis).

7.40 The following paragraphs explain the rules that apply whenever figures involved in the calculation of HB and CTB (including second adult rebate) have to be converted to weekly amounts. The final paragraph describes rounding. Further rules apply if the claimant has rent-free periods (paras. 7.14-15). For the equivalent rules for rates in Northern Ireland, see chapter 11.

RENT

HB 80
HB60+ 61
NIHB 77
NIHB60+ 60

7.41 Whenever a weekly figure is needed for rent, the following rules apply (and the same rules apply to service charges):

- for rent due in multiples of weeks, divide the rent by the number of weeks it covers;
- for rent due calendar monthly (or in multiples of calendar months), divide by the number of months (if necessary) to find the monthly figure, then multiply by 12 to find the annual figure, then divide by 52 to find the weekly figure. This is a new rule applying from April 2006. Dividing

by 52 (a figure which cannot be varied) intentionally gives a slightly generous weekly figure;

- for rent due daily (or, any case other than above, in multiples of days), divide by the number of days (if necessary) to find the daily figure, then multiply by seven to find the weekly figure.

COUNCIL TAX

7.42 Whenever a weekly figure is needed for council tax liability, the following rules apply: CTB 57(1)(b) CTB60+ 40(1)(b)

- for annual figures, divide the council tax by 365 (or 366 in financial years ending in a leap year) to find the daily figure, and then multiply the daily figure by seven;
- for figures which do not relate to a whole year, divide the council tax by the number of days it covers to find the daily figure, and then multiply the daily figure by seven.

INCOME

7.43 Whenever a weekly income figure is needed, the following rules apply: HB 33(1) HB60+ 33(1) NIHB 30(1) NIHB60+ 31(1) CTB 23(1) CTB60+ 23(1)

- for an amount relating to a whole multiple of weeks, divide the amount by the number of weeks it covers;
- for an amount relating to a calendar month, multiply the amount by 12 to find the annual figure, then divide the annual figure by 52 (or, if the claimant and any partner are under 60, 53 if appropriate);
- for an amount relating to a year (this typically applies only to self-employed income), divide the amount by 52 (or, if the claimant and any partner are under 60, divide the amount by 365 or 366 as appropriate to find the daily figure, and then multiply the daily figure by seven);
- for an amount relating to any other period, divide the amount by the number of days it covers to find the daily figure, then multiply the daily figure by seven.

ROUNDING

7.44 In HB, the authority may 'if appropriate' round any amount involved in the calculation to the nearest penny, halfpennies being rounded upwards. In CTB, there is no similar rule: indeed the DWP recommends that entitlement should be calculated to at least six decimal places (GM para. B3.300). This is to avoid reconciliation errors at the end of the financial year. Notifications sent to claimants about their HB/CTB entitlement may be rounded to the nearest penny. HB 80(8) HB60+ 61(7) NIHB 77(8) NIHB60+ 60(8)

8 Second adult rebate

8.1 This chapter, which applies only in England, Wales and Scotland, explains the types of CTB known as 'second adult rebate' (also sometimes called 'alternative maximum CTB'). It covers:

- who is eligible for second adult rebate;
- how to calculate second adult rebate;
- the 'better buy' comparison; and
- notifications about second adult rebate.

8.2 There are two types of second adult rebate:

- the student only type (para. 8.3) is new from 1st April 2006. It is designed to compensate for the loss of council tax exemption caused by the presence of the 'second adult';
- the general type (para 8.4) is for when the claimant has a 'second adult' in his or her home who is on JSA(IB), IS or guarantee credit or is on a low income. It is worth up to 25% of the council tax, and was designed to compensate for the loss of council tax discount caused by the present of the 'second adult'.

The level of the claimant's own income and capital (and that of any partner) is irrelevant. But because of the 'better buy' comparison (para. 8.29), second adult rebate is only awarded if the claimant does not qualify for main CTB, or qualifies for more second adult than main CTB.

Eligibility for second adult rebate

'STUDENT ONLY' SECOND ADULT REBATE

CBA 131(1) (3),(6),(7),(9) CTB 62(1) sch 2 para 1(c) CTB60+ 46(1) sch 6 para 1(c)

8.3 The rule about who is eligible for 'student only' second adult rebate is straightforward. It is awarded if the following condition is met, and is always worth 100% of the council tax liability on the dwelling (so there is nothing to pay at all by way of council tax while it is awarded):

- the dwelling is wholly occupied by students who are not in the eligible groups;
- but for the presence of one or more second adults on JSA(IB), IS or CTB.

Table 8.1: Eligibility for general second adult rebate

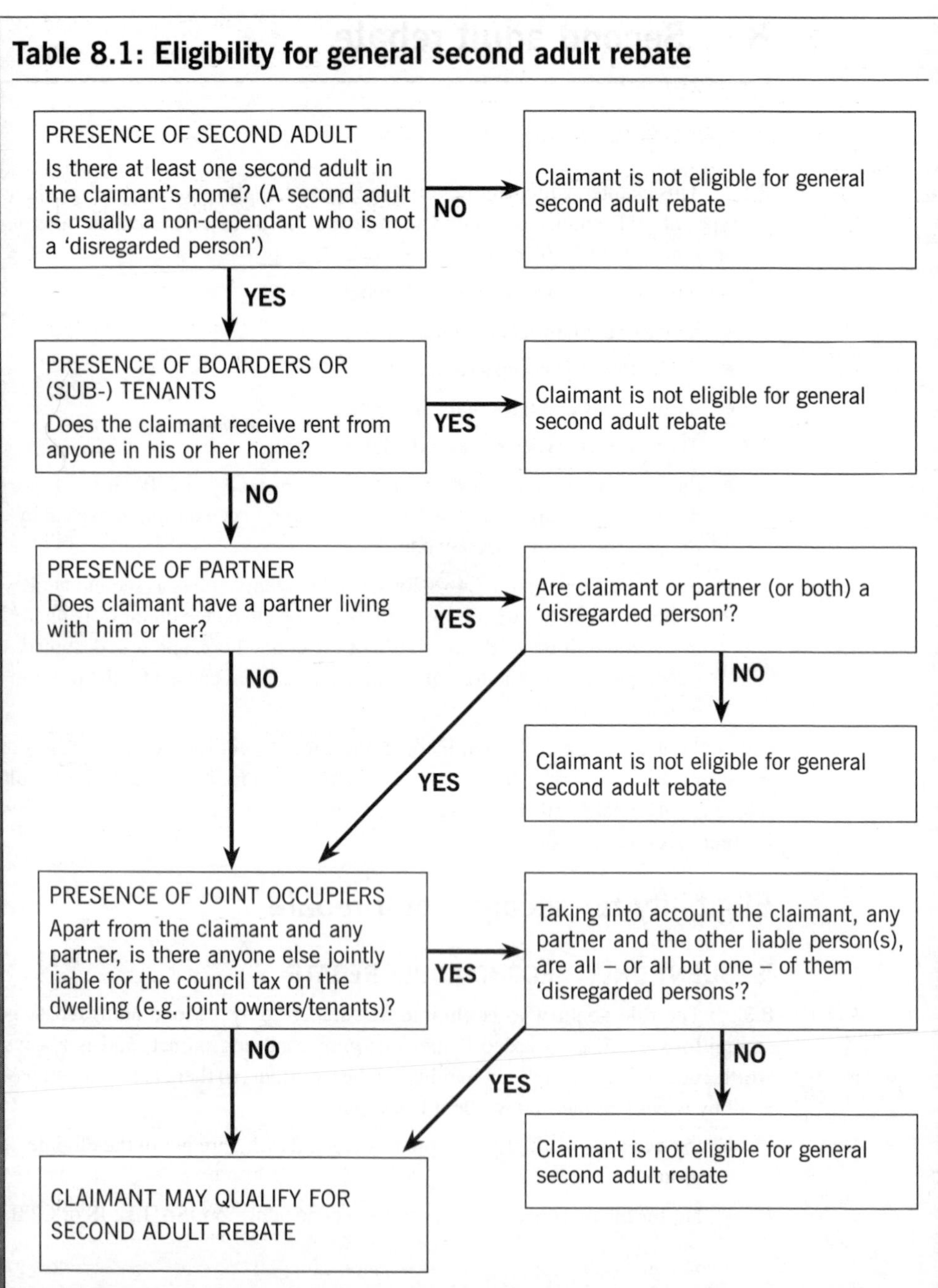

For these purposes, 'student' is defined using HB/CTB law (para. 21.5); and the 'eligible groups' means the groups who are eligible to claim HB/CTB as listed in table 21.1.

CBA 131(1) (3),(6),(7),(9) CTB 62(1) sch 2 para 1(a),(b) CTB60+ 46(1) sch 6 para 1(a),(b)

GENERAL SECOND ADULT REBATE

8.4 The information needed to establish whether a claimant is eligible for general second adult rebate is summarised in the flow chart in table 8.1 and described in more detail below.

PRESENCE OF SECOND ADULT

CBA 131(6)(b) (7)(a),(11) CTB 63(a),(c) CTB60+ 47(a),(c)

8.5 A claimant can only qualify for second adult rebate (of either type) if there is at least one 'second adult' in his or her home. A person is a 'second adult' if he or she:

- is a non-dependant or in certain circumstances someone else (paras. 8.6-7); and
- is not a 'disregarded person' (para. 8.8).

There may be two or more 'second adults' in the claimant's home: the claimant can still qualify for second adult rebate.

8.6 A non-dependant is by far the most common kind of second adult so long as he or she is not a 'disregarded person'. Typical non-dependants are adult sons, daughters, other relatives or friends who live in the claimant's household on a non-commercial basis (paras. 4.41-43).

8.7 A person can also be a second adult if he or she is the type of carer who is defined in law as not being a non-dependant (para. 4.51), so long as he or she is not a 'disregarded person'. This is not common because many carers are 'disregarded persons' (categories 14 to 17 in appendix 6). There may be other categories who count as a second adult, such as paid companions or live-in employees of the claimant or partner – so long as they are not a 'disregarded person' (and do not pay rent: para. 8.9).

8.8 A 'disregarded person' cannot be a second adult. This means a person who falls within any of the groups which are disregarded for council tax discount purposes (para. 9.17). The main groups are summarised in table 8.2. Appendix 6 defines all the relevant categories of people and gives the detailed rules about whether they are 'disregarded persons'.

PRESENCE OF BOARDERS OR (SUB-)TENANTS

CBA 131(6)(a),(11) CTB 2(1) CTB60+ 2(1)

8.9 A claimant who receives rent from any resident in his or her home is not eligible for second adult rebate (even if all the other conditions are fulfilled). Typically, this means that home-owner claimants with boarders or tenants, and tenant claimants with boarders or sub-tenants, cannot get second adult rebate.

Table 8.2: 'Disregarded Persons': simplified summary

See appendix 6 for more detailed definitions.

- People under 18, or aged 18 if child benefit is payable.
- Education leavers under 20.
- Various students, foreign language assistants and student nurses.
- Youth Training trainees under 25.
- Apprentices on NCVQ/SVEC courses.
- People who are severely mentally impaired.
- Carers.
- People in prison or other forms of detention.
- People who normally live elsewhere.
- Members of religious communities.
- Diplomats and members of international bodies or of visiting forces.

8.10 The exclusion from entitlement applies only if the person paying rent is 'resident' in the claimant's dwelling. A 'resident' means a person aged 18 or more who has 'sole or main residence' there. Therefore, rent received from an under-18-year-old or a holiday-maker does not prevent entitlement.

8.11 The exclusion appears in the Act of Parliament rather than the regulations. The Act does not, however, define 'rent'. The regulations give a definition of 'rent' for other purposes as being (in broad terms) a payment which could be met by HB, and this definition seems appropriate here.

8.12 The exclusion is worded in such a way that it applies only if someone is liable to pay rent to the claimant. It does not apply if someone is liable to pay rent to the claimant's partner (or any other resident).

CLAIMANT'S INCOME AND CAPITAL

8.13 None of the rules about eligibility for second adult rebate takes into account the amount of a claimant's (or partner's) income or capital in any way.

8.14 The £16,000 capital limit (which applies for HB and main CTB) does not apply when second adult rebate is being considered. Millionaires can get second adult rebate (so long as they fulfil the appropriate conditions).

Examples: Second adult rebate

SINGLE CLAIMANT

A single claimant is liable for council tax on her home. The level of her income means she cannot qualify for main CTB. Only her son lives with her. He is aged 20 and is on JSA(IB).

The claimant's son is her second adult. The claimant qualifies for second adult rebate of 25% of her council tax liability.

COUPLE

A couple are jointly liable for council tax on their home. Only their daughter lives with them. The woman in the couple is a student nurse (and is thus a 'disregarded person'). The couple's income is too great for them to qualify for main CTB. The daughter works part-time for a gross income of £100 per week.

The couple's daughter is their second adult. They qualify for second adult rebate of 15% of their council tax liability.

STUDENTS

A student rents his home, and is not in one of the eligible groups for HB/CTB. His parents live with him; they are on pension credit.

If his parents did not live with him, his home would be exempt from council tax. But because they do live with him, they are his second adults. Because they are on pension credit, the student qualifies for second adult rebate of 100% of his council tax liability.

CLAIMANT'S AND PARTNER'S OTHER CIRCUMSTANCES

CBA 131(7)(b) **8.15** If the conditions mentioned earlier are satisfied, the final condition about eligibility for second adult rebate, which applies for general second adult rebate only (para. 8.4), depends on whether the claim is made by:

- a single claimant or a lone parent (with no joint occupiers);
- a couple (with no joint occupiers); or
- a claimant who has joint occupiers.

SINGLE CLAIMANTS AND LONE PARENTS

8.16 There is no further condition if the claimant is single or a lone parent. It does not matter whether he or she is or is not a 'disregarded person' (para. 8.8). But if the claimant is jointly liable for council tax, see paragraph 8.18.

COUPLES

8.17 There is a further condition for general second adult rebate (para. 8.4) if the claimant is in a couple. Couples are eligible for second adult rebate only if at least one partner is a 'disregarded person' (para. 8.8). It does not matter whether this is the claimant or the partner – and so long as one of them is a 'disregarded person' it does not matter whether the other one is or is not a 'disregarded person'. But if the couple are jointly liable for council tax with some other person, see paragraph 8.18. A polygamous marriage is eligible for general second adult rebate if all – or all but one – of the partners are 'disregarded persons'. CTB 63(b) CTB60+ 47(b)

JOINT OCCUPIERS

8.18 There is also a further condition for general second adult rebate (para. 8.4) if the claimant is jointly liable for the council tax on his or her home with at least one other person (other than just his or her partner if the claim is made by a couple). In such cases, information is needed about all of these joint occupiers. Each one who makes a claim is eligible for general second adult rebate so long as either: CTB 63(d) CTB60+ 47(d)

- all the joint occupiers are 'disregarded persons'; or
- all but one of the joint occupiers are 'disregarded persons'.

8.19 This rule typically applies to joint owners and joint tenants. For example, if two sisters jointly own their home (and they have a second adult), each of them is eligible for general second adult rebate so long as at least one of them is a 'disregarded person' (para. 8.8). Or if three single people jointly rent their home (and they have a second adult), each of them is eligible for general second adult rebate so long as at least two of them are 'disregarded persons'.

8.20 In all such cases, each joint occupier who makes a claim qualifies for his or her share of the total amount of second adult rebate. This share must always be equal between all the joint occupiers, including any who are students. CTB 62(2),(3) CTB60+ 46(2),(3)

Amount of second adult rebate

8.21 Having established that the claimant is eligible for second adult rebate, the authority needs the following information in order to calculate the amount on a weekly basis:

- the claimant's weekly eligible council tax liability (para. 8.23); and
- for general second adult rebate only (para. 8.4) details of the second adult's income or, if the claimant has more than one second adult, details of all the second adults' incomes (paras. 8.24 onwards).

8.22 'Student only' second adult rebate (para 8.3) is always 100 per cent of the claimant's weekly eligible council tax. As shown in table 8.3, the amount of general second adult rebate (para. 8.4) may be 25 per cent, 15 per cent or 7½ per cent of the claimant's weekly eligible council tax – depending on the income of the second adult(s). No matter how many second adults a claimant has, the claimant can only get one amount of second adult rebate.

Table 8.3: Amount of general second adult rebate

CTB 2(4),62(1), sch 2 para 1
CTB60+ 2(4),46(1), sch 6 para 1

FOR CLAIMANTS WITH ONE SECOND ADULT

If the second adult is on JSA(IB)*, IS or pension credit	25%
If the second adult is not on those benefits and his or her gross income** is:	
under £150.00 per week	15%
between £150.00 and £193.99 per week	7½%
£194.00 per week or more	nil

FOR CLAIMANTS WITH TWO OR MORE SECOND ADULTS

If all the second adults are on JSA(IB)*, IS or pension credit	25%
If at least one of the second adults is not on those benefits and the combined gross income of all the second adults*** is:	
under £150.00 per week	15%
between £150.00 and £193.99 per week	7½%
£194.00 per week or more	nil

Notes

* For these purposes a person counts as receiving JSA(IB) if he or she is entitled to JSA(IB) but not receiving it because of a sanction, or in the 'waiting days' before JSA(IB) starts (or would start apart from a sanction).

** If the second adult has a partner, the partner's gross income is added in.

*** For each second adult who has a partner, the partner's gross income is added in. But if any of the second adults is on JSA(IB), IS or pension credit (or has a partner who is), then his or her income (and any partner's) is disregarded.

8.23 The amount of a claimant's eligible council tax liability is described in chapter 9. Paragraph 7.42 explains how to convert council tax figures to a weekly amount. Examples of the calculations of general second adult rebate follow. The last example illustrates how a 25 per cent discount is dealt with in calculations. The example at the end of this chapter illustrates the calculation of second adult rebate for joint occupiers.

Examples: Calculating second adult rebate

SINGLE CLAIMANT WITH SECOND ADULT ON JSA(IB)

A single claimant is the only person liable for council tax on his home. The only person living with him is his adult daughter, who is on JSA(IB). Neither the claimant nor his daughter is a 'disregarded person'. His eligible council tax liability is £20.00 per week.

Eligible for second adult rebate?

As a single claimant, he is eligible for second adult rebate because:

- he has a second adult living with him (his daughter); and
- he does not receive rent from a boarder or (sub-)tenant.

Amount of second adult rebate

His daughter is on JSA(IB) so the weekly amount is:

25% of weekly eligible council tax (25% x £20.00)	£5.00

COUPLE WITH TWO SECOND ADULTS

A couple are the only people liable for council tax on their home. The only people living with them are their two adult sons. One son is on JSA(IB). The other son is working and his gross pay is £133 per week. He also has savings which generate a weekly gross interest of £5 per week. One partner in the couple is a full-time mature university student. The other partner and the sons are not 'disregarded persons'. The couple's eligible council tax liability is £24.00 per week.

Eligible for second adult rebate?

As a couple, they are eligible for second adult rebate because:

- they have at least one second adult living with them. In fact they have two second adults (the sons); and
- they do not receive rent from a boarder or (sub-)tenant; and
- at least one of the couple is a 'disregarded person' (the student).

Amount of second adult rebate

If there is more than one second adult, their gross incomes are combined. But in this case the income of the son on JSA(IB) is disregarded. So only the other son's income counts. That son's gross weekly income is £133 (from the job) plus £5 (interest), which amounts to £138, so the weekly amount of second adult rebate is:

15% of weekly eligible council tax (15% x £24.00)	£3.60

DISCOUNT PLUS SECOND ADULT REBATE

A single woman is the only person liable for council tax on her home. The only other person living with her is her father, who is on income support. The woman is a carer who counts as a 'disregarded person'. Her father is not a 'disregarded person'. The council tax for the dwelling (before any discount is granted) is £730 per year – which is £14 per week.

Discount

When calculating council tax discounts, 'disregarded persons' are ignored (appendix 6). So for discount purposes, this dwelling has one resident. The woman qualifies for a 25% discount which, on a weekly basis, is:

25% of the weekly amount for the dwelling (25% x £14.00)	£3.50

Eligible for second adult rebate?

As a single claimant her own circumstances are immaterial. She is eligible for second adult rebate because:

- she has a second adult living with her (her father); and
- she does not receive rent from a boarder or (sub-)tenant.

Amount of second adult rebate

Her father is on income support so she qualifies for second adult rebate of 25% of her weekly eligible council tax. This means 25% of liability for council tax before the discount is subtracted, which is:

25% of weekly eligible council tax (25% x £14.00)	£3.50

She qualifies for both the discount and the second adult rebate, the total of the two being £7.00 per week.

Better buy

It turns out in this particular case that, because of her own low income, the woman qualifies for main CTB of £4.00 per week. Since her main CTB is greater than her second adult rebate, she gets only her main CTB. The final result is that she qualifies for main CTB of £4.00 plus the discount of £3.50, so in total her council tax bill is reduced by £7.50 per week.

ASSESSING SECOND ADULTS' GROSS INCOME

8.24 To calculate the amount of general second adult rebate (para. 8.4 and table 8.3), it is necessary to assess the gross income of any second adult who is not on JSA(IB), IS or pension credit (or treated as receiving JSA(IB): table 8.3). If the second adult has a partner, the partner's income is added in with the second adult's income (even if the partner is a 'disregarded person' and so could not be a second adult in his or her own right). CTB sch 2 paras 2,3 CTB60+ sch 6 paras 2,3

8.25 If a claimant has more than one second adult, it is necessary to combine the income of all of them, apart from any who are on income support or JSA(IB) (or treated as receiving JSA(IB): table 8.3) – adding in the income of the partner of each second adult.

8.26 It is gross, not net, income which is relevant, and it is calculated in exactly the same way as a non-dependant's income is calculated for the purposes of main CTB, as outlined in paragraphs 7.25-27. The authority is entitled to require the same level of evidence, proof, etc, as when it assesses a claimant's income (paras. 5.17-19 and 5.22-23).

8.27 Providing details of second adults' income (and that of their partners) can pose several difficulties for claimants. They may not be able to obtain these details, or may not wish to ask. However, if the authority does not know how much the gross income is, it cannot award a general second adult rebate.

DISCRETIONARY HOUSING PAYMENTS

8.28 If a claimant qualifies for second adult rebate only, no discretionary housing payment (para. 22.5) may be awarded.

The 'better buy'

8.29 A claimant cannot be awarded both main CTB and second adult rebate at the same time. Deciding which one the claimant is actually awarded is often called a 'better buy' comparison: CBA 131(9)

- a claimant who only qualifies for main CTB is awarded that;
- a claimant who only qualifies for second adult rebate is awarded that;
- a claimant who qualifies for both is awarded whichever of the two is higher or, if the two are the same, main CTB. This is decided entirely according to the amounts themselves and entirely by the authority. A claimant cannot choose to have the lower figure.

Some examples of the better buy calculation are given below.

JOINT OCCUPIERS AND THE BETTER BUY

CBA 131(9)
CTB 62(2),(3)
CTB60+ 46(2),(3)

8.30 If a dwelling has two or more joint occupiers and one or more of them claims CTB, each joint occupier's entitlement to main CTB and second adult rebate is assessed separately, and the better buy comparison is done separately for each joint occupier. This can mean that one joint occupier is awarded main CTB, another second adult rebate. The second of the examples below illustrates this.

Notifications

8.31 Table 8.4 shows the information the authority must notify to the claimant when second adult rebate is awarded (or when it cannot be awarded).

Table 8.4: Information to be notified in second adult rebate cases

The general matters in table 16.1 must always be notified (including the right to a written statement, the right to request a reconsideration, and the right to appeal).

IF SECOND ADULT REBATE IS AWARDED

- The normal weekly amount of council tax rounded to the nearest penny.
- The normal weekly amount of second adult rebate rounded to the nearest penny.
- The fact (if true) that the claimant is better off on second adult rebate than on main CTB and the lesser amount of main CTB.
- The rates of second adult rebate and related gross income levels.
- The first day of entitlement.
- The gross income of any second adult or the fact that the second adult is on JSA(IB), IS or pension credit.
- The claimant's duty to notify the authority of changes of circumstance and examples of the kinds of change that should be reported.
- Details of any rounding of figures.

IF SECOND ADULT REBATE IS NOT AWARDED

- The normal weekly amount of council tax rounded to the nearest penny.
- The rates of second adult rebate and related gross income levels.
- The gross income of any second adult or the fact that the second adult is on JSA(IB), IS or pension credit.
- The fact (if true) that the claimant is better off on main CTB and the lesser amount of second adult rebate.
- Any other reason why the claimant is not entitled.

Example: Better buy

LONE PARENT WITH ONE NON-DEPENDANT/SECOND ADULT

A lone parent is the only person liable for the council tax on her home. She is not on income support and has excess income for main CTB purposes of £25.00. The only people living with her are her daughter of 15 and her son of 21. The son works 12 hours per week for a gross pay of £180 per week (and has no other income). Only the daughter (because of being under 18) is a 'disregarded person'. The lone parent's eligible council tax liability is £16.00 per week. Her circumstances means that she is eligible for second adult rebate (the son is her second adult) as well as main CTB (taking the son into account as a non-dependant).

Main CTB

Weekly eligible council tax	£16.00
minus non-dependant deduction for son (he is not in remunerative work, so the lowest deduction applies: table 7.3)	£2.30
minus 20% of excess income (20% x £25.00)	£5.00
equals weekly main CTB	£8.70

Second adult rebate

The level of the son's gross income means that the claimant qualifies for a 7½% second adult rebate:

weekly second adult rebate (7½% x £16.00)	£1.20

Better buy comparison

Her entitlement to main CTB is greater than her entitlement to second adult rebate, so she is awarded main CTB only.

Example: Better buy for joint occupiers

TWO JOINT HOME-OWNERS WITH ONE NON-DEPENDANT/SECOND ADULT

The only residents of a (d)well(ing) are three sisters, Elsie, Lacie and Tillie. Elsie and Lacie jointly own it, and are jointly liable for the council tax there. Tillie lives there rent-free. She is their non-dependant. The eligible council tax for the whole dwelling is £20.00 per week.

Elsie is a full-time university student (learning, as it happens, to draw) and is therefore a 'disregarded person'. She has capital of £20,000.

Lacie is working (as a treacle operative, in fact). She is not a 'disregarded person'. For main CTB purposes she has excess income of £30.00 (and capital under £3,000).

Tillie is on income support. She is not a 'disregarded person'. She is therefore a second adult.

Elsie's claim for CTB

Elsie is not eligible for main CTB – she has too much capital (and, in any case, most full-time students are not eligible for main CTB, though they are eligible for second adult rebate: para. 21.25).

Elsie is eligible for second adult rebate (para. 8.18). Tillie is on income support, so the second adult rebate for the whole dwelling is 25 per cent of the council tax. Because there are two joint occupiers, Elsie qualifies for half of this,

which is (½ of 25% x £20.00)	£2.50

Lacie's claim for CTB

Lacie is eligible for main CTB. Because there are two joint occupiers, it is worked out on half the council tax for the dwelling. Because Tillie is on income support, there is no non-dependant deduction for her.

Lacie's entitlement to main CTB is:

weekly eligible council tax (½ x £20.00)	£10.00
minus 20% of excess income (20% x £30.00)	£6.00
which is	£4.00

Lacie's entitlement to second adult rebate is the same as Elsie's,

which is (½ of 25% x £20.00)	£2.50

Better buy comparisons

Elsie: No better buy comparison is required.

She is awarded second adult rebate of £2.50

Lacie: A better buy comparison is required.

Her main CTB (£4.00) is greater than her second adult rebate (£2.50).

She is awarded main CTB of £4.00

The total weekly CTB awarded on the dwelling is therefore £6.50

With apologies to Lewis Carroll

9 Eligible council tax

9.1 CTB is worked out by reference to the claimant's 'eligible council tax'. This chapter, which applies only in England, Wales and Scotland, explains this term, and gives the details of how to work out eligible council tax in all cases. It covers:

- the council tax itself, and who has to pay it;
- the exemptions, disability reductions, discounts, etc, which can reduce or eliminate council tax liability;
- eligible council tax for both main CTB and second adult rebate purposes.

COUNCIL TAX OVERVIEW

9.2 The council tax is the means by which local people help meet the cost of local public services. It is a tax on residential properties known as dwellings. Local councils, known in England and Wales as billing authorities and in Scotland as local authorities, are responsible for the billing and collection of the tax. (Scottish authorities are also responsible for collecting the council water charge.) Table 9.1 lists the key considerations that arise when considering council tax liability, etc. Fuller details of the council tax are in CPAG's *Council Tax Handbook* (6th edition, Alan Murdie and Martin Ward, Child Poverty Action Group, 2005), which covers many matters not included in this guide (such as billing, payment, penalties, appeals, and so on).

Table 9.1: Council Tax: key considerations

- Which dwelling is being considered?
- What valuation band does it fall into?
- How much is the council tax for that band?
- Who is liable to pay the council tax there?
- Is the dwelling exempt from council tax altogether?
- Do they qualify for a disability reduction?
- Do they qualify for a discount?
- Do they qualify for main CTB or second adult rebate?
- Should the council use its power to reduce liability?

DWELLINGS AND VALUATION BANDS

9.3 One council tax bill is issued per dwelling, unless the dwelling is exempt (para. 9.11). A dwelling means a house, a flat, etc, whether lived in or not, and also houseboats and mobile homes that are used for domestic purposes.

9.4 The amount of tax depends first on which valuation band a dwelling has been allocated to, and this is shown on the bill. The lower the valuation band, the lower the tax. An amount for each band is fixed each year by the billing or local authority, and often includes amounts for other bodies (such as a county council, a parish council, the police, etc).

9.5 In England and Scotland, dwellings are currently valued as at 1st April 1991 (taking effect from 1st April 1993), and there are eight valuation bands – band A to band H. In Wales, dwellings have been re-valued as at 1st April 2003 (taking effect from 1st April 2005); and there are nine valuation bands – band A to band I. However, transitional provisions in Wales mean that no dwelling should go up by more than one band per year (in the first three years) as a result of the re-valuation.

9.6 The valuation list holds current details of which band dwellings are in. In England and Wales it can be seen at either the local valuation office or the billing authority's main office or viewed on-line at the Valuation Office Agency's site, *www.voa.gov.uk*. In Scotland it may be seen at the local authority's main office.

WHO IS LIABLE TO PAY COUNCIL TAX?

9.7 Council tax is normally payable by someone resident in the dwelling (but there are also exceptions described in the next paragraph). A 'resident' is someone aged 18 or over, solely or mainly resident in the dwelling. Where there is more than one resident the liable person is the one with the greatest legal interest in the dwelling. So if a resident home-owner has a lodger, the home-owner is liable, not the lodger. If a resident council, housing association or private tenant has a lodger, the tenant is liable, not the lodger.

9.8 The most common exceptions to the above rule are that the owner (or other landlord) is liable for council tax on:

- a 'house in multiple occupation'. This means a house which was originally constructed or subsequently adapted for occupation by more than one household;
- many hostels and care homes; and
- unoccupied dwellings (unless they are exempt).

In other words, the residents (in the first two cases) are not liable, but many owners pass on the cost of paying the council tax (along with any other overheads) when fixing the rent.

JOINT LIABILITY

9.9 There are two ways in which joint liability (or 'joint and several liability') arises:

- if there is more than one resident with the greatest (or only) legal interest in the dwelling they are jointly liable for the council tax. For example two sisters who jointly own their home, or three friends who jointly rent their home, are jointly liable;
- if the liable person has a partner living with him or her, then the partner is jointly liable (even if he or she has no legal interest in the property). This applies to couples and polygamous arrangements.

For exceptions see the next paragraph. For how jointly liable residents are dealt with in CTB, see paragraphs 9.26-30. There are further rules (not in this guide) about joint liability for unoccupied properties.

STUDENTS AND PEOPLE WITH SEVERE MENTAL IMPAIRMENT

9.10 The exceptions to these rules on joint liability relate to students and people who are severely mentally impaired. A person counts as 'severely mentally impaired' as described in category 13 in appendix 6; and as a student (for these purposes) as described in categories 5, 6 or 7 of that appendix. Such a person is not jointly liable if there is another resident with the same legal interest in the dwelling who is neither severely mentally impaired nor a student. See the next paragraph if they are all severely mentally impaired, or all students.

EXEMPTIONS

9.11 The following occupied dwellings are exempt from council tax:

- dwellings where all the residents are students, including in England and Wales where that dwelling is only occupied during term time;
- halls of residence mainly occupied by students;
- dwellings where all occupants who would otherwise be liable for the council tax are severely mentally impaired, including cases where the only other occupiers are students;
- dwellings occupied only by persons under 18 years of age;
- armed forces accommodation;
- in England and Wales only, annexes or similar self-contained parts of a property which are occupied by an elderly or disabled relative of the residents living in the rest of it; and
- in Scotland only, certain dwellings used as trial flats by registered housing associations for pensioners and disabled people.

Examples: Council tax liability, exemptions and discounts

Unless specifically stated none of the following are students, severely mentally impaired, etc.

A COUPLE WITH A LODGER

A couple live in a house which the man owns in his name only. They have children in their 20s living at home, and a lodger who rents a room and shares facilities.

The couple are jointly liable for the council tax, because the man is the resident with the greatest legal interest in the dwelling and the woman is jointly liable with him by being his partner. There is no reason to suppose they qualify for exemption, or a disability reduction or a discount.

A LONE PARENT

A lone parent owns her home and lives there with her three children, all under 18.

The lone parent is solely liable for the council tax, because she is the resident with the greatest legal interest in the dwelling. She is the only (adult) resident so she qualifies for a 25% discount.

THREE SHARERS

Three friends jointly rent a house (in other words all their names are on the tenancy agreement). No-one else lives with them.

They are all jointly liable for the council tax, because they are all residents with the greatest legal interest in the dwelling. There is no reason to suppose they qualify for exemption, or a disability reduction or a discount.

THE SHARERS' CIRCUMSTANCES CHANGE

One of the sharers leaves and is not replaced. One of the others becomes a full-time university student.

The remaining non-student resident is now the only liable person, and qualifies for a 25% discount because the student is disregarded when counting the residents.

9.12 Various unoccupied dwellings are also exempt. For example, an unoccupied dwelling which is substantially unfurnished is exempt for six months – and there are many other categories.

DISABILITY REDUCTIONS

9.13 The council tax bill is reduced if a dwelling has at least one disabled resident and provides:

- an additional bathroom or kitchen for the use of the disabled person;
- a room, other than a bathroom, kitchen or toilet, used predominantly to meet the disabled person's special needs such as a downstairs room in a two storey house which has to be used as a bedroom by the disabled person because of the nature of the disability; or
- sufficient floor space to enable the use of a wheelchair required by the disabled person within the dwelling.

9.14 In each case the authority must be satisfied that the facility in question is either essential, or of major importance, for the disabled person (who may be an adult or a child) in view of the nature and extent of the disability. Disability reductions are not limited to specially adapted properties.

9.15 The effect of the reduction is that the person is liable for the amount that would be due if his or her dwelling was in the next lowest valuation band (or in the case of a band A dwelling, one-sixth less than normal).

DISCOUNTS

9.16 The council tax bill is reduced if:

- there is only one resident in the dwelling. In this case the discount is always 25 per cent; or
- there are no residents in the dwelling (unless the dwelling is exempt). In this case, the discount can be 50% or any lower amount or even nil (in other words in some cases there is no discount).

9.17 When considering the number of people in the dwelling certain people including students, apprentices, carers, severely mentally impaired people and under-18-year-olds are disregarded. Appendix 6 describes the categories of person who are disregarded. A person can be disregarded for the purpose of awarding a discount but still liable to pay the tax.

OBTAINING AN EXEMPTION, DISABILITY REDUCTION OR DISCOUNT

9.18 An authority is expected to take reasonable steps to ascertain whether exemptions, disability reductions and discounts apply to the dwellings in its area. These can be awarded on the basis of information available to it, or someone can write requesting this. There is no time limit on obtaining exemptions, disability reductions or discounts, though the authority is entitled to seek appropriate evidence.

OTHER REASONS WHY LIABILITY MAY BE LOWER

9.19 In addition to the disability reductions and discounts mentioned above, authorities can offer a discount for prompt payment of the tax or the adoption of certain payment methods. In some areas council tax may be 'capped' by the government to a lower figure, and in a few areas there may be a 'transitional reduction' in liability because of recent re-organisation of authority boundaries. The following describes the final method of reducing liability in England only.

POWER TO REDUCE COUNCIL TAX LIABILITY

9.20 In England only an authority may reduce any liability for council tax. This is a wide power (some would call it a discretion) which permits the authority to reduce liability 'to such extent as it thinks fit' and 'includes power to reduce an amount to nil'. This can be done 'in relation to particular cases or by determining a class of case in which liability is to be reduced to an extent provided by the determination.'

9.21 This power exists under section 13A of the Local Government Finance Act 1992, as inserted by section 76 of the Local Government Act 2003 (itself brought into force by section 128(2) of the 2003 Act). No further rules are given about how to get such a reduction, so a person could write in and ask, or an authority could design its own rules without any such request. Similarly, no mention is made of any kind of appeals mechanism, though presumably these matters could be judicially reviewed.

IMPACT ON DISCRETIONARY HOUSING PAYMENTS

9.22 The power to reduce council tax liability is separate from the power to make discretionary housing payments (para. 22.2). The government contributes to awards of DHPs, which can be granted only to people on HB/CTB. Neither of those points apply to the above power.

Eligible council tax

9.23 A claimant's 'eligible council tax' is the figure used in calculating his or her entitlement to main CTB and/or second adult rebate. The eligible council tax figure used in calculating main CTB can differ from that used in calculating second adult rebate, as mentioned in the appropriate places below. An example is at the end of the chapter.

9.24 A claimant's weekly eligible council tax is calculated by working through the following steps: CTB 57(1),(2),62(1 CTB60+ 40(1),(2), 46(1)

1. Start with the council tax due on his or her home.
2. If the claimant is entitled to a disability reduction, use the council tax figure after that reduction has been made.

3. If the claimant is entitled to a discount, use the council tax figure after that discount has been made.
4. Apportion the result if the claimant is a joint occupier (see below).
5. Convert it to a weekly figure (as described in para. 7.39).

9.25 All the above steps apply when calculating eligible council tax for main CTB purposes and student second adult rebate purposes. But steps 3 and 4 are omitted when calculating eligible council tax for general second adult rebate purposes (see para. 9.30). See also paragraph 9.31 about other items which can affect a council tax bill.

APPORTIONMENT FOR JOINT OCCUPIERS

CTB 57(3),(4)
CTB60+ 40(3),(4)

9.26 A joint occupier is one of two or more people who are jointly liable to pay the council tax on a dwelling, other than just a couple or polygamous arrangement. In such cases, the figures used in calculating eligible council tax are apportioned between the joint occupiers for main CTB purposes (but not second adult rebate: para. 9.30).

9.27 This apportionment is found by dividing the total council tax liability by the number of people who are jointly liable.

9.28 If amongst several jointly liable people some are a couple or polygamous marriage, the law is unclear. The DWP advises (GM para. B2.36) that if there are three jointly liable people, two of whom are a couple, then the couple are eligible for main CTB on two-thirds of the council tax liability and the other person on one-third.

9.29 It is also worth noting here that, in most cases, students and people who are severely mentally impaired are not jointly liable for council tax (para. 9.10) so the apportionment ignores them.

VARIATIONS WHEN CALCULATING GENERAL SECOND ADULT REBATE

9.30 As mentioned earlier, there are two differences in the rules for calculating eligible council tax for general second adult rebate purposes:

- Step 3 in paragraph 9.24 does not apply. In other words, a claimant's eligible council tax is calculated as though he or she did not qualify for any council tax discount. This is mainly for mathematical reasons. As illustrated in the following example, a claimant who qualifies for a discount does not lose it.
- Step 4 in paragraph 9.24 does not apply. In other words, there is no apportionment between joint occupiers. Instead, the apportionment will be done after the calculation of second adult rebate is otherwise complete (as described in para. 8.20).

OTHER ITEMS AFFECTING ELIGIBLE COUNCIL TAX

9.31 The following additional rules apply to main CTB and also to second adult rebate:

- in the case of an authority which offers discounts against its council taxes for people who pay in a lump sum or by a method other than cash (e.g. direct debit), CTB is calculated on liability before those discounts are subtracted;
- if lower council taxes are set as a result of council tax 'capping' procedures, these apply from the beginning of the financial year, and CTB is calculated (throughout the financial year) on the lower amount;
- if a council tax bill is increased to recover an earlier overpayment of CTB or of community charge benefit, CTB is calculated before those amounts are added;
- if a penalty is added to a council tax bill, CTB is calculated as if that penalty was not included; and
- if council tax liability is reduced (paras. 9.13 and 9.16), CTB is calculated on the reduced amount.

Example: Eligible council tax

THE CLAIMANT AND HIS HOUSEHOLD

A claimant's dwelling falls in band D, which in his area is £900 per year. With him lives only his cousin (as his non-dependant). The claimant is a full-time student with income from several sources, including a grant towards his disablement needs. His cousin is on income support. The claimant qualifies for:

- a disability reduction, because he has a large enough house to use his wheelchair indoors. This is worth £100 per year; and
- a 25% council tax discount, because he is a full-time student, so there is only one countable resident in his home, his daughter. This is worth £200 per year.

ELIGIBLE COUNCIL TAX FOR MAIN CTB

In calculating main CTB his eligible council tax is the figure obtained by deducting both the disability reduction and the discount from the amount for the dwelling. This is (£900 – £100 – £200 =) £600, the weekly equivalent of which is (to the nearest penny) £11.51.

It turns out, though, when the authority assesses his entitlement to main CTB, that he does not qualify because he has too much capital.

ELIGIBLE COUNCIL TAX FOR SECOND ADULT REBATE

In calculating second adult rebate his eligible council tax is the figure obtained by deducting the disability reduction from the amount for the dwelling but not the discount (para. 9.30). This is (£900 – £100 =) £800, the weekly equivalent of which is (to the nearest penny) £15.34.

Because his cousin is on income support, he qualifies for second adult rebate equal to 25% of the last figure (table 8.3). This is (to the nearest penny) £3.84. On an annual basis this is £200.

HIS RESULTING LIABILITY FOR COUNCIL TAX

The following are the annual figures:

The council tax for the dwelling is	£900
He is granted his disability reduction of	– £100
He is granted his discount of	– £200
He is granted second adult rebate of	– £200
So his resulting liability is	= £400

10 Eligible rent

10.1 HB is worked out by reference to the claimant's 'eligible rent'. This chapter explains this term, and gives the details of how to work out 'eligible rent' in all cases. It covers:

- what counts as 'rent' for HB purposes and how this differs from 'eligible rent';
- eligible rent for council (and in Northern Ireland, NIHE) tenants;
- eligible rent for housing association tenants;
- eligible rent for private tenants under the 'New Scheme' (also sometimes known as 'maximum rent' in these cases);
- eligible rent for private tenants under the 'Old Scheme';
- eligible rent for registered rent cases;
- eligible rent for other cases; and
- which service charges are eligible to be met through HB.

10.2 The chapter does not apply in areas where the local housing allowance applies (para. 22.22 and table 22.1).

'Rent' and 'eligible rent'

'RENT'

HB 11(1),13(1)
HB60+ 11(1),13(1)
NIHB 11(1),13(1)
NIHB60+ 11(1),13(1)

10.3 The term 'rent' has various meanings in different branches of the law. As far as HB is concerned, all the types of payment shown in table 10.1 count as rent. In this chapter, the term 'actual rent' is used to mean the total of all the payments shown in that table which a claimant is liable to pay on his or her normal home.

10.4 Charges for services are also included in the legal definition of 'rent' for HB purposes. This does not means that HB will necessarily pay for them (paras. 10.75 onwards). Note that certain categories of claimant and certain types of dwelling are not eligible for HB even where the claimant is liable for rent (paras. 2.14 onwards); that some housing costs which do not count as rent for HB purposes can be met through JSA(IB), income support or guarantee credit (paras. 2.24-25); and that further rules apply in relation to increases to cover arrears of rent; to garages and land; and to business premises (paras. 10.106-108).

Table 10.1: Payments counted as rent for HB purposes

- Rent in its ordinary sense, whether under a tenancy or licence, including board and lodging payments and payments for 'use and occupation'.
- 'Mesne profits' in England, Wales and Northern Ireland or 'violent profits' in Scotland (paid after a tenancy or right to occupy is terminated).
- Houseboat mooring charges and berthing fees and caravan and mobile home site charges (even if owned by the claimant, and in addition to rental if not owned).
- Payments made by residents of charitable almshouses.
- Payments under rental purchase agreements.
- Payments for crofts and croft land in Scotland.

'ELIGIBLE RENT'

10.5 A claimant's 'eligible rent' is the figure used in calculating his or her entitlement to HB (para. 7.4). It could be exactly equal to his or her actual rent (this happens in some council tenant cases, for example), but often it is different. The three main reasons for this are: HB 12(3) HB60+ 12(3) NIHB 13(3) NIHB60+ 13(3)

- many service charges cannot be met by HB: for example water charges, meals and most fuel (and, in Northern Ireland, any rates element included in the rent must be identified: chapter 11);
- in the case of much privately rented accommodation (and some housing association and similar accommodation), the rent officer's or NIHE's valuations are used to work out the eligible rent rather than the landlord's figures;
- in some cases the eligible rent may be restricted to a lower figure.

This chapter explains all the rules about working out 'eligible rent'. A summary of the main points may be found in tables 10.3 and 10.4.

APPORTIONMENT FOR JOINT OCCUPIERS

10.6 In the case of a claimant who is a joint occupier (para. 4.47), many of the figures used in calculating eligible rent are apportioned between the joint occupiers. In doing this, the authority must determine how much of the actual rent on the dwelling is fairly attributable to each of the joint occupiers, taking into account the number of people paying towards the rent, the proportion of rent paid by each, HB 12(5) HB60+ 12(5) NIHB 13(5) NIHB60+ 13(6) and any relevant other circumstances – such as the size and number of rooms each occupies, and whether there is any written or other agreement between them. The authority must then apportion the figures used in calculating the claimant's eligible rent on the same basis. Unlike CTB (para. 9.26), the rent is apportioned amongst all of the joint occupiers even if one of them (or more than one) is a student, a rule confirmed by the Court of Appeal *(Naghshbandi v LB Camden and the Secretary of State for Work and Pensions)*.

In *CH/3376/2002,* the commissioner dealt with a case where there were two joint tenants, one of whom was absent. He held that the proportion of rent paid is not necessarily the predominant factor (though in appropriate cases it can be), and apportioned the whole of the rent to the tenant who was present, taking account of a wide range of personal factors including his age, health, sick mother, local connections, attempts to ameliorate the situation and lack of control over the other tenant's (his step-son's) failure to pay the rent and whether it was appropriate to expect the claimant to seek alternative accommodation. The example illustrates a similar situation.

Example: Joint occupiers

TOM, DICK AND HARRY

Three unrelated friends in their thirties, Tom, Dick and Harry, jointly rent a two-bedroom housing association house, where the rent for the whole house is £150 per week (and this does not include any service charges). Dick and Harry have a bedroom each. Tom uses the living room as a bedroom. They share the kitchen and all other facilities. They have each contributed one-third of the rent in the past. Harry loses his job and claims HB, saying that his share remains one-third.

Harry's eligible rent is very likely to be regarded as £50 per week. It is possible that a fairer split would be something other than one-third each, but unlikely based on the information given.

TOM MOVES OUT

Tom moves out. He is not replaced. Dick and Harry keep their own bedrooms and begin to share the living room. They agree between them that they should contribute equally to the rent.

Harry's eligible rent is now very likely to be regarded as £75 per week – unless the authority considers that the new rent is unreasonable and has the power to restrict it (as described in later parts of this chapter).

Definitions

'OLD SCHEME' CASES *versus* 'NEW SCHEME' CASES

10.7 Especially in the private rented sector, the amount of a claimant's eligible rent depends very much on whether his or her case falls within the 'Old Scheme' or the 'New Scheme'. (Strictly speaking, the distinction applies to all types of HB case – including council tenants, NIHE tenants and housing association tenants – but the greatest impact is on private sector tenants.) 'Old Scheme' and 'New Scheme' are defined below. In broad terms, all claimants who have been on HB since before 2nd January 1996 (and some claimants who have more recently taken over an HB claim from someone who has been on HB since before then) fall within the 'Old Scheme'. So do claimants in certain kinds of accommodation where care, support or supervision is provided.

CPR sch 3 para 4(1) NICPR sch 3 para 4(1)

10.8 Terminology varies widely across the country. 'Old Scheme Cases' are also known as 'Old Cases' or 'Exempt Cases' (because they were exempt from the January 1996 changes). 'New Scheme Cases' are also known as 'New Cases' or 'Non-exempt cases'.

10.9 As described below, a person falls within the Old Scheme if he or she:

- is (personally) an 'exempt claimant'; or
- has had exemption transferred to him or her; or
- is claiming HB in respect of 'exempt accommodation'.

Otherwise, he or she falls within the New Scheme.

'EXEMPT CLAIMANTS'

10.10 A claimant is an 'exempt claimant' (and therefore falls within the 'Old Scheme') if he or she:

CPR sch 3 para 4(2)-(4),(8),(10) NICPR sch 3 para 4(1)(a),(9)

- was 'entitled to' HB on Monday 1st January 1996 in Great Britain or Monday 1st April 1996 in Northern Ireland; and
- has remained 'entitled to and in receipt of' HB continuously since that date (disregarding breaks in HB entitlement/receipt of up to 52 weeks in the case of a 'welfare to work beneficiary': table 12.2; or in any case disregarding breaks of four weeks or less); and
- has not moved home since that date, or has moved only because a fire, flood, explosion or natural catastrophe made his or her former home uninhabitable.

10.11 Note that, without there being any apparent reason for it, the above rules are different from rules protecting people against other changes (e.g. para. 10.31).

TRANSFERRING EXEMPTION: DEATH, DEPARTURE AND DETENTION

CPR sch 3 para 4(5)-(8),(10) NICPR sch 3 para 4(2)-(6)

10.12 Exemption is transferred in the following three ways from one claimant ('A') to another claimant ('B') (who therefore falls within the 'Old Scheme'). 'Partner' and 'member of the household' have their specific HB meanings (paras. 4.3 onwards):

- A dies; and B was (until then) his or her partner or any other member of the household;
- A leaves the dwelling; and B was (until then) his or her partner;
- A is 'detained in custody pending sentence upon conviction or under a sentence imposed by a court' (and is not entitled to HB under the rules about absences from home: chapter 3); and B is (or was until then) his or her partner.

10.13 Additionally, in all three cases:

- At the date of his or her death, departure or detention, A must be in receipt of HB (or a 'welfare to work beneficiary' – table 12.2 – who was in receipt of HB no more than 52 weeks previously);
- B must occupy the dwelling as a home on that date (or be treated as occupying it: para. 3.3 onwards);
- B's claim for HB must be made within four weeks of that date (or awarded to fall within those four weeks: paras. 5.51-54);
- B's claim is then treated as having been made on that date;
- B then continues to be exempt for as long as he or she:
  - remains 'entitled to and in receipt of' HB continuously (disregarding breaks in HB entitlement/receipt of up to 52 weeks in the case of a 'welfare to work beneficiary': table 12.2; or in any case disregarding breaks of four weeks or less): this includes renewal claims so long as they run continuously or are backdated to run continuously (disregarding breaks as just mentioned), and
  - does not move to occupy a new dwelling as his or her home, or moves only because a fire, flood, explosion or natural catastrophe makes his or her home uninhabitable;
- B's exemption is then transferred to any other claimant in the same way as described above (para. 10.12). There is no limit to the number of transfers of exemption so long as the above conditions are complied with in each case.

Example: Old Scheme cases: exempt claimants and transferring exemption

Mrs Sawable is a magician's assistant. Her husband lives with her. She is in receipt of HB on 1st January 1996.

- So she is an exempt claimant from 2nd January 1996.

Mrs Sawable remains continuously entitled to and in receipt of HB.

- So she continues to be an exempt claimant.

Mrs Sawable dies in May 2006. Mr Sawable makes a claim for HB within four weeks of her death.

- So, because of the rules about 'transferred exemption', he is an exempt claimant.

'EXEMPT ACCOMMODATION'

10.14 Any claimant in 'exempt accommodation' falls within the 'Old Scheme', no matter when his or her claim for HB is made. 'Exempt accommodation' is:

CPR sch 3 para 4(1),(10)
NICPR sch 3 para 4(1)(b),(9)

- any accommodation 'provided by':
  - a housing association, whether registered or unregistered,
  - a registered charity,
  - a non-profit-making voluntary organisation,
  - a non-metropolitan county council, or
  - any other registered social landlord,

  where (in each of the cases) 'that body or a person acting on its behalf also provides the claimant with care, support or supervision'; or
- in Great Britain only, any resettlement place.

10.15 For the purposes of the first type of exempt accommodation, there is no definition of 'care', 'support' or 'supervision': these terms take their ordinary English meanings and are open to appeal (chapter 19). Also, what it means for accommodation to be 'provided by' the body concerned is open to debate, though it is not restricted to cases where the claimant pays rent to that body. (For example, if a registered charity makes arrangements with a private landlord to use accommodation owned by him for its clients, and the landlord collects the rent but the charity retains the right to say who will live in the accommodation, it may be argued that the accommodation is 'provided by' the charity.)

'REGISTERED RENT CASE'

CPR sch 3 para 4
NICPR sch 3 para 4
NICPR sch 3 para 4
NIHB60+ sch 3 para 4

10.16 'Registered rent case' is not a term used in the law. It is used in this guide to mean all pre-January 1989 tenancies in Great Britain, and most pre-October 1978 tenancies in Northern Ireland, which are still subject to the Rent Acts whether or not the rent has been registered (i.e. fixed) by the rent officer. (The Rent Acts were the Acts that governed landlord and tenant law at that time, and people who have had the same tenancy since then still fall within those Acts.)

'HOUSING ASSOCIATION' AND 'REGISTERED HOUSING ASSOCIATION'

HB 2(1)
HB60+ 2(1)
NIHB 2(1)
NIHB60+ 2(1)

10.17 For HB purposes, a 'housing association' means the same as in section 1(1) of the Housing Associations Act 1985 or, in Northern Ireland, article 114 of the Housing (Northern Ireland) Order 1981 No.156 as amended by SI 1986 No.1035. These define a housing association as a society, body of trustees, or company:

- whose objects or powers include the power to provide, manage, construct or improve housing; and
- which does not trade for profit or, if it does, is limited by its constitution not to pay interest or dividends above a limit (currently 5%) set by the Treasury or, in Northern Ireland, the Department of Finance and Personnel.

A 'housing association' may (or may not) also be a charity, registered with the Charity Commissioners.

HB 14(10)
HB60+ 14(10)
NIHB 16(5)
NIHB60+ 16(5)

10.18 For HB purposes, a 'registered housing association' means a housing association which is registered with the Housing Corporation (in England), Welsh Assembly (in Wales), Communities Scotland (in Scotland) or the Department for Social Development (in Northern Ireland). In Great Britain (but not Northern Ireland) associations so registered are also known as registered social landlords.

'HAMA' AND 'HAL' SCHEMES

10.19 Housing Associations sometimes act as managing agents for private landlords: these are known as 'HAMA' schemes (Housing Associations as Managing Agents). In these cases the Housing Association is not the landlord so claims from rent-payers in such accommodation count as private tenant cases (paras. 10.31 onwards).

10.20 Sometimes housing associations lease accommodation from private landlords and in turn rent it out to tenants: these are known as 'HAL' schemes (Housing Association Leasing). In these cases the housing association is the tenant's landlord so claims from rent-payers in such accommodation count as housing association cases (paras. 10.25 onwards).

Eligible rent for council and NIHE tenants

10.21 The eligible rent of a council tenant (or in Northern Ireland a tenant of the NIHE) is simply:

HB 12(3)
HB60+ 12(3)
NIHB 13(3)
NIHB60+ 13(3)

- the actual rent;
- minus amounts for service charges which are ineligible for HB (paras. 10.75 onwards).

10.22 This applies in all rent rebate cases (para. 1.16): it applies whether it is the claimant or a partner (or both) who rents from the council. (Different rules apply to people renting from county councils: paras. 10.71.)

10.23 In all these cases:

- non-weekly rents need to be converted to a weekly figure (para. 7.39);
- adjustments must be made in the case of joint occupiers (para. 10.6);
- it is always the authority (not, say, the rent officer) which determines how much the eligible rent is and deals with all matters relating to service charges.

10.24 In theory at least, it is possible for the authority to reduce the eligible rent below the figure described above, depending on whether the case falls within the Old Scheme or New Scheme (para. 10.7). For an Old Scheme case, the same rules and protections apply as for a private sector Old Scheme case (para. 10.51). For a New Scheme case, the general power in paragraph 10.48 applies. In practice, council tenants' eligible rents are rarely if ever restricted, though the Court of Appeal has recognised this as a possibility *(Burton v Camden London Borough Council).*

HB 12(7)
HB60+ 12(7)
NIHB 13(7)
NIHB60+ 13(7)

Eligible rent for housing association and stock transfer tenants

10.25 The eligible rent of a housing association tenant, or former public sector tenant whose property has since been transferred to a new landlord, depends first on whether the claimant falls within the Old Scheme or the New Scheme (para. 10.7). This applies in all cases in which the landlord is a housing association (para. 10.17), whether or not the housing association is a registered housing association, or registered social landlord: it applies whether it is the claimant or a partner (or both) who rents from them. The rules on rent officer (or NIHE) referrals for New Scheme cases for stock transfer property are similar to but slightly more generous than the rules for referring registered housing association New Scheme cases (para. 10.29). The circumstances in which the rent is referred for both these types of landlord in New Scheme cases are dealt with in table 10.2, and further rules are then given in paragraphs 10.28-30. The rules for housing association

HB 2(1),12(3)
HB60+ 2(1),12(3)
NIHB 2(1),13(3)
NIHB 2(1),13(3)

and stock transfer property Old Scheme cases are given in paragraph 10.27. Note that property of both registered and unregistered housing associations, including transferred stock, counts as Old Scheme if 'care, support or supervision is provided' (paras. 10.14-15).

Example: Eligible rent for a council tenant

A claimant rents a council flat. His actual rent is £65 per week. This figure includes £5 per week for the cleaning and lighting of communal areas and £12 per week for the use of an emergency alarm service.

His eligible rent is calculated as follows. The charge for the communal areas is eligible for HB. However, the charge for emergency alarm service is not eligible, so this has to be deducted from his actual rent to find his eligible rent. His eligible rent is therefore £53 per week.

NIHB sch 3 paras 1,3,4
NIHB60+ sch 3 paras 1,3,4

10.26 There are some drafting problems with the law in Northern Ireland which can be interpreted as meaning that all housing association tenants (without exception) should be treated as 'registered rent cases'. It is assumed that this is not the intention of those who drafted the law and that this error will if necessary be corrected.

OLD SCHEME CASES

CPR sch 3 para 5
NICPR sch 3 para 5

10.27 In Old Scheme cases (regardless of whether the landlord is a registered or unregistered housing association or stock transfer or not), the claimant's eligible rent is worked out in the same way as for a private sector Old Scheme case (para. 10.51). For example:

- the authority could restrict the eligible rent on grounds of unreasonableness (but must have comparables demonstrating this and cannot rely on figures provided by the rent officer);
- however, there are rules preventing all or part of such a restriction in the case of certain protected groups.

NEW SCHEME CASES

HB 2(1),12(3), sch 2 para 3
HB60+ 2(1),12(3), sch 2 para 3
NIHB 2(1),13(3), sch 3 para 3
NIHB60+ 2(1),13(3), sch 3 para 3

10.28 In New Scheme cases, everything depends on whether the authority refers the rent to the rent officer on the grounds that it considers the rent or size to be unreasonable (table 6.1). In Northern Ireland, if the Housing Executive considers the rent or size unreasonable it is obliged to apply the rent restriction rules in the same way that rent officers do in Great Britain. The circumstances in which the rent is referred for all New Scheme housing association and stock transfer cases are shown in table 10.2. Note that in Great Britain (and possibly Northern Ireland:

para. 10.26) the concessions on automatic referrals in New Scheme cases only apply to stock transfer tenants and tenants of registered housing associations, not unregistered housing associations (paras. 10.17-18).

10.29 If the authority does make a referral to the rent officer, the claimant's eligible rent is worked out in the same way as for a private sector New Scheme case (para. 10.33). For example:

HB 13(1),14
HB60+ 13(1),14
NIHB 14(1),15
NIHB60+ 14(1),15

- the rent officer's figures are binding and a 'maximum rent' will apply – which often results in the eligible rent being restricted;
- and once the case has been referred to the rent officer, a further restriction could be applied (para. 10.48);
- however, there are rules preventing all or part of such a restriction in the case of certain protected groups.

10.30 If the authority does not make a referral to the rent officer, the claimant's rent is worked out in the same way as for a council tenant (para. 10.21) – but the resulting eligible rent cannot be restricted in any way (because if the authority considers the rent to be unreasonable, it must refer the rent to the rent officer – table 6.1 – and the previous paragraph will then apply).

HB 12(3)
HB60+ 12(3)
NIHB 13(3)
NIHB60+ 13(3)

Eligible rent for private tenants

10.31 There are two main ways of working out a private tenant's eligible rent, depending on whether the claimant falls within the New Scheme or the Old Scheme (as defined in paras. 10.7-15). Rules for those two types of cases are dealt with in turn below, and are followed by some further rules which apply in registered rent cases and other special cases.

10.32 This applies in all cases in which the landlord is a private individual or company: it applies whether it is the claimant or a partner (or both) who rents from them.

Eligible rent for New Scheme private sector cases

10.33 In New Scheme private sector cases, the claimant's eligible rent is always the 'maximum rent' applying in his or her case (as described in the following paragraphs), unless:

HB 13(1),14
HB60+ 13(1),14
NIHB 14(1),15
NIHB 14(1),15

- the claimant and/or other occupiers could formerly afford the accommodation (para. 10.38); or
- the claimant has had a bereavement (para. 10.41); or

- the claimant's rent details change during his or her award of HB (para. 10.45); or
- the authority reduces the eligible rent to below the maximum rent in certain cases (para. 10.48); or
- the claimant has a registered rent (para. 10.67).

Table 10.2: Eligible rent: concessions for housing associations and stock transfer landlords

HB 2(1),13(5), sch 2 paras 3,12
HB60+ 2(1),13(5), sch 2 paras 3,12
CPR sch 3 para 4
NIHB 2(1),14(5),16(5)
NIHB60+ 2(1),14(5),16(5)
NICPR sch 3 para 4(1)(r),(9)

ALL HOUSING ASSOCIATION PROPERTY INCLUDING TRANSFERRED STOCK

(a) The following rules apply all housing association stock in Great Britain & NI* regardless of whether the property is also former local authority/ NIHE transferred stock.

- All housing association property where 'care support or supervision' is provided is 'exempt accommodation' (paras. 10.14-15) and is dealt with as an Old Scheme case (para. 10.27). This rule applies whether the housing association is registered or unregistered (paras. 10.17-18).
- In New Scheme Cases (para. 10.28), except where the home is also stock transfer property in which case the appropriate rule below applies, tenants of registered housing associations can only have their rents referred to the rent officer (in NI to the NIHE for a rent decision*), if the authority considers that either the rent is unreasonably high or the accommodation is unreasonably large.
- The single room rent does not apply to tenants of registered housing associations (para. 6.12).
- Special rules about the timing of referrals apply to hostels where the accommodation is owned or managed by a registered housing association (paras. 6.9-10).

NEW SCHEME CASES: STOCK TRANSFER LANDLORDS IN GREAT BRITAIN AND NORTHERN IRELAND

(b) All former local authority or NIHE stock where the stock transfer took place on or after 7th October 2002 (whether or not transferred to a housing association) where the claim is not an Old Scheme case (paras. 10.7-15).

◆ These properties can only have their rents referred if there has been a rent increase since the transfer took place and the authority considers that the rent is unreasonably high (but not if it considers the property unreasonably large).

(c) All former local authority, new town or NIHE stock where the transfer took place before 7th October 2002 (whether or not transferred to a housing association) where the claim is not an Old Scheme case (paras. 10.7-15).

◆ These properties can only have their rents referred if there has been a rent increase since the transfer took place and the authority considers that either: the rent is unreasonably high; or the accommodation is unreasonably large (table 6.1).

HOUSING ACTION TRUSTS AND FORMER SCOTTISH HOMES PROPERTY

(d) All Housing Action Trust (HAT) and former HAT properties.

◆ All current HAT properties are exempt from referral to the rent officer and so are dealt with in the same way as local authority tenants (paras. 10.21-24). There are no special concessions for property which is subsequently transferred from a HAT to another landlord. However, transfer is likely to be to a housing association in which case apply the appropriate rule above.

(e) All former Scottish Homes property.

◆ There are no special concessions for former Scottish Homes property which has subsequently transferred to another landlord. However, transfer is likely to be to a housing association in which case apply the appropriate rule above.

* Tenants of housing associations in NI: see para. 10.26.

MAXIMUM RENT: THE GENERAL RULE

HB 2(1),13
HB60+ 2(1),13
NIHB 2(1),14
NIHB60+ 2(1),14

10.34 The claimant's 'maximum rent' is the lowest of the figures provided by the rent officer (chapter 6) in his or her case (or the only figure if the rent officer provides only one). But before deciding which is lowest, the figures must be adjusted in certain cases. Table 10.3 describes the rent officer's figures and shows how to calculate maximum rent.

10.35 There are two exceptions: different rules can apply to awards of HB continuing from before 6th October 1997 (para. 10.36), and to lettings begun in or before January 1989 (para. 10.67).

MAXIMUM RENT: THE '50% TOP-UP' FOR CERTAIN OLDER CLAIMS

CPR sch 3 para 8
NICPR sch 3 para 5

10.36 As described in the next paragraph, the calculation of a claimant's maximum rent is different in the case of any claimant who meets the following conditions:

- the claimant was 'entitled to and in receipt of' HB on Sunday 5th October 1997; and
- the claimant has remained 'entitled to and in receipt of' HB continuously since that date (disregarding breaks of up to 52 weeks in the case of a 'welfare to work beneficiary': table 12.2; but in any other case with no breaks whatsoever); and
- the claimant has not moved to occupy a new dwelling as his or her home since that date (regardless of the reason for the move); and
- the claimant has qualified for a '50% top-up' continuously since that date; and
- the rent officer has provided a local reference rent in the claimant's case.

10.37 If a claimant meets all the above conditions, he or she must be considered for a 50% top-up, calculated by working through the following steps:

- Start with the rent officer's figures and make all the adjustments exactly as in steps 1 and 2 in table 10.3.
- The claimant's maximum rent is then the average of (i.e. half-way between) the local reference rent and the claim-related rent; unless the single room rent is lower than that, in which case the maximum rent is that single room rent.

Table 10.3: Calculating 'maximum rent' for New Scheme cases

HB 13
HB60+ 13
NIHB 14
NIHB60+ 14

1. START WITH THE RENT OFFICER'S FIGURES

The authority needs all the figures provided by the rent officer, which could be one or more of the following:

- a claim-related rent determination;
- a local reference rent determination;
- a single room rent determination (only in the case of a 'young individual': para. 6.12).

Convert these to a weekly figure at this stage (para. 7.39). Work through Step 2 separately for each figure.

2. ADJUSTMENTS MADE BY THE AUTHORITY *

(a) Deduction for meals

Deduct an amount for meals – but only if the claimant's actual rent includes meals. Use the amounts shown in table 10.7. There are two exceptions:

- do not deduct anything for meals in the case of the single room rent;
- do not deduct anything for meals in the case of the claim-related rent if the rent officer has notified the authority that it does not include meals.

(b) Apportionment for joint occupiers

If the claimant is a joint occupier, apportion the resulting figures (para. 10.6). Do not, however, apportion the single room rent.

3. CALCULATE MAXIMUM RENT

The claimant's 'maximum rent' is the lowest of the resulting figures (or if there is only one figure, it is that one).

* **Note:**
No adjustment is made for water charges, fuel or any service charges other than those in this table: if those are included in the claimant's actual rent, the rent officer takes this into account when fixing his or her figures (chapter 6).

Examples: Calculating maximum rent

EXAMPLE ONE: A STRAIGHTFORWARD CASE

A private tenant over the age of 25 makes a first claim for HB. Her actual rent is £80 per week including water charges and fuel charges. She is not a joint occupier. The rent officer has provided the following figures:

- a claim-related rent determination of £70 per week;
- a local reference rent determination of £65 per week;
- no single room rent determination (because the claimant is not a 'young individual')

Because none of the adjustments in table 10.3 apply in this case, her maximum rent is simply the lower of the above two figures, i.e. £65 per week.

EXAMPLE TWO: A JOINT OCCUPIER AGED UNDER 25

A private tenant under the age of 25 makes a first claim for HB. He is a joint occupier with two others: they share their rent equally. The actual rent for the whole property is £180 per week including water charges and fuel charges. The rent officer has provided the following figures:

- a claim-related rent determination of £150 per week;
- a local reference rent determination of £135 per week;
- a single room rent determination of £42 per week.

The only adjustment in table 10.3 which applies is the apportionment for joint occupiers:

- the adjusted claim-related rent is (£150 ÷ 3 =) £50 per week;
- the adjusted local reference rent is (£135 ÷ 3 =) £45 per week;
- the single room rent is not adjusted; it is £42 per week.

The claimant's maximum rent is the lowest of the resulting figures, i.e. £42 per week.

Note: In both cases, further rules apply if the claimant could afford the accommodation when he or she took on the rent commitment (para. 10.38).

Example: Maximum rent with a '50% top-up'

A private tenant over the age of 25 was on HB on 5th October 1997. She has not moved since then and she meets all the other conditions to be considered for a 50% top-up. Her actual rent is £100 per week including water charges and fuel charges. She is not a joint occupier. Her case is referred to the rent officer in July 2005 and the rent officer provides the following figures:

- a claim-related rent determination of £90 per week;
- a local reference rent determination of £70 per week;
- no single room rent determination (because she is not a 'young individual).

Because she qualifies for a 50% top-up (paras. 10.36-37), and because none of the adjustments in table 10.3 applies, her maximum rent is the average of (i.e. half-way between) the local reference rent and the claim-related rent, which is £80 per week.

MAXIMUM RENT: PROTECTION FOR PEOPLE WHO COULD FORMERLY AFFORD THEIR ACCOMMODATION

10.38 This is the first of the two 'protected groups' – people who are protected against the effect of the rules about maximum rents (and various other rent restrictions: para. 10.58). A claimant falls within this protected group if:

HB 13(14)-(16)
HB60+ 13(14)-(16)
CPR sch 3 para 5
NIHB 14(14),(15)
NIHB60+ 14(14),(15)
NICPR sch 3 para 5

- he or she or any combination of the occupiers of his or her home (para. 10.43) could afford the financial commitments there when the liability to pay rent was entered into (no matter how long ago that was); and
- the claimant has not received HB for any period in the 52 weeks prior to his or her current claim. Receipt of CTB during those weeks is ignored.

10.39 In such a case, the protection lasts for the first 13 weeks of his or her entitlement to HB. During those weeks, his or her eligible rent is worked out in the same way as for a council tenant (para. 10.21) – but the resulting eligible rent cannot be restricted in any way.

10.40 This protection gives the claimant time to move, without the additional pressure of having insufficient HB. In the case of a couple, so long as the claimant has not received HB during the past 52 weeks, it is immaterial whether his or her partner has. In some cases it therefore makes a substantial difference which person in a couple makes the claim for HB (para. 5.4).

MAXIMUM RENT: PROTECTION FOR PEOPLE WHO HAVE HAD A BEREAVEMENT

HB 13(11),(12),(16)
HB60+
13(11),(12),(16)
CPR sch 3 para 5
NIHB 14(11),(12)
NIHB60+
14(11),(12)
NICPR sch 3 para 5

10.41 This is the second of the two 'protected groups' – people who are protected against the effect of the rules about maximum rents (and various other rent restrictions: para. 10.58). A claimant falls within this protected group if:

- any of the occupiers of his or her home (para. 10.43) has died within the last 12 months (including occupiers who were temporarily absent); and
- the claimant has not moved home since the date of that death.

10.42 In such a case, the protection lasts until 12 months after that death. During that period it works as follows. If the claimant was on HB at the date of the death, his or her eligible rent must not be reduced to below whatever was his or her eligible rent immediately before that date (it is, however, increased if any rule requires this). If the claimant was not on HB at the date of the death, his or her eligible rent is worked out in the same way as for a council tenant (para. 10.21) – but the resulting eligible rent cannot be restricted in any way.

Examples: The protected groups

BEREAVEMENT

A claimant makes a claim for HB after the death of her husband. She has not moved since her husband's death. Her actual rent is high.

Because of the protection for people who have had a bereavement, her eligible rent must not be restricted in any way until the first anniversary of her husband's death. Until then, her eligible rent is her actual rent minus amounts for any ineligible services.

REDUNDANCY

A claimant makes a claim for HB after he is made redundant. His actual rent is high. He moved to this address when he was in a well-paid job and could easily afford the rent and outgoings. He has not been on HB in the last year.

Because of the protection for people who could formerly afford their accommodation, his eligible rent must not be restricted in any way for the first 13 weeks of his entitlement to HB. During those weeks, his eligible rent is his actual rent minus amounts for any ineligible services.

DEFINITIONS: 'OCCUPIER' AND 'RELATIVE'

10.43 For the purposes of the above two protected groups, the only 'occupiers' taken into account are:

HB 13(16)
HB60+ 13(16)
CPR sch 3 para 5
NIHB 14(16),(17)
NIHB60+ 14(6),(7)
NICPR sch 3 para 5

- the claimant;
- any member of his or her family (partner, child, young person: paras. 4.7-40);
- any 'relative' (para. 10.44) of the claimant or partner (including non-dependants, boarders, tenants, sub-tenants and joint occupiers) who has no separate right to occupy the dwelling.

10.44 A 'relative' is defined for the above (and all other HB) purposes as:

HB 2(1)
HB60+ 2(1)
NIHB 2(1)
NIHB60+ 2(1)

- a parent, daughter, son, sister or brother;
- a parent-in-law, daughter-in-law, son-in-law, step-daughter or step-son, including equivalent relations arising through civil partnership;
- a partner (para. 4.8) of any of the above (i.e. by marriage or civil partnership, or by living together as husband and wife or civil partners); or
- a grandparent, grandchild, aunt, uncle, niece or nephew.

MAXIMUM RENT IF THE CLAIMANT'S RENT CHANGES

10.45 Once a claimant's maximum rent has been calculated as above, it applies throughout his or her award of HB – except as described in the following two paragraphs.

HB 13(8)-(10),(13)
HB60+ 13(8)-(10),(13)
NIHB 14(7),(9),(10),(18)
NIHB60+ 14(7),(9),(10),(18)

10.46 If the claimant's details have to be re-referred to the rent officer (paras. 6.6-11), a new maximum rent must be calculated as above and used for the remainder of his or her award of HB (whether it is higher or lower than – or the same as – the initial maximum rent). Not all rent increases (indeed very few) trigger a re-referral to the rent officer.

10.47 If the claimant's actual rent reduces to below the maximum rent, the law is a little unclear. It appears to mean that, over-riding all the above rules, the most a person's eligible rent can ever be is what he or she actually pays minus the authority's valuation of amounts for ineligible service charges. If this is not the effect of the law, it would seem reasonable for the authority to use its general power to restrict the eligible rent (para. 10.48) to that figure.

REDUCING MAXIMUM RENT IN CERTAIN CASES

10.48 In private sector New Scheme cases, the authority has a general power to reduce any claimant's eligible rent to below the 'maximum rent' calculated as above if 'it appears to the authority that in the particular circumstances of the case the eligible rent... is greater than it is reasonable to meet by way of housing

HB 12(7)
HB60+ 12(7)
NIHB 13(7)
NIHB60+ 13(7)

benefit.' (The same power applies in council tenant New Scheme cases: para. 10.24, and in housing association cases only if the case has been referred to the rent officer: paras. 10.29-30.)

10.49 In such a case, the eligible rent is reduced to 'such lesser sum as seems to that authority to be an appropriate rent in that particular case'. In doing this an authority must have regard to factors such as personal circumstances: *R v HBRB of the City of Westminster ex parte Laali.*

10.50 In practice, reductions under this provision are uncommon. They can be made only if the authority makes a proper judgment about the above matters (para. 1.33). This means that the authority should have evidence and an objective justification before making a reduction (GM para. A10.440-41).

Eligible rent for Old Scheme private sector cases

CPR sch 3 para 5
NICPR sch 3 para 5

10.51 In Old Scheme private sector cases (para. 10.31), the claimant's eligible rent is worked out in the same way as for a council tenant (para. 10.21) unless:

- the authority restricts the eligible rent to a lower figure (paras. 10.52 onwards); or
- the claimant has a registered rent or other fixed rent (paras. 10.66-69).

ELIGIBLE RENT RESTRICTIONS

10.52 The rules about eligible rent restrictions in Old Scheme cases are summarised in table 10.4. In applying them, authorities:

- must not take a blanket approach (GM para. A4.277): each step must be considered in the individual circumstances of each case and each step is open to appeal;
- must not restrict a claimant's eligible rent just because of the subsidy rules. The requirements of the HB regulations (described below) are the only test that is relevant in deciding whether or not benefit should be restricted.

There has been much case law about these matters, well explained in *Housing Benefit and Council Tax Benefit Legislation,* by Lorna Findlay and others, published annually by the Child Poverty Action Group. The key points are referred to below. Because of the difficulties in applying the law, the DWP is currently reviewing the Old Scheme rules (*Housing Benefit Direct,* August 2005).

Table 10.4: HB restrictions for Old Scheme cases: a simplified summary

STEP ONE: IS THE RENT OR SIZE UNREASONABLE?

The claimant's HB can be restricted only if, compared with suitable alternative accommodation:

- the rent is unreasonably high; or
- the dwelling is unreasonably large; or
- a rent increase is unreasonable.

STEP TWO: IS THE CLAIMANT IN A PROTECTED GROUP?

Protections against HB restrictions can apply for claimants:

- who could afford their accommodation when their letting began; or
- who have had a death in their home; or
- who have children or young persons, or are aged 60 or more, or are sick or disabled.

STEP THREE: SHOULD THE ELIGIBLE RENT BE RESTRICTED?

If the rent is unreasonable (step one) and none of the protections applies (step two), the authority must decide how much (if at all) the claimant's eligible rent should be reduced.

DECIDING WHAT IS 'UNREASONABLE' BY FINDING COMPARABLES

10.53 The first question is whether: CPR sch 3 para 5 NICPR sch 3 para

- the rent is unreasonably high, or
- the accommodation is unreasonably large for all the occupiers, or
- a rent increase is unreasonably high, or
- a rent increase is unreasonably soon after another increase during the previous year.

10.54 As regards size, the question of who counts as an occupier is open to interpretation (since 'occupier' is not further defined for these purposes) and appeal (chapter 19), but it is not limited to the groups listed in paragraph 10.43. Though the *Swale and Marchant* case (para. 6.26) may affect how some authorities interpret 'occupier' for these purposes, there is an argument that that case was about the definition of 'occupier' in a different context and so is not binding here.

10.55 In all the above cases, authorities:

- must make a comparison (as regards the rent, size or rent increase, as appropriate) with suitable alternative accommodation (paras. 10.56-57);
- may additionally take account of figures provided by the rent officer (if the case was referred to the rent officer: chapter 6) – and the DWP advises that they 'must' do this (GM para. A4.274), bearing in mind that the rent officer's function is different;
- must not, at this stage, take into account the impact of the subsidy rules on their own finances (para. 10.64).

10.56 Authorities should make the comparison by working through the following questions:

(a) what is the rent (including all eligible and ineligible services) for the claimant's dwelling?

(b) what type of alternative accommodation is suitable for the claimant? and, in order to determine this, what services are requisite in order to regard the alternative accommodation as suitable and what other factors need to be taken into account (para. 10.57)?

(c) what rent (including all eligible and ineligible services) would be payable for such accommodation?

(d) is the rent in (a) unreasonably high by comparison with the rent in (c)?

The above is based on *R v Beverley BC HBRB ex p Hare*. As regards (d) above, 'unreasonably high' means more than just 'higher': *Malcolm v Tweeddale DC HBRB*. Commissioners have confirmed this wide approach *(CH/4306/2003)* and have confirmed *(CH/2214/2003)* that it applies to unreasonable rent increases (as well as to unreasonably high rents/large accommodation).

CPR sch 3 para 5
NICPR sch 3 para 5

10.57 In deciding what alternative accommodation would be suitable for the claimant (question (b) above), authorities:

- must take account of the nature of the alternative accommodation and the exclusive and shared facilities provided, having regard to the age and state of health of all the occupiers (as defined in para. 10.43). 'For example, a disabled or elderly person might have special needs and require more expensive or larger accommodation' (GM para. A4.290);
- must only take into account alternative accommodation with security of tenure which is reasonably equivalent to what the claimant currently has (GM A4.289);

- 'must have a sufficiency of information to ensure that like is being compared with like... Unless that can be done, no safe assessment can be made of the reasonableness of the rent in question or the proper level of value': *Malcolm v Tweeddale DC HBRB;*
- may take account of alternative accommodation outside the authority's own area if there is no comparable accommodation within it. But if this is necessary, it is unreasonable to 'make comparisons with other parts of the country where accommodation costs differ widely from those which apply locally' (GM para. A4.291).

PROTECTED GROUPS

10.58 Three groups of claimants are protected against the effect of the above rules about HB restrictions. The first two groups, and the rules applying to them, are the same as those described in paragraphs 10.38-41; the details of the third group, and the rules applying to it, are described below.

CPR sch 3 para 5
NICPR sch 3 para 5

VULNERABLE PEOPLE

10.59 A claimant falls within this protected group if any of the occupiers of his or her home (as defined in paras. 10.43-44) is:

CPR sch 3 para 5
NICPR sch 3 para 5

- aged 60 or more; or
- responsible for a child or young person in the household (paras. 4.26-40); or
- incapable of work for social security purposes (para. 12.15). This is decided by the DWP, not the authority; and is decided by reference to the present-day definition of 'incapable of work' *(CH/4424/2004).*

In such a case, the authority must not reduce the claimant's eligible rent unless there is suitable alternative accommodation available (para. 10.60) and it is reasonable to expect the claimant to move (para. 10.61).

10.60 What counts as suitable alternative accommodation was described earlier (para. 10.57). The point here is that it must be available. For example, accommodation the claimant has recently left, or an offer of accommodation the claimant has refused, may be available – but only while it actually remains available to the claimant, and not after it has been let to someone else. In *R v East Devon DC HBRB ex p Gibson,* the judge emphasised that the authority was not an accommodation agency, and said: 'It is... quite sufficient if an active market rent is shown to exist in houses in an appropriate place at the appropriate level of rent to which the [eligible] rent is restricted. There must, however, be evidence at least of that... otherwise the recipient, if he had to move, would have nowhere to go. It is, however, sufficient, as I wish to stress, to point to a range of properties, or a bloc of property, which is available without specific identification of particular

CPR sch 3 para 5
NICPR sch 3 para 5

dwelling houses'. The DWP follows this and emphasises that 'authorities should regard accommodation as not available if, in practice, there is little or no possibility of the claimant being able to obtain it, for example because it could only be obtained on payment of a large deposit which the claimant does not have' (GM para. A4.299).

CPR sch 3 para 5
NICPR sch 3 para 5

10.61 In deciding whether it is reasonable to expect the claimant to move, authorities must take into account:

- the claimant's prospects of retaining employment; and
- the effect on the education of a child or young person who would have to change school (this means any child or young person mentioned in para. 10.43).

In *R v Sefton MBC ex p Cunningham,* the judge emphasised the authority's duty to take individual circumstances into account when considering 'suitability', 'availability' and 'reasonableness'. In that case, the authority's decision was overturned because there was no evidence that it had considered the effect of a move on the claimant's eight-year-old child's education.

RESTRICTING THE ELIGIBLE RENT

CPR sch 3 para 5
NICPR sch 3 para 5

10.62 The final question (if it applies at all, considering the above points) is of how much to restrict the eligible rent. In considering this, the authority must work through the following questions:

(a) is it appropriate to make a reduction in the claimant's eligible rent? and if it is

(b) what is the appropriate amount for the reduction? and

(c) how was that appropriate amount arrived at?

The above is based on the judgments in *Mehanne v Westminster CC HBRB,* and *R v Beverley BC HBRB ex p Hare.* As regards (b) above, the authority must not reduce the claimant's eligible rent below the cost of comparable alternative accommodation: *R v Brent LBC ex p Connery.*

10.63 As regards all the above questions, authorities must consider what is appropriate in the individual circumstances of each case. There are cases in which no reduction is appropriate. There are also cases in which no reduction is appropriate for the time being but may become appropriate later on. In practice in such cases some authorities still tend to restrict claimants' eligible rents to what the rent officer has recommended (in cases which have been referred to the rent officer: chapter 6). However, the rent officer's figures do not take into account personal circumstances at all, whereas the question of what is 'appropriate' places a duty on authorities to do so.

THE IMPACT OF SUBSIDY

10.64 In *R v Brent LBC ex p Connery,* it was held that: 'An authority was entitled, except when acting in those cases where an absolute duty was to be fulfilled, to take into account the implications for its own financial situation [e.g. subsidy] when exercising its discretion' (as quoted in *The Times,* 25.10.89). As described earlier, there are three main questions to be considered in applying the rules about HB restrictions:

- whether the rent, size or rent increase is unreasonable;
- whether people fall within the protected groups; and
- whether to reduce the eligible rent or disallow a rent increase and, if so, by how much.

10.65 The first two are questions of fact. Subsidy considerations cannot therefore play a part in answering them. The DWP's opinion is that the authority may take subsidy into account in answering the third question, though not as the only consideration (GM para. A4.292).

IF A RENT HAS BEEN FIXED AS BINDING ON THE LANDLORD

10.66 In addition to the other Old Scheme rules, if a claimant's rent has been fixed by a rent officer, rent tribunal or rent assessment committee (so that it is binding on the landlord), the claimant's eligible rent must not exceed that fixed figure. This applies for one year from the date on which the fixed figure takes effect. (If, however, the letting began in or before January 1989, see below.)

CPR sch 3 para 5
NICPR sch 3 para 5

Eligible rent for registered rent cases

10.67 The following rules apply to:

- tenancies in England and Wales which were entered into before 15th January 1989;
- tenancies in Scotland which were entered into before 2nd January 1989;
- tenancies in Northern Ireland which are protected or statutory tenancies to which article 3 of the Housing (Northern Ireland) Order 1978 applies, i.e. their rent is fixed by a rent officer;
- tenancies granted on or after those dates in which the landlord is required to preserve the tenant's rights (typically because the landlord has moved a tenant whose tenancy began before those dates).

HB 12(3)(b)
HB60+ 12(3)(b)
CPR sch 3 para 5
NIHB 13(3)(b)
NIHB60+ 13(3)(b)
NICPR sch 3 para 5

These are referred to in this guide as 'registered rent cases'. They are sometimes also called protected tenancies, regulated tenancies, fair rent tenancies, Rent Act tenancies, and even 'Old, Old Scheme' cases.

10.68 In registered rent cases, the claimant's eligible rent is worked out as follows (but see also the next paragraph):

- if the claimant's rent has been fixed by a rent officer, rent tribunal or rent assessment committee (so that it is binding on the landlord), the claimant's eligible rent equals that figure minus any ineligible service charges included within it;
- in any other case, it is worked out in the same way as for a council tenant (para. 10.21).

HB 12(7)
HB60+12(7)
CPR sch 3 para 5
NIHB 13(7)
NIHB60+ 13(7)
NICPR sch 3 para 5

10.69 In either of the above cases, it is possible for the authority to restrict the eligible rent – though this is in practice rare. The rules are as follows:

- if the case falls within the 'Old Scheme' (para. 10.7), it is dealt with in the same way as any other Old Scheme private sector case (paras. 10.51 onwards);
- if the case falls within the 'New Scheme', the only way in which the rent can be restricted is if the authority uses its general power described in para. 10.48.

Eligible rent for other cases

TENANTS OF CHARITIES AND VOLUNTARY ORGANISATIONS

10.70 The eligible rent of a claimant renting from a registered charity or a non-profit making voluntary organisation is worked out in the same way as for private sector cases (paras. 10.31 onwards); unless the charity or voluntary organisation is a registered housing association, in which case the rules for housing association tenants apply (paras. 10.25-30 and table 10.2).

TENANTS OF ENGLISH COUNTY COUNCILS

AA 134(1B),191
HB 14(1)
HB60+ 14(1)

10.71 The eligible rent of a claimant renting from an English county council (a typical example would be when a claimant rents from a county council social services department) is worked out in the same way as for private tenant cases (para 10.31). This does not apply where the council is a unitary authority, in which case the landlord is the same body as pays HB and its tenants are treated in the same way as other council tenants (para. 10.21).

TENANTS OF PROBATION OR BAIL HOSTELS

HB sch 2 para 11
HB60+
sch 2 para 11

10.72 In Great Britain only, tenants of probation hostels and bail hostels are treated in the same way as registered rent cases (paras. 10.67).

TENANTS IN RESETTLEMENT PLACES

10.73 The eligible rent of a claimant renting a resettlement place is worked out in the same way as for a private sector Old Scheme case (paras. 10.51 onwards) – unless it is a rent rebate case, in which case it is dealt with as such (para. 10.21).

TENANTS IN HOSTELS AND NIGHT SHELTERS

10.74 There are no rules about eligible rent specifically for hostels or night shelters. The various rules given in the rest of this chapter apply. For example, a hostel might also be a registered housing association, a registered charity, etc; in which case the rules for that type of accommodation apply.

Service charges

10.75 The remainder of this chapter deals with service charges (and related charges) which may be included in a claimant's actual rent, or payable as well as the rent. It applies to all HB claims and explains which charges are eligible for HB and which are not. The section covers:

HB 12,13, sch 1
HB60+ 12,13, sch 1
NIHB 13,14, sch 1
NIHB60+ 13,14, sch 1

- which service charges are and are not eligible for HB; and
- whether the authority or the rent officer is responsible for valuing the various kinds of services.

This section is relevant only in the calculation of HB for rent (not CTB or HB for rates in Northern Ireland).

THE IMPORTANCE OF SERVICE CHARGES

10.76 Many tenants pay for services either in with their rent (in which case it is immaterial whether they are mentioned in their letting agreement) or separately. As illustrated in the examples, there are two main methods of showing service charges in letting agreements:

- a claimant's rent may be shown as so much per week (or month, etc) including certain services; or
- it may be shown as so much per week (or month, etc) with an amount for service charges being due on top of the rent.

10.77 Whether a service charge is eligible for HB affects the amount of a claimant's eligible rent (para. 10.5), which in turn affects the amount of his or her HB.

- If a charge is 'eligible for HB', this means that it is a charge which can be included in a claimant's eligible rent. With certain exceptions (mentioned below as they arise), it does not need to be valued; and no deduction is made for it at any stage in deciding the amount of a claimant's eligible rent unless the charge for it is excessive (para. 10.86).

- If a charge is 'ineligible for HB', this means that it is a charge which cannot be included in a claimant's eligible rent. With certain exceptions, it needs to be valued and deducted at some point in deciding the amount of a claimant's eligible rent (para. 10.78).

Councils, housing associations and many other landlords provide details of service charges to their tenants (and in many cases, tenants have a right to this information: for good information on this, see *Housing Rights Guide* by Geoffrey Randall, published by Shelter). It is in their interests as well as their tenants' to bear in mind the detailed rules when deciding what services to provide and how much to charge for them.

Examples: Service charges

1. A council tenant claimant's rent is expressed as being £100 per fortnight including £20 per fortnight for fuel for the claimant's own room and £10 per fortnight for heating, lighting, cleaning and maintaining communal areas. In this case the eligible rent is £80 per fortnight (£40 per week). The ineligible charge for fuel for the claimant's own room is deducted.
2. A housing association claimant's rent is expressed as being £70 per fortnight plus £20 per fortnight for fuel for the claimant's own room and £10 per fortnight for heating, lighting, cleaning and maintaining communal areas. In this case the eligible rent is £80 per fortnight (£40 per week). The eligible charge for the communal areas is added.

Notes

- The facts in the two examples are the same but are expressed differently.
- Information about the service charges illustrated is given later in this chapter.
- The terms 'net rent' and 'gross rent' are sometimes used to distinguish between different methods of expressing a rent figure. But they are used in different ways nationally and are best avoided for HB purposes.

WHO DEALS WITH SERVICE CHARGES

10.78 In Great Britain, service charges may be dealt with by the authority or the rent officer (or both of them) in assessing a claimant's eligible rent. In Northern Ireland, service charges are always dealt with by the NIHE. Fuller details are given in the remainder of this chapter, but in general terms:

- when a 'maximum rent' applies in assessing the claimant's eligible rent (as in many private tenant cases, for example), the rent officer provides the council with figures which are already adjusted to take account of most service charges: in effect, the rent officer values them;

- when a 'maximum rent' does not apply (as in all council, most housing association and some private tenant cases), it is the authority which assesses all matters relating to service charges.

'Maximum rent' is explained in paragaph 10.34. Details of which rules apply for various service charges are given at the relevant places throughout this chapter.

DEFINITION OF 'SERVICES'

10.79 The law defines 'services' as 'services performed or facilities... provided for, or rights made available to, the occupier...' and 'service charge' as any periodical charge for any such service.

HB 12(8)
HB60+ 12(8)
CPR sch 3 para 5
NIHB 13(8)
NIHB60+ 13(8)
NICPR sch 3 para 5

Which service charges are eligible?

10.80 Service charges are eligible for HB, so long as they:

HB 12(1),(3),(8)
HB60+ 12(1),(3),(8)
CPR sch 3 para 5
NIHB 13(1),(3),(8)
NIHB60+ 13(1),(3),(8)
NICPR sch 3 para 5

- have to be paid as a condition of occupying the dwelling as a home; and
- are not listed in the regulations as ineligible (as described in the following paragraphs); and
- are not excessive in relation to the service provided (para. 10.86).

The rules about individual service charges, and whether they are eligible for HB, are in paragraphs 10.87 onwards.

10.81 The first of these conditions need not have applied from the date the letting agreement began. A service charge is eligible for HB (subject to the other conditions) whenever the claimant agreed to pay it, if the only alternative would have been to lose his or her home. (Note also that a different rule applies in the case of charges for garages, land, etc: para. 10.107.)

10.82 Details of which service charges are eligible for HB (subject to the above points) follow, and are summarised in table 10.5. Helpful advice on services is given by the DWP (GM paras. A4.170-192).

10.83 Sometimes services are provided free to a claimant. The DWP points out in relation to hostel residents (thought the point is relevant to all claims) that 'HB should be based only on items included in the resident's charge. [Authorities] must confirm which services are included in the hostel charge.' (GM para. A4.129).

VALUING INELIGIBLE SERVICE CHARGES

10.84 When the authority has the duty of valuing ineligible service charges (para. 10.78), this is done as follows:

HB 12(3) sch 1 para 3
HB60+ 12(3) sch 1 para 3
NIHB 13(3) sch 1 para 3
NIHB60+ 13(3) sch 1 para 3

- if the amount can be identified from the letting agreement or in some other way, the authority uses the amount so identified as the value;

- but if this identified amount is unrealistically low for the service provided, or if the amount cannot be identified, the authority must decide what amount is fairly attributable to the value;
- however, different rules can apply for water charges, fuel and meals (paras. 10.87-96).

VALUING ELIGIBLE SERVICE CHARGES

HB 12, sch 1
HB60+ 12, sch 1
NIHB 13, sch 1
NIHB60+ 13, sch 1

10.85 If (unusually) it is necessary to value eligible service charges, the authority values them as follows:

- if the amount can be identified from the letting agreement or in some other way, the authority uses the amount so identified as the value;
- but if this identified amount is excessive, or if the amount cannot be identified, the authority must decide what amount is fairly attributable to the value.

HB 12(7)
sch 1 para 4
HB60+ 12(7)
sch 1 para 4
NIHB 13(7)
sch 1 para 4
NIHB60+ 13(7)
sch 1 para 4

EXCESSIVE ELIGIBLE SERVICE CHARGES

10.86 In deciding whether an eligible service charge is excessive, the authority must take account of the cost of comparable services. If it is excessive, the authority must decide how much would be reasonable for that service and disallow the excess.

WATER CHARGES

HB 2(1),12(3),(6)
HB60+
2(1),12(3),(6)

10.87 In Great Britain, water charges (including any sewerage or environmental charges) are not eligible for HB. So if such charges are included in a claimant's rent, an amount must be deducted for them. (No deduction is made at any stage if the claimant pays water charges direct to the water company, since in such a case the water charges are not included in the claimant's rent.) In Northern Ireland water charges are eligible for HB through the rates element of HB (though they are not separately identifiable). However the rates element is deducted from the rent as in Great Britain (paras. 11.11-15).

10.88 In cases in which a maximum rent applies, the rent officer deducts an amount for such charges (para. 6.16 onwards). In other cases, the authority decides the value as follows:

- if the water charge varies according to consumption, either the actual amount or an estimate;
- otherwise, if the claimant's accommodation is a self-contained unit, the actual amount of the water charge;
- otherwise, a proportion of the water charge for the self-contained unit. The proportion should equal the floor area of the claimant's accommoda-

tion divided by the floor area of the self-contained unit (but in practice, authorities sometimes use different, simpler methods).

Table 10.5: Service charges summary

As described throughout this chapter, further details apply in many of the following cases.

HB sch 1 paras 1,5
HB60+
sch 1 paras 1,5
NIHB
sch 1 paras 1,5
NIHB60+
sch 1 paras 1,5

TYPE OF SERVICE CHARGE	ELIGIBLE FOR HB?
Water charges	NO
Provision of a heating system	YES
Fuel for communal areas	YES
Other fuel	NO
Meals	NO
Furniture/household equipment	YES
Communal window cleaning	YES
Other exterior window cleaning which the occupier(s) cannot do	YES
Other window cleaning	NO
Communal cleaning	YES
Other cleaning	NO
Emergency alarm systems	NO
Counselling and support	NO
Medical/nursing/personal care	NO
Day-to-day living expenses	NO
Most communal services relating to the provision of adequate accommodation	YES

FUEL, ETC

10.89 Charges for fuel (such as gas, electricity, etc, and also any standing charges or other supply costs) are not eligible for HB. So if such charges are included in a claimant's rent, an amount must be deducted for them. (No deduction is made at any stage if the claimant pays fuel charges direct to the fuel company, since in such a case the fuel charges are not included in the claimant's rent.)

HB 12(3)
sch 1 paras 5-8
HB60+ 12(3)
sch 1 paras 5-8
NIHB 13(3)
sch 1 paras 5-8
NIHB60+ 13(3)
sch 1 paras 5-8

10.90 There are two exceptions to the above:

- a charge for the provision of a heating system is eligible for HB, but only if it is separate from the fuel charge;
- a fuel charge for communal areas is eligible for HB, but only if is it separate from the fuel charge for the claimant's own accommodation. Communal areas are areas of common access (e.g. halls, stairways, passageways) and, in sheltered accommodation only, they also include common rooms (e.g. a dining room or lounge).

HB sch 1 para 6
HB60+ sch 1 para 6
NIHB sch 1 para 6
NIHB60+ sch 1 para 6

Table 10.6: Standard weekly fuel deductions

Amounts are added together if fuel is provided for more than one of the purposes shown.

IF THE CLAIMANT AND ANY FAMILY OCCUPY MORE THAN ONE ROOM	
Fuel for heating	£11.95
Fuel for hot water	£1.40
Fuel for lighting	£0.95
Fuel for cooking	£1.40
Fuel for any other purpose	NIL
Fuel for all the above	£15.70
IF THE CLAIMANT AND ANY FAMILY OCCUPY ONE ROOM ONLY	
Fuel for heating	£7.15
Fuel for hot water:	
if fuel for heating is also provided	NIL
if fuel for heating is not also provided	£1.40
Fuel for lighting:	
if fuel for heating is also provided	NIL
if fuel for heating is not also provided	£0.95
Fuel for cooking	£1.40
Fuel for any other purpose	NIL
Fuel for all the above: £7.15 for heating + £1.40 for cooking (+ NIL for hot water and lighting)	£8.55

10.91 In cases in which a maximum rent applies, the rent officer deducts an amount for such charges (para. 6.16 onwards). In other cases, the rules depend on whether the amount of the fuel charge is known to the authority, as described below.

10.92 If the amount of a fuel charge is identifiable, the authority uses this figure as the value of the fuel charge. However, if this is unrealistically low or includes an element for communal areas which cannot readily be separated out, the fuel charge is treated as unidentifiable.

10.93 If the amount of a fuel charge is not identifiable (or not 'readily identifiable'), the authority decides its value by reference to standard amounts depending on what the fuel is for, as shown in table 10.6. As shown there, the standard amounts are lower for claimants who occupy one room only. If the authority uses these standard amounts, it must invite the claimant to provide evidence on which the 'actual or approximate' amount of the charge may be estimated; and, if reasonable evidence is provided, the authority must estimate the value of the fuel charge.

MEALS (INCLUDING FOOD)

10.94 Charges for meals are not eligible for HB. So if such charges are included in a claimant's rent, an amount must be deducted for them.

HB 12(3)
sch 1 paras 1(a)(i),2
HB60+ 12(3)
sch 1 paras 1(a)(i),(2)
NIHB 13(3)
sch 1 paras 1(a)(i),(2)
NIHB60+ 13(3),
sch 1 paras 1(a)(i),(2)

10.95 For these purposes, 'meals' includes the preparation of meals (e.g. where meals are prepared somewhere else and then delivered) and also the provision of unprepared food (e.g. cereal, bread still in its wrappings).

10.96 In cases in which a maximum rent applies, the rent officer (or NIHE) does not deduct an amount for such charges, though there are uncommon exceptions to this (para. 6.16 onwards). So both in these cases and in all other cases, the authority decides the value by reference to standard amounts depending on what meals are provided, as shown in table 10.7. Those amounts cannot be varied; the actual amount the landlord charges for meals is never used. As shown in the table, one deduction applies for each person whose meals are paid for in the claimant's rent (whether this is the claimant, a member of the family or some other person such as a non-dependant). No deduction applies for anyone whose meals are not included (for example, a baby). When appropriate, deductions are calculated separately for each person (for example fewer meals may be provided for someone who goes out to work than for someone who does not).

FURNITURE AND HOUSEHOLD EQUIPMENT

HB 12(3)
sch 1 para 1(b)
HB60+ 12(3)
sch 1 para 1(b)
NIHB 13(3)
sch 1 para 1(b)
NIHB60+ 13(3)
sch 1 para 1(b)

10.97 Charges for the use of these are eligible for HB; unless there is an intention that they will become part of the claimant's personal property, in which case they are ineligible. Ineligible amounts are valued by the rent officer in maximum rent cases, otherwise by the authority.

Table 10.7: Standard weekly meals deductions

HB sch 1 para 2
HB60+ sch 1 para 2
NIHB sch 1 para 2
NIHB60+ sch 1 para 2

A separate amount is assessed and deducted for each person whose meals are provided.

IF AT LEAST THREE MEALS ARE PROVIDED EVERY DAY	
For the claimant, and each other person from the first Monday in September following his or her 16th birthday	£20.50
For each other person	£10.35
IF BREAKFAST ONLY IS PROVIDED	
For the claimant, and each other person of any age	£2.50
ALL OTHER CASES	
For the claimant, and each other person from the first Monday in September following his or her 16th birthday	£13.65
For each other person	£6.85

CLEANING AND WINDOW CLEANING

HB 12(3)
sch 1 para 1(a)(iv)
HB60+ 12(3)
sch 1 para 1(a)(iv)
NIHB 13(3)
sch 1 para 1(a)(iv)
NIHB 13(3)
sch 1 para 1(a)(iv)

10.98 Charges for the following are eligible for HB; unless the cost is met by Supporting People (para. 10.103) – in which case they are not eligible for HB:

- cleaning of communal areas;
- communal window cleaning; and
- cleaning the outsides of windows which no-one in the household can do.

Any other cleaning and window cleaning (such as cleaning the insides of windows and cleaning the claimant's own accommodation) is never eligible for HB (but may be met by Supporting People).

OTHER COMMUNAL SERVICES, ETC

HB 12(3)
sch 1 para 1(a)
HB60+ 12(3)
sch 1 para 1(a)
NIHB 13(3)
sch 1 para 1(a)
NIHB60+ 13(3)
sch 1 para 1(a)

10.99 Charges for the following are eligible for HB:

- children's play areas;
- TV and radio relay (though not normally of satellite or cable services);
- communal laundry facilities;
- other services which are related to the provision of adequate accommodation.

10.100 The DWP advises (GM para. A4.177, and see chapter A4 generally) that the last item includes:

- portering and refuse removal;
- lifts, communal telephones and entry phones; and
- the time people such as scheme managers and caretakers spend on eligible services.

OTHER DAY-TO-DAY LIVING EXPENSES, ETC

10.101 Charges for the following are not eligible for HB. So if charges for them are included in a claimant's rent, an amount must be deducted for them. The amount is valued by the rent officer in maximum rent cases, otherwise by the authority:

HB 12(3) sch 1 para 1(a),(g)
HB60+ 12(3) sch 1 para 1(a),(g)
NIHB 13(3) sch 1 para 1(a),(g)
NIHB60+ 13(3) sch 1 para 1(a),(g)

- laundry (e.g. washing sheets, etc, for the claimant);
- transport;
- sports facilities;
- TV and radio rental and licence and (in most cases) satellite and cable service charges;
- any other leisure items or day-to-day living expenses; or
- any other services which 'are not related to the provision of adequate accommodation'.

SUPPORT CHARGES

10.102 Support charges are never eligible for HB. This includes charges for:

HB 12(3) sch 1 para 1(c)-(f)
HB60+ 12(3) sch 1 para 1(c)-(f)
NIHB 13(3) sch 1 para 1(c)-(f)
NIHB 13(3) sch 1 para 1(c)-(f)

- cleaning and window cleaning over and above that mentioned in paragraph 10.98;
- emergency alarm systems;
- counselling and support; and
- medical, nursing and personal care.

10.103 Claimants who need such services may be able to have the cost met by Supporting People, a goverrnment programme for funding support services administered by local authorities (in Northern Ireland by the NIHE) and independent of HB/CTB.

10.104 In some situations there remain difficulties in distinguishing what constitutes a support charge as above (which is not eligible for HB) and what is merely part of the rent as any landlord would charge it (and which would therefore be eligible for HB: para. 10.105). Chasing rent arrears would usually be an example of the latter: most landlords would regard it as part and parcel of their day-to-day work. But it might become an example of the former if it formed a substantial part of the work of staff in a hostel for residents with difficulty budgeting.

OVERHEADS INCLUDING MANAGEMENT COSTS AND COUNCIL TAX

10.105 Whether the landlord's normal overheads (such as maintenance, insurance and repair costs) count as 'services' or simply as part of the claimant's rent is an arguable point. But in either case they are eligible for HB. In particular, this includes any part of the rent towards the landlord's liability for council tax (e.g. if the claimant has a resident landlord or lives in a house made up of bedsits). No amount is deducted for these items at any stage, so they do not normally need to be valued.

INCREASES TO COVER ARREARS OF RENT

HB 11(3)
HB60+ 11(3)
NIHB 11(3)
NIHB60+ 11(3)

10.106 If a claimant's rent has been increased in order to recover arrears of rent or other charges, that part of the rent is ineligible for HB. This rule applies only if an individual claimant's rent is increased to cover his or her own arrears on a current or former home. It does not apply when landlords increase rents on all their properties as a result of arrears generally.

GARAGES, LAND, ETC

HB 2(4)(a)
HB60+ 2(4)(a)
NIHB 2(4)(a)
NIHB60+ 2(4)(a)

10.107 The rent on a garage (or any other buildings, gardens or land included in the claimant's letting agreement) is eligible for HB if:

- they are used for occupying the dwelling as a home; and
- the claimant acquired them at the same time as the dwelling; and
- the claimant has no option but to rent them at the same time.

They are also eligible for HB if the claimant has made or is making reasonable efforts to end liability for them.

BUSINESS PREMISES

HB 12(4)
HB60+ 12(4)
NIHB 13(4)
NIHB60+ 13(4)

10.108 Rent on any part of a property which is used for business, commercial or other non-residential purposes is not eligible for HB. For example, if a claimant rents both a shop and the flat above it, only the rent relating to the flat is eligible for HB. If the rent on the business premises is not specified separately from the rent on the home, it is necessary for the authority to decide how much relates to each. For self-employed claimants who work from home, see paragraph 15.23.

11 Help with rates in Northern Ireland

11.1 This chapter deals with rate rebates which, in Northern Ireland only, are available as part of the HB scheme. Council tax and CTB do not exist in Northern Ireland and, while rate rebates appear similar to CTB there are, nevertheless, significant differences. Rate rebates can be paid by either the Northern Ireland Housing Executive (NIHE) or the Rate Collection Agency (RCA) although not by both simultaneously. The tenure of the property will, in the main, govern which of these organisations will deal with the claim but, as always, there are some exceptions to the general rules. This chapter covers:

- the background to this significant difference between the HB scheme in Northern Ireland compared to the rest of the UK;
- the legislative authority and administrative arrangements in place;
- who can get a rate rebate;
- which organisation will process the rate rebate application;
- what restrictions, if any, apply to the amount of eligible rates;
- conversion to weekly amounts (where necessary) and;
- how much rate rebate will be paid;
- payment of benefit by rebate or allowance.

Background

CURRENT POSITION

11.2 The arrangements for local government in Northern Ireland are currently under review and following the recent publication of a paper on the Reform of Public Administration there are likely to be significant and far-reaching changes in the future. This will almost certainly result in a major reduction in the number of councils and changes to the functions they will carry out. For the moment however there are 26 district, borough and city councils which, unlike their counterparts elsewhere in the UK, have comparatively few powers and many of the functions associated with local government in Great Britain are carried out by non-departmental public bodies and departments of the Northern Ireland Executive. Part of the funding of these services is by means of a domestic rate system, which comprises two elements. The first of these elements is the local rate, which is set by the local district council to fund the services it delivers, such as street cleansing and leisure facilities. The second element is the regional rate set by the

Department of Finance and Personnel to fund other services, such as roads and water treatment. The property owner or occupier, however, receives only one rate demand and makes payment to the RCA, which passes the local element on to the local district council. If the property is tenanted the landlord will normally include rates charges in the overall amount payable by the tenant.

11.3 In Northern Ireland, assistance with domestic rates charges is available as part of the HB scheme by means of a rate rebate processed either by the NIHE or RCA. Rate rebates, while having some similarities with CTB are, nevertheless, significantly different. Although the administrative arrangements are very different, the scheme which applies in Northern Ireland today is essentially the same as that which applied in Great Britain prior to the introduction of the community charge (poll tax) and its successor council tax.

THE FUTURE

11.4 The system of domestic rates is also undergoing a process of major change, which is due to take effect from April 2007. Full details of the changes are not yet available; however the general direction is now clear and this will involve:

- a change to the basis of valuation for rating from a rental value to a capital value; however, unlike in Great Britain, each property (with the possible exception of those owned by social landlords such as the NIHE and Housing Associations) will have an individual capital value on which rates will be assessed;
- the introduction of a reliefs scheme for certain people who are most likely to be affected by the overall increase in rates following the implementation of the new scheme. Rates relief will be payable in addition to any rate rebate payable under the Housing Benefit scheme; however, it may be possible for a person to qualify for rate relief even if there is no entitlement to rate rebate.

At this stage the indications are that the rate relief scheme will be administered by the NIHE for tenants and the RCA for owner-occupiers along with Housing Benefit. Full details of the amounts which will be paid, the qualifying conditions and the method of payment are not yet available but will be included in the 2007-08 edition of this Guide.

Legislative authority and administrative arrangements

11.5 The legislative authority to administer HB in Northern Ireland is derived from the Social Security Administration Act (Northern Ireland) 1992 which sets out the arrangements for the administration of the HB scheme in Northern

Ireland. The NIHE is required by section 126(3)(a) of the Act to administer all claims for HB from tenants. In carrying out its functions the NIHE can award rent allowances, rent rebates and rate rebates provided that the claimant is not an owner-occupier. If the claimant is an owner-occupier section 126(3)(b) of the Act places a similar responsibility on the RCA but only in respect of rate rebates. Both organisations use the same framework of regulations, that is Housing Benefit Regulations (Northern Ireland) 2006 (as amended); the Housing Benefit (Persons who have attained the qualifying age for state pension credit) Regulations (Northern Ireland) 2006 (as amended); and the Housing Benefit (Decisions and Appeals) (Northern Ireland) Regulations 2001 SR 2001 No. 213 (as amended).

RATE COLLECTION AGENCY (RCA)

11.6 The RCA is an executive agency within the Department of Finance and Personnel, a Department of the Northern Ireland Executive. As well as HB the RCA's other core function is to collect the rates levied on the owners and/or occupiers of all domestic and commercial properties in Northern Ireland. The RCA administers its HB service from one central location in Belfast although five local RCA offices (primarily dealing with receiving rates payments) will accept claim forms and documents from members of the public. Claim forms can be requested or downloaded from the RCA's website *(www.ratecollectionagencyni.gov.uk)*; alternatively the HB central unit can be contacted at Londonderry House, 21-27 Chichester Street, Belfast, BT1 4JJ (028 9025 2525).

11.7 Although the HB regulations apply equally to the RCA clearly any regulation dealing with the amount of rent eligible for HB (chapters 6 and 10) will not be relevant when processing claims. Additionally the fact that all applicants have a rate liability and account considerably simplifies payment, as there is no necessity to issue cheques: the rate rebate is simply credited to the account and overpayments are recovered by simply debiting the rate account.

Who can get a rate rebate

NICBA 129(1)(a) HBR 8(1)(a), 9(1) **11.8** With very few exceptions, and subject to the usual rules on income and household circumstances, anyone with a rate liability (either directly or as part of an overall charge payable to a landlord) is potentially entitled to a rate rebate. Rate rebates are, therefore, payable to all of the following groups of claimants (NB: this list is not exhaustive):

- owner occupiers;
- tenants;
- boarders;
- lodgers;

- people living in houses in multiple occupation;
- people living in bed and breakfast accommodation;
- hostel residents.

11.9 There are, however, a few situations where a rate rebate cannot be paid even though the claimant has a rates liability. These are:

IAA99 115
NIHB 9(1)(b), (l),10(1), 53(1)
NIHB60+ 9(1)(b),(l),10(1)

- The claimant is a full time student who does not fall within one of the groups which can qualify for HB (paras. 21.24-33).
- The claimant is a recent migrant who is disqualified (para. 20.1).
- The rates liability is deemed to have been created to take advantage of the HB scheme (paras. 2.47-52). This is, however, more theoretical than actual as in practice it is difficult to see how this could occur.

In all these situations the NIHE/RCA is obliged to treat that person as not liable to make payments and consequently cannot pay a rate rebate.

11.10 There is one further situation in which the NIHE/RCA cannot pay a rate rebate: this is where the landlord is a registered charity and the property occupied is exempt from rates charges. Where this is the case there is simply no rates charge to rebate.

MUST THERE ALWAYS BE A RATES ELEMENT?

11.11 In some instances tenants (and also occasionally landlords) state that they are not being charged rates. Unless the tenant has to make rates payments directly to the RCA this is incorrect as, in the great majority of cases, the landlord is recovering the rates element as part of the overall charge paid by the tenant as 'rent'. If the tenant has to pay rates directly the RCA will issue a rates demand, which will easily establish liability and the amount to be paid. This is the only situation where the NIHE should accept that the amount payable to a landlord is exclusive of rates. Otherwise it must assume that rates are included within the overall charge paid by the tenant. This also applies to a new property where the rates have not yet been assessed. If this is the case a payment on account (based on the rates payable on a similar property) should be issued pending receipt of the actual amount of rates payable.

NIHB 12(2), 13(3)(b),(6)
NIHB60+ 12(2), 13(3)(b),(6)

11.12 Generally a rates element should be included as otherwise the HB assessment could well be incorrect. This is particularly likely if non-dependant deductions have to be made or if the claimant has income in excess of his applicable amount. This is because different non-dependant deductions and excess income tapers apply to rates than those used for rent rebates and allowances. The exception to this general rule concerns tenanted properties where an NAV has not yet been assessed; this usually only occurs with newly built properties. In these circumstances there is no liability for rates; consequently a rate rebate is not appropriate. Once the NAV has been assessed the rate rebate should be paid retrospectively provided the claimant notifies the NIHE within one month of receiving the rate demand from the RCA.

CALCULATING THE RATES PAYABLE

11.13 Where the rates element is not separately identified the NIHE must calculate the amount of rates by reference to the Net Annual Valuation (NAV) of the dwelling and the amount of rates payable in the District Council area in which the dwelling is located. It is unusual for an NAV to change from year to year unless there is an improvement to the property requiring it to be reassessed. In contrast, the amount of rates payable in a district council area will vary, usually upwards, each year.

11.14 Annual rates payable are calculated by multiplying the NAV by the rate in the pound for the district council area in which the dwelling is located. This is illustrated in the example below. The NAV can be obtained from the VLA's valuation list. NAVs for a particular property can now be accessed on-line at the VLA's website by searching on the address details *(www.vla.nics.gov.uk)*. The current rate in the pound for each of the 26 districts (including the regional rate) can be viewed on-line at the RCA site at *www.ratecollectionagencyni.gov.uk/poundages.htm*

Example – Calculation of annual rates payable

A property in Belfast district is listed on the VLA valuation list as having a NAV of £250.

1. NAV of dwelling	=	£250
2. Amount of rates per £1 of NAV in Belfast District for 2006-07	=	3.7360
3. Annual rates (1 x 2) = £250 x 3.7360	=	£934.00

NIHB 83(2)(a)
NIHB60+ 66(2)(a)
NIDAR 7(2)(a),(3),8(2)

11.15 If, as is almost always the case, the rates payable change each year the NIHE must recalculate the rates element. If the overall charge has not been increased this will result in a reduction in the amount of the rent element. The NIHE should not wait either until the overall charge is increased or until it is advised by the tenant (or landlord). This is because there is no duty to notify changes in the amount of rates payable.

Which organisation processes the rate rebate application

GENERAL RULE

11.16 In general rate rebate claims from tenants will be processed by the NIHE and those from owner-occupiers will be processed by the RCA. While there are some exceptions to this general rule relating to rent liability (for example, partners of tenants are treated as if they are liable for rent) in practice these present little difficulty, as they are clearly identifiable. There is sometimes a degree of confusion as to as to which agency should process the claim which largely arises because a person perceives that he or she is an owner occupier when this is not in fact the case. The exceptions and the areas of confusion are discussed in the following paragraphs and are summarised in table 11.1.

NIAA 126(3)(a),(b)
NIHB 2(4)(a)-(c)
NIHB60+ 2(4)(a)-(c)

PEOPLE WITH A LIFE INTEREST

11.17 This is probably the most common area of confusion and usually arises following the death of the former owner of a property. The terms of the will may leave ownership of the property to any other person (but usually a son or daughter) subject to the right of a named person to live in that property for as long as they wish or until they die. This is also known as 'having your day in the house'.

NIAA 126(3)(b)
NIHB 2(1),(4)(a)
NIHB60+ 2(1),(4)(a)

11.18 The person having a life interest is not an owner occupier despite the fact that the person may have lived in the property for many years and, indeed, may have been the partner of the former owner. Equally the person cannot be described as a tenant in the accepted sense. Indeed, even if this person is being charged rent no rent allowance can be paid as the person has an absolute right to occupy the property for the rest of their life rent-free. Despite this, there is still a rates liability and in these circumstances it falls on the NIHE to process the claim.

PARTICIPANTS IN CO-OWNERSHIP SCHEMES

11.19 The other main area of confusion relates to participants in an equity-sharing scheme operated by the Northern Ireland Co-ownership Housing Association. Such people are commonly considered to be owner-occupiers but despite this cannot claim a rate rebate from the RCA and should instead claim through the NIHE. This is because the participants will rent the part of the property they do not own; therefore it is administratively convenient that claimants should only have to deal with one agency processing both the rent allowance and the rate rebate.

RENTAL PURCHASE SCHEMES

NIHB 11(1)(a), 13(1)(h) NIHB60+ 11(1)(a), 13(1)(h)

11.20 There is one further anomaly, which relates to people buying their homes through rental purchase schemes, i.e. where ownership does not transfer until the final instalment has been paid. Such people would also be commonly regarded as owner-occupiers but can receive assistance with both rental purchase instalments (as if they were rent) (para. 2.29) and with rates from the NIHE.

EXCEPTIONS: PERSONS TREATED AS IF THEY ARE OWNER OCCUPIERS

NIHB 8(1)(b)-(e) NIHB60+ 8(1)(b)-(e)

11.21 Although the tenure of the property largely governs which agency will deal with the rate rebate claim, it is important to note that this is not absolute. As well as the circumstances previously noted, the general provision, which allows the NIHE to accept a rent rebate or allowance claim from a person other than the liable person (para. 11.16), this rule applies equally to rate rebate only claims made to the RCA. Therefore it is possible for a rate rebate application to be accepted from and paid to the following persons:

- the partner of the person liable for rates (para. 2.36) including partners of full time students;
- a person whose liability has been waived by their landlord in return for doing repairs (para. 2.36);
- the former partner of the person liable for rates;
- some other person it is reasonable to treat as liable.

In the last two cases the conditions in paragraph 11.22 must also apply.

NIHB 8(1)(c) NIHB60+ 8(1)(c)

11.22 In order to treat a former partner or some other person as liable for rates it is also necessary to demonstrate that:

- the person left in occupation is required to make payments in order to continue to live there; and
- the person liable to make payments is not doing so; and
- it must also be 'reasonable to treat [that person] as liable'; in practice this means that that person must have been living in the home before the person liable for making rates payments stopped doing so.

11.23 This provision allows, for example, the RCA to accept and process a rate rebate claim from the partner of a sole owner who has had to move into residential care accommodation on medical grounds.

11.24 Table 11.1 summarises which agency will deal with rate rebate claims from particular types of occupiers.

Table 11.1: Which agency deals with claims

Owner occupier	RCA
Housing association tenant	NIHE
NIHE tenant	NIHE
Tenant of private landlord	NIHE
Co-ownership participant	NIHE
Buying through rental purchase	NIHE
Person with a life interest	NIHE
Partner of sole owner	RCA
Former partner of sole owner	RCA
Former non-dependant	RCA

What restrictions, if any, apply to the amount of eligible rates

GENERAL RULE: POWER TO RESTRICT ELIGIBLE RATES

11.25 Prior to April 1996 the amount of eligible rates could be restricted by the NIHE and RCA on the same grounds as those which applied to rents; that is, a restriction could be applied if the rates were deemed to be unreasonably high or if the property was over-large. NIHB 12(1),(3) NIHB60+ 12(1),(3)

11.26 Since April 1996, however, neither the NIHE nor the RCA have had any power to restrict the amount of eligible rates. With only a few exceptions the amount of rates eligible for HB is the full amount of rates charged on that property expressed on a weekly basis.

EXCEPTIONS TO GENERAL RULE

11.27 There are three exceptions to this rule. The first applies to both the NIHE and the RCA while the second and third will normally only apply to cases being dealt with by the NIHE. These are as follows: NIHB 12(2),(4),(5)

- If the rateable unit includes non-residential accommodation (such as a shop or commercial workshop) only that proportion of the rates which relates to residential accommodation is eligible.

- If the person occupies only part of a rateable unit (for example a boarder, lodger or someone living in a multi-occupied property) only the proportion of the total rates payable on the property which appears appropriate is eligible. For example if a person has exclusive occupancy of one room in an eight-bedroom house, sharing kitchen, bathroom and living room: then 1/8th of the total rates on the property as a whole would be eligible. Similarly, if that person had exclusive use of three of the eight rooms, the eligible rates would be 3/8th of the total rates on the property as a whole.
- If there is joint liability to pay rates (for example in a joint tenancy) eligible rates will normally be the total rates on the property divided by the number of people with a liability to pay. Exceptionally, however, unlike the GB rule relating to council tax benefit (paras. 9.26-29), if there is a difference in the proportions of the total rates paid this must be taken into account. This could mean, for example, that there would be a 2/3rd to 1/3rd split of the total rates payable.

Conversion to weekly amounts

NIHB 77(2),(3) NIHB60+ 60(2),(3)

11.28 HB is a weekly benefit and it is therefore necessary to convert the annual rates charge to a weekly figure before calculating entitlement. Previously there were two alternative methods of conversion but from April 2006 this has been simplified and only one method is now used. The frequency of the tenancy or whether the rates are included in the overall charge paid to the landlord or paid directly to the RCA is no longer relevant. Unless the tenant has rent free weeks the annual rates charge is now converted to a weekly amount by simply dividing the total annual rates charge by 52. This applies even if there are 53 Mondays in that particular year. Benefit is then calculated in the normal way, deducting any non-dependant charges and any tapered excess income as appropriate (paras. 11.31-34). Where the tenancy has 'rent free' weeks an adjustment is necessary so that benefit is paid in the weeks in which they are charged rent (paras. 11.35-36).

Example – Eligible rates based on annual rates bill of £650

Annual amount of eligible rates	£650
£650 divided by 52	= £12.50 – weekly eligible rates

ROUNDING

NIHB 77(8) NIHB60+ 60(8)

11.29 Any amount which as a result of the conversion to weekly amounts does not exactly equal a whole penny can be rounded down to the nearest whole penny if the remainder is less than half a penny, or up to the next whole penny if it is equal to or more than half a penny.

How much rate rebate will be paid?

11.30 As with rent rebates and allowances, the amount of rate rebate payable depends on the type and amount of the claimant's income as well as whether or not any non-dependants live in the household.

INCOME SUPPORT CASES

11.31 If the claimant receives income support, income-based jobseeker's allowance or the guarantee credit, or is treated as if they do (para. 7.6), they will receive the maximum rebate, which is the full amount of eligible rates expressed on a weekly basis less any non-dependant charges that apply (para. 11.34 and table 11.2).

NICBA 129(3)(a)
NIHB 3(2),67(b)
sch 6 paras 4,5
sch 7 paras 5,6
NIHB60+
3(2),24,48

CLAIMANTS WHO LOST IS/JSA(IB) AS A RESULT OF SUPPORTING PEOPLE

11.32 In addition, those claimants who lost all entitlement to IS/JSA(IB) as a result of the introduction of Supporting People (para. 10.103) (mainly long leaseholders with service charges) continue to be treated as entitled to the maximum rebate indefinitely (para. 13.48) as if they were still entitled to income support (para. 11.31).

ALL OTHER CASES

11.33 If the claimant does not receive income support, JSA(IB) or the guarantee credit then it is necessary to calculate entitlement. This is done on the same basis as claims for rent rebates and allowances (paras. 7.8-11) but note that there are two different methods depending on whether the claimant (or their partner if they have one) is aged at least 60 or younger (chapters 13 to 15). If they are aged at least 60 a further differentiation applies depending on whether or not they receive the savings credit (chapter 13). If the claimant's income is less than or equal to the applicable amount, the maximum rebate is awarded (paras. 7.4 and 11.31). If the claimant's income is greater than his or her applicable amount a taper of 20 per cent of the excess income is applied. Once again this is expressed on a weekly basis, as illustrated in the example.

NICBA 129(3)(b)
NIHB 24(1),
67(b), 68(a)
NIHB60+ 24,25,
28(1),48(b),49(a)

Example: Effect of taper where income exceeds applicable amount

A couple (both aged over 18 but under 60) with one child aged 14, income of £170 per week (after disregards) and a weekly rate liability of £12.50.

1. Deduct applicable amount from income (after disregards) i.e.

Income	£170.00
Applicable amount	£151.93
Excess	£18.07

2. Take 20% of excess income and deduct from weekly eligible rates i.e.

Weekly eligible rates	£12.50
Less 20% of excess	£3.61
Weekly rate rebate	£8.89

NON-DEPENDANT DEDUCTIONS

NIHB 71
NIHB60+ 53

11.34 As with rent rebates and allowances a non-dependant in the household can affect the amount of rate rebate payable. The normal rules concerning when a non-dependant deduction is made to rent rebates/allowances apply equally to rate rebates (paras. 7.17-38 and table 7.2); in particular, no deduction is made if the claimant receives the care component of disability living allowance, attendance allowance or is registered blind (paras. 7.19-22). The rules as to the treatment of non-dependant couples and joint occupiers are the same as for rent allowances/ rebates (paras. 7.35-38). Only the rate of deduction and the circumstances in which they apply are different. These are given in table 11.2.

ADJUSTMENT AND PAYMENT FOR RENT FREE PERIODS

11.35 In rare cases tenants who pay their rates as part of their gross rent may also have 'rent free' periods. If this is the case an adjustment is necessary so that benefit is paid only in the periods in which rent is charged.

11.36 A period is 'rent free' if the rent is set over a longer period (e.g. 52 weeks) but the landlord then opts to collect it in regular instalments over shorter periods (e.g. weekly) some of which are rent free, but only if the true rental period is an exact multiple of the instalment period (e.g. 52 weeks and weekly, but not yearly and weekly).

Table 11.2: Weekly non-dependant deductions for rates

Non-dependant working 16 hours or more per week* with a gross income of:	
£338 per week or more	£6.95
between £271 and £337.99 per week	£5.80
between £157 and £270.99 per week	£4.60
under £157.00 per week	£2.30
Non-dependant not in work or working less than 16 hours* per week	
On income support or income-based jobseeker's allowance	NIL
All other cases (regardless of income level)	£2.30

* Strictly speaking what matters is whether the non-dependant is in remunerative work (see paras. 7.29-34).

Example: Effect of non-dependant deduction

Using the same example in paragraph 11.33 but this time with a non-dependant working over 16 hours with gross income of £195 per week

1. Deduct non-dependant charge from weekly eligible rates i.e.

Weekly Eligible Rates	£12.50
Less Non Dependant Charge	£4.60
Maximum Rate Rebate	£7.90

2. Deduct applicable amount from income (after disregards) i.e.

Income	£170.00
Applicable Amount	£151.93
Excess	£18.07

3. Take 20% of excess income and deduct from maximum Rate Rebate i.e.

Maximum Rate Rebate	£7.90
Less 20% of Excess	£3.61
Weekly Rate Rebate	£4.29

NIHB 78(2)
NIHB60+ 61(2)

11.37 The weekly benefit is calculated in the normal way (para.11.28) including any deductions which apply as a result of the taper or non-dependant charges (paras. 11.33-34) to give the 'true' weekly benefit. From this the total benefit for the whole period is calculated by multiplying the true weekly figure by the total number of weeks in the period to which it relates (including any rent free period), which unless liability commences part way through the year will be 52. This is then divided by the number of weeks in which the rent is charged (i.e. the whole period less any rent free weeks) and paid in equal instalments in each of those weeks together with any HB in respect of the rent. No HB is payable during any 'rent free' week.

MINIMUM RATE REBATE

NIHB 72
NIHB60+ 54

11.38 Unlike rent rebates and allowances, where no HB is payable if entitlement is less than 50p per week, there is no minimum rate rebate figure. Hence if a claimant is entitled to only 1p per week this has to be deducted from the rates account by the RCA, credited to the rent account or paid by the NIHE.

EXTENDED PAYMENTS AND CONTINUING PAYMENTS OF RATE REBATE

11.39 These are dealt with in paragraphs 17.81-99 and table 17.6 of the guide.

Payment of rate rebate as a rent allowance

NIHB
86(2),87,88(5)
NIHB60+
69(2),70,71(5)

11.40 In the vast majority of cases, HB for rates is paid as rebate. However, a rate rebate can be paid as if it was a rent allowance in the following circumstances:

- the claimant is a tenant who is entitled to a rent allowance, or would be but for any non-dependant charges or the application of the taper; and
- the claimant pays rates to his or her landlord as part of the rent (whether or not the charge is separately identified) rather than directly to the RCA.

Note that this does not apply to owner-occupiers, because they pay their rates directly to the RCA, or NIHE tenants, because they are paid by rebate. The decision to pay benefit as an allowance is at the discretion of the NIHE. Any allowance so payable can be paid to the tenant or directly to the landlord in accordance with the rules for rent allowances (paras. 16.12-40); in particular, where the total benefit is £2 per week or less payment can be four-weekly, or where it is less than £1 per week every six months.

12 Applicable amounts

12.1 An applicable amount is the figure used in calculating HB and main CTB to reflect the basic living needs of the claimant and family. This chapter covers:

- personal allowances;
- general rules about premiums;
- the detailed rules for each premium in turn; and
- further rules and special cases.

CBA 135
NICBA 131
HB 22
HB60+ 22
NIHB 20
NIHB60+ 20
CTB
CTB60+

12.2 A claimant's applicable amount is the same for both HB and main CTB purposes. It is the total of any personal allowances and premiums which apply in their case. All claimants have an applicable amount but for those in receipt of income support, income-based job seeker's allowance or the guarantee credit this is a technicality as they are treated as having no income and capital and are therefore entitled to maximum HB/CTB (para. 7.2). Consequently, this chapter does not apply to these claimants for the purpose of calculating HB/CTB.

HB 5
HB60+ 5
NIHB 5
NIHB60+ 5
CTB 5
CTB60+ 5

12.3 As described in the relevant places in this chapter, there are some differences in the law depending on whether:

- the claimant or any partner is aged 60 or over; and
- the claimant and any partner are both under the age of 60.

HB 22(a),(b),
sch 3 paras 1,2
HB60+ 22(a),(b)
sch 3 paras 1,2
NIHB 20(a),(b)
sch 4 paras 1,2
IHB60+ 20(a),(b)
sch 4 paras 1,2
CTB 12(a),(b)
sch 1, paras 1,2
CTB60+ 12(a),(b)
sch 1, paras 1,2

Personal allowances

SINGLE PEOPLE, COUPLES, LONE PARENTS AND CHILDREN

12.4 Personal allowances are awarded for the claimant and any other family members (para. 4.7). There are different amounts for single claimants, couples and lone parents. Additions are made for children and young persons (sometimes known as dependants' allowances). The amounts, which vary with age, are given in table 12.1.

POLYGAMOUS MARRIAGES

HB 23
60+ sch 3 para 1
NIHB 21
NIHB60+
sch 4 para 1
CTB 13
CTB60+
sch 1 para 1

12.5 The applicable amount for a claimant in a polygamous marriage (para. 4.23) is the sum of the following. If the following could combine to produce more than one result, the result which is most favourable to the claimant applies:

- where none of the partners in a polygamous marriage is aged 60 or over:
  - the personal allowance of £90.10, unless (in HB only) all the members of the polygamous marriage are under 18, in which case £68.65; and

  - £32.65 for each spouse in excess of two;
- where at least one of the partners in a polygamous marriage is aged 60 or over but none of the members of the marriage have attained the age of 65:
  - the personal allowance of £174.05; and
  - £60.00 for each spouse in excess of two;
- where at least one of the members of a polygamous marriage is aged 65 or over:
  - the personal allowance of £197.65; and
  - £65.70 for each spouse in excess of two;
- additions to the personal allowance for any child or young person as in any other case including, if appropriate, any premiums in respect of them.
- family premium if there is at least one child or young person;

Any special rules with respect to premiums for partners in polygamous marriages are dealt with as they arise in this chapter.

Table 12.1: Weekly applicable amounts

A claimant's applicable amount is the total of each of the figures in this table which applies.

PERSONAL ALLOWANCES

Single claimant	aged under 25	£45.50
	aged 25+ but under 60	£57.45
	aged 60+ but under 65	£114.05
	aged 65+	£131.95
Lone parent	aged under 18 (HB only)	£45.50
	aged 18+ but under 60	£57.45
	aged 60+ but under 65	£114.05
	aged 65+	£131.95
Couple	both aged under 18 (HB only)	£68.65
	at least one aged 18+ but both under 60	£90.10
	at least one aged 60+ but both under 65	£174.05
	at least one aged 65+	£197.65
Child		£45.58
Young person		£45.58

PREMIUMS

1. 'Any age premiums'

(premiums that do not depend on claimant's or partner's age)

Family	baby rate (at least one child under 1)	£26.75
	normal rate	£16.25
	(protected lone parent rates: see para.12.10)	
Disabled child	each dependent child	£45.08
Enhanced disability	each dependent child	£18.13
Severe disability	single rate	£46.75
	double rate	£93.50
Carer	claimant or partner or each	£26.35

2. 'Under 60 premiums'

(premiums that apply only if claimant and any partner are under 60)

Disability	single claimant/lone parent	£24.50
	couple (one/both qualifying)	£34.95
Enhanced disability	single claimant/lone parent	£11.95
	couple (one/both qualifying)	£17.25

EXAMPLES: APPLICABLE AMOUNTS

Except for the lone parent in the fourth example, none of the following qualifies for any of the premiums for disability or for carers.

SINGLE CLAIMANT AGED 23

Personal allowance:	
Single claimant aged under 25	£45.50
No premiums apply	
Applicable amount	£45.50

COUPLE WITH TWO CHILDREN AGED 13 AND 17

The older child is still at school so still counts as a dependant of the couple.

Personal allowances:	
Couple at least one over 18 (and both under 60)	£90.10
Child aged 13	£45.58
Child aged 17	£45.58
Premium: family premium (normal rate)	£16.25
Applicable amount	£197.51

COUPLE AGED 38 AND 65

Personal allowance:	
Couple at least one aged 65	£197.65
Applicable amount	£197.65

DISABLED LONE PARENT WITH BABY

The lone parent is in receipt of the highest rate of the care component disability living allowance and so qualifies for a disability premium and enhanced disability premium. Her baby is aged under one year.

Personal allowances:	
Lone parent aged over 18 (and under 60)	£57.45
Child	£45.58
Premiums:	
Family premium ('baby' rate)	£26.75
Disability premium (single rate)	£24.50
Enhanced disability premium (single rate)	£11.95
Applicable amount	£166.23

Premiums

HB 22(c),(d) sch 3 paras 3-6, 12-17
HB60+ 16(c),(d) sch 3 paras 3-9
IHB 20(c),(d) sch 4 paras 3-6,12,17
NIHB60+ 20(c),(d) sch 4 paras 3-9
CTB 12(c),(d) sch 1 paras 3-6, 12-17
CTB60+ 12(c),(d) sch 1 paras 3-9

12.6 Many claimants – but not all – qualify for one or more premiums. Table 12.1 lists the premiums available and gives their amounts. A premium is awarded if its conditions of entitlement are satisfied. Some of the conditions are straightforward, some more complicated and less well known. Claimants may therefore miss entitlement unless authority staff are fully trained and claim forms are carefully designed. In particular, entitlement to many of the premiums is triggered by being in receipt of certain state benefits. General points and special rules such as when a person can be treated as being in receipt of a qualifying benefit are given in paragraphs 12.32-37. Paragraphs 12.8-30 set out the specific conditions for each premium.

HOW MANY PREMIUMS AT ONCE?

HB sch 3 paras 5-6
HB sch 4 paras 5-6
TB sch 1 paras 5-6

12.7 Apart from as described in the remainder of this chapter, there are no limitations on how many premiums can be awarded at a time. However, as indicated in the table, certain premiums are 'under 60 premiums' (in other words, they can be awarded only if the claimant and any partner are both under the age of 60) whereas others are 'any age premiums' (in other words, they can be awarded regardless of whether the claimant and any partner are under or over 60). This is mentioned again wherever relevant in the following description of the conditions for qualifying for premiums.

FAMILY PREMIUM

HB sch 3 para 3
B60+ sch 3 para 3
NIHB sch 4 para 3
NIHB60+ sch 4 para 3
CTB sch 1 para 3
CTB 60+ sch 1 para 3

12.8 The condition for this premium is that there is at least one child or young person in the claimant's family – whether the claimant is in a couple or is a lone parent. The terms 'child', 'young person', 'family', 'couple' and 'lone parent' are used in the specific senses defined for HB and CTB (paras. 4.6-40). In particular, a child or young person need not be the natural child of the claimant but could, for example, be a grandchild living as part of the claimant's family.

12.9 There are two main rates of this premium (and see also para. 12.10):

- the 'baby' rate is awarded to couples and lone parents with at least one child aged under one year;
- the normal rate is awarded to other couples and lone parents (with at least one child or young person).

HB sch 3 para 3(3)-(5)
NIHB sch 4 para 3(3)-(5)
CTB sch para 3(3)-(5)

12.10 Where the claimant is under the age of 60, higher 'protected rates' of family premium apply to certain lone parents (never couples). They are £32.70 ('baby' protected rate) and £22.20 (normal protected rate). The conditions are in the next paragraph. There is no equivalent protected rate where the claimant is aged 60 or over.

12.11 A lone parent under age 60 qualifies for the protected rates of the family premium if, and for as long as, all the following conditions apply:

- on 5th April 1998, they were entitled to HB or CTB and satisfied the conditions for the (then existing) lone parent rate of the family premium or would have done so but for the fact that 5th April 1998 fell within a rent-free period;
- they have remained entitled to HB or CTB continuously since that date (ignoring breaks due only to rent-free periods);
- they have not ceased to be a lone parent at any time since that date;
- they have not become entitled to income support or to income-based jobseeker's allowance, or ceased to be entitled to both those benefits, at any time since that date; and
- they have not reached the age of 60 or become entitled to a disability premium at any time since that date.

As soon as any of the last four conditions ceases to apply, the person ceases permanently to qualify for the protected lone parent rate (but may still qualify for the basic rate).

DISABILITY PREMIUM

12.12 A disability premium may be awarded where the claimant and any partner are under age 60. To receive this premium the claimant (or in the case of a couple, either partner) must count as 'disabled or long-term sick' in one of the ways described in paragraphs 12.13-14 (but note that it must be the claimant, not the partner, in the cases described in para. 12.15). In the case of a couple, the couple rate is awarded even if only one partner fulfils the conditions.

HBR sch 3 para 12
NIHB sch 4 para 1
CTB sch 1 para 12

'DISABLED OR LONG-TERM SICK'

12.13 The following are the ways of counting as 'disabled or long-term sick' in order to qualify for a disability premium (para. 12.12). They are that the claimant or any partner:

HB sch 3 para 13(4),(2)
NIHB sch 4 para 13(4),(2)
CTB sch 1 para 13(4),(2)

(a) is registered or certified blind (this means with the social services or social work department or in Northern Ireland with the Health and Social Services Board); or

(b) ceased to be registered or certified blind within the past 28 weeks because of regaining sight; or

(c) receives disability living allowance (either component payable at any rate), including where all or part of the mobility component is paid to the Motability fund; or

(d) receives a benefit which is treated as attendance allowance (para. 12.35); or

(e) receives the disability element or severe disability element of working tax credit; or

(f) has an invalid vehicle supplied by the NHS or gets DWP payments for car running costs; or

(g) is incapable of work and satisfies the further conditions in either of the next two paragraphs.

In the case of items (c) and (d) special rules apply where the qualifying benefit is lost after a period in hospital – see paragraph 12.37 and table 12.3 for details.

PEOPLE WHO ARE INCAPABLE OF WORK: THE MAIN RULE

HB sch 3 para 13(1)(a)(i),(7) NIHB sch 4 para 13(1)(a)(i),(7) CTB sch 1 para 13(1)(a)(i),(7)

12.14 For the above purposes, the claimant or any partner counts as 'disabled or long-term sick' if they are 'in receipt' of (para. 12.32) severe disablement allowance or incapacity benefit payable at the long-term rate (which starts after 52 weeks of incapacity for work), or are terminally ill and receive it at the short-term higher rate (which starts after 28 weeks of incapacity for work). See also paragraph 12.36 where a person was previously incapable of work immediately before starting on a government training scheme.

PEOPLE WHO ARE INCAPABLE OF WORK: THE '28/52-WEEK RULE'

HB sch 3 para 13(1)(b) NIHB sch 4 para 13(1)(b) CTB sch 1 para 13(1)(b)

12.15 Additionally, for the purposes of qualifying for a disability premium, the claimant (but not the claimant's partner) counts as disabled or long-term sick if they:

- are incapable of work; and
- have been incapable of work for a 'qualifying period' (calculated as described below) of:
  - 28 weeks (196 days) if they are terminally ill, or
  - 52 weeks (364 days) in any other case.

After the qualifying period is completed, there are further 'linking rules' (described below). See also paragraph 12.36 where a person was previously incapable of work immediately before starting on a government training scheme.

12.16 This way of qualifying for a disability premium 'fills the gap' for people who are incapable of work but do not get incapacity benefit. For couples, it must be the claimant – not their partner – who fulfils this rule. It can therefore be important which partner makes the claim (para. 5.4).

12.17 'Incapable of work' means the same here as it does for incapacity benefit purposes. Broadly, during the first 28 weeks the person must satisfy an 'own occupation test', and thereafter (or from the outset if they have no normal occupation) an 'all work test'. Broadly, a person is 'terminally ill' if their death can be expected within six months. The decision about whether a claimant is capable or incapable of work will always be made by a Decision Maker at the Jobcentre Plus office (DWP GM, para. C4.138).

THE 'QUALIFYING PERIOD' AND THE 'LINKING RULES'

12.18 In the following, a 'gap' means a period during which the person either is capable of work or is disqualified from incapacity benefit. The qualifying period (para. 12.15) need not be continuous. Any number of periods can be added together so long as the gap between each is eight weeks or less (52 weeks or less, in the case of a 'welfare to work beneficiary' (table 12.2)). Once a person has completed the qualifying period, there are linking rules as follows:

HB sch 3 paras 11(5), 13(3),(4),(6),(8)
NIHB sch 4 paras 11(5), 13(3),(4),(6),(8)
CTB sch 1 paras 11(5), 13(3),(4),(6),(8)

- the claimant does not qualify for a disability premium during a gap;
- after a gap of eight weeks or less (52 weeks or less, in the case of a 'welfare to work beneficiary'(table 12.2)), the person qualifies for a disability premium straight away;
- after a gap of more than eight weeks, the person does not qualify for a disability premium until they have completed a fresh qualifying period.

Breaks in entitlement to HB or CTB during the qualifying period or after it have no effect on this rule.

Table 12.2: Definition of 'welfare to work beneficiary'

For all HB/CTB purposes, this means a person who:

SI 1998 No 2231
NISR 1998 No 324

- has been incapable of work for at least 28 weeks (196 days); and
- has stopped (on or after 5th October 1998) receiving a benefit or advantage which was dependent on his or her being incapable of work (the relevant benefits and advantages for HB/CTB purposes are those described in paragraphs 10.10, 10.36 and 12.18 of this guide); and
- has – within 7 days of ceasing to be incapable of work – started:
  - remunerative work (in broad terms, 16 hours or more per week: paras. 7.29 onwards), or
  - Work Based Training for Adults (in England and Wales), or
  - Training for Work (in Scotland); and

- has notified the DWP of the fact that he or she has started work, and has done so within one month of the date on which he or she ceased to claim that he or she is incapable of work (or, in certain cases, has won a social security appeal relating to this).

Such a person counts as a welfare to work beneficiary for 52 weeks only. The DWP should inform authorities if someone is a welfare to work beneficiary (GM para. C4.149).

DISABLED CHILD PREMIUM

HB sch 3 para 16
HB60+ sch 3 para 8
NIHB sch 4 para 16
NIHB60+ sch 4 para 8
CTB sch 1 para 16
CTB60+ sch 1 para 8

12.19 The condition for this premium is that a child or young person in the family:

- is registered or certified blind (this means with the social services or social work department or in Northern Ireland with the Health and Social Services Board); or
- ceased to be registered or certified blind within the past 28 weeks because of regaining sight; or
- receives disability living allowance (either component payable at any rate).

A disabled child premium is awarded for each child or young person to whom this applies. If the child/young person dies the premium should continue for eight weeks following the death. Special rules apply if the child is in hospital – see paragraph 12.37 and table 12.3 for details.

ENHANCED DISABILITY PREMIUM

HB sch 3 para 15
HB60+ sch 3 para 7
NIHB sch 4 para 15
NIHB60+ sch 4 para 7
CTB sch 1 para 15
CTB60+ sch 1 para 7

12.20 Where the claimant and any partner are aged under 60 this premium can be awarded in respect of the claimant or partner and/or in respect of a child or young person in the family. Two or more of these premiums are awarded if appropriate – for example, if a claimant or partner qualifies and also one or more children or young persons. Where the claimant or any partner is aged 60 or over, this premium can only be awarded in respect of a child or young person in the family. Special rules apply where disability living allowance is lost following a period in hospital (para. 12.37 and table 12.3).

12.21 The condition in the case of the claimant or partner is that:

- the claimant is (or in the case of a couple, both partners are) aged under 60; and
- the claimant (or in the case of a couple, either partner) receives the highest rate of the care component of disability living allowance. (The

mobility component of disability living allowance is not sufficient, nor is the middle or low rate of the care component.)

In the case of a couple, the couple rate is awarded even if only one partner fulfils the second condition.

12.22 The condition in the case of a child or young person is that they receive the highest rate of the care component of disability living allowance. (The mobility component of disability living allowance is not sufficient, nor is the middle or low rate of the care component.)

SEVERE DISABILITY PREMIUM

12.23 There are three conditions for this premium:

HB sch 3 para 14(HB60+ sch 3 para 6(2) NIHB sch 4 para 14(2) NIHB60+ sch 4 para 6(2) CTB sch 1 para 14 CTB60+ sch 1 para 6(2)

- the claimant must be receiving one of the following qualifying benefits:
  - the middle or highest rate of the care component of disability living allowance, or
  - attendance allowance at either rate, or
  - a benefit which is treated as attendance allowance (para. 12.35); and
- they must have no non-dependants (but see paragraph 12.25 below for exceptions); and
- no-one must be receiving carer's allowance in respect of them (but see paragraphs 12.26 and 12.32 for circumstances where the carer will be treated as either in receipt or not in receipt of carer's allowance).

In the case of a couple, except where their partner is blind (para. 12.24), both members must be in receipt of a qualifying benefit. Special rules apply where a qualifying benefit is lost following a period in hospital (paras. 12.24, 12.26, 12.37 and table 12.3).

HB sch 3 para 14(HB60+ sch 3 para 6(3) NIHB sch 4 para 14(3) NIHB60+ sch 4 para 6(3) CTB sch 1 para 14 CTB60+ sch 1 para 6(3)

12.24 A single claimant or lone parent who satisfies all three conditions gets the single rate of severe disability premium. In the case of a couple or a polygamous marriage, a severe disability premium is awarded as follows:

- if both members of a couple satisfy all three conditions, they get the double rate;
- if both members of a couple satisfy the first two conditions but only one satisfies the third condition, they get the single rate;
- if, in a couple, the claimant only satisfies all three conditions, and their partner is registered or certified blind or ceased to be within the past 28 weeks, they get the single rate. In this case, if the 'wrong' partner makes the claim, they should be advised to 'swap the claimant role';

- if a couple have been getting the double rate, but one partner then ceases to satisfy the first condition because of having been in hospital for four weeks, they get the single rate from that point.
- in the case of a polygamous marriage, the double rate of severe disability premium if all members of the marriage satisfy all three conditions in paragraph 12.23; the single rate if all members of the marriage satisfy the first two of those conditions but someone receives a carer's allowance for caring for at least one of them; and the single rate if the claimant satisfies all three conditions and all the other members of the marriage are registered or certified blind or ceased to be within the past 28 weeks.

HB sch 3 para 14(4) HB60+ sch 3 para 6(6) NIHB sch 4 para 14(4) NIHB60+ sch 4 para 6(6) CTB sch 1 para 14(4) CTB60+ sch 1 para 6(6)

12.25 For the purposes of the above rule, the following non-dependants do not count (i.e. do not prevent the award of a severe disability premium):

- non-dependants under 18 (para. 7.20);
- non-dependants who are registered or certified blind or who ceased to be within the past 28 weeks;
- non-dependants receiving:
  - the middle or highest rate of the care component of disability living allowance, or
  - attendance allowance, or
  - a benefit which is treated as attendance allowance (para. 12.35).It should also be borne in mind that a number of categories of people are excluded from the definition of a non-dependant (paras. 4.42-43).

HB sch 3 paras 14(5)-(7),19 HB60+ sch 3 paras 14(7)-(8),11 NIHB sch 4 paras 14(5)-(7),19 NIHB60+ sch 4 paras 14(7)-(8),11 CTB sch 1 paras 14(5)-(7),19 CTB60+ sch 1 paras 14(7)-(8),11

12.26 For the purpose of determining whether the severely disabled person has a carer receiving carer's allowance in respect of them (para. 12.23) the following considerations apply:

- the carer will not be in receipt of carer's allowance if it overlapped by other benefits (paras 12.32 and 12.34);
- a backdated award of carer's allowance is ignored as regards any period before the award was made: in other words the backdated part does not cause an overpayment;
- in the case of couples or polygamous marriages the carer will be treated as in receipt of a carer's allowance if they have lost it because the claimant or the partner they are caring for has been in hospital for four weeks or more. This will ensure that a couple in receipt of the single rate will continue to receive it at the same rate when one member goes into hospital (paras 12.23-25);
- the carer will be treated as if they are in receipt of carer's allowance if it is not awarded because of the loss of benefit rules following certain benefit fraud convictions.

Example: Severe disability premium, etc

A husband and wife are both under 60 and both receive the middle rate of the care component of disability living allowance. Neither of them is or has recently been registered or certified blind. Their daughter of 17 is in full-time employment and lives with them. Their son lives elsewhere and receives carer's allowance for caring for the husband. No-one receives carer's allowance for the wife.

Disability premium: Because of receiving disability living allowance, they are awarded the couple rate of disability premium.

Enhanced disability premium: Because they get the middle (not the highest) rate of the care component of disability living allowance, this cannot be awarded.

Severe disability premium:

- Both receive the appropriate type of disability living allowance.
- Although their daughter is a non-dependant, she is under 18.
- Someone receives carer's allowance for caring for only one of them.

So they are awarded the single rate of severe disability premium (for the second reason in para. 12.24).

CARER PREMIUM

12.27 The condition to qualify for this premium is that the claimant (or, in the case of a couple, either partner) is entitled to (paras. 12.29, 12.32) carer's allowance or was entitled to carer's allowance within the past eight weeks.

HB sch 3 paras 7(2),17
HB60+ sch 3 paras 5(2),9
NIHB sch 4 paras 7(2),17
NIHB60+ sch 4 paras 5(2),9
CTB sch 1 paras 7(2),17
CTB60+ sch 1 paras 5(2),9

12.28 A single claimant who satisfies the condition gets one carer premium. A couple will get one or two carer premiums, one if one of them fulfils the condition, two if both do. In the case of a polygamous marriage a carer premium will be awarded for each partner that satisfies the conditions.

12.29 A claimant only has to be 'entitled' and not 'in receipt' so where carer's allowance is overlapped by another benefit (see examples) that would be sufficient. Further, once a person has claimed carer's allowance and their entitlement has been established (whether or not they receive it) it continues indefinitely until they no longer satisfy the conditions for it (e.g. the person being cared for dies or the carer starts work). Note that it does not matter whether their original claim for carer's allowance was made before their claim for HB/CTB: they will continue to be 'entitled' to carer's allowance and qualify for the premium without the need to make a further claim for carer's allowance (see CIS/367/2003). This in fact has been the position since 3rd April 2000 when the regulations were amended.

12.30 It is also worth noting that since 28th October 2002, many older people (often caring for their partner) may qualify for this premium for the first time.

Before that date the rules for carer's allowance were such that no-one who first started caring after reaching age 65 could be entitled to carer's allowance and so qualify for the premium.

INTERACTION OF CARER AND SEVERE DISABILITY PREMIUM

HB sch 3 para 19
HB60+ sch 3 para 11
NIHB sch 4 para 19
NIHB60+ sch 4 para 11
CTB sch 1 para 19
CTB60+ sch 1 para 11

12.31 It is worth noting that although entitlement to carer's allowance means the award of a carer premium for the carer, the person cared for may lose a severe disability premium (though not retrospectively: para. 12.26). However this happens only if the carer's allowance (or part of it) is actually being paid to the carer (para. 12.32) – and not in the situation illustrated in the examples. It is therefore not impossible for a couple who care for each other to qualify for a severe disability premium and also for two carer premiums.

Example: Carer premium and overlapping benefits

CLAIMANT OVER AGE 65

A claimant and her partner are both aged over 80 and in receipt of retirement pension. She looks after her partner who has been in receipt of attendance allowance since 6th November 2002. On 11th November 2002 she made a claim for carer's allowance and was notified by the DWP that she was entitled to carer's allowance but it could not be paid because it was overlapped by her retirement pension (in other words, payment of the latter prevents payment of the former).

On 10th April 2006 she makes a claim for HB/CTB for the first time. They are awarded HB/CTB from 11th April 2005 (para. 5.51) the award includes the carer premium. If her partner subsequently dies, she would no longer be entitled to carer's allowance, but the premium would continue for a further eight weeks.

CLAIMANT UNDER 65

A claimant aged 33 is in receipt of incapacity benefit. He cares for his severely disabled sister who receives the high care rate of disability living allowance. She lives alone in her own flat. He claims carer's allowance and is entitled to it but it cannot be paid because it is overlapped by his incapacity benefit. Once having claimed carer's allowance he remains 'entitled' to it indefinitely until such time as he no longer meets the conditions for it (e.g. he starts work, becomes a student or his sister dies or no longer qualifies for disability living allowance). Whilst he remains entitled to carer's allowance he should be awarded the carer premium on his HB/CTB without the need for a further claim for carer's allowance even if there are breaks in his HB/CTB award. Note that his sister would also be entitled to the severe disability premium because although he is 'entitled' to carer's allowance he is not 'in receipt' of it (para 12.32).

General rules and special cases

BEING 'IN RECEIPT' OF A BENEFIT

12.32 Receipt of a state benefit forms part of the condition for many of the premiums. For these purposes, a person is 'in receipt' of a benefit only if it is paid in respect of himself or herself, and only during the period for which it is awarded. Except as described in paragraph 12.34 below, a person will not be in receipt where they are entitled to that benefit but it cannot be paid due to the overlapping benefit rules.

HB sch 3 para 19
HB60+ sch 3 para 11
NIHB sch 4 para 19
NIHB60+ sch 4 para 11
CTB sch 1 para 19
CTB60+ sch 1 para 11

DWP CONCESSIONARY PAYMENTS

12.33 For the purpose of entitlement to any premium, a DWP concessionary payment compensating for non-payment of any state benefit is treated as if it were that benefit.

HB sch 3 para 18
HB60+ sch 3 para 10
NIHB sch 4 para 18
NIHB60+ sch 4 para 10
CTB sch 1 para 18
CTB60+ sch 1 para 10

OVERLAPPING SOCIAL SECURITY BENEFITS

12.34 Where a claimant is entitled to a qualifying benefit but does not receive it because of the rules about overlapping social security benefits (for example if widow's pension is payable instead of incapacity benefit) then the claimant will not normally be treated as being in receipt of the qualifying benefit except in the following circumstances:

- if they qualify for the carer's premium (para. 12.27);
- if they qualified for that premium before the relevant qualifying benefit was overlapped. In such cases they will continue to be treated as in receipt of the qualifying benefit during any period in which they would be in receipt of that benefit but for the overlapping benefit rules. The purpose of this rule is that it protects claimants from a reduction in their benefit merely because they became entitled to an overlapping benefit at some later date;
- if the qualifying benefit is only partially overlapped (i.e. the overlapping benefit is paid at a rate which is less than the qualifying benefit).

HB sch 3 paras 7,19
HB60+ sch 3 paras 5,11
NIHB sch 4 paras 7,19
NIHB60+ sch 4 paras 5,11
CTB sch 1 paras 7,19
CTB60+ sch 1 paras 5,11

BENEFITS TREATED AS ATTENDANCE ALLOWANCE

12.35 A person will be treated as in receipt of attendance allowance (paras. 7.21, 7.25, 12.13, 12.23 and 12.25) if they receive any type of increase for attendance or mobility paid with an industrial disablement benefit or war disablement benefit (including constant attendance allowance, 'old cases' attendance payments, mobility supplement, severe disablement occupational allowance and exceptionally severe disablement allowance).

HB 2(1)
HB60+ 2(1)
NIHB 2(1)
NIHB60+ 2(1)
CTB 2(1)
CTB60+ 2(1)

PEOPLE ON TRAINING COURSES OR IN RECEIPT OF A TRAINING ALLOWANCE

HB sch 3 para 7(1)(b), 13(5) HBR 60+ sch 3 para 5(1)(b) NIHB sch 4 para 7(1)(b), 13(5) NIHB60+ sch 4 para 5(1)(b) CTB sch 1 para 7(1)(b), 13(5) CTB60+ sch 1 para 5(1)(b)

12.36 Once a person qualifies for the disability premium by virtue of being incapable of work (paras. 12.14 and 12.15) or the carer premium by virtue of being in receipt of carer's allowance (para. 12.27), if they go on a government-run or approved training course (para. 13.64) or receive a training allowance, the premium does not cease just because they no longer satisfy those conditions. The objective of this rule is that otherwise there would be a disincentive to undertake such training.

PEOPLE IN HOSPITAL

12.37 Despite the abolition of the hospital down-rating rule (para. 12.39) certain premiums (severe disability and carer) may be lost as a result of a period in hospital – see table 12.3 for details. In addition, after a continuous period in hospital (as opposed to a linked period, paragraph 12.39) of 52 weeks the claimant's right to benefit will be lost (paras. 3.3, 3.32), or in the case of any dependants (adults or children) they are unlikely to be treated as a member of the family (paras. 4.24, 4.31). In both cases this will override any special rules in table 12.3.

Table 12.3: Loss of certain premiums after a period in hospital

HB sch 3 paras 13(1)(a)(iii)(6), 15(1),16(a) HBR 60+ paras 7,8(a) NIHB sch 4 paras 13(1)(a)(iii)(6), 15(1),16(a) NIHB60+ sch 4 paras 7,8(a) CTB sch 1 paras 13(1)(a)(iii)(6), 15(1),16(a) CTB60+ paras 7,8(a)

DISABILITY, DISABLED CHILD AND ENHANCED DISABILITY PREMIUM (PARAS. 12.15 AND 12.19-22)

- Where the claimant/partner/child loses their disability living allowance (including in the case of the disability premium one of the benefits in paragraph 12.35) solely because they have been in hospital for four weeks* (12 weeks in the case of a child) or more the relevant premium will continue or, in the case of a new claim, is still awarded.

HB sch 3 para 14(5)(a) HBR 60+ sch 3 para 6(7)(a) NIHB sch 4 para 14(5)(a) NIHB60+ sch 4 para 6(7)(a) CTB sch 1 para 14(5)(a) CTB60+ para 6(7)(a)

SEVERE DISABILITY PREMIUM (PARA. 12.23)

- In the case of a single claimant or a lone parent where payment of a qualifying benefit is lost because they have been in hospital for four weeks* then the premium will be lost.
- In the case of couples or polygamous marriages where one or more members would be in receipt of a qualifying benefit but for the fact they have been in hospital for four weeks* they will continue to be treated as in

receipt of that benefit and the premium will continue be awarded – see also paragraph 12.26.

CARER PREMIUM (PARA. 12.27)

- Where a carer goes into hospital, entitlement to carer's allowance is not normally lost until after 12 weeks, after which the carer premium will continue for a further eight weeks (making 20 in total).
- Where a disabled person has been in hospital for four weeks* (12 in the case of a child) they will lose their disability living allowance/attendance allowance or equivalent benefit with the result that their carer will lose entitlement to carer's allowance. The carer premium will continue for a further eight weeks (para. 12.27).

* The four/twelve week period may not be continuous but may be made up of two or more distinct periods which are less than 29 days apart.

Abolition of certain premiums and other rules

PENSIONER AND BEREAVEMENT PREMIUMS

12.38 The following premiums have either been abolished or ceased to be relevant in the calculation of the applicable amount:

- the bereavement premium from 10th April 2006 (by which time all the previous beneficiaries have reached age 60 or over); and
- the pensioner premiums from 6th October 2003 – although these still technically exist in the legislation they are no longer relevant to the calculation of the applicable amount.

See past editions of this guide for details of the rules prior to abolition.

PEOPLE IN HOSPITAL AND CHILDREN WITH CAPITAL

12.39 The following special rules have been abolished:

- amount of a child's or young person's capital no longer affects the award of any personal allowance or premium. The rules were different before 4th April 2005 (see 2004-05 edition of this guide for details);
- the hospital down rating rule was abolished with effect from 10th April 2006. Under this rule the personal allowance was reduced if the claimant or their partner was in hospital for a period totaling 52 weeks made up of two or more periods which were separated by breaks of four weeks or less (see 2005-06 edition of this guide for details). However, benefit may still be affected by a period in hospital (para. 12.37).

13 Income and capital

13.1 This and the following two chapters describe how income and capital are dealt with in the assessment of HB and main CTB. Chapters 14 and 15 give additional information relating to employed earners and the self-employed. This chapter covers:

- how different rules apply for different groups of claimants;
- general matters;
- benefits, pensions, and other state help;
- the home, property and possessions;
- savings and investments;
- trust funds and awards for personal injury;
- other items of income and capital;
- notional income and capital; and
- the separate rules used for claimants on savings credit.

13.2 The claimant is treated as having the income and capital of any partner and all references in this chapter to the income or capital of a claimant, should be read as also referring to the income or capital of a partner (para. 13.6). The income and capital of a child or young person is always disregarded (para. 13.146).

13.3 Income and capital are assessed differently for all purposes relevant to second adult rebate (para. 8.24) and to non-dependant deductions (paras. 7.24-27); this chapter does not apply in such cases.

The different rules for different groups of claimants

CLAIMANTS ON JSA(IB), IS OR GUARANTEE CREDIT

HB sch 5 paras 4,5,
sch 6 paras 5,6
HB60+ 26
IIHB sch 5 para 12,
sch 6 paras 4,5,
sch 7 paras 5,6
NIHB60+ 24
TB sch 4 paras 4,5,
sch 5 paras 5,6
CTB60+ 16

13.4 If a claimant is on JSA(IB), IS or guarantee credit (or his or her partner is), the whole of his or her (and any partner's) income and capital is fully disregarded. There are no exceptions whatsoever. The remainder of this chapter therefore does not apply in such cases. (Paras. 7.4-5 show how their entitlement to HB/main CTB is assessed.)

CLAIMANTS ON SAVINGS CREDIT

13.5 If a claimant is on savings credit (or his or her partner is), there are special rules for assessing income and capital. The rules for people on savings credit are in paragraphs 13.150-159 and the other parts of this chapter do not apply.

OTHER CASES: WHOSE INCOME AND CAPITAL COUNTS

13.6 In all cases other than the above (paras. 13.3-5), for the purposes of assessing HB and main CTB, a claimant is treated as possessing any income and capital belonging to:

HB 25,45
HB60+ 25
NIHB 22,42
NIHB60+ 23
CTB 15,35
CTB60+ 15

- the claimant themself; and
- any partner.

DIFFERENCES IN ASSESSMENT DEPENDING ON AGE

13.7 The rules for people aged 60+ (or whose partner is) are different from those for people aged under 60 (and whose partner is). Whilst the two sets of regulations frequently produce the same effect, there are some differences (e.g. the amount of disregard for income from (sub-)tenants: table 13.2). The rules and differences are given at the relevant places in the remainder of this and the next two chapters.

HB60+ 28
NIHB60+ 26
CTB60+ 18

13.8 In particular the approach to which types of income do and do not count in the assessment of HB/CTB is different for the two age groups:

HB 31(1)
HB60+ 29(1)
NIHB 28(1)
NIHB60+ 29(1)
CTB 21(1)
CTB60+ 19(1)

- if the claimant or any partner is aged 60+, nothing counts as income unless the law says it does (an approach which suits computers);
- if the claimant and any partner are under 60, everything counts as income unless the law says it does not (an approach which makes it pointless to create imaginative new kinds of income).

WHEN A CLAIMANT IS TREATED AS HAVING A NON-DEPENDANT'S INCOME AND CAPITAL

13.9 A special rule applies if:

HB 26
HB60+ 24
NIHB 23
NIHB60+ 22
CTB 16
CTB60+ 14

- it appears to the authority that the claimant and non-dependant have entered into arrangements to take advantage of the HB or CTB scheme; and
- the non-dependant has both more income and more capital than the claimant; and
- the claimant is not on JSA(IB), IS or guarantee credit.

13.10 The rule in such cases is that:

- the claimant is treated as having the income and capital of the non-dependant; and
- the claimant's own income and capital is completely disregarded.

For the purposes of considering the amount (if any) of the non-dependant deduction, the non-dependant is treated as having his or her own income and capital (not the income and capital of the claimant).

Definitions and general matters

DISTINGUISHING CAPITAL FROM INCOME

13.11 The distinction between income and capital is usually straightforward. Typical examples of each are given in table 13.1. If a difficulty arises in deciding whether a payment is income or capital, the DWP advises (GM paras. C2.20-22): 'As a general rule, capital includes all categories of holdings which have a clear monetary value... A payment of capital can normally be distinguished from income because it is (i) made without being tied to a period, and (ii) made without being tied to any past payment, and (iii) not intended to form part of a series of payments.'

In a recent case, a commissioner has confirmed that the HB/CTB regulations do not (except in the case of income for 60+s: para. 13.8) provide a definition of income or capital; instead the regulations 'operate at the stage after the money has been classified' *(CH/1561/2005)*. In considering how income can turn into capital, the commissioner (agreeing with *R(SB) 2/83* and *R(IS) 3/93*) held that this happens as follows: 'A payment of income is treated as income when received. It remains income for the period in which it is paid. Any surplus remaining at the end of that period metamorphoses [changes] into capital.' (The case was about certain social security benefits but probably applies equally to other regular payments of income: para. 13.93.)

WHICH TYPES OF INCOME AND CAPITAL COUNT

13.12 As described in the later parts of this chapter, some types of income and capital are wholly disregarded; some are partly disregarded; and some are counted in full (table 13.1). Also, in some cases a claimant can be treated as having income or capital he or she does not in fact possess: this is known as 'notional' income or capital (para. 13.132).

Table 13.1: Examples of capital and income

CAPITAL WHICH IS (WHOLLY OR PARTLY) TAKEN INTO ACCOUNT FOR HB/MAIN CTB PURPOSES

- Savings in a bank, building society, etc
- National Savings Certificates, stocks and shares
- Property (unless it falls within one of the numerous disregards)
- Redundancy pay (with some exceptions)
- Tax refunds

CAPITAL WHICH IS DISREGARDED FOR HB/MAIN CTB PURPOSES

- The home a claimant owns and lives in
- A self-employed claimant's business assets
- Arrears of certain state benefits
- Certain compensation payments
- A life insurance policy which has not been cashed in

INCOME WHICH IS (WHOLLY OR PARTLY) TAKEN INTO ACCOUNT FOR HB/MAIN CTB PURPOSES

- Earnings from a job or from self-employment
- Pensions
- Certain state benefits (e.g. contribution-based jobseeker's allowance, retirement pension)
- Rent received from a sub-tenant or boarder in the claimant's home
- Tariff income from capital

INCOME WHICH IS DISREGARDED FOR HB/MAIN CTB PURPOSES

- Reimbursement of expenses wholly incurred in the course of a job
- Certain state benefits (e.g. disability living allowance, attendance allowance)
- Charitable or voluntary payments
- Payments (e.g. 'keep') received from a non-dependant
- Fostering payments

These examples are simplified. The detailed rules are given later in this chapter.

WHY CAPITAL IS ASSESSED

HB 43,52
HB60+ 29(2),43
NIHB 40,49
NIHB60+ 27(2),41
CTB 33,42
CTB60+ 19(2),33

13.13 A claimant's capital is first assessed under the rules in this chapter, then taken into account as follows:

- if it amounts to more than £16,000, the claimant is not entitled to HB or main CTB at all; otherwise
- the first £6,000 is completely ignored in the assessment of HB and main CTB (before 1st April 2006, this figure was £3,000 for under 60s);
- the remainder up to £16,000 is treated as generating 'tariff income' (para. 13.14).

The £6,000 and £16,000 figures are called the 'lower capital limit' and 'upper capital limit'. (See para. 13.15 for when the lower capital limit can be a different figure.)

13.14 'Tariff income' is assessed as follows (and illustrated in the examples):

- deduct £6,000 from the total amount of assessed capital;
- then divide the remainder by 250 if the claimant and any partner are aged under 60, but 500 if the claimant or any partner is aged 60+;
- then, if the result is not an exact multiple of £1, round the result up to the next whole £1. This is the claimant's weekly tariff income.

HB 52
HB60+ 29(2)
NIHB 43
NIHB60+ 27(2)
CTB 42
CTB60+ 19(2)

13.15 In HB only, the lower capital limit is £10,000 (instead of £6,000) in the following types of residential accommodation:

- a care home or independent hospital (in Scotland, care home services) where the claimant has pre-1993 preserved rights (paras. 2.21 and 2.23);
- local authority Part III accommodation (in Northern Ireland, accommodation provided by the Health and Social Services Board) so long as board is not provided (paras. 2.22-23);
- an unregistered Abbeyfield Home;
- accommodation which is not a care home (in Scotland, care home services), but is provided together with both board and personal care under an Act of Parliament or Royal Charter. This can apply, for example, to accommodation provided by the Salvation Army (para. 2.23) or under the Polish Resettlement Act.

13.16 For HB for people aged 60+, the £10,000 lower capital limit continues regardless of absences of up to 52 weeks from such accommodation (or, in the case of Polish Resettlement Act accommodation, up to 13 weeks, so long as the person, with the consent of the manager, intends to return). For under-60s, there is no similar rule.

13.17 In CTB there is never a £10,000 lower capital limit because a resident in the above types of accommodation cannot be liable for council tax.

Examples: Calculating tariff income

CLAIMANT UNDER 60

A single claimant aged 59 is a home owner and has capital, assessed under the rules in this chapter, of £8,085.93.

This first £6,000 is disregarded, leaving a remainder of £2,085.93. Divide the remainder by 250 and round the answer up to the next whole £1. The claimant has tariff income of £9.

CLAIMANT AGED 60+

A single claimant aged 61 is a council tenant and has capital, assessed under the rules in this chapter, of £8,085.93.

This first £6,000 is disregarded, leaving a remainder of £2,085.93. Divide the remainder by 500 and round the answer up to the next whole £1. The claimant has tariff income of £5.

HOW CAPITAL IS ASSESSED

13.18 The whole of a claimant's capital is taken into account, including certain types of income which are counted as capital, but excluding capital which is disregarded. The general rules about how capital is valued are given below. Other rules about this, about which types of income are counted as capital, and about which types of capital are disregarded, are mentioned in the relevant places in this chapter. Authorities may seek the assistance of the Valuation Office Agency in London in valuing capital items such as dwellings or other property. Forms authorities may use for this purpose appear in the Guidance Manual (chapter C2 annex E). HB 44 HB60+ 44 NIHB 41 NIHB60+ 42 CTB 34 CTB60+ 34

VALUING CAPITAL IN GENERAL

13.19 The following rule applies whenever a property, shares, or anything else (except for national savings certificates: para. 13.95) has to be valued for HB/main CTB purposes. Other parts of this chapter mention considerations that also have to be taken into account for specific items. The rule has three steps: HB 47(a) HB60+ 45(a) NIHB 44(a) NIHB60+ 43(a) CTB 37(a) CTB60+ 35(a)

- take the current market or surrender value of the capital item;
- then disregard 10% if selling it would involve costs;
- then disregard any mortgage or other 'encumbrance' (e.g. a loan) secured on it.

In practice, a claimant's capital is usually valued at his or her date of claim and revalued only if there is a reasonably large change. But it should be revalued whenever there is a change which affects entitlement to HB/CTB.

VALUING JOINTLY HELD CAPITAL

HB 51
HB60+ 49
NIHB 48
NIHB60+ 47
CTB 41
CTB60+ 39

13.20 The following rule applies when a capital item (e.g. a property) is held jointly by two or more people. An example is given below:

- first assume that all the joint owners own an equal share in the capital item;
- then value the person's resulting assumed share (as in para. 13.19) and count that as his or her capital.

It was held in an income support case, which is persuasive for HB and CTB purposes, that the above rule does not apply when an item is held in distinct, known shares (e.g. one person holds a one-third share and the other a two-thirds share) and that in such cases the actual share should be valued (as in para. 13.19) and counted as the person's capital *(Secretary of State for Work and Pensions v Hourigan)*.

Examples: Valuing capital

SHARES WHOLLY OWNED BY A CLAIMANT

A claimant owns 1,000 shares in a company. The sell price is currently £0.50 each.

For HB/main CTB purposes, from the current market value (1,000 x £0.50 = £500) deduct 10% (£50) giving £450. Assuming no loan or other incumbrance is secured on the shares, the value for HB/main CTB purposes is therefore £450.

A JOINTLY OWNED PROPERTY

A claimant and her sister inherit some land from their father. In his will, he stipulated that it was a joint inheritance. The land has recently been valued by the Valuation Office Agency, and the authority accepts their valuations, which are as follows:

- if the whole of the land was sold, it would fetch £10,000;
- if a half-share in the land was sold, the half-share would fetch only £4,000 (because of certain covenants which affect the use of the land).

The claimant has recently taken out a loan for £2,000 using the land as security (and none of the loan has yet been repaid).

For HB/main CTB purposes, the claimant's share of the capital in the land is valued as follows:

- first the claimant is treated as owning half of the land;
- then this half share is valued. Using the Valuation Office Agency's figure, the authority values the half share at £4,000;

- then 10% is deducted towards sales costs: £4,000 minus £400 leaves £3,600;
- then the claimant's loan is deducted: £3,600 minus £2,000 leaves £1,600.

So for HB/main CTB purposes, the claimant has capital of £1,600 (plus any other capital she may have).

WHY INCOME IS ASSESSED

13.21 A claimant's earned and unearned income, assessed under the rules described in this chapter and chapters 14 and 15, is compared with his or her applicable amount in calculating how much HB or main CTB he or she is entitled to (paras. 7.8-11).

HOW INCOME IS ASSESSED

13.22 The whole of a claimant's income is taken into account (though for people aged 60+, what counts as income in the first place is limited: paras. 13.7-8), including tariff income from capital (para. 13.14) and certain types of capital which are counted as income, but excluding income which is disregarded. General points about income are given below. Other rules about this, about which types of capital are counted as income, and about which types of income are disregarded in whole or in part, are mentioned in the relevant places in this chapter. HB 27,31,40 HB60+ 30 NIHB 24,28,37 NIHB60+ 28 CTB 17,21,30 CTB60+ 20

13.23 The HB and main CTB rules distinguish earned income (i.e. earnings received by employed earners or by the self-employed) from unearned income (e.g. pensions, benefits, rent received by the claimant, and so on). Chapter 14 deals with earnings from a job, chapter 15 with self-employed earnings. The rules about unearned income are in this chapter.

DECIDING WHICH WEEKS INCOME BELONGS TO

13.24 The general objective for HB/main CTB purposes is '[calculating or] estimating the amount which is likely to be [the claimant's] average weekly income'. However, there are many specific rules and these are given in this and the next two chapters as they arise. Where there is no specific rule, it is usually straightforward to decide according to the facts of the case which week or weeks a claimant's income belongs to for HB/main CTB purposes. HB 27(1) HB60+ 30(1) NIHB 24(1) NIHB60+ 28(1) CTB 17(1) CTB60+ 20(1)

ARREARS OF INCOME

13.25 In broad terms, it is usually the case that if a claimant receives arrears of income, then those arrears are treated as being income belonging to the week or weeks to which they relate (except to the extent that they are income which is HB 31(2),79(6),(7) NIHB 28(2),76(8),(9) CTB 21(2),67(8),(9) disregarded). It is because of this that certain arrears of income are disregarded as capital (*CH/1561/2005,* and see para. 13.11). Exceptions to this and further specific rules are given in this and the next chapter as they arise.

INCOME TAX

HB sch 5 para 1
HB60+ 33(12)
NIHB sch 6 para 1
NIHB60+ 31(11)
CTB sch 4 para 1
CTB60+ 23(12)

13.26 The income tax payable on any kind of income, even income not listed elsewhere in this guide, is disregarded in the assessment of that income.

CONVERTING INCOME TO A WEEKLY FIGURE

13.27 For HB/main CTB purposes, income must be converted (if necessary) to a weekly figure. The details are given in paragraph 7.43.

State benefits, tax credits, pensions, etc

13.28 This section gives the rules about the assessment for HB/main CTB purposes of state benefits and tax credits, state, war and other pensions, and other payments from state, local authority and related sources. Paragraphs 13.29-34 give general rules, paragraphs 13.35 onwards give rules for individual benefits.

STATE BENEFITS: GENERAL RULE FOR CURRENT PAYMENTS

HB 31(1)
HB60+ 29(1)
NIHB 28(1)
NIHB60+ 27(1)
CTB 21(1)
CTB60+ 19(1)

13.29 Except when indicated, state social security benefits and pensions are counted in full as unearned income. All the following are counted in full:

- working tax credit;
- child tax credit (but see also paras. 13.44-45);
- child benefit (but see also para. 13.43);
- maternity allowance;
- carer's allowance (but see also para 13.53);
- contribution-based jobseeker's allowance;
- incapacity benefit and severe disablement allowance;
- industrial injuries benefit;
- retirement pensions;
- bereavement allowance, including widow's pensions.

HB 31(2)
HB60+ 33(6)
NIHB 28(2)
NIHB60+ 31(6)
CTB 21(2)
CTB60+ 23(6)

Except in the case of working tax credit and child tax credit (para. 13.44), the period over which these are taken into account is 'the period in which that benefit is payable'.

Example: Arrears of incapacity benefit

A claimant, who has been receiving HB and main CTB for many years, has been receiving incapacity benefit since January 2005. It has been taken into account as her income for HB/main CTB purposes from that date. In June 2006, following a successful appeal, she is paid arrears of incapacity benefit for the period from September 2004 to January 2005.

The arrears are her income for the period from September 2004 to January 2005. The authority may therefore reassess her entitlement to HB /main CTB for that period, which may result in an overpayment (chapter 18).

STATE BENEFITS: GENERAL RULE FOR ARREARS

13.30 Except when indicated in the following paragraphs (and there are many exceptions: see in particular para. 13.31), arrears of state benefits and pensions are counted as unearned income for the period they cover and there is no disregard of their capital value.

HB 79(7)
HB60+ 33(6)
NIHB 76(9)
NIHB60+ 31(6)
CTB 67(9)
CTB60+ 23(6)

STATE BENEFITS: LARGE ARREARS DUE TO OFFICIAL ERROR

13.31 In the case of several benefits (e.g. DLA: para 13.36), arrears are disregarded as capital for 52 weeks from the date of payment. In those cases (and they are identified throughout this section as they arise), there is a lengthened disregard if:

- the underpayment was due to official error; and
- the amount of the arrears is £5,000 or more; and
- the award of the arrears is made on or after 14th October 2002.

In such cases, the arrears are then disregarded (if this would be longer than the 52 weeks) for as long as the claimant or any partner remain continuously entitled to HB/CTB (including periods for which the partner remains continuously entitled after the claimant's death).

HB sch 6 para 9
HB60+ sch 6
paras 18,21,22
NIHB sch 7 para 9
NIHB60+ sch 7
paras 18,21,22
CTB sch 5 para 9
CTB60+ sch 4
paras 18,21,22

REDUCED STATE BENEFITS

13.32 If the amount of a state benefit received by a claimant has been reduced due to a Child Support Agency 'reduced benefit direction' (or if the claimant or any partner is aged 60+, due to a reduction for hospitalisation), the net amount (i.e. after the reduction) is counted as unearned income. Similarly, if it is reduced due to the overlapping social security benefit rules, the net amount is counted as unearned income (a rule which is laid down in the law only if the claimant or any partner is aged 60+, but must logically be true for all age groups).

HB 40(5)
HB60+ 29(3),(4)
NIHB 37(3)
NIHB60+ 27(3),(4)
CTB 30(5)
CTB60+ 19(3),(4)

However (except as in para. 13.33) if the amount of a state benefit received by a claimant has been reduced for any other reason (for example, in order to recover a previous overpayment), the gross amount (i.e. before the reduction) is counted as unearned income.

REDUCED TAX CREDITS

HB 2(1),40(6)
NIHB 2(1),37(4)
CTB 2(1),30(6)

13.33 If the amount of working tax credit (WTC) or child tax credit (CTC) (para. 13.44) has been reduced to recover an overpayment which arose in a previous tax year, the net amount of WTC or CTC (i.e. after the deduction) is counted as unearned income. Apart from that, reduced amounts of WTC and CTC are dealt with as above (para. 13.32).

INCREASES IN STATE BENEFITS FOR DEPENDANTS

HB sch 5 para 52
HB60+ 29(1)(j)
NIHB sch 6 para 54
NIHB60+ 27(1)(h)
CTB sch 4 para 52
CTB60+ 19(1)(j)

13.34 With some state benefits, an increase can be added for a dependent partner, or other dependent adult(s) or child(ren). These are dealt with as follows:

- If the claimant and any partner are under 60, count an increase as unearned income if the benefit it is paid with counts as unearned income – unless the dependant is not a member of the family (para. 4.7), in which case disregard it.
- If the claimant or any partner is aged 60+, count the increase as unearned income if it is for a partner: all other increases are disregarded.

HB 2(1), sch 5 paras 6-9,50
HB60+ 2(1),29(1)(j), sch 6 para 21
NIHB 2(1), sch 6 paras 6-9,52
NIHB60+ 2(1),27(1)(h)
CTB 2(1), sch 4 paras 7-10
CTB60+ 2(1),19(1)(j), sch 4 para 21

DISABILITY LIVING ALLOWANCE AND OTHER BENEFITS FOR ATTENDANCE AND MOBILITY

13.35 Current payments of the following are disregarded in full as income:

- disability living allowance;
- attendance allowance and constant attendance allowance;
- exceptionally severe disablement allowance;
- severe disablement occupational allowance; and
- payments compensating for non-receipt of the above.

HB sch 6 para 9
NIHB sch 7 para 9
CTB sch 5 para 9

13.36 Arrears of the above are disregarded in full as income. They are also disregarded as capital for 52 weeks from the date of payment, or longer for some large awards of arrears (para. 13.31).

HB sch 5 para 43, sch 6 para 39
HB60+ 29(1)(d)-(f), sch 6 paras 21,22
NIHB sch 6 para 46, sch 7 para 39
NIHB60+ 27(1)
CTB sch 4 para 44, sch 5 para 39
CTB60+ 19(1)(d)-(f), sch 4 paras 21,22

'PRE-1973' WAR WIDOW'S AND WAR WIDOWER'S PENSIONS

13.37 There are special payments paid to 'pre-1973' war widows, widowers and surviving civil partners, the amount, from April 2006, being £68.42 per week. If the claimant or any partner is aged 60+, these payments are assessed in the same way as in paragraph 13.39. If the claimant and any partner are under 60:

- current payments are disregarded in full as income;
- arrears of such payments are disregarded in full as income;
- arrears are also disregarded as capital for 52 weeks from the date of payment, or longer for some large overpayments (para. 13.31). The same applies to payments compensating for non-receipt of such pensions.

OTHER PENSIONS FOR BEREAVEMENT AND DISABLEMENT

13.38 The following rules apply to:

(a) war widow's, war widower's and war disablement pensions, war pensions for surviving civil partners, and also guaranteed income payments under the Armed Forces and Reserve Forces Compensation Scheme;

(b) payments to compensate for non-payment of those;

(c) analogous payments from Governments outside the UK.

HB sch 5 paras 15,52-54
HB60+ 29(1), sch 5 paras 1-6, sch 6 paras 21,22
NIHB sch 6 paras 13,14,55-57
NIHB60+ 27(1), sch 6 paras 1-7
CTB sch 4 paras 16,52-54
CTB60+ 19(1), sch 3 paras 1-6, sch 4 paras 21,22

13.39 In Northern Ireland, all the above are disregarded in full as income. In England, Wales and Scotland, disregard as income:

- if the claimant or partner is aged 60+, all amounts granted for constant attendance or exceptionally severe disablement;
- regardless of age, any other amounts for attendance or mobility; and
- in all cases, £10.00 per week (subject to the rules on aggregation in para. 13.148; and see also para. 13.42).

13.40 In Northern Ireland, arrears of these payments are disregarded in full as income. In England, Wales and Scotland, they are counted as unearned income for the period they cover apart from the £10.00 per week disregard.

13.41 Arrears of amounts granted for constant attendance or exceptionally severe disablement are also disregarded as capital for 52 weeks from the date of payment, or longer for some large overpayments (para. 13.31). The same applies to payments compensating for non-receipt of such amounts.

13.42 It should be noted that many councils in England, Wales and Scotland operate a 'local scheme' whereby a larger amount or all of war widows', war widowers' and war disablement pensions, and war pensions for surviving civil partners, (para. 13.38(a)) are disregarded currently and/or in arrears (para. 22.10). See also the rules for second world war payments, etc (para. 13.148).

CHILD BENEFIT AND GUARDIAN'S ALLOWANCE

13.43 If the claimant and any partner are under 60, child benefit counts in full as income (para. 13.29) but guardian's allowance is disregarded. If the claimant or any partner is aged 60+, both are disregarded.

HB sch 5 para 50
HB60+ 29(1)(j)
NIHB sch 6 par 52
NIHB60+ 29(1)(h)
CTB sch 4 para 51
CTB60+ 19(1)(j)

WORKING TAX CREDIT AND CHILD TAX CREDIT

HB 2(1),27(1),(2), 32,34(e),46(9), sch 5 para 56, sch 6 para 9
HB60+29(1)(b), 32,44(3), sch 5 para 21
NIHB 2(1),24(1),(2), 29,31(e),43(8), sch 6 para 58, sch 7 para 9
NIHB60+ 27(1)(b), 30,42(3), sch 6 para 22
CTB 2(1),17(1),(2), 22,24(e),36(9), sch 3 para 56, sch 4 para 9
CTB60+ 19(1)(b), 22,34(3), sch 3 para 21

13.44 Working tax credit (WTC) and child tax credit (CTC) are assessed as follows for HB/CTB purposes. If the claimant or any partner is aged 60+, CTC is disregarded (but WTC is counted) as unearned income. For under 60s, both are counted as unearned income. In each case, the period over which they are taken into account is simply the period they cover, as follows:

(a) in the case of a daily instalment, the one day in respect of which it is paid;

(b) in the case of a weekly instalment, the period of seven days ending on the day on which it is due to be paid;

(c) in the case of a two-weekly instalment, the period of 14 days commencing six days before the day on which the instalment is due to be paid (because two-weekly instalments of WTC/CTC are due at the end of the first week of the two weeks they cover);

(d) in the case of a four-weekly instalment, the period of 28 days ending on the day on which it is due to be paid.

There are four further rules for special circumstances:

- If WTC/CTC are reduced (e.g. to recover an overpayment) see paragraphs 13.32-33.
- Legislative changes in the amount of WTC/CTC (such as the April up-rating) may be disregarded for up to 30 benefit weeks.
- Certain recipients of WTC qualify for a disregard from their earnings of £14.90 per week (para. 14.30). If (uncommonly) their earnings are insufficient for this £14.90 disregard to be made in full from them (as described in para. 14.32), £14.90 is instead disregarded from their WTC.
- Certain claimants with child care costs qualify for a disregard from their earnings (para. 14.21). If (uncommonly) their earnings are insufficient for this disregard to be made in full from them, any balance of the disregard is made from their WTC.

13.45 The way arrears of WTC and CTC are assessed for HB/CTB purposes has changed this year (from 1st and 3rd April 2006), and is now much simpler. Such arrears are never counted as income; and are disregarded as capital for 52 weeks from the date of payment, or longer for some large overpayments (para. 13.31). (The effect of this rule is that the arrears themselves cannot create an overpayment of HB/CTB.) The same rule applies to predecessor benefits (working families' tax credit, disabled person's tax credit, family credit, disability working allowance and family income supplement) and payments compensating for non-payment of any of these items.

JSA(IB), IS, HB, CTB AND PENSION CREDIT

13.46 Current payments of:

- savings credit count in full as unearned income – but there are special rules for assessing HB/CTB from anyone on savings credit (paras. 13.150-159);
- guarantee credit, JSA(IB), IS, HB and CTB are not counted as income.

13.47 Arrears of all the above benefits are never counted as income; and are disregarded as capital for 52 weeks from the date of payment, or longer for some large overpayments (para. 13.31). The same rule applies to predecessor benefits (community charge benefit, housing benefit supplement and supplementary benefit) and payments compensating for non-payment of any of these items.

It is worth noting that the further rules about the date an award, change or end of entitlement to pension credit takes effect can also operate in a way that effectively causes payments of pension credit to be disregarded as income (para. 17.27 and table 17.5).

HB sch 5 paras 4,7, 36,37,40,48,51, sch 6 paras 5,9, 29,30,36
HB60+ 29(1)(j),44(3), sch 5 paras 21,22
NIHB sch 6 paras 4,5,39,40,43,53, sch 7 paras 5,6,36,37
NIHB60+ 27(1)(h),42(30, sch 6 paras 22,25
CTB sch 4 paras 4,8,38,39,49 sch 5 paras 9,29,30,36,37
CTB60+ 19(1)(j),34(3), sch 3 paras 21,22

CERTAIN FORMER SUPPORTING PEOPLE CLAIMANTS

13.48 The whole of a claimant's unearned income is disregarded if he or she lost entitlement to JSA(IB) or IS on 1st April 2003, and the only reason for this was that the assessment of his or her JSA(IB) or IS no longer included support charges because they became payable by Supporting People (para. 10.103). This applies only if the claimant and any partner are under 60, only to CTB and HB for rates in Northern Ireland (but not to HB for rent anywhere in the UK), and is rare.

CTB sch 4 para 6
NIHB sch 6

DISCRETIONARY HOUSING PAYMENTS

13.49 Discretionary housing payments (para. 22.2) are disregarded in full as income; and are disregarded as capital for 52 weeks from the date of payment, or longer for some large overpayments (para. 13.31).

HB sch 5 para 62, sch 6 para 9
HB60+ 29(1), sch 6 para 21
NIHB sch 6 para 62, sch 7 para 9
NIHB60+ 27(1) sch 7 para 21
CTB sch 4 para 62, sch 5 para 9
CTB60+ 19(1) sch 4 para 21

WIDOWED MOTHER'S ALLOWANCE AND WIDOWED PARENT'S ALLOWANCE

13.50 From current payments of these benefits, disregard £15 per week (subject to the rules on aggregation in para. 13.147). Arrears of these payments are counted as unearned income for the period they cover apart from the £15.00 per week disregard and there is no disregard of the capital value of arrears.

HB sch 5 para 16
HB60+ sch 5 paras 7,8
NIHB sch 6 para 15
NIHB60+ sch 6 paras 8,9
CTB sch 4 para 17
CTB60+ sch 3 paras 7,8

BEREAVEMENT PAYMENT

13.51 Bereavement payment is a lump-sum, one-off payment and so counts as capital (not income).

HB60+ 29(1)(j)
NIHB60+ 27(1)(h)
CTB60+ 19(1)(j)

STATUTORY SICK, MATERNITY, PATERNITY AND ADOPTION PAY

HB 35(1)(i)
HB60+ 29(1)(j)
NIHB 32(1)(i)
NIHB60+ 27(1)(h)
CTB 25(1)(i)
CTB60+ 19(1)(j)

13.52 Statutory sick, maternity, paternity and adoption pay count as earnings (as described in para. 14.52). There is no disregard of the capital value of arrears of any of these items.

CARER'S ALLOWANCE

HB60+ sch 6 paras 21,22
NIHB60+ sch 7 paras 21,22
CTB60+ sch 3 paras 21,22

13.53 Carer's allowance counts in full as unearned income. If the claimant or any partner is aged 60+, arrears are disregarded as capital for 52 weeks from the date of payment. If the claimant and any partner are under 60, there is no disregard of the capital value of arrears.

AGE-RELATED PAYMENTS; CHRISTMAS BONUS

HB sch 5 para 32
HB60+ 29(1)(j)
NIHB sch 6 para 34
NIHB60+ 27(1)(h)
CTB sch 4 para 33
CTB60+ 19(1)(j)
SI 2005/1983 reg 8(b)

13.54 The lump-sum 'age-related payments' of £50, £100 or £200, which were introduced in late 2005 to help people aged 65+ pay their council tax or meet other household costs, are wholly disregarded for all HB/CTB purposes. The 'Christmas bonus' of £10, which is awarded each year to certain people, is disregarded as income.

FOSTERING, BOARDING OUT AND RESPITE CARE PAYMENTS

HB sch 5 paras 26,27
HB60+ 29(1)
NIHB sch 6 paras 27,28
NIHB60+ 27(1)
CTB sch 4 paras 27,28
CTB60+ 19(1)

13.55 If the claimant or any partner is aged 60+ disregard all such payments in full as income: there are no further conditions. If the claimant and any partner are under 60, disregard these payments in full as income if they are received from a local authority or voluntary organisation or (in the case of respite care payments) a primary care trust; and also disregard (in the case of respite care payments), contributions required from the person cared for.

ADOPTION AND CUSTODIANSHIP ALLOWANCES

HB 2(1), sch 5 para 25
HB60+ 29(1)
NIHB 2(1), sch 6 para 25
NIHB60+ 27(1)
CTB sch 4 para 26
CTB60+ 19(1)

13.56 If the claimant or partner is aged 60+ disregard all such payments in full as income: there are no further conditions. If the claimant and partner are under 60:

- disregard any amount in excess of the dependant's allowance and any disabled child premium for the child or young person concerned; and
- count any balance as unearned income.

COMMUNITY CARE, SPECIAL GUARDIANSHIP AND OTHER SOCIAL SERVICES PAYMENTS

HB sch 5 paras 26,28,57,
ch 6 paras 19,58-60
HB60+ 29(1)
NIHB sch 6 paras 27,29,50,
ch 7 paras 19,55-59
NIHB60+ 27(1)
CTB sch 4 paras 27,28,57,
sch 5 paras 19,62
CTB60+ 19(1)

13.57 If the claimant or partner is aged 60+ disregard all such payments in full (as income): there are no further conditions. If the claimant and partner are under 60, disregard in full (both as income and capital):

- any social services payment made for the purposes of avoiding taking children into care or to children and young persons who are leaving or have left care;

- any special guardianship payment (for support services); and
- any social services community care payment.

HB sch 5 para 63, sch 6 para 57
HB60+ 29(1)
NIHB sch 6 para 63, sch 7 para 54
NIHB60+ 27(1)
CTB sch 4 para 63, sch 5 para 59
CTB60+ 19(1)

SUPPORTING PEOPLE PAYMENTS

13.58 Supporting people payments (usually administered by social services to assist people with certain support costs in their home) are disregarded in full as income.

HB sch 5 para 31, sch 6 para 20
HB60+ 29(1)
NIHB sch 6 para 33, sch 7 para 20
NIHB60+ 27(1)
CTB sch 4 para 33, sch 5 para 20
CTB60+ 19(1)

SOCIAL FUND PAYMENTS AND LOANS

13.59 Disregard payments and loans from the social fund in full (both as income and capital) – including winter fuel payments.

THE MACFARLANE TRUSTS, THE FUND, THE EILEEN TRUST, THE INDEPENDENT LIVING FUNDS, THE SKIPTON FUND

HB 2(1), sch 5 para 35, sch 6 paras 24,34
HB60+ 29(1)
NIHB 2(1), sch 6 para 38, sch 7 paras 24,34
NIHB60+ 27(1)
CTB sch 4 para 36, sch 5 paras 24,34
CTB 60+ 19(1)

13.60 The Macfarlane Trust, the Macfarlane (Special Payments) Trust, the Macfarlane (Special Payments) (No. 2) Trust, 'the Fund', and the Eileen Trust were all set up to assist certain people with HIV. The Independent Living Fund, the Independent Living (Extension) Fund, and the Independent Living (1993) Fund were all set up to enable severely disabled people to live independently. The Skipton Fund was set up to assist certain people with hepatitis C. Any payment from any of these is disregarded in full (both as capital and income). Payments in kind from any of these are also disregarded. If money from any of these is passed on to a third party, it is usually also disregarded in the assessment of the third party's income and capital (and always disregarded if that third party or his or her partner is aged 60+).

HB sch 6 para 55
HB60+ sch 6 para 14
NIHB sch 7 para 51
NIHB60+ sch 7 para 14
CTB sch 5 para 57
CTB60+ sch 4 para 14

THE CREUTZFELDT-JACOB DISEASE TRUST

13.61 Disregard payments to sufferers of variant Creutzfeldt-Jacob disease and their families (as capital).

THE NEW DEAL AND OTHER GOVERNMENT TRAINING SCHEMES

HB 2(1),46(7), sch 5 paras 13,49, 58,60,61
sch 6 paras 8,35, 43,44,49
HB60+ 29(1)
NIHB 2(1),43(7), sch 6 paras 12,51,6[illegible]
sch 7 paras 8,35,4[illegible]
NIHB60+ 27(1)
CTB 2(1),36(7), sch 4 paras 14,50, 58,60,61,
sch 5 paras 8,35,4[illegible] 45,51
CTB60+ 19(1)

13.62 The following is about payments received by people on the New Deal or on other schemes run by the DWP. There are three possibilities in the assessment of HB/CTB:

- If the claimant or any partner is aged 60+, all such payments are disregarded as income: there are no further conditions; but if they form part of the claimant's capital (which is improbable) they count as capital.
- In most other cases, people on such schemes remain entitled to JSA(IB) or IS, so their income and capital are disregarded.
- In any other case, the income and capital is assessed as in paragraph 13.64.

13.63 The full details of the assessment depend on the nature of the training scheme concerned. More detail may be found in DWP guidance (GM paras C3.583-601 and circular HB/CTB A6/2004).

13.64 The main rules are as follows:

- Payments on the New Deal and similar schemes are ignored as income unless they are made as a substitute for JSA(IB), IS, IB or SDA, or are for basic day-to-day maintenance.
- Training grants under the New Deal 50-plus Employment Credit Scheme are disregarded as capital for 52 weeks from the date of payment.
- Access to Work payments (to enable disabled people to gain or retain employment) and payments under the Blind Homeworkers' Scheme are disregarded as both income and capital.
- Earnings received whilst undergoing Work Based Training for Young People, Work Based Training for Adults, Training for Work or Community Action, are counted as earnings in the normal way (chapter 14).
- Payments on the Employment Retention and Advancement Scheme, the Return to Work Credit Scheme, the Lone Parent Work Search Scheme, the Lone Parent In-work Credit Scheme, and most other schemes under section 2 of the Employment and Training Act 1973, the Enterprise and New Towns (Scotland) Act 1990 or, in Northern Ireland, the Employment and Training Act (Northern Ireland) 1950, are disregarded both as income and as capital.

CAREER DEVELOPMENT LOANS

HB 41(4)
HB60+ 29(1)
CTB 31(4)
CTB60+ 19(1)

13.65 In Great Britain only, career development loans are paid under arrangements between the DWP and national banks. If the claimant or any partner is aged 60+, they are disregarded as income. If the claimant and any partner are under 60, they count in full as income.

HEALTH BENEFITS AND PRISON VISITS PAYMENTS

HB sch 5 paras 44-46, sch 6 paras 40-42
HB60+ 29(1)
NIHB sch 6 paras 47-49, sch 7 paras 40-42
NIHB60+ 27(1)
CTB sch 4 paras 45-47, sch 5 paras 40-42
CTB60+ 19(1)

13.66 If the claimant or any partner is aged 60+, all the following payments are disregarded in full as income, but arrears are not disregarded as capital. If the claimant and any partner are under 60, all the following are disregarded in full as unearned income and also disregarded as capital for 52 weeks from the date of payment:

- payments for travel for hospital visits;
- health service supplies or payments in lieu of free milk and vitamins;
- Home Office payments for travel for prison visits.

STATE RETIREMENT PENSION: PAYMENTS AND DEFERRAL

13.67 State retirement pension counts in full as income. Since 6th April 2006, a person who chooses to defer their state retirement pension can choose between a lump sum now, or increased payments later, and can change their mind about this (subject to conditions). The law is peculiar but appears to mean that the amount of a lump sum is disregarded as capital (until and unless the person opts to have increased payments rather than a lump sum). Increased payments count in full as income.

SI 2005/2677
NISR 2006 No 104

OCCUPATIONAL AND PERSONAL PENSIONS

13.68 These count in full as unearned income, after deducting tax. However, disregard as capital any amount held in a pension scheme and the value of the right to receive money from it (para. 13.91).

Payments under the Pension Protection Fund are counted as unearned income (and for 60+s this is because of the definition of 'retirement pension income'). These are government payments to people who have lost out on their occupational pension scheme because it was under-funded when it began to be wound up and because the employer is now insolvent or has ceased to exist (and so cannot make up the shortfall).

HB 35(2),40(10), sch 5 para 1, sch 6 para 31
HB60+ 29(1)(x),33(12), sch 6 para 24
NIHB 32(2),37(8), sch 6 para 1, sch 7 para 31
NIHB60+ 27(1)(v),37(11), sch 7 para 24
CTB 25(2),30(11), sch 4 para 1, sch 5 para 31
CTB60+ 19(1)(x),23(12), sch 5 para 24

The home, property and possessions

13.69 This section is about how things the claimant owns affect his or her entitlement to HB and main CTB, including the home, a former or future home, other property and rent received by the claimant.

HOMES AND OTHER PROPERTY

13.70 The claimant's current, former or future home can be disregarded and so can a home or other property (including non-domestic property) which the claimant has never occupied, if the conditions in the following paragraphs apply. The disregards described below can apply one after another, so long as the relevant conditions are met (as illustrated in the example).

THE CLAIMANT'S HOME

13.71 Disregard the capital value of the dwelling normally occupied as the claimant's home, and any land or buildings (including in Scotland croft land) which are part of it or are impracticable to sell separately. There is no time limit. This disregard is limited to one home per claim but see the other headings below.

HB sch 6 para 1
HB60+ 2(1) sch 6 para 26
NIHB sch 7 para 1
NIHB60+ 2(1), sch 7 para 27
CTB sch 5 para 1
CTB 60+ 4 para 2

A RELATIVE'S HOME

HB sch 6 para 4(a)
HB60+ sch 6 para 4(a)
NIHB sch 7 para 4(a)
NIHB60+ sch 7 para 4(a)
CTB sch 5 para 4(a)
CTB60+ sch 4 para 4(a)

13.72 Disregard the capital value of the home of a partner or relative of anyone in the claimant's family, if that partner or relative is aged 60+ or incapacitated. There is no time limit. The property may be occupied by others as well as the partner or relative. Any number of properties may be disregarded under this rule. 'Relative' is defined in paragraph 10.44. 'Incapacitated' is not defined for this purpose; in particular, it is not linked to premiums or state benefits.

AN INTENDED HOME

HB sch 6 paras 2,27,28
HB60+ sch 6 paras 1-3
NIHB sch 7 paras 2,27,28
NIHB60+ sch 7 paras 1-3
CTB sch 5 paras 2,27,28
CTB60+ sch 4 paras 1-3

13.73 Disregard the capital value of a property which the claimant intends to occupy as a home as follows:

- in all cases, for 26 weeks from the date of acquisition or such longer period as is reasonable; and/or
- if the claimant is taking steps to obtain possession (e.g. if there are squatters or tenants), for 26 weeks from the date the claimant first seeks legal advice or begins legal proceedings, or such longer period as is reasonable; and/or
- if the property requires essential repairs or alterations, for 26 weeks from the date the claimant first takes steps to render it fit for occupation or reoccupation as his or her home, or such longer period as is reasonable. This could apply for example to the normal home of a claimant in temporary accommodation

A FORMER HOME

13.74 There is no disregard of the capital value of a claimant's former home as such. However, a former home may well fall within one of the following headings (which also apply to other property): if it does not, then it is taken into account as capital.

PROPERTY FOR SALE

HB sch 6 para 26
HB60+ sch 6 para 7
NIHB sch 7 para 26
NIHB60+ sch 7 para 7
CTB sch 5 para 26
CTB60+ sch 4 para 7

13.75 Disregard the capital value of any property the claimant intends to dispose of, for 26 weeks from the date when the claimant first takes steps to dispose of it, or for such longer period as is reasonable. This can apply to a former or second home or any other property. It can apply to more than one property.

COUPLES AND POLYGAMOUS MARRIAGES: DIVORCE, DISSOLUTION AND ESTRANGEMENT

HB sch 6 para 25
HB60+ sch 6 para 6
NIHB sch 7 para 25
NIHB60+ sch 7 para 6
CTB sch 5 para 25
CTB60+ sch 4 para 6

13.76 If a claimant has divorced their partner, dissolved their civil partnership with them or become estranged from them, disregard the whole capital value of the claimant's former home (and any land or buildings which are part of it or are impracticable to sell separately) as follows:

- for any period when it is occupied by the former partner if he or she is now a lone parent. This could begin straight after the divorce/estrangement, or later on, and there is no time limit in this case;
- in any other case, for 26 weeks from the date of divorce or estrangement (e.g. if the former partner is not a lone parent at the time, or the property is empty). The time limit in this case cannot be extended, but the property may fall within one of the other disregards afterwards.

Note that (unlike in the next paragraph) the claimant must have formerly lived there as his or her home for this disregard to apply. 'Divorce' (in the case of married couples) and 'dissolution' (in the case of civil partners) carry their ordinary meaning. 'Estrangement' means more than just physical separation, namely that the couple in question consider their relationship to be over *(CH/117/2005)*.

COUPLES AND POLYGAMOUS MARRIAGES: SEPARATION

13.77 If a claimant has not divorced their partner, dissolved their civil partnership with them, or become estranged from them, but the HB/CTB rules treat him or her as no longer being in a couple or polygamous marriage (e.g. because of the rules about absence of a partner: para. 4.24), disregard the whole capital value of any property currently occupied as a home by the former partner. There is no time limit. Note that (unlike in the previous paragraph) it is irrelevant who used to live there.

HB sch 6 para 4(b)
HB60+
sch 6 para 4(b)
NIHB sch 7 para 4(b)
NIHB60+
sch 7 para 3(b)
CTB sch 5 para 4(b)
CTB60+
sch 4 para 4(b)

DISPUTED ASSETS WHEN A RELATIONSHIP ENDS

13.78 When a relationship ends, ownership of a property may be in dispute. This can sometimes mean the current market value of the property (paras. 13.19-20) is nil until ownership of the property is settled.

HOUSING ASSOCIATION DEPOSITS

13.79 If the claimant and any partner are under 60, disregard in full as capital any amount deposited with a housing association (para. 10.17) in order to secure accommodation. There is no such disregard if the claimant or any partner is aged 60+.

HB sch 6 para 11(a)
NIHB
sch 7 para 11(a)
CTB sch 5 para 11(a)

MONEY FROM SELLING A HOME

13.80 If the claimant and any partner are under 60, disregard in full as capital:

- money from the sale of the claimant's former home, including in Northern Ireland any compensation paid resulting from compulsory purchase; and
- money refunded by a housing association with which it was deposited (para. 13.79),

but only if it is intended for purchasing another home within 26 weeks, or such longer period as is reasonable. (However, interest accrued on the money is counted as capital in the normal way: para. 13.94.) If the claimant or any partner is aged 60+, a different rule applies (para. 13.81).

HB
sch 6 paras 3,11(b)
NIHB
sch 7 paras 3,11(b)
CTB
sch 5 paras 3,11(a)

Example: The capital value of a property following relationship breakdown

- A married couple jointly own the house they live in. They do not own any other property. They have one child at school. They claim CTB. The man is the claimant.

  The value of the house is disregarded as capital: it is their normal home (para. 13.71). However, they turn out not to qualify for CTB because they have too much income.

- The couple separate (but are not estranged).The man leaves and rents a room in a shared house. He does not intend to return (and so they no longer count as a couple: para. 4.24). He claims HB and CTB for the flat.

  In the man's claim, his share of the house is disregarded: it is the home of his former partner from whom he is separated (para. 13.77).

- They divorce. The terms of the divorce are that the man retains a one-third share in the house; but that the house cannot be sold until their child is 18. The man notifies the council of this.

  In his claim, his share of the house is disregarded: it is his former home and is occupied by his former partner from whom he is divorced and who is a lone parent (para. 13.76).

- More than 26 weeks after their divorce, their child leaves school. The house is not put up for sale and the man does not seek his share of its value.

  In his claim, his interest in the house must now be taken into account (para. 13.76). As a joint owner, he is treated as possessing one-half of its value (and the other points in para. 13.20 are taken into account in valuing it).

- The house is put up for sale.

  In the man's claim, his interest in the house is now disregarded as capital for 26 weeks (or longer if reasonable: para. 13.75).

- The house is sold, and the man puts his share into a building society account and starts trying to raise a mortgage using the money. It seems likely that he will be able to buy somewhere within the next two or three months.

  In his claim, this money is disregarded: it is the proceeds of the sale of his former home and he plans to use it to buy another property within 26 weeks (para. 13.80).

MONEY FOR BUYING A HOME

13.81 If the claimant or any partner is aged 60+, payments (or amounts deposited in the claimant's name) for the sole purpose of buying a home are disregarded for one year from the date of receipt. Apart from lasting longer, this is wider than the rule for under 60s (para. 13.80). It includes home sale proceeds and money refunded by a housing association, but also (for example) money given or loaned by a relative for that purpose.

HB60+
sch 6 paras 18,20(a
NIHB60+
sch 7 paras 18,20(a
CTB60+
sch 4 paras 18,20(a

VALUING PROPERTY GENERALLY

13.82 The general rules about valuing capital apply to a property which has to be taken into account as capital for HB/main CTB purposes (paras. 13.19-20). In such cases, an authority can get a free valuation of property from the Valuation Office Agency (and a form which can be used for this purpose is in GM chapter C2 annex E).

VALUING PROPERTY WHICH IS RENTED OUT

13.83 Unless it forms part of the capital assets of a business (or in certain circumstances a former business: para. 15.7), property a claimant owns and has rented out is valued as described earlier (paras. 13.19-20). However, the fact that it is rented out will affect its market value; for example, the presence of a sitting tenant can reduce it. For information about rental income see the following.

HB sch 6 para 7
HB60+ sch 6 para
NIHB sch 7 para 7
NIHB60+
sch 7 para 5
CTB sch 5 para 7
CTB60+
sch 4 para 5

Table 13.2: Rent received from people in the claimant's home

RENT, KEEP, ETC, FROM HOUSEHOLD MEMBERS

- Disregard the whole of any rent, 'keep', etc, received from a child or young person in the family (paras. 4.26-40) or from a non-dependant (para. 4.44).

HB sch 5 para 21
HB60+ 29(1)
NIHB sch 6 para 2
NIHB60+ 27(1)
CTB sch 4 para 21
CTB60+ 19(1)

RENT FROM BOARDERS (AS DEFINED IN PARA. 4.46)

- Disregard the first £20.00 of that rent.
- Count only half the rest as unearned income.
- A separate £20.00 is disregarded for each individual boarder who is charged for – even a child – regardless of whether they have separate agreements.

HB sch 5 para 41
HB60+ sch 5 para
NIHB sch 6 para 4
NIHB60+
sch 6 para 10
CTB sch 4 para 23
CTB60+
sch 3 para 9

RENT FROM (SUB-)TENANTS (AS DEFINED IN PARAS. 4.48-49)

HB sch 5 para 22 HB60+ sch 5 para 10 NIHB sch 6 para 23 NIHB60+ sch 6 para 11 CTB sch 4 para 23 CTB60+ sch 3 para 10

- Disregard the first £20.00 of that rent if the claimant or any partner is aged 60+ (regardless of whether the rent includes heating).
- Disregard the first £15.95 of that rent if the claimant and any partner are under 60 and the rent includes heating.
- Disregard the first £4.00 of that rent if the claimant and any partner are under 60 and the rent does not include heating.
- Count all the rest as unearned income.
- A separate £20.00, £15.95 or £4.00 is disregarded for each (sub-) tenancy.

RECEIVING RENT

13.84 Table 13.2 shows how rent received by the claimant from people living in his or her home is taken into account. See also the example. Table 13.3 shows how rent received from property other than the claimant's home is taken into account.

HB sch 6 para 33 HB60+ sch 6 para 28 NIHB sch 7 para 33 NIHB60+ sch 7 para 30 CTB sch 5 para 33 CTB60+ sch 4 para 28

13.85 The value of the right to receive rent is disregarded as capital.

Example: Letting out a room

A couple in their 20s are on HB and CTB. They have a spare room and they let it out to a man for £50.00 per week inclusive of fuel for heating etc, and water charges (but not meals). He is their sub-tenant.

For the purposes of their HB/CTB, their income from this sub-tenant is £50.00 minus £14.55, which is £35.45 per week.

Later, the same couple agree with the man that if he increases what he pays to £65.00 per week, they will feed him. He is now their boarder.

For the purposes of their HB/CTB, their income from this boarder is £65.00 minus £20.00, which is £45.00, the result being divided in two, which is £22.50 per week.

Note that the rules therefore mean that a claimant is usually better off renting out a room to a boarder than to a (sub-)tenant.

Table 13.3: Rent received on property other than the claimant's home

IF THE CLAIMANT OR ANY PARTNER IS AGED 60+

Rent received on property (other than the claimant's home) is disregarded in full as income in all circumstances.

HB 60+ 29(1), sch 5 para 22
NIHB60+ 27(1), sch 6 para 25
CTB60+ 19(1), sch 3 para 24

IF THE CLAIMANT AND ANY PARTNER ARE UNDER 60 AND THE PROPERTY'S VALUE IS DISREGARDED AS CAPITAL

This applies to rent received on one of the types of property (other than the claimant's home) whose capital value is disregarded (as described in paras. 13.71-77 and 15.7):

HB sch 5 para 17(2)
NIHB sch 6 para 18(2)
CTB sch 4 para 18(2

- Take the amount of the rental income for an appropriate period (e.g. a month, a year).
- Disregard any payment towards mortgage repayments (both interest and capital repayments) or any council tax or water charges the claimant is liable to pay during that period on the property (note that other outgoings cannot be disregarded).
- Count the balance (converted to a weekly figure) as the claimant's unearned income.

IF THE CLAIMANT AND ANY PARTNER ARE UNDER 60 AND THE PROPERTY'S VALUE COUNTS AS CAPITAL

This applies to rent received on one of the types of property (other than the claimant's home) whose value is taken into account as his or her capital (even if for some reason the capital value is nil for HB/main CTB purposes):

HB 46(4), sch 5 para 17(1)
NIHB 43(4), sch 6 para 18(1)
CTB 36(4), sch 4 para 18(1)

- Take the amount of the rental income for an appropriate period (e.g. a month, a year).
- Deduct any outgoings incurred in respect of the letting (e.g. agents' fees, tax due on the income, repairs, cleaning, council tax, water charges, repayments of mortgages/loans, etc.).
- The balance (if any) is capital (not income) for HB/main CTB purposes.

PAYMENTS FOR WORK ON THE HOME

HB sch 6 paras 10,38 HB60+ sch 6 paras 18,20(b) NIHB sch 7 paras 10,38 NIHB60+ sch 7 paras 7,20(b) CTB sch 5 paras 11,38 CTB 60+ sch 4 paras 18,20(b)

13.86 The following disregard applies, for example, to money paid by a council to assist a tenant to buy a property, a home improvement grant, a loan from a bank or similar institution or from a friend or relative, or any other loan or payment. It works as follows:

- If the claimant and any partner are under 60:
  - payments solely for essential repairs or improvements to the home, and
  - grants from a local authority to purchase, alter or repair an intended home

  are disregarded as capital for 26 weeks from the date of payment, or such longer period as is reasonable.
- If the claimant or any partner is aged 60+:
  - payments (or amounts deposited in the claimant's name) solely for essential repairs or improvements to the home or an intended home are disregarded for one year from the date of receipt.

TAX REFUNDS FOR MORTGAGE INTEREST

HB sch 6 para 21 HB60+ 29(1) NIHB sch 7 para 21 NIHB60+ 27(1) CTB sch 5 para 21 CTB60+ 19(1)

13.87 If the claimant and any partner are under 60, tax refunds for interest on a mortgage taken out for purchasing a home, or for carrying out home repairs or improvements, are disregarded in full as capital. There is no such disregard for 60+s.

MORTGAGE AND LOAN PROTECTION POLICIES

HB sch 5 para 29 HB60+ 29(1) NIHB sch 6 para 31 NIHB60+ 27(1) CTB sch 4 para 30 CTB60+ 19(1)

13.88 The following applies if a claimant has taken out insurance against being unable (perhaps because of sickness) to pay his or her mortgage or some other loan (for example a car loan), and is now receiving payments under that insurance policy. In such cases, if the claimant or any partner is aged 60+, all payments received under that insurance policy are disregarded as unearned income. If the claimant and any partner are under 60 they are disregarded only insofar as they cover the cost of:

- the repayments on the mortgage or other loan; and
- any premiums due on the policy in question; and
- (only in the case of a mortgage protection policy) any premiums on another insurance policy which was taken out to insure against loss or damage to the home and which was required as a condition of the mortgage.

COMPENSATION AND INSURANCE PAYMENTS FOR THE HOME OR POSSESSIONS

13.89 Such payments are disregarded as capital if they are for repair or replacement following loss of, or damage to, the claimant's home or personal possessions. If the claimant and any partner are under 60, they are disregarded for 26 weeks from the date of payment, or such longer period as is reasonable. If the claimant or any partner is aged 60+, they are disregarded for one year from the date of receipt.

HB sch 6 para 10
HB60+ sch 6 paras 18,19
NIHB sch 7 para 1
NIHB60+ sch 7 paras 18,19
CTB sch 5 para 10
CTB60+ sch 4 paras 18,19

PERSONAL POSSESSIONS

13.90 Disregard in full as capital the value of the claimant's personal possessions. If the claimant and any partner are under 60, the law specifically mentions that if they were purchased for the purpose of obtaining or increasing entitlement to HB/CTB, their capital value should be taken into account. If the claimant or any partner is aged 60+, the same applies, but under the deprivation of capital rule (para. 13.133).

HB sch 6 para 12
HB60+ sch 6 para
NIHB sch 7 para 1
NIHB60+ sch 7 para 8
CTB sch 5 para 12
CTB sch 4 para 8

Savings, investments and private income

13.91 This section is about savings, investments etc. When these are taken into account, they are valued as described in paragraphs 13.19-20. (But for national savings certificates, see para. 13.95.) The following terms are used below:

- the 'surrender value' (of an insurance policy, for instance) means what the claimant would be paid (by the insurance company, for instance) if he or she cashed it in now (rather than waiting for it to mature, for instance);
- the 'value of the right to receive income' (from an annuity, for instance) means what the claimant would be paid in return for transferring the right to receive the income to someone else.

SAVINGS AND CASH

13.92 These count in full as capital. For example, money in a bank or building society account (or under the mattress) is counted as capital (but see the next paragraph).

HB 44(1)
HB60+ 44(1)
NIHB 41(1)
NIHB60+ 42(1)
CTB 34(1)
CTB60+ 34(1)

INCOME PAID REGULARLY INTO AN ACCOUNT

13.93 Regular payments of income (e.g. earnings, benefits, pensions) into a claimant's bank, building society or similar account should not be counted as capital for the period they cover (para. 13.11). For example, if earnings are paid in monthly, only what is left at the end of the month is capital. In practice, authorities often do not do this unless claimants specifically ask them to.

INTEREST

HB 46(4) HB60+ 29(1), sch 5 paras 22,24 NIHB 43(4) NIHB60+ 27(1), sch 6 paras 24,25 CTB 36(4) CTB60+ 3 paras 23,24

13.94 Except where other rules in this chapter state otherwise, interest or other income derived from capital (such as interest on a bank or building society account) is counted not as income but as capital. If the claimant and any partner are under 60, the law spells out that this is done from the date it is due to be credited to the claimant, and it seems logical that this would also apply to 60+s.

NATIONAL SAVINGS AND ULSTER SAVINGS CERTIFICATES

HB 47(b) HB60+ 45(b) NIHB 44(b) NIHB60+ 43(b) CTB 37(b) CTB60+ 35(b)

13.95 These count as capital, but the following applies instead of the normal rules about valuing capital. From 1st July in any year to 30th June in the next year, the capital amount for HB/main CTB purposes is their value as at 1st July in the first of those years. For current issues, this means their purchase price. The DWP usually issues a circular with valuation tables each year – usually in July.

INVESTMENTS

13.96 These count as capital. They are valued as described in the general rules (paras. 13.19-20), with the effect that:

- shares are valued at their 'sell' price. Then disregard 10% towards the cost of their sale;
- unit trusts are valued at their 'sell' price. Normally this already allows for notional sales costs. If it does not, disregard 10% for this;
- income bonds count in full.

LIFE INSURANCE POLICIES

HB sch 6 para 17 HB60+ sch 6 para 11 NIHB sch 7 para 17 NIHB60+ sch 7 para 11 CTB sch 5 para 17 CTB60+ sch 4 para 11

13.97 Disregard as capital the surrender value of a life insurance policy. (This includes instruments, such as bonds, which have a life insurance element: *CIS/733/1995* reported as *R(IS)7/98*.) But count as capital any money actually received from it (e.g. if the claimant actually cashes in all or part of it).

FUNERAL PLAN CONTRACTS

HB60+ sch 6 para 12 NIHB60+ sch 7 para 12 CTB60+ sch 4 para 12

13.98 If the claimant or any partner is aged 60+, disregard the value of a funeral plan contract. To qualify the contract provider (which would normally be a firm or company but need not be so) must contract to provide or secure the provision of a funeral in the UK, and that must be the sole purpose of the contract. There is no such disregard if the claimant and any partner are under 60.

ANNUITIES

HB sch 6 para 13 HB60+ 29(1), sch 6 para 25 NIHB sch 7 para 13 NIHB60+ 27(1), sch 7 para 25 CTB sch 5 para 13 CTB60+ 19(1), sch 4 para 25

13.99 If the claimant has an annuity, it means he or she has invested an initial lump sum with an insurance company which, in return, pays the claimant a regular income. Count this in full as unearned income. Disregard as capital the surrender value of the annuity, and also the value of the right to receive income from it (para. 13.91).

HOME INCOME PLANS

13.100 If the claimant has a home income plan, it means he or she raised a loan using his or her home as security, has invested the loan as an annuity and, in return, gets a regular income: part of this income is used to repay the loan, part may be used to repay the claimant's mortgage, and part may be left over for the claimant to use. Count the income received by the claimant as unearned income, but only after deducting (if they have not been deducted at source):

- any tax payable on that income;
- any repayments on the loan which was raised to obtain the annuity; and
- any mortgage repayments made using the income (using the figures for the repayments which apply after tax has been deducted from them).

Disregard as capital the surrender value of the annuity, and the value of the right to receive income from it (para. 13.91).

HB 41(2), sch 5 para 18, sch 6 para 13
HB60+ 29(1), sch 5 para 11, sch 6 para 29
NIHB 38(2), sch 6 para 19, sch 7 para 13
NIHB60+ 27(1), sch 6 para 12, sch 7 para 31
CTB 31(2), sch 5 para 13
CTB60+ 19(1), sch 3 para 11, sch 4 para 29

EQUITY RELEASE SCHEMES

13.101 If the claimant is in an equity release scheme, it means that he or she receives (loaned) payments which are advanced by a lender at regular intervals and are secured on his or her home. If the claimant or any partner is aged 60+, such payments, if made at regular intervals, count in full as income (even though they are a loan). If the claimant and any partner are under 60, there is no specific rule in the law but, since the payments are loans, the authority should probably disregard them (but see para. 13.126).

HB60+ 29(1)(w),(8)
NIHB60+ 27(1)(u),(8
CTB60+ 19(1)(w),(8)

LIFE INTEREST AND LIFERENT

13.102 If a claimant has a life interest or (in Scotland) liferent, it means he or she has the right to enjoy an asset during his or her or someone else's lifetime, after which it will pass to someone else. The actual value to the claimant (if any) of the life interest or liferent is counted as capital; and any actual income the claimant receives from it is counted as earned or unearned income as appropriate. Disregard as capital the value of the right to receive income from it (para. 13.91).

HB sch 6 para 15
HB60+ sch 6 para 27
NIHB sch 7 para 15
NIHB60+ sch 7 para 29
CTB sch 5 para 15
CTB60+ sch 4 para 27

REVERSIONARY INTEREST

13.103 If a claimant has a reversionary interest, it means he or he has an interest in property but will not possess it until some future event (for example, the death of a relative). Disregard in full the capital value of a reversionary interest. For HB and main CTB purposes, however, a property the claimant has rented out is not disregarded as a reversionary interest: the rules for dealing with such property are explained in table 13.3.

HB sch 6 para 7
HB60+ sch 6 para 5
NIHB sch 7 para 7
NIHB60+ sch 7 para 5
CTB sch 5 para 7
CTB60+ sch 4 para 5

Personal injury payments, trust funds, etc

SUMMARY

13.104 This section is about payments for personal injury and similar matters (these rules changed on 10th November 2005) and trust funds (whether for personal injury or not). The general rules are:

- any payment of income for a personal injury is disregarded;
- personal injury money held in a court or trust is disregarded as capital;
- any other payment of capital for a personal injury counts as capital if the claimant and any partner are under 60, but is disregarded for 60+s;
- other money held in a trust is disregarded as capital if the trust (not the claimant) controls when it makes payments.

But there are exceptions, as described below (and see also paras. 13.60-61 in the case of trust funds relating to people with HIV and people with Creutzfeld-Jacob disease).

HB sch 6 paras 45,46
HB60+ sch 6 para 17
NIHB sch 7 para 44
NIHB60+ sch 7 para 17
CTB sch 5 paras 47,48
CTB60+ sch 4 para 17

PERSONAL INJURY PAYMENTS ADMINISTERED BY A COURT

13.105 Compensation for personal injury, if paid into a court and administered by the court on the compensated person's behalf, is disregarded in full as capital without time limit. The same applies to compensation for the death of a parent, but in this case only if the compensated person is under 18.

PERSONAL INJURY PAYMENTS UNDER A COURT ORDER OR OUT-OF-COURT SETTLEMENT

HB 41(5)
HB60+ sch 5 paras 14,15
NIHB 38(4)
NIHB60+ sch 6 paras 15,16
CTB 31(5)
CTB60+ sch 3 paras 14,15

13.106 If the claimant or any partner is 60+, the following are disregarded as income:

- any payment made under a court order for accident, injury or disease of the claimant, partner or child;
- any periodic payment made in an out-of-court settlement for injury of the claimant or partner.

If the claimant and any partner are under 60, and a court orders that any part of a personal injury payment is to be paid periodically, then that part counts as unearned income (not capital) for HB/CTB purposes.

HB sch 6 para 14
HB 60+ sch 6 para 17
NIHB sch 7 para 14
NIHB60+ sch 7 para 18
CTB sch 5 para 14
CTB60+ sch 4 para 17

PERSONAL INJURY MONEY HELD IN A TRUST

13.107 Any money for personal injury which is held in a trust fund is disregarded in full as capital without time limit (and if the claimant and any partner are under 60, so is the value of the right to receive income from it: para. 13.91). If the claimant or any partner is aged 60+, the law makes it clear that the particular money need not be kept track of. If, say, the award was £20,000 then £20,000 is disregarded from the person's capital for ever more. (If the trust pays the claimant income, see para. 13.108.)

HB sch 5 para 14
HB60+
sch 5 para 12
NIHB sch 6 para 16
NIHB60+
sch 6 para 13
CTB sch 4 para 15
CTB60+
sch 3 para 12

PERSONAL INJURY MONEY PAID AS INCOME

13.108 Payments of income for a personal injury, whether from a trust or not, are disregarded in full as income.

PROPERTY HELD IN A TRUST

13.109 If the claimant or any partner is aged 60+, a property held in a trust for the claimant's or partner's benefit (other than a charitable trust, or a trust for people with HIV as described in para. 13.60) is disregarded – so long as the trust makes payments or has a discretion to make payments to the claimant or partner. There is no such disregard if the claimant and any partner is under 60.

HB60+
sch 6 para 30
NIHB60+
sch 7 para 32
CTB60+
sch 4 para 30

DISCRETIONARY TRUSTS: INCOME

13.110 Payments of income from any discretionary trust (one which the claimant has no absolute right to take money from) are disregarded in full as income.

HB60+
sch 5 para 12
NIHB60+
sch 6 para 13
CTB60+
sch 3 para 12

Other items of income and capital

MAINTENANCE

13.111 Disregard £15 of maintenance received, but only if there is at least one child or young person in the family, and only if the maintenance is paid to the claimant by one of the following:

- if the claimant or any partner is aged 60+, from a current or former married partner or civil partner of either of them; but
- if the claimant and any partner are under 60, from:
  - a former partner of either of them, or
  - a parent of any child or young person in the claimant's family (so long as that parent is not in the claimant's family), or
  - the Secretary of State (under child support provisions) in lieu of maintenance.

HB sch 5 para 47
HB60+ 29(1),
sch 5 para 20
NIHB sch 6 para 50
NIHB60+ 27(1),
sch 6 para 21
CTB sch 4 para 48
CTB60+
sch 3 para 20

13.112 The definitions of 'partner', 'child', 'young person', 'family' are in chapter 4. The £15 disregard applies whether the maintenance is payable to the claimant or to a child or young person. If two or more maintenance payments are received in any week, the maximum disregard is £15 per week.

CHARITABLE AND/OR VOLUNTARY PAYMENTS

HB 46(6), sch 5 para 14, sch 6 para 34
HB60+29(1)
NIHB 43(6), sch 6 para 16, sch 7 para 34
NIHB60+ 27(1)
CTB 36(6), sch 4 para 15, sch 5 para 34
CTB60+ 19(1)

13.113 Payments which are charitable and/or voluntary (such as payments from family, friends or charities) are assessed as follows:

- since 10th November 2005, payments of income are fully disregarded in all circumstances;
- lump sum payments in kind are fully disregarded as capital;
- other payments of capital are fully disregarded if the claimant or any partner is aged 60+, but count in full as capital if the claimant and any partner are under 60.

PAYMENTS IN KIND

HB 40(1), sch 5 para 23
HB60+ 29(1)
NIHB 37(1), sch 6 para 24
NIHB60+ 27(1)
CTB 30(1), sch 4 para 24
CTB60+ 19(1)

13.114 A 'payment in kind' is a payment made in goods (e.g. fuel, food) rather than in money (e.g. cheques, cash). Regular payments in kind are dealt with as follows. If the payments are voluntary or charitable, see paragraph 13.113. If the payments are earned income they are usually disregarded (para. 14.39). If the payments are made in the course of business to a self-employed claimant, their value counts in full as self-employed income (because there is no specific disregard in such a case). If the payments are unearned (i.e. in any other case), their value is disregarded.

CONCESSIONARY COAL AND CASH IN LIEU

HB 40(1), sch 5 para 23
HB60+ 29(1)
NIHB 37(1), sch 6 para 24
NIHB60+ 27(1)
CTB 30(1), sch 4 para 24
CTB60+ 19(1)

13.115 Concessionary coal, and cash in lieu of it, are disregarded as income *(R v Doncaster Metropolitan Borough Council and Another ex p Boulton)*.

SECOND WORLD WAR PAYMENTS

HB sch 6 para 54
HB60+ sch 6 para 13
NIHB sch 7 para 50
NIHB60+ sch 7 para 13
CTB sch 5 para 56
CTB60+ sch 4 para 13

13.116 Disregard in full as capital, without time limit, the ex gratia payments of £10,000 made by the Secretary of State in respect of imprisonment or internment of the claimant or his or her deceased partner, or the claimant's or partner's deceased spouse or civil partner, by the Japanese during the Second World War. The DWP (circular HB/CTB A1/2001) has recommended that authorities need not attempt to identify the particular £10,000, but that £10,000 should simply be disregarded from the capital the claimant has.

HB sch 6 para 56
HB60+ sch 6 para 15
NIHB sch 7 para 53
NIHB60+ sch 7 para 15
CTB sch 5 para 58
CTB60+ sch 4 para 15

Also disregard in full as capital, without time limit, any payment (apart from a war pension) made to compensate for the fact that, during the Second World War, the claimant or partner or either's deceased spouse or civil partner:

- was a slave labourer or a forced labourer; or
- had suffered property loss or personal injury; or
- was a parent of a child who had died.

THE LONDON BOMBINGS CHARITABLE RELIEF FUND

13.117 All payments from the above fund (set up to assist victims of the bombings on 7th July 2005) are fully disregarded as both income and capital.

HB 2(1), sch 5 para 35, sch 6 para 25
HB60+ 29(1), sch 6 para 16
NIHB 2(1), sch 6 para 38, sch 7 para 25
NIHB60+ 27(1), sch 7 para
CTB 2(1), sch 4 para 36, sch 5 para 24
CTB60+ 19(1), sch 4 para 1

COMPENSATION FOR THE FAMILIES OF THE DISAPPEARED

13.118 In Northern Ireland only, compensation payments to the families of the disappeared are disregarded in full for 52 weeks from the date of receipt.

NIHB sch 7 para 52
NIHB60+ sch 7 para 26

GALLANTRY AWARDS

13.119 Disregard in full as unearned income:

- Victoria Cross and George Cross payments;
- the lump sum payments of up to £6,000 for those who have agreed not to receive any further payments of income from those; and
- analogous awards for gallantry from this country or another country.

These amounts are disregarded as capital if the claimant and any partner are under 60. There is no such disregard for 60+s.

HB sch 5 para 10, sch 6 para 47
HB60+ 29(1)
NIHB sch 6 para 10, sch 7 para 45
NIHB60+ 27(1)
CTB sch 4 para 11, sch 5 para 49
CTB60+ 19(1)

PARENTAL CONTRIBUTIONS TO STUDENTS

13.120 The following rules apply to contributions made by claimants to a student son or daughter ('student' is defined in paras. 21.5-19):

- If a claimant has been assessed as being able to make a contribution to the student's grant (other than a discretionary grant) or student loan, the whole amount of the assessed contribution is disregarded in the assessment of the claimant's income.
- If a claimant contributes towards the maintenance of a student under the age of 25, who has a discretionary grant or no grant, the amount of the contribution is disregarded in the assessment of the claimant's income – but only up to a maximum weekly figure. The maximum weekly figure is £45.50 minus the amount of any discretionary grant.

So far as possible the above are disregarded from unearned income, then any balance is disregarded from earned income.

HB sch 4 para 11, sch 5 paras 19,20
HB60+ sch 4 para 6, sch 5 paras 18,19
NIHB sch 5 para 11, sch 6 paras 20,21
NIHB60+ sch 5 para 6, sch 6 paras 19,20
CTB sch 3 para 11, sch 4 paras 19,20
CTB60+ sch 2 para 6, sch 3 paras 18,19

EDUCATION MAINTENANCE ALLOWANCES

HB sch 5 para 11
HB60+ 29(1)
NIHB sch 6 para 11
NIHB60+ 27(1)
CTB sch 4 para 12
CTB60+ 19(1)

13.121 Disregard Education Maintenance Allowances or Awards (including Assisted Places Allowances) in full as unearned income. These include payments under the national scheme for 16- to 18-year-olds in non-advanced education and also payments towards a child's travel to school.

HB sch 6 para 51
NIHB sch 7 para 49
CTB sch 5 para 53

13.122 If the claimant and any partner are under 60, disregard Education Maintenance Allowance bonuses in full as capital for 52 weeks from the date of payment. There is no such disregard for 60+s.

ASSISTANCE WITH REPAYING STUDENT LOANS

HB sch 5 para 12
HB60+ 29(1)
CTB sch 4 para 13
CTB60+ 19(1)

13.123 Disregard (as unearned income) any payment made to a former student to help with repaying his or her student loan. This applies whether the payer pays it direct or via the ex-student. It includes payments by the DfES under the Teacher Repayment Loan Scheme, but also includes any other case.

SPORTS AWARDS

HB 2(1),
sch 5 para 59,
sch 6 para 50
HB60+ 29(1)
NIHB 2(1),
sch 6 para 61,
sch 7 para 48
NIHB60+ 27(1)
CTB 2(1),
sch 4 para 59,
sch 5 para 52
CTB60+ 19(1)

13.124 If the claimant or any partner is aged 60+, these are disregarded if paid as income but counted if paid as capital. If the claimant and any partner are under 60, they are dealt with as follows:

- Any amounts awarded in respect of the claimant's or a member of the family's food (excluding vitamins, minerals or other special performance-enhancing dietary supplements), ordinary clothing or footwear (excluding school uniform and sportswear), household fuel, rent, council tax, or water charges, are counted in full as income or capital as appropriate.
- Any other amounts are disregarded in full as unearned income, and as capital for 26 weeks from the date of payment.

JURORS' ALLOWANCES

HB sch 5 paras 39
HB60+ 29(1)
NIHB sch 6 para 42
NIHB60+ 27(1)
CTB sch 4 para 41
CTB60+ 19(1)

13.125 If the claimant or any partner is aged 60+ these are disregarded in full. If the claimant and any partner are under 60, they are disregarded in full except in so far as they compensate for loss of earnings or loss of a social security benefit.

LOANS

13.126 A genuine loan usually increases a person's capital (until and to the extent that he or she spends it, perhaps on the thing it was lent for), though it is at least possible for a loan to be income (*Morrell v Secretary of State for Work and Pensions,* and see para 13.11) depending on the circumstances of the case, and the law requires this in the case of student loans (paras. 21.37-43) and career development loans (para. 13.65). For equity release schemes, see para. 13.101.

OUTSTANDING INSTALMENTS OF CAPITAL

13.127 There are no specific rules for outstanding instalments of capital if the claimant or partner is aged 60+, in whose case they count as capital when received.

13.128 If the claimant and any partner are under 60 and if, at the claimant's date of claim for HB/CTB (or at the date of any subsequent reconsideration of the claim), he or she is entitled to outstanding instalments of capital (i.e. instalments due after that date), the authority must consider whether the sum of the outstanding instalments and the claimant's other capital exceeds £16,000,

HB 41(1), sch 6 para 18 NIHB 38(1), sch 7 para 17 CTB 31(1), sch 5 para 18

- If it does, the outstanding instalments are ignored as capital but are counted as income. The law does not lay down any particular way of doing this.
- If it does not, the outstanding instalments are counted in full as capital from the date of claim (or reconsideration).

CAPITAL OUTSIDE THE UK

13.129 The following rules apply if a claimant possesses capital in a country outside the UK.

HB 48, sch 6 para 23 HB60+ 46, sch 6 para 23 NIHB 45, sch 7 para 23 NIHB60+ 44, sch 7 para 23 CTB 38, sch 5 para 23 CTB60+ 36, sch 4 para 23

- If there is no prohibition in that country against bringing the money to the UK, value it at its market or surrender value in that country; then disregard 10% if selling it would incur costs; then disregard any mortgage or other incumbrance secured on it; then disregard any charge which would be incurred in converting it into sterling; and count the remainder as capital.
- If there is such a prohibition, value it at what a willing buyer in the UK would give for it; then disregard 10% if selling it would incur costs; then disregard any mortgage or other incumbrance secured on it; and count the remainder as capital.

INCOME OUTSIDE THE UK

13.130 The following rules apply if a claimant is entitled to income payable in a country outside the UK.

HB sch 5 paras 24,33, sch 6 para 16 HB60+ sch 5 paras 16,17 NIHB sch 6 paras 25,35, sch 7 para 16 NIHB60+ sch 6 paras 17,18 CTB sch 4 paras 25,34 sch 5 para 16 CTB60+ sch 3 paras 16,17

- If there is no prohibition in that country against bringing the money to the UK, treat it as income in the normal way, allowing any disregard which may apply (including any earnings disregard in the case of earned income); also disregard any charge for converting it into sterling.
- If there is such a prohibition, disregard it in full; also (but only if the claimant and any partner are under 60) disregard as capital the value of the right to receive income from it (para. 13.91).

HB sch 5 para 2
HB60+ 29(1)
NIHB sch 6 para 2
NIHB60+ 27(1)
CTB sch 4 para 2
CTB60+ 19(1)

EXPENSES FOR UNPAID WORK

13.131 Expenses for unpaid work (whether for a charity, voluntary organisation, friend or neighbour) are disregarded. (For expenses for paid work, see para. 14.45.)

Notional income and capital

HB 42(11),(12),49(7)
HB60+ 47(5)
NIHB 39(11),(12),46(7)
NIHB60+ 45(5)
CTB 32(11),(12)
CTB60+ 37(5)

13.132 In the situations described below a claimant is treated, for HB/main CTB purposes, as possessing income and/or capital he or she does not in fact possess – known as 'notional' income and/or capital. The notional income or capital is assessed as if it was actual income or capital and any relevant disregards must be applied.

DEPRIVATION

HB 42(1),49(1)
HB60+ 41(8),47(1)
NIHB 39(1),46(1)
NIHB60+ 39(8),45(1)
CTB 32(1),39(1)
CTB60+ 31(8),37(1)

13.133 If a claimant deliberately deprives himself or herself of capital or income in order to qualify for HB (or for more HB), he or she is treated as still having it for HB purposes. The same applies independently for CTB. It is the claimant's intention which must be taken into account (not the item he or she spent the money on).

Authorities sometimes (wrongly) confuse what the money was spent on with what the claimant's intentions were. A recent commissioner's decision illustrates this *(CH/3169/2004)*. The claimant was a schizophrenic man without an appointee who lived in 'an intolerable level of chaos'. He had a very big windfall and telephoned the authority to arrange for his HB to be stopped. When he re-claimed 4 months later, he had almost none of this capital left. It was agreed by the parties that the money had gone on 'alcohol and high living'. The authority said he had deprived himself of this money. The commissioner was satisfied that it had not been shown that the claimant appreciated what he was doing, or the consequences of it, and held that the test whether someone spent capital 'for the purpose of' getting (more) HB is subjective. The commissioner remitted the case to a differently constituted tribunal with various directions including that the tribunal take proper account of the claimant's mental state and capabilities.

HB60+ 47(2)
NIHB60+ 45(2)
CTB60+ 37(2)

13.134 If the claimant or any partner is aged 60+, one special rule applies. It is that repaying or reducing a debt, or purchasing goods or services reasonable in the claimant's circumstances is never deprivation. The rule is automatic, and applies regardless of the claimant's intention. For any other question of deprivation in the case of this age group, and for all questions of deprivation in the case of under 60s, the claimant's intention is the only determining factor.

DIMINISHING NOTIONAL CAPITAL

13.135 If a claimant is treated as having notional capital for the above reason (paras. 13.133-134), the amount of notional capital taken into account is reduced each week, broadly speaking, by the amount of any HB, CTB, JSA(IB) or IS (but not WTC or CTC), lost as a result of the claimant being treated as having notional capital. The rules for doing this are so complicated that the DWP is iunderstood to be planning to simplify them – perhaps by disregarding a fixed percentage from the notional capital instead. For further details, see GM paras. C2.328-381.

HB 50
HB60+ 48
NIHB 47
NIHB60+ 48
CTB 40
CTB60+ 38

AVAILABLE ON APPLICATION

13.136 If the claimant or any partner is aged 60+, the claimant is treated as having any amount of state retirement pension which he or she has not claimed, but might reasonably be expected to be entitled to. This does not apply to deferred state retirement pension or to the increased state retirement pension a person does not get if they choose a lump sum instead (para. 13.67). Different rules apply to potential income from a private pension scheme (para. 13.145). Apart from that, no other type of income or capital can be treated as available on application for 60+s.

HB60+ 2(1),41
NIHB 2(1),39
CTB60+ 2(1),31

13.137 If the claimant and any partner are under 60, any income or capital which the claimant could have on application (in other words, simply by applying for it) is treated as possessed by him or her from the date it could be obtained. This rule does not apply to:

HB 42(2),49(2)
NIHB 39(2),43(2)
CTB 32(2),39(2)

- working tax credit or child tax credit;
- income which could be obtained in the form of a DWP rehabilitation allowance;
- payments (of income or capital) made to a provider of a New Deal arrangement;
- income or capital which could be obtained from a discretionary trust or a trust for personal injury (paras. 13.104-110);
- capital which could be obtained from the London Bombings Charitable Relief Fund (para. 13.117); or
- any kind of disregarded capital.

Also the DWP advises that this rule should not be applied in the case of income from any other social security benefit unless the authority is sure about the amount the person could receive (GM para. C3.755).

PAYMENTS TO OR FOR THIRD PARTIES

HB 42(a),(13), 49(4),(8)
HB60+ 42
NIHB 39(a),(14), 46(4),(8)
NIHB60+ 40
CTB 32(a),(13), 39(4),(8)
CTB60+ 32

13.138 If income (including goods or other payments in kind) is paid in A's name but used by B for food, household fuel, clothing or footwear (other than school uniform and sportswear), eligible rent (apart from any non-dependant deduction), council tax or water charges, it is treated as belonging to B. If the claimant and any partner are under 60, the rule applies also to capital (but not for 60+s).

13.139 This rule must not be used in relation to occupational or personal pensions (including payments from the Pension Protection Fund: para. 13.68) if the intended beneficiary is bankrupt or sequestered, and payment is made to a trustee (or similar) for him or her, and any family have no other income.

UP-RATINGS

HB 42(8)
HB60+ 41(9)
NIHB 39(8)
NIHB60+ 39(11)
CTB 32(8)
CTB60+ 31(9)

13.140 If the April up-rating date for social security benefits or tax credits is different from that for HB/CTB, they are generally treated as up-rated on the same date as HB/CTB (paras. 17.34-35 and table 17.1).

WORK PAID AT LESS THAN THE GOING RATE

HB 42(9),(10)
NIHB 39(9),(10)
CTB 32(9),(10)

13.141 This rule applies only if the claimant and any partner are under 60. If the claimant is paid less than the going rate for a job, he or she is treated as having whatever additional pay is reasonable in the circumstances.

13.142 The means of the employer must be taken into account; and this rule does not apply to voluntary work, to claimants provided with a New Deal arrangement (para. 13.62) or to claimants on an 'approved work' training programme (e.g. work trials or work placements).

13.143 When this rule is used, disregard notional tax and national insurance contributions and apply the earnings disregards (paras. 14.20-32).

RELATIONSHIP TO A COMPANY

HB 49
NIHB 49
CTB 39

13.144 This rule applies only if the claimant and any partner are under 60. It applies to a claimant who is not the sole owner of, or a partner in, a company, but whose relationship to that company is analogous to someone who is. In such cases, the claimant's share of the capital of that company is assessed as though he or she was the sole owner or partner and any actual share of the company he or she possesses is disregarded.

PENSION SCHEMES

HB 42
HB60+ 41
NIHB 39
NIHB60+ 39
CTB 32
CTB60+ 31

13.145 If a claimant or partner aged 60+ could get income from his or her pension scheme, but has failed to do so or chosen not to do so, then he or she is treated as having that income.

INCOME AND CAPITAL OF A CHILD OR YOUNG PERSON

13.146 The income and capital of a child or young person is wholly disregarded.

The over-riding £20 disregard from certain income

13.147 In any particular claim for HB/main CTB, the maximum weekly disregard per claim is £20 from any or all of the following:

HB sch 5 para 34
HB60+
sch 5 para 12(3)
NIHB sch 6 para 36
NIHB60+
sch 6 para 13(3)
CTB sch 4 para 35
CTB60+
sch 3 para 12(3)

- certain war pensions for bereavement or disablement (para. 13.38);
- widowed mother's allowance and widowed parent's allowance (para. 13.50);
- if the claimant and any partner are under 60, student loan and access fund income (chapter 21).

Since this rule is almost never needed, the DWP intends to abolish it during 2006.

13.148 If two (or more) members of the family get any of these types of payment, the maximum weekly disregard is £20 for the whole family. In such cases, the disregard is used in whatever way is most favourable to the claimant.

13.149 Nothing in the above prevents an authority in Great Britain from running a local scheme whereby more than £10 (or all) of a war pension for bereavement or disablement is disregarded (para 22.10).

Assessing income and capital for people on savings credit

13.150 This section explains how income and capital are assessed if the claimant or any partner is on savings credit. It over-rides the rules described earlier in this chapter. If, however, the claimant qualifies for second adult rebate, the 'better buy' (para. 8.29) still applies once main CTB has been assessed as follows.

INCOME AND CAPITAL IS ASSESSED BY THE DWP

13.151 A claimant on savings credit has had his or her income and capital assessed by the DWP (i.e. the pensions service). With the exceptions mentioned below, the authority must use the DWP's assessment of income and capital in assessing the claimant's HB/CTB. Table 17.5 gives more information about the date these figures take effect.

HB60+ 27(1)
NIHB60+ 25(1)
CTB60+ 17(1)

Table 13.4: Claimants on savings credit: adjustments to the DWP's assessed income figure (AIF)

All the amounts mentioned in this table are weekly.

(a) Start with the DWP's assessed income figure

(b) Add the amount of savings credit payable

(c) If the claimant receives the following, deduct the amount shown*:

• earned income if the claimant is a lone parent	£5 (table 14.1)
• earned income if the claimant meets the conditions for the additional earnings disregard	£14.90 (para. 14.30)
• earned income if the claimant meets the necessary conditions for the child care disregard	the whole amount, up to the appropriate limit (para. 14.21)
• maintenance received from a current or former married partner or civil partner	£15 (para. 13.111)
• pensions for war bereavement or disablement	any amount disregarded under a local scheme (i.e. any amount over £10: para. 22.10)

(d) Make the following (very rare) adjustments if appropriate:

- add the income of any partner who was ignored in assessing pension credit but has to be taken account in HB/CTB
- if the authority determines that the income and capital of a non-dependant should be used instead of the income and capital of the claimant and partner (para 13.9), use this income instead of the DWP's assessment

* In each case the deduction equals the difference between what is disregarded in the assessment of pension credit and what is disregarded in HB/CTB.

THE DWP MUST NOTIFY THE AUTHORITY

13.152 The DWP must provide the authority with details of its assessment of income and capital within two working days of the following (or in either case as soon as reasonably practicable thereafter): HB60+ 27(2),(3) NIHB60+ 25(2),(3) CTB60+ 17(2),(3)

- the date the DWP did the assessment, if the person has already claimed or is already on HB/CTB by that time; or
- the date the authority informs the DWP that the claimant or partner has claimed HB/CTB, in all other cases.

In particular, the DWP must include in the notification its 'assessed income figure' ('AIF') for the claimant. 'Assessed income figure' is the term used in the law (and by most HB/CTB staff) to mean the DWP's assessment of the person's net weekly income – which includes any tariff income (even though the DWP separately notifies the authority of the capital figure it has used to determine that tariff income). Misleadingly, the DWP (i.e. the pensions service) rarely uses the term 'assessed income figure', but refers instead to 'net income' (or some other term).

13.153 If the DWP notifies the authority of new figures at any time, this is implemented as a change of circumstances (supersession) in the HB/CTB claim (table 17.1 and para. 17.4).

WHEN THE AUTHORITY ADJUSTS THE DWP'S ASSESSED INCOME FIGURE

13.154 Once the DWP has notified the authority of the claimant's assessed income figure, it is adjusted by the authority – but only if one (or more) of the things in table 13.4 applies. This is simply to reflect differences in assessing income for pension credit purposes as opposed to HB/CTB purposes. In making such adjustments, the authority uses (where necessary) the rules earlier in this chapter. HB60+ 27(4),(5) NIHB60+ 25(4),(5) CTB60+ 17(4),(5)

WHEN THE AUTHORITY ADJUSTS THE DWP'S CAPITAL FIGURE

13.155 The capital figure notified by the DWP is never (apart from the one exception below) adjusted. In particular, if the DWP notifies a figure above £16,000, the claimant is not entitled to HB/CTB. HB60+ 27(6),(7) NIHB60+ 25(6),(7) CTB60+ 17(6),(7)

13.156 The one exception works as follows. If the DWP notified the authority that the claimant's capital was £16,000 or lower and then the claimant's capital rises above £16,000 during the course of the DWP's 'assessed income period' (the period during which the DWP does not reconsider the amount of a claimant's income or capital) then the authority must itself reassess capital using the rules earlier in this chapter. HB60+ 27(8) NIHB60+ 25(8) CTB60+ 17(8)

13.157 If the authority's assessment is that the claimant's capital is now over £16,000, entitlement to HB/CTB ends. If the authority's assessment is that the claimant's capital is £16,000 or lower (whether different or the same as the DWP's assessment), there is no change to the amount of the claimant's HB/CTB.

DISPUTES AND APPEALS

DAR sch para 6
NIDAR sch 6

13.158 If a claimant disagrees with the DWP's assessed income figure (and any other income or capital figures notified by the DWP), this is something to take up using the DWP's disputes and appeals procedure. The claimant has no right to appeal to a social security tribunal via the authority about these figures.

13.159 If a claimant disagrees with an adjustment to the assessed income figure (table 13.4) or a re-assessment of capital (para. 13.157), he or she may ask the authority to reconsider (para. 17.55) and/or appeal to a tribunal via the authority (chapter 19).

Example: A war widow on savings credit

INFORMATION

A war widow aged 81 gets savings credit of £12.00 per week. She also gets a war widow's pension of £57.00 per week and retirement pension and an occupational pension, and has some capital.

The DWP notifies the authority of its assessed income figure (AIF) of £202.00 and notifies her capital as being £7,000. The authority dealing with her claim has a local scheme whereby it disregards the whole of a war widow's pension.

ASSESSMENT

The authority (table 13.4) starts with the DWP's assessed income figure (£202.00) and adds her savings credit (£12.00), giving a total of £214.00. It then disregards all but £10.00 of the war widow's pension of £57.00 (in other words, it disregards £47.00). This gives her net income for HB/CTB purposes as being £167.00 per week. It must use this figure in calculating her entitlement to HB/CTB.

The authority must accept that her capital is £7,000 at the outset. If evidence later arises of an increase in her capital, perhaps taking it above £16,000, it then becomes the authority's duty to re-assess her capital; but no action is taken upon this re-assessment unless the amount is greater than £16,000.

14 Employed earners

14.1 This chapter describes the rules for assessing income (and capital) received by employed earners in connection with their employment. It covers:

- the assessment of earnings;
- earned income disregards generally;
- the child care disregard;
- the additional earnings disregard (for people working at least 16/30 hours per week);
- particular kinds of earnings and expenses; and
- starting work, absences from work and ending work.

14.2 This chapter applies only if the claimant or any partner are not on JSA(IB), income support or pension credit. Apart from that, it applies to the assessment of a claimant's earnings and those of any partner; and in some cases the rules are different depending on whether they are under 60 or aged 60+. All earnings (and all other income and capital) of children and young persons are disregarded in full. Income of non-dependants and second adults are assessed differently. For more information on these points, and other general considerations, see paragraphs 13.2-10.

WHO IS AN 'EMPLOYED EARNER'?

HB 2(1) **14.3** The term 'employed earner' means a person who is gainfully employed in
CTB 2(1)
NIHB 2(1) Great Britain either under a contract of service, or in an office (including elective
NIHB60+ 2(1) office) with emoluments (forms of gain) chargeable to income tax under Schedule E (PAYE). This definition most obviously includes an employee who works for a wage or salary but it also includes directors of limited companies, clergy and local authority councillors.

The assessment of earnings

14.4 The key steps for assessing employed earnings for HB/main CTB purposes are:

- identifying earned income;
- establishing the gross earnings;
- deducting tax and national insurance contributions;
- deducting half of any approved pension contribution;

- converting the result, if necessary, to a weekly figure;
- deducting a fixed 'earned income disregard' and, if appropriate, amounts for child care costs and for certain people working 16/30 hours or more per week.

In certain circumstances, notional (rather than actual) earnings are used but this does not apply where the claimant or any partner is aged 60 or over (para. 13.141).

ESTABLISHING GROSS EARNINGS

14.5 The authority must first identify an appropriate assessment period that can be used as the basis for calculating or estimating the gross earned income. The aim is to identify the period that provides the most accurate basis on which to estimate average weekly earnings.

HB 2(1),29
HB60+ 2(1),33
NIHB 2(1),26
NIHB60+ 3(1),32
CTB 2(1),19
CTB60+ 2(1),23

GROSS EARNINGS OF UNDER-60s

14.6 Where the claimant and any partner are under age 60 and earnings have not fluctuated, the earnings are averaged over the five weeks immediately preceding the date of claim if the claimant is paid weekly; or the two months immediately preceding the date of claim if the claimant is paid monthly. But if averaging the earnings over some other period would produce a more accurate estimate of what will be the claimant's earnings, they should be averaged over that period. (See also para. 13.141 in the case of work paid at less than the going rate.)

HB 29
NIHB 26
CTB 19

14.7 If the claimant has not been employed for long enough to assess earnings on the above basis, but has received some earnings that are likely to represent average weekly earnings, then the authority should use those earnings to estimate average weekly earnings.

14.8 In any other circumstance, the authority should ask the claimant to provide an estimate from their employer of likely weekly earnings over an appropriate period. Most authorities have standard certificate of estimated earnings forms that can be used for this purpose.

14.9 Where the amount of a claimant's earnings changes during an award, the authority should estimate average weekly earnings by reference to the likely earnings from the employment over an appropriate period not exceeding 52 weeks.

GROSS EARNINGS OF 60+s

14.10 Where the claimant or any partner are aged 60 or over, and they work the same hours each week, and their income does not fluctuate, the rules with regard to establishing earnings are less prescriptive. Where the period for which a payment of earnings is made is a week or less, the weekly amount will be the amount of the payment and there are rules for the conversion of non-weekly to

HB60+ 33
NIHB 31
CTB60+ 23

weekly amounts (paras. 7.40 and 7.43). Where, however, the claimant's regular pattern of work means that they do not work the same hours every week, or where the claimant's earnings fluctuate and have changed more then once, the authority should average the claimant's weekly earnings as described in the following paragraphs.

14.11 Where the claimant does not work the same hours every week and there is a recognised cycle of work, the authority should work out the average weekly earnings over the period of the complete cycle (including any periods where the claimant does no work, but not including any other absences).

14.12 Where the claimant does not work the same hours every week but there is no recognizable cycle of work or where the claimant's earnings fluctuate and have changed more than once, the authority should work out the claimant's average earnings on the basis of:

- the last two payments before the date of claim or supersession if those payments are one month or more apart; or
- the last four payments if the last two payments are less then one month apart; or
- some other number of payments if this means a more accurate average weekly amount can be calculated.

Calculation of net earnings

HB 36 HB60+ 36 NIHB 33 NIHB60+ 34 CTB 26 CTB60+ 26

14.13 Net earnings are gross earnings less:

- income tax;
- Class 1 National Insurance contributions;
- half of any sum paid by the employee towards an occupational or personal pension scheme.

GROSS EARNINGS

14.14 Gross earnings means the amount of earnings after the deduction of expenses wholly and exclusively and necessarily incurred in the performance of the employment *(R(IS) 16/93)* (para. 14.46) but before any authorised deductions by the employer for tax, etc.

DEDUCTING INCOME TAX AND NATIONAL INSURANCE CONTRIBUTIONS

HB 36 HB60+ 36 NIHB 33 NIHB60+ 34 CTB 26 CTB60+ 26

14.15 If the claimant's actual gross earnings were used as described above, any income tax or Class 1 National Insurance contributions actually paid (or made from them) must be deducted from those earnings.

14.16 If the claimant's gross earnings were estimated, notional amounts for the income tax payable (using only the lower and basic rate of tax as appropriate and less only the personal allowance for a person aged under 65, whatever the claimant's actual circumstances) and Class 1 National Insurance contributions must be deducted from those estimated earnings on a pro-rata basis.

HB 36
HB60+ 36
NIHB 33
NIHB60+ 34
CTB 26
CTB60+ 26

14.17 Where, in Northern Ireland, the claimant works in the Republic, the amounts deducted are those which the NIHE estimates would have been deducted if they worked in Northern Ireland.

DEDUCTING HALF OF PENSION CONTRIBUTIONS

14.18 Where the claimant's actual or estimated gross earnings are used, half of any contributions they make or which would be payable on the estimated earnings to an occupational or personal pension scheme, must be deducted from the gross earnings figure.

HB 36
HB60+ 36
NIHB 33
NIHB60+ 34
CTB 26
CTB60+ 26

CONVERSION TO A WEEKLY FIGURE

14.19 If a claimant's earnings are paid other than weekly, they must be converted to a weekly figure as described in paragraph 7.43.

Earned income disregards generally

14.20 An earned income disregard must be deducted from each claimant's earnings. The amount depends on the type of case: the figures are given in table 14.1 (which also applies to self-employed earners). As shown in that table, only one of the amounts shown there is deducted from the combined earnings of a couple or polygamous marriage. (In certain cases, there are further disregards: paras. 13.120, 14.21 and 14.30.)

HB 36(2), sch 4
HB60+ 36(1), sch
NIHB 33(2), sch 5
NIHB60+ 34(1), sch 5
CTB 26(2), sch 3
CTB60+ 26(1), sch 2

Table 14.1: Weekly earned income disregards

£25 – LONE PARENTS

The weekly disregard is for anyone who counts as a lone parent for HB/CTB purposes.

£20 – CERTAIN PEOPLE WHO ARE DISABLED OR LONG-TERM SICK

This weekly disregard (per single claimant or per couple) applies in all the following cases:

- where the claimant and any partner are under 60 and the claimant's applicable amount includes a disability premium (para. 12.12) or severe disability premium (para. 12.23)
- where the claimant or any partner are 60+ and in receipt of:
  - long-term incapacity benefit
  - severe disablement allowance
  - attendance allowance
  - disability living allowance
  - a mobility supplement;
  - the disability or severe disability element of working tax credit

  or are

  - registered blind
  - treated as incapable of work (para. 12.15) for a continuous period of:
    - 196 days if terminally ill; or
    - 364 days in any other case.

Note: If the claimant or any partner to whom a £20 disregard applies becomes 60 and either had an award of HB/CTB within 8 weeks of becoming 60 then they re-qualify for the £20 disregard provided that:

- they qualified for the £20 disregard under the previous award; and
- continued in employment after that award ended, and
- there is no break of more than 8 weeks in HB/CTB entitlement or employment.

£20 – CERTAIN CARERS AND CERTAIN PEOPLE IN SPECIAL OCCUPATIONS

Except where the preceding disregards of £25 or £20 apply, this weekly disregard (per single claimant or per couple) applies in the following cases:

- single claimants and couples who are awarded a carer premium.
- single claimants and couples employed in the special occupations listed in paragraph 14.37.

OTHER SINGLE CLAIMANTS AND COUPLES

In any case not mentioned above, the weekly disregard is:

- £10 per couple;
- £5 per single claimant.

Note

Other earned income disregards are described in paragraph 14.21 and 14.30.

The child care disregard

14.21 In addition to the disregards in table 14.1, up to £175.00 (for one child) or £300 (for two or more children) per week per HB/main CTB claim is disregarded for child care costs in the circumstances described below. HB 28 HB60+ 31 NIHB 25 NIHB60+ 29 CTB 18 CTB60+ 21

WHO CAN QUALIFY?

14.22 The following groups qualify for the child care disregard in the circumstances described: HB 28 HB60+ 31 NIHB 25 NIHB60+ 29 CTB 18 CTB60+ 21

- lone parents in remunerative work;
- couples if both are in remunerative work;
- couples if one of them (claimant or partner) is in remunerative work and the other one incapacitated (para. 14.24), or in hospital, or in prison (whether serving a sentence or on remand).

REMUNERATIVE WORK

14.23 In general terms, 'remunerative work' means at least 16 hours per week. The full details are given in paragraphs 7.29 onwards. However, for the purposes of the child care disregard, a person on maternity leave, paternity leave or adoption leave from remunerative work still counts as being in remunerative work. For these purposes, a person who has been in remunerative work continues to count as such for up to 28 weeks (immediately following the last day of actually being in remunerative work) during which he or she: HB 28 HB60+ 31 NIHB 25 NIHB60+ 29 CTB 18 CTB60+ 21

(a) is paid statutory sick pay;

(b) is paid incapacity benefit at the short-term lower rate (which applies during the first 28 weeks of incapacity);

(c) is paid income support on the grounds of incapacity for work;

(d) is credited with earnings on the grounds of incapacity for work; or

(e) any combination of the above.

In case (c) the first day of the 28 weeks is the day on which the first person is first paid income support, and in case (d) the first day of the 28 weeks is the first day for which the person is credited with earnings.

INCAPACITATED

HB 28 **14.24** The other member of the couple is 'incapacitated' where:

HB60+ 31 NIHB 25 NIHB60+ 29 CTB 18 CTB60+ 21

- they are aged 80 or over;
- the claimant's applicable amount includes a disability premium on account of the other member's incapacity;
- they are aged less than 80 and apart from the age criteria would satisfy the conditions for the disability premium (para. 12.12) or would satisfy one of those conditions but have not been treated as incapable of work because the DWP has decided that their incapacity has arisen from their own misconduct or failure to take up medical treatment;
- the claimant's applicable amount would include a disability premium (para. 12.12) on account of the other member's disability but they have been disqualified by the DWP;
- the claimant has been treated as incapable of work (para. 12.15) for a continuous period of at least 196 days (breaks in continuity of 56 days should be ignored in calculating the 196 days);
- they receive (in GB) the NI equivalent of the following, or (in NI) the GB equivalent:
  - short-term higher rate or long-term incapacity benefit,
  - attendance allowance (AA),
  - severe disablement allowance (SDA),
  - disability living allowance (DLA),
  - industrial injuries constant attendance allowance, or
  - an increase of a war pension or disablement pension analogous to AA, DLA or an increase in disablement pension;
- any of the above pensions or allowances, except short-term higher rate or long-term incapacity benefit, have ceased because of hospitalisation; or
- the claimant has an invalid carriage or other vehicle provided under the relevant legislation.

HB 28 IN WHAT CIRCUMSTANCES DO THEY QUALIFY?

HB60+ 31 NIHB 25 **14.25** The above groups qualify for the disregard if the claimant or partner pays
NIHB60+ 29 CTB 18 one or more of the following to care for at least one child in their family (so long
CTB60+ 21 as that child satisfies the age condition – see below):

- a registered child-minder, nursery or play scheme; or
- a child-minding scheme for which registration is not required (e.g. run by a school, local authority or, in Northern Ireland, Crown property); or
- child care approved for working tax credit purposes; or
- any other out-of-school-hours scheme provided by a school on school premises or by a local authority (in Northern Ireland an education and library board or HSS trust) – but, in this case only, the child must be aged 8 or more.

The disregard does not, however, apply to payments in respect of compulsory education, nor to payments made by a claimant to his or her partner (or *vice versa*) if the child is the responsibility of at least one of them (para. 4.33), nor to payments for care provided by a relative (para. 10.44) for care wholly or mainly in the child's home.

THE AGE CONDITION

14.26 A child satisfies the age condition until:

HB 28
HB60+ 31
NIHB 25
NIHB60+ 29
CTB 18
CTB60+ 21

- the first Monday in September after their 15th birthday; or
- if the child meets the conditions for a disabled child premium (para. 12.19), or would do so apart from having regained sight, the first Monday in September after their 16th birthday.

AMOUNTS, ETC

14.27 The amount of the disregard equals what the claimant or partner pays, up to a maximum of:

HB 28
HB60+ 31
NIHB 25
NIHB60+ 29
CTB 18
CTB60+ 21

- £175.00 per week per HB/main CTB claim for claimants with one child who meets the above criteria (paras. 14.25-26); or
- £300.00 per week per HB/main CTB claim for claimants with two or more children who meet those criteria.

14.28 The disregard is made as far as possible from the earnings (from employment or self-employment) of a claimant and/or partner who satisfies the conditions in paragraph 14.22. Any balance, if the earnings are insufficient, is disregarded from any working tax credit or child tax credit the claimant or partner receives (para. 13.44). Apart from that, it cannot be disregarded from unearned income.

HB sch 4 para 17
HB60+ sch 4 para 9
NIHB sch 5 para 17
NIHB60+
sch 5 para 9
CTB sch 3 para 16
CTB60+
sch 2 para 9

14.29 The amount the claimant or partner pays is averaged over whichever period, up to a year, gives the most accurate estimate of the charges, taking account of information supplied by the person providing the care.

The additional earnings disregard

14.30 In addition to the earned income disregards mentioned above, a disregard of £14.90 per week is made if at least one of the following conditions is met (but see para. 14.32 for the exception to this rule):

- the claimant, or any partner receives the working tax credit 30 hours element; or
- the claimant or any partner is aged at least 25 and that person is engaged in remunerative work for on average at least 30 hours per week; or
- the claimant is in a couple who have at least one dependent child or young person and at least one member of the couple is engaged in remunerative work for on average at least 16 hours per week; or
- the claimant is a lone parent who is engaged in remunerative work for on average at least 16 hours per week; or
- the claimant's applicable amount includes a disability premium because of their disability and the claimant is engaged in remunerative work for on average at least 16 hours per week;
- the claimant's applicable amount includes a disability premium because of their partner's disability and the partner is engaged in remunerative work for on average at least 16 hours per week;
- the claimant or any partner receives the 50-plus element of working tax credit (DWP HB/CTB A3/2004, para 15, advises that this is shown on the tax credit award notice or can be confirmed by the Inland Revenue);
- the claimant or any partner would qualify for the 50-plus element of working tax credit if they were to make an application (Regulation 18 of the Working Tax Credit (Entitlement and Maximum Rate) Regulations 2002 sets out the entitlement conditions for the 50-plus element and DWP A3/2004 Appendix A provides the procedures to help identify this group);
- the claimant is aged at least 60, meets the conditions for the disabled/ long-term sick earned income disregard (table 14.1) and does paid work averaging at least 16 hours per week;
- The claimant or partner is aged at least 60, one of them does paid work averaging at least 16 hours per week and that person's circumstances meet the condition for the disabled/long-term sick earned income disregard (table 14.1).

14.31 For the above purposes, the question of whether anyone works 16 hours or more per week on average is decided as in paragraphs 7.29 onwards; and the question of whether anyone works 30 hours or more per week on average is decided in the same way (apart from the different number of hours).

14.32 The above £14.90 earned income disregard is not made if it (along with the other earned income disregard(s) which apply in any particular case) would result in a negative earned income figure. In such a case, a similar disregard is instead made from working tax credit (para. 13.44).

Particular kinds of earnings and expenses

BONUSES, TIPS AND COMMISSION

14.33 All forms of bonuses, tips and commission derived from the employment are included in the assessment of gross earnings. HB 35(1) HB60+ 35(1) NIHB 32(1) NIHB 33(1) CTB 25(1) CTB60+ 25(1)

ARREARS OF EARNINGS

14.34 Where the claimant or any partner is aged under 60, any arrears of pay count as capital. HB 79(7) NIHB 76(9) NIHB60+ 58(9) CTB 67(9)

TAX REFUNDS

14.35 Where the claimant and any partner are aged under 60, tax refunds on earnings count as capital (not earnings) including in Northern Ireland any analogous payments from the Irish Republic. HB 46(2) NIHB 43(2) CTB 36(2)

EARNINGS PAID IN A LUMP SUM

14.36 Where the claimant and any partner are aged under 60 and have earnings that are paid in a lump sum (or in any other form which could in broad terms be characterised as capital), they are nonetheless counted as earnings. They are averaged over the period they cover. HB 41(3) NIHB 38(3) CTB 31(3)

SPECIAL OCCUPATIONS ANNUAL BOUNTY

14.37 Where the claimant (and any partner) is aged under 60 and receives a bounty paid by the special occupations this counts as capital (not earnings) if it is paid annually or at longer intervals. For these purposes the 'special occupations' means part-time fire-fighters, auxiliary coast guards, part-time life-boat workers, and members of the Territorial Army or similar reserve forces. HB 46(1) NIHB 43(1) CTB 36(1)

NON-CASH VOUCHERS

14.38 If an employee receives non-cash vouchers that are taken into account for the purposes of calculating National Insurance contributions, their value is counted as employed earnings. The value of such vouchers should appear on pay slips (circular HB/CTB A17/99). HB 35(1)(k) HB60+ 35(1)(g) NIHB 32(1)(l) NIHB60+ 33(1)(g) CTB 25(1)(k) CTB60+ 25(1)(g)

PAYMENTS IN KIND

HB 35(2)(a) HB60+ 35(2)(a) NIHB 32(2)(a) NIHB60+ 33(2)(a) CTB 25(2)(a) CTB60+ 25(2)(a)

14.39 With the exception of certain non-cash vouchers (para. 14.38), payments in kind (i.e. payments of goods rather than money) are completely disregarded in the assessment of earnings. (For unearned payments in kind, see para. 13.114.) The DWP advises (GM paras. C3.99-101) that credits received via Local Exchange Trading Schemes ('LETS') do not count as payments in kind, but should be given a cash value as earnings.

COUNCILLORS' ALLOWANCES

14.40 Councillors' allowances, apart from expenses payments, count as employed earnings. (For general advice on these, see GM paras. C3.83-95.)

ROYALTIES ETC

HB60+ 33(4),(5),(8) NIHB60+ 31(4),(5),(8) CTB60+ 23(4),(5),(8)

14.41 The following two paragraphs apply to:

- any royalty or similar payment for use of a copyright, patent or trademark;
- any Public Lending Right Scheme payment for authors etc;
- any other (earned or unearned) occasional payment.

14.42 If the claimant or any partner is aged 60+:

- the first two items are included in the assessment of gross earnings if the recipient is the first owner of the copyright, patent or trademark or author of the book in question;
- the last item is included in the assessment of gross earnings in all cases (in other words, even if it is unearned).

14.43 If the claimant and any partner is under 60, the law lays down no particular way of assessing such payments, though in most cases it could well be appropriate to apply the rules for 60+s (except that unearned occasional payments should probably count as charitable or voluntary payments: para. 13.113).

COMPANY DIRECTORS

14.44 In the case of a claimant who is a director of a company registered with Companies House:

- the income paid by the company to the director is assessed as earned income under the usual rules;
- his or her interest (or share of it) in the company is assessed as capital.

WORK EXPENSES

14.45 The treatment of work expenses met by an employer is as follows:

- if they are for travel to work, or for the cost of caring for a child or other dependant, these must be added in as part of the employee's earnings;
- if they are for other items necessary for performance of the job, these are disregarded in full.

HB 35(1)(f),(2)(b), sch 5 para 3
HB60+ 29(1)(f),(2)(b)
NIHB 32(1)(f),(2)(b), sch 6 para 3
NIHB60+ 33(1)(f),(2)(b)
CTB 25(1)(f),(2)(b), sch 4 para 3
CTB60+ 19(1)(f),(2)(b)

14.46 Work expenses met by an employee and not reimbursed by the employer may not be disregarded against the employee's earnings (but see paragraph 14.21 as regards child care expenses); but where they are wholly and exclusively and necessarily incurred in the performance of the employment (e.g. travel costs between work places as opposed to travel to work costs) they should be deducted from the earnings figure to arrive at the gross earnings figure that is used as the starting point for the calculation of net earnings (*R(IS) 16/93* followed in *CIS 507/94*).

EXPENSES IN UNPAID WORK

14.47 Expenses received by a person doing unpaid work are disregarded in full if they are paid by a charitable organisation or non-profit-making voluntary organisation.

HB sch 5 para 2
HB60+ 29(1)
NIHB sch 6 para 2
NIHB60+ 27(1)
CTB sch 4 para 2
CTB60+ 19(1)

Starting work

14.48 Although in HB and main CTB there are no specific rules about the period to which earned income should be attributed, the general principle is that, when a claimant starts work, earnings should be taken into account from the beginning of the job – not (if different) the first pay day. (However, for Access to Work and similar schemes, see para. 13.64; for 'extended payments', see para. 17.81; and for the general rules about when changes of circumstances are taken into account, see chapter 17.)

ADVANCES OR LOANS FROM AN EMPLOYER

14.49 Advances and loans from an employer do not count as earnings. They count as capital if (and for as long as) the person has the money.

HB 46(5)
NIHB 43(5)
CTB 36(5)

Absences from work and ending work

14.50 The general rules are described below but note that where the claimant or any partner is aged 60 or over any earnings (other than royalties, etc) derived from employment which ended before the first day the claimant becomes entitled to HB/CTB, are disregarded. More details are in tables 14.2 and 14.3. These rules may appear complicated. This is because (for example) during a holiday a person may get

HB 35
HB60+ 35 sch 4 para 8
NIHB 32
NIHB60+ 33 sch 5 para 8
CTB 25
CTB60+ 25 sch 2 para 8

sick pay, or while on sick leave a person may get holiday pay. (For the general rules about when changes of circumstances are taken into account, see chapter 17.)

HOLIDAY PAY

HB 35(1)(d),46(3) HB60+ 35(1)(d), sch 4 para 8 NIHB 32(1)(d),43(3) NIHB60+ 33(1)(d), sch 5 para 8 CTB 25(1)(d),36(3) CTB60+ 25(1)(d), sch 2 para 8

14.51 Holiday pay counts as earnings (but see tables 14.2 and 14.3). Where the claimant or any partner is aged 60 or over, any holiday pay from employment which ended before the first day of HB/CTB entitlement is disregarded. Where the claimant and any partner are aged under 60, any holiday pay payable more than four weeks after the following event counts as capital:

- the beginning of an absence or break from work (table 14.2), or
- ending work (table 14.3).

HB 2(1), 35(1)(i),36(3) HB60+ 35(1)(h)-(j) NIHB 2(1), 32(1)(i),33(2) NIHB60+ 33(1)(h)-(j) CTB 2(1)25(1)(i), 26(3) CTB60+ 25(1)(h)-(j)

SICK PAY, MATERNITY PAY, PATERNITY PAY AND ADOPTION PAY

14.52 Statutory sick, maternity, paternity and adoption pay and employer's sick, maternity, paternity and adoption pay, and corresponding Northern Ireland payments (or in Northern Ireland, corresponding GB payments), count as earnings (but see table 14.2).

RETAINERS

HB 35(1)(e) HB60+ 35(1)(e) NIHB 32(1)(e) NIHB60+ 33(1)(e) CTB 25(1)(e) CTB60+ 25(1)(e)

14.53 Retainers are payments made for a period when no actual work is done, for example to employees of school meals services during the school holidays. These count as earnings (but see table 14.2).

STRIKE PAY

HB60+ 29(1) NIHB60+ 27(1) CTB60+ 19(1)

14.54 Strike pay does not count as earned income (since it is not paid by an employer). If the claimant and any partner are under 60, it counts as unearned income (but see tables 14.2 and 14.3). If the claimant or any partner are aged 60-plus, it is disregarded because it is not defined as income for HB/CTB purposes.

REDUNDANCY PAYMENTS

HB 35(1)(b),(g) HB60+ 35(1)(b) NIHB 32(1)(b),(g) NIHB60+ 33(1)(b) CTB 25(1)(b),(g) CTB60+ 25(1)(b)

14.55 Redundancy payments (including those paid periodically rather than in a lump sum) do not count as earnings. Redundancy payments count as capital if (and for as long as) the person actually has the money (but see table 14.3 for the treatment of other payments which may be made on redundancy – such as payments in lieu of notice and compensation payments).

Table 14.2: Absences from work

PERIODS WHILST SOMEONE RECEIVES A RETAINER

- ◆ Reassess earnings if they change (for example, if the person is paid less during the summer holidays).

HOLIDAYS, ABSENCES WITHOUT GOOD CAUSE, AND STRIKES

- ◆ Reassess earnings if they change (for example, if the person is paid less during holidays, or nothing during a strike). (See also the general rule about holiday pay: para. 14.51.)

SICK LEAVE, MATERNITY LEAVE, PATERNITY LEAVE, ADOPTION LEAVE, LAY OFF, SUSPENSION AND OTHER ABSENCES WITH GOOD CAUSE

The following rules apply so long as the employment has not terminated.

- ◆ If the absence for any of these reasons began before the person's 'date of claim' (para. 5.33). Count only the following as earnings (and only if they are received during the absence):
  - holiday pay – but only if it is an absence from remunerative work (paras. 7.29 onwards). (See also the general rule about holiday pay: para. 14.51.)
  - retainers;
  - statutory or employer's sick, maternity, paternity or adoption pay;
- ◆ If the absence for any of these reasons begins on or after the person's 'date of claim' (para. 5.33). Reassess earnings if they change (for example if the person receives a lower rate of pay for any of these reasons). (See also the general rule about holiday pay: para. 14.51.)

Table 14.3: Ending work

'Remunerative work' is described in paragraphs 7.29 onwards.

ENDING REMUNERATIVE WORK

Where the claimant or any partner is aged 60 or over any earnings (other than royalties) derived from employment which ended before the first day the claimant becomes entitled to HB/CTB are disregarded.

Where the claimant and any partner are aged under 60:

- If the termination of employment occurred before the person's 'date of claim' (para. 5.33) for any reason other than retirement. During the period following termination disregard all earnings except:
    - payments in lieu of remuneration (but periodic redundancy payments count as capital: para. 14.55);
    - payments in lieu of notice or compensating for loss of income;
    - holiday pay (see also the general rule about holiday pay: para. 14.51);
    - retainers;
    - compensation awards made by industrial tribunals for unfair dismissal. Other compensation payments count as capital (not earnings).
    - a sum payable in respect of: arrears of pay following an order for reinstatement or re-engagement under the Employment Rights Act 1996, or following an order under that Act or the Trade Union and Labour Relations (Consolidation) Act 1992 for the continuation of a contract of employment, or by way of remuneration following a protective award under the Trade Union and Labour Relations (Consolidation) Act 1992.
- If the termination occurs on or after the person's 'date of claim' (para 5.33). Reassess to take changes and ending of earnings into account. There are no special rules.

ENDING WORK WHICH IS NOT REMUNERATIVE WORK (PART-TIME WORK)

- If the termination occurred before the person's 'date of claim' (para. 5.33) disregard all earnings apart from retainers.
- If the termination occurs on or after the person's 'date of claim' (para. 5.33). Reassess to take changes and ending of earnings into account. There are no special rules.

15 The self-employed

15.1 This chapter describes the rules for assessing self-employed income (and capital). It covers:

- deciding who is self-employed;
- deciding what assessment period to use;
- assessing the total income during that period;
- assessing allowable expenses during that period;
- calculating pre-tax profit (chargeable income) for that period;
- allowing for tax and national insurance;
- allowing for half of any pension contributions;
- calculating net profit.

15.2 This chapter applies only if the claimant or any partner are not on JSA(IB), income support or pension credit. Apart from that, it applies to the self-employed income of a claimant and those of any partner; and in some cases the rules are different depending on whether they are under 60 or aged 60+. For more information on these points, and other general considerations, see paragraphs 13.2-10.

15.3 This chapter does not apply to the self-employed income of a non-dependant or second adult: the law does not lay down any particular way of assessing income from self-employment in such cases, although it must be gross (not net) of tax and national insurance; and in practice, most authorities assess their income under the rules in this chapter, but using the pre-tax profit figure rather than the net income figure.

15.4 For self-employed people on the New Deal, please see paragraph 15.41.

Who is self-employed?

CBA 2(1)(b)
NICBA 2(1)(b)
HB 2(1)
HB60+ 2(1)
NIHB 2(1)
NIHB 60+ 2(1)
CTB 2(1)
CTB60+ 3(1)

15.5 A 'self-employed earner' means someone who is gainfully employed in Great Britain (or in Northern Ireland gainfully employed in NI or the Republic) except anyone employed under a contract of service (i.e. an employee) or employed in an office (e.g. a company director of a limited liability company para. 14.44). A person may be a sole trader or in a business partnership (para. 15.28), and therefore be a self-employed earner. The DWP advises that the claimant's word should generally be accepted as to whether they are self-employed unless there are grounds for uncertainty (GM para. C3.311).

15.6 The following are not self-employed income:

- fostering and respite care payments (para. 13.55);
- Sports Council awards (para. 13.124);
- rent received by the claimant on their home (table 13.2);
- rent received by the claimant on property other than their home (table 13.3) *(R(FC) 2/92)*, unless the renting of property constitutes gainful self-employment (perhaps because of the number of properties rented out).

HB 37(2)
HB60+ 38(2)
NIHB 34(2)
NIH60+ 38(2)
CTB 27(2)
CTB60+ 28(2)

Capital

15.7 Assets of a business wholly or partly owned by a claimant are disregarded as capital whilst he or she:

- is self-employed in that business - so long as the assets are held in the course of self-employment *(CH/4258/2004)*; or
- has ceased to be self-employed. In this case, the assets are disregarded for as long as is reasonably needed for him or her to dispose of them; or
- is not self-employed because of sickness or disability, but intends to be afterwards. In this case, the assets are disregarded for 26 weeks from the date of any claim for HB/CTB, and then for whatever period is reasonable to enable him or her to return to self-employment.

HB sch 6 para 8
HB60+ sch 6 paras 9,10
NIHB sch 7 para 8
NIHB60+ sch 7 paras 9,10
CTB sch 5 para 8
CTB60+ sch 4 paras 9,10

15.8 It is sometimes necessary to decide whether capital is personal or part of the business. In general, the test depends on whether the capital is employed and risked in the business. For example, an amount in a self-employed claimant's personal bank account would not be disregarded as a business asset if it is neither employed nor risked in the business.

The assessment period

15.9 The income and expenses of a self-employed person are estimated by reference to an 'assessment period'. This should be whatever period is appropriate to enable the most accurate estimation of average weekly earnings *(CH/329/2003)*. Where the claimant and any partner are aged under 60 the period must not be longer than one year. Surprisingly, where the claimant or any partner is aged 60+ it must be for a one year period unless the circumstances are as set out in paras. 15.12-14. The year does not need to be the year immediately before the claim or the date the claim is looked at. The general principle is that income and expenses in the past (in the assessment period) are used to calculate HB and CTB in the future.

HB 2(1),30
HB60+ 37
NIHB 24(1),27
NIHB60+ 35
CTB 2(1) 20
CTB60+ 27

PEOPLE WHO HAVE BEEN SELF-EMPLOYED FOR AT LEAST A YEAR

15.10 For people who have been self-employed for some time the DWP advises that the assessment period should normally be that of the last year's trading accounts, but that a shorter or different period may be used if that period is more representative of the currrent trading position (GM para. C3.330).

15.11 A person who claims HB/CTB during the course of self-employment should usually have evidence of his or her recent actual income and expenses from that self-employment. It would usually be reasonable in such cases for the council to ask for the claimant's most recent accounts showing income and expenses (regardless of whether these are prepared by an accountant or other professional or by the claimant).

PEOPLE WHO HAVE BEEN SELF-EMPLOYED FOR LESS THAN A YEAR

15.12 If someone has been self-employed for less than a year, the assessment period is whatever period (during which they have been self-employed) that will give the most accurate assessment.

PEOPLE SETTING UP IN BUSINESS

15.13 A person who claims HB/CTB when he or she is just setting up in self-employment cannot possibly have evidence of his or her actual income and expenses from that self-employment. In such cases, the DWP (in their HB/CTB Guidance Manual) recommends that councils should estimate the claimant's income and expenses based on information provided by the claimant. Many councils have forms claimants can fill in giving their estimates. These estimates (unless they are unreasonable) are typically used to assess the claimant's HB/CTB for a short period, say 13 weeks. The claimant should then be advised to keep proper records of income and expenses during that period, so that he or she can send them in to be used as evidence for the following period.

IF THE NATURE OF A BUSINESS CHANGES

15.14 If the nature of a claimant's business changes in such a way as to affect the normal pattern of business, e.g. the loss of a major customer or changing from full-time to part-time self-employment, the authority should again identify an assessment period that allows it to calculate the earnings with the greatest accuracy, e.g. starting with the date the change occurred and ending on the date for which the most recent figures regarding earnings and expenditure are available *(CH/329/2003)*.

CAN THE FIGURES BE ALTERED LATER?

15.15 Once the various figures have been assessed as described above, they can be altered later if they were based on a mistake of fact or law or there was an official error, or if there has subsequently been a relevant change of circumstances (e.g. as in para. 15.14). It is incorrect in any other case to revise the figures.

A NOTE ON ACCOUNTING METHODS

15.16 Self-employed people commonly account for their income and expenditure using one of the following methods:

- a 'cash' basis – counting income as being received on the day they receive the money and counting expenses as being incurred on the day they pay the money out; or
- an 'on paper' basis – counting income as being received on the day they issue their bill or invoice for it and counting expenses as being incurred on the day they receive a bill or invoice for them; or
- the basis required (roughly speaking) for income tax purposes – counting income as being received on the day they issue their bill or invoice or the day they receive the money, whichever happens first and counting expenses as being incurred on the day they receive a bill or invoice or the day they pay the money out, whichever happens first.

15.17 In relation to the rules that operate where the claimant and any partner are under age 60, there is a body of opinion that HB and CTB entitlement should reflect the claimant's cash flow – the first method above. On the other hand, there is evidence that the HB and CTB regulations were drafted on the assumption that income and expenditure should be dealt with under the second or third method above. For example, the rules about debts referred to in items (k) and (l) of table 15.1 would not be needed if income and expenditure were dealt with on a purely cash flow basis. The rules that operate where the claimant or any partner is aged 60-plus are drafted on the assumption that income and expenditure is to be dealt with on a cash flow basis – note the absence of the previously mentioned items in table 15.1 for these claimants. Consequently, where accounts 'on a paper basis' have been submitted for such claimants the information they contain needs to be converted to a cash flow basis, i.e. to reflect gross receipts actually received – not money owed to the business, and expenses actually paid – not unpaid bills.

Assessing total earnings

HB 37(1),38(1),(3)
HB60+38(1)
NIHB 34(1),35(1),(3)
NIHB60+ 36(1)
CTB 27(1),28(1),(3)
CTB60+ 28(1)

15.18 The total earnings of the employment means all the income/receipts of the business during the assessment period. There are two general points to bear in mind.

- Only payments of income are taken into account. A payment of capital into a business (e.g. an investment in the business by, say, a relative) is not a payment of income. It is disregarded under the general rule about disregarded capital (para. 15.7).
- Only income 'derived from' the employment is taken into account. Income from some other source (e.g. as described in para. 15.19) falls under whatever rules apply to that kind of income (chapter 13).

GRANTS, LOANS AND THE ACCESS TO WORK SCHEME

15.19 The following additional points apply:

- Typically, but not always, grants are not 'derived from' self-employment. If not, they should be regarded as a separate source of income or capital – typically voluntary or charitable (para. 13.113).
- Genuine loans are not income (para. 13.126). Money from a loan forms part of the claimant's capital. If it is a loan to the business it is therefore disregarded (para. 15.7).
- Disabled people setting up in self-employment can get payments under the government's Access to Work scheme: these are disregarded as income (para. 13.64).

SINGLE REGENERATION BUDGET (BUSINESS START-UP ALLOWANCES)

HB 37(1)
HB60+38(1)
NIHB 34(1)
NIHB60+ 36(1)
CTB 27(1)
CTB60+ 28(1)

15.20 The Single Regeneration Budget (SRB) has replaced various employment related national schemes and programmes including the Business Start up Allowance (GM para. C3.340-42). Any regular payments to the business from the SRB received by the claimant during the assessment period (except for capital payments) must be counted as part of the total income of the employment. They must not be counted as a separate source of income. But they are not included as income if payments ceased before the date of claim for HB or CTB. In Northern Ireland any equivalent allowance under legislation of the Irish Republic is treated in the same way.

Assessing allowable expenses

HB 38(3)(a),(7)
HB60+ 39(2)(a),(6)
NIHB 35(3)(a),(7)
NIHB60+ 37(2)(a)
CTB 28(3)(a),(7)
CTB60+ 34(3),(7)

15.21 Having worked out the total income in the assessment period, the next step is to allow for the expenses incurred in running the business during the assessment period. The two general principles are:

- expenses are allowed for so long as they are 'wholly and exclusively incurred' for the purpose of the business; but
- the authority cannot allow for an expense if it is not satisfied, given the nature and the amount, that it has been 'reasonably incurred'.

15.22 The law contains rules about special kinds of expenses. These are summarised in table 15.1.

WORKING FROM HOME

15.23 A rent-paying claimant who works from home may regard part of their rent as a business expense. Whether it is an allowable expense depends on the circumstances of the case. It is clear that if part of the home is exclusively used for the business (e.g. an annexe), then the rent on this is an allowable expense but is also disregarded in the assessment of the claimant's eligible rent (paras. 10.5 and 10.108). In all cases, however, an allowance should be made for a reasonable proportion of heating the home and of similar overheads.

DRAWINGS TAKEN BY THE CLAIMANT FROM THE BUSINESS

15.24 Claimants may take 'drawings' from their business as a kind of wages or salary for themselves. These must not be allowed as a business expense.

COUPLES WHERE ONE EMPLOYS THE OTHER

15.25 If the claimant pays their partner to work for the business, this is allowable as a business expense. It will then count as the partner's earnings. The rules are different if the couple are in a business partnership (para. 15.28).

SELF-EMPLOYED CHILDMINDERS

15.26 For claimants who are self-employed childminders, instead of working out what their actual expenses are, two-thirds of their total earnings are disregarded in lieu of expenses. No actual expenses can be allowed for.

HB 38(9)
HB60+ 39(8)
NIHB 35(9)
NIHB60+ 37(8)
CTB 28(9)
CTB60+ 29(8)

Pre-tax profit

15.27 The next step is to work out the claimant's 'pre-tax profit' (referred to in the regulations as 'chargeable income'):

HB 38(1)(a),(3)
HB60+ 39(1)(a),(3)
NIHB 35(1)(a),(3)
NIHB60+ 37(1)(a),(
CTB 28(1)(a),(3)
CTB60+ 29(1)(a),(3)

Total earnings (paras. 15.18-20)

MINUS

- allowable expenses (paras. 15.21-26)

= pre-tax profit.

BUSINESS PARTNERSHIPS

15.28 If the claimant is self-employed in a partnership, the pre-tax profit (as defined above) should be assessed for the partnership and then split between the business partners. This split should reflect how the business partners actually split their income. This split is required even if the business partners are a couple because it will ensure the correct calculation of notional tax and national insurance

HB 38(1)(b),(4)
HB60+ 39(1)(b)
NIHB 35(1)(b),(4)
NIHB60+ 37(1)(b)
CTB 28(1)(b),(4)
CTB60+ 29(1)(b)

Table 15.1 Special types of expenses

		Allowable?
(a)	Interest payments on any business loan	Yes
(b)	Sums (other than interest payments) employed or intended to be employed in setting up or expanding the business	No
(c)	Income spent on repairing an existing business asset (except to the extent that any sum is payable under an insurance policy for this)	Yes
(d)	Capital repayments on loans for repairing an existing business asset (except to the extent that any sum is payable under an insurance policy for this)	Yes
(e)	Capital repayments on loans for replacing business equipment or machinery	Yes
(f)	Capital repayments on any other business loans	No
(g)	Any other capital expenditure	No
(h)	Depreciation of any capital asset	No
(i)	Losses incurred before the beginning of the assessment period	No
(j)	Excess of VAT paid over VAT received in the assessment period	Yes
(k)	Proven bad debts	Yes/NA*
(l)	Other debts	No/NA*
(m)	Expenses incurred in the recovery of any debt	Yes
(n)	Business entertainment	No
(o)	Any sum for a domestic or private purpose	No

* Not applicable where the claimant or any partner is aged 60 or over (para. 15.17)

Example: Expenses

A self-employed technical writer's accounts include the following expenditure. Before the purchase of her computer and laser printer, she used to do all her writing by hand. The references (a), (b), etc, are to table 15.1.

A cash payment to buy her computer.	Not allowable (g).
Repayments on the loan she took out to buy her printer.	The capital element of the repayments is not allowable (f). The interest element is allowable (a).
Repayments on a smaller loan covering half the cost of repairing her printer, which was not insured.	Capital and interest elements are both allowable (d), (a).
A cash payment covering the other half of the cost of the printer repair.	Allowable (c)
Repayments on a general purpose business loan to help with her cash-flow.	The interest element of the repayments is allowable (a). The capital element is not (f).
A figure for depreciation in the value of the computer and printer.	Not allowable (h).

Example: A self-employed childminder

A claimant earns £120 per week from working as a self-employed childminder. She is a lone parent with no other form of earned income. She does not make pension contributions. She does not use a childminder for her own children. Her income from childminding is assessed as follows:

- From the gross amount, two-thirds (£80) is disregarded. The remaining amount is £40.00
- £40 per week is too low for a deduction to be made for notional tax and national insurance (tables 15.2, 15.3).
- She qualifies for an earned income disregard. For a lone parent (table 14.1) this is £25.00
- So her assessed weekly earned income for HB/main CTB purposes is £15.00

(para. 15.34). The rules are different if one partner in a couple employs the other (para. 15.25).

15.29 The rules regarding the business partner's share of the net profit also apply to 'share fishermen'.

NIL INCOME FROM SELF-EMPLOYMENT

15.30 If the claimant's allowable expenses exceed his or her total income, then pre-tax profit is nil. So his or her income from the self-employment is nil.

HB 38(10) HB60+ 39(9) NIHB 35(1) NIHB60+ 37(9) CTB 28(10) CTB60+ 29(9)

MORE THAN ONE EMPLOYMENT

15.31 If a self-employed claimant is engaged in any other employment or self-employment, the losses from one cannot be set against the income from the other.

IF THE PRE-TAX PROFIT APPEARS UNREPRESENTATIVE

15.32 If the pre-tax profit appears unlikely to represent the claimant's income, the authority should consider whether selecting a different assessment period would produce a more accurate estimate (para. 15.9).

Notional income tax and notional NICs

HB 39 HB60+ 40 NIHB 36 NIHB60+ 38 CTB 29 CTB60+ 30

15.33 Allowances are made for income tax and national insurance contributions ('NICs'). However, the authority must work these out itself, based on the claimant's pre-tax profit. The figures calculated by the authority are known as 'notional income tax' and 'notional NICs'. They usually differ from the actual income tax and NICs paid by the claimant. One reason for the difference is that an amount for depreciation and certain expenses which are allowed by the Inland Revenue cannot be allowed for HB/CTB purposes. In Northern Ireland, if the claimant is employed in the Republic the authority deducts what it considers would have been deducted had they worked in Northern Ireland.

THE CALCULATIONS

HB 39 HB60+ 40 NIHB 36 NIHB60+ 38 CTB 29 CTB60+ 30

15.34 The calculations are given in tables 15.2 and 15.3. An example is given near the end of this chapter. The tables apply to annual amounts of pre-tax profit. If a claimant's assessment period was a different length (e.g. three months), convert pre-tax profit into an annual figure before doing the calculations (para. 7.43). In the case of a couple, work through the calculations separately for each one who has self-employed income.

HB 34 HB60+ 34 NIHB 31 NIHB60+ 32 CTB 24 CTB60+24

15.35 Tables 15.2 and 15.3 give the figures for the tax year from 6th April 2006 to 5th April 2007. The law changed on 10th November 2005 to say authorities should use the tax and national insurance figures 'applicable to the assessment period'. This is intended broadly to reflect the way real tax assessments work. For example, if a claim is made or reconsidered in December 2006, then (although the assessment period might have been partly in one tax year and partly in another) the figures 'applicable to the assessment period' are nonetheless the 2006-07 tax year's. In other words the figures in the tables apply whenever the date of claim or date of reconsideration falls between 6th April 2006 and 5th April 2007, both dates included. Having said that, the law also allows the authority to ignore changes in tax and national law (such as the Budget) for up to benefit 30 weeks – though this is something authorities seldom do.

Table 15.2: Calculating notional income tax (2006-07 tax year)

(a) Start with the annual pre-tax profit figure.

(b Subtract £5,035*.

(c) If there is a remainder:
multiply the first £2,150 (or all, if it is under £2,150) by 10%;
multiply the rest (if any) by 22%, and add to the result of the above.**

(d) The result is the amount of notional tax.

Notes

* £5,035 is the personal allowance.

** The 40% tax rate is not used in assessing notional income tax, nor are any allowances taken into account other than as above.

Pension contributions

15.36 An allowance is made for half of any pension contributions payable by self-employed claimants towards: HB 38(11),(12) HB60+ 36(11),(12 NIHB 35(11),(13) NIHB60+ 37(10),(11) CTB 28(11),(12) CTB60+ 29(11),(1

- a self-employed personal pension scheme if they are payable on a periodical basis (e.g. monthly). No allowance is made for the lump sum payments some self-employed people make (often for tax purposes); or
- an annuity for a retirement pension for the claimant or a dependant (including husbands, wives and unmarried partners) – if the scheme is approved by the Inland Revenue as eligible for tax relief. People can no longer enter such schemes, but those who entered them in the past may still be in them.

Table 15.3: Calculating notional NI contributions (2006-07 tax year)

CLASS 2 NICS

If the annual pre-tax profit figure is £4,465* or more, then the amount of notional class 2 NICs is £109.20.**

CLASS 4 NICS

(a) Start with the annual pre-tax profit figure (unless this is greater than £33,540***, in which case start with £33,540).

(b) Subtract £5,035.***

(c) If there is a remainder, multiply it by 8%. The result is the amount of notional class 4 NICs.

Notes

The person may have class 2 notional NICs alone, or may have both class 2 and class 4 notional NICs.

* £4,465 is the lower threshold for class 2 NICs. If the person's pre-tax profit is lower, then the notional class 2 NICs figure is nil (regardless of whether the claimant has in fact applied to the Inland Revenue for exemption).

** £109.20 is 52 times £2.10 (the weekly rate of class 2 NICs), there being 52 Sundays in the 2006-07 tax year (6 April one year to 5 April the following year).

*** £5,035 is the lower threshold, and £33,540 the upper threshold, for class 4 NICs. The 1% class 4 NIC rate for income above £33,540 is not used in assessing notional NICs. (The regulations have not been amended to keep them up-to-date with NIC rules, but this appears to be their intention.)

15.37 The allowance applies only while the claimant is making such payments. So if a claimant starts or ceases making such payments while he or she is on HB or CTB (or the amount of the payments changes), this is taken into account as a change of circumstances and HB and/or CTB must be reassessed.

15.38 To find the annual equivalent of pension contributions:

- for contributions payable calendar monthly, multiply the monthly contribution by 12;
- in any other case, divide the contribution by the number of days it covers (e.g. in the case of a weekly contribution, divide by 7) and multiply by 365.

Example: Pension contributions

When a claimant claims HB and CTB, he is paying pension contributions of £50 per month. The annual equivalent is 12 x £50 = £600. Half of this (£300) is allowable in calculating his annual net profit.

After making three monthly payments, he reduces his payments to £40 per month. The annual equivalent is 12 x £40 = £480. Half of this (£240) is allowable in calculating his annual net profit. His claim must be reassessed taking his new annual net profit into account from the Monday after the day on which the first payment of £40 was due.

Net profit

15.39 The final step is to work out the claimant's net profit. It is always advisable to work this out initially on an annual basis.

HB 38(1)-(3)
HB60+ 36(1)-(3)
NIHB 35(1)-(3)
NIHB60+ 37(1)-(3)
CTB 28(1)-(3)
CTB60+ 29(1)-(3)

Pre-tax profit (paras. 15.27-32)

MINUS

- notional income tax and notional NI contributions (paras. 15.33-35)
- half of pension contributions (paras. 15.36-38)

= net profit.

CONVERSION TO A WEEKLY FIGURE

15.40 The result must be converted to a weekly figure. Divide the annual figure by 365 and then multiply the result by 7. This weekly figure is the one used in calculating entitlement to HB and main CTB (subject to the earned income disregards: paras. 14.20-32).

Example: Notional tax and NI contributions and net profit: 2006-07

A married woman's annual pre-tax profit is £9,000. She contributes £480 per year to a personal pension scheme. Her husband has no source of earned income.

NOTIONAL INCOME TAX (TABLE 15.2)

(a)	Start with the annual pre-tax profit figure. This is	£9,000
(b)	Subtract the personal allowance of £5,035. This leaves	£3,965
(c)	Of this,	
	multiply the first £2,150 by 10%	
	10% of £2,150 is:	£215.00
	multiply the rest (£3,965 – £2,150 = £1,815) by 22%	
	22% of £1,815 is	£399.30
	Adding these together gives:	£614.30
(d)	So her notional tax is:	£614.30

NOTIONAL CLASS 2 NICS (TABLE 15.3)

The annual pre-tax profit figure (£9,000) is greater than £4,465, so the amount of her notional class 2 NICs is £109.20.

NOTIONAL CLASS 4 NICS (TABLE 15.3)

(a) Start with the annual pre-tax profit figure (which is not greater than £33,540). This is £9,000.

(b) Subtract £5,035.

(c) Multiply the remainder (which is £3,965) by 8%.

This is £317.20 – which is the amount of her notional class 4 NICs.

NET PROFIT

Annual pre-tax profit	£9,000.00
minus notional income tax	£614.30
minus notional class 2 NICs	£109.20
minus notional class 4 NICs	£317.20
minus half of annual contributions to pension scheme	£240.00
Equals annual net profit:	£7,959.30
On a weekly basis this is (£7,959.30 ÷ 365 x 7 =)	£152.64
She qualifies for an earned income disregard of	£10.00
So her weekly net profit (after the disregard) is	£142.64

People on the self-employed employment option of the New Deal

15.41 People on the 'self-employment route' of the New Deal, and people assisted with pursuing self-employment on an Employment Zone programme or on the 'intensive activity period' of the New Deal (paras. 13.62-64) are nearly all entitled to income support or income-based jobseeker's allowance: in their case, all their income and capital is disregarded for HB and main CTB purposes (paras. 7.5, 13.3). In the rare cases of such people not on either of those benefits, there are special rules, given in the 2005-06 edition of this Guide.

16 Decisions, notices and payment

16.1 This chapter describes the process of decision-making, notices and payment. It covers the following:

- how quickly a should claim be dealt with and benefit paid;
- who must be notified of the authority's decision;
- information that must be provided to the claimant and others;
- how, and when, HB/CTB should be paid;
- the requirement to make a payment of HB in 14 days (a payment on account) for rent allowance claimants;
- how often a rent allowance should be paid;
- when HB can be paid direct to a landlord (except for pathfinder authorities: see paras. 22.53-62);
- who else may receive payment of a rent allowance/CTB.

Dealing with claims and changes

HOW QUICKLY SHOULD THE CLAIM BE DEALT WITH AND BENEFIT PAID?

HB 89(3), 90(1)(a),91(3)
HB60+ 70(3), 71(1)(a),72(3)
NIHB 84(3), 85(1)(a),86(3)
NIHB60+ 67(3), 68(1)(a),69(3)
CTB 75(3),76(1)(a)
CTB60+ 60(3), 61(1)(a)

16.2 Once the authority has received a claim and all the information and evidence it reasonably requires from the claimant it must:

- reach a decision on the claim within 14 days or as soon as reasonably practicable after that;
- notify persons affected (para. 16.7) as soon as the claim is decided; and
- in the case of HB, make payment within 14 days of the receipt of the claim or as soon as possible after that.

In all rent allowance cases if the authority is unable to meet the 14 day decision-making timetable it must normally make a payment on account (para. 16.16).

EXCEPTIONS TO THE REQUIREMENT TO DECIDE

16.3 The authority does not have to meet the above time limits however where a claim: HB 89(2) HB60+ 70(2) NIHB 84(2) NIHB60+ 67(2) CTB 75(2) CTB60+ 60(2)

- is not made in the proper time and manner (para. 5.8 and 5.25); or
- is not supported by reasonably required information or evidence from the claimant (para. 5.17); or
- has been withdrawn (para. 5.16).

TIME PERIOD IN WHICH OTHER DECISIONS SHOULD BE MADE

16.4 From time to time authorities have to make other decisions on a claim, e.g. to supersede an original decision following a change of circumstance. Notice of their decisions must be made within 14 days or as soon as possible after that. Notice is not required, however, where a change in CTB entitlement relates solely to a reduction in the council tax where government 'tax-capping' or a delayed award of a disability reduction or discount leads to an overpayment of CTB. HB 90(1)(b) HB60+ 71(1)(b) NIHB 85(1)(b) NIHB60+ 68(1)(b) CTB 76(1)(b) CTB60+ 61(1)(b)

REMEDIES FOR DELAYS

16.5 Authorities are expected to meet the time limits in the majority of cases. Delays are normally only justifiable, for example, in periods of peak pressure such as the annual up-rating or while handling a high level of enquiries following a take-up campaign. Many authorities fail to meet the time limit and it may be necessary to place pressure on them through campaigns and other remedies to ensure that they meet this obligation in the future. Remedies include:

- complaints to the local government ombudsman;
- action in the High Court or Court of Session in Scotland for judicial review to require authorities to make a determination; and
- action in the County Court or Sheriff Court to require authorities to make a payment if they have agreed that the claimant is entitled.

16.6 In *R v Liverpool CC ex parte Johnson No. 1* the court held that authorities have a duty to allocate sufficient resources according to their caseload such that the vast majority of claims can be processed within the 14 day time limit. The court also found that the fact that many authorities fail to meet this standard is not an excuse but rather makes the need for judicial intervention 'all the greater'.

Who should be notified and how?

PERSONS AFFECTED

HB 2(1),90
HB60+ 2(1),71
NIHB 2(1),85
NIHB60+ 2(1),68
CTB 2(1),76
CTB60+ 2(1),61
DAR 3
NIDAR 3

16.7 The authority is required to notify all persons affected by a decision. A 'person affected' means any of the following where their rights, duties or obligations are affected by a decision:

- the claimant;
- where a claimant, or would-be claimant, is unable to act on his or her own behalf:
  - a receiver appointed by the Court of Protection;
  - an attorney with a general power or a power to claim or as the case may be receive benefit appointed under the Powers of Attorney Act 1971 or the Enduring Powers of Attorney Act 1985;
  - a person appointed by the council to act on behalf of someone who is unable to act on his or her own behalf;
  - a person appointed by the Secretary of State (in practice a manager at the DWP office) to act on behalf of someone who is unable to act on his or her own behalf;
- the landlord – but only in relation to a decision (not) to make direct payments (where the payment is made to an agent acting for the landlord the agent is the person affected)(paras. 16.29-30 and 16.34); or
- anyone – including the landlord – from whom the authority has decided that an overpayment is recoverable (para. 18.25).

16.8 There may be more than one person affected by any decision made by the authority. For example, where the authority decides to recover an overpayment from the claimant's landlord, both the landlord and the claimant are 'persons affected' and both should be notified of the relevant decisions. The term 'person affected' is not confined to people; it also applies to corporate bodies such as housing associations and letting companies.

INFORMATION TO BE PROVIDED IN A NOTICE

HB 90 sch 9
HB60+ 71 sch 8
NIHB 85 sch 10
NIHB60+ 68 sch 10
CTB 76 sch 8
CTB60+ 61 sch 7

16.9 The authority must send a written notice to the claimant or other person affected by a decision (paras.16.41 and 18.83) which in all cases must contain the information set in paragraph 16.11. Table 16.1 sets out the additional minimum information that a notice must contain following a decision on a claim for HB and/or CTB. In practice, some notices do not meet these minimum requirements and/or are difficult to understand. Further, some authorities do not keep copies of their notices, thereby placing their staff in the impossible position of being unable to explain to claimants what they have said to them.

16.10 A decision notice is also required where: rent allowance is to be paid direct to the landlord (paras. 16.30, 16.34 and 16.41); the income of a non-dependant is treated as the claimant's (para. 13.9); and there is a recoverable overpayment (paras. 18.10 and 18.83-90).

HB 90 sch 9 paras 11-13,15
HB60+ 71 sch 8 paras 11-13,15
NIHB 85 sch 10 paras 11-13,15
NIHB60+ 68 sch 10 paras 11-13,15
CTB 76 sch 8 paras 11,16
CTB60+ 61 sch 7 paras 11,16

16.11 All notices (whatever the type of decision and regardless of whether the claimant is entitled) must include statements explaining the right of the person affected to:

- obtain a written statement of the authority's reasons for the decision and the time and manner in which this can be requested (17.16); and
- request a reconsideration of a decision (para. 17.55) and, where appropriate, to appeal against that decision (i.e. where it is an appealable decision – paras. 19.17-19).

HB sch 9 paras 1-8
HB60+ sch 8 paras 1-8
NIHB sch 10 paras 1-8
NIHB60+ sch 10 paras 1-8
CTB sch 8 paras 1-8
CTB60+ sch 7 paras 1-8

Table 16.1: Information to be notified following decisions on a claim

(Separate notices are required for HB and CTB decisions)

WHERE THE CLAIMANT IS ENTITLED TO HB AND/OR CTB

Items to be included in all decision notices where the claimant is entitled

(a) The matters to be notified in every case (para. 16.11).

(b) The claimant's duty to notify the authority of changes of circumstance and examples of the kinds of change that should be reported.

(c) The weekly eligible rent/council tax/rates (and in the case of CTB the details of any rounding of figures*).

(d) The normal weekly amount of benefit (and in the case of CTB the details of any rounding of figures).

(e) The first day of entitlement.

Additional items where the claimant is entitled to HB and/or main CTB

(f) The amount and category of any non-dependant deductions.

(g) Except where the claimant is on IS/JSA(IB)/guarantee credit the applicable amount and how it is worked out.

(h) Except where the claimant is on IS/JSA(IB)/state pension credit the weekly earnings and unearned income.

HB sch 9 paras 1-10,14
HB60+ sch 8 paras 1-10,14
NIHB sch 10 paras 1-10,14
NIHB60+ sch 10 paras 1-10,14
CTB sch 8 paras 1-10,13-15
CTB60+ sch 7 paras 1-10,13-15

(i) Where the claimant is entitled to the savings credit only

- the amount of income and capital notified to the authority by the DWP (para. 13.151) or where appropriate the capital figure calculated by the authority (13.156); and
- any adjustment of the DWP's income and capital figures; and
- the amount of savings credit.

(j) HB only, the amount of any deductions for fuel where the amounts in table 10.6 have been applied and the fact that they may be varied if they supply evidence.

(k) HB only, where payment is by rent allowance, the date of payment and period for which payment is being made.

Additional item where the claimant is entitled to both types of CTB

(l) Where the claimant is entitled to both main CTB and second adult rebate, the fact that they are better off on the type of CTB that has been awarded and the amount of alternative CTB that would otherwise have been payable.

Additional items where the claimant is entitled to second adult rebate

(m) Rates of second adult rebate and related gross income levels.

(n) Gross income of any second adult or the fact that the second adult is on IS/JSA(IB)/state pension credit.

WHERE THE CLAIMANT IS NOT ENTITLED TO HB OR CTB

(o) Items (a) and (c)* in all cases.

(p) Where HB or main CTB is not payable because of income or, in the case of HB only, the minimum payment rule (para. 7.12):

- items (f) and (j); and
- where the claimant is not on IS/JSA(IB)/guarantee credit, items (g) and (h); and
- where appropriate, the fact that HB is not payable because the minimum payment rule applies and the weekly HB that would otherwise be payable.

(q) Where HB and/or main CTB is not payable for any reason other than in (p) above, the reason why it is not payable.

(r) Where second adult rebate is not payable because the income of the second adults is too high or some other reason:

- in the case where the income of the second adults is too high: items (m) and (n); or
- in any other case the reason why it is not payable.

* Details of CTB rounding figures are not required if the claimant is not entitled

Time and manner of payment

PAYMENT OF HB

16.12 Authorities may decide on the time and manner in which to make payments of HB on the basis of the circumstances of the individual case. They are expected to have regard to the reasonable needs and convenience of the person they are paying, as well as the time and frequency with which the liability to make payments arises. Decisions on payment method/frequency are not appealable but a person affected can request the authority to reconsider its decision at any time (para. 17.55).

HB 91(1)
HB60+ 72(1)
NIHB 86(1)
NIHB60+ 69(1)
DAR sch para 1
NIDAR sch para 1

16.13 The requirement to consider the needs and convenience of the person receiving payment they are paying means that authorities should not make unreasonable demands, such as collection from a place not easily accessible, or insist on payment by crossed cheques or credit transfer arrangements when the payee does not have a bank account (GM para. A6.120).

PAYMENT OF RENT REBATES FOR COUNCIL AND NIHE TENANTS

16.14 Except as described below where the landlord is the NIHE or a housing authority (para. 1.20) (including where the dwelling is located outside their area) payment must be in the form of a rebate applied to the rent account. However, where the landlord is a housing authority payment must take the form of a rent allowance (para. 16.15) if the claimant's dwelling is the subject of:

AA 134(1A), NIAA 126(1)(b)
HB 91A
HB60+ 72A

- in England and Wales, an interim management order, a final management order, an interim empty dwelling order or a final empty dwelling order made by that authority under section 102, 113, 133 or 136 of the Housing Act 2004;
- in Scotland; a management control order made by that authority under section 74 of the Antisocial Behaviour etc. (Scotland) Act 2004.

PAYMENT OF RENT ALLOWANCE FOR ALL OTHER CASES

AA 134(1B)
NIAA 126(1)(c)
HB 91(1),94(1)
HB60+ 72(1),75(1)
NIHB 86(1),90(1)
NIHB60+ 69(1), 73(1)

16.15 In all other cases, including tenants of: private landlords, housing associations (para. 10.17), stock transfer landlords (para. 10.25) and other types of landlord (paras. 10.70-74), the tenant will be paid by rent allowance. Payment is normally made direct to the tenant, though in certain circumstances a rent allowance may be paid to the landlord (paras. 16.30 and 16.34). The rules about payment to landlords are different in pathfinder authorities (paras. 22.53-62).

PAYMENTS ON ACCOUNT (INTERIM PAYMENTS)

HB 93(1)
HB60+ 74(1)
NIHB 89(1)
NIHB60+ 72(1)

16.16 A payment on account, sometimes known as an interim payment, must be paid within 14 days if the following circumstances are met:

- the tenant is to be paid by rent allowance (para. 16.15); and
- the authority is unable to make a decision on the amount of benefit payable within 14 days of receipt of the claim; and
- that inability has not arisen out of the claimant's failure, without good cause, to provide necessary information or evidence (which the authority has requested from the claimant in writing).

The authority must pay an amount it considers reasonable on the basis of whatever information is available to it about the individual claimant's circumstances, such as sources of income, and any relevant determination made by a rent officer (para. 23.43). Note there is no equivalent rule for tenants who are to be paid by rent rebate (para. 16.14).

16.17 Payments on account are not discretionary and provided that the claimant has done all that is required of them a payment must be made within 14 days. This position was confirmed in the case *R v Haringey LBC ex parte Ayub,* where it was also held that no separate claim or request for a payment on account is required. The fact that no request is necessary is reinforced in DWP Guidance (GM A6.137).

16.18 Many authorities fail to make payments on account or only make such payments when the claimant's tenancy is at risk. These practices are unlawful and may expose the authority to judicial review or a complaint to the local government ombudsman. Where an authority fails to make a payment the ombudsman is likely to find maladministration and recommend that compensation be paid *(www.lgo.org.uk)*.

16.19 Good cause for the claimant failing to provide necessary information and evidence would include, for example, a landlord's unwillingness to provide evidence of rent payments. DWP guidance (GM A6.140) advises that a claimant cannot be held responsible for delays in receiving confirmation of IS entitlement from the local DWP office. A claimant cannot be held responsible for a failure to supply information which they have not been asked specifically to provide and must also be given a reasonable time to provide any information which has been requested. The authority is obliged to make initial payment on account on the 14th day following receipt of the claim based on the information originally available to it. This is the case even when the post-1996 payment rules (para. 16.21) apply.

16.20 Following a decision to make a payment on account the notice must advise the claimant that if the payment turns out to be more than their actual entitlement it will be recoverable from the person to whom it was paid. If when the claim is finally decided this turns out to be the case future rent allowance payments will be adjusted to allow for any under or overpayment made. Decisions relating to payment on account, except those relating to adjustments, are not appealable (table 19.1).

HB 93(2),(3)
HB60+ 74(2),(3)
NIHB 89(2),(3)
NIHB60+ 72(2),(3)
DAR sch para 1(b)
NIDAR sch para 1(b)

FREQUENCY OF RENT ALLOWANCE PAYMENTS

16.21 Following any 'payment on account', or first payment, the authority may choose to pay a rent allowance at intervals of two or four weeks or one calendar month or, with the consent of the person entitled to payment, at intervals greater than one month. Except for certain pre-1997 transitionally protected claims (para. 16.23), the authority must make payments to claimants at the end of the period to which they relate as follows:

- where payment is being made direct to the landlord every four weeks (or, at the authority's discretion, monthly where there is a monthly rent liability); or
- in any other case every two weeks or other period in accordance with paragraph 16.24.

HB 92(1)-(3)
HB60+ 73(1)-(3)
NIHB 88(1)-(3)
NIHB60+ 71(1)-(3)

16.22 Where the authority is paying benefit direct to a landlord for more than one claimant the first payment to a new claimant may be made at a shorter interval than four weeks if it is 'in the interest of efficient administration'. In practice this allows the authority to align any new claimants of a landlord whom they already pay direct into the same payment cycle as their other claimants.

FREQUENCY OF RENT ALLOWANCE CASES FOR CERTAIN PRE-1997 CASES

16.23 The rules in paragraphs 16.21-22 do not apply to claimants who:

- were in receipt of HB before 7th October 1996; and
- have been on HB continuously since without any breaks; and
- have not moved home since that date.

CPR sch 3 para 7
NICPR sch 3 para 7

Except where the claimant dies and their surviving partner makes a claim within four weeks, any break in the claim no matter how short results in the payment cycle reverting to the ordinary (post-1996) rules (para. 16.21). In all other cases where the pre-1997 rules apply authorities have a duty, as far as possible, to make payments two weeks before the end of the period covered in accordance with the same rules about frequency of payment as described in paragraph 16.24. So a fortnightly rent liability should be paid in advance, while four-weekly or monthly liabilities should be met midway through the period. However, where the tenancy allows for rent to be paid in arrears the authority has the discretion to make payments at the end of the period.

CLAIMANT'S RIGHT TO FORTNIGHTLY PAYMENTS

HB 91(2),92(5),(7)
HB60+ 72(2), 73(5),(7)
NIHB 86(2), 88(5),(7)
NIHB60+ 69(2), 71(5),(7)

16.24 Where payment is being made to the claimant they can require the authority to make payments every two weeks if their weekly HB is greater than £2. Where the amount of weekly benefit is £2 or less, the authority may pay HB according to the following rules:

- if they are a student once a term (para 21.34);
- where the amount of weekly HB is less than £1 per week, every six months;
- in any other case the authority may choose to pay either at intervals of two weeks, four weeks, one month or, where the claimant has given their consent, any other interval greater than a month.

In all these cases the authority retains discretion to pay the claimant weekly where the circumstances in paragraph 16.25 apply.

AUTHORITY'S DISCRETION TO PAY WEEKLY

HB 92(6)
HB60+ 73(6)
NIHB 88(6)
NIHB60+ 71(6)

16.25 Except where HB is paid direct to a landlord, authorities have discretion to pay HB weekly if it considers that:

- paying HB over a longer period would lead to an overpayment; or
- the claimant pays rent weekly and it is in his or her interest (or that of the family) to receive weekly payments.

The first instance covers cases where there is only a short period of entitlement to HB, or where a change of circumstance is anticipated in the near future. The second instance may be helpful in cases where claimants have difficulty in budgeting over a longer period. DWP guidance suggests that 'authorities are not expected to make special enquiries as to whether this applies' but if, for example, the social services advise that they have difficulty then payment can be made (GM A6.127).

PAYMENT OF HB FOR RATES IN NORTHERN IRELAND

16.26 In Northern Ireland payment of HB for rates is normally by rebate; further details can be found at (paras. 11.11 and 11.40). NIHB 87 NIHB60+ 70

PAYMENT OF CTB

16.27 In Great Britain payment of CTB is normally by means of a rebate (credit) to the individual's council tax account, so reducing their overall liability for the tax. Where the rebate is greater than the tax liability the authority may reduce the liability for the tax in subsequent years. However, any outstanding CTB must be paid direct to the claimant where: CTB 77 CTB60+ 62

- the tax has been paid for the year, and the claimant requests it;
- the account has been paid and closed (e.g. because the claimant has moved out of the area);
- in any other case, where the claimant is liable for the tax and the authority considers it appropriate.

Where the claimant is to be paid direct payment should normally be made within 14 days or as soon as reasonably practicable after that.

To whom should the payment be made?

16.28 HB for council and NIHE tenants and CTB (in Northern Ireland HB for rates (para.11.40)) is normally paid by way of a rebate to their rent/council tax/ rates account (paras. 16.26 and 16.27). In all other cases the normal requirement is that the benefit is paid to the claimant. However, in particular circumstances: AA 134(1A),(1B), 138(1) NIAA 126(1) HB 94 HB60+ 75 NIHB 90 NIHB60+ 73 CTB 78 CTB60+ 63

- a rent allowance can be paid to the claimant's landlord, or someone else to whom rent is payable (paras. 16.29-40), e.g. a lettings agent, or a nominee (note that these rules are different in the pathfinder areas (paras. 22.53-62)); and
- a rent allowance or CTB is paid to an appointee or, in the case of a claimant who has died, a personal representative or next of kin aged 16 or over (paras. 16.43-45).

Subject to a landlord's right to refuse direct payments (para. 16.40), when an amount of rent allowance is paid to a landlord or lettings agent this discharges the claimant's liability to pay that amount of rent, unless the authority recovers any overpayment from that landlord or lettings agent (para. 18.62).

FIRST PAYMENT OF A RENT ALLOWANCE MADE PAYABLE TO A LANDLORD OR LETTINGS AGENT BUT SENT TO THE CLAIMANT

HB 96(2) HB60+ 77(2) NIHB 92(2) NIHB60+ 75(2)

16.29 The authority has the discretion to make the first payment of a new or renewed rent allowance claim by sending the claimant a cheque or other instrument of payment payable to the landlord for part or all of the amount due. The DWP advises that this 'is to avoid the possibility of a claimant misusing a first payment covering several weeks' entitlement' (GM A6.142). The authority is, however, only able to make the first cheque, etc, payable to the landlord where:

- the authority is of the opinion that the claimant has not already paid the landlord for the period in respect of which any payment is to be made; and
- it is in the interests of the efficient administration of housing benefit.

The DWP has advised authorities (GM A6.145) to consider using this power where:

- the amount due is £100 or more; or
- it has reason to think that the claimant might default; or
- there is a rent debt but the case is not appropriate for longer term direct payment arrangements.

However, this amount seems low when compared with the guidance on discretionary direct payments (para. 16.34) or the eight weeks worth of rent arrears which are required for mandatory direct payments (para. 16.30).

MANDATORY DIRECT PAYMENTS TO LANDLORDS

HB 95(1) HB60+ 76(1) NIHB 91(1) NIHB60+ 74(1)

16.30 Except where the authority decides that the landlord is not a 'fit and proper person' to receive direct payments (paras. 16.37-39), they must make direct payments of a rent allowance to a landlord where:

- an amount of income support, state pension credit or either kind of JSA payable to the claimant, or partner, is being paid direct to the landlord to meet arrears, or to meet the cost of ineligible services of a hostel resident (para. 16.33 and appendix 7); or
- the claimant has rent arrears equivalent to eight weeks or more, except where the authority considers it to be in the overriding interest of the claimant not to make direct payments.

16.31 In *R v Haringey LBC ex parte Ayub* it was held that the duty to pay a landlord direct once the claimant is eight weeks or more in rent arrears only arises if the landlord or someone else informs the authority that there are eight weeks or more arrears. It is not up to the authority to find this out for itself. If the tenant disputes that there are eight weeks' arrears the authority must consider the available evidence and come to a finding of fact on the balance of probability. Either party (the claimant or landlord) can appeal about the authority's decision.

16.32 Where the authority is making direct payments because the claimant is eight or more weeks in rent arrears, the direct payment should cease once the arrears fall below the eight-week level, unless one of the circumstances in paras. 16.30 (first bullet), 16.34 or 16.36 applies.

16.33 Where deductions are being made from IS/JSA/pension credit to meet the ineligible costs of certain hostel residents or rent arrears (appendix 7), direct payments of HB to the landlord should continue until such time as the DWP ceases to make the relevant deductions. DWP local offices should advise authorities of appropriate cases (GM A6.154). Note that in certain circumstances it is possible for direct payment of IS/JSA/pension credit to be made after the tenant's arrears are equivalent to only four weeks rent, or in the case of certain hostel residents without there being any rent arrears at all (appendix 7).

DISCRETIONARY DIRECT PAYMENTS TO LANDLORDS

16.34 Direct payments may be made at the discretion of the authority where: HB 96(1),(2) HB60+ 77(1),(2) NIHB 92(1),(2) NIHB60+ 75(1),(2)

- the claimant requests, or consents to, such an arrangement (but not in the pathfinder areas where different rules apply (paras. 22.53-62)); or
- the authority considers it to be in the interest of the claimant and family (for example, 'serious rent arrears' of over £200 or equivalent to six weeks rent (GM A 6.157)); or
- benefit is owing to a claimant who has left a dwelling with rent arrears (in which case direct payment is limited to the amount of rent owing); or
- the authority has decided that the landlord is not a 'fit and proper person' (para. 16.37) to receive direct payments but nevertheless considers that it is in the overriding interests of the claimant to pay the landlord direct (para. 16.39).

16.35 Authorities might use their power to pay direct in the interest of the claimant and family where, for example, the claimant has a history of rent arrears at a previous address or where social or medical problems (such as mental illness or drug addiction) indicate that help with budgeting is needed.

DIRECT PAYMENT TO LANDLORD FOLLOWING TENANT'S DEATH

16.36 If the claimant dies but the authority has already decided to make payment direct to the landlord, any benefit up to the amount of any rent outstanding must be paid to the landlord. To qualify, the landlord must make a written request to the authority within 12 months of the claimant's death (see also para. 16.45). HB 96(1),(2) HB60+ 77(1),(2) NIHB 92(1),(2) NIHB60+ 75(1),(2

REQUIREMENT OF LANDLORDS TO BE A 'FIT AND PROPER PERSON'

HB 95(3),96(3) HB60+ 76(3),77(3) NIHB 91(4),92(3) NIHB60+ 74(4),75(3)

16.37 Except where the authority considers that it is in the overriding interests of the claimant for payments to be made to the landlord (para. 16.39), in order to receive direct payments the authority must be satisfied that the landlord is a 'fit and proper person' to receive them. The test enables the authority to refuse direct payments in cases where the landlord is involved in fraudulent acts related to HB. The DWP suggests (GM A6.166) that the authority might also consider whether the landlord has regularly failed to:

- report changes in tenants' circumstances which he or she might reasonably be expected to know might affect entitlement; or
- repay an overpayment which the authority has decided is recoverable – despite the fact that a proper notice was issued and that the rights of review had been exercised or made available.

16.38 In deciding whether the landlord is 'fit and proper', the authority should not base its judgment on:

- the landlord's undesirable activity in non-HB matters (such as contravention of the Housing Acts)(GM para. A6.163); or
- the fact that the landlord makes use of the right to request a revision or appeal before repaying any recoverable overpayment; or
- the fact that the landlord has made complaints of maladministration to the local government ombudsman.

The DWP also advises that the 'fit and proper' test should only be applied where the authority is 'doubtful about the landlord's honesty in connection with HB' (GM para. A6.164).

HB 96(3) HB60+ 77(3) NIHB 92(3) NIHB60+ 75(3)

16.39 Where the authority is satisfied that the landlord is not a 'fit and proper person' but it appears to be in the overriding interest of the claimant to pay the landlord direct, then discretionary direct payments can still be made (para. 16.34). This would apply, for example, where the risk to the claimant of not paying the landlord outweighs any risk associated with direct payment (GM A6.159).

LANDLORD'S RIGHT TO REFUSE DIRECT PAYMENTS FROM A NON-TENANT

16.40 A landlord has the right to refuse to accept HB direct as payments of rent in respect of anyone who not a party to the tenancy agreement *(Bessa Plus Plc v Lancaster)*, typically, for example, the tenant's partner, or possibly the claimant's nominee (para. 16.44). This may cause difficulties particularly where the non-tenant member of a couple should be the claimant (paras. 12.15-16, 12.24 and 21.26). In such cases the authority should pay the claimant. It is also arguable that a landlord can refuse direct payments in respect of their tenant (but not retrospectively), because this will leave them open to overpayment recovery (paras. 18.35-38 and 18.50-53).

INFORMATION TO BE PROVIDED TO CLAIMANTS AND LANDLORDS OR LETTINGS AGENTS

16.41 When a decision has been made that HB is to be paid direct to the landlord, both the claimant and landlord should be notified of that fact within 14 days (para. 16.2). The notice must include the date from which the arrangement will commence and their right to obtain a written statement of reasons and make written representations. The notification must also inform both the landlord and claimant that where:

HB 90 sch 9 paras 11-12
HB60+ 71 sch 8 paras 11-12
NIHB 85 sch 10 paras 11-12
NIHB60+ 68 sch 10 paras 11-12

- an overpayment is recoverable from the landlord (para. 18.35); and
- the overpayment is recovered from direct payments made on behalf of a tenant to whom the overpayment does not relate (para. 18.51),

that tenant's rent must be treated as paid to the value of the amount recovered.

16.42 The landlord must also be informed of his or her duty to report any change of circumstances which might affect the claimant's amount of, or right to, HB and the kind of change which should be notified.

Other people who may receive a rent allowance or CTB

APPOINTEE

16.43 Where an appointee acts on behalf of a claimant who is incapable of managing his or her own affairs (para. 5.5) then payment may be made to that person. In most cases, however, CTB will be paid by rebating the claimant's tax liability. The authority should also consider whether the claimant's property should be exempt from the council tax on grounds that all the occupiers have severe mental impairment (para. 9.11).

HB 94(2)
HB60+ 75(2)
NIHB 90(2)
NIHB60+ 73(2)
CTB 78(2)
CTB60+ 63(2)

NOMINEE

16.44 In the case of HB, if the claimant requests in writing that the authority makes payment to another person (who must be 18 or more), the authority may make payments to that person. The DWP incorrectly refers to this person as an agent and advises that the claimant must be unable to collect the money himself or herself (GM para. A6.148). This is not the case, however, as the relevant regulation specifically identifies that the claimant may be able to act on their own behalf.

HB 94(3)
HB60+ 75(3)
NIHB 90(3)
NIHB60+ 73(3)

A DEAD CLAIMANT'S PERSONAL REPRESENTATIVE OR NEXT OF KIN

HB 97(1)-(3)
HB60+ 78(1)-(3)
NIHB 93(1)-(3)
NIHB60+ 76(1)-(3)
CTB 80(1)-(3)
CTB60+ 65(1)-(3)

16.45 Following a claimant's death, the authority must, if a written application is received within 12 months (or such longer period as the authority may allow), pay a rent allowance – or any CTB above the dead claimant's residual council tax liability – to his or her personal representative or, if there is none, the next of kin. The next of kin take priority in the following order: spouse, issue (children, grandchildren), other relatives (parents, brothers, sisters or their children); and must be aged 16 or over. However, note that if the claimant died with rent arrears payment can be made to their landlord to clear the debt (para. 16.36).

17 Changes to entitlement

17.1 This chapter explains how a claimant's entitlement to HB or CTB can change or end – typically because of a change in the claimant's circumstances or because the claimant has asked the authority to reconsider its decision. It covers:

- how a decision can be changed;
- general rules about 'revisions' and 'supersessions';
- the duty to notify a change of circumstances;
- when changes of circumstances take effect from;
- how mistakes and errors are corrected;
- asking the authority to reconsider a decision and how the authority deals with this; and
- the rules about 'extended payments' and 'continuing payments'.

How a decision can be changed

CPSA sch paras 2,11 NICPSA sch 7 paras 2,11

17.2 Once an authority has decided a claim (para. 16.2), its decision cannot be changed unless:

- the authority changes the decision by 'revising' it – usually because it was wrongly decided in the first place; or
- the authority changes the decision by 'superseding' it – usually because there has been a change of circumstances; or
- the authority corrects an accidental error in the decision; or
- an appeal tribunal, Commissioner, tribunal of Commissioners, or court alters the decision on appeal.

The first three are described in this chapter; appeals are described in chapter 19.

TERMINOLOGY

17.3 The terms 'revise', 'revision, 'revised decision', 'supersede', 'supersession' and 'superseding decision' are explained in the next few paragraphs. Table 17.1 summarises which applies in which circumstances, and gives the date from which it applies. Accidental errors are explained in paragraph 17.45.

Table 17.1: Revisions and supersessions: main points

SITUATION	REVISION OR SUPERSESSION? AND DATE IT TAKES EFFECT
CHANGES OF CIRCUMSTANCES	
A change which the claimant had a duty to notify and which he or she notified to the authority more than one month after it occurred (this time limit can be extended) and the claimant qualifies for more HB/CTB	**Supersession:** From the Monday following the day when the authority receives the notification (or for some rent increases, earlier)
Any other change of circumstances	**Supersession:** From the Monday following the day the change occurs (or for some rent increases, earlier)
OFFICIAL ERROR	
An official error arising at any time (whether resulting in an overpayment or an underpayment)	**Revision or supersession:** From the date the decision took effect or should have
OVERPAYMENTS (OTHER THAN AS ABOVE)	
A mistake of fact meaning the claimant was overpaid	**Revision or supersession:** From the date the decision took effect or should have
SUCCESSFUL REQUESTS BY PERSON AFFECTED	
A person affected requests the authority to reconsider its decision within one month (which can be extended)	**Revision:** From the date the decision took effect or should have
A person affected requests this outside the above time limits	**Supersession:** From the Monday of the week in which the authority received the request
A person affected appeals within the time limits for appeal and the authority chooses to revise instead	**Revision:** From the date the decision took effect or should have

RENT OFFICER RE-DETERMINATIONS (APPEALS)	
A rent officer re-determination is in the claimant's favour	**Revision:** From the date the decision took effect or should have
A rent officer re-determination is against the claimant's favour	**Supersession:** From the Monday following the rent officer re-determination
OTHER MISTAKES OF FACT OR LAW	
Other mistake of fact arising within one month of the decision	**Revision:** From the date the decision took effect or should have
Any other mistake of fact or law	**Supersession:** From the Monday of the benefit week in which the authority was notified of it or became aware of it

Examples: Revisions and supersessions when there is a change or dispute

A CHANGE RESULTING IN A SUPERSESSION

A claimant writes to tell the authority that her wages went down some months after she was awarded HB/CTB. Her letter gets to the authority within one month of the change, and she provides acceptable evidence.

The authority should make a superseding decision, so that the increase in her HB/CTB is awarded from the Monday following the date her wages went down.

A LATE-NOTIFIED CHANGE RESULTING IN A SUPERSESSION

The same as the above story, except that the claimant took six months to inform the authority (and has no reason for her delay).

The authority should make a superseding decision, so that the increase in her HB/CTB is awarded from the Monday following the date it received the information from her.

A DISPUTE RESULTING IN A REVISION

A claimant has been awarded HB/CTB on the basis that the maximum non-dependant deduction is to apply in respect of her son (because he works full-time but she has been unable to provide evidence of his income). Within one month of notification of the decision on her claim, she writes in with acceptable evidence of his true (low) income.

The authority should revise its decision, so that the lower non-dependant deduction applies from the beginning of her claim.

A DISPUTE RESULTING IN A SUPERSESSION

The same as the last story, except that the claimant took eight months to provide the evidence (and has no reason for her delay).

The authority should make a superseding decision, so that the lower non-dependant deduction applies from the Monday of the week it received the evidence from her.

'REVISION', 'SUPERSESSION' AND 'RECONSIDERATION'

17.4 'Revision' and 'supersession' are the legal terms for what is more commonly called in day-to-day work a 'reconsideration'. Generally speaking the distinction between them is as follows:

- **Revision:** A revision is typically required when a decision was wrong from the outset. When a decision is revised, the revision goes back to the beginning (to the date of the decision in question).
- **Supersession:** A supersession is typically required when there has been a change of circumstances. When a decision is superseded, the supersession does not go right back: there will always be a 'before' and an 'after'.

17.5 Depending on the circumstances (described in the next sections of this chapter), the authority may have to revise or supersede a decision:

- because a claimant or other person affected requests this (para. 17.55) – in which case he or she does not have to get the terminology right; or
- because the authority has the power to do so without such a request; or
- because the regulations require it.

In each case there are rules about what factors are relevant to a revision or supersession and how to obtain the information and evidence needed (paras. 17.65-66).

DAR 7(4)
NIDAR 7(4)

17.6 If more than one event occurs in a case (such as a two successive changes in circumstances), each is dealt with in turn. However, if a single event apparently requires both a revision and a supersession, it is dealt with as a revision. For example, a claimant may request a reconsideration so late that it can only be dealt with as a supersession (para. 17.60), but the authority realises it has made an official error (para. 17.46) which has to be treated as a revision: the revision 'wins'.

CPSA sch 7 paras 1(2),3(1),4(1),(2),
NICPSA sch 7 para 1(2),3(1),4(1),(2),
DAR 7(1)
NIDAR 7(1)

17.7 Once a decision has been revised or superseded, the result is a decision itself, which can in turn be revised or superseded in the same way as an original decision can be. This applies also to a decision imposed by an appeal tribunal, a Commissioner, or a tribunal of Commissioners.

Duty to notify a change of circumstances

HB 88(1),(4)
HB60+ 69(1),(4)
NIHB 83(1),(3)
NIHB60+ 66(1),(3)
CTB 74(1),(4)
CTB60+ 59(1),(4)

17.8 The claimant has a duty to notify the authority's 'designated office' (para. 5.9), in writing, of any 'relevant' change of circumstances (though if the claimant or any partner is on pension credit this duty is very limited: tables 17.2, 17.3). What counts as a 'relevant' change is in the next paragraph. The duty to notify begins on the date the claim is made and continues for as long as the person is in receipt of HB or CTB (except in relation to 'extended payments' and 'continuing payments': paras. 17.81 and 17.94). If HB/CTB is payable to someone other than the claimant (e.g. a landlord or an appointee), that person is also required to notify relevant changes.

HB 88(1)
HB60+ 69(1)
NIHB 83(1)
NIHB60+ 66(1)
CTB 74(1)
CTB60+ 59(1)

17.9 For these purposes a 'relevant' change is one which the claimant (or other person) could reasonably be expected to know might affect:

- entitlement to HB/CTB; or
- amount of HB/CTB; or
- method of payment (e.g. whether to pay HB to the landlord rather than the claimant or *vice versa*).

17.10 Whether a claimant (or other person) could reasonably be expected to know a change might affect HB or CTB, is of importance if failure to notify a change results in an overpayment and the question of recovering the overpayment arises (chapter 18), or results in an underpayment and the question of whether it should be awarded arises (para. 17.37).

17.11 Apart from the specific rules mentioned in the next paragraph, the following are a selection of things the claimant should inform the authority of:

- changes in rent, including changes of address (unless the claimant is a council or NIHE tenant);
- changes in rates if they are not collected by the RCA (Northern Ireland only);
- changes in the status of non-dependants/second adults;
- changes in family circumstances affecting the applicable amount;
- changes in capital and/or income;
- changes relating to payment of HB direct to a landlord.

17.12 The law lists certain things which the claimant must inform the authority of (table 17.2) and certain other things which the claimant need not inform the authority of (table 17.3).

Table 17.2: Changes the claimant must notify*

HB 88
HB60+ 69
NIHB 83
NIHB60+ 66
CTB 74
CTB60+ 59

CLAIMANT AND ANY PARTNER UNDER 60

- The end of his or her (or any partner's) entitlement to JSA(IB) or IS
- Changes where a child or young person ceases to be a member of the family: for example, when child benefit stops or he or she leaves the household

CLAIMANT OR ANY PARTNER AGED 60+

- Changes in the details of their letting (HB rent allowances only)
- Changes affecting the residence or income of any non-dependant
- Absences exceeding or likely to exceed 13 weeks

ADDITIONAL MATTERS FOR CLAIMANTS ON SAVINGS CREDIT

- Changes affecting any child living with the claimant (other than age) which might affect the amount of HB/CTB
- Changes to capital which take it (or may take it) above £16,000
- Changes to a non-dependant if the non-dependant's income and capital was treated as being the claimant's (para. (d) of table 13.4)
- Changes to a partner who was ignored in assessing savings credit but is taken into account for HB/CTB (para. (d) of table 13.4)

ADDITIONAL MATTERS FOR CLAIMANTS ON SECOND ADULT REBATE

- Changes in the number of adults in their home
- Changes in the total gross incomes of the adults in their home
- The date any adult in their home ceases to receive JSA(IB) or IS

Notes

* This is a list of the items specifically mentioned in the law. The claimant's duty is wider (paras. 17.9-11).

Table 17.3 Changes the claimant need not notify*

HB 88
HB60+ 69
NIHB 83
NIHB60+ 66
CTB 74
CTB60+ 59

- Beginnings or ends of awards of pension credit (either kind) or changes in the amount
- Changes which affect JSA(IB) or IS but do not affect HB/CTB
- Changes in rent (HB rent rebates only)
- Changes in council tax
- Changes in rates paid direct to the RCA (Northern Ireland only)
- Changes in the age of any member of the family or non-dependant
- Changes in the HB or CTB regulations

Notes

* In the first case, it is the DWP's duty (and no-one else's) to notify the authority of the change. In the second, the change has no impact on HB/CTB. In the third, fourth and fifth, the authority has made the changes, and so should not need to be informed of them. In the last two cases, the authority should implement the change automatically.

Changes of circumstances which are notified on time or do not require notification

17.13 This section describes how authorities should deal with changes of circumstances which:

- are notified to the authority on time ('on time' means within a month of the occurrence of the change – or longer in special circumstances: para. 17.40); or
- do not require to be notified to the authority (table 17.3).

In each case, in broad terms the general principle is that the change is taken into effect from a date at or very near to the occurrence of the change. Late-notified changes are dealt with in the next section (para. 17.36 onwards).

17.14 The authority may alter a decision if there has been a change of circumstances or one is anticipated. The effect of this may be to:

- alter the claimant's entitlement to HB/CTB; or
- end the award of HB/CTB.

17.15 This is normally a supersession (in the second case a supersession at nil) but in limited circumstances it can be a revision (paras. 17.46 and 17.49). The following paragraphs explain which option is available to the authority in each circumstance.

NOTIFYING THE OUTCOME

17.16 The claimant and any other person affected must be notified in writing of the alteration in entitlement (or of the end of the award), within 14 days or as soon as reasonably practicable, including the following matters:

HB 90(1)(b), sch 9
HB60+ 71(1)(b), sch 8
NIHB 85(1)(b), sch 10
NIHB60+ 68(1)(b), sch 10
CTB 76(1)(b), sch 8
CTB60+ 61(1)(b), sch 7

- a statement of what the authority has altered;
- the person's right to request a written statement, to request a reconsideration, and to appeal to an appeal tribunal, and how and when to do these things.

THE DATE THE CHANGE ACTUALLY OCCURS

17.17 The date a change actually occurs is an important concept: it affects the date on which the change is implemented in HB/CTB (which may be before, on, or after the date of claim, depending on the other circumstances of the case, as described later in this chapter).

17.18 Determining the date a change actually occurs can be straightforward (e.g. in the case of a claimant's birthday) or difficult (e.g. in the case of acquiring a partner). In four cases there are specific rules:

- If entitlement to any social security benefit ends, the date the change actually occurs is defined as being the day after the last day of entitlement to that benefit. (But this is over-ridden when the claimant qualifies for an extended payment: paras. 17.22-23 and para. 17.81 onwards.)

HB 79(1)
HB60+ 59(1)
NIHB 76(1)
NIHB60+ 58(1)
CTB 67(1)
CTB60+ 50(1)

- If there is a change in tax, national insurance or the maximum rate of working tax credit or child tax credit, and this is caused by a change in the law (e.g. the Budget), it may be disregarded (i.e. treated as not occurring) until up to 30 benefit weeks later. This applies to the income of a claimant, partner, non-dependant or second adult.

HB 34
HB60+ 34
NIHB 31
NIHB60+ 32
CTB 24
CTB60+ 24

- If the claimant or partner is aged 65+, changes in non-dependant deductions are delayed for 26 weeks (paras. 7.37-38);
- There are special rules about arrears of income (para. 13.25).

HB60+ 59(9)-(12)
NIHB60+ 58(10)-(13)
CTB60+ 50(10)-(13)

> **Example: A claimant's birthday**
>
> A claimant receiving HB and CTB (but not income support or JSA(IB)) reaches the age of 60 on Wednesday 5th July 2006. The effect is that her HB and CTB increase.
>
> She has no duty to notify the authority of this. The authority should alter her entitlement to HB and CTB.
>
> The new amounts of HB and CTB are awarded from the Monday following the change, i.e. Monday 10th July.
>
> This is a supersession.

IMPLEMENTING CHANGES: THE GENERAL RULE

17.19 The following general rule applies for all changes other than those mentioned in the remainder of this chapter. Typical examples are changes in income, capital, age or household composition.

HB 79(1)
HB60+ 59(1)
NIHB 76(1)
NIHB60+ 58(1)
CTB 67(1)
CTB60+ 50(1)
DAR 7(2)(a)(i),8(2)
NIDAR 7(2)(a)(i),8(2)

17.20 So long as the result of a change is that entitlement to HB/CTB continues, the authority alters the claimant's entitlement to HB/CTB. The new amount of HB/CTB is awarded from the Monday after the date the change occurs, even if the change occurs on a Monday. This is a supersession. (If the result of the change is that entitlement ends, see paragraph 17.21.)

CHANGES ENDING AN AWARD OF HB/CTB

HB 79(1)
HB60+ 59(1)
NIHB 76(1)
NIHB60+ 58(1)
CTB 67(1)
CTB60+ 50(1)
DAR 8(2)
NIDAR 8(2)

17.21 If the result of a change of circumstances is that the claimant no longer satisfies all of the basic conditions of benefit (paras. 2.4 and 2.6) then (for example, a claimant dies or a claimant not on guarantee credit becomes a millionaire through the lottery), the authority must end the award of HB/CTB. In such cases:

- the last week of HB/CTB entitlement is the benefit week (para. 5.32) in which the claimant's circumstances change; and
- in the last week, the claimant is entitled to a full week's HB/CTB (i.e. calculated as if the change had not occurred).

This is a supersession. Different rules apply to moves and changes in rent or council tax (paras. 17.29-32) and to certain other changes (paras. 17.23 and 17.25).

WHEN JSA(IB), IS, IB OR SDA CEASE AFTER 26 WEEKS OR MORE

17.22 The following rule applies to people who have been on income-based jobseeker's allowance (JSA(IB)), income support (IS), incapacity benefit (IB) or severe disablement allowance (SDA) for 26 weeks or more, and who have found a job or similar. The full details are in table 17.4.

Table 17.4: Ending an award of HB/CTB when someone has been on certain benefits for 26 weeks or more

CLAIMANTS WHO HAVE BEEN ON JSA(IB) AND/OR IS

AN AWARD OF HB/CTB MUST END IF:

- the claimant or any partner starts employment or self-employment, or increases his or her hours or earnings; and
- this is expected to last for at least five weeks; and
- the claimant or partner has been entitled to JSA or IS continuously for at least 26 weeks (or any combination of those two benefits in that period*); and
- entitlement to JSA(IB) or IS ceases as a result**

HB 77,78
HB60+ 58
NIHB 74,75
NIHB60+ 56,57
CTB 65,66
CTB60+ 49

CLAIMANTS WHO HAVE BEEN ON IB AND/OR SDA

AN AWARD OF HB/CTB MUST END IF:

- the claimant or any partner starts employment or self-employment, or increases his or her hours or earnings; and
- this is expected to last for at least five weeks; and
- the claimant is not on income support or pension credit and nor is any partner; and
- the claimant or partner has been entitled to IB or SDA continuously for at least 26 weeks (or any combination of those two benefits in that period*); and
- entitlement to IB or SDA ceases as a result.

Notes

* A combination of JSA/IS over the 26 weeks is sufficient, or a combination of IB/SDA is sufficient.

** Over the 26 weeks no distinction is made between JSA(IB) and JSA(Cont), but the claimant must be on JSA(IB) (not JSA(Cont)) for at least one day before starting the job, etc.

HB 77,78(1) HB60+ 58 NIHB 74,75 NIHB 56,57 CTB 65,66 CTB60+ 49

17.23 In such cases, the award of HB/CTB ends. It does so at the end of the benefit week which contains the last day of entitlement to JSA(IB), IS, IB or SDA. (This is a different rule from the one in paragraph 17.25. Although the two rules sound similar, they have different effects – as illustrated in the examples, 'When JSA(IB) ends'.)

17.24 In such cases, subject to further conditions, the claimant qualifies for a four-week 'extended payment', as explained in paragraphs 17.81 onwards. But the award of HB/CTB must end even if the claimant does not meet those further conditions (for example does not notify the fact that he or she has begun work, etc) and even if the claimant has no entitlement to an extended payment. If the claimant wishes to be awarded HB/CTB thereafter, he or she must re-claim.

WHEN JSA(IB), IS, IB OR SDA CEASE FOR OTHER REASONS

HB 79(1) HB60+ 59(1) NIHB 76(1) NIHB60+ 58(1) CTB 67(1) CTB60+ 50(1)

17.25 If JSA(IB), IS, IB or SDA cease in any circumstances other than as above (para. 17.22), the general rule applies (para. 17.19). In other words:

- if the claimant continues to qualify for at least some HB/CTB, this is awarded from the Monday following the first day of non-entitlement to JSA(IB), IS, IB or SDA;
- if the claimant no longer qualifies for any HB/CTB, the former amount continues until the end of the benefit week containing the first day of non-entitlement to JSA(IB), IS, IB or SDA.

17.26 This applies if, for example, the claimant gets a job but has not been on JSA/IS/IB/SDA for 26 weeks, or simply does not sign on, etc. When JSA(IB) or IS cease because the claimant or partner starts getting pension credit, the claimant may qualify for a four-week 'continuing payment' (paras. 17.94 onwards). In other circumstances, until the authority obtains the details of the claimant's new circumstances, it is likely to suspend HB/CTB (para. 17.67).

CHANGES RELATING TO PENSION CREDIT

17.27 If a change in either guarantee credit or savings credit, whether due to a change in the claimant's circumstances or due to an official error (as defined in para. 17.46), affects the claimant's entitlement to HB/CTB, this takes effect from the date shown in table 17.5. These are supersessions.

Examples: When JSA(IB) ends

PERSON QUALIFYING FOR EXTENDED PAYMENT

A woman on HB/CTB gets a job which starts on Monday 6th November 2006. She has been on JSA(IB) for more than 26 weeks and meets the relevant conditions in table 17.4. Her last day of entitlement to JSA(IB) is Sunday 5th November.

Her award of HB/CTB ends. It ends at the end of the benefit week containing her last day of entitlement to JSA(IB), i.e. it ends on Sunday 5th November. (The claimant will then get a four weeks extended payment, and can also reclaim HB/CTB.)

PERSON NOT QUALIFYING FOR EXTENDED PAYMENT

A man on HB/CTB gets a job which starts on Monday 6th November 2006. He has been on JSA(IB) for less than 26 weeks and so does not meet the conditions in table 17.4. His last day of entitlement to JSA(IB) is Sunday 5th November. He informs the authority promptly of these matters and provides all the information and evidence reasonably required.

His award of HB/CTB continues. The new amount of HB/CTB (based on his new income) takes effect from the Monday following the first day of non-entitlement to JSA(IB), Monday 13th November.

These are both supersessions.

Table 17.5: When pension credit starts, changes or ends

HB60+ 41(9),60
NIHB60+ 59(11)
CTB60+ 31(9),51
DAR 8(2),(3)
NIDAR 8(2),(3)

WHAT THE CHANGE IS	WHEN IT TAKES EFFECT IN HB/CTB*
Pension credit starts, increasing entitlement to HB/CTB	The Monday following the first day of entitlement to pension credit
Pension credit starts, reducing entitlement to HB/CTB	The Monday following the date the authority receives notification from the DWP about the change (or, if later, the Monday following the date of the pension credit change)
Pension credit changes or ends, increasing entitlement to HB/CTB	The Monday of the benefit week in which pension credit changes
Pension credit changes or ends, reducing entitlement to HB/CTB:	

◆ if this is due to a delay by the claimant in notifying a change in circumstances to the DWP	The Monday of the benefit week in which pension credit changes
◆ in any other case	The Monday following the date the authority received notification from the DWP about the change (or, if later, the Monday following the pension credit change)
The 'assessed income figure' (AIF) (para. 13.152) changes:	
◆ if the AIF changes during 1st to 15th April in any year	The date the annual HB/CTB up-rating takes effect (para. 17.34)
◆ if the AIF changes at any other time	The Monday following the date the AIF changes

Note

* If any of the above would take effect during a claimant's 'continuing payment' period (para. 17.94), the change is instead deferred until afterwards.

RETROSPECTIVE CHANGES TO SOCIAL SECURITY BENEFITS

DAR 4(7B),(7C), 7(2)(i),8(14) NIDAR 4(6B),(6C), 7(2)(h),8(11)

17.28 Changes relating to social security benefits (other than those described above) fall within the general rule (paras. 17.19-20). However, for mainly technical reasons it is made clear in the law that:

- if a social security benefit, or an increase in a social security benefit, is awarded back to a date before the start of an HB/CTB award, that award is revised as necessary;
- if a social security benefit, or an increase in a social security benefit, is awarded back to a date after the start of an HB/CTB award, that award is superseded as necessary;
- if an award of HB/CTB ended due to the end of an award of a social security benefit, but that social security benefit is reinstated, then the decision to end HB/CTB is revised as necessary (to reinstate the award of HB/CTB if appropriate).

Arrears of working tax credit and child tax credit are dealt with as in paragraphs 13.44-45.

MOVES AND CHANGES IN RENT OR COUNCIL TAX LIABILITY

17.29 The rules about moves and changes in liability are described below. In each case these are supersessions (at nil if there is no further entitlement). Unlike in former years, moves no longer require a fresh claim (though some authorities have their own special forms for moves) unless they are from one authority area to another.

17.30 The CTB rules for implementing a move, or a change in liability for council tax, are always that the amount of CTB alters on the exact day that the change occurs, and in the benefit week of the change CTB is calculated on a daily basis (the daily amount being one-seventh of the weekly eligible council tax). This is true whether entitlement to CTB continues after the change or reduces to nil.

CTB 57(1),67(2),(3),(5),(6)
CTB60+ 40(1),61(2),(3),(5),(6)

17.31 The HB rules for implementing a move, or a change in liability for rent, have changed this year. There are two general rules, and an exception for hostels, as follows:

HB 79(2),(2A)(a),80(4)(b),(c),(10)
HB60+ 59(2),(2A)(
61(4)(b),(c),(11)
NIHB 76(2)(3)(a),(1
77(4)(b),(c),(9)
NIHB60+ 58(2),(3)
(14),80(4)(b),(c),(9)

- If a change in rent or move means that entitlement to HB continues, the amount of HB alters on the exact day that the change occurs, and in the benefit week of the change HB is calculated on a daily basis (the daily amount being one-seventh of the weekly eligible rent).
- If a change in rent or move means that entitlement to HB reduces to nil, HB continues until the end of the benefit week (para. 5.32) in which the change occurs, so in the last benefit week, the claimant gets a whole week's HB.
- But in the case of a hostel (para. 6.10) where payments fall due on a daily basis, a change a move (as well as a change in rent) is always implemented from the exact day of the change (so residents get HB only for the exact days when payments are due).

17.32 The following changes also take effect on a daily basis:

HB 79(2A)(b),(2B),80(11),81(2)
HB60+ 59(2A)(b),(2B),61(12),62(2)
NIHB 76(3),(4),(11
77(10),78(12)
NIHB60+ 58(3),(4
(15),60(10),61(2)

- the beginning or end of a rent-free period;
- starting or stopping being eligible for HB on a former home, or on two homes, including stopping being eligible because the (4 weeks or 52 weeks) time limit runs out. These are described in chapter 3.

17.33 And whenever a claimant is eligible for HB on two homes, eligible rent in each benefit week is calculated by adding together the daily eligible rent for the two address for the appropriate number of days (as illustrated in the last of the examples).

Examples: Moves and changes in liability

MOVING WITHIN AN AUTHORITY'S AREA

A man moves from one address to another within an authority's area on Monday 4th September 2006. He is liable for rent and council tax at his old address up to and including Sunday 3rd September and at his new address from Monday 4th September.

- His HB and CTB change on and from Monday 4th September to take account of his new eligible rent and eligible council tax.

A woman moves from one address to another within an authority's area on Thursday 1st June 2006. She is liable for rent and council tax at her old address up to and including Sunday Wednesday 31st May and at her new address from Thursday 1st June.

- His HB and CTB change on and from Thursday 1st June (on a daily basis) to take account of her new eligible rent and eligible council tax.

A HOSTEL RESIDENT

A man moves to a hostel for three nights and is liable for rent on a daily basis on Tuesday 4th, Wednesday 5th and Thursday 6th April 2006.

- His HB is awarded for those exact three days (on a daily basis).

MOVING OUT OF AN AUTHORITY'S AREA

A woman moves out of an authority's area on Saturday 22nd July 2006. She is liable for rent and council tax at her old address (which is not a hostel) up to and including Friday 21st July.

- Her HB ends at the end of the benefit week containing her last day of liability for rent, in other words her last day of HB is Sunday 23rd July.
- Her CTB ends on the last day of her liability for council tax. In other words her last day of CTB is Friday 21st July.

CHANGES IN RENT AND COUNCIL TAX

A woman's rent goes up on Saturday 20th May 2006.

- If her entitlement to HB changes as a result, it changes on and from Saturday 20th May 2006 (on a daily basis).

A man's council tax goes down on Tuesday 4th April 2006, because from that day he becomes entitled to a discount.

- If his entitlement to CTB changes as a result, it changes on and from Tuesday 4th April 2006 (on a daily basis).

HB ON TWO HOMES

A woman flees violence on Wednesday 7th June 2006. She leaves a council tenancy at which the eligible rent is £70 pw. She goes to a hostel where the eligible rent is £140 pw, payable on a daily basis. Her intention to return to the council tenancy means that she is eligible for HB on both homes.

- In benefit week commencing Monday 5th June 2006 her eligible rent is a full week's eligible rent at the council tenancy (£70.00) plus five-sevenths of a week's eligible rent at the hostel (£120), totalling £190.

CHANGES IN THE REGULATIONS

17.34 When regulations relevant to HB/CTB are amended, the authority alters the claimant's entitlement to HB/CTB from the date on which the amendment takes effect (unless entitlement reduces to nil, in which case para. 17.21 applies). But in HB only, for claimants whose rent is due weekly or in multiples of weeks, the annual HB/CTB up-rating (which for everyone else takes effect on 1st April) takes effect from the first Monday in April (3rd April in 2006). These are supersessions.

HB 79(3)
HB60+ 60(3)
NIHB 76(5)
NIHB60+ 58(5)
CTB 67(4)
CTB60+ 50(4)
DAR 8(10)
NIDAR 8(12)

WHEN THERE IS MORE THAN ONE CHANGE

17.35 Each change in circumstances is dealt with separately. But the following applies when changes which actually occur in the same benefit week would have an effect (under the earlier rules in this chapter) in different benefit weeks:

HB 79(4),(5)
HB60+ 59(4),(5)
NIHB 76(6),(7)
NIHB60+ 58(6),(7)
CTB 67(7)
CTB60+ 50(7)

- In HB only, if one of the changes is in:
  - the annual up-rating (when it takes effect on the first Monday of April as described in the previous paragraph);
  - the amount of liability for rent on a dwelling;
  - moving into a new dwelling;
  - starting or stopping being eligible for HB on a former home or on two homes, including stopping being eligible because the (4 weeks or 52 weeks) time limit runs out,

  the other changes in entitlement instead apply when that applies. And for this rule, the first item in the above list takes priority over the other four.
- For HB in all other cases, all the changes take effect from the Monday of the benefit week in which the changes actually occur.
- For CTB in all cases, work out the various days on which the changes have an effect (under the earlier rules): all the changes instead apply from the earliest of these dates.

These are supersessions.

Changes of circumstances which are notified late

LATE NOTIFICATION OF CHANGES WHICH REDUCE ENTITLEMENT

DAR 8(2)
NIDAR 8(2)

17.36 If a claimant delays (no matter how long) notifying the authority of a change which would have the effect of reducing his or her entitlement to HB or CTB, the authority must nonetheless implement the change according to the rules in the previous section. This is a supersession. It creates an overpayment (which may or may not be recoverable: chapter 18). The authority's duty to notify the outcome is the same as in paragraph 17.16. An example appears below.

Example: Late notified change reducing entitlement

A claimant's wages went up four months ago, but the claimant did not inform the authority until today.

The change is implemented from the Monday following the day the wages went up – thus creating an overpayment (which will very likely be recoverable).

This is a supersession.

LATE NOTIFICATION OF CHANGES WHICH INCREASE ENTITLEMENT

DAR 7(2)(a),(3),8(3),(5)
NIDAR 7(2)(a),(3),8(3),(5)

17.37 The rules in the previous section do not, however, apply if the claimant delays notifying the authority of a change which would have the effect of increasing his or her entitlement to HB or CTB (or would otherwise be 'advantageous' to the claimant) – and which he or she had a duty to notify (para. 17.9 and table 17.2). A claimant counts as having delayed notifying a change if his or her written notification is received by the authority more than one month after the change occurred (though this time limit can be extended: para. 17.40).

17.38 In such cases the change is instead deemed to have occurred on the date the authority received the written notification – and then the change is taken into account using the rules in the previous section but based on that date. In other words, the claimant loses money (as in the first example below). This is a supersession. The authority's duty to notify the outcome is the same as in paragraph 17.16.

17.39 The following points are worth noting in connection with this rule.

- The rule applies only to changes which the claimant has a duty to notify, and therefore does not apply to the changes mentioned in paragraphs 17.8-9 (and see also para. 17.10 for what a claimant could be expected to know he or she had to notify).
- A claimant cannot be held to have a duty to notify something which he or she cannot know.

- The effect of the rule can be mitigated by the rule about underlying entitlement (para. 18.16).
- The claimant can take longer to provide the notification if the circumstances in the next paragraph apply.

Example: Late notified changes

A claimant's wages went down four months ago, but the claimant did not inform the authority until today. The authority asks why she delayed, but she has no special circumstances.

The change is implemented from the Monday following the day the claimant's written notification of the change was received by the authority. The claimant does not get her arrears. (However, if the claimant has 'special circumstances', she may get her arrears: para. 17.40). This is a supersession.

EXTENDING THE TIME LIMIT FOR NOTIFYING A CHANGE THAT INCREASES ENTITLEMENT

17.40 In the case of a change of circumstances which increases entitlement, the one month time limit for notifying it is extended (and the claimant does not lose money) if: DAR 9(1)-(5) NIDAR 9(1)-(5)

- the notification is received by the authority within 13 months of the date on which the change occurred; and
- the claimant, when writing to notify the change, also notifies the authority of the reasons for his or her failure to notify the change earlier; and
- the authority is satisfied that the change of circumstances is relevant; and
- the authority is satisfied that there are or were 'special circumstances' as a result of which it was not practicable to notify the change within the one month time limit. The longer the delay (beyond the normal one month), the more compelling those special circumstances need to be; and
- the authority is satisfied that it is reasonable to grant the claimant's request. In determining this, the authority may not take account of ignorance of the law (not even ignorance of the time limits) nor of the fact that a Commissioner or tribunal of Commissioners or court has taken a different view of the law from that previously understood and applied.

17.41 If the authority refuses the claimant's request, the claimant has no right to ask it again to accept late notification of the same change. However, the authority DAR 9(60 NIDAR 9(6) must implement the change from some date (the late date: para. 17.38) – which is a supersession. That supersession (and the date it is to apply from) is a decision itself (para. 17.7), and so the claimant has the right to ask the authority to reconsider (para. 17.55) or to appeal (chapter 19).

Implementing rent officer re-determinations

DAR 4(3),7(2)(c), 8(6),10

17.42 The following rules apply (in England, Wales and Scotland only) if the claimant or an authority appeals to the rent officer and he or she issues a re-determination, or if the authority applies for a correction in a rent officer determination or re-determination and he or she issues a substitute determination or substitute re-determination (paras. 6.41-50). In such cases, the new rent officer figures apply as follows.

- If the effect of the new figures would be to increase the amount of the claimant's eligible rent, the authority alters its original decision from the date it took effect (or should have). So the claimant gets his or her arrears. This is a revision.
- If the effect of the new figures would be to reduce the amount of the claimant's eligible rent, the authority alters its original decision from the Monday following the rent officer's re-determination, substitute determination or substitute re-determination. So the claimant (if the authority acts promptly) does not suffer from an overpayment. This is a supersession.

In either case, the authority's duty to notify the outcome is the same as in paragraph 17.16.

17.43 The above rules do not apply in Northern Ireland, since decisions about restricting the eligible rent are made by the NIHE and unlike in Great Britain there is no special procedure for appealing (paras. 6.40 and 6.51). The equivalent situation is where the claimant asks the NIHE to reconsider its decision. Except where as a result of the request the NIHE decides to restrict the rent still further, where the request is made within the one month time limit (paras. 17.55 and 17.59) any increase in benefit will be payable from the date of the original decision (para. 17.58). This is a revision. Where the request is made outside one month and it results in an increase in benefit the new decision will take effect from the date of the request (paras 17.51-52). This is a supersession. If the request is made within the one month time limit but the new decision is that the rent should be restricted still further, then normal NIHE practice, except perhaps in the case of misrepresentation or fraud, is to treat the request as a change of circumstances (i.e. a change in the housing market conditions) from the date of the request (paras. 17.51-52) and not to restrict benefit from the date of the original decision. This is a supersession.

Mistakes and errors

17.44 This section is about what an authority can or must do when there has been a 'mistake of fact' or a 'mistake of law' in a decision – or an 'accidental error' or other 'official error' in it. These four terms are distinguishable as follows:

- A 'mistake of fact' means that the decision was based (at least partly) on an incorrect fact (without at this stage saying that it was necessarily anybody's fault).
- A 'mistake of law' means that the decision was based (at least partly) on an incorrect understanding of the law.
- An 'accidental error' is something on the lines of a slip of the pen – a failure by the authority to put into action (or to record) its true intentions.
- An 'official error' is defined independently (para. 17.46) and can include one or a combination of the above (*CH/943/2003*).

The example contrasts the first two.

Example: 'Mistake of fact' and 'mistake of law'

In deciding a claim for HB/CTB, an authority determined that a man and a woman were not a couple.

This would be a mistake of fact if the authority made its decision not knowing that they were actually married (e.g. because the claimant had lied or the authority misread the application form).

It would be a mistake of law if the authority wrongly believed that two unmarried people could never be a couple.

CORRECTING ACCIDENTAL ERRORS

17.45 The authority may correct an accidental error in any decision (including a revised or superseding decision), or the record of any decision, at any time. The correction is deemed to be part of the decision or record, and the authority must give written notice of the correction as soon as practicable to the claimant and any other person affected.

DAR 10A(1),(2)
NIDAR 10A(1),(2)

CORRECTING OTHER OFFICIAL ERRORS

17.46 The authority may revise or supersede a decision at any time if the decision arose from an 'official error'. An 'official error' means an error by an authority, a contractor to an authority, or an officer of the DWP or the Commissioners of Inland Revenue acting as such. However, something does not count as an 'official error' if it was caused wholly or partly by any person or body other than the above,

CPSA sch 7 paras 1(1),23(1)
NICPSA sch 7 paras 1(1),23(1)
DAR 1(2),4(2)
NIDAR 1(2),4(2)

nor if it is an error of law which is shown to have been an error only by a subsequent decision of a Commissioner or tribunal of Commissioners.

17.47 The effect may be that there has been an underpayment of HB/CTB (in which case the arrears must be awarded – no matter how far back they go) or an overpayment (which may or may not be recoverable: chapter 18).

BECOMING AWARE THAT AN APPEAL DECISION APPLIES TO A CASE

DAR 4(7)
NIDAR 4(6)

17.48 The authority may revise a decision at any time to take account of an appeal decision in the same case (by an appeal tribunal, Commissioner, tribunal of Commissioners or court) which the authority was not aware of at the time it made the decision.

MISTAKES OF FACT RESULTING IN AN OVERPAYMENT

DAR 4(2)
NIDAR 4(2)

17.49 The authority may revise or supersede a decision at any time if the decision was made in ignorance of, or was based on a mistake as to, some material fact – and the decision was, as a result, more favourable than it would otherwise have been. This creates an overpayment (which may or may not be recoverable: chapter 18).

MISTAKES OF FACT DISCOVERED WITHIN ONE MONTH

17.50 The authority may revise a decision if, within one month of the date of notifying it, the authority has information sufficient to show that it was made in ignorance of, or was based on a mistake as to, some material fact. This is something the authority may do without a request from anyone else. This one month time limit cannot be extended (though the person affected could write asking the authority to reconsider and ask for this to be considered late because of special circumstances: para 17.59).

OTHER MISTAKES OF FACT – SUPERSESSION RATHER THAN REVISION

CPSA sch 7 para 4(5),(6)
NICPSA sch 7 para 4(4),(5)
DAR 7(2)(b),8(4)(5)
NIDAR 7(2)(b), 8(4),(5)

17.51 If none of the previous rules in this section apply, the authority may supersede a decision at any time if the decision was made in ignorance of, or was based on a mistake as to, some material fact. This could arise only in the case of increases to entitlement (because decreases are all covered by the earlier rules). This is something the authority may do because the claimant or other person affected has asked it to, or without anyone asking it to. An example follows.

Example: Mistake of fact resulting in a supersession

A claimant with a non-dependant in remunerative work was unable to provide the authority with details of the non-dependant's income. So the authority applied the highest level of non-dependant deduction in assessing her HB and CTB (para. 7.27). Now, four months later, the claimant provides evidence which is acceptable to the authority. It means a lower deduction applies.

Because this is outside the time limit for a revision (para. 17.57), the authority alters the amount of the claimant's HB/CTB from the Monday of the benefit week in which it received the evidence. The claimant does not get her arrears.

Note that the outcome would be different if the claimant wrote giving her reasons for the delay and the authority accepted that these amounted to special circumstances (para. 17.59). She would then get her arrears.

17.52 The supersession in such a case takes effect from the Monday at the beginning of the benefit week in which:

- the request was received from the claimant or other person affected (if a request was indeed made); or
- the authority first had information to show that the original decision was made in ignorance or mistake of fact (in any other case).

OTHER ERRORS OF LAW

17.53 A final rare rule applies if a decision was based on an error of law but was not due to 'official error' (para. 17.46). (This could arise if the Commissioners or courts interpret the law in an unexpected way.) The authority may supersede the decision at any time. This is something the authority may do because the claimant or other person affected has asked it to, or without anyone asking it to. In such a case, the supersession takes effect from the date on which it is made (or, if earlier, from the date the person's request was received).

CPSA sch 7 para 4(5),(6)
NICPSA sch 7 para 4(4),(5)
DAT 7(2)(b)
NIDAR 7(2)(b)

NOTIFYING THE OUTCOME

17.54 Whenever the authority alters a decision under the above rules (except in the case of correcting accidental errors, for which a different rule applies: para. 17.45), it must write notifying the claimant and any other person affected, of the same matters as in paragraph 17.16.

DAR 10
NIDAR 10
HB sch 9
HB60+ sch 8
NIHB sch 10
NIHB60+ sch 10
CTB sch 8
CTB60+ sch 7

Asking the authority to reconsider a decision

GENERAL RULES

SA sch 7 para 4(1)
NICPSA sch 7 para 4(1)
DAR 4(1),(8),(9), 7(2),(6),(7)
IDAR 4(1),(8),(9), 7(2),(6),(7)

17.55 This section is about requests to the authority to reconsider its decision. Such requests must be in writing and may be made either by the claimant or by any other 'person affected' (para. 16.7). This could be done either instead of or before making an appeal to the appeal tribunal (chapter 18). Although the law refers to requests for a 'revision' or 'supersession', the person does not have to remember to use either term in his or her request, and it does not matter if he or she uses those terms wrongly. The authority should treat any letter raising queries about entitlement as a request to reconsider its decision (unless the claimant is simply asking for a written statement of reasons: para. 19.24).

TIME LIMIT FOR REQUESTS

17.56 If the request for a reconsideration is received:

- within the time limit, the authority must consider revising its decision (para. 17.58);
- outside the time limit, the authority must consider superseding its decision (para. 17.60).

DAR 4(1),(4), 10A(3)
NIDAR 4(1),(4), 10A(3)

17.57 A request is within the time limit if it is received by the authority within one calendar month of the date the decision was notified. In calculating this time limit:

- any time is ignored from the date the authority received a request for a statement of reasons (para. 19.24) to the date the authority provided the statement (both dates inclusive); and
- any time is ignored before the date on which the authority gave notice of the correction of an accidental error (para. 17.45); and
- the time limit may be extended by the authority as described below (para. 17.59).

REQUESTS RECEIVED WITHIN THE TIME LIMIT

SA sch 7 para 3(3)
NICPSA sch 7 para 3(3)
DAR 6
NIDAR 6

17.58 If the request for reconsideration is received within the time limit, and the authority alters entitlement to HB/CTB, this takes effect from the date of the original decision – unless the authority determines that the original decision took effect from a wrong date, in which case it takes effect from the correct date. This is a revision. Whether or not the authority alters entitlement, the outcome must be notified (para. 17.61).

EXTENDING THE TIME LIMIT FOR REQUESTS

17.59 The one-month time limit is extended if: DAR 4(8),5(1)-(6) NIDAR 4(7),5(1)-(6)

- the request is received in writing by the authority within 13 months of the date on which the decision was notified; and
- the request says that the person is asking for it to be accepted late, and gives the reasons for his or her failure to request a reconsideration earlier; and
- the person gives sufficient details to identify the disputed decision; and
- the request for revision 'has merit'; and
- the authority is satisfied that there are or were 'special circumstances' as a result of which it was not practicable to request a reconsideration within the one month time limit. The longer the delay (beyond the normal one month), the more compelling those special circumstances need to be; and
- the authority is satisfied that it is reasonable to grant the claimant's request. In determining this, the authority may not take account of ignorance of the law (not even ignorance of the time limits) nor of the fact that a Commissioner or tribunal of Commissioners or court has taken a different view of the law from that previously understood and applied.

REQUESTS RECEIVED OUTSIDE THE TIME LIMIT

17.60 If the request for reconsideration is received outside the one month time limit, and the authority refuses to extend this limit, the person affected has no right to ask it to accept a further late request to reconsider the same matter. However, the authority should nonetheless reconsider its decision and should consider making a superseding decision instead: the details are in paragraph 17.51. DAR 5(7),7(2)(b) NIDAR 5(7),7(2)(b)

Example: Late request for the authority to reconsider its decision

In May 2006, the authority notified a claimant of its decision on his claim. Amongst other things, the decision depended upon an assessment of the claimant's self-employed income.

In September 2006, the claimant asks the authority to reconsider its decision, as he forgot to tell them about part of his expenditure. He has no special circumstances for his delay. However, the authority accepts that (if it had known) it would have allowed that additional expenditure (and he would therefore have qualified for more HB/CTB).

The change is implemented from the Monday following the day the claimant's written notification of the change is received by the authority. The claimant does not get his arrears. This is a supersession. (However, if the claimant has 'special circumstances', he may get his arrears: para. 17.59).

NOTIFYING THE OUTCOME

DAR 10
NIDAR 10
HB sch 9
HB60+ sch 8
NIHB sch 10
NIHB60+ sch 10
CTB sch 8
CTB60+ sch 7

17.61 In all the circumstances described in this section, the authority must notify the claimant of the outcome of his or her request for reconsideration, including the following matters

- whether it has changed its decision;
- if it has not changed its decision, the reasons why it has refused the claimant's request;
- if it has changed its decision, the same matters as in paragraph 17.16.

Revisions prompted by an appeal

PSA sch 7 para 3(6)
NICPSA
sch 7 para 3(6)
DAR 4(1),(6)
NIDAR 4(1),(6)

17.62 The authority may revise a decision if an appeal to an appeal tribunal is made against it within the relevant time limits, and the appeal has not yet been determined. This takes effect from the date of the original decision – unless the authority determines that the original decision took effect from a wrong date, in which case it takes effect from the correct date. Generally speaking, if the authority does revise a decision in these circumstances, the appeal lapses. More information is in paragraph 19.6.

Information and evidence

WHAT MATTERS ARE TAKEN INTO ACCOUNT

CPSA sch 7
paras 3(2),4(3),5,16
NICPSA sch 7
paras 3(2),4(2),5,16

17.63 When considering revising or superseding any decision, the authority need not consider any matter which was not raised in the request (if a request was made) or did not cause it to act on its own initiative. An authority may ask experts for help when considering any decision it has made (in order to decide whether it should be revised or superseded).

DAR 4(10)
NIDAR 4(9)

17.64 In considering revising a decision, the authority must ignore any change of circumstances which has occurred since the decision was made and must ignore any future change of circumstances which may be about to occur. (In relation to these, the authority must consider supersession instead.) This rule ensures that decisions relating to different events do not become muddled up.

REQUESTS FOR INFORMATION AND EVIDENCE

17.65 When a revision or supersession is being considered as a result of a request from a claimant or other person affected, and the authority requires further evidence or information in order to consider all the issues raised, the authority has a duty to request this in writing from the person affected. Then:

AA 5(1)(hh),6(1)(hh)
NIAA 5(1)(hh)
DAR 4(5),7(5),13
NIDAR 4(4),7(5),13

- if the information or evidence is provided within one calendar month of the date of the authority's request – or within such longer period as the authority may allow – the authority must consider the revision or supersession taking it into account;
- if the information or evidence is not provided within the above time limit, the authority must consider the revision or supersession on the basis of the original request from the claimant or other person affected.

In the second case, if doubt arises about entitlement to HB/CTB, the authority may suspend HB/CTB (paras. 17.67 onwards).

17.66 When a revision or supersession is being considered without a request, but because the authority has the power to do so, it has the same rights to require information, evidence, documents and certificates as in the case of a claim (para. 5.17). If the claimant fails to provide these, the authority may suspend HB/CTB (paras. 17.67 onwards).

HB 86(1)
HB60+ 67(1)
NIHB 81(1)
NIHB60+ 64(1)
CTB 72(1)
CTB60+ 57(1)
DAR 13
NIDAR 13

Suspending, restoring and terminating HB/CTB

17.67 The authority may suspend HB/CTB in the circumstances set out in the following paragraphs. To suspend simply means stopping making payments for the time being, in order to seek information and evidence or for other reasons. Eventually, entitlement to HB/CTB will either be restored (as described at all the relevant places below) or terminated (para. 17.79). The claimant has a right of appeal to a social security tribunal (para. 19.17) about a decision terminating HB/CTB, or restoring HB/CTB at a different amount or for a different reason (which is a supersession) but not about a decision suspending HB/CTB, or restoring HB/CTB at the same amount for the same reasons.

SI 2001/1605
NISR 2000/215
DAR part III
NIDAR part III

DOUBT REGARDING ENTITLEMENT

17.68 The authority may suspend, in whole or in part, any payment of HB/CTB where there is doubt as to whether the conditions for entitlement are or were fulfilled. The authority may also suspend, in whole or in part, any HB/CTB payment where it is considering whether a decision about an award should be revised or superseded. Obviously where a revised or superseded decision would result in an increase in entitlement, there is no need for the authority to consider suspension.

DAR 11(1),(2),12
NIDAR 11(1),(2),12

17.69 Payments should be made in both cases once the authority is satisfied that the suspended benefit is properly payable and no outstanding issues remain to be resolved. This should be done so far as practicable within 14 days of the decision to make or restore the payment.

AN APPEAL IS PENDING IN THE CASE IN QUESTION

DAR 11(1),(2)(b)
NIDAR 11(1),(2)(b)

17.70 The authority may suspend, in whole or in part, any payment of HB/CTB where an appeal is pending (in that case) against a decision of an appeal tribunal, a Commissioner or a court.

17.71 An appeal is pending where an appeal against the decision has been made, but not determined, or an application for leave to appeal against the decision has been made, but not yet determined.

DAR 12(2)
NIDAR 12(2)

17.72 Payments should be made when the appeal is no longer pending and the suspended benefit remains payable following the decision of the appeal. This should be done so far as practicable within 14 days of the decision to make or restore payment.

AN APPEAL IS PENDING AGAINST A DECISION IN A DIFFERENT CASE

DAR 11(2)(b)
NIDAR 11(2)(b)

17.73 The authority may suspend, in whole or in part, any payment of HB/CTB where an appeal is pending against a decision given by a Commissioner or a court in a different case, and it appears to the authority that if the appeal were to be determined in a particular way an issue would arise as to whether the award of HB/CTB in the case under consideration ought to be revised or superseded.

DAR 12(1)(b),(2)
NIDAR 12(1)(b),(2)

17.74 Payments should be made when the appeal is no longer pending and the benefit suspended remains payable following the determination of the appeal. This should be done so far as practicable within 14 days of the decision to make or restore payment.

POSSIBLE OVERPAYMENTS

DAR 11(2)(c)
NIDAR 11(2)(c)

17.75 The authority may suspend, in whole or in part any payment of HB/CTB when an issue arises as to whether an amount of HB/CTB is recoverable. Again once resolved payment of any outstanding amount should be made. Again, so far as practicable, this should be done within 14 days of the decision to make or restore payment.

FAILURE TO FURNISH INFORMATION ETC

DAR 13(1),(2)
NIDAR 13(1),(2)

17.76 The authority may suspend in whole or in part any payment of HB/CTB that relates to someone who fails to comply with the requirements to provide information or evidence needed by the authority in deciding whether a decision should be revised or superseded.

17.77 The authority must notify the person concerned of this power. The person concerned must: DAR 13(3)-(5) NIDAR 13(3)-(5)

- furnish the information or evidence required within:
  - one month beginning with the date on which the notification was sent to them; or
  - such longer period as the authority considers necessary to enable them to comply with the requirement; or
- satisfy the authority within the relevant period that:
  - the information or evidence required does not exist; or
  - it is not possible for them to obtain the required information or evidence.

17.78 Where a person satisfies the requirements the authority must, so far as practicable, make, or restore, payment within 14 days of making the decision to make or restore payment.

TERMINATING HB/CTB

17.79 When someone's HB/CTB has been suspended and he or she has failed to comply with the information requirements (para. 17.77), HB/CTB entitlement is terminated (in other words, simply ends). This is done from: DAR 14 NIDAR14

- the date on which the payments were suspended (i.e. no further payments are made); or
- whatever earlier date HB/CTB entitlement ended. In this case the authority should have a justification for choosing that earlier date. Terminating back to an earlier date causes an overpayment. Whether and how much of that overpayment is recoverable depends on the rules in chapter 18. Terminating back to an earlier date also means that the claimant has no current award of HB/CTB and must make a fresh claim if he or she wants HB/CTB for the future.

A decision to terminate HB/CTB must be notified, and is open to appeal (chapter 19). The result of an appeal may be to alter the date from which the termination takes effect or, indeed, to undo the termination (i.e. restore the HB/CTB award at an appropriate level of payment).

17.80 The law about termination (and the terminology) can be difficult. For example:

- It is unclear whether and how CTB can be suspended. The DWP considers (circular HB/CTB A31/2004) that suspending CTB does not necessarily require the issuing of a new council tax bill. This appears wrong, but it is hard to reconcile council tax law with council tax benefit law to understand when, and in what sense, an authority 'pays' CTB to itself.

- It is unclear how termination works when only part of the HB/CTB was suspended. This is largely theoretical, as suspension in part almost never happens in practice; but if it did occur, it would be perfectly possible to go on to suspend in full (under the ordinary rules, paras. 17.67 onwards) and then terminate as above (para. 17.79).
- Terminating an award of HB/CTB (because of failure to provide information or evidence) is done under different rules from superseding HB/CTB at nil (because it is known that the claimant is no longer entitled to HB/CTB). However the concept of termination may be unnecessary, since the authority could instead supersede at nil having drawn a negative inference (as in para. 5.28 in connection with claims). Indeed the law appears to acknowledge this in the second case in paragraph 17.79, where there must also have been a supersession at nil (to take account of the change of circumstances that justified terminating from an earlier date).
- Finally, the so-called 'cooling-off period' (which added a one-month delay to the right of appeal about a termination decision) has without doubt ceased to exist since amendments were made to the law on 10th November 2005.

Example: Suspending, restoring and terminating HB/CTB

The authority obtains information that a man on HB/CTB has got a new job.

The authority suspends his award immediately, and writes to him allowing him one month to respond.

If he responds and provides the necessary information and evidence within the month, the authority restores his HB/CTB from the appropriate date (and makes any supersession needed to take account of his new income), probably thereby creating an overpayment from that date until the date HB/CTB were suspended.

If the claimant refuses to respond, or responds insufficiently, the authority terminates the award of HB/CTB. In this case, the authority needs to establish when the termination should occur.

HB 72,73 sch 7, sch 8 HB60+ 52,53, sch 7 NIHB 69,70 NIHB60+ 50,51, sch 8 CTB 60,61, sch 6, sch 7 CTB60+ 41,42, sch 5

Extended payments

17.81 The following rules are designed to help long-term unemployed people who are returning to work, by giving them an 'extended payment' of four weeks extra HB/CTB.

ENTITLEMENT TO EXTENDED PAYMENTS

17.82 A claimant is entitled to an extended payment ('EP') if:

- the claimant's award of HB/CTB ends in the circumstances described in paragraph 17.23 and table 17.4 (in broad terms, because he or she has been on JSA(IB)/IS/IB/SDA for 26 weeks or more and this has ceased because of a new job, etc); and
- the claimant or partner remains liable (or treated as liable) for rent or liable for council tax/rates (at the same or a new address).

CLAIMS, ETC

17.83 There is no requirement for a written claim. Instead, a person who fulfils the conditions is treated as having claimed an EP so long as he or she notifies the authority or the DWP of the matters in table 17.4. This must be done within four weeks of the day the new job, new hours or new rate of pay, began. Although it could be done in person or by telephone, it is wise for claimants to follow this up with written confirmation.

17.84 The authority has a duty to determine EP claims and notify the outcome – even if a claimant does not qualify for an EP – and even if the only reason is that the DWP has said that the claimant does not satisfy the '26-week condition' (table 17.4). Unlike the other conditions (in that table and para. 17.82), it is for the Secretary of State (via the DWP) to 'certify' whether or not the claimant fulfils this condition – and this is binding on the authority. If the claimant disagrees with this particular matter he or she may negotiate with the DWP, but the only formal method of appeal would be to seek judicial review.

17.85 As regards whether the claimant satisfies the other conditions (in para. 17.82) the DWP's advice is that authorities should normally accept what the claimant has said – though, of course, an authority may well not accept it if a claimant said, in late December, that his new job impersonating Father Christmas would last five weeks.

PERIODS AND AMOUNTS OF EXTENDED PAYMENTS

17.86 An EP is awarded for the four weeks following the Sunday on which the authority ends the HB/CTB benefit period as a result of the claimant ceasing to be entitled to JSA(IB)/IS/IB/SDA(para. 17.23) or (if relevant) moving (para 17.91).

17.87 An EP is treated as though it was ordinary HB/CTB for other purposes (such as whether the claimant falls within the New Scheme or Old Scheme for eligible rent purposes: chapter 10). Also it may be replaced, later, by a new ongoing HB/CTB benefit period as described in paragraph 17.89.

17.88 In each of those four weeks, the amount of HB/CTB EP equals the amount awarded in the last benefit week of the (recently ended) award of HB/CTB – ignoring any part-week of entitlement and ignoring any rent-free period in that week. The one exception is that no HB EP is awarded in a rent-free week. (For example, if the normal four-week EP period contains one rent-free week, the claimant will get only three weeks' worth of EPs.) Otherwise all changes of circumstances are ignored.

FURTHER AWARDS OF HB/CTB FOLLOWING EXTENDED PAYMENTS

17.89 Claimants may remain entitled to HB/CTB despite their (or their partner's) new job or increase in hours or earnings. A further claim (by the claimant or partner) for ongoing HB/CTB runs consecutively as follows:

- If the claimant is entitled to less ongoing HB/CTB than the amount of the EP (or exactly the same amount), the new amount is awarded from the benefit week immediately following the end of the EP period.
- If the claimant is entitled to more ongoing HB/CTB than the amount of the EP, the balance is awarded for the EP period, and the whole amount is awarded thereafter. (This could arise, for example, if a non-dependant left the household and the increase in entitlement due to this was greater than the decrease in entitlement due to the new income of the claimant or partner.)

Table 17.6: Extended payments for movers

HB: A MOVE FROM RENT ALLOWANCE TO RENT ALLOWANCE

The amount of HB at the new address is exactly equal to the amount of HB at the old address (including any rate rebate in NI*).

If the move is to a new authority area, the old authority makes this payment.

HB: A MOVE FROM RENT ALLOWANCE TO RENT REBATE

The amount of HB at the new address is calculated using:

- the eligible rent (and rates*) at the new address, but
- the non-dependant deduction(s) (if any) at the old address.

If the move is to a new authority area, the new authority makes this payment.

HB: A MOVE FROM RENT REBATE TO RENT REBATE

The amount of HB at the new address is calculated using:

- the eligible rent (and rates*) at the new address, but
- the non-dependant deduction(s) (if any) at the old address.

If the move is to a new authority area, the new authority makes this payment.

HB: A MOVE FROM RENT REBATE TO RENT ALLOWANCE

The amount of HB at the new address is exactly equal to the amount of HB at the old address (including any rate rebate in NI*).

If the move is to a new authority area, the new authority makes this payment.

CTB: ALL CASES

The amount of CTB at the new address is calculated using:

- the eligible council tax liability at the new address, but
- the non-dependant deduction(s) (if any) at the old address.

If the move is to a new authority area, the new authority makes this payment.

RATE REBATE ONLY PAYABLE

The amount of HB at the new address is calculated using

- the eligible rates at the new address, but
- the non-dependant deduction(s) (if any) at the old address.

* In Northern Ireland, where a rate rebate is paid together with HB in respect of rent, follow the appropriate rent rebate or allowance category. Where a rate rebate only is payable, including cases where the claimant is a tenant but does not qualify for any HB in respect of their rent, follow the table as for 'Rate Rebate only'.

MISCELLANEOUS MATTERS

17.90 The following are the main further matters relating to EPs.

- A separate determination should be made (and notified) about whether to recover recoverable overpayments of HB by deduction from an EP for HB.
- The question of whether an EP has been overpaid depends on who has to notify and/or determine what. For example, if a claimant said that his new job would last at least five weeks and then the employer (unforeseeably) closed down, the extended payment was correctly paid: there has been no overpayment.

EXTENDED PAYMENTS FOR MOVERS

17.91 Claimants who are entitled to an EP are entitled to it even if they move home during the week before, or the week in which, they or a partner take up employment or self-employment – but not in cases of increasing hours or earnings.

17.92 The amount of the EP for HB at the new address (during the EP period) depends on whether the claimant's entitlements at the old and new addresses are to a rent allowance or a rent rebate, as shown in table 17.6, which also shows the amount of the EP for CTB at the new address.

17.93 In any case when the claimant moves to a new authority area, the law allows authorities to exchange information relevant to extended payments. The DWP advises that the old authority should keep all the documentation and write to the new authority confirming the details.

Continuing payments

HB60+ 54 **17.94** The following rules are designed to 'tide someone over' when he or she
NIHB60+ 52 CTB60+ 45 transfers from JSA(IB) or IS to pension credit. The person has no need to claim a continuing payment: it is awarded automatically.

ENTITLEMENT TO CONTINUING PAYMENTS

17.95 Someone on HB/CTB and either JSA(IB) or IS is entitled to a continuing payment if:

- he or she reaches 60 (or 65 if he has stayed on JSA(IB) beyond age 60); and
- the DWP certifies to the authority that the claimant has claimed or is treated as having claimed pension credit, and IS or JSA(IB) has therefore stopped.

17.96 Someone on HB/CTB and either JSA(IB) or IS is also entitled to a continuing payment if:

- he or she has a partner and the partner claims pension credit; and
- the DWP certifies this to the authority.

PERIODS AND AMOUNTS OF CONTINUING PAYMENTS

17.97 In such cases the person (so long as he or she otherwise remains entitled to HB/CTB) gets four weeks of HB/CTB, starting on the day after his or her last day of entitlement to IS/JSA(IB), calculated as follows:

- he or she is treated as having no income or capital;
- his or her eligible rent and/or council tax are treated as being the same as they were immediately beforehand – except in the case of an increase (in either) in which case the increased amount is used;
- but non-dependant deductions are done according to the actual circumstances of the case.

17.98 If the four weeks in question would not run out on a Sunday, the continuing payment is lengthened by up to six days to ensure that it does end on a Sunday.

17.99 The idea behind continuing payments is that the award of HB/CTB can then continue seamlessly. The amount awarded during the continuing payment period is not an overpayment (unless, say, the claimant lied about his or her age, perhaps).

Example: Continuing payments

A man is on HB/CTB and JSA/(IB) when he reaches 65. He reaches 65 on Tuesday 18th April 2006. The DWP tells the authority that he has been treated as having claimed pension credit.

His continuing payment of HB/CTB is awarded from Tuesday 18th April 2006 to Sunday 21st May 2006 – a total of four weeks and six days.

By then the authority knows the claimant qualifies for guarantee credit from his birthday.

He is awarded HB/CTB based on this from Monday 22nd May 2006.

18 Overpayments

18.1 This chapter explains:

- what an overpayment is;
- why the cause of an overpayment is important;
- when an overpayment is recoverable;
- how the amount of the overpayment is worked out;
- when, from whom, how, and at what rate an overpayment should be recovered;
- whether recovered overpaid benefit results in rent arrears;
- how far recovery of an overpayment may be pursued;
- when an administrative penalty may be added to a fraudulent overpayment; and
- the information that should be provided to the claimant and any other person affected.

AA 75(1),76(1)
NIAA 73(1)
HB 99
HB60+ 80
NIHB 95
NIHB60+ 78
CTB 82
CTB60+ 67

18.2 Where more HB is paid than someone is entitled to, this is referred to as an 'overpayment'. The term includes any overpayment by way of a rebate to a rent account and in Northern Ireland a rates account. Where more CTB is paid than a claimant is entitled to, this is referred to as 'excess benefit'. As most of the rules relating to 'overpayments' and 'excess benefit' are the same, the term overpayment is used in this chapter to refer to both.

18.3 The overpayment and recovery of benefit has caused major difficulties for claimants, landlords and authorities. Claimants and landlords have had their rights denied and unnecessary debts created. Many authorities have failed to follow the correct decision-making process, notify claimants, keep adequate records, or account for overpayments properly. As a consequence they have made inaccurate subsidy claims and created rent and council tax arrears for themselves and debts for landlords.

What is an overpayment?

AA 75(1),76(1)
NIAA 73(1)
HB 99
HB60+ 80
NIHB 95
NIHB60+ 78
CTB 82
CTB60+ 67

18.4 Overpayments are established through revision or suspension (table 17.1) of benefit entitlement. They are amounts of benefit which have been paid but to which there is no entitlement under the regulations. They include any overpayment of:

- a rent allowance paid on account (para. 16.16);
- CTB due to a backdated award of a council tax discount (para. 9.16), or council tax disability reduction (para. 9.13).

The importance of making the necessary revisions and supersessions, in order to establish that there has been an overpayment, must not be overlooked (CH/27794/2004).

18.5 Having identified that an overpayment has occurred the authority must:

- establish the cause of each overpayment;
- decide whether or not the overpayment is recoverable;
- identify the period and calculate the amount of the overpayment;
- consider whether or not recovery should be sought;
- decide from whom the recovery should be sought;

and, within 14 days (para. 18.83), notify the claimant and other persons affected accordingly, for example, where recovery is sought from the landlord.

Example: An overpayment

The claimant receives HB and CTB from 10th April 2006. On 11th May 2006 her adult son comes to live with her. The claimant has a duty to inform the authority of this change of circumstances but does not do so until 9th August 2006. The authority determines that a non-dependant deduction should have been made for the son from the benefit week commencing Monday 15th May 2006 (the date from which the change of circumstances should have taken effect). The claimant has received benefit up to and including the benefit week commencing 14th August 2006. An overpayment of benefit has occurred for 14 weeks.

Establishing the cause of the overpayment

18.6 The authority must establish the cause of an overpayment in order to:

- decide whether or not it is recoverable;
- correctly notify the claimant, the person the authority is seeking to recover from (if not the claimant), and any other person affected;
- claim the correct amount of subsidy;
- in some cases, determine the method of recovery.

18.7 An overpayment might arise due to:

- local authority error, e.g. the authority fails to act on notification of a change of circumstances provided by the claimant;

- Job Centre Plus or Pensions Service error, e.g. the Job Centre Plus office makes a mistaken award of income support or income-based JSA;
- claimant error or claimant fraud, e.g. the claimant fails to inform the authority of a change in circumstance which he or she has a duty to report, such as the end of entitlement to income support or income-based JSA; or
- other reasons, e.g. the claimant obtains a retrospective award of a council tax discount and this reduces the council tax liability for that period.

Technical and advance overpayments are amounts of CTB or rent and rate rebates (but not rent allowances) that are paid in advance by way of a rebate to an account.

18.8 Consecutive overpayments may result from different causes. For example, the claimant may fail to notify the authority that their earnings have increased. The authority may then delay acting on that information once it is informed, in which case that part of the overpayment would be classified as authority error (OG para. 2.41). In such a case the cause and amount of each overpayment must be separately identified.

Recoverable overpayments

OVERPAYMENTS THAT CAN BE RECOVERED

HB 93(2),100(1),(2)
HB60+ 74(2), 81(1),(2)
NIHB 89(2),96(1),(2)
NIHB60+ 72(2), 79(1),(2)
CTB 83(1),(2)
CTB60+ 68(1),(2)

18.9 Except to the extent that it forms part of a bankruptcy debt (para. 18.10) the following overpayments are recoverable:

- an overpayment of a rent allowance payment on account which is being recovered by deductions from ongoing benefit (regardless of the cause of the overpayment);
- an overpayment of CTB caused by a retrospective reduction in the claimant's council tax as a result of a delayed award of a discount or disability reduction;
- the overpayment was caused by an 'official error' (para. 18.11) and it is an amount of rent rebate or CTB that has been overpaid in respect of a period following the date on which the revision took place that identified the overpayment;
- in Northern Ireland, the overpayment was caused by an 'official error' (para. 18.11) and it is an overpayment of rate rebate which has arisen as a result of reduction in the regional rate;
- the overpayment was caused by an 'official error' (para. 18.11) and the appropriate person realised that they were being overpaid (para. 18.12).

BANKRUPTCY DEBTS

18.10 The Court of Appeal has dealt with the question of whether an overpayment is recoverable when someone has been discharged from bankruptcy *(Secretary of State for Work and Pensions v Steele)*. The Court pointed out that, in bankruptcy law, only debts or liabilities (including 'contingent liabilities') existing at the commencement of the bankruptcy are cancelled by the discharge of the bankruptcy. Even if an overpayment period began before then, the overpayment does not exist (and so cannot be a 'contingent liability') until the decision is made to recover. This case is about JSA but applies equally to HB/CTB.

MEANING OF OFFICIAL ERROR

18.11 An official error is a mistake, whether in the form of an act or omission made by the authority, the DWP, the Inland Revenue, or any of these bodies' contractors. It does not include circumstances where the claimant, or someone acting on the claimant's behalf, or the person to whom payment has been made, caused or materially contributed to that error. The failure of the DWP to notify the authority that IS has ceased is not an official error because the claimant has a duty to notify the authority of this type of change *(R v Cambridge CC ex parte Sier)*. However, the DWP advises that this does not apply to pension credit cases because the authority relies on the Pensions Service to report any changes (OG para. 2.41). A mistaken award of IS by the DWP is an official error as is a decision which is based on the wrong award of another benefit or tax credit made by the authorities which has since been successfully challenged and is final because any further appeal rights have been exhausted (including a failure to appeal within the time limits) *(CH/943/2003)*.

HB 100(3)
HB60+ 81(3)
NIHB 96(3)
NIHB60+ 79(3)
CTB 83(3)
CTB60+ 68(3)

AWARENESS OF BEING OVERPAID

18.12 Where the overpayment arose due to official error it will nevertheless still be recoverable if either at the time the payment was received, or at the time of any notice relating to it, the claimant, a person acting on his or her behalf, or the person to whom the payment has been made, could reasonably have been expected to realise that it was an overpayment. The test is whether there was a reasonable expectation that there was an overpayment not whether there might be one *(R v Liverpool CC ex parte Griffiths)*. The purpose of this rule is to provide a degree of protection to the claimant who has relied on being entitled to the payment *(CH/1176/2003)*.

HB 100(2)
HB60+ 81(2)
NIHB 96(2)
NIHB60+ 79(2)
CTB 83(2)
CTB60+ 68(2)

18.13 The test of whether a person should have been expected to realise that there was an overpayment is individual and will vary according to the knowledge, experience and capacity of the claimant (or their representative). Therefore it will require an examination of all the facts, so for example if the claimant has learning difficulties or has been overpaid in similar circumstances before then that will be relevant. DWP guidance also points out that a person may not be expected to realise they were being overpaid if they were 'wrongly advised by an official source' (OG para. 2.100).

18.14 The following points in this paragraph arise from the decision *CH/1176/2003*. The time that a payment is received is the time it is credited to that person's account and not the time the cheque was received or presented at the bank. The time the payment is received should be interpreted as meaning a period (probably any time during that day) and not as the exact instant. Whether the relevant person has received notice is not restricted to the formal decision notice (paras. 16.7-11) and could be by other means such as a telephone call, provided it is sufficiently clear that it is associated with the payment being made. Whether or not the person has received notice refers to notice about the payment in question and not any subsequent overpayment notice, otherwise the rule would be meaningless.

Working out the amount of a recoverable overpayment

UNDERLYING ENTITLEMENT

HB 104(1)
HB60+ 85(1)
NIHB 100(1)
NIHB60+ 83(1)
CTB 89(1)
CTB60+ 71(1)

18.15 When calculating the amount of a recoverable overpayment, any amount 'which should have been determined to be payable' must be deducted. This means whatever would have been awarded if the authority had known the true facts of the case throughout, all changes of circumstances had been notified on time, and any necessary claims had been made. Money kept by a claimant (i.e. not recovered from him or her) under this rule is often called 'underlying entitlement' to distinguish it from an actual award of HB/CTB. Underlying entitlement must be deducted (if there is any) in all situations in which an overpayment occurs *(Adan v London Borough of Hounslow and Another)*.

Example: Underlying entitlement in a straightforward case

A claimant has been doing undeclared work while signing on, and JSA is cancelled back to the time he began this.

Because of underlying entitlement, the recoverable overpayment of HB/CTB is only the difference between what he or she was awarded and what he or she would have been awarded if the true facts had been known throughout. This might be all of the HB/CTB he was paid in this period (if he was well paid in the job) or none of it (if he was paid less than he was getting on JSA) or any amount in between.

18.16 When the authority deals with a recoverable overpayment for a particular period, there are three stages at which underlying entitlement is considered:

- Any underlying entitlement for that period which has already been identified as belonging to that period must be used to reduce the overpayment. This arises if the claimant had been late notifying a change of circumstances and had thus not been awarded arrears of entitlement for all or part of that period (para. 17.36).
- The authority should invite the claimant (or other overpaid person) to provide information which may establish underlying entitlement. This is part of the process of determining the amount of the overpayment. In day-to-day work, the authority may use the rules about suspension, restoration and termination (paras. 17.67-80) while considering possible underlying entitlement.
- Once the authority has decided and notified the amount of the overpayment, the claimant (or other overpaid person) may ask the authority to reconsider (para. 17.55) or appeal to a tribunal (chapter 19), and in doing so may include information which would establish underlying entitlement.

8.17 Also, the following calculation rules apply when considering underlying entitlement (and are illustrated in the examples):

- only underlying entitlement falling (in whole or part) within the period of the overpayment is used to reduce the overpayment;
- although underlying entitlement (within that period) is used to reduce an overpayment – maybe even to nil – it can never be used to actually pay money out.

18.18 It is for the claimant to establish the underlying amount they are entitled to for the period in question *(CH/2588/2003)* but it is for each authority to decide what level of evidence it will require to prove the matter on the balance of probabilities (para. 1.35). In particular, the Verification Framework does not apply to the assessment of underlying entitlement.

WHERE THE CLAIMANT HAS CONTINUED TO PAY RENT OR COUNCIL TAX TO THE AUTHORITY

18.19 During the period of the overpayment the claimant may have paid money into a local authority rent or council tax/rates account above their erroneous liability. If this is the case such payments may be deducted for the purpose of working out the amount of the recoverable overpayment.

HB 104(2)
HB60+ 85(2)
NIHB 100(2)
NIHB60+ 83(2)
CTB 89(2)
CTB60+ 71(2)

Examples: Underlying entitlement: calculation rules

UNDERLYING ENTITLEMENT PERIOD FALLS WHOLLY WITHIN OVERPAYMENT PERIOD

Information: In a particular case, there is a recoverable overpayment of £15 per week for weeks 1 to 20 inclusive (20 x £15 = £300), and only in weeks 6 to 15 inclusive is there underlying entitlement of £20 per week (10 x £20 = £200).

Assessment: The whole of the underlying entitlement (£200) is used to reduce the overpayment (£300). So the recoverable overpayment is £100.

UNDERLYING ENTITLEMENT PERIOD FALLS PARTLY WITHIN OVERPAYMENT PERIOD

Information: In a particular case, there is a recoverable overpayment of £5 per week for weeks 1 to 20 inclusive (20 x £5 = £100), and underlying entitlement (because the claimant did not notify a beneficial change on time) in weeks 11 to 30 inclusive of £15 per week.

Assessment: Only the underlying entitlement in weeks 11 to 20 inclusive (10 x £15 = £150) is used to reduce the overpayment (£100). It is enough to reduce the recoverable overpayment to nil. The remainder of the underlying entitlement cannot be awarded. (It lurks instead.)

ONE CHANGE WITH TWO EFFECTS

Information: Six months ago, a claimant (not on JSA(IB), IS or pension credit) had a baby and started to receive child benefit but did not report these things to the authority, simply because she did not get round to it.

Assessment: The recoverable overpayment (caused by her income from child benefit) is smaller than the underlying entitlement (caused by the increase in her applicable amount to take account of the baby). The recoverable overpayment is therefore nil (but the remainder of the underlying entitlement cannot be awarded).

ANOTHER CHANGE WITH TWO EFFECTS

Information: Three months ago, the claimant's daughter moved in with him as his non-dependant, but he did not report this to the authority because he hoped he would get away with it. He rents from a private landlord.

Assessment: The recoverable overpayment (caused by the presence of the non-dependant) is in this case bigger than the underlying entitlement (caused by the increase in his eligible rent because he now requires a room for his daughter). The recoverable overpayment is only the net amount (i.e. the difference between the two figures).

Example: Diminishing capital rule

The claimant has been in receipt of a £5.73 rent allowance each week since 22nd May 2006. She visits the authority's housing benefit office on 12th October 2006, to query the amount of benefit she is receiving.

During the course of her interview it emerges that she had accidentally forgotten to include on her original application form £250 which she has retained throughout the period in a building society account. When this amount is added to her previously declared and still existing capital of £15,783 it brings the amount that counts for HB purposes to £16,033. With capital above the maximum limit there has been no entitlement to benefit from the start of the claim.

The overpayment arose due to the claimant's failure to disclose a material fact relating to capital and is recoverable. The overpayment has taken place over 21 benefit weeks so the diminishing capital rule applies. There is only one complete 13-week period.

The amount of HB overpaid by the end of 13 benefit weeks is:

£5.73 x 13 =	£74.49

With the application of the diminishing capital rule for the rest of the period of payment – and for the sole purpose of calculating the overpayment – the claimant's capital is assumed to be £15,958.51, i.e.

Claimant's capital	£16,033.00
MINUS amount of overpaid HB during 13-week period	£74.49
Claimant's assumed capital for purpose of calculating overpaid HB =	£15,958.51

The original calculation of HB had taken into account the declared capital of £15,783. The tariff income from the actual and 'diminished' capital amount is the same. Therefore, under the diminishing capital rule, no overpayment has occurred between the 14th and last week in which the benefit has been paid. The total amount of recoverable overpayment is £74.49.

The claimant still actually has capital of £16.033. She is not entitled to HB until such time as the amount of her capital falls below £16,000.01 (as would be the case if, for example, she repaid the overpayment).

DIMINISHING CAPITAL RULE

HB 103(1) HB60+ 84(1) NIHB 99(1) NIHB60+ 82(1) CTB 88(1) CTB60+ 70(1)

18.20 Where the overpayment arose as:

- a result of a misrepresentation or failure to disclose relevant information relating to the claimant's capital, or that of a child or young person; or
- an error relating to capital (other than a non-recoverable official error); and in either case
- the overpayment is in respect of more than 13 weeks;

the authority must treat the amount of the capital as having been reduced by the amount overpaid during the first and each subsequent period of 13 benefit weeks for the purpose of working out the overpayment.

18.21 The reasoning behind this rule is that if the capital had been taken into account, so that the benefit was reduced or not awarded, the claimant's capital would in all probability have been reduced to meet his or her housing costs, council tax liability, or day-to-day living expenses.

HB 103(2) HB60+ 84(2) NIHB 99(2) NIHB60+ 82(2) CTB 88(2) CTB60+ 70(2)

18.22 This notional reduction of capital does not count for any other purpose, e.g. calculating entitlement. This rule is entirely separate from, and should not be confused with, the diminishing notional capital rule (para. 13.135).

When should a recoverable overpayment be recovered?

18.23 A recoverable overpayment may be recovered at the authority's discretion. The law says that such overpayments are recoverable and not that they must be recovered. The DWP advises authorities to note that the question of whether an overpayment is recoverable is quite separate from the question of whether to recover it. Due regard should be given to the circumstances relating to individual cases when deciding if recovery is appropriate (OG para. 2.77).

18.24 The authority is not obliged to make recoveries. The exercise of the discretion is governed by a number of legal principles that are long established (paras. 1.56-58). Every case must be decided on its merits. This means that the authority must be satisfied that it is reasonable to make a recovery in the individual case. A person affected can ask the authority to revise its decision to recover a recoverable overpayment but there are no appeal rights against a decision as to the exercise of discretion to recover an overpayment. An authority which acted unreasonably or irrationally would be susceptible to judicial review. However, a decision will not be unreasonable merely because it is not the most reasonable course of action but only if it is so unreasonable that no reasonable authority could have reached that conclusion.

From whom may recovery be sought?

RECOVERY OF OVERPAID COUNCIL TAX BENEFIT

18.25 A recoverable overpayment of CTB (also known as 'excess benefit') may be recovered from the claimant or (if different) the person who received the CTB. (The law also allows overpaid CTB to be deducted, subject to limitations, from ongoing payments of CTB to a partner, but in practice this never happens.) AA 76(3) CTB 86

RECOVERY OF OVERPAID HOUSING BENEFIT

18.26 The law about recovery of overpaid HB has changed this year, mainly to provide the authority with clearer choices about who to recover from. In the following description, references to 'landlord/agent' mean the landlord if the money was paid to the landlord but the agent if the money was paid to the agent. For appeals about who overpaid HB should be recovered from, see paragraph 18.39.

The DWP appears to view the changes in the law this year as making it less likely that recovery will be made from a landlord in certain circumstances (circular HB/CTB A4/2006). While it remains true that many authorities take seriously their duty to weigh up the pros and cons of recovery from one party (such as a landlord) rather than another (such as a claimant), it is not the case that they are absolutely banned from recovering from a landlord (to whom a payment was made) in any circumstances. An amendment would be required to the Social Security Administration Act 1992 for this to be the case (and it is possible that the DWP will include this in legislation this year).

18.27 The first rule is that a recoverable overpayment of HB may in all cases be recovered from the person who was paid the HB – including, for example, a claimant, a landlord/agent or an appointee. AA 75(3) NIAA 73(3)

18.28 The second rule is that an alternative (nearly) always exists – so that the authority has a choice whether to recover from the payee (as above) or from whichever of the following applies in a particular case: HB 101(2)-(4) HB60+ 82(2)-(4) NIHB 97(2)-(4) NIHB60+ 80(2)-(

(a) if the overpayment was caused by (paras. 18.29-32) someone other than the payee, that person;

(b) if the overpayment was due to official error and someone other than the payee could reasonably have been expected to realise it was an overpayment, that person;

(c) if neither (a) nor (b) applies, and the HB was paid to the landlord/agent (or anyone else other than the claimant, such as an appointee), the claimant (but not a partner);

(d) if neither (a) nor (b) applies, and the HB was paid to the claimant, a partner.

The effect of these rules is described in paragraphs 18.32-38.

WHEN A PERSON HAS CAUSED THE OVERPAYMENT

HB 101(2)(a)
HB60+ 82(2)(a)
NIHB 97(2)(a)
NIHB60+ 80(2)(a)

18.29 An overpayment of HB will be considered to be 'caused by' a particular person if it arose as a result of their misrepresentation or failure to disclose a relevant fact and at that time they were the claimant, acting on behalf of the claimant, or a person to whom the overpaid benefit was paid.

18.30 A misrepresentation is a statement that is untrue or misleading. A misrepresentation could be a written or verbal statement.

18.31 A failure to disclose occurs where a person has a duty to disclose information (paras. 17.8-12), they do not disclose it and there was some 'failure' on that person's part because there was a reasonable expectation that they should disclose it having regard to all the circumstances. A person may not be expected to disclose if they were given clear advice to the contrary by an official of the authority or the DWP (Commissioners decision R(SB) 3/89).

18.32 A person will be liable for recovery even if the misrepresentation or failure to disclose was unintentional. Neither does the misrepresentation or failure to disclose have to be the sole cause of the overpayment; the fact that it was a contributing factor will be sufficient to make that person liable to recovery (CSB/64/1986).

RECOVERY OF HB FROM THE CLAIMANT

HB 101(2)(c)
HB60+ 82(2)(c)
NIHB 97(2)(c)
NIHB60+ 80(2)(c)

18.33 Overpaid HB can always be recovered from the claimant; and if the claimant dies, this means recovery from their estate (if they have any). (The only exception is rare, and is when the rules in paras. 18.27-28 identify two other parties an overpayment can be recovered from, such as a landlord/agent and an appointee.)

RECOVERY OF HB FROM CLAIMANT'S PARTNER

HB 101(2)(b),(4)
HB60+ 82(2)(b),(4)
NIHB 97(2)(b),(4)
NIHB60+ 80(2)(b),(4)

18.34 Overpaid HB can be recovered from a partner only in the following circumstances:

- the partner caused the overpayment; or
- the partner could (in the case of an official error overpayment) reasonably have been expected to realise there was an overpayment; or
- the claimant (not the landlord) received the HB, and no other person caused the overpayment, and no other person could (in the case of an official error overpayment) reasonably have been expected to realise there was an overpayment.

Furthermore, if the authority wishes to recover from the partner's ongoing HB (para. 18.43), it can do this only if the claimant and partner are members of the same household (paras. 4.3, 4.24) both at the date of the overpayment and the date it is recovered. Obviously this test is not met if the claimant has died or gone away.

RECOVERY OF HB FROM LANDLORDS AND AGENTS

18.35 Overpaid HB can be recovered from the landlord/agent unless all the following are true:

HB 100(3),101(2)(a)
HB60+ 81(3),82(2)(a)
NIHB 96(3),97(2)(a)
NIHB60+ 79(3),80(2)(a)

- the landlord/agent did not receive the HB; and
- the landlord/agent did not cause the overpayment; and
- the landlord/agent could not (in the case of an official error overpayment) reasonably have been expected to realise there was an overpayment.

So if the landlord/agent received the HB, the mere fact that they knew nothing of the overpayment does not prevent recovery from the landlord/agent *(Warwick DC v Freeman)*. There is, however, an important exception (para. 18.37; and see also para. 18.26).

18.36 Note that recovery from ongoing payments of HB does not count as recovery from the landlord/agent (even if the HB in question is being paid to the landlord/agent). It counts as recovery from the claimant (para. 18.43), and so only the claimant, not the landlord/agent, has the right of appeal (CSHB/615/2003).

BAN ON RECOVERY FROM LANDLORDS OR AGENTS

18.37 Overriding the above rules, an authority must not recover HB overpayments from the landlord/agent who received the HB if:

HB 101(1)
HB60+ 82(1)
NIHB 97(1)
NIHB60+ 80(1)

- the landlord/agent has notified the authority or the DWP in writing that they suspect there has been an overpayment; and
- it appears to the authority that:
  - there are grounds for instituting proceedings against any person for an offence of making dishonest or false representations for obtaining benefit, or
  - there has been a deliberate failure to report a relevant change of circumstances (para. 18.38) and the overpayment occurred as a result of that deliberate failure; and
- the authority is satisfied that the landlord has not:
  - colluded with the claimant so as to cause the overpayment, nor
  - acted, or neglected to act, in such a way so as to contribute to the period, or the amount, of the overpayment.

18.38 The relevant change of circumstances mentioned above can be any change which affects entitlement to, or the amount of, HB – except for the claimant leaving the dwelling in respect of which HB was payable. So if a claimant leaves and the landlord writes notifying his or her departure, the authority may nonetheless recover from the landlord (or the claimant) any overpaid HB relating to the period after the move.

APPEALS ABOUT WHO TO RECOVER FROM

18.39 The following points apply regardless of whom the authority seeks to recover an overpayment from (CH/1129/2004), but most commonly arise when the authority seeks recovery from a landlord/agent.

18.40 The person from whom an authority seeks to recover an overpayment (e.g. a landlord/agent or claimant) is a 'person affected' and so has the right to challenge the authority's decision (*Secretary of State for Work and Pensions v Chiltern District Council and Warden Housing Association* and CH/5216/2001) – by asking the council to reconsider or applying to a social security appeal tribunal (chapter 19).

18.41 However, any such challenge is limited (CH/5216/2001) to challenging:

- the factual basis on which the decision was made (e.g. the amount of the overpayment); or
- the legality of the decision to recover from the person.

The second is possible only if the authority has exceeded its powers in choosing who to recover from (e.g. it attempts to recover from someone from whom it is not permitted to recover). It does not include a challenge about whether the decision was the most reasonable course of action, provided action taken is within the margin of discretion allowed to authorities by the courts (which is wide). The courts will only consider a decision to be unlawful if it was so unreasonable that no reasonable authority could have reached that conclusion.

Method of recovery

AA 75(4),(5), 76(2)(b),(3)
NIAA 73(4),(5)
HB 102,105,107
HB60+ 83,86,88
NIHB 98,101,103
NIHB60+ 81,84,86
CTB 86,90
CTB60+ 71,75

18.42 Authorities may recover a recoverable overpayment by any lawful method but an overpayment of HB cannot be recovered from a payment of CTB or *vice versa*. The following are the main methods adopted by authorities:

(a) in the case of HB only, by deduction from any on-going benefit payable to them (subject to maximum amounts, paras. 18.64-66) in every case;

(b) from arrears of HB or CTB which becomes payable while there is an outstanding overpayment in every case;

(c) by deduction from certain social security benefits payable to the claimant in certain circumstances;

(d) in the case of HB only, where the overpaid benefit was paid direct to the landlord on behalf of one of their tenants, from any benefits including HB to which the landlord themselves may be personally entitled;

(e) in the case of HB only, where the overpaid benefit was paid direct to the landlord on behalf of one of their tenants, from any ongoing HB payable to that landlord in respect of their other tenants (e.g. by deduction from a bulk payment schedule);

(f) by setting up a sundry debtors' account and billing for the overpayment;

(g) in the case of CTB, by adding the overpaid CTB on to the claimant's council tax account as an amount of council tax owing, or in the case of HB paid by way of rent rebate by adding a charge to the claimant's rent account – but if this is the case the debt will not normally constitute rent arrears and will simply be a separate debt owed to the landlord (paras. 18.61-62).

The particular method used will be a determining factor as to whether the recovery creates rent arrears in respect of the tenant to whom the overpayment relates (paras. 18.61-62).

RECOVERY BY DEDUCTIONS FROM ON-GOING HB, INCLUDING HB PAID DIRECT TO A LANDLORD

18.43 Where the authority is recovering an overpayment by deduction from the claimant's on-going benefit (including any offsetting against any underpayment) paid direct to a landlord or, in the case of a council tenant, in the form of a reduced rebate, the position is no different than if the reduced HB was paid to the claimant. With the sole exception of rent allowance claims, to which paragraph 18.45 applies, the reduced HB payments represent part payment of the rent and so the claimant must make up the subsequent shortfall in HB to avoid rent arrears accruing (OG para. 4.48). This method represents recovery from the claimant, not the landlord, and consequently the landlord is not a 'person affected' and does not have any right to apply for a revision of the decision or appeal against it *(R(H) 7/04)*.

18.44 Note that in the case of council/NIHE tenants paid by rent rebate a distinction should be made between a reduction in an on-going rebate (i.e. an increase in the rent payable each period as it arises) and a charge added to the rent account representing the overpayment. Such a charge will not normally constitute rent arrears as it is an addition to the rent that has already been paid (paras. 18-61-62) (albeit by overpaid HB). Charges of this kind will be easily identifiable, since the total charge for the rental period in which it is made will be more than the gross un-rebated rent. In the case of CTB, any overpayment can be added to the council tax account and be charged as additional council tax.

18.45 Where a rent allowance claim is paid direct to the landlord and the cause of the overpayment is landlord fraud which has resulted in a conviction or the landlord agreeing to pay a penalty as an alternative to prosecution (18.78), then any arrears of rent which result from the reduced housing benefit cannot be pursued by the landlord. If this rule is applied, then both the landlord and the tenant must

AA 75(5)(b)
NIAA 73(5)(b)
HB 107
HB60+ 88
NIHB 103
NIHB60+ 86

be notified (paras. 18.84 and 18.86) and the landlord would be able to appeal. In practice however, this rule is hardly ever used. The DWP advises (OG appendix 1, para. 16) that where this rule is applied the legislation imposes no penalty on landlords who attempt to recover or evict a tenant due to the non-closure of their rent liability, but that the courts have been advised that landlords would be in breach of the relevant legislation if they attempted this action.

RECOVERY FROM ARREARS OF BENEFIT OWED

HB 102(1) HB60+ 83(1) NIHB 98(1) NIHB60+ 81(1) CTB 86(1) CTB60+ 71(1)

18.46 An existing overpayment can be recovered at some future date by offsetting it against any underpaid benefit. Any underpaid benefit in excess of the overpayment will constitute a payment towards any rent owed for the period to which it relates. If the tenant fails to make up any shortfall for that period then it will result in rent arrears. If the underpayment is not sufficient to meet the full debt, the question of whether the remaining debt creates rent arrears will depend on the method employed to recover it (para. 18.42).

RECOVERY FROM OTHER SOCIAL SECURITY BENEFITS

HB 105 HB60+ 86 NIHB 101 NIHB 84 CTB 90 CTB60+ 84

18.47 In the case of HB where methods (a), (b) or (d) in paragraph 18.42 are not possible because the person from whom the recovery is being sought is not entitled to HB, or in the case of CTB methods (a), (b) or (g) are not possible, the authority may request the DWP to recover any overpayment from any person identified in paragraph 18.29 by deductions from certain social security benefits payable to them (para. 18.48).

18.48 The benefits from which recovery can be made referred to in paragraph 18.47 include: income support, jobseeker's allowance, state pension credit, attendance allowance, disability living allowance and carer's allowance. Recovery can also be made from: retirement pension, incapacity benefit, widow's and bereavement benefits, maternity allowance and industrial injuries benefits; or from any equivalent of these benefits paid to that person by a European Union member state. Recovery is not permitted from guardian's allowance, child benefit, war pensions, statutory sick pay, statutory maternity pay, child tax credit or working tax credit.

18.49 The DWP will recover overpayments from social security benefits where it is:

- requested by the authority to do so; and
- satisfied that the overpayment arose as a result of a misrepresentation or failure to disclose a material fact by, or on behalf of, the claimant, or by some other person to whom a payment of HB/CTB has been made; and
- that person is receiving sufficient amounts of one or more benefits to enable deductions to be made.

RECOVERY FROM THE LANDLORD BY DEDUCTIONS FROM THE LANDLORD'S PERSONAL BENEFIT

18.50 In a rent allowance case the authority may, in appropriate circumstances, decide to recover the overpayment from the landlord by deduction from any benefit to which the landlord is personally entitled (e.g. the landlord's income is low enough to qualify for HB in their own right). Where the overpayment arose from the landlord's misrepresentation or failure to disclose but the landlord does not qualify for HB in their own right, recovery can be made from the landlord's other social security benefits as described in paragraphs 18.47-49. In either case, the landlord will normally wish to recover their loss by recharging the tenant (paras. 18.60-62). In practice, recovery from a landlord's personal benefits is rare.

AA 75(5)(a)
NIAA 73(5)(a)
HB 106(2)
HB60+ 87(2)
NIHB 102(2)
NIHB60+ 85(2)

RECOVERY FROM THE HB OF TENANT(S) UNRELATED TO THE OVERPAYMENT (DEBIT OF BULK PAYMENT SCHEDULE)

18.51 Where the overpaid benefit was paid to the landlord and the landlord receives on-going direct payments of rent allowance in respect of other ('innocent') tenants to whom the overpayment does not relate, the authority may recover the overpayment by deducting from the direct payments of other tenants to whom the overpayment does not relate. This method is often employed by authorities to recover from landlords who have substantial numbers of tenants on HB who are all paid in the same payment cycle by a single payment (e.g. cheque) accompanied by a bulk payment schedule. Recovery is made by deducting the overpayment from the gross HB owed in respect of all its tenants.

18.52 Any amount recovered by this method from 'innocent' tenants will be deemed to have been paid as rent by them to the value of the recovered sum. In these circumstances, the landlord is a 'person affected' and should be notified (para. 18.84-85) but the 'innocent' tenant/claimant from whose benefit the deductions are being made is not. Consequently such tenants/claimants should not receive an overpayment notification and do not have the right to appeal or request a decision. The authority should, however, have notified all claimants and landlords at the time direct payments commenced that:

HB sch 9 para 11(c)
HB60+ sch 8 para 11(c)
NIHB sch 10 para 11(c)
NIHB60+ sch 10 para 11(c)

- it had the power to make deductions from the amount paid to the landlord in order to recover an overpayment of benefit relating to another tenant; and
- in such a case the claimant's rent liability will have been discharged to the full value of their HB entitlement.

18.53 Where this method has been employed, the landlord will wish to recover their loss from the tenant to whom the overpayment relates. Whether this consequent recovery constitutes rent arrears will be determined by the rules in paragraphs 18.61-62.

RECOVERY BY SETTING UP A SUNDRY DEBTORS ACCOUNT

HB 102(1)
HB60+ 83(1)
NIHB 98(1)
NIHB60+ 81(1)
CTB 86(2)(a)
CTB60+ 71(2)(a)

18.54 An authority may implement a recovery by simply sending a demand for payment to any person liable to recovery. Recovery can be enforced by registering the debt in the courts as described by paragraphs 18.70-73 below.

18.55 A bill sent directly to the tenant paid by rent allowance does not constitute rent arrears. A bill sent to a local authority/NIHE tenant paid by rent rebate from their landlord may create rent arrears if their tenancy agreement so stipulates (paras. 18.60-62).

RECOVERY BY CHARGING THE CLAIMANT'S RENT/COUNCIL TAX ACCOUNT

HB 102(1)
HB60+ 83(1)
NIHB 98(1)
NIHB60+ 81(1)
CTB 86(2)(b)
CTB60+ 71(2)(b)

18.56 Authorities are able to recover any overpaid CTB by simply adding the debt to the council tax and issuing a new bill. They will then be able to enforce this debt by the usual council tax enforcement procedures.

18.57 This method is not available for tenants paid HB by rent allowance, although where the recovery has been made from their landlord the landlord will probably wish to recover their loss from the tenant. For the circumstances in which the landlord may pass this charge on as rent arrears, see paras. 18.60-62.

18.58 Except in the circumstances described in paragraphs 18.61-62, authorities who recover overpaid rent rebates by debiting the rent account of the claimant cannot claim that the debt constitutes rent arrears. Instead, the debt created is separate housing benefit debt which cannot be enforced by possession proceedings as it is not an amount of rent lawfully due (para. 18.61) and the claimant would have a defence against any such action.

18.59 Authorities may, however, use their rent accounting systems to collect contributions towards overpayment debts and some tenants may prefer this as being the most convenient way to pay. The DWP advises that authorities should be able to distinguish 'recovered' overpaid HB from arrears of rent. Authorities should also make it clear to claimants that the payments being sought represent overpaid HB (OG para. 4.97-101) and should be able to distinguish payments the claimant makes to cover the overpayment and payments of rent. Where the tenant is not on full HB or has existing rent arrears, authorities would be well advised to issue the tenant with a separate HB overpayment account so that when the tenant makes a payment there can be no doubt against which debt the payment is to be attributed, otherwise over time the true position is likely to become increasingly difficult to unravel. Common law rules stipulate that where a person owes more than one debt they may elect to attribute any payments they make towards each debt in the proportions they choose (OG para. 4.102). If they do not so specify, then the payment will be attributed to the earliest debt first.

METHODS BY WHICH THE LANDLORD MAY RECOVER THE REPAID OVERPAYMENT FROM THE CLAIMANT

18.60 The landlord may seek to recover the sum repaid to the authority from the claimant to whom the overpayment relates. Landlords are perfectly entitled to recover their losses under general legal principles; however, where they do so the question often arises as to whether this constitutes rent arrears.

CIRCUMSTANCES IN WHICH A LANDLORD RECHARGE CREATES RENT ARREARS

18.61 The general rule is that once rent has been paid, even though it was paid by benefit to which the claimant was not entitled, any liability for it has been extinguished for all time *(R v Haringey LBC ex p Ayub)*. The fact that the authority can recover it is merely a consequence of a power it has been given by legislation and does not alter this position. Therefore, if the landlord recharges the tenant for the past period to which the overpaid benefit relates, any charge that they make cannot be 'rent' because in effect the tenant would be charged twice for the same period. However, this general rule has been modified by legislation and may also be modified by contractual agreement (para. 18.62).

18.62 The general rule against the creation of retrospective rent arrears is modified in the following circumstances:

- the tenancy agreement expressly stipulates that overpaid HB recovered from the landlord can be recharged as 'additional rent' – this applies equally to claimants paid by rent rebate as well as rent allowance; or
- the claimant is a non-local authority tenant (i.e. paid by rent allowance, not rent rebate) and the overpayment relates to a period after 6th April 1997: the landlord is able to treat the sum it has repaid to the authority as rent arrears. HB 95(2) HB60+ 76(2) NIHB 91(2) NIHB60+ 74(2)

In both cases the landlord has the ultimate sanction of eviction to secure payment. However, these exceptions can never be applied to 'innocent' tenants to whom the overpayment does not relate (paras. 18.51-52). AA75(6) NIAA 73(6)

18.63 Where the claimant to whom the overpayment relates is no longer the landlord's tenant, the landlord may invoice the former tenant and then pursue the debt through normal civil debt recovery procedures.

Rate of recovery from ongoing HB

18.64 Where benefit is to be recovered by deductions from ongoing HB the regulations set a maximum rate. The maximum rate is tied to a formula based on a single person's personal allowance. There are two maximum permitted rates of deduction depending on whether or not the overpayment has arisen as a result of fraud.

18.65 Where the claimant has been found guilty of fraud; or admitted fraud after caution; or agreed to pay a penalty (para. 18.78); the maximum permitted weekly deduction is £11.60 plus 50% of any of the earned income disregards shown in table 14.1 or any disregarded regular charitable or voluntary payments (para. 13.113) or war disablement pension or war widow's pension (para. 13.38) if they apply to the claim. In any other case the maximum permitted weekly deduction is £8.70 plus 50% of the income disregards previously identified if they apply to the claim. In both cases the amounts are subject to an overall maximum deduction which does not reduce the balance of benefit payable to less than 50p. The council should deduct less than the maximum permitted amount in any case where, after considering all of the claimant's circumstances, this is justified in order to avoid undue hardship.

18.66 In deciding the rate of recovery from organisations, the authority has the power to effect large recoveries in a single lump sum (para. 18.51) but it will often not be appropriate to do so. The authority should act reasonably in deciding a rate of recovery. In particular, as a matter of good practice, the authority should discuss the rate of recovery with the organisation concerned to ensure the rate of recovery does not undermine that organisation's financial stability or essential activities.

Pursuing and enforcing recovery

18.67 The DWP advises (OG para. 7.40) that 'it is for authorities to decide how far to pursue recovery…' In the past, many authorities have failed to pursue recovery actively if legal proceedings were required. Where an authority has decided an overpayment is recoverable, exercised its discretion and decided to recover, the DWP expects it to make a serious attempt at recovery. The OG (para. 7.42) advises that at least two letters requesting payment should be issued, that an interview will often be appropriate and that a home visit might be cost-effective. As a matter of good practice, authorities should include in their recovery work procedures that ensure that the claimant is receiving all the HB/CTB and other benefits to which they may be entitled, with the aim of reducing the overpayment and increasing resources to meet the debt.

18.68 The authority may take civil proceedings for debt in an appropriate court but the simplified debt recovery procedure described in paragraph 18.70 is more appropriate.

LIMITATION ON RECOVERY THROUGH THE COURTS

18.69 Once an authority has decided that an overpayment is recoverable a debt is created which the authority may choose to pursue in the County Court. Any such action must be brought within six years (five years in Scotland) from the date of decision (OG paras. 7.20-21). This limitation only applies to recovery through the courts and not any other method of recovery (such as by deductions from ongoing HB) (OG para. 7.22). Note that there is no limit on how far back the decision that there has been a recoverable overpayment may go; the restriction is only on pursuing recovery in the courts from the date the authority made its decision. However, in extreme cases the authority may find it difficult to obtain evidence to make and support their calculations and therefore be unable to 'prove' the overpayment (OG para. 7.00).

SIMPLIFIED DEBT RECOVERY PROCEDURE

18.70 The authority has the power to recover HB overpayments by execution in the County Court in England and Wales as if under a court order; and in Scotland as if it were an extract registered decree arbitral.

AA 75(7),76(6)
NIAA 73(7)

18.71 In England and Wales, this procedure allows an HB overpayment determination to be registered directly as an order of the court without the need to bring a separate action. The authority applies to the court on a standard county court form (N 322A), attaching a copy of the overpayment decision notice and accompanied by the relevant fee. The DWP advises (OG para. 7.49) that the decision notice must comply fully with the legislative requirements of the benefit regulations (para. 18.84-86). An officer of the court then makes an order and a copy is sent to the authority and the debtor. Once an order has been made, the normal methods of enforcement are available to the authority, i.e. attachment of earnings, a garnishee order allowing the authority to obtain money owed to the debtor by a third party, a warrant of execution against goods executed by the county court bailiff, or a charging order, normally against land.

18.72 There is no provision for any appeal against an order made by the 'proper officer' of the court. Consequently, where the claimant or landlord disputes the determination that there is a recoverable overpayment or from whom it should be recovered, this is a matter which can only be taken up by applying for a revision of, or appealing, the relevant decision(s) (chapter 19). However where, for example, the overpayment notice is defective or appeal rights ignored by the authority an application for the setting aside of the order can be made to the court.

18.73 In Scotland, the HB determination is immediately enforceable as if it were an extract registered decree arbitral. There is no requirement to register the overpayment determination with the Sheriff Court. The usual methods of enforcement are available, i.e. arrestment of earnings; poinding and warrant sale; arrestment of moveable property and inhibition of heritable property.

Overpayments and fraud

18.74 The subject of HB/CTB fraud and the authority's response goes beyond the remit of this guide. The interested general reader is referred to the Audit Commission's *Countering housing benefit fraud: a management handbook* (1997) while officers working for an authority should also refer to the DWP *Local authority fraud investigators manual* and the DWP fraud circulars. Overpayments are, however, often related to charges of fraud. The effective recovery of overpayments is one tool in the authority's anti-fraud strategy and as anti-fraud work increases, in the short term at least, the number and amount of overpayments that are identified by the authority increases.

THE ADMINISTRATIVE PENALTY

AA 115A NIAA 109A **18.75** Authorities have power to levy an administrative penalty (a fine) as an alternative to bringing a prosecution for fraud. This power can be used in respect of any period from 18th December 1997 (whether or not the overpayment started before that date).

WHEN WILL A PENALTY APPLY?

18.76 Where the overpayment is substantial or there are other aggravating factors (such as being in a position of trust) the person suspected will not normally be offered the alternative of a penalty instead of prosecution.

18.77 The question of a penalty cannot arise until the authority has decided that an overpayment is recoverable under the regulations and the person from whom recovery is sought has been properly notified. The authority then has the discretion to invite a person to pay a penalty where it is satisfied that:

- the overpayment was caused by an 'act or omission' on the part of that person; and
- there are grounds for bringing a prosecution against that person for fraud relating to that overpayment under the Social Security Administration Act or any other enactment.

18.78 Where the conditions for a penalty apply, it can only be levied with the agreement of the person concerned. However, if that person refuses to agree to pay a penalty they could be liable to fraud proceedings instead.

CALCULATION OF THE PENALTY

18.79 The penalty is equivalent to 30% of the recoverable overpayment due or 30% of the overpayment which accrued from 18 December 1997 if the overpayment started before that date.

AGREEING TO PAY A PENALTY

18.80 It is up to the authority to decide how any agreement to pay a penalty will be made. However, where the authority considers that a penalty may be appropriate in any particular case it must give a written penalty notice to the person liable for prosecution. SI 1997/2813 NISR 1997/514

18.81 This notice advises them:

- that they may be invited to agree to pay a penalty; and
- that if they make the agreement to do this in the manner specified by the authority (e.g. by signing a standard written undertaking) no fraud proceedings will be brought against them for the overpayment in question.

18.82 The penalty notice must contain certain minimal information about the penalty system such as their right to withdraw from an agreement within 28 days and to repayment if the amount of recoverable overpayment is successfully challenged on appeal or revision. For more details about the information to be contained in the notice see the DWP guidance (OG para. 4.382).

Overpayment decision notices

18.83 When the authority decides to recover an overpayment of HB/CTB a decision notice should be sent to the person from whom recovery is sought and any other person affected by the decision. So, for example, if the authority decides to recover from the landlord, it must send letters to both the claimant and the landlord. This should happen within 14 days of the decision being made or as soon as reasonably practicable thereafter. HB 90(1)(b) HB60+ 71(1)(b) NIHB 85(1)(b) NIHB60+ 68(1)(b) CTB 76(1)(b) CTB60+ 61(1)(b)

18.84 The notice must contain the following information: HB sch 9 para 15(1) HB60+ sch 8 para 15(1) NIHB sch 10 para 15(1) NIHB60+ sch 10 para 15(1) CTB sch 8 para 16(1) CTB60+ sch 7 para 16

- the fact that there is a recoverable overpayment;
- the reason why there is a recoverable overpayment;
- the amount of the recoverable overpayment;
- how the amount was calculated;
- the benefit weeks to which the recoverable overpayment relates;
- where recovery of HB is to be made by deduction from future HB, the amount of that deduction;
- in the case of overpaid CTB, the method of recovery to be adopted;

- the person's right to request a written statement setting out the authority's reasons for its decision on any matter set out in the letter and the manner and time in which to do so; and
- the person's right to request a revision or appeal the decision and the manner and time in which to do so; and
- any other appropriate matter, e.g. the opportunity to make representations with regard to hardship.

HB sch 9 para 15(2) HB60+ sch 8 para 15(2) NIHB sch 10 para 15(2) NIHB60+ sch 10 para 15(2)

18.85 Where the authority is seeking to recover an overpayment of HB from another claimant's direct payments to the landlord (para. 18.51), the decision notice to that landlord must also identify both:

- the original claimant on whose behalf the recoverable amount was paid to that landlord; and
- the other claimant(s) from whose benefit recovery is going to be made.

HB 107(3) HB60+ 88(3) NIHB 103(3) NIHB60+ 86(3)

18.86 Where the authority has decided to recover an overpayment from a rent allowance paid direct to the landlord by the method described in paragraph 18.45 (as a result of landlord fraud) the authority must also notify both the landlord and the tenant that:

- the overpayment which it has recovered, or decided to recover, is one for which the landlord has been convicted of fraud or has agreed to pay a penalty; and
- any tenant from whose benefit the recovery is made must be deemed to have paid his or her rent to the value of the amount recovered.

18.87 The DWP advises (OG para. 5.05) that overpayment notices should include an invitation to the person in question to either make a full repayment or negotiate some other arrangement within 28 days. A more appropriate period in fact is the one month normally allowed for a request for revision/appeal to be made.

DEFECTIVE NOTICES

18.88 Failure by authorities to notify persons affected clearly and correctly of decisions about overpayments has caused problems for claimants, landlords and authorities. Experience has shown that overpayment notices, particularly those to landlords, are often defective. Many fail to give an adequate reason why the overpayment is recoverable or advise landlords of their appeal rights. For example, the phrase 'change of circumstances' is not itself an adequate explanation as it covers a multitude of possibilities and so does not give not the person affected sufficient information to be able to judge whether they have grounds for an appeal *(R v Thanet DC ex parte Warren Court Hotels Ltd)*. The failure to issue an adequate notice which includes all the information required by the regulations constitutes maladministration. An authority that issues a deficient notice may undermine the legal basis of its debt recovery action *(Warwick DC v Freeman)*. There is no legally recoverable debt until such time as the authority makes the appropriate decision and issues the required notice.

18.89 However, where a defect in a notice is only trivial and no substantial harm is caused as a result, the authority may still nevertheless be entitled to recover the overpaid benefit *(Haringey LBC v Awaritefe)*.

18.90 Where an authority has recovered benefit from a person before issuing them with a valid notice, for example, by making a deduction from a bulk payment schedule (para. 18.51), then that recovery will be unlawful. The person affected will have the right to apply to the court for repayment of any benefit which has been recovered *(Waveney DC v Jones)*. However, where a person has been overpaid, and voluntarily makes a repayment following a demand made by the authority (para. 18.54) they will not be able to seek repayment of the money that they have repaid even where the authority has failed to follow the correct procedure (e.g. issue a valid notice) *(Norwich CC v Stringer)*. The difference is that in the second case the landlord could have resisted recovery should they have chosen to dispute the decision.

19 Appeals

19.1 This chapter describes what can be done if a claimant (or in certain cases other people such as a landlord or a landlord's agent) disagrees with a decision made by the authority or simply does not understand it. There is a right of appeal from the authority's decisions to an independent, legally qualified appeal tribunal. This tribunal replaced the former HB/CTB review board from 2nd July 2001. The current HB/CTB appeal arrangements are similar and in many instances identical to the arrangements that apply to other social security benefits.

Overview of the Appeal Service

APPEAL TRIBUNALS AND THE APPEALS SERVICE

19.2 The tribunals that decide HB/CTB appeals are part of an independent tribunal body responsible for hearing appeals on decisions on social security, child support, vaccine damage, tax credit and compensation recovery. From April 2006 appeal tribunals are expected to obtain their administrative support from the Tribunals Service with the Department for Constitutional Affairs (Appeal Service Annual Report and Accounts 200405 p. 67. For more on the Tribunals Service Programme see *www.dca.gov.uk/legalsys/tribunals.htm*). Information on the Appeal Service, the appeal process and the venues at which appeals are heard can be found on the web at *www.appeals-service.gov.uk*.

THE DISPUTES PROCESS

19.3 While not a term contained in the legislation, the matters described in this chapter are often referred to as part of a 'disputes process'. In the first instance the claimant or other 'person affected' (para. 19.15) may seek to have a disputed decision changed via one of two routes:

- by requesting the authority to look at it again (i.e. apply for a revision or supersession); or
- by appealing against it.

19.4 Whichever route is chosen applications must be made in writing and sent to the authority. This should normally be done within one calendar month of the date the authority notified the relevant decision. If the first route is taken, once the person affected has the result of their application for revision they normally have one calendar month from the date that was sent out in which to appeal. If the second route is taken, the authority normally takes the opportunity provided by the receipt of an appeal to reconsider the disputed decision prior to referring it on to the Appeal Service.

19.5 There are three ways in which the authority may change a disputed decision. It can be:

- revised (i.e. changed normally from its original date – see para 17.4);
- superseded (i.e. changed but from a later date – see para 17.4);
- changed on appeal.

19.6 As mentioned above, when an appeal is received, the authority may consider whether the decision can be revised. If it can be revised to the advantage of the person affected, the authority should revise the decision and the appeal lapses. This applies even though the person affected may not receive all that has been asked for in the appeal. Where a decision has been revised to the advantage of the person affected there is then a fresh decision with a fresh dispute period, and fresh rights to apply for a revision or appeal.

19.7 The appeal should automatically proceed to an independent appeal tribunal if:

- the decision is not revised by the authority; or
- the decision is revised, but not in favour of the person affected; or
- the decision is superseded by the authority.

19.8 Where the authority revises the decision but not in favour of the person affected the appeal is deemed to be against the revised decision and the person affected is given an additional month in which to make further representations. DAR 17(3),(4) / NIDAR 17(3),(4)

How quickly should appeals be dealt with?

19.9 There are no statutory performance standards relating to how quickly:

- an authority should refer an appeal to the Appeal Service; or
- a tribunal should hear the appeal once it has been lodged with the Appeal Service.

THE REFERRAL OF APPEALS TO THE APPEAL SERVICE

19.10 Between April 2003 and March 2004 the Appeal Service received 3,960 housing benefit appeals. This may be compared with the 19,015 income support appeals received in the same period from a similar benefit caseload (*Hansard,* Written Answers, 25 Oct 2004).

19.11 The Local Government Ombudsmen have described how a 'pattern of delays by some councils in the referral of housing benefit appeals to the Appeal Service is a particular concern…' (Foreword to Advice and guidance on arrangements for forwarding housing benefit appeals to the Appeals Service, 2004, The Commission for Local Administration in England – *www.lgo.org.uk/pdf/sp-2-web.pdf*).

19.12 The DWP's suggested Service Level Agreement between authorities and the Appeal Service (A20/2003 appendix B, para. A65 – the 2003-04 SLA has been carried forward into subsequent years – see also U6/2005) indicates that the authority should aim to complete its submission to the tribunal and issue it to all parties within four calendar weeks. Where the appeal is particularly complex or more information is required, it is accepted that this timescale may be exceeded. The suggested service level agreement also indicates that the authority should inform the Appeal Service of all cases that have been outstanding for more than three months where a submission has not been issued. The authority should explain the reasons for the delay and confirm when the submission will be provided.

19.13 The Local Government Ombudsmen's publication identified above advises authorities how they might go about meeting the four-week target. It also illustrates the remedies available to complainants, including recommendations regarding compensation.

THE SETTING OF AN APPEAL HEARING DATE BY THE APPEAL SERVICE

19.14 The Secretary of State sets the Appeals Service a number of targets in relation to the administration of appeals. In 2005-06 the target for the time between the Appeal Service receiving the completed enquiry form (TAS 1) from the person affected (paras. 19.42-43) and the date of the tribunal hearing was no more than 11 weeks (*Hansard* 24th March 2005: Col. 97WS).

Who may appeal

DAR 3 NIDAR 3 **19.15.** The people who have a right to appeal against an HB/CTB decision are referred to as 'persons affected'. Someone is a 'person affected' by a decision where their rights, duties or obligations are affected by it. Additionally, to be a 'person affected' they must be:

- a claimant;
- in the case of a person who is unable for the time being to act:
  - a receiver appointed by the Court of Protection with power to claim, or as the case may be, receive benefit on the claimant's behalf;
  - in Scotland, a tutor, curator, judicial factor or other guardian acting or appointed in terms of law administering that person's estate; or

- an attorney with a general power or a power to receive benefit appointed by the person liable to make those payments under the Powers of Attorney Act 1971 or the Enduring Powers of Attorney Act 1985;

- a person appointed by the authority to act for the claimant;
- a landlord/agent where a decision has been made by the authority to pay HB to them (paras. 16.29, 16.30, 16.34, 16.36); or
- a person from whom the authority decides that an HB/CTB 'overpayment' is recoverable (para. 18.25).

19.16 There may be more than one 'person affected' by a decision. For example, where the authority decides to recover an overpayment from the landlord both the landlord and claimant are 'persons affected' by the decision. Such decisions can give rise to tripartite appeals.

Decisions that may be appealed

19.17 Except in relation to certain decisions relating to the claims process, payments, overpayments and other matters (table 19.1), a person affected has a right of appeal against any relevant decision (whether as originally made or as revised or superseded) the authority makes on a claim for, or on an award of, HB/CTB.

CPSA sch 7 para 6(1)(a),(b)
NICPSA sch 7 para 6(1)(a),(b)

DEFECTIVE CLAIMS

19.18 Claims that are not properly completed are referred back to the claimant as defective (para. 5.24). The DWP now considers that there are appeal rights against the decision that a claim is defective under the European Convention on Human Rights (following *R(IS) 6/04* see *U9/2004 para 31*). The HB and CTB (Decisions and Appeals) Regulations 2001 have been amended accordingly.

NON-APPEALABLE DECISIONS

19.19 There is no right of appeal against an authority's refusal to carry out an 'any time' revision on the grounds of an official error (see para. 17.46-47) (*Beltekian v Westminster CC*). Certain types of decision relating to the claims process, payment of benefit and overpayments are generally not appealable – although there are exceptions. These are set out in table 19.1. All other types of decision are appealable (para. 19.17).

19.20 In relation to overpayment decisions the Court of Appeal has confirmed that included in the appealable decisions is a right of appeal against the decision as to from whom the authority should recover an overpayment (*Secretary of State for Work and Pensions v Chiltern DC and Warden Housing Association*). A subsequent Tribunal of Commissioners (*CH/5216/2001 et al*) concluded that where the authority was seeking to recover an overpayment from a landlord the

CPSA sch 7 para 6
DAR 16(1) and sch
NICPSA sch 7 para 6 and sch
NIDAR 16(1) and sch

Table 19.1 Decisions which cannot be appealed and related appealable decisions

DECISIONS RELATING TO THE CLAIM PROCESS

Non-Appealable

- Decisions about which partner in a couple may claim (para. 5.4);
- Decisions about who can claim for people unable to act for themselves (para. 5.5).

Appealable

- Decisions that a claim is incomplete (para. 5.28);
- Decisions regarding the time and manner in which a claim is made (para. 5.8 onwards);
- Decisions regarding the date of claim (paras. 5.33-47) including decisions regarding the backdating rule (para. 5.33).

PAYMENT DECISIONS

Non-Appealable

- Decision about the time and manner of payment of benefit (para. 16.12);
- Decision about the frequency of payment of a rent allowance to private tenants; (paras. 16.21-25);
- Decision about making a payment on account (para. 16.16) (but see the exception identified below);
- Decisions about making payment to a person entitled (para. 16.28);
- Decisions about who should get any outstanding payment following the death of the person entitled (para. 16.45);
- Decisions relating to the suspension of benefit or payment following a suspension (para. 17.67) but the decision to terminate benefit entitlement is appealable.

Appealable

- Decisions regarding adjustments to payment on account of rent allowance to take account of an under or overpayment (para. 16.20);

- Decisions regarding when payment is to be made to a landlord/agent (paras. 16.30-40) including decisions on whether the landlord/agent is a 'fit and proper person' (paras. 16.37-39).

OVERPAYMENT DECISIONS

Non-Appealable

- Decisions about the meaning of an overpayment/excess CTB (para. 18.4);
- Decisions made about the method of recovery (para. 18.42);
- Decisions about recovery from prescribed social security benefits (para. 18.47);
- A decision as to the exercise of discretion to recover an 'overpayment' (paras. 18.23-24).

Appealable

- Decisions regarding the recoverability of an overpayment/excess CTB (paras. 18.9-14);
- Decisions regarding the person from whom recovery may be sought (paras. 18.25-41) (*Secretary of State for Work and Pensions v Chiltern DC* and *CH/5216/2001 et al*);
- Decisions relating to the diminution of capital rule (paras. 18.20-22);
- Decisions regarding the sums to be deducted in calculating the recoverable overpayment/excess CTB (paras. 18.15-22).

OTHER NON-APPEALABLE DECISIONS

- A decision involving issues that arise on appeal to the Commissioners or the courts in other cases;
- The assessed income figure (AIF) provided by the Pension Service that the authority must use (subject to prescribed modifications) where the claimant or any partner is in receipt of the pension savings credit only (paras. 13.151-153). Any modification the authority makes to that figure is appealable (para. 13.154 and table 13.4).
- Any decision made by the authority as to the application or operation of a local scheme (i.e. disregard of war disablement and war widows' pensions) (para. 22.10);
- Any decision made by the authority that adopts a decision of a rent officer (i.e. the authority's decision regarding the maximum rent where

the authority is bound by the figures produced by the rent officer) (para. 10.34);

- Any decision terminating or reducing the amount of HB/CTB made under the regulations for work-focused interviews.
- Any decision as to the amount of HB/CTB to which a person is entitled where the amount is determined by the rate of benefit provided for by law.

landlord had an unqualified right of appeal against the authority's decisions that there was an overpayment, the amount and recoverability of that overpayment. It also concluded, however, that the decision as to from whom the authority should recover the overpayment, e.g. the landlord rather than the claimant, could only be challenged on judicial review grounds, i.e. that the authority had acted in bad faith, for an improper purpose, unreasonably or in breach of a legitimate expectation.

APPEALS AGAINST NON-APPEALABLE DECISIONS

19.21 If an appeal is made against a non-appealable decision (table 19.1) the authority should identify it as 'out of jurisdiction' on its referral to the Appeal Service. It should be struck out by the appeal tribunal clerk or member. For example, as table 19.1 indicates, there is no right of appeal via the authority to the tribunal against the assessed income figure (AIF). This is the figure the authority must use in the calculation of HB/CTB in a savings credit only case (paras. 13.151-153). If the authority receives an appeal that is clearly about the AIF, it should advise the claimant that the correct thing to do is to lodge an appeal with the Pension Service. The claimant should also be advised that the appeal lodged with the authority will be processed, but as there is no right of appeal via the authority against the AIF, it will be treated as 'out of jurisdiction' and the Appeals Service will be asked to strike it out (DWP, *Pension Credit Handbook,* para. 1103). The claimant does, however, have a right of appeal via the authority to the tribunal against any modification the authority may or may not make of the Pension Service's AIF (table 13.4).

19.22 In appropriate cases, certain of the non-appealable decisions set out in table 19.1 can be revised or superseded on request. For example, the claimant or landlord could request the authority to revise its discretionary decision to recover a recoverable overpayment in a case of hardship. Were the authority to act irrationally, unreasonably or in bad faith in relation to many of these non-appealable decisions it would be susceptible to a complaint of maladministration or judicial review.

NOTIFICATION OF APPEALABLE DECISIONS TO PERSONS AFFECTED

19.23 The authority has an obligation to notify its appealable decisions (para. 19.17) to all persons affected. The notification should set out: DAR 10 NIDAR 10

- the decision against which the right of appeal lies;
- the right to request the authority to provide a written statement of the reasons for that decision – in a case where the notice does not include a statement of reasons; and
- the right of appeal against that decision.

OBTAINING A WRITTEN STATEMENT EXPLAINING THE DECISION

19.24 If no explanation is included in the notification of the decision, a person affected may request a statement of reasons at any time. The authority must then, 'so far as practicable', provide one within 14 days. DAR 10(2) NIDAR 10(2)

Making an appeal

19.25 Authorities are expected to make available forms on which an appeal may be made. The council may design its own leaflet/appeal form or may prefer to use the DWP's leaflet GL24 'If you think our decision is wrong' as a template (*www.dwp.gov.uk/publications/dwp/2004/gl24_oct.pdf*). The authority also has the power to accept an appeal that takes the form of a letter. Where an appeal form is not used, the person seeking the appeal is advised to head their letter 'Appeal' and use the phrase 'I wish to appeal against…' in the body of the letter. In this way the authority should not mistake it for an application for revision (para. 19.5). DAR 18(1),19(2),(4),20(1),(4) NIDAR 18(1),19(2),(4),20(1),(4)

TIME LIMITS

19.26 Appeals should normally be made within one month of the date of notification of the decision against which it is made. Where a statement of reasons (para. 19.24) has been requested during this time the one month period is extended by the time taken between the receipt of the request and the date on which the statement is provided. Out of time appeals may be accepted in particular circumstances but must be made at the latest within 13 calendar months of the date a valid decision notice was sent out by the authority (para. 19.31). Out of time applications should describe reasons for the delay. DAR 18(2) NIDAR 18(2)

ATTRIBUTES OF A VALID APPEAL

19.27 To be properly made an appeal should meet the conditions set out in table 19.2. DAR 20(1) NIDAR 20(1)

Table 19.2 Necessary attributes of a valid appeal

The appeal must:

- be in writing on a form approved for the purpose by the authority or in such other form (e.g. letter) as the authority may accept; and
- be signed by the person who has a right of appeal; and
- be delivered, by whatever means (e.g. post, fax, e-mail) to the authority; and
- contain details of the grounds on which it is made (it is not enough, for example, for the claimant to say that they are unhappy with the decision – they must state why they think the decision is wrong); and
- contain sufficient particulars of the decision to enable that decision to be identified.

DAR 20(7)(b) NIDAR 20(7)(b) **19.28** An appeal signed by someone who is not a 'person affected' is not 'duly made' and should be identified as such by the authority. Arguably this applies where a solicitor for example signs the appeal request (*R v Lambeth ex p Crookes*). The authority should make a copy of the appeal form or letter and return the original to the sender with appropriate advice, e.g. have the claimant, landlord or other person affected sign the form. If the appeal is not returned with 14 days or such longer period as appropriate the authority should send a copy of the appeal to the Appeal Service. It should be turned down by the tribunal member if they agree that it fails to satisfy the legal requirement. The tribunal member should inform the appellant and the authority of the determination.

WITHDRAWING AN APPEAL

DAR 20(9) NIDAR 20(9) **19.29** An appeal may be withdrawn by an appellant in writing at any time before it is decided. If the authority has not sent the appeal to the Appeal Service any request to withdraw can be accepted by the authority. If the authority has referred the appeal to the Appeal Service any request from the appellant to withdraw the appeal must be sent to the Appeal Service.

WHAT HAPPENS IF THE APPELLANT DIES DURING THE APPEAL PROCESS?

DAR 21(1) NIDAR 21(1) **19.30** If the appellant dies during the appeal process the authority may appoint anyone it thinks fit to proceed with the appeal in the place of the deceased.

Out of time appeals

19.31 An appeal should normally be made to the authority within one month of the date of notification of the decision against which it is made or in particular circumstances 13 months. The decision is considered to be notified on the date it is posted or handed to the person affected. The authority should ensure that it has an accurate record of when notifications are actually posted (as opposed to the date on the letter) or handed to persons affected. An appeal is treated as made on the day that it is received by the authority. If the authority's decision notice is invalid because it fails to meet the relevant legal requirements (paras. 16.9-11, 18.83-90) the time for appealing does not start until the authority issues a valid notice (*CH/1129/04* paras. 2-4). DAR 2(a),18(1),19 NIDAR 2(a),18(1),1

19.32 Beyond the normal one month period an application for an extension of the time limit within a further 12 months should be successful where either: DAR 19(5) NIDAR 19(5)

- the authority, or if not the authority the tribunal member, is satisfied that it is in the 'interests of justice' for the application to be granted; or
- a tribunal member is satisfied that if the application is granted there are reasonable prospects that the appeal will be successful.

19.33 Under the first bullet point the authority may admit an appeal without involving the Appeals Service. The DWP (Circular A28-2002, para. 31) advises that the authority should make sure that the Appeal Service knows that it has admitted the late appeal by including the following paragraph in its appeal submission: 'The appeal was made on [date] but the reason(s) for the late application has been accepted by the relevant authority under regulation 32 of the SS&CS (D&A) Regs. Accordingly, the issue does not need to be considered by the tribunal.' Presumably the legal reference should in fact be to regulation 19 of DAR. DAR 19(5)(b) NIDAR 19(5)(b)

19.34 If the authority does not admit the late appeal the question must be referred to the Appeal Service for consideration. The authority should advise the Appeal Service why it does not support the 'out of time' appeal. As soon as practicable, a copy of the decision on the out of time appeal made by the tribunal member must be sent or given to principal parties to the proceedings.

NECESSARY CONDITIONS FOR AN OUT OF TIME APPEAL TO BE ACCEPTED BY THE TRIBUNAL MEMBER

19.35 An application for an out of time appeal may be granted if the tribunal member is satisfied that: DAR 19(5) NIDAR 19(5)

- there are reasonable prospects that the appeal will be successful; or
- it is in the interests of justice for the application to be granted.

Note that it is sufficient if the application satisfies one of the two tests and that the first test (which can only be considered by a tribunal member) is not a particularly challenging one!

The 'interests of justice'

DAR 19(60(a),(7)
NIDAR 19(6)(a),(7)

19.36 The regulations prescribe that it is not in the interests of justice to grant an application unless the authority or tribunal member is satisfied that one of the following circumstances exists and is relevant to the application:

- the applicant or a spouse or dependant of the applicant has died or suffered serious illness; or
- the applicant is not resident in the United Kingdom; or
- normal postal services were disrupted; or
- some other special circumstances exist which are wholly exceptional and relevant to the application.

Additionally, it must be as a result of those special circumstances that it was not practicable for the application to be made within the time limit.

GUIDING PRINCIPLE

DAR 19(8)
NIDAR 19(8)

19.37 In determining whether it is in the interests of justice to grant the application, the authority or tribunal member must have regard to the principle that the later the application for the extension of time the more compelling the special circumstances for lateness must be. Remember, however, that unlike the authority the appeal tribunal may accept an out of time appeal if there are reasonable prospects that the appeal will be successful (para. 19.35) without there being special circumstances.

FACTORS THAT CANNOT BE TAKEN INTO ACCOUNT

DAR 19(9)(a),(b)
NIDAR 19(9)(a),(b)

19.38 In determining whether it is in the interests of justice to grant an application, the authority or tribunal member cannot take account of the following factors:

- that the applicant was unaware of or misunderstood the law or the time limits; or
- that a Commissioner or a court has taken a different view of the law from that previously understood and applied.

The authority's action on receipt of an appeal

19.39 On receipt of an appeal the authority should:

- consider revising the decision appealed against (para. 19.4);
- classify the appeal (i.e. not duly made, out of time and/or involves a third party) if not revised to the advantage of the person affected;
- send the appropriate forms (the pre-hearing enquiry form (TAS1 HB) to the appellant, (TAS1 HB R) to any third party and the notification of appeal (AT37) to the Appeal Service) and its submission to:
  - the appellant;
  - any third party; and
  - the Appeal Service.

19.40 The authority must send all appeals to the Appeals Service unless the appeal lapses following an advantageous revision or is withdrawn by the appellant. The authority should indicate on the notification of appeal form (AT37) sent to the Appeal Service if it knows that eviction proceedings have begun. Such cases can be heard urgently by tribunals.

19.41 The previous category of 'misconceived appeal' (i.e. an appeal which is frivolous or vexatious, or obviously unsustainable and has no prospect of success) and related procedures were suspended in March 2002 (DWP A10/2002, A32/2002). The regulations relating to misconceived appeals have now been abolished (SI 2004 No. 3368).

The pre-hearing enquiry form (TAS1 HB)

19.42 The pre-hearing enquiry form (TAS1 HB or Welsh equivalent TAS1 W HB) that the authority sends to the person affected includes questions as to whether that person:

- wants to withdraw their appeal;
- wants an oral hearing (at which they and/or their representative can be present) or paper hearing (which does not require their attendance);
- agrees to having less than 14 days notice where they have opted for an oral hearing;
- has an outstanding appeal against another benefit decision; and/or
- needs an interpreter or signer.

NORMALLY 14 DAYS TO RETURN ENQUIRY FORM TO THE APPEAL SERVICE

DAR99 39(2),(3)
NIDAR99 39(2),(3)

19.43 The person affected should normally return the pre-hearing enquiry form (TAS1) to the appropriate regional office of the Appeal Service within 14 days of the date it was sent out by the authority. If it is not returned within 14 days the Appeal Service may assume that the person affected does not wish to continue with the appeal and the appeal will be struck out. The tribunal clerk may give a longer period for reply, for example where the appellant is in hospital or some other reason exists which would prevent the appellant from replying on time. If the form cannot be returned within 14 days the regional office of the Appeal Service should be advised. If the authority is aware of any reason that might prevent the appellant from replying on time, this should be clearly marked on the notification of appeal (AT37) it sends to the Appeal Service.

The submission

19.44 The nature of the submissions that may be produced for the appeal tribunal is not detailed in legislation but guidance on the writing of submissions can be found in GM paras C.11.410-428. A well prepared submission assists the tribunal to arrive at a correct decision based on the law and the facts relating to the appeal.

The appeal hearing

MEMBERSHIP OF TRIBUNAL

DAR 22(1),(2)
NIDAR 22(1),(2)

19.45 All tribunal members are independent of the authority. In the case of an appeal concerning HB/CTB the tribunal normally consists of just one person who is legally qualified. In rare instances where financial questions are raised, e.g. regarding a difficult question relating to a self-employed claimant's accounts, there may also be a financially qualified tribunal member. An additional member may also be present to provide that member with experience or to assist with the monitoring of standards.

VENUES

19.46 The hearing normally takes place at a tribunal venue near to the appellant. The Appeal Service has a network of around 140 tribunal venues that it uses to hear cases across England, Wales and Scotland. Information on venue locations in England, Scotland and Wales and available facilities can be found on the web at: *www.appeals-service.gov.uk/venue_information.asp* The Appeal Service (Northern Ireland) currently holds appeal hearings at 19 venues in towns and cities throughout the province.

FUNCTION

19.47 The tribunal's task is to reconsider the specific decision that has been appealed. It does not have to consider any issue that has not been raised in the appeal but is does have the power to do so. The tribunal should not shut its eyes to things where to do so would cause an injustice. It cannot however take into account any circumstances that did not exist at the time the decision appealed against was made.

CPSA sch 7 para 6(9)
NICPSA sch 7 para 6(9)

An oral hearing

NOTICE

19.48 At least 14 days before the hearing (beginning with the day on which the notice is given and ending on the day before the hearing of the appeal is to take place) notice of the time and place of any oral hearing should be given to every party to the proceedings. If notice has not been given to someone who should have been given it, the hearing may proceed only with the consent of that person.

DAR99 49(2)
NIDAR99 49(2)

POSTPONEMENT

19.49 A tribunal member or the clerk may at any time before the beginning of the hearing postpone the hearing. Where a person affected wishes to request a postponement of the hearing they should do so by writing to the clerk stating the reasons for the request. If it is too late to request a postponement, an adjournment may be requested at the hearing. The clerk or tribunal member may grant or refuse the request as they think fit.

DAR99 51(1)
NIDAR99 51(1)

PUBLIC OR PRIVATE HEARINGS

19.50 The initial presumption is that a hearing will be in public. In practice of course normally only the people involved in the hearing are present. Should there be people in attendance who are not involved in the hearing a (part) private hearing may be held:

- in the interests of national security, morals, public order or children;
- for the protection of the private or family life of one of the parties; or
- in special circumstances, because publicity would prejudice the interests of justice.

DAR99 49(6)
NIDAR99 49(6)

19.51 Certain persons such as trainee panel members or trainee clerks are entitled to be present at an oral hearing (whether or not it is otherwise in private). They must not take part in the proceedings.

DECIDING TO PROCEED IN THE ABSENCE OF ANY OF THE PARTIES

DAR99 49(4)
NIDAR99 49(4)

19.52 If one of the parties to whom notice has been given fails to appear at the hearing the chair may, having regard to all the circumstances including any explanation offered for the absence:

- ◆ proceed with the hearing; or
- ◆ give such directions with a view to the determination of the appeal as they think proper.

DAR99 49(5)
NIDAR99 49(5)

19.53 If one of the relevant parties has waived the right to be given 14 days notice of the hearing, the chair may proceed with the hearing despite the absence.

THE PARTIES' RIGHTS AT THE HEARING

DAR99 49(1),(7)
NIDAR99 49(1),(7)

19.54 The procedure for an oral hearing is determined by the chair. The parties to the proceedings however have certain rights which the chair must respect. Each party is entitled to:

- ◆ be present; and
- ◆ be heard at an oral hearing.

DAR99 49(8)
NIDAR99 49(8)

19.55 In law parties entitled to be present at a hearing do not have to be physically present, but can attend by a live television link, e.g. a video conference facility, but only where the chair gives permission. The Appeal Services is working to extend the use of the video-link in tribunal hearings (*Annual Report and Accounts 2003-2004,* page 17). One of the principal aims is to enable appellants to attend their hearing from remote or rural areas.

19.56 A person who has the right to be heard at a hearing:

- ◆ may be accompanied; and
- ◆ may be represented by another person whether they have professional qualifications or not.

DAR99 49(8)
NIDAR99 49(8)

19.57 For the purposes of the proceedings at the hearing, any representative has all the rights and powers to which the person represented is entitled.

DAR99 49(11)
NIDAR99 49(11)

19.58 Any person entitled to be heard at an oral hearing may:

- ◆ address the tribunal;
- ◆ give evidence;
- ◆ call witnesses; and
- ◆ put questions directly to any other person called as a witness.

Order of the hearing

19.59 The procedure for an oral hearing is determined by the chair within the framework set in the regulations, e.g. the need to ensure that the parties have the opportunity to put their case. Failure to observe proper procedures or the rights of the parties may leave the tribunal's decision open to appeal on grounds of natural justice (GM para C11.451) or the right to a fair hearing *(CJSA/5100/2001)*. DAR99 49(1) NIDAR99 49(1)

19.60 The way in which the tribunal actually hears the appeal varies according to the issue that the tribunal has to decide. Each chair has their own way of conducting a hearing. Nevertheless the appellant should expect to have those present in the room introduced and their function explained at the start. The chair should also explain the procedure they wish to follow and seek the agreement of the parties to going ahead in that way. The chair may wish the appellant to start by explaining why they think the decision is wrong. If there is a Presenting Officer for the authority in attendance, they will be asked to explain the basis of the authority's decision. At some point the chair is likely to ask questions of the parties. Usually the appellant is offered the opportunity of having the final word before the tribunal goes on to consider its decision.

DIRECTIONS

19.61 The chair may at any stage of the proceedings, either of their own motion or on a written application made to the clerk by any party to the proceedings: DAR 38(2) NIDAR 38(2)

- give such directions as they consider necessary or desirable for the just, effective and efficient conduct of the proceedings; and
- direct any party to the proceedings to provide such particulars or to produce such documents as may be reasonably required.

ADJOURNMENT

19.62 An oral hearing may be adjourned by the chair at any time on the application of any party to the proceedings or of their own motion. This might be, for example, to allow new evidence to be looked at. Where a hearing has been adjourned and it is not practicable, or would cause undue delay, for it to be resumed before a tribunal with the same tribunal member(s) there must be a complete rehearing (DWP A17/2002, para. 33). DAR99 51(4) NIDAR99 51(4)

WITHDRAWING AN APPEAL

19.63 An appeal may be withdrawn by the appellant at the oral hearing. If this happens the clerk must send a notice in writing to any party to the proceedings who is not present when the appeal or referral is withdrawn, informing them that the appeal has been withdrawn. DAR99 40(1)(a),(2) NIDAR99 40(1)(a),(2)

The tribunal's decision

19.64 The tribunal reaches a decision once it has considered all the evidence from an oral or paper hearing. In reaching it decision the tribunal should:

- consider the relevant law applicable to the decision in question;
- identify the relevant facts - and where these are in doubt or dispute find them (if necessary on the balance of probability); and
- apply the law to the relevant facts to arrive at a reasoned decision.

DUTY TO FOLLOW DECISIONS OF THE COURTS AND COMMISSIONERS

19.65 In its consideration of the legal issues the tribunal has a duty to follow past decisions of the Courts and Commissioners (para. 19.94) unless the case before the tribunal is distinguishable (R(U)23/59). Northern Ireland decisions are of persuasive authority only in England, Wales and Scotland (R(I) 14/63) and *vice versa*. Decisions of appeal tribunals themselves do not set any precedent.

19.66 There is an order of precedence to Commissioners decisions (R(I)12/75(T)). This is as follows:

- decisions of Tribunals of Commissioners (i.e. three Commissioners sitting together to decide cases of particular importance) are the most authoritative – whether reported or unreported;
- reported decisions (which are given serial numbers by the year and identified by having the prefix 'R', e.g. R(H)1/02)) come next;
- then come unreported decisions (which are identified by the Commissioner's file number, e.g. CH/1502/2004).

19.67 If there appears to be conflict between two or more Commissioners' decisions the above hierarchy should be applied (R(I)12/75(T)). If the conflicting decisions are of equal rank, the tribunal is free to choose between them. More recent decisions should be preferred to older decisions. If a more recent unreported decision has fully considered all the earlier authorities, and given reasons for disapproving one or more earlier reported decisions, the tribunal should generally follow the more recent unreported decision (R(IS) 13/01).

19.68 Details regarding the accessing of Commissioners' decisions on-line can be found in appendix 2. Reported cases are kept at tribunal venues but unreported cases are not. If an appellant, representative or presenting officer wishes to use an unreported decision in support of their case a copy should, where possible, be sent in advance, otherwise an adjournment may be necessary.

THE WRITTEN DECISION NOTICE

19.69 If the appellant attends an oral hearing they may be given the decision on the day. It should be confirmed in writing as soon as practicable by the chair. Every decision of an appeal tribunal must be recorded in summary by the chair. The decision notice must be in the written form approved by the President of Appeal Tribunals *(www.appeals-service.gov.uk/506.htm)*. The chair must sign it. Where there was a legally qualified member and a financially qualified member the decision notice should state if the decision is unanimous or not.

DAR99 53(1),(2),(5)
NIDAR99 53(1),(2),(5)

COMMUNICATION OF THE DECISION

19.70 As soon as practicable after an appeal has been decided, a copy of the decision notice must be sent or given to every party to the proceedings. They must also be informed of:

DAR99 53(3)
NIDAR99 53(3)

- the right to apply for a statement of reasons; and
- the conditions governing appeals to a Commissioner.

The Appeal Service aims to issue a copy of the tribunal's decision to the authority, appellant and appellant's representative, where one exists, within two days of the tribunal hearing (A20/2003, appendix B, para. A59).

19.71 The decision notice is the legal document that enables the authority to correct and pay benefit in line with the tribunal's decision.

A 'STATEMENT OF REASONS'

19.72 A statement of reasons sets out the findings of fact and the reasons for the decision. If an appeal to the Social Security Commissioners is being considered, a statement of reasons must be asked for.

TIME LIMIT FOR APPLICATION FOR STATEMENT OF REASONS

19.73 A party to the proceedings may apply to the clerk for a statement of the reasons for the tribunal's decision. A statement of reasons can be asked for at the tribunal. Otherwise the application must normally be made within one month of the date the decision notice was given or sent. If this is not asked for in time the chance of appealing may be lost.

DAR99 53(4)
NIDAR99 53(4)

19.74 Late applications for the statement of reasons can only be accepted if the application is made in writing to the clerk within three months of the date the decision note was sent. In calculating this three month period no account should be taken of time that elapses before the day on which notice was given of:

DAR99 54(1),(13)
NIDAR99 54(1),(12A)

- a correction of a decision or the record of a decision; or
- a decision to refuse to set aside.

Where a correction is made, or where set-aside is refused, the three month period is counted from the day notice of the correction or refusal is given.

DAR99 54(2)-(5)
NIDAR99 54(2)-(5)

19.75 The application must explain why the application is late, including details of any relevant special circumstances. A legally qualified panel member considers the application and decides the matter. Similar considerations apply as to those that apply to late appeals.

REQUIREMENT TO SUPPLY WRITTEN STATEMENT OF REASONS

DAR99 54(11)
NIDAR99 54(11)

19.76 Following receipt of an accepted application for a written statement of reasons the tribunal member must:

- record a statement of the reasons; and
- send or give a copy of that statement to every party to the proceedings as soon as practicable.

The Appeal Service aims to issue a full statement of reasons within four weeks of a request being received (A20/2003, appendix B, para. A61).

RECORD OF TRIBUNAL PROCEEDINGS

DAR99 55(1),(2)
NIDAR99 55(1),(2)

19.77 A record of the proceedings at an oral hearing, which is sufficient to indicate the evidence taken, must be made by the tribunal member. This record, together with the decision notice, and any statement of the reasons for the tribunal's decision, must be preserved by the Appeal Service for six months from the date it was created. Any party to the proceedings may within that six month period apply in writing for a copy of the appropriate document, which should be supplied on request.

Implementing the tribunal's decision

19.78 The authority should action the tribunal's decision as soon as practicable. The DWP indicates that the authority should seek to complete the necessary actions within four calendar weeks (A20/2003, appendix B, para. A70).

What actions can be taken if a tribunal's decision is wrong?

19.79 Once a tribunal has made and communicated its decision the decision may be:

- altered if the authority supersedes the decision;
- corrected, where there is an accidental error;
- set aside on certain limited grounds;
- appealed to the Social Security Commissioners.

WHEN MAY THE AUTHORITY SUPERSEDE THE TRIBUNAL'S DECISION?

19.80 A decision of a tribunal may be superseded, either on application or on the authority's own initiative, where: DAR 7(2)(a),(d) NIDAR 7(2)(b),(c)

- the decision was made in ignorance of a material fact; or
- the decision was based on a mistake as to a material fact; or
- there has been a relevant change of circumstances since the decision had effect.

WHEN MAY A TRIBUNAL'S DECISION BE CORRECTED?

19.81 The clerk, or a tribunal member, may at any time correct accidental errors such as a typing mistake, misspelling of a name or omission about which both sides agree *(CI/3887/99 para. 8)*. A correction made to, or to the record of, a decision is deemed part of the decision or record of that decision. Any of the parties to the appeal can ask for a correction to be made. A written notice of the correction must be given as soon as practicable to every party to the proceedings. There is no right of appeal against a correction or a refusal to make a correction. DAR99 56(1),(2) NIDAR99 56(1),(2)

SETTING ASIDE DECISIONS

19.82 If a tribunal decision is 'set aside' this means that the decision is cancelled and a new tribunal must be arranged. Any party to the proceedings may apply for a decision of an appeal tribunal to be set aside by a legally qualified tribunal member. The member may set the decision aside where it appears just on the ground that: DAR99 57(1) NIDAR99 57(1)

- a document relating to the proceedings was not sent to, or was not received at an appropriate time by, any of the parties to the proceedings or their representatives or was not received at an appropriate time by the person who made the decision;
- any party to the proceedings or their representative was not present at the hearing.

19.83 In determining whether it is just to set aside a decision on the ground that someone was not present, the tribunal member must consider whether the party making the application gave notice that they wished to have an oral hearing. If not the decision cannot be set aside unless the tribunal member is satisfied that the interests of justice obviously support acceptance of the set aside application. DAR99 57(2) NIDAR99 57(2)

19.84 An application for a set aside must:

- be made within one month of the date on which:
  - a copy of the decision notice is sent or given to the parties; or
  - the statement of the reasons for the decision is given or sent in,

whichever is the later;

- be in writing; and
- signed by a party to the proceedings or, where the party has provided written authority to a representative to act on their behalf, that representative;
- contain particulars of the grounds on which it is made; and
- be sent to the clerk to the appeal tribunal.

EXTENSION OF THE TIME LIMITS IN WHICH TO APPLY FOR A SET ASIDE

DAR99 57(6) NIDAR99 57(6)

19.85 Late applications for set aside may be accepted up to one year after the end of the one month time limit.

DAR99 57(7) NIDAR99 57(7)

19.86 An application for an extension of time must include details of any relevant special circumstances. It must be determined by a legally qualified panel member.

DAR99 57(8) NIDAR99 57(8)

19.87 An application for an extension of time cannot be granted unless the panel member is satisfied that:

- if the application is granted there are reasonable prospects that the application to set aside will be successful; and
- it is in the interests of justice for the application for an extension of time to be granted.

AR99 57(9)(b),(10) NIDAR99 57(9)(b),(10)

19.88 It is not in the interests of justice to grant an application for an extension of time unless the panel member is satisfied that:

- the applicant or a spouse or dependant of the applicant has died or suffered serious illness;
- the applicant is not resident in the United Kingdom; or
- normal postal services were disrupted; or
- some other special circumstances exist which are wholly exceptional and relevant to that application,

Additionally it must be as a result of those special circumstances that it was not practicable for the application to set aside to be made within the one month time limit.

DAR99 57(11) NIDAR99 57(1)

19.89 In determining whether it is in the interests of justice to grant an application for an extension of time, the panel member must have regard to the principle that the greater the amount of time that has elapsed between the expiry of the time within which the application to set aside is to be made and the making of the application for an extension of time, the more compelling should be the special circumstances on which the application for an extension is based.

19.90 Where an application to set aside a decision is entertained every party to the proceedings must be sent a copy of the application. They must also be afforded a reasonable opportunity of making representations on it before the application is determined. DAR99 57(4) NIDAR99 57(4)

COMMUNICATION OF THE DECISION ON THE APPLICATION TO SET ASIDE

19.91 Every party to the proceedings must receive a written notice of the decision on an application to set aside as soon as practicable. The notice must contain a statement giving the reasons for the decision. DAR99 57(5) NIDAR99 57(5)

19.92 There is no right of appeal against the outcome of a set aside request. If the request is refused, however, the time limit for appealing to the Commissioner does not start until the notification of the set aside decision has been issued and the application to set aside may be treated as an application for a statement of the reasons (19.72) for the tribunal's decision, subject to the normal time limits (19.73-74). DAR99 57A(2) NIDAR99 57A(2)

19.93 An application under this regulation for an extension of time which has been refused may not be renewed. DAR99 57(12) NIDAR99 57(12)

Appeals to Social Security Commissioners

19.94 The Social Security Commissioners are appointed to decide appeals on questions of law from appeal tribunals. The Commissioners' role is to give interpretations of the law which are binding on all decision makers and appeal tribunals. The Commissioners are barristers, solicitors or advocates of not less than ten years' standing who are specialists in social security law. Commissioners have a legal status comparable to that of a High Court judge in their specialised area. Any appeals from their decisions are to the Court of Appeal or the Inner House of the Court of Session, and from there to the House of Lords. Cases involving European Union law are referred by the Commissioners direct to the European Court of Justice.

19.95 Chapter C11 of the GM provides guidance on appeals to Commissioners. Most appeals are determined on paper without a hearing. Parties make their submissions in writing. However, parties may ask for an oral hearing. Hearings take place at the Commissioners' offices in London (Harp House, 83-86 Farringdon Street, London EC4A 4DH – correspondence should be sent to 5th Floor, Newspaper House, 8/16 Great New Street, London EC4A 3NN) and Edinburgh (23 Melville Street, Edinburgh EH3 7PW). In Northern Ireland the address for the Commissioners is Headline Building, 10-14 Victoria Street, Belfast, BTI 3GG. Hearings may take place at other locations in particular circumstances.

WHEN CAN AN APPEAL BE MADE TO THE COMMISSIONERS?

CPSA sch 7 paras 8(1),(2), (7)(c),(8)
NICPSA sch 7 paras 8(1),(2), (7)(c),(8)
DAR99 58(1),(3)
NIDAR99 58(1),(3)
SSCPR 9,10,12,13
SSCPR 9,10,12,13

19.96 An appeal can only be made to the Social Security Commissioners where the following points are satisfied:

- the ground for seeking an appeal is that the appeal tribunal made an error on a point of law (para. 19.98) in arriving at its decision; and
- the appeal is being made by someone entitled to make it (para. 19.100); and
- the appellant has applied to the tribunal – preferably on form OSSC1 (or OSSC2 for authorities) for leave to appeal to the Commissioner; and
- the application for leave to appeal is made within one month of the date the tribunal's statement of reasons was sent; or a late application made within 13 months of that date is accepted by the chair; and
- the tribunal chair accepts the application for leave to appeal; or
- where a tribunal chair has rejected an application for leave:
- an application has been made directly to a Commissioner (again on Form OSSC1/OSSC2) normally within one month (though out of time applications may be considered if there are special reasons) of the tribunal chair's rejection of the application for leave being sent; and
- the Commissioner considers that there are special reasons to accept the application for leave; and
- the appellant has submitted the appeal, together with all the necessary accompanying documents, to the Commissioner within one month (or longer if there are special reasons) of the date the tribunal's decision granting leave was sent.

19.97 Where the Commissioner grants leave to appeal the appellant does not normally have to a make a separate appeal. Detailed advice on appealing to the Commissioners in England and Wales and Forms OSSC1/OSSC2 can be found on the Social Security and Child Support Commissioners' web site: *www.osscsc.gov.uk* The equivalent advice and forms in use in Scotland can be found on the Scottish Commissioners' web site *www.ossc-scotland.org.uk* and in Northern Ireland on the Northern Ireland Court Service web site: *www.courtsni.gov.uk/en-GB/Services/Tribunals/OfficeOfSSC/HowTo/*

What is an error in a point of law?

19.98 An appeal to a Commissioner can only be made on an error in a point of law.

CPSA sch 7 para 8 NICPSA sch 7 para 8(1)

19.99 An error in a point of law is where, for example *(R(IS) 11/99)*, the appeal tribunal:

- failed to apply the correct law;
- wrongly interpreted the relevant Acts or Regulations;
- followed a procedure that breached the rules of natural justice;
- took irrelevant matters into account, or did not consider relevant matters, or did both of these things;
- did not give adequate reasons in the full statement of its decision (para. 19.69);
- gave a decision which was not supported by the evidence;
- decided the facts in such a way that no person properly instructed as to the relevant law, and acting judicially, could have come to the decision made by the tribunal.

Who can apply for leave to appeal?

19.100 Where the disputed decision relates to housing benefit, the following can apply for leave to appeal to the Commissioners:

SSCPR 4(1) NISSCPR 4(1)

- the claimant;
- any other 'person affected' by the decision (para. 19.15.) provided that they are an appellant against the tribunal's decision or a party to the appeal tribunal proceedings;
- the authority against whose decision the appeal to the appeal tribunal was brought;
- the Secretary of State (the Department for Social Development in Northern Ireland).

Appeals against a Commissioner's decision

19.101 There is a right to appeal against a Commissioner's decision to the Court of Appeal or the Court of Session in Scotland. An appeal can only be made on a point of law. Leave to appeal must be obtained from the Commissioner or, if the Commissioner refuses, from the relevant Court. The time limit for applying for leave to appeal to the Commissioner is three months. The time limit may be extended by the Commissioner. If leave to appeal is refused the application may

SSCPR 33 NISSCPR 33

be renewed in the relevant Court within six weeks. If the Commissioner grants leave the appeal must be made to the relevant Court within six weeks.

Errors of law: restrictions on entitlement

CPSA sch 7 para 18
NICPSA sch 7 para 18

19.102 The rules that restrict entitlement in other cases when an error of law by an authority has been identified apply when:

- the result of an appeal to a Commissioner or court is that the authority's decision was erroneous in point of law (including cases where all or part of a Regulation or Order has been held to be invalid); and
- after the date of the determination of that appeal, that authority or another authority has to make a decision in accordance with it; and
- the authority's decision would be about:
  - a claim (regardless of whether the claim was made before or after the appeal determination), or
  - a revision (and if this is as a result of an application to do so, regardless of whether the application was made before or after the appeal determination), or
  - a supersession following an application for one (regardless of whether the application was made before or after the appeal determination).

In such cases, in respect of the period before the appeal determination, the authority must make the decision as though it had not been found to be wrong in law. This does not, however, apply where the decision would have been made before the appeal determination.

20 Recent migrants

20.1 There are two quite distinct mechanisms by which recent migrants can be excluded from HB/CTB entitlement: either as a person subject to 'immigration control' (para. 20.17) or as a 'person from abroad'. However, whether a claimant is a 'person from abroad' is determined by a two stage test, (in which the claimant first has to show they have a 'right to reside' (para. 20.30) and additionally if they succeed that they are 'habitually resident' (para. 20.56). In effect there are three different tests, each of which can exclude a claimant from HB/CTB.

20.2 The government's powers to exclude nationals of a foreign state from benefit are constrained by its treaty obligations (often in return for reciprocal rights for UK citizens abroad). The result is that the rules which exclude recent migrants are a synthesis of benefit, immigration, European and international law, making them especially complex and their interpretation notoriously difficult.

DECIDING WHICH OF THE THREE TESTS TO APPLY

20.3 Not all the tests affect every category of claimant and deciding which tests are relevant is not straightforward. Some categories of claimant automatically pass, or are exempt from the operation of one or all of the three tests. Generally, those who are subject to the immigration status test will not also be subject to the right to reside test and *vice versa* (this is because a person who has a right to reside in the UK under EU law is not subject to immigration control). All claimants are also subject to the habitual residence test unless they are otherwise exempt (20.56).

20.4 To assist the reader in determining which of the three tests apply, this chapter has been set out according to the following categories of claimant:

- asylum seekers, refugees, and other persons granted leave on humanitarian grounds;
- non-EEA foreign nationals;
- EEA nationals (i.e. nationals from member states of the European Economic Area (table 20.2)).

Asylum-seekers, refugees and other persons granted leave on humanitarian grounds

20.5 The section sets out the rules for people who have entered the UK and who are claiming the right to, or have been granted, asylum; or people who have applied for, or been granted, the right to remain in the UK for other humanitarian reasons (such as escaping a war or a natural disaster). Most applicants for asylum are excluded from HB/CTB (para. 20.6) whilst their application is processed, and also following a decision if it is refused. If asylum is granted or the authorities grant permission to stay in the UK for other reasons then benefit can be awarded (paras. 20.11-14).

EXCLUSION OF ASYLUM SEEKERS

20.6 An asylum seeker is someone who applies to be recognised as a refugee under the United Nations Convention on the grounds of a fear of persecution if they are returned to their country of origin. Whilst their asylum application is processed they will be granted 'temporary admission' by the immigration authorities (table 20.1). Except where they are transitionally protected (para. 20.9), or where their country of origin is an EEA, ECSMA or CESC member state (table 20.1), a person whose asylum application has not yet been finally determined will be 'subject to immigration control' (para. 20.17) and so excluded from HB/CTB. Their only rights to support are through the Home Office asylum support scheme managed by the National Asylum Support Service (NASS).

IAA99 115(1),(3),(

ASYLUM SEEKERS FROM EEA, ECSMA OR CESC STATES

20.7 Although all EEA nationals are defined as being exempt from immigration control, an asylum seeker who is an EEA national will have to show that they have a 'right to reside' (paras. 20.30-55) and pass the habitual residence test (paras. 20.56-69) in the same way as any other EEA national in order to qualify for HB/CTB.

IAA99 115(1),(3),(
SI 2000 No. 636 sch para 4
NISR 2000 No. 71 sch para 4

20.8 Asylum seekers from ECSMA or CESC states which are not also EEA states (table 20.2) (i.e. as at 1st April 2006 Turkey, Croatia and Macedonia) will be entitled to HB/CTB if they are 'lawfully present' (paras. 20.24-25) and pass the habitual residence test (paras. 20.56-69).

TRANSITIONALLY PROTECTED ASYLUM SEEKERS

20.9 A small number of asylum seekers are transitionally protected in certain circumstances if either:

CPR sch 3 para 6(1)-(3)
NICPR sch 3 para 6(1)-(2)

- they were entitled to HB/CTB as an asylum seeker before 5 February 1996 (GM C7.700-754); or

- their claim for asylum was made before 3rd April 2000 either at the port of entry, or in-country if they were nationals of country on the upheaval list (GM C7.760-871).

20.10 In both cases protection is lost as soon as the applicant receives their first negative decision (whether or not it is being appealed) on their asylum claim. See previous editions of this guide for details.

PERSONS GRANTED ASYLUM – REFUGEES

HB 10(1)(3B)(g)
B60+ 10(1)(4A)(g)
NIHB 10(1)(5)(g)
NIHB60+ 10(1)(5)(g)
CTB 7(1)(4A)(g)
TB60+ 7(1)(4A)(g)
PR sch 4 paras 2-4
NICPR sch 4 paras 2-4

20.11 An asylum seeker whose application for asylum is accepted will be granted refugee status. All refugees together with their dependants are granted leave (table 20.1) without a public funds restriction and so are not 'subject to immigration control' (para. 20.17). They are also exempt from the habitual residence test and so are entitled to benefit from the date their refugee status is confirmed. For the time being, refugees are also entitled to retrospective benefit for the whole of their exclusion period immediately prior to their refugee status being confirmed (GM C7.890-892). A strict four-week time limit applies. This right will be abolished when section 12 of the Asylum and Immigration (Treatment of Claimants, etc) Act 2004 is brought into force.

PERSONS GRANTED HUMANITARIAN PROTECTION OR DISCRETIONARY LEAVE

HB 10(3B)(h)
HB60+ 10(4A)(h)
NIHB 10(5)(h)
NIHB60+ 10(5)(h)
CTB 7(4A)(h)
CTB60+ 7(4A)(h)

20.12 A person whose claim for asylum has been refused (i.e. is not a refugee) may nevertheless be granted one of the two forms of exceptional leave known as 'Humanitarian Protection' and 'Discretionary Leave' if there are other humanitarian or exceptional reasons why they should not be returned to their country of origin. Both types of leave are granted at the discretion of the Home Secretary.

20.13 Humanitarian protection is granted to those whose life would be at risk or who would be at risk of degrading treatment if they returned to their country of origin. Discretionary leave is granted to those who do not fit the criteria for humanitarian protection and is only granted in exceptional circumstances. Persons granted either form of leave are not 'subject to immigration control' (para. 20.17) and are exempt from the habitual residence test and so entitled to HB/CTB from the date their status is confirmed. However, unlike refugees, their status does not confer rights on their family members to come to live with them.

IAA99 115(9)
HB 10(3B)(h),(j)
B60+ 10(4A)(h),(j)
NIHB 10(5)(h),(j)
NIHB60+ 10(5)(h),(j)
CTB 7(4A)(h),(j)
TB60+ 7(4A)(h),(j)

EVACUEES (MONTSERRAT, KOSOVO ETC)

20.14 Occasionally the government will grant 'leave' to persons evacuated to the UK to escape a specific humanitarian crisis (e.g. war, famine or natural disaster). Normally evacuees will be granted either humanitarian protection or discretionary leave (para. 20.12) and so be entitled to HB/CTB (e.g. Kosovo evacuees (GM

C7 Annex E)). Government policy is to grant Montserrat evacuees who left the island after 1st November 1995 due to the volcanic eruption indefinite leave not exceptional leave, however Montserrat evacuees are specifically exempted from the habitual residence test and so are also entitled to HB/CTB (see GM C7 Annex D, Appendix 16, paras. 34-38 for details).

Non-EEA nationals

WHO IS A NON-EEA NATIONAL

20.15 This section (paras. 20.16-26) sets out rules for foreign nationals who have not made a claim for asylum and who are not nationals of an EEA member state, Switzerland or the common travel area (table 20.2). In this section these claimants are referred to as non-EEA nationals.

ENTITLEMENT TO HB/CTB FOR NON-EEA NATIONALS

20.16 A non-EEA national will only be entitled to HB/CTB if they are: IAA99 115(9) HB 10 HB60+ 10 NIHB 10 NIHB60+ 10 CTB 7 CTB60+ 7

- not 'subject to immigration control'; and
- either habitually resident in the common travel area or exempt from the habitual residence test (paras. 20.56-69).

PERSONS WHO ARE SUBJECT TO IMMIGRATION CONTROL

20.17 Except where they are exempted by the regulations (para. 20.23) a non-EEA national will be subject to immigration control and excluded from HB/CTB if they are a person who: IAA99 115(1),(9)

- requires leave (table 20.1) to enter or remain in the UK but does not have it (i.e. an illegal entrant or overstayer);
- has leave to enter or remain in the UK but which is subject to a public funds condition (e.g. most visitors or students);
- has leave to enter or remain in the UK given as a result of a maintenance undertaking (i.e. a UK resident has formally agreed to sponsor him or her);
- has leave to enter or remain in the UK only while waiting for the outcome of an appeal against a decision to vary, or to refuse to vary, any limited leave.

MEANING OF LEAVE AND SPONSORED IMMIGRANT, ETC

20.18 Whether a person requires 'leave' (legal permission) to enter the UK by the immigration authorities is determined by immigration law. Nearly all non-EEA nationals will require leave to enter the UK. Leave can be granted for a fixed period or open ended ('indefinite') and with or without a public funds condition (i.e. ' no recourse to public funds'). Most immigrants with limited leave to enter the UK (including those allowed to work) will do so on the clear understanding that they support themselves during their stay without the need for support from public funds (GM C7.52). Table 20.1 describes the meaning of 'leave' and some other forms of immigration status.

20.19 The immigration authorities sometimes grant indefinite leave to a person to enable them to join a family member on the understanding that their relatives are prepared to support them (GM C7.400). These people are known as 'sponsored immigrants' and are mostly aged over 65 (GM C7.403). In certain cases the immigration authorities will require the supporting relatives (known as sponsors) to sign a legally binding agreement (known as an undertaking) to maintain and accommodate that person as a condition of granting them leave.

20.20 For HB/CTB purposes a sponsored immigrant will only be 'subject to immigration control' if their sponsor has signed a formal undertaking to support them. A signed statement will only amount to an 'undertaking' if it is a clear promise to support that person in the future. A statement of ability and willingness to support that person is not sufficient to amount to an undertaking (*Secretary of State for Work and Pensions v Ahmed,* confirming CIS/426/2003) but a written undertaking not given on an official form my still be a formal undertaking affecting benefit entitlement (*R v Secretary of State ex parte Begum* reported as R(IS)11/04).

Table 20.1 Some immigration terminology

Illegal entrant	A person who enters the UK without leave and who has not been granted temporary admission.
Leave	Legal permission to be in the UK granted by the immigration authorities (or in exceptional circumstances at the discretion of the Home Secretary (paras. 20.12 and 20.60). Leave can be for a fixed period (limited leave) (e.g. a visa) or open ended (indefinite leave). Temporary admission is not a form of leave.
Overstayer	A person whose leave has expired and has not been renewed and for whom no appeal is pending.
Public funds	A claim for any of the following benefits or assistance: • income support; income-based jobseeker's allowance; state pension credit; housing benefit or council tax

	benefit (and most other non-contributory state benefits) or; • re-housing by the local authority as homeless under part 7 of the Housing Act 1996.
Settled status	A person who is a national of a foreign state who has been granted the right to reside in the UK by the immigration authorities. Their passport will be endorsed as such and accompanied by an authenticating stamp issued by the Home Office Immigration and Nationality Directorate.
Sponsored immigrant	A person who has been granted leave to remain in the UK to join a family member as a result of a sponsor giving a formal undertaking for their maintenance and accommodation (para. 20.19).
Temporary admission	The period of grace allowed a person who has entered the UK while their application for leave or for asylum is determined. Temporary admission is not a form of leave but person who has been granted it will be 'lawfully present' (para. 20.25).

PEOPLE WHO SATISFY THE IMMIGRATION CONTROL TEST

IAA99 115(1),(3),(9) SI 2006 No. 1003 Reg 14 SI 2000 No. 636 sch NISR 2000 No. 71 sch

20.21 The following people satisfy the immigration control test:

- nationals of an EEA member state (including the A8 states);
- non-EEA nationals who are family members of EEA nationals;
- British passport holders who are British Citizens or who have right of abode in the UK;
- citizens of countries in the Common Travel Area (table 20.2);
- holders of passports containing a Certificate of Entitlement to the right of abode in the UK (GM C7.60);
- persons who have settled status (table 20.1) (GM C7.60).

20.22 In addition to those persons who satisfy the immigration control test, a number of other categories of persons are specifically exempted from the test (para. 20.23). A person who satisfies, or who is exempt from, immigration control will also have a right to reside in the UK (para. 20.30).

PEOPLE WHO ARE EXEMPT FROM THE IMMIGRATION CONTROL TEST

AA99 115(1),(3)(9)
I 2000 No. 636 sch
NISR 2000
No. 71 sch

20.23 For HB/CTB purposes all EEA nationals (table 20.2) are defined as not being subject to immigration control. Certain other categories of claimant who would otherwise be subject to the test are exempted from it by regulations. These are:

- ECSMA or CESC nationals who are 'lawfully present' (paras. 20.24-25);
- people admitted to the UK as sponsored immigrants, as a result of a maintenance undertaking, who have been resident for less than five years and whose sponsor (or all of their sponsors if there is more than one) has died;
- people admitted to the UK as sponsored immigrants, as a result of a maintenance undertaking, who have been resident for five years or more;
- people with limited leave whose funds have been temporarily disrupted (para.20.26).

ECSMA/CESC NATIONALS

SI 2000 No. 636
sch para 4
NISR 2000 No. 71
sch para 4

20.24 A national of a non-EEA state which has ratified either the European Convention on Social and Medical Assistance (ECSMA) or the Council of Europe Social Charter (CESC) and who is 'lawfully present' in the UK will be exempt from the immigration control test. ECSMA and CESC member states as at 1st April 2006 are identified in table 20.2. An up-to-date list of countries that have ratified these treaties can be found on-line at *http://conventions.coe.int* (treaties 14 and 35 on the full list).

20.25 A person will be lawfully present in the UK if they have any form of 'leave' or if they have been granted 'temporary admission' (table 20.1) *Szoma (FC) v Secretary of State for Work and Pensions.*

CLAIMANTS WITH LIMITED LEAVE – FUNDS DISRUPTED

HB 10(4)
HB 10(5)
NIHB 10(6)
NIHB60+ 10(6)
CTB 7(5)
CTB60+ 7(5)
SI 2000 No. 636
sch para 1
NISR 2000 No. 71
sch para 1

20.26 Claimants with limited leave to remain in the UK (and thus normally ineligible for HB/CTB: para. 20.18), but whose funds have been temporarily interrupted, are entitled to HB/CTB for up to 42 days in any one period of leave provided that there is a reasonable expectation that the funds will be resumed.

EEA nationals

WHO IS AN EEA NATIONAL

20.27 This section (paras. 20.29-55) sets out rules for citizens (and their family members) of the common travel area, EEA member states and Switzerland (table 20.2), who have not made a claim for asylum. The guide refers to these claimants as EEA nationals. Changes to the rights of residence test came into force on 30th April 2006 as a result of EC Directive 2004/38/EC. The new Directive updates and consolidates the right to reside previously contained in numerous other Directives. The Directive is given effect in the UK by the Immigration (European Economic Area) Regulations 2006. The rules which are described below are those that apply from 30th April 2006. SI 2006 No 1003

Table 20.2 Member states of certain European treaties

GROUP	MEMBER STATES
Common Travel Area	The UK, the Republic of Ireland, the Channel Islands and the Isle of Man.
EEA states (excluding Ireland and the UK)	Austria; Belgium; Cyprus; Denmark; Finland; France; Germany; Greece; Iceland[1]; Italy; Liechtenstein[1 2]; Luxembourg; Malta; Netherlands; Norway[1]; Portugal; Spain; Sweden; Switzerland[3].
EEA accession states (A8 states)	Czech Republic; Estonia; Hungary; Latvia; Lithuania[2]; Poland; Slovakia; Slovenia[2].
EEA accession states from 2007	The following states are expected to join the EU (and thus the EEA) on the 1 January 2007: Bulgaria[2]; Romania[2].
ECSMA or CESC states (excluding EEA states)	As at 1 April 2006 the only states other than the EEA member states that have ratified either of the treaties are: Croatia; Macedonia; Turkey.

1. Indicates not a member of the European Union.
2. Indicates has not ratified either ECSMA or CESC.
3. Switzerland is treated as part of the EEA by the EEA-Swiss agreement (para. 20.28).

SI 2006 No 1003 Reg 2(1)

20.28 The Directive applies only to nationals of member states in the European Union. However, the regulations that give it legal effect in the UK (para. 20.27) apply its provisions to EEA and Swiss nationals (table 20.2) giving them the same freedom of movement rights as other EC nationals.

ENTITLEMENT TO HB/CTB FOR EEA NATIONALS

20.29 An EEA national will only be entitled to HB/CTB if they:

- are a person who is exempt from the habitual residence test (paras. 20.57-58);
- have 'right to reside' in the UK (para. 20.33) other than the right of residence during their first three months of their stay or the right to reside as a work-seeker under Article 39 of the EC treaty (para. 20.34); and are habitually resident in the common travel area (paras. 20.61-69).

THE RIGHT TO RESIDE TEST

20.30 In order to qualify for HB/CTB a claimant will have to show that they have a right of residence in the UK, the Channel Islands, Isle of Man or the Republic of Ireland (collectively known as the Common Travel Area). Claimants without a right to reside are treated as not being habitually resident and so disqualified from HB/CTB. The test is intended to complement the habitual residence test by guarding against the possibility that a person who has no intention of working could otherwise acquire rights to benefit simply by living in the UK for a reasonably lengthy period. Strictly speaking the test applies to all claimants not just EEA nationals. However, any non-EEA national who satisfies the immigration status test clearly has right to be resident in the UK (by virtue of their leave or being 'lawfully present').

PERSONS WHO SATISFY THE RIGHT TO RESIDE TEST

HB 10(3B) HB60+ 10(4A) NIHB 10(5) NIHB60+ 10(5) CTB 7(4A) CTB60+ 7(4A)

20.31 A person will satisfy the right to reside test if they:

- are exempt from the habitual residence test (paras. 20.57-58);
- satisfy or are treated as satisfying the immigration control test (paras. 20.21-23);
- have the right to reside in the common travel area as a British or Irish Citizen (para. 20.32);
- are an EEA national from one of the 19 EEA states (excluding A8 states) identified in table 20.2 who have a right to reside as described in paragraph 20.33;
- are an EEA national from one of the accession (A8) states identified in table 20.2 who has a right to reside as described in paragraph 20.48;
- are a claimant who has transitional protection from the test (paras. 20.52-53).

BRITISH AND IRISH CITIZENS

20.32 All British and Irish citizens have the right to reside in the Common Travel Area (table 20.2). This right applies regardless of economic status or whether they were born or brought up in the Common Travel Area. Consequently the only test that will apply to these claimants is the habitual residence test (para. 20.56). Once such a person has established habitual residence they will be deemed to be habitually resident immediately on their return if they are returning to the UK after a period of absence in an EC member state (para. 20.69). The test is only therefore likely to disqualify such an applicant if they are visiting the UK for the first time (e.g. born abroad to British parents). See also paragraph 20.40 for the circumstances in which a British citizen can acquire EEA worker status and become exempt from the habitual residence test.

HB 10(2),(3)
HB60+ 10(2),(3)
NIHB 10(2),(3)
NIHB60+ 10(2),(3
CTB 7(2),(3)
CTB60+ 7(2),(3)

EEA NATIONALS WITH A RIGHT TO RESIDE WHO ARE ENTITLED TO HB/CTB

20.33 This paragraph applies to nationals of the 19 EEA states (excluding A8 nationals, for which see paragraph 20.48) identified in table 20.2. These nationals will have a right to reside and claim HB/CTB if they are:

HB 10(3B)(a)-(f)
HB60+ 10(4A)(a)-
NIHB 10(5)(a)-(f)
NIHB60+ 10(5)(a)-
CTB 7(4A)(a)-(f)
CTB60+ 7(4A)(a)-(

(a) economically active (i.e. self-employed, a worker, or treated as a worker (paras. 20.36-41));

(b) a person who has acquired a right of permanent residence (paras. 20.42-44);

(c) a work-seeker who is entitled to JSA(IB) (para. 20.35);

(d) economically inactive but considered to be self sufficient (paras. 20.54-55) and are habitually resident in the common travel area.

Note that in the case of items (a)-(c) these claimants are also exempt from the habitual residence test and so entitled to HB/CTB.

EEA NATIONALS WITH A RIGHT TO RESIDE WHO ARE NOT ENTITLED TO HB/CTB

20.34 EC Directive 2004/38/EC gives a right of residence to all economically inactive EC nationals and their family members for the first three months of their stay in the UK. In addition under Article 39 of the EC treaty work-seekers have the right to reside in a member state while actively seeking work. However, 2004/38/EC permits member states to exclude the beneficiaries of both these rights from social assistance (HB/CTB/IS/JSA(IB)/SPC), except work-seekers who are entitled to claim JSA(IB) (para. 20.35). These rules are contained in the HB/CTB regulations and apply to nationals of the EEA member states identified in table 20.2 as well as nationals of EC states (para. 20.28). Therefore, unless an

HB 10(3A)
HB60+ 10(4)
NIHB 10(4)
NIHB60+ 10(4)
CTB 7(4)
CTB60+ 7(4)

economically inactive EEA national has some other right to reside (paras. 20.41-45) or is self-sufficient (para. 20.54) they will be excluded from HB/CTB.

EEA WORK-SEEKERS

20.35 In paragraph 20.34 'work-seeker' means a national from one of the 19 EEA member states who enters the UK seeking work, rather than someone who starts work in the UK and is subsequently made unemployed (in which case see paragraph 20.41). Although work-seekers are excluded from most forms of social assistance they are entitled to JSA(IB) – a right which is established by EC case law (and which DWP concedes). A work-seeker will be entitled to HB/CTB if they are in receipt of JSA(IB). A8 nationals who are work-seekers do not have a right to reside under Article 39 of the EC treaty as work-seekers and their right is subject to self-sufficiency.

SELF-EMPLOYED EEA NATIONALS AND EEA WORKERS

HB 10(3B)(a),(b)
B60+ 10(4A)(a),(b)
NIHB 10(5)(a),(b)
HB60+ 10(5)(a),(b)
CTB 7(4A)(a),(b)
TB60+ 7(4A)(a),(b)

20.36 A self-employed person (and members of their family) who is a national of an EEA member state (including the A8 accession states) has a right to reside in the UK.

20.37 EEA nationals and their family members who are in paid employment, including nationals of the A8 accession states who are registered on the worker registration scheme, have right to reside in the UK as EEA 'workers'. The definition of 'worker' is exceptionally complex and an area of rapidly developing case law. The description which follows in paragraphs 20.38-40 below can only be regarded as a broad summary. Further, except in the case of A8 nationals (for which see paras. 20.49-50), in certain circumstances persons temporarily out of work are treated as workers (para. 20.41).

20.38 To be classed as an 'EEA worker' a person must be currently, or in certain circumstances previously have been (para. 20.41), engaged in remunerative work in the UK which is:

- 'effective and genuine'; and
- not 'on such a small scale as to be purely marginal and ancillary' *(Levin v Staatssectaris van Justitie)*.

20.39 European case law has established that no-one should be denied EEA worker status simply because they are working part-time or because they are low paid and need to supplement their income with social security benefits *(Raulin v Minister van Ondervijsen Wetenschappen)*. The DWP suggests (GM C7 Annex B para. 6) that a number of factors should be considered before the authority decides whether any work done by the claimant is 'effective and genuine'. These include:

- the period of employment;
- the number of hours worked;
- the level of earnings;
- whether the work is regular or erratic; and
- whether the person has become voluntarily unemployed.

These factors are meant to be considered as a whole. The presence or absence of any one factor is not, by itself, conclusive.

20.40 The definition of an EEA worker does not include a UK citizen who is working in the UK *(Raulin)*. Such individuals do not need to exercise rights under European law in order to be able to work in their home state. However British citizens can obtain the status of EEA worker by living and working in another EEA country and then returning to the UK.

PERSONS WHO RETAIN THEIR WORKER STATUS WHILST TEMPORARILY OUT OF WORK

20.41 EEA nationals and their family members will retain their EEA worker status if they have worked in the UK and they are:

EC/38/2004 Art 7(3)
SI 2006 No 1003
Reg 6(2)
HB 10(3B)(c)
HB60+ 10(4A)(c)
NIHB 10(5)(c)
NIHB60+ 10(5)(c)
CTB 7(4A)(c)
CTB60+ 7(4A)(c)

(a) temporarily unable to work as a result of an illness or accident;

(b) involuntarily unemployed and have embarked on a course of vocational training;

(c) unemployed (whether or not voluntarily) and have embarked on a course of vocational training related to their previous employment;

(d) registered as a job-seeker whilst involuntarily unemployed after having been employed in the UK for more than one year;

(e) registered as a job-seeker whilst involuntarily unemployed after completing a fixed term employment contract of less than one year;

(f) registered as a job-seeker whilst involuntarily unemployed after becoming unemployed during the first 12 months.

In the case of items (e) and (f) only, the worker status is retained for at least six months, in all other cases for so long as they continue to meet the conditions.

PERSONS WHO HAVE ACQUIRED A RIGHT OF PERMANENT RESIDENCE

20.42 An EEA national and a member of their family (para. 20.47) will have a right of permanent residence in the UK if:

EC/38/2004 Art 16
SI 2006 No 1003
Regs 5,15
HB 10(3B)(c)
HB60+ 10(4A)
CTB 7(4A)
CTB60+ 7(4A)

- they have lawfully resided in the UK for a continuous period (para. 20.43) of five years;
- they were working in UK until they retired from the labour market and one of the conditions in paragraph 20.44 applies.

20.43 A period of residence will count as continuous if the total length of absence from the UK in any one year does not exceed six months or longer if the absence is due to compulsory military service. A single period of absence of up to 12 consecutive months can also be treated as continuous residence if it is for important reasons such as pregnancy, child birth, serious illness, study, vocational training or a posting in another country. Once acquired, the right of permanent residence can only be lost after a period of absence from the UK which exceeds two years.

RETIRED WORKERS WITH A RIGHT OF PERMANENT RESIDENCE

2004/38/EC Art 17
SI 2006 No 1003 Reg 5
HB 10(3B)(e)
HB60+ 10(4A)(e)
NIHB 10(5)(e)
NIHB60+ 10(5)(e)
CTB 7(4A)(e)
CTB60+ 7(4A)(e)

20.44 In certain circumstances an EEA national and member of their family can acquire a right of permanent residence before completing five years employment or other lawful residence in the UK. An EEA national will acquire this right if:

- they were working in the UK and retired on or after reaching pension age (60 for a woman, 65 for a man);
- they were working in the UK prior to taking early retirement and their spouse or registered civil partner is (or was before marrying) a UK national;
- they were working in the UK for at least 12 months prior to taking early retirement and have continuously resided (or worked) in the UK for more than three years;
- they stopped working because of permanent incapacity and their spouse or registered civil partner is a UK national;
- they stopped working because of permanent incapacity and have continuously resided (or worked) in the UK for more than two years;
- they stopped working because of permanent incapacity arising from an accident at work or occupational disease for which UK incapacity or industrial injuries benefit is paid;
- they are a worker or self-employed person who after three years continuous employment in the UK, now works in another EEA state but who retains their home in the UK and returns to it at least once a week.

Note that (A8) accession state nationals can only acquire these rights after one year's continuous employment (para. 20.50).

20.45 In calculating the length of employment with respect to one of the rights above any period of involuntary unemployment registered with the Jobcentre, or period out of work due to illness, accident or some other reason 'not of [their] own making' will be treated as a period of employment.

20.46 Once the right of permanent residence has been acquired it will also apply to any family member (para. 20.47) who lives with them regardless of their nationality. A family member will also acquire a right of permanent residence if the worker or self employed person dies and either:

- the worker or self-employed person had, at the time of death, resided continuously in UK for two years;
- the death resulted from an accident at work or occupational disease;
- the surviving spouse or registered civil partner only lost their UK nationality as a result of the death of their partner.

MEANING OF FAMILY MEMBER

20.47 Where an EEA citizen has a right to reside as described in paragraphs 20.36-44 and 20.54 that right will also extend to any member of their family. In this context member of family means: 2004/38/EC Art 2(2), 3(2) SI 2006 No 1003 Reg 7,8

(a) their spouse or registered civil partner;

(b) their direct descendants who are aged under 21;

(c) the dependants of their spouse or their registered civil partner;

(d) their dependent direct relatives in ascending line (i.e. parents, grand-parents, etc) and those of their spouse or their registered civil partner;

(e) any other family members, irrespective of nationality, not included above, who in their country of origin, are dependants or members of the household of that EEA citizen, or where serious health grounds strictly require the personal care of the family member by the EEA citizen;

(f) any partner with whom the EEA citizen has a 'durable relationship, duly attested'.

A8 NATIONALS WITH A RIGHT TO RESIDE

20.48 This paragraph applies to nationals of the eight EEA accession states (A8) identified in table 20.2. These nationals will have a right to reside if: HB 10(3B)(f) HB60+ 10(4A)(f) NIHB 10(5)(f) NIHB60+ 10(5)(f) CTB 7(4A)(f) CTB60+ 7(4A)(f)

(a) they have worked legally in the UK for a uninterrupted period of at least 12 months and are economically active as described in item (a) of paragraph 20.33 above (other EEA nationals);

(b) they were granted indefinite leave to remain in the UK before 1st May 2004;

(c) they are currently self-employed in the UK;

(d) they are currently working as an employee in the UK and are registered under the Home Office 'worker registration scheme' (para. 20.49) or have applied to go on to it within the first 30 days of starting their job;

(e) they are transitionally protected (para. 20.52);

(f) they are a work-seeker or former self-employed person who is self-sufficient (paras. 20.54-55);

(g) they have worked legally in the UK for a uninterrupted period of at least 12 months and have acquired a right of permanent residence as described in paragraphs 20.42 and 20.50.

In the case of items (a) to (e) they are also exempt from the habitual residence test and so entitled to HB/CTB.

A8 NATIONALS WITH RIGHTS TO WORK IN THE UK

SI 2004 No 1219 Reg 2

20.49 Except the self-employed and those who completed a 12 month uninterrupted period of work before 1st May 2004, A8 nationals who wish to work in the UK are required to register with the Home Office under 'worker registration scheme' within 30 days of starting work (a process which is a formality). A8 nationals who are registered will qualify for HB/CTB so long as they continue to work (and for up to 30 days after finishing work). Workers who finish work and who do not find work within 30 days will be required to re-register if they start back at work again at some later date. The requirement to register will cease when they have been working in the UK for an uninterrupted period of 12 months (para. 20.50). To count as an 'uninterrupted period' the worker must not be out of work for more than a total of 30 days in the last 12 month period.

20.50 Following 12 months' uninterrupted employment in the UK (including those who were legally working in the UK prior to 1st May 2004 and who had completed an uninterrupted period of 12 months' legal work before that date), A8 nationals are treated as other EEA nationals and can acquire the same rights (e.g. the right of permanent residence (para. 20.42)).

20.51 A8 nationals who have not completed 12 months' continuous employment in the UK and who are not in work (e.g. students, pensioners, others incapable of work through sickness or disability) or who are seeking work will not have the right to reside in the UK unless they are self-sufficient (para. 20.54).

TRANSITIONAL PROTECTION FROM THE RIGHT TO RESIDE TEST

;PR sch 3 para 6(4) NICPR sch 3 para 6(3)

20.52 A claimant will be transitionally protected from the rights of residence test if they were entitled to HB/CTB on 30th April 2004 (including a claim backdated to that date) and have remained continuously entitled to at least one of the following benefits: HB, CTB, IS, JSA(IB) or the guarantee credit, since. Note that continuous entitlement to HB or CTB will likewise preserve protection for IS, JSA or the guarantee credit.

20.53 The main beneficiaries of transitional protection are expected to be nationals from the 19 EEA states who entered the UK while economically inactive (e.g. students, people incapable of work).

STUDENTS AND OTHER SELF-SUFFICIENT EEA NATIONALS

20.54 Most economically inactive EEA citizens including students not covered by a right described in paragraphs 20.41-44 above are excluded from HB/CTB. An EEA citizen, or their family member, will however, have the right to reside in the common travel area and so are not excluded from HB/CTB if they are self sufficient. Students will however be excluded unless they are a member of an eligible group (para. 21.24 and table 21.1).

EC/38/2004 Art 7(1),(2)
SI 2006 No 1003 Reg 4(1)(c), 6(1)(d),14(1)
HB 10(3)
HB60+ 10(3)
CTB 7(3)
CTB60+ 7(3)

20.55 A person will be considered self-sufficient if they have comprehensive sickness insurance and they can persuade the benefit authorities that they have sufficient resources for themselves and their family not to become 'a burden on the social assistance system'. Whether a person is a burden will depend on the personal circumstances of the applicant (GM C7.238). The guidance manual states that persons 'who have no prospect of finding work or becoming self sufficient' will normally be considered a burden (GM C7.239). DWP guidance also suggests that a person who first claims benefit after having been in the UK for some time, the fact that they have been self sufficient will be a factor in the decision, as will the length of time they are likely to be claiming benefits (GM C7.239).

The habitual residence test

20.56 Unless they are exempt (paras. 20.57-58) all claimants, irrespective of their nationality, have to satisfy the authority that they are 'habitually resident' in the United Kingdom, the Channel Islands, the Isle of Man or the Republic of Ireland to be entitled to HB/CTB. A person who is not habitually resident is a 'person from abroad' and not entitled to HB/CTB.

HB 10(2)
HB60+ 10(2)
NIHB 10(2)
NIHB60+ 10(2)
CTB 7(2)
CTB60+ 7(2)

EXEMPT CLAIMANTS

20.57 The following claimants, whether or not they are EEA nationals, are exempt from the habitual residence test:

- a person aged under 60 in receipt of income support or income-based jobseeker's allowance;
- a person aged 60 or over in receipt of state pension credit;
- a refugee;
- a person granted exceptional leave (including humanitarian protection or discretionary leave) (paras. 20.12 and 20.60);
- a person who left the territory of Montserrat after 1st November 1995 because of the volcanic eruption;

HB 10(3B)(g)-(k),(4
HB60+ 10(4A)(g)-(k),(5)
NIHB 10(5)(g)-(k),(
NIHB60+ 10(5)(g)-(k),(6)
CTB 7(4A)(g)-(k),(5
CTB60+ 7(4A)(g)-(k),(5)

- a person not subject to immigration control and who is in the UK as a result of their deportation, expulsion or removal by compulsion of law from another country to the UK;
- persons whose funds have been temporarily disrupted.

HB 10(3B)(a)-(f)
HB60+ 10(4A)(a)-(f)
NIHB 10(5)(a)-(f)
NIHB60+ 10(5)(a)-(f)
CTB 7(4A)(a)-(f)
CTB60+ 7(4A)(a)-(f)

20.58 In addition, the following EEA nationals (para. 20.33, items a-c) are also exempt:

- a person who is self-employed, a 'worker' (paras. 20.36-37) or a former worker who has retained worker status while temporarily out of work (para. 20.41);
- a person who is a 'family member' (para. 20.47) of any person referred to in item (a) above;
- a person who has acquired a right of permanent residence (para. 20.42);
- a person who is an A8 national who is working in the UK (or was within the last 30 days) and is registered under the Home Office Worker Registration Scheme.

20.59 DWP guidance suggests that the test should be applied to anyone who has entered the Common Travel Area in the last two years (GM C7.100). However, the guidance also stresses that in deciding whether a person is habitually resident authorities should take account of a number of factors (para. 20.64) the result of which may be that the test is satisfied immediately on entry to the country (see GM C7.172).

PERSONS WITH EXCEPTIONAL LEAVE TO ENTER OR REMAIN

20.60 Exceptional leave is a form of leave granted by the Home Secretary outside the normal immigration rules on humanitarian grounds to persons who have not also made a claim for asylum. (Asylum seekers instead may be granted humanitarian protection or discretionary leave – which technically are also forms of exceptional leave (para. 20.12)).

The meaning of 'habitual residence'

20.61 The term 'habitual residence' is not defined in the regulations. The DWP (GM C7.170) described the term as 'intended to convey a degree of permanence in the [claimant's] residence in the Common Travel Area'. The term 'habitual residence' arises in European legislation, in particular EEC Regulation 1408/71 dealing with social security for migrant workers, and in family law.

'HABITUAL RESIDENCE' IN EUROPEAN SOCIAL SECURITY LAW

20.62 In *Angenjeux v. Hakenberg* the court ruled that 'the place where one habitually resides must be understood in the case of a business representative

[…] as the place in which he has established the permanent centre of his interests and to which he returns in the intervals between his tours'. In *Di Paolo v Office National de l'Emploi* the court ruled that where a person habitually resides also corresponds with where the habitual centre of his interests is situated. The court also ruled that account should be taken of the length and continuity of residence before the person concerned moved, the length and purpose of his absence, the nature of the occupation found in the other member state and the intention of the person concerned as it appears from all the circumstances.

20.63 The judgment in the Di Paolo case emphasised that whenever a worker has stable employment in a member state there is a presumption that he resides there, even if he has left his family in another state.

20.64 The authority must establish the relevant facts on which it can make a decision as to whether or not someone is 'habitually resident'. Drawing on the relevant European case law, the DWP suggests (GM C7.175) that the authority, in deciding this question, should consider the following factors:

- length and continuity of residence;
- future intentions;
- employment prospects;
- reasons for coming to the UK; and
- centre of interest (i.e. the intention to follow a settled way of life in the UK and the ties they have formed (GM C7.220)).

'HABITUAL RESIDENCE' IN FAMILY LAW

20.65 The prime authority on the ordinary and natural meaning of 'habitual residence' is the speech of Lord Brandon in *Re J (A Minor) (Abduction)*. This was a case on the Convention on the Civil Aspects of International Child Abduction. Lord Brandon emphasised that 'there is a significant difference between a person ceasing to be habitually resident in country A, and his subsequently becoming habitually resident in country B. A person may cease to be habitually resident in country A in a single day if he or she leaves it with a settled intention not to return to it but to take up long-term residence in country B instead. Such a person cannot, however, become habitually resident in country B in a single day. An appreciable period of time and a settled intention will be necessary to enable him or her to become so.'

PERSUASIVE COMMISSIONER'S DECISIONS

20.66 There are a number of Commissioner's decisions relating to the test of habitual residence within the income support scheme that must be considered persuasive for HB/CTB purposes. These decisions have adopted the key criteria of 'an appreciable period of time' and a 'settled intention'. The following key points arose from CIS 1067/1995:

- residence implies a more settled state than mere physical presence, thereby excluding short stay visitors;
- to be a resident the claimant must be seen to be making a home here;
- the home need not be his or her only home, nor need it be intended to be a permanent one, but it must be a genuine home for the time being;
- the length, continuity and general nature of a claimant's actual residence are more important than his or her intentions as to the future;
- a person may abandon habitual residence in a single day but this does not mean that he or she becomes a habitual resident of another country to which he or she intends to move;
- an appreciable period of time, as well as a settled intention, is necessary to enable the claimant to become habitually resident; and
- what counts as an 'appreciable period of time' must depend on the facts in each case; it must, however, be the kind of period which demonstrates a settled and stable pattern of living as a resident.

20.67 Commissioner's Decision CIS/2326/1995 agreed with the main points of CIS 1067/l995. It emphasised, however, that no particular periods should be mentioned as amounting to an appreciable period of time except in relation to actual cases that arise for decision. The Commissioner considered that the question in each individual case must be whether, in all the circumstances, including the settledness of the person's intentions as to residence, the residence has continued for a sufficient period for it to be said to be habitual.

UK COURT DECISIONS

20.78 The House of Lords upheld the Commissioner decision in CIS 2326/1995. It found that an appreciable period of time of actual residence is needed to establish habitual residence for people coming to the UK for the first time *(Nessa v Chief Adjudication Officer)* whereas the European Court of Justice in *Swaddling v Chief Adjudication Officer* has ruled that a UK claimant who had returned to Britain after living and working in France for several years could not have his right to benefit made subject to any period of actual residence here after his return by the 'habitual residence' test.

20.69 The DWP accepts that people returning to the UK from an EU member state and re-establishing their ties here should be treated as habitually resident immediately upon their return (GM C7.150). Authorities should do the same. Indeed, the DWP has gone further than the principle established in the European Court case. The DWP advises authorities (GM C7.151) to extend the effect of the judgment to people of any nationality returning from any country overseas and re-establishing their ties in the UK, Republic of Ireland, Channel Islands or Isle of Man. In other words, they should be treated as habitually resident immediately on return. However, this advice conflicts with other DWP Guidance (Decision Makers Guide 071209-071211) and with other case law, and is probably wrong.

21 Students

21.1 This chapter describes the rules used in assessing HB and CTB for students. It covers:

- who is a 'student';
- which students can get HB and CTB;
- how their income is assessed; and
- other special rules applying in their case.

21.2 The student figures in this chapter (for loans, grants and disregards) are for the 2005-06 academic year and are taken from DWP circular HB/CTB A13/2005. Figures for the 2006-07 academic year are expected to be published in about August 2006.

21.3 As described in this chapter, the student rules vary between HB and CTB, and also between main CTB and second adult rebate.

Who counts as a 'student'?

21.4 For the HB/CTB student rules to apply, the person in question must be a 'student'. The definition is given below. Other important terms are defined after that. Paragraph 21.22 compares these with the definitions used in council tax law – which are different.

DEFINITION OF 'STUDENT'

HB 2(1),53,54,58
NIHB 2(1),50,51,55
CTB 2(1),43,44

21.5 For HB and CTB purposes, a student is defined as any person 'who is attending or undertaking a course of study at an educational establishment… [or a New Deal qualifying course]'. This includes:

- study at any level (from school onwards) whether full-time or part-time;
- students with or without loans or grants;
- both state-funded and private establishments; and
- both term-times and vacations.

Some special cases are mentioned below.

21.6 Once a course has started, a person carries on counting as a student until their course finishes or they abandon it or are dismissed from it. So someone does count as a student during the Christmas and Easter vacations and any summer vacation(s) occurring within the course, even if they take up full-time work then.

But someone does not count as a student during the summer vacation after the end of a course or between two different courses.

STUDENTS WITH PARTNERS

21.7 In the case of a couple, the HB and CTB rules vary depending on whether one or both are students and which partner makes the claim. Details are given as each rule is described (and see table 21.2). HB 54,58 NIHB 51,55 CTB 44

INTERCALATED PERIODS

21.8 Although the general rule is that a person must be 'attending or undertaking' the course to count as a 'student', a person continues to count as a 'student' during 'intercalated periods': *O'Connor v Chief Adjudication Officer.* An intercalated period is one during which a student temporarily suspends attendance, for example because of sickness or for personal reasons, but still remains registered with his or her educational establishment.

SANDWICH COURSES

21.9 People on sandwich courses do count as students – both when they are studying and during their periods of work experience. HB 53(1) NIHB 50(10 CTB 43(1)

HEALTH CARE STUDENTS

21.10 The following count as students if (as is almost always the case) they fit the definition given above (para. 21.5):

- students undertaking nursing and midwifery diploma courses;
- NHS-funded students undertaking degree programmes.

QUALIFYING COURSES UNDER THE NEW DEAL

21.11 Studying on a 'qualifying course' is one of the options under the New Deal (paras. 13.62-63) for certain people. Such people count as students.

21.12 Most people on a 'qualifying course' receive income-based jobseeker's allowance: in their case, all their income and capital is disregarded for HB and main CTB purposes (and they are eligible for HB and CTB: table 21.1). In the case of someone on a qualifying course not getting JSA(IB) or IS, please see the 2005-06 edition of this Guide.

TRAINING SCHEMES

21.13 People on the New Deal (except as described above) do not count as students; nor do people on other government training schemes. The question of whether anyone else on a training scheme counts as a student is decided by reference to the definition of 'student' quoted above: they usually do not count as a student. HB 53(1) NIHB 50(1) CTB 43(1)

'Full-time' *versus* 'part-time' students

21.14 Some of the HB and CTB rules apply to both full-time and part-time students; some apply only to full-time students. Details are given as each rule is described.

GENERAL CASES

HB 53(1) NIHB 50(1) CTB 43(1)

21.15 There is no general-purpose definition of 'full-time' (or 'part-time'). Some special cases do have definitions (as in the next few paragraphs). In any other case, the law goes no further and authorities usually rely on factors such as how the educational establishment and local education authority treat the course. DWP advice (GM chapter C5, annex A, para. C5.08) is to consult the educational establishment or be guided by receipt of a student loan.

FURTHER EDUCATION COURSES

HB 53(1) NIHB 50(1) CTB 43(1)

21.16 A student studying at a further education college counts as a full-time student if (and only if) their course involves:

- in England, more than 16 hours per week of 'guided learning', as set out in the 'learning agreement' obtainable from their college;
- in Wales, more than 16 hours per week of 'guided learning', as set out in a college document;
- in Scotland:
  - more than 16 hours of classroom-based or workshop-based 'guided learning', or
  - more than 21 hours per week of a combination of that and additional hours using structured learning packages,

as set out (in either case) in a college document. There is no such specific rule in Northern Ireland.

SANDWICH COURSES

HB 53(1) NIHB 50(1) CTB 43(1)

21.17 All students on sandwich courses count as full-time.

MODULAR COURSES

HB 53(2),(4) NIHB 50(2),(4) CTB 43(2),(4)

21.18 A modular course is one which contains two or more modules, a specified number of which have to be completed in order to complete the course. They often permit full-time, part-time or mixed attendance. In such cases, a student counts as full-time only during the parts of the course for which he or she is registered as full-time (so a student in fact changing from full-time in, say, her second year to part-time in her third would count for HB/CTB purposes as part-time in her third year).

RETAKES ON MODULAR COURSES

21.19 The following applies only to the parts of modular courses that count as full-time for HB/CTB purposes. If someone fails a module or an exam in such a case, he or she continues to count as full-time for any period in which he or she continues to attend or undertake the course for the purposes of retaking the exam or module (including any vacations within that period other than vacations after the end of the course). HB 53(3) NIHB 50(3) CTB 43(3)

Other definitions

HIGHER EDUCATION

21.20 Whether a student is in higher education or not is one of the main descriptions used in HB and CTB to distinguish different levels of education. Higher education is defined as meaning: HB 53,56 NIHB 50,53 CTB 43,45

- first degree, postgraduate and higher degree courses;
- courses for the further training of teachers and youth and community workers;
- courses for the Diploma of Higher Education, the BTEC/SVEC Higher National Diploma (HND) or Higher National Certificate (HNC), the Diploma in Management Studies, or the Certificate in Education;
- any other courses at a level higher than GCE A level or BTEC/SVEC Ordinary National Diploma (OND) or Ordinary National Certificate (ONC), whether or not leading to a qualification.

PERIOD OF STUDY AND SUMMER VACATION

21.21 Some of the rules refer to a student's period of study: HB 53(1) NIHB 50(1) CTB 43(1)

- the period of study for any course requiring more than 45 weeks study in a year (e.g. for many postgraduate courses) runs from the first day of the academic year to the day before the first day of the next academic year. The course is treated as not having a summer vacation;
- for courses of less than one year, the period of study is the whole of the course;
- in all other cases, the period of study runs from the first day of the academic year to the last day before the summer vacation (or in the final year of a course of more than one year, to the last day of the course). This usually means three terms plus the Christmas and Easter vacations;
- subject to the above points, for students on sandwich courses, periods of work experience are included in the period of study.

HB AND CTB DEFINITIONS *VERSUS* COUNCIL TAX DEFINITIONS

21.22 For council tax purposes, four groups of people – including certain foreign language assistants and student nurses – are defined in the law as being 'students' (categories 5 to 8 in appendix 6). These council tax definitions are relevant for considering whether a dwelling is completely exempt from council tax (para. 9.11) whether a council taxpayer can get a discount (para. 9.16) and who can get 'student only' second adult rebate (para. 8.3). The council tax definitions rather than the HB and CTB definitions are also used for certain purposes to do with second adult rebate (chapter 8). But for all the HB and CTB rules described in this chapter, the council tax definitions are irrelevant: only the definitions given earlier are relevant.

21.23 There is some overlap between the council tax definitions and the HB and CTB definitions. For example, a person who counts as a 'student' in council tax law (apart from a foreign language assistant) is usually a 'student' in HB and CTB law. However, this does not guarantee that he or she will count as a 'full-time student' (category 10 in appendix 6). (For example, there are small but growing numbers of further education students who count as full-time for council tax purposes but not for HB/CTB purposes – usually because of the nature of their studies.) Matters such as these depend on the individual circumstances of the case.

Which students can get HB and CTB?

21.24 To be eligible for HB or main CTB a student must satisfy the following rules. None of the rules affects eligibility for second adult rebate.

WHICH STUDENTS ARE ELIGIBLE?

HB 8(1)(e),56 **21.25** Students cannot get HB or main CTB unless they fall within certain groups.
NIHB 8(1)(e),53 This rule does not apply to second adult rebate. The rule works as follows:
CTB 45

- Students aged 60 or more (or who have a partner who is) are always eligible for HB and main CTB.
- Students who are single claimants are eligible for HB and main CTB only if they are in one (or more) of the groups in table 21.1.
- Students who are lone parents are in all cases eligible for HB and main CTB.
- Couples are eligible for HB and main CTB in all cases unless both are students and neither of them is in any of the groups in table 21.1. (Information about which partner should claim is given below.)

Table 21.1: HB and main CTB eligible groups

- All students who are currently receiving income support or income-based jobseeker's allowance (but student eligibility for IS and JSA(IB) is also restricted).
- All part-time students.
- Students under 19 not in higher education.
- Students under 20 for whom child benefit is payable.
- Students aged 60 or more or whose partners are.
- Students (couples or lone parents) who are responsible for a child or young person.
- Single students who are responsible for a foster child.
- Students who qualify for a disability premium (para. 12.12).
- Students who are disqualified from incapacity benefit.
- Students who have been incapable of work for 28 weeks or more.*
- Students whose grant assessment (if made by an English, Welsh, Scottish or Northern Ireland grant-awarding body) includes a disabled student's allowance for deafness.
- Students who were absent, with the consent of their educational establishment, due to illness or because of providing care for another person, and who have now ceased to be ill or providing care, and who are now not eligible for a grant or loan – but in this case only from the date of ceasing to be ill or providing care until the day before resuming the course (or, if earlier, the day their establishment agrees they can resume it) – and only up to a maximum of one year.

Note

* 'Incapable of work' means what it does for incapacity benefit purposes (para. 12.17). The student is not eligible during the first 28 weeks of incapacity for work – referred to here as a 'qualifying period'.

In calculating the qualifying period, periods of incapacity for work are added together if they are separated by gaps of eight weeks or less.

Once the qualifying period is completed, the student is eligible. After a gap (i.e. a period in which the student is capable of work or is disqualified from incapacity benefit) of eight weeks or less, the student does not have to start a new qualifying period: he or she becomes eligible again straightaway. But after a gap of more than eight weeks, the student is not eligible until he or she has completed a fresh qualifying period.

WHICH PARTNER IN A COUPLE SHOULD CLAIM?

HB 8(1)(e),56
NIHB 8(1)(e),53
CTB 45

21.26 Table 21.2 explains which partner in a couple is eligible to claim HB and main CTB on behalf of both. In all cases where a claim may be made, it takes into account the income, capital and applicable amount relating to them both. Authorities which receive claims from the 'wrong partner' (i.e. in the cases in the second and fifth rows of the table) should return the application form with an explanation and a suggestion that the other partner should be the claimant.

STUDENTS WHO MAINTAIN TWO HOMES

HB 7(3),(5)(b)
NIHB 7(3),(6)(b)

21.27 Some students have to maintain two homes, one near their educational establishment and one elsewhere. There are special rules for students in these circumstances which apply for HB purposes only:

- students without partners (i.e. single claimants and lone parents) can, if they are in one of the eligible groups in table 21.1, get HB on only one home (paras. 3.26);
- for couples, the rules are given in table 21.2 and paragraph 3.28.

There are other rules about HB on two homes (para. 3.6) which apply in addition to these. For CTB there are no special rules for students maintaining two homes.

HALLS OF RESIDENCE, ETC

HB 53,57
NIHB 50,54

21.28 In addition to the previous rules, students are eligible for HB on halls of residence and any other accommodation where the rent is payable to the establishment they attend only as follows:

- Full-time students (including couples, whether one or both is a full-time student) can get HB on such accommodation (so long as they are in an eligible group: table 21.1). This applies at any point in the year.
- Part-time students (including couples so long as the other one is not a full-time student) cannot get HB on such accommodation unless:
  - it is their summer vacation; or
  - they would fall into one of the eligible groups (table 21.1) if they were full-time students; or
  - the establishment genuinely collects the rent merely on behalf of, or rents the accommodation itself from, some other person or body.

Table 21.2: Summary: student couples: HB and main CTB

The 'eligible groups' referred to in this table are those listed in table 21.1

Partner A	Partner B	Who can claim HB and main CTB?	HB on two homes?
◆ Student in the eligible groups	Student in the eligible groups	Either	Yes on both, if reasonable, and if maintaining two is unavoidable
◆ Student in the eligible groups	Student not in the eligible groups	Partner A only *(see notes 1, 2)*	Only on the home occupied by partner A
◆ Student in the eligible groups	Non-student	Either	Yes on both, if reasonable, and if maintaining two is unavoidable
◆ Student not in the eligible groups	Student not in the eligible groups	Neither *(see note 1)*	Not on either
◆ Student not in the eligible groups	Non-student	Partner B only *(see notes 1, 3)*	Only on the home occupied by partner B
◆ Non-student	Non-student	Either	Student rules do not apply

Notes

1. But (in each of these cases) if either partner is aged 60+, either may claim.
2. 'A' must also be liable for council tax to get main CTB.
3. 'B' must also be liable for council tax to get main CTB.

21.29 This rule applies to any accommodation which the establishment owns, leases under a lease granted for more than 21 years, or rents from another educational establishment or an education authority. It does not apply (i.e. the students are eligible for HB) if the establishment itself rents accommodation on a temporary basis from a council, housing association or private landlord and then sublets it to its students – unless it has arranged this in order to take advantage of the HB scheme.

21.30 There is no equivalent rule in CTB. This is because halls of residence are exempt from council tax (para. 9.11).

ABSENCE DURING THE SUMMER VACATION

HB 55 NIHB 52 **21.31** Finally, full-time students are not eligible for HB on their term-time accommodation if they are absent from it during the summer vacation. The rule does not apply unless the student is absent for at least one Sunday/Monday midnight. Once the rule applies, it continues to apply (but only during the summer vacation) until the end of the benefit week in which the student returns to the accommodation. (This is because of the ordinary rules about start of entitlement to HB: chapter 5.) This rule never applies to part-time students, and for couples it applies only if both are full-time students.

21.32 Furthermore the rule applies only if the student's main purpose in occupying the accommodation during his or her period of study is to facilitate attendance on the course. Authorities should take into account any other relevant factor in reaching a decision. For example, if the student lived in the accommodation before starting the course, or moved to the area to be near relatives, or is a council or housing association tenant, it is unlikely that the main purpose of occupying the home is to attend the course.

21.33 There is no equivalent rule in CTB. There may therefore be rare cases in which a student is eligible only for CTB during a period of absence from his or her term-time accommodation.

TERMLY PAYMENT OF HB

HB 92(5),(7) NIHB 88(5),(7) **21.34** The authority may pay a student's HB once a term. However, if the student is entitled to more than £2.00 HB per week, he or she can insist on being paid under the normal rules about frequency of payment (paras. 16.21-25). This rule applies to full-time and part-time students, and to couples where either or both are students. In practice it is never used.

Assessing HB and main CTB for students

STUDENTS OR PARTNERS AGED 60+

21.35 In the case of a student who is aged 60 or more, or a student whose partner is aged 60 or more, all student income (grants, loans, hardship funds, etc) is disregarded in the assessment of HB and main CTB. (Such students are always eligible for HB and main CTB: para. 21.25.) HB60+ 29(1) NIHB60+ 27(1) CTB60+ 19(1)

OTHER STUDENTS

21.36 For any other student who is eligible (paras. 21.24-33) there are special rules about the assessment of student loans as income and about how grant and other student income is assessed for HB and main CTB purposes. This chapter describes these.

Student loan income

WHO CAN GET A STUDENT LOAN?

21.37 With the exceptions mentioned in the following paragraph, all full-time UK students in higher education are eligible to apply for a student loan. Parents, partners and students themselves may, depending on the circumstances, be assessed as having to make a contribution to a student loan.

21.38 Part-time students and students undertaking nursing and midwifery diploma courses (para. 21.10) are never eligible for a student loan; and the following are not normally eligible for a student loan:

- postgraduates (except that students studying for a Postgraduate Certificate of Education (PGCE) are eligible for a student loan);
- students aged 50 or more.

The situation is complex in these two cases, and it is advisable for an authority to enquire of the student himself or herself as to whether he or she can get a student loan, and to seek supporting documentation as appropriate.

AMOUNTS

21.39 In the 2005-06 academic year, for students living away from home, the maximum student loan is shown in table 21.3. The figures for NHS-funded students are lower (and may be found in DWP circular HB/CTB A13/2005).

ASSESSMENT

21.40 In calculating HB and main CTB, all students who are eligible to apply for a student loan are treated as receiving one at the maximum level applicable to HB 64 NIHB 61 CTB 51 them (as shown in table 21.3) if they ‘could acquire [a student loan] in respect of that year by taking reasonable steps to do so’. This is done regardless of whether they actually apply for a student loan and/or actually receive one. In the case of a couple this means taking up to two student loans into account as appropriate.

HB 53,59,64
NIHB 50,56,61
CTB 43,47,51

21.41 The student loan is then assessed for HB and main CTB purposes as shown in table 21.3 (and an example also follows). Table 21.3 covers all the main types of student course. Further variations are given in paragraphs 21.52 onwards, covering students who fall within the ‘old rules’, courses that start other than in autumn and students who leave part way through their course.

HB 66(1),67
NIHB 63(1),64
CTB 53,54

21.42 If a student loan is assessed on the assumption that the student, or his or her partner, will make a contribution, the amount of that contribution is disregarded from the student’s or partner’s other income. (There may also be circumstances in which a parent who makes a contribution can have that amount disregarded in the assessment of his or her own HB and main CTB: para. 13.120.)

REPAYING A STUDENT LOAN

HB sch 5 para 12
CTB sch 4 para 13

21.43 If someone else repays a former student’s student loan, that payment (whether made to the student or direct to the Student Loans Company) is disregarded as that student’s income. This includes DfES payments under the ‘Teacher Repayment Loan Scheme’ – and any other such payments. However, when a student himself or herself repays a student loan this is not disregarded from his or her other income for HB/CTB purposes; also, there is no similar rule in Northern Ireland.

Student grant income

HB 59(1)
NIHB 63(1)
CTB 46(1)

21.44 The rules for assessing grant income apply to any kind of educational grant, award, scholarship, studentship, exhibition, allowance or bursary, whether paid by an education authority or anyone else. In the 2005-06 academic year, the main grant figures for education authority grants may be found in DWP circular HB/CTB A13/2005.

ASSESSMENT

HB 53,59,63,64
NIHB 50,56,60,61
CTB 43,46,50,51

21.45 Grant income is assessed for HB and main CTB purposes as shown in table 21.4.

HB 66(1),67
NIHB 63(1),64
CTB 53,54

21.46 If a student’s grant is assessed on the assumption that the student, or his or her partner, will make a contribution, the amount of that contribution is disregarded from the student’s or partner’s other income. (Similarly, a parent who makes a contribution has that amount disregarded in the assessment of his or her own HB and main CTB: para. 13.120.)

Other income

ACCESS FUND PAYMENTS OR HARDSHIP FUND PAYMENTS

21.47 'Access fund payments' (also known as 'hardship fund payments') are administered by educational establishments, who may make payments to: HB 53(1) NIHB 50(1) CTB 43(1)

- students who fall within the student loan scheme (para. 21.37);
- postgraduates (of all kinds); and
- students aged 19 or more in further education.

The rules about access fund payments apply identically to payments from the Welsh Assembly's financial contingency funds.

21.48 Access fund payments are treated as follows: HB 65,68(2)-(4), sch 5 para 34 NIHB 62,65(2)-(4), sch 6 para 36 CTB 52,55(2)-(4), sch 4 para 35

- if they meet costs which are not met through a grant, but would be disregarded if they were met through a grant (as in table 21.4), they are disregarded in full;
- any other regular payments towards certain necessities (defined below) are:
  - disregarded in full as income if they are made before the student's course begins and are made in anticipation of the person becoming a student;
  - disregarded in full as income if they are made on or after 1st September (or the first day of the course if later) to tide a student over till receipt of his or her student loan;
  - in any other case, treated as income (averaged over the period they cover), then £20 per week is disregarded (subject to the over-riding £20.00 limit on certain disregards: para. 13.147).
- regular payments towards any other amount are completely disregarded;
- single lump sum payments are treated as capital; but if they are for certain necessities (defined below), the capital is disregarded for 52 weeks from the date of payment.

21.49 The 'certain necessities' mentioned above are food, ordinary clothing and footwear, household fuel, eligible rent (apart from any amount attributable to non-dependant deductions), council tax or water charges – of the claimant or any member of the family.

Table 21.3: Student loans: 2005-06 academic year

AMOUNTS	**Final year**	**Other years**	**Per extra week**
Courses in London:	£4,490	£5,175	£96
Courses outside London:	£3,645	£4,195	£75

Note: Figures are for English, Welsh and Scottish students living away from home in the 2005-06 academic year. In each case, they are the maximum amount a student could obtain. The figures do not apply to NHS-funded courses or to nursing and midwifery diploma students. Figures are taken from DWP circular HB/CTB A13/2005.

TREATMENT FOR HB/MAIN CTB PURPOSES

(a) Take the whole amount into account as income (even though it is in fact a loan). Include any amount from extra weeks. Treat any parental or partner's assumed contribution to it as being received (even if not actually paid).

(b) Disregard £632 in all cases. This is a standard amount including £280 towards travel and £352 towards books and equipment.

(c) Average the resulting amount over the period described below.

(d) Then disregard £10 from the weekly figure (in the case of a couple, disregard £10 from each one's weekly figure), subject to the over-riding £20 limit on certain disregards (para. 13.147).

PERIOD OVER WHICH THE LOAN IS AVERAGED

General rule

Average over the period from the first Monday in September to the last Sunday in June. (In 2005-06 this is 42 weeks: 5.9.05 to 25.6.06.)

Exceptions

First years only: If the course begins after the first Monday in September, still average over the period described above, but then ignore it as income for the week(s) before the course begins.

Final years and one-year courses only: Average over the period from the first Monday in September to the last Sunday in the course.

All years (but likely to apply only in Scotland): If any year of the course starts before the first Monday in September, average over the period from the first Monday in the course to the last Sunday in June (or, in final year and one-year courses, the last Sunday in the course).

Further exceptions and special cases are given in paras. 21.52 onwards.

Example: A student loan

In the 2005-06 academic year, a student in his second year of a degree course in Wales could get a student loan of £4,195. (He is not in receipt of a grant of any kind.) His wife is not a student and has claimed HB and CTB for them both. His student loan is assessed as follows in the assessment of his wife's HB/CTB claim.

Whether or not he applies for or receives it, he is treated as receiving it and it is assessed as follows (see also table 21.3):

(a) Treat the whole £4,195 as income (even though it is in fact a loan).

(b) Disregard £632 for books and equipment and travel, leaving £3,563.

(c) Average this over the 42 weeks from 5.9.05 to 25.6.06, which is £84.83 per week.

(d) Disregard £10, which gives £74.83 per week.

So this student has student loan income of £74.83 per week from 5.9.05 to 25.6.06. This is the case even if his second year did not start until a date in October 2005. (But if he had been a first year, the £74.83 per week would have been ignored as income until the first Monday in his first year.)

Table 21.4: Student grants: 2005-06 academic year

TREATMENT FOR HB/MAIN CTB PURPOSES

(a) Treat any parental or partner's assumed contribution to it as being received (even if not actually paid).

(b) No standard disregard is made for travel or for books and equipment – unless the student neither receives nor is treated as receiving a student loan, in which case disregard £632. (But see also step (c).)

(c) Disregard any amount included in the grant for the following:

- all amounts because the student has a disability;
- all amounts for books and equipment and/or for travel (in addition to the standard £632 if appropriate);
- all amounts for child care (including, for example, parents learning allowance, child care grant, dependants' additions for children, allowance for lone parents with formal childcare costs, etc);
- education maintenance awards (para. 13.121);
- the higher education grant;
- the National Assembly for Wales' learning grant;
- the adult learner's grant;
- tuition or examination fees;
- expenses for term-time residential study;
- two homes grant;
- additions for anyone outside the UK so long as the student's applicable amount does not include an amount for that person.

(d) Average the resulting amount over the period described below.

PERIOD OVER WHICH THE GRANT IS AVERAGED

Awards for adult dependant(s) from an education authority or government department

Average over the same period as the student loan (table 21.3: the general rule and exceptions all apply).

Care leavers grant

Average over the summer vacation only, ignoring any part weeks.

Grants for day-to-day maintenance and any other amount (other than the disregarded amounts)

If it is attributable to the student's period of study (para. 21.21): Average over the period from the first Monday to the last Sunday in that period of study omitting, for sandwich students, any benefit weeks falling wholly or partly within the period of work experience.

If it is attributable to any other period: Average over the period from the first Monday to the last Sunday in that period.

Exceptions

Nursing and midwifery diploma students: They may get a bursary towards their maintenance (and cannot get a student loan). Their bursary (after any appropriate disregards) is averaged over the full calendar year (52/53 weeks).

NHS-funded students on degree courses: They may get a bursary towards their maintenance (and can get a student loan at a lower rate than other students). Their bursary (after any appropriate disregards) is averaged over the full calendar year (52/53 weeks) – and their loan is dealt with as in table 21.3.

OTHER INCOME

21.50 If a full-time or part-time student receives earned or unearned income other than (or as well as) grant or covenant income or a student loan, the ordinary earned and unearned income disregards apply to it (chapters 13-15).

THE EXTRA STUDENT INCOME DISREGARD

21.51 In addition to the above points, there is a further disregard for student expenditure, which works as follows. If the student has loan or grant income, certain amounts are disregarded from it, as shown in tables 21.3 and 21.4. If the student necessarily spends more on those items than the amounts indicated in the tables, the excess is disregarded from his or her other income (as illustrated in the example). This important disregard is often overlooked: students are advised to check that it has been applied properly. HB 63 NIHB 60 CTB 50

Example: The extra student income disregard

A student receives a student loan. In the assessment of the loan for HB/CTB purposes, £352 is disregarded towards books and equipment and £280 towards travel. She is not in receipt of any grant for travel, but can satisfy the authority that her actual travel costs for the year will be £700 (£420 more). She uses money from a part-time job to pay for this.

The additional £420 per year for travel is disregarded in assessing her income from her part-time job (as well as any other earned income disregards which may apply: paras. 14.20-21 and 14.30). There is no particular rule for which weeks to allow this in. Since her loan income has to be averaged over 42 weeks, it may be fair to average this £420 over those 42 weeks.

Special cases

COURSES THAT START OTHER THAN IN AUTUMN

HB 53(1),64(2) NIHB 50(1),61(3) CTB 43(1),51(2)

21.52 The following rules cater for courses that do not start in the autumn. They use the concepts 'academic year' (as defined in para. 21.56) and 'quarter' (as defined in para. 21.55) in ways that do not always match day-to-day expectations.

21.53 For students whose 'academic year' (para. 21.56) begins on 1st September, their loan is averaged over the benefit weeks falling wholly within the ten months from 1st September to 30th June, both dates inclusive (as described in table 21.3).

21.54 But for students whose 'academic year' (para. 21.56) begins on 1st January, 1st April or 1st July, their loan is averaged over the benefit weeks falling wholly within:

- the whole academic year beginning on that date;
- but excluding the whole of the 'quarter' (para. 21.55) in which, 'in the opinion of the Secretary of State', the longest of any vacation is taken.

DEFINITION OF 'QUARTER'

HB 64(2)(b) NIHB 61(3)(B) CTB 51(2)(b)

21.55 For the purposes of the above rules, the following (despite the fact that they are of different lengths in two cases) are the four 'quarters':

- 1st January to 31st March (3 months);
- 1st April to 30th June (3 months);
- 1st July to 31st August (2 months);
- 1st September to 31st December (4 months).

DEFINITION OF 'ACADEMIC YEAR'

21.56 For the purposes of the above rules, 'academic year' means the twelve months beginning on: HB 53(1) NIHB 50(1) CTB 43(1)

- 1st January if the course begins in the winter;
- 1st April if the course begins in the spring;
- 1st July if the course begins in the summer – but see below for an exception;
- 1st September if the course begins in the autumn.

But if a student is required to begin attending a course during August or September and continue attending through the autumn, his or her academic year is the one beginning on 1st September.

21.57 The seasons are not in turn defined in the law, but the following is believed to be correct (indeed the last three lines in para. 21.56 would not work in law if the following were wrong):

- winter starts on the winter solstice in late December;
- spring starts on the spring equinox in late March;
- summer starts on the summer solstice in late June;
- autumn starts on the autumn equinox in late September.

An alternative view is that the seasons start on the traditional 'quarter days' (HB/CTB G13/2005), so that:

- winter starts on 25th December;
- spring starts on 25th March;
- summer starts on 24th June;
- autumn starts on 29th September.

LOAN INCOME AND DEPENDANT INCOME OF STUDENTS LEAVING PART WAY THROUGH A COURSE

21.58 A student who leaves part way through his or her course is treated for HB and main CTB purposes as having income from a student loan or dependant grant – but only if a payment of a student loan and/or a dependant grant has actually been paid to the student in the 'academic year' (defined as in para. 21.56) in question. In such cases there are four steps: HB 40(7)-(9) NIHB 37(5)-(7) CTB 30(8)-(10)

(a) Take the total amount of student loan and/or grant for dependants which he or she would have received if he or she had remained till the end of the academic term in which he or she left. Then deduct the standard amount for travel and books and equipment (£632). In the law (and guidance) the result is 'A'.

(b) Calculate how much student loan income and/or dependant grant has been taken into account already in that academic year (up to – and including – the benefit week in which he or she left) under the normal rules (table 21.3) but pretending that there was no £10 disregard. In the law (and guidance), the result is 'B x C' (B being the number of weeks and C the weekly amount in those weeks).

(c) Subtract B x C from A. Average the result over the benefit weeks from (and including) the benefit week following that in which the student abandoned or was dismissed from the course up to (and including) the final benefit week in the last 'quarter' (as defined in para. 21.55) for which the student loan and/or dependant grant was paid to that student. In the law (and guidance) the number of weeks in this period is 'D'; and the amount taken into account as income in each of those weeks is the formula:

$$\frac{A - (B \times C)}{D}$$

(d) This counts as the ex-student's income only from (and including) the benefit week following that in which the student abandoned or was dismissed from the course up to (and including) the final benefit week in the last 'quarter' (para. 21.55) for which a student loan or a grant for dependants was paid to the student.

THE 'OLD' RULES

21.59 There are variations for students who (in the 2005-06 academic year) are in at least their eighth year. They are in the 2005-06 edition of this guide.

Example: Student income assessment: 2005-06 academic year

INFORMATION

Student claimant	Single woman, student aged 20, lives alone. She is eligible for HB because of her disability (table 21.1).
Course	2005-06, outside London, first year of course, full-time, undergraduate.
Period of study	Thursday 6.10.05 to Wednesday 14.6.06 inclusive.
Student loan	She receives £4,195 (the maximum amount available in her case).
Grant	She gets a disabled student's grant only.
Other income	Net earnings (after all appropriate disregards) of £50 per week at all material times; no capital.

INCOME FROM LOAN

She qualifies for a student loan, and is treated as receiving one at the maximum level available – which in her case is £4,195. (In fact she actually receives this amount.)

Disregard £632 for books and equipment and travel, leaving £3,563.

Average this (£3,563) over the 42 weeks from 5.9.05 to 25.6.06, giving £84.83 per week.

Disregard £10.00, giving £74.83 per week.

INCOME FROM GRANT

Her disabled student's grant is disregarded completely.

HB: ASSESSED INCOME*

Monday 5.9.05 to Sunday 9.10.05: She is not yet a student and the income from her loan is ignored. So her assessed income is £50.00 per week (from the job alone).

Monday 10.10.05 to Sunday 25.6.06: Her assessed income is £124.83 per week which is £74.83 from the loan and £50 from earnings.

Monday 26.6.06 to Sunday 3.9.06: This is outside the period over which her loan is averaged. So her assessed income is £50.00 (from the job alone).

Monday 4.9.06 to Sunday 24.6.07: Figures not yet available, but this is the 42-week period over which her loan is averaged.

* Not applicable in CTB because her home is exempt.

22 Discretionary housing payments, local schemes, pilots and pathfinders

22.1 This chapter sets out the various local variations to the HB and CTB schemes permitted by the law, including government pilot schemes that from time to time are introduced to test future reforms. Although the sections on 'pathfinders' describe what is in effect an entirely separate housing benefit scheme within the areas in which they operate, they may be of interest to the general reader, professional adviser or benefit administrator as they are likely to form the basis on which the HB scheme will operate in the future. This chapter covers:

- discretionary housing payments;
- 'local schemes', that is authorities' powers in Great Britain to operate schemes in their areas which disregard the whole of any war pension or war widows pension as income;
- government powers to vary the HB and CTB schemes locally;
- the HB 'pathfinders' operating in 18 local authority areas in Great Britain in which the eligible rent is based on standard flat rate allowance – known as the local housing allowance.

Discretionary housing payments

SI 2001 No. 1167
SI 2001 No. 2340
NISR 2001 No. 216
NISR 2001 No. 80

22.2 In Great Britain the Secretary of State's power to make regulations to provide for a scheme of discretionary housing payments is set out in section 69 of the Child Support, Pensions and Social Security Act 2000. By section 70 of the same Act the Secretary of State can pay grants to local authorities (i.e. subsidy) for the cost of the scheme. In Northern Ireland the equivalent powers for the DSD to make regulations and pay grants to the NIHE for the costs of administering the scheme are contained in sections 60 and 61 of the Child Support, Pensions and Social Security (Northern Ireland) Act 2000.

22.3 These payments are an independent scheme administered by authorities which also administer HB/CTB. However, they are not a form of HB or CTB, and so the HB/CTB appeals procedures (chapter 19) do not apply.

22.4 Discretionary housing payments (DHPs) are available to claimants who:

- in Great Britain are entitled to HB or CTB and 'appear to [the] authority to require some further financial assistance... in order to meet housing costs'; or

- in Northern Ireland are entitled to HB in respect of their rent which has been restricted under the New Scheme rules (paras. 10.33 onwards) and 'appear to [the] authority to require some further financial assistance... in order to meet housing costs'.

22.5 Discretionary housing payments cannot be awarded towards any of the following:

- ineligible service or support charges (chapter 10);
- in Great Britain any rent liability if the claimant is entitled to CTB only;
- in Great Britain any council tax liability if the claimant is entitled to HB only or to second adult rebate only;
- in Northern Ireland any liability to meet rates;
- increases to cover rent arrears which are not eligible for HB (para. 10.106);
- reductions in any benefit as a result of Jobseeker's sanctions, Child Support sanctions or sanctions following certain benefit related offences (para. 7.16);
- HB/CTB that is suspended (paras. 17.67-80).

22.6 Furthermore the total weekly amount of the award, taken together with the claimant's award of HB or CTB, must not exceed:

- the claimant's eligible rent calculated as though he or she were a council tenant (paras. 10.21-24);
- the claimant's liability for council tax.

22.7 So, for example, DHPs could be used for such things as the following:

- to make up the shortfall in eligible rent in a 'New Scheme' case caused by the rent officer's/NIHE figures being used;
- in Great Britain only, to make up the shortfall in eligible rent in an 'Old Scheme' case where the authority considers there is no other way of doing this;
- to make up for the effect of the 65 per cent and 20 per cent tapers used in the calculation of benefit;
- to make up for the effect of non-dependant deductions.

22.8 DWP guidance to local authorities on making DHPs is contained in a circular letter (not part of the normal HB/CTB series), 'Discretionary Housing Payments' of 16th March 2001, which can be viewed on-line at *www.dwp.gov.uk/housingbenefit/manuals/dhpguide.pdf.* There is no requirement for the claimant's family circumstances to be 'exceptional' – nor does there to have to be 'hardship'(circular letter, paragraph 2). The payments are, however, entirely discretionary and authorities vary in their willingness to award them. While it may well be worth enquiring about and/or claiming a DHP, no claimant should rely on his or her authority actually awarding him or her payment in the above (or any other) circumstances. Note that there is no time limit for making a claim for DHP (circular letter, paragraph 19).

SI 2001 No 2340
SI 2005 No 2052

22.9 The DWP partially reimburses local authorities for the cost of DHPs through a system of grants (separate from the system for HB/CTB described in chapter 23). Local authorities must make their grant claim by 31st May of each year. Claims for grants of less than £50,000 do not need to be audited.

Local schemes

AA 134(8),(10), 139(6),(8)
HB 40(3)-(4)
HB60+ 33(10)-(13)
CTB 30(3)-(4)
TB60+ 23(10)-(13)

22.10 The HB and CTB schemes as described in this guide are those which authorities are required by law to operate. However, authorities in England, Wales and Scotland (not Northern Ireland) may grant extra benefit under a 'local scheme' – that is, an improved version of the scheme. The only improvement authorities are permitted, however, is to disregard war disablement pensions, war widows' pensions and war widowers' pensions, in whole or part, over and above the fixed disregard required by law (usually £10: paras. 13.38-39). The vast majority, but not all, authorities have decided to do this. In April 2003, of the 408 authorities 393 were disregarding the whole of any excess above the statutory minimum £10, a further four authorities were applying a partial further disregard and only 11 were not taking advantage of a local scheme (and so applying the statutory minimum £10) (*Hansard* 14/04/2003, col. 513W). The decision to run a local scheme is made by a resolution of the authority. A separate resolution is required for HB and CTB. The question of whether or not an authority should run a local scheme is not open to the appeal procedure.

AA 134(12), 139(10)
SI 1995 No. 2793

22.11 When an authority does apply a local scheme its 'permitted total' for HB expenditure is set at 100.7% of its total HB expenditure after the cost of any local scheme has been deducted. However, this should have no effect on an authority's power to operate a local scheme (see DWP *Subsidy Guidance Manual* paragraph 1270). Further information on subsidy payments for local schemes can be found in paragraphs 23.16-18 of this guide.

Miscellaneous government powers to vary HB and CTB schemes locally

CBA 175(6)
NICBA 171(6)

22.12 Unlike other welfare benefits the Government possesses wide powers to vary both the HB and CTB regulations to make different rules for different areas. This power has been exercised to set the rules for local housing allowance pathfinders.

22.13 Powers exist in the Jobseekers Act 1995 (s29) to run pilot schemes. These powers allow the government to vary the rules for HB, CTB, IS and JSA within a particular area or to a particular class of claimant provided it will test whether the change will improve work incentives. However, these schemes have a maximum life of one year and do not permit variation of the maximum eligible rent or council tax. There are no such schemes currently in place.

22.14 From time to time specific legislation is passed to facilitate a new policy initiative which cannot be accommodated by existing powers. For example, s79 of the Welfare Reform and Pensions Act 1999 allowed payments to be made to HB claimants who trade down if their home was larger than they require. A small scheme was piloted but wound up after it proved ineffective.

Local housing allowance pathfinders

22.15 In November 2002 the government published its proposals for major reform of the housing benefit scheme in its paper *Building choice and responsibility: a radical agenda for housing benefit* (DWP 2002). The intention is to test these reforms, initially to tenants of private landlords only (para. 22.22), in a number of local authority areas. These areas are known as 'pathfinders'. The reform package consists of three main elements:

- instead of HB being calculated on the actual rent subject to a cap (i.e. the eligible rent in a non-pathfinder authority), the eligible rent is based on a flat rate allowance determined by the rent officer. Each month a set of allowances is fixed for each category of dwelling (within a defined geographic area). Each category of dwelling is appropriate to a particular household size and the rate for each category of dwelling is the eligible rent for all similar claims within that area. The set rate is payable even if the claimant's actual rent is lower;
- instead of the practice which applies outside the pathfinder areas whereby the majority of payments of HB are made direct to the landlord, payment of HB in the pathfinder areas will, except in exceptional circumstances, normally be made to the claimant;
- claims are no longer referred to the rent officer for individual assessment. Instead the rent officer will publish a set of allowances for each category of dwelling size within a defined 'broad rental market area'.

22.16 In authorities where these reforms are piloted, transitional protection will apply so that no claimant will receive less HB than they were entitled to immediately before the change in the rules. If the new allowance is more generous then they will benefit from the increase as soon as their claim is revised.

LEGISLATIVE AUTHORITY, REFERENCES AND GUIDANCE

22.17 The power to make changes to the HB regulations for pathfinder schemes are a pre-existing feature of the Benefit Acts (para. 22.12) as are the powers to change the rent officer rules (s122 of the Housing Act 1996). Under these powers the regulations for the pathfinder authorities are contained within separate schedules to the housing benefit regulations (schedule 10 in the working age regulations, schedule 9 in the 60+ regulations). For the most part these schedules work by inserting 'ghost' regulations within the main regulations, for example regulation 12A deals with eligible rent and regulation 13A the maximum rent (compare regulation 12 (para. 10.5) and regulation 13 (para. 10.34) in non-pathfinder areas). Therefore throughout the remainder of this chapter the marginal references are expressed as such, with the exception of transitional rules (para. 22.50) and amendments to the non-pathfinder regulations which otherwise would be 'invisible' (para. 22.63). The DWP has published separate Guidance for the Local Housing Allowance (Housing Benefit Local Housing Allowance Guidance Manual). References to it are included where appropriate (GLHA, followed by paragraph number).

LOCAL HOUSING ALLOWANCE AND MAXIMUM RENT STANDARD LOCAL RATE

22.18 Strictly speaking, the term 'local housing allowance' (LHA) is a determination made by the rent officer in a pathfinder area instead of the determinations made in non-pathfinder authorities (paras. 6.16-6.34), whereas the 'maximum rent (standard local rate)' is the equivalent in the pathfinder area to the 'maximum rent' (paras 10.33-35). In a non-pathfinder authority the maximum rent is the lowest of the various rent officer determinations, whereas in a pathfinder authority the 'maximum rent (standard local rate)' is simply the same as the appropriate (published) local housing allowance for the area in which the claimant's home is situated. Therefore in a pathfinder area the local housing allowance will be, subject to any transitional protection that may apply, identical to the figure used by the authority to calculate the eligible rent. In the remainder of this chapter the term local housing allowance (LHA) is used interchangeably to refer to both the LHA and the maximum (standard local rate).

22.19 The appropriate local housing allowance determination will depend on the area in which the claimant's home is situated and the number of occupiers in their household (para. 6.25). The local housing allowance is largely modeled on the local reference rent (paras. 6.28-30), that is, it is the mid-point (excluding exceptionally high or low rents) of the range of rents for similar sized dwellings. However, the defined area over which the rent officer makes his or her determination is known as the broad rental market area (para. 22.20) and subtly different from the local reference rent concept of locality (para. 6.19). For further details about the assumptions on which each determination is made, see paragraph 22.48.

22.20 In the pathfinder areas the broad rental market area replaces the concepts of 'locality, vicinity and neighbourhood' (paras. 6.18-21 and 22.48) which are centred on the claimant's dwelling. Instead the broad rental market area is a definite geographical area which can be demarcated by a boundary line drawn on a map (but which may change over time as markets change).

EXTENT OF THE PATHFINDERS

22.21 As at 1st April 2006 there are 18 local authorities in Great Britain participating as pathfinders. Each pathfinder had its own start date (table 22.1) but all started between November 2003 and July 2005. There is no set time limit for the life of a pathfinder but each is expected to run for a minimum of two years. Where the authority takes part, the HB regulations are modified for those types of tenancy which come within the scope of the scheme (para. 22.22). There are two basic types of pathfinder scheme, 'phased' or 'big bang' (these are not terms used in the regulations but are the accepted jargon in the pathfinder areas). In 'big bang' authorities the whole of the qualifying caseload is converted to the new scheme on the date the pathfinder starts. In 'phased' authorities all new claims go straight to the local housing allowance but existing claims are converted as and when the claim comes up for renewal. Table 22.1 sets out the 18 pathfinder authorities, their start date and whether they are phased or big bang.

HB 13A(1)(a),(b)
HB60+ 13A(1)(a),(b

Table 22.1: Pathfinder authorities and start dates

Authority	Start date	Pathfinder type
Argyll and Bute	30 May 2005	Big Bang
Blackpool	17 November 2003	Phased
Brighton and Hove	2 February 2004	Big Bang
Conwy	9 February 2004	Phased
Coventry	12 January 2004	Phased
East Riding of Yorkshire	18 April 2005	Big Bang
Edinburgh	9 February 2004	Big Bang
Guildford	4 July 2005	Big Bang
Leeds	9 February 2004	Phased
Lewisham	1 December 2003	Phased

HB 122, sch 10
HB60+ 103, sch 9
ROO sch 3A part 2

North East Lincolnshire	9 February 2004	Big Bang
Norwich	13 June 2005	Big Bang
Pembrokeshire	20 June 2005	Big Bang
St Helens	23 May 2005	Big Bang
Salford	25 July 2005	Big Bang
South Norfolk	6 June 2005	Big Bang
Teignbridge	12 January 2004	Phased
Wandsworth	11 April 2005	Big Bang

22.22 The pathfinder scheme only applies to certain types of letting within a pathfinder authority area, broadly lettings by private sector landlords. Within a pathfinder authority, the scheme will apply to any letting which is not listed in the following exceptions:

- the tenant is a council tenant paid by rent rebate (paras. 10.21-22);
- the 'rent' payable includes a mooring or site charge for a houseboat, caravan or mobile home (for guidance see GLHA paras. 1.28-29);
- the landlord is a registered social landlord (para. 10.18) or a housing action trust;
- the claimant occupies 'exempt accommodation' (para. 10.14) (for guidance see GLHA para. 1.20);
- the tenancy is let on a pre-1989 agreement (para. 10.67);
- the claim relates to rent payable in a hostel (para. 6.10), bail hostel or probation hostel (para. 10.72);
- the rent officer has determined that a substantial part of the rent is attributable to board and attendance (paras. 22.49-52).

22.23 If any of these exceptions apply then the claim will be treated in the same way as if it was not in a pathfinder authority (chapter 10 and paras. 16.28-40). A special procedure applies if a substantial part of the rent is attributable to board and attendance (paras. 22.49-52).

Eligible rent in pathfinder authorities

LOCAL HOUSING ALLOWANCE CASES

HB 12A(1), 13A(3),(8) HB60+ 12A(1), 13A(3),(8)

22.24 Except where the claimant is entitled to the protected rate because it is higher (paras. 22.26-34), the eligible rent in the pathfinder area will be the same as the rate for the appropriate local housing allowance (para. 22.41). In these cases the eligible rent is technically known as the maximum rent (standard local rate).

22.25 Unlike non-pathfinder claims the maximum rent (standard local rate) cannot be reduced to take account of the fact that: HB 13A(3),(8) HB60+ 13A(3),(8) ROO sch 3A para 2(3)

- the actual rent the claimant pays to the landlord is lower (paras. 10.5, 10.21, 10.33, 10.51);
- the claimant is a joint tenant (10.6);
- part of the property is used for business purposes (10.108);
- the rent includes an amount for ineligible services such as fuel or water (para. 10.75 onwards) because the rent officer is bound to exclude these in their determination of the local housing allowance (para. 22.48);
- the authority considers the rent officer's determination to be unreasonable and decides to restrict the rent still further (paras 10.48-49).

TRANSITIONALLY PROTECTED CASES

22.26 There are three types of protected claims.

- Existing claimants who were in receipt of housing benefit at the start of the pathfinder. Except where the claimant qualifies for one of the other types of protection (para. 22.29), these types of claim can be protected for an unlimited period. However, protection takes the form of the claimant's eligible rent being frozen.
- Claimants who have had a death in their household can be protected for up to 12 months.
- Claimants who were previously paying their own rent who have not claimed HB in the previous year can be protected for the first 13 weeks of their claim.

PROTECTION FOR EXISTING CLAIMANTS

22.27 Existing claimants will be protected if: HB 12A(2),(3) HB60+ 12A(2),(3)

- they have been continuously in receipt of housing benefit since the start of the pathfinder (table 22.1); and
- their eligible rent which applied immediately prior to the first revision of their claim following the start of the pathfinder is higher than the maximum rent (standard local rate) (para. 22.24) which applies in their case.

In such circumstances their eligible rent is frozen until their local housing allowance is equal to or higher than their protected rate. The eligible rent will continue at the frozen rate indefinitely until the local housing allowance catches up with it or the circumstances in para. 22.29 apply. All protection is lost as soon as the claimant moves home or loses entitlement to HB altogether. There are no linking rules which ignore short breaks in entitlement or because the claimant takes part in a welfare to work scheme.

22.28 The frozen rate includes any eligible rent calculated as an 'Old Scheme' case (paras. 10.51-10.66) because the claimant has been on HB since January 1996, but not as a result of the claimant living in 'exempt accommodation' (para. 10.14) as these cases are not subject to the local housing allowance (para. 22.22).

HB 12A(3)(b),(c), (9)(b),(c) HB60+ 12A(3)(b),(c), (9)(b),(c)

22.29 There are two exceptions to the frozen rate being applied indefinitely:

- where an existing claimant first claimed HB following the death of a household member, their eligible rent will be based on their actual rent for the first 12 months of their claim (para. 22.30); or
- they are an existing claimant whose eligible rent is based on their actual rent during the first 13 weeks of their claim (para. 22.33).

In both cases, their eligible rent continues for the remainder of their 12 month or 13 week protection period as appropriate. At the end of this period their eligible rent reverts to what it would have been without any protection except where a relevant change of circumstance has occurred (para. 22.39) which has triggered a higher maximum rent (standard) local rate than the one that applied at the beginning of the protection period.

PROTECTION FOR HOUSEHOLDS FOLLOWING A DEATH

HB 12A(4),(9)(d) HB60+ 12A(4),(9)(d)

22.30 Except where the claimant's maximum rent (standard local rate) is equal to or higher than the claimant's actual rent, then the eligible rent will be protected following the death of a household member. The circumstances when these rules apply are identical to those in paras. 10.41-44. The protected rate will be their actual rent, subject only to a reduction if the property is partly used for business (para. 10.108) or if the authority applies a restriction using its general powers (para. 10.48).

22.31 The protected rate will continue for 12 months from the date of the death or until such time as the authority determines a local housing allowance which is greater than the protected rate. The authority can only determine a new local housing allowance if it is notified of a further relevant change of circumstances.

HB 13A(1)(b)(iv) HB60+ 13A(1)(b)(iv)

22.32 A relevant change of circumstances only occurs if the circumstances in paragraph 22.39 apply or there is a further death of a household member (other than the claimant) but one which does not affect the category of dwelling (para. 22.42 and table 22.2) which applies in their case.

PROTECTION FOR HOUSEHOLDS DURING THE FIRST 13 WEEKS OF THEIR CLAIM

HB 12A(6),(7), (9)(e),(10) HB60+ 12A(6),(7), (9)(e),(10)

22.33 Except where local housing allowance would be higher, where the authority is satisfied that the claimant could previously afford to pay their rent, then their eligible rent is worked out in the same way as a council tenant's (para. 10.21).

These rules mirror the protection in non-pathfinder authorities (paras. 10.38-40). Note that this protection only applies in the 'phased' pathfinders (para. 22.21 and table 22.1) to claims made after the pathfinder start date; this is because in the 'big bang' pathfinders all claims will be covered by the rules in paragraph 22.29.

22.34 Protection continues until the earliest of either

- the end of the 13 week protection period; or
- until a relevant change of circumstance occurs (para. 22.39) which results in a maximum rent (standard local rate) being applied which is equal to or higher than the protected rate.

At the end of the 13 week period the eligible rent will be the relevant local housing allowance that would have applied had they not been protected, except where there has been a relevant change of circumstance during the 13 week protection period in which case the eligible rent will be equivalent to the maximum rent (standard local rate) (i.e. local housing allowance) which would have otherwise applied on the date the change occurred.

TRANSFER OF CASES IN PATHFINDER AREAS

22.35 In big bang pathfinders (para. 22.21 and table 22.1) the entire caseload is transferred to the local housing allowance or the protected rate if higher on the pathfinder start date. HB 13A(1)(a) HB60+ 13A(1)(a)

22.36 In phased pathfinders (para. 22.21 and table 22.1) cases are transferred to the local housing allowance or the protected rate as appropriate from the pathfinder start date on the earliest of the following dates which occurs: HB 13A(1)(b)(i)-(iii),(c) HB60+ 13A(1)(b)(i)-(iii),(c)

- when a new claim is made;
- the claimant moves home at any time on or after 9th April 2004;
- there has been a relevant change of circumstances which would have led to referral to the rent officer in a non-pathfinder authority (table 6.3);
- the date on which their claim would next be referred to the rent officer if they were not in a pathfinder area (para. 6.6) (i.e. 52 weeks after the previous referral).

22.37 In both the big bang and phased pathfinders, on transfer the eligible rent will either be equivalent to the appropriate local housing allowance that applies in their case (paras. 22.42 and table 22.2) or the 'frozen' protected rate (paras. 22.26-34) if that is higher.

LENGTH OF AWARD FOLLOWING TRANSFER TO LHA AND SUBSEQUENT AWARDS

22.38 Where the claimant's eligible rent has been based on the local housing allowance instead of the protected rate, it will continue until the claimant has a HB 11A HB60+ 11A relevant change of circumstances (para. 22.39) or until the anniversary date after the claim was made, at which point the LHA will expire and be replaced by the latest appropriate rate. Note it is the anniversary of the date of claim, not the start of the award (i.e. ignoring any backdating). If the anniversary date falls on a Monday the effective date for the new rate will be the same day, in any other case it will be the following Monday. If that benefit week falls in the following month, the LHA rate will be that of the previous month, that is the month in which the anniversary date fell (GLHA para. 3.11).

RELEVANT CHANGE OF CIRCUMSTANCES FOLLOWING LHA AWARD

HB 13A(1)(b)(iv)
HB60+ 13A(1)(b)(iv)

22.39 Once an award based the local housing allowance has been made it will remain in force for one year unless a relevant change of circumstance has occurred. A relevant change of circumstance only occurs if:

- there has been a change in the category of dwelling which applies in determining the local housing allowance (para. 22.42);
- there has been a rent increase under a term of the tenancy which was part of the tenancy agreement when the claim was made.

22.40 The revised award or new award will be based on the appropriate local housing allowance for the claimant's household which was in force during the month in which the decision on the claim is made. It is therefore possible that the award is revised following the notification of a rent increase but that the eligible rent falls because the local housing allowance rates for that month are lower than the rates that applied when the original claim was made.

Rate of local housing allowance

22.41 In all cases the eligible rent will be equivalent to the appropriate local housing allowance set by the rent officer for the month in which the award is made. Technically this is known as the maximum rent (standard local rate) – but this is misleading because it is also the minimum eligible rent. The appropriate local housing allowance will be determined by the 'broad rental market area' in which the property is situated (paras. 22.20 and 22.48) and the appropriate category of dwelling (by number of rooms) which applies to the claimant's household (para. 22.42 and table 22.2).

APPROPRIATE CATEGORY OF DWELLING FOR EACH HOUSEHOLD TYPE

HB 13A(3)
HB60+ 13A(3)

22.42 The appropriate category of dwelling is determined by the rent officer size criteria (table 6.5) except where:

Table 22.2: Appropriate category of dwelling and rate of LHA for each household type within a broad rental market area

Household type	Category of Dwelling/ Rate of LHA
(a) single claimant (para. 4.6) aged under 25 except where: ◆ a non-dependant lives with them; ◆ they are paid the severe disability premium; ◆ they are a care leaver aged under 22 (para. 6.12 cases (d) and (e)).	Shared room rate
(b) couple or single claimant aged at least 25 or single claimant aged under 25 who falls within the exceptions in (a) above; and the dwelling in which they live does not provide them with either: ◆ the exclusive use of at least two living rooms; or ◆ exclusive use of one room, a bathroom, toilet and either a kitchen or cooking facilities.	Shared room rate
(c) Any couple or single person to whom (b) applies but who lives in accommodation which provides them with the exclusive use of at least two rooms; or the exclusive use of one room, a bathroom, toilet and either a kitchen or cooking facilities.	Two room rate
(d) Any household entitled to three living rooms (including bedrooms) as defined by the size criteria (table 6.5).	Three room rate
(e) Any household entitled to four living rooms (including bedrooms) as defined by the size criteria (table 6.5).	Four room rate
(f) Any household entitled to five living rooms (including bedrooms) as defined by the size criteria (table 6.5).	Five room rate
(g) Any household entitled to six living rooms (including bedrooms) as defined by the size criteria (table 6.5).	Six room rate
(h) Any household entitled to seven or more living rooms as defined by the size criteria (table 6.5)	The appropriate rate already determined for that sized household or determined following an application to the rent officer (para. 22.46)

a. the claimant is a 'young individual' (para. 6.12) who is not also a person to which either one of cases c, d, e or f in paragraph 6.12 of this guide applies (claimant with a non-dependant, severe disability premium, care leaver);

b. the claimant is part of a couple without dependent children; or is single and aged at least 25; or is single and aged under 25 but falls within one of the four exceptions in (a) above (i.e. cases c-f in para. 6.12).

In the case of (a): the category of dwelling will be the standard allowance for a room in 'shared accommodation'. In the case of (b) the category of dwelling will be the allowance for a two-roomed property except where the property in which they have chosen to live is shared accommodation (para. 22.45). A summary of the household type, appropriate category of dwelling and rate of LHA is provided in table 22.2. Note that although the appropriate rate is determined by the rent officer size criteria, the decision as to the size of the household is made by the local authority, not the rent officer and so is appealable (para. 22.64).

COUNTING OCCUPIERS

HB 13A(3)(b)(iii),(9) HB60+ 13A(3)(b)(iii),(9)

22.43 In deciding the appropriate rate of LHA (other than the shared rate) the same rules apply as for counting the number of occupiers when applying the size criteria in a non-pathfinder authority (paras. 6.25-26 and table 6.5) except that the rules make it expressly clear that 'occupier' includes anyone who the authority 'is satisfied occupy as their home the dwelling to which the claim relates' but does not include 'any joint tenant who is not a member of the claimant's household'. In counting the number of occupiers the local authority should include persons in the household (including the partner of the claimant) who are excluded from benefit by the rules on nationality or residence as described in chapter 20 (GLHA paras. 2.15-16).

RATE OF LOCAL HOUSING ALLOWANCE AND ITS PUBLICATION

HB 13B HB60+ 13B ROO 4B(1)

22.44 The rates of the local housing allowance for each category of dwelling in a specific broad rental market area (paras. 22.20 and 22.48) are set by the rent officer each month. Each local housing allowance will apply for the month following the month in which it is set. Normally only allowances up to six roomed accommodation will be set unless the rent officer and authority agree that allowances for larger properties are regularly needed. Where the household requires accommodation of seven rooms or more and no LHA exists a special procedure applies (para. 22.46). The authority is required to take 'such steps as appropriate' to ensure that the rates of the LHA for any broad rental market area(s) in its boundary are 'brought to the attention' of potential claimants.

HOUSEHOLDS NORMALLY ENTITLED TO THE TWO ROOM RATE BUT WHO LIVE IN ACCOMMODATION WHICH ONLY QUALIFIES FOR THE SHARED RATE

22.45 A household in case (b) in paragraph 22.42 above is entitled to receive the two room rate of the local housing allowance; however if they choose to occupy certain smaller accommodation then they may not be entitled to the two room rate. The type of accommodation that will qualify them for the two room rate will be one which provides them with:

HB 13A(3)(b)
HB60+ 13A(3)(b)

- the exclusive use of at least two living rooms; or
- the exclusive use of one living room, a bathroom and toilet and either a kitchen or cooking facilities.

In any other case they will only be entitled to the LHA rate for shared accommodation. Official DWP guidance states that accommodation will qualify the claimant for the two room rate if it is 'a one-bedroom flat or studio or other kind of self-contained accommodation' but that the accommodation will not qualify if it is 'a property where all or some of the facilities are shared' (GLHA paras. 2.40-41). Note that the descriptive terms 'shared accommodation', 'studio' and 'self-contained accommodation' are not terms which appear in the legislation. In deciding which rooms count as a living room, see paragraph 22.47.

RATE OF LHA FOR SEVEN ROOMED OR LARGER PROPERTIES

22.46 Each month the rent officer will determine the LHA for each category of dwelling up to six roomed accommodation for each broad rental market area (or part of) within the pathfinder authority. They will only normally set the LHA for larger dwellings if they agree with the authority that the rates for larger dwellings are regularly required (para. 22.44). The rent officer will also set the LHA for larger dwellings if it relates to a specific claim and no LHA exists – a process which is initiated by the authority applying to the rent officer for one to be set. Similarly the authority must also apply for a determination where it receives a request on an approved form from a prospective tenant who is likely to claim housing benefit – in effect a type of pre-tenancy determination (para. 6.52) but one which does not require the consent of the landlord. In both cases the rent officer will be required to supply the LHA for the appropriate category of dwelling for each broad rental market area within the authority boundary. If a 'one off' LHA is set it will apply to any other similar claims made later in the same month.

HB 13A(4),(5)
HB60+ 13A(4),(5)

COUNTING ROOMS

22.47 In counting the number of rooms in the dwelling for any category of dwelling other than the shared rate (table 22.2) 'room' means a bedroom or 'a

HB 13A(9)
HB60+ 13A(9)
ROO sch 3A para 1(2)

room suitable for living in' except a room which is shared with any other person unless that person is:

- a member of the tenant's household;
- a non-dependant;
- a person who pays rent to the tenant.

The rent officer's determinations

LOCAL HOUSING ALLOWANCE DETERMINATIONS

ROO 4B(1)-(5), sch 3A paras 2-4

22.48 Local housing allowance determinations for each category of dwelling are broadly modelled on the local reference rent (para 6.28) and single room rent (para. 6.31) determinations and the formula for setting them is similar (para. 22.20) but with certain modifications to the valuation assumptions. These are:

- The hypothetical dwelling on which LHA determination is based is assumed to be situated within the 'broad rental market area' as the claimant's dwelling rather than being in the same locality (paras. 6.19 and 22.20).
- Unlike a locality which is centred on the claimant's dwelling a broad rental market area has a defined geographical boundary and so will not overlap with any other broad rental market area. Any boundary should be co-terminous with postcodes.
- Since the boundary of the broad rental market area is fixed, the LHA determination for each category of dwelling within it will be the same for any dwelling within that category.
- Unlike localities which comprise two or more neighbourhoods (para. 6.19) a broad rental market area is comprised of 'two or more distinct areas of residential accommodation' and there is no requirement that the facilities in paragraph 6.19 are '[...] in or accessible from the neighbourhood of the dwelling'.
- Instead of a single room rent for 'young individuals', a determination based on shared accommodation is set which is applicable to a wider group of claimants (para. 22.42) and is based on the rents of dwellings that have modestly more generous facilities than the single room rent (paras. 6.32 and 22.45).
- In setting the LHA (all categories of dwelling) the rent officer must exclude rental evidence attributable to 'services', 'facilities (including the use of furniture) provided for the tenant' and 'rights made available to the tenant', if any of these are ineligible to be met by housing benefit. Since the LHA is set with this assumption the authority should not

deduct any amount from the LHA in determining the eligible rent even if the tenancy includes ineligible services (para. 22.25).

- The LHA determinations for two roomed or larger dwellings will be based on evidence of dwellings in the same category. Therefore there is no need for the assumption that they match the appropriate size criteria (para. 6.29). The claimant's eligible rent will simply be the LHA for the category of dwelling which is applicable to them.
- A complete set of LHA determinations for each category of dwelling (up to six rooms) is made at the end of each month and will be in force on the first working day of the next month. The rent officer must also make determinations for any category of larger dwellings which they 'believe are likely to be required for the purpose of calculating housing benefit'. In practice this will be after discussion with the authority (para. 22.46). Any other determinations for larger dwellings are made as and when requested or a claim needs to be determined (paras. 22.44) and take effect for the remainder of that month and apply to any similar claim.
- The limits of each broad rental market area (or part of) which falls within the authority's boundary are determined when the pathfinder goes live (strictly speaking the rent officer determines these in the month before) and are changed when, in the rent officer's opinion, it is necessary. The postcodes within any broad rental market area that fall within the authority's boundary must be notified.

In all other aspects the assumptions in paragraphs 6.19, 6.29, 6.30 and 6.32 apply.

BOARD AND ATTENDANCE DETERMINATIONS

22.49 Where the authority receives a claim from a private sector tenant and it appears that a substantial part of the rent is attributable to board and attendance, it must refer the claim to the rent officer stating that it believes that to be the case. The referral should be made within the same time limits and accompanied by the same information as if a referral was being made in a non-pathfinder area (paras. 6.14-15).

HB 13A(6),(7)
HB60+ 13A(6),(7
ROO 4C

22.50 Where such a referral has been made, the rent officer will decide whether a substantial part of the rent is attributable to board and attendance. Where the rent officer decides that this is the case he/she will make a determination on the same basis as if the claim had been referred to them in a non-pathfinder authority except that if the claim was previously an old scheme case (paras. 10.7 and 10.51-66) it will be treated as a new scheme case (paras. 10.7 and 10.33-50).

CPR sch 3 para 4(

22.51 Where the rent officer determines that a substantial part of the rent is not attributable to board and attendance then he/she will notify the authority which will be obliged to treat the claim as it would any other pathfinder case (i.e. apply the appropriate LHA or the protected rate if that is higher).

CPSA sch 7 para 6(2)(c)

22.52 Since the decision as to whether or not a substantial part of the rent is attributable to board and attendance is made by the rent officer this cannot be appealed to a tribunal (table 19.1) but the authority can ask for this decision, or any decisions where there is a board and attendance determination, to be redetermined. These 'appeal' procedures are described in paragraphs 22.63-67.

Payment of benefit in pathfinder areas

HB 96(3A)(a),(b) HB60+ 77(3A)(a),(b)

22.53 In pathfinder areas the authority will no longer have discretion to make direct payments purely on the grounds that the claimant has consented to them (para. 16.34) if the claim is one to which the pathfinder scheme applies (para. 22.22). Instead, direct payments will only be permissible in certain set circumstances when the claimant is considered to be at risk or for purely transitional purposes during the early months of the pathfinder (para. 22.55). In both cases these conditions are subject to the landlord being a 'fit and proper person' (para. 16.37-39) and to any maximum payment (para. 22.56). These rules apply even if benefit is payable at the protected rate.

22.54 The circumstances when claimants can be considered to be at risk are limited to the following cases:

- the claim is one to which mandatory direct payments would apply if was not in a pathfinder area (paras. 16.30-31);
- the first payment of the claim is yet to be made and the authority considers that the first payment should be made to the landlord (para.16.29);
- the claimant has moved owing rent (para.16.34);
- the authority considers that the claimant 'is likely to have difficulty managing his/her affairs' (para 22.57) – in the language of DWP guidance the claimant is 'vulnerable' (GLHA para. 5.10);
- the authority considers that it 'is improbable that the claimant will pay his/her rent' (para. 22.62).

For DWP guidance on the last two cases see paragraphs 22.57-62.

HB 96(3A)(b)(i),(iv) HB60+ 77(3A)(b)(i),(iv)

22.55 In addition, for transitional purposes during the start of the pathfinder, the authority will be able to make direct payments to a landlord where:

- in 'big bang' pathfinders (para. 22.21 and table 22.1) the authority may continue to make direct payments for up to six months from the start of the pathfinder or until the next (i.e. second) LHA determination, whichever is the sooner, provided they have been continuously in receipt of HB since the start of the pathfinder;

- in 'phased' pathfinders (para. 22.21 and table 22.1) where direct payments were already being made on an award which was in force at the start of the pathfinder (table 22.1). In this case payments can continue until the first LHA determination is made (including any case where the claim is protected).

MAXIMUM AMOUNT OF HB WHICH CAN BE PAID TO A LANDLORD

22.56 Under the LHA scheme it is possible for the amount of HB to be greater than the claimant's actual rent. Where direct payments are being made to a landlord the maximum amount of benefit which can be paid to the landlord where the tenant is not in rent arrears is limited to the rent due. If the tenant has arrears, the authority can decide whether to pay any excess towards the arrears, but only up to the level of those arrears. HB 95(2A) HB60+ 95(2A)

GUIDANCE ON VULNERABLE CLAIMANTS

22.57 In DWP guidance claimants who 'are likely to have difficulty in managing their affairs' are referred to as vulnerable. The guidance stresses the importance of grounding a decision on evidence although it states that authorities are not expected to be proactive in identifying potential cases (GLHA, 5.22, 5.30-39).

22.58 The guidance suggests that the sources of evidence will often be the typical causes or effects of vulnerability. Potential causes include: people with learning difficulties; people with poor literacy skills or unable to speak English; people addicted to drugs, alcohol or gambling; women fleeing domestic violence; single homeless care leavers; and people leaving prison. The guidance also suggests that the risk that a person is likely to be vulnerable will increase where the claimant lives alone and has no support (GLHA para. 5.41). Potential effects include: severe debt problems, DWP direct payments to utilities, the person is in receipt of support from a homeless charity, the person is receiving help through Supporting People, the person is unable to obtain a bank account or even that the person is incapable of providing evidence to support their claim of vulnerability (GLHA para. 5.42). In the last case, the guidance suggests that the authority may be able 'to use evidence from personal interviews and local knowledge' however; it warns authorities that they should try and avoid rewarding the claimant for their 'laziness or apathy'.

22.59 The guidance suggests that the authority should always seek to interview the claimant and obtain written evidence from any relevant person (GLHA para. 5.31-32). All evidence should be weighed but any evidence from social services, a doctor, the DWP, the courts or a 'reputable financial institution' should be accepted without question (GLHA para. 5.33-44). Evidence can also be accepted from families, friends and landlords but should be treated with caution (GLHA 5.36-37). Evidence from welfare groups such as Citizens Advice Bureaux 'should normally be accepted' and authorities should always 'consider' evidence from a rent deposit guarantee scheme (GLHA para. 5.35).

22.60 Somewhat controversially perhaps, the guidance stresses that payment should not be delayed pending the outcome of a decision and that 'how the claimant handles initial payments may, in fact help [the authority] reach a decision on vulnerability'. However, it also suggests that where a landlord is currently being paid this would continue pending a decision on vulnerability (GLHA para. 5.51).

22.61 The guidance states that someone who acts on behalf of the claimant as an appointee or agent (paras. 5.6 and 16.56-7) should not be considered vulnerable (GLHA para. 4.20).

22.62 The guidance stresses the importance of collecting, verifying, and considering evidence before reaching a decision that a claimant is 'unlikely to pay their rent' (see GLHA 6.30-55). However, the guidance points out that this test 'is likely to be based on past behaviour to a greater degree than a [vulnerability decision]' (GLHA para. 6.41). Authorities are warned against making decisions on the basis of self serving statements that the claimant will not pay their rent without finding out why this is the case (GLHA paras. 6.42-43). The guidance suggests that evidence of past behaviour 'must be compelling' and 'show a sustained period of non-payment' rather than 'the odd missed payment here and there' (GLHA para. 6.44). On the other hand the guidance also points out that a person may legitimately withhold their rent, for example 'in a dispute with their landlord over repairs and maintenance' (GLHA para. 6.45).

Appeals and errors

CPSA sch 7 para 6(2)(c) HB 16(1)(b),(5), sch 10 para 10 HB60+ 16(1)(b),(5), sch 9 para 10

22.63 As in non-pathfinder areas there is no right of appeal against a decision which adopts a rent officer determination (para. 6.40). In addition, in pathfinder authorities there is also no right to seek a redetermination about the level of the LHA or the broad rental market area on which it is based. This is because, unlike non-pathfinder authorities where the rent officer's determinations relate to individual properties, a LHA determination in a pathfinder area relates to all claims within that category of dwelling and would trigger a review of all other claims. However, there are special procedures to allow for:

ROO 4D

- authorities to ask for a redetermination of the rent officer's decision that a claim is a board and attendance case and any subsequent board and attendance determinations (para. 22.65). All exempted cases (para. 22.22) can have redeterminations;
- correction of accidental errors made by the rent officer (such as a typing mistake) which are not errors of professional judgment in the determination of an LHA or of a broad rental market area (para. 22.48).

An example might be that the rent officer notified the authority of a broad rental market area but notified the authority of the wrong postcode districts to which it applies. Errors as to whether a particular claim is a board and attendance case can also be included in this type of appeal.

22.64 As in non-pathfinder areas, claimants can appeal decisions (chapter 17) made by the authority which are not made as a direct consequence of adopting a rent officer's determination. This may happen for example where:

- the household size has been incorrectly assessed resulting in the wrong category of LHA being applied (note that, unlike non-pathfinder authorities, the authority applies the size criteria, not the rent officer, who simply sets the rates of the LHA each month);
- the authority has incorrectly decided that the claimant is a 'young individual';
- the authority has incorrectly assessed the use of facilities resulting in the shared rate of LHA being applied instead of the two room rate (this is also a decision of the authority and not the rent officer);
- the authority has failed to apply the protected rate when the claimant is entitled to it;
- the decision as to whether the claim is exempt from the LHA (para. 22.22) is wrong (except where this is a direct consequence of a rent officer's determination that it is a board and attendance determination);
- the decision involves the payment of benefit (paras. 22.53-62) but see also table 19.1.

BOARD AND ATTENDANCE REDETERMINATIONS

22.65 The authority may apply to the rent officer for a redetermination as to their determination that a particular case is a board and attendance case; the procedure mirrors the procedure in paragraphs 6.44-46 of this guide. HB 15 HB60+ 15 ROO 4D

ERRORS

22.66 Where there has been an accidental error, as described in paragraph 22.63 above, a similar procedure as in paragraphs 6.48-50 of this guide applies for substitute determinations. HB 16 HB60+ 16 ROO 4E, 7A(2)-(3)

DATE ON WHICH CHANGES TAKE EFFECT FOLLOWING REVISIONS

22.67 In the limited circumstances where the rent officer is able to correct their error (i.e. where it is not an error of professional judgment) and their determination has been amended as a result, the rules in paragraph 17.42 apply. HB 16,18A HB60+ 16,18A

23 Subsidy

23.1 This chapter provides an overview of the various subsidies that are available to meet local authority HB and CTB related expenditure in 2005-06 and 2006-07. It applies to Great Britain only.

The importance of subsidy

LOST INCOME

23.2 Authorities have sometimes overlooked the importance of central government HB and CTB related subsidies and have lost income as a consequence. This may be because they:

- failed to claim their full subsidy entitlement;
- were unable to substantiate their subsidy claims; or
- had followed incorrect procedures.

AA 140C(3) **23.3** Where it appears that subsidy has been overpaid to an authority, or that there has been a breach of subsidy rules, the Secretary of State has the discretion to recover appropriate amounts. The criteria that the Secretary of State considers when exercising this power are set out in DWP Circular S1/2002 (para. 3).

THE TENSION BETWEEN SUBSIDY RULES AND THE PROPER ADJUDICATION OF CLAIMS

23.4 Not only do subsidy payments form a significant proportion of most authorities' total income: they are also a vital factor in determining the quality, effectiveness and style of HB and CTB administration. Over the years studies of HB and CCB/CTB administration have highlighted the tension between proper decision-making and some of the perverse penalties and incentives built into the subsidy arrangements (see, for example, *Remote-Control: The National Administration of Housing Benefit,* Audit Commission, 1993 and *Housing Benefit: the National Perspective,* Audit Commission, 2002). While the changes to the subsidy rules that occurred in 2004-05 removed some of these tensions, such as the rules on backdated claims (para. 23.28), others, such as applying the appropriate category to overpayments, remain (para. 23.42).

Legislation and guidance

23.5 The Social Security Administration Act 1992 (sections 140A-140G) provides the outline legal framework relating to the payment of subsidies to authorities. The detailed legal rules are set out in the Income-related Benefits (Subsidy to Authorities) Order 1998 (SI 1998 No 562) as amended each year. The rules and rates relating to 2006-07 will be incorporated in an amendment to this order. This will be made, in accordance with established practice, after the end of the 2006-07 year.

23.6 The DWP issues guidance on the subsidy arrangements in the form of the Subsidy Guidance Manual. This is reissued each year (normally in December) to reflect the subsidy arrangements applicable for that year. The DWP also issues the S series of circulars with the aim of keeping authorities up to date with subsidy-related proposals and developments. Both sets of guidance are available on-line at *www.dwp.gov.uk/housingbenefit/manuals*

April 2004 revision of the subsidy arrangements

23.7 The Local Government Act 2003 provided for rent rebates to be taken out of the housing authority's housing revenue account (HRA). As a result responsibility for payment of rent rebate subsidy was transferred from the Office of the Deputy Prime Minister (ODPM) and National Assembly for Wales to the DWP from 2004-05. The DWP took the opportunity to make wide-ranging changes to the way authorities have been subsidised for their HB/CTB related expenditure from April 2004 and to the rates and rules that apply to benefit subsidy (DWP Circular S9-2003).

Authority expenditure

23.8 An authority's expenditure on different aspects of the HB and CTB schemes may be categorised under the following headings:

- benefit payment costs, i.e. the money paid out in the form of HB or CTB;
- ongoing administrative costs, which include staff salaries, accommodation costs, postage and computer running costs;
- additional administrative costs that may be incurred as a result of changes to related benefit schemes, for example, the introduction of the new tax credit and pension credit arrangements; and
- the setup and operating costs associated with specific arrangements such as those incurred as a result of the adoption of the Verification Framework.

23.9 Money to meet these costs comes from either:

- DWP subsidies; or
- the authority's own general fund, or in Wales the council fund.

23.10 Prior to April 2004, in England and Wales, housing revenue account (HRA) rent rebate expenditure (essentially rent rebates for council tenants) fell as a cost to the authority's housing revenue account. The housing revenue account (HRA) records income and expenditure relating primarily to council housing. Since April 2004 the cost of HRA rent rebates has fallen as a cost to the general fund or in Wales the council fund. To the extent that this expenditure fails to attract benefit subsidy, e.g. certain local authority error overpayments, this is a new cost to fall on the general fund or council fund. In England and Wales, authorities had the option of phasing this change in over two years. Full details of the transitional arrangements were in the consultation packages accompanying the draft HRA subsidy determination 2004-05. These continue for 2005-06 to allow authorities to adjust to the impact of the new regime. Transitional arrangements will not apply after 31st March 2006 (ODPM, Letter to Chief Finance Officers/Chief Accountants of Local Housing Authorities, dated 16th December 2004).

Central government subsidies

23.11 Since 2004-05 all central government subsidies relating to HB/CTB have been under the control of the DWP.

BENEFIT EXPENDITURE SUBSIDY

23.12 Benefit subsidy is available to meet 100% of an authority's expenditure on:

- rent rebates;
- rent allowances; and
- council tax benefit.

It should be noted, however, that this 100% subsidy 'entitlement' is subject to the transitional protection arrangements described in para. 23.25 and specific exceptions identified in the rest of this chapter and summarised in table 23.1.

ADDITIONAL SUBSIDIES

23.13 In addition to benefit subsidy, additional DWP subsidies were available in 2005-06 to:

- assist with authorities' HB/CTB administration costs (administration subsidy) (para. 23.55);

- assist with the increased administrative costs associated with the new tax credit and pension credit schemes (included within administration cost subsidy);
- set up and operate the Verification Framework (para. 23.59);
- introduce data-matching and reviews from April 2004 (included within administration cost subsidy);
- encourage authorities to apply sanctions and prosecute fraudsters (the sanctions and prosecutions reward scheme under the SAFE arrangements – para. 23.60);
- encourage authorities to identify specific categories of overpayment and error – the Weekly Incorrect Benefit (WIB) (para. 23.62) element of the Security Against Fraud and Error Scheme (SAFE); and
- help authorities tackle the barriers to improved performance (Performance Standards Fund – para. 23.64).

23.14 From 2006-07 the separate subsidy arrangements relating to the setting up and operation of the Verification Framework, the Weekly Incorrect Benefit scheme and the Sanctions and Prosecutions reward scheme have been abolished and the sums previously allocated through these mechanisms incorporated into an authority's administration cost subsidy (DWP S2/2006).

Qualifying expenditure

23.15 Benefit expenditure that counts for subsidy purposes is known as qualifying expenditure.

DISCRETIONARY LOCAL SCHEMES

23.16 Most authorities operate some form of discretionary local scheme for War Pensioners. This allows an authority to disregard some or all of any war disablement and war widow's or widower's pension (paras. 13.42, 13.149 and 22.10).

23.17 Benefit expenditure attributable to a local scheme does not count as qualifying expenditure and is therefore not eligible for HB or CTB subsidy but from April 2004 an authority running such a scheme receives an addition of 0.2% to its annual subsidy up to the value of 75% of the cost of the scheme to the authority.

23.18 An authority's discretionary expenditure on modified schemes to enhance the mandatory disregards of Navy and Army war widows' pensions should be contained within the relevant permitted total.

Table 23.1: Summary of benefit expenditure subsidy arrangements 2005-07

COMPONENT	ARRANGEMENTS	RATE
Basic rate	HB/CTB In England and Wales the 100% subsidy on HRA rent rebates is subject to HRA rent increases having kept to Government guidelines	100% Subject to transitional protection arrangements
LA error OPs	Where LA error OPs equal to or less than 0.48% of correct payments	100% on all LA error OPs
	Where LA error OPs above 0.48% but equal to or less than 0.54% of correct payments	40% on all LA error OPs
	Where LA error OPs above 0.54% of correct payments	Nil on all LA error OPs
OPs caused by fraud	HB/CTB	40%
Rebate credited in advance of entitlement	Rent rebate/CTB	Nil
DWP/IR error OPs	HB/CTB	100% Recovered amounts are deducted from subsidy entitlement
Excess CTB due to delayed award of transitional relief/budget substitution	CTB	Nil
Claimant error/other OPs	HB/CTB	40%
Duplicate payments where original alleged to have been lost/stolen/not received and later found to be cashed	Rent allowance	25%

Disproportionate increases in LA rents	Rent rebate Applies in Scotland and Wales only	Nil
Unreasonable rents – deregulated private sector tenancies not subject to a maximum rent calculation	Rent allowance where authority is unable to restrict the eligible rent under 'old' regulation 11 Subsidy on HB attributable to rent above the Rent Officer's determination	60%
	Rent allowance where authority is able to restrict the eligible rent under 'old' regulation 11 Subsidy on HB attributable to rent above the Rent Officer's determination	Nil
Homeless in board and lodging accommodation	Non-HRA rent rebate Subsidy on HB attributable to rent above authority's cap	Nil
	Subsidy on HB attributable to rent above authority's threshold figure up to level of authority's cap	10%
Homeless in accommodation held on licence by LAs	Non-HRA rent rebate Subsidy on HB attributable to rent above authority's cap	Nil
Short term leased accommodation	Rent rebate Subsidy on HB attributable to rent above authority's cap	Nil
Modular Improvement rule	HRA rent rebate rules in England and Wales	Nil
Extended payments	HB/CTB	100%
Discretionary local schemes	HB/CTB	0.2% addition to authority's annual benefit subsidy, capped at 75% of the total benefit cost of the local scheme to the authority

RENT REBATE SUBSIDY LIMITATION SCHEME (ENGLAND AND WALES)

23.19 Subsidy is not paid on any additional rent rebate expenditure that results from an authority increasing its average actual rents by more than its central government guideline rent increase. The DWP has been responsible for this Rent Rebate Subsidy Limitation Scheme since April 2004.

23.20 Deductions are calculated following the rules as previously set out by ODPM/NAW and remain a charge on the HRA. This necessitates a transfer from the HRA to the General Fund. An authority may apply for special determinations to disapply the rule where it can show that it faces exceptional circumstances outside its control. The details of the rules are described in *Rent Rebate Subsidy Limitation: Derogations in 2006-2007,* England (ODPM December 2005) *(www.odpm.gov.uk/pub/418/RentRebateSubsidyLimitationDerogations20062007EnglandPDF49kb_id1161418.pdf)*

RENT REBATE ATTRIBUTABLE TO MODULAR IMPROVEMENT SCHEMES

23.21 Modular Improvement Schemes allow council tenants to choose to pay increased rents in return for additional rights, services or facilities such as a door entry system or improved heating. For the purpose of rent rebate subsidy in England and Wales, rent rebate expenditure attributable to modular or menu improvement schemes is not eligible for subsidy.

23.22 Authorities are exempt from the reduction, however, where the rights, services or facilities:

- were made available with the sole purpose either of improving the physical condition of the dwellings or of meeting the needs of tenants or both; and
- were available for tenants to choose regardless of whether the tenants were or were not in receipt of rebates; and
- were not an influence on the authorities' letting policies and practices in the current and two proceeding financial years in relation to tenants eligible to receive rebates; and
- were made available at reasonable cost.

CERTAIN CASH PAYMENTS AND PAYMENTS IN KIND

23.23 Qualifying rent rebate expenditure is also reduced by the amount of any cash payments or payments in kind made to a local authority tenant by the authority except:

- payments made that are unrelated to the fact that the claimant is a tenant of the local authority, e.g. educational maintenance awards;
- awards required by law;
- discretionary payments made under section 137 of the Local Government Act 1972 or section 83 of the Local Government (Scotland) Act 1973;
- reasonable compensation for repairs or redecorating carried out by the tenant which would normally have been carried out by the landlord; and
- one-off compensation payments for the loss, damage or inconvenience caused because the tenant occupies a particular property.

This provision catches, for example, certain rent payment incentive schemes.

Subsidy on qualifying HB/CTB benefit expenditure

23.24 In 2005-06 and 2006-07 the normal subsidy rate on benefit expenditure is 100%. A lower rate is payable in specific circumstances.

TRANSITIONAL PROTECTION

23.25 The introduction of the new subsidy rates and rules across the whole HB system in April 2004 resulted in subsidy 'winners and losers'. To minimise and cushion the effects of the new subsidy regime on authorities, any subsidy losses are limited to 0.5% in 2004-05, 1% in 2005-06 and 2% in 2006-07 (DWP S2-2006). Authorities that are subsidy winners under the new arrangements have to meet some of the costs from the increased subsidy they would otherwise receive.

Penalised benefit expenditure

23.26 To provide authorities with a firm incentive to monitor and control costs, the following areas of benefit expenditure are penalised in 2005-06 and 2006-07:

- identified overpayments (para. 23.36);
- disproportionately high increases in rents for local authority tenants in Scotland and Wales (para. 23.44);
- rent allowances claims subject to rent officer referral that have not been referred in the appropriate year (para. 23.49);
- rent allowances claims subject to rent officer referral that are exempt from a maximum rent calculation but where the rent used in the calculation of HB is above the rent officer's claim related rent (para 23.53); and

- rent rebates paid for certain homeless families in bed and breakfast accommodation and occupants of certain short-term leased accommodation where the rent payment is above a certain level (para. 23.45).

23.27 Authorities must apply the benefit rules fairly, objectively and impartially. They must not allow the subsidy penalties to interfere with this duty, though where the authority has a discretion one factor it may take into account is its own financial position *(R v Brent LBC HBRB ex parte Connery).*

Backdating of claims

23.28 Since April 2004 the subsidy rate for HB/CTB awards that have been backdated where the claimant has 'continuous good cause' for a late claim (para. 5.53) has been 100%. Prior to this date such benefit expenditure incurred a penalised rate of subsidy. It should be noted, however, that subsidy claims on backdated benefit are subject to the external auditor's certification that good cause has been established (S9-2003, para. 13).

Overpayments/excess CTB

23.29 The subsidy payable on benefit overpayments/(excess CTB) varies with the category of the overpayment as shown in table 23.1.

CATEGORIES

23.30 An 'authority error overpayment' means an overpayment caused by a mistake made, whether in the form of an act or omission, by an authority. It does not apply, however, where the claimant, a person acting on the claimant's behalf or any other person to whom the payment is made, caused or materially contributes to that mistake.

23.31 A 'fraudulent overpayment' means an overpayment in respect of a period falling wholly or partly after 31st March 1993 that:

- is classified as such by an officer of the authority, whom the authority has designated for the purpose, after that date; and
- occurs as a result of the payment of benefit arising in consequence of:
  - dishonest or false representations for the purpose of obtaining benefit (i.e. a breach of section 111A or 112(1) of the Social Security Administration Act 1992);
  - someone knowingly failing to report a relevant change of circumstances, (contrary to the requirements of the regulations (paras. 17.8-12)) with the intention to obtain or retain the benefit for themselves or another.

23.32 A 'technical overpayment' means that part of an overpayment which occurs as a result of a rent rebate or CTB being awarded in advance of the payment when:

- a change of circumstances, which occurs subsequent to that award, reduces or eliminates entitlement to that rebate or benefit; or
- the authority identifies, subsequent to that award, a recoverable overpayment which does not arise from a change in circumstances.

23.33 It does not include, however, any part of that overpayment occurring before the benefit week following the week in which the change is disclosed to the authority or it identifies that overpayment.

23.34 A 'departmental error' overpayment means an overpayment caused by a mistake made, whether in the form of an act or omission

- by an officer of the DWP or of HM Revenue & Customs, acting as such, or a person providing services to that Department or to HM Revenue & Customs; or
- in a decision of an appeal tribunal or a Commissioner,

23.35 The category of 'departmental error' does not apply, however, where the claimant, a person acting on the claimant's behalf, or any other person to whom the payment is made, caused or materially contributes to that mistake. The definition also excludes any mistake of law that is shown to have been an error only by virtue of a subsequent decision of a Commissioner or a court.

SUBSIDY ON OVERPAYMENTS

23.36 In the case of overpayments the subsidy arrangement acts, at least in part, as an incentive to authorities. Subsidy is paid on the identified overpayments. Amounts recovered, except in the case of 'departmental error' overpayments, are not deducted from the authority's subsidy entitlement. For example, if the authority recovers a fraudulent overpayment or claimant error overpayment it receives 40% subsidy and keeps the money it has recovered.

LOCAL AUTHORITY ERROR OVERPAYMENTS

23.37 Prior to April 2004 the authority received nil subsidy on all overpayments categorised as 'authority error'. Since April 2004 the authority receives subsidy for 'authority error' overpayments in a way that rewards it for reducing the creation of such overpayments against the DWP's estimate of its expected 'authority error' overpayments. This is done via a threshold system. The thresholds are expressed as a percentage of the correct payments made by the council.

23.38 Correct payments are defined as those for which full (100%) subsidy is payable. This includes rent rebates, non-HRA rent rebates, rent allowances and council tax benefit. It also incorporates any backdating that has been properly undertaken. All elements of benefit expenditure that attract subsidy at lower rates are excluded from the calculation of 'correctly paid benefit'.

23.39 In 2005-06 and 2006-07 the thresholds – expressed as a percentage of the authority's correct payments – are:

- 0.48% – the lower threshold; and
- 0.54% – the upper threshold.

23.40 The authority receives:

- 100% subsidy on all local authority error overpayments – if the level of error does not exceed the lower threshold;
- 40% subsidy on all local authority error overpayments – if the level of error is greater than the lower threshold but does not exceed the upper threshold;
- nil subsidy on all local authority error overpayments – if the level of error is greater than the upper threshold.

23.41 Where the 'authority error' overpayment is recoverable the authority keeps any amount actually recovered without any loss of subsidy.

23.42 The reduced rate of subsidy on 'authority error' overpayments above the lower threshold acts as a penalty on the authority and unfortunately also as an unintended 'incentive' to misclassification. The authority's external auditors are alerted to the need to pay particular attention to the possibility that local authority error overpayments have been declared as eligible overpayments (Audit Commission, Certification Instruction BEN01 (04-05) para. 33).

INDICATIVE RENT LEVELS

23.43 Rent officers supply authorities with indicative rent levels (IRLs). These are supplied on the first working day of each month for eight types of property. As the authority is unable to decide rent allowance entitlement under the January 1996 rules until the rent officer has made a full determination, IRLs can be used by the authority in working out the amount of a payment on account. Where the authority is unable to recover all or part of an overpaid payment on account caused by the difference between the final determination (and consequent maximum rent) and the IRL, full subsidy is payable on the unrecovered amount providing the IRL used was the correct one and provided the authority applies the final determination in the HB assessment by the Monday following the date it was received.

Disproportionate rent increase rule

23.44 The disproportionate rent increase rule is intended to discourage authorities in Scotland and Wales from loading rent increases onto council tenants to unfairly generate increased subsidy income. An authority can gain exemption if it can convince its auditors that the authority has not deliberately targeted rent increases at tenants getting HB and that its rents during the year in question have increased by a common percentage with no subsidy deduction having been incurred in the previous year.

Homeless people in B & B, licensed and short-term leased accommodation outside the HRA

23.45 Reduced subsidy applies to rent rebates paid to people in:

- board and lodging (including bed and breakfast) accommodation where the liability arises under the relevant homeless persons' legislation (i.e. section 206(2)(b) of the Housing Act 1996 or section 35(2)(b) of the Housing (Scotland) Act 1987);
- accommodation held by the authority on licence (e.g. hotel annexes) where the liability arises under the relevant homeless persons' legislation; and
- accommodation held by the authority on a lease not exceeding ten years, i.e. short-term leased (STL) accommodation.

23.46 Each authority is notified of:

- a cap; and
- a threshold.

For 2006-07 these caps and thresholds are shown in Appendix 2 of S2/2006. The equivalent figures for 2005-06 are set out in Appendix 1 of S1/2005.

23.47 Benefit attributable to that part of the eligible rent that exceeds the authority's cap attracts nil subsidy entitlement. In licensed and short-term leased accommodation, the remainder attracts 100% subsidy. However, in the case of board and lodging accommodation, benefit attributable to that part of eligible rent between the threshold and the cap attracts only 10% subsidy – with the aim of making the use of such accommodation by housing authorities less attractive. The Government's stated policy intention is that no family with children should remain in bed and breakfast accommodation – except in an emergency – after March 2004 (para. 12, S4-2003).

Example of reduced subsidy available on rent rebates awarded on bed and breakfast accommodation (2005-07)

Using an illustrative threshold and cap as follows:

Threshold = £100

Cap = £140

(The difference is £40.)

The application of the threshold and cap is as follows:

Weekly eligible rent used to calculate HB is £200.

Since the weekly eligible rent exceeds the cap by £60 the first £60 of any HB paid would not attract subsidy.

If claimant's HB entitlement were £150 (due to other income, etc) , subsidy would be:

- nil on £60;
- 10% on £40; and
- 100% on £50.

If claimant's HB entitlement were £110, subsidy would be:

- nil on £60;
- 10% on £40; and
- 100% on £10

Subsidy and rent allowance awards

23.48 The basic rate of subsidy payable on rent allowance expenditure has been 100% since April 2004.

23.49 Rent officer arrangements apply to HB awarded in respect of deregulated tenancies. Where the authority is required under regulations to apply for a rent officer determination during the relevant year but fails to do so the relevant rent allowance expenditure attracts nil subsidy. A number of authorities have lost a significant amount of subsidy due to a failure to refer relevant cases to the Rent Service (see *R (Isle of Anglesey County Council) v Secretary of State for Work and Pensions* and also *R (L. B. Lambeth) v Secretary of State for Work and Pensions*).

23.50 Where a rent allowance claim falls within the rent officer referral arrangements but is not subject to a maximum rent calculation (i.e. referred to as old scheme cases – pre-January 1996) then in general no subsidy is payable on the rent allowance attributable to the rent above the rent officer's claim related rent determination, but there are exceptions to this general rule (para. 23.54).

23.51 Where rent officer's determinations are used directly to calculate the maximum rent on which a rent allowance can be assessed, full subsidy is normally payable. This entitlement to maximum subsidy includes those cases where the authority cannot restrict the rent because there has been bereavement in the household or where the rent could be afforded when the tenancy was taken up and the claimant has not been in receipt of HB for 52 weeks prior to the current claim (paras. 10.38-42).

23.52 Discretionary Housing Payments (paras. 22.2-9) do not count as qualifying expenditure for HB subsidy purposes (though authorities do receive a sometimes underspent DWP contribution towards such expenditure (para. 22.9).

OLD SCHEME CASES – PRE-JANUARY 1996

23.53 In most cases falling under the pre-January 1996 rules, no subsidy is payable on any rent allowance equal to or less than the amount by which the eligible rent exceeds the rent officer's significantly high rent figure or exceptionally high rent determination.

23.54 The exception to the general rule is where the authority is unable to treat a claimant's eligible rent as reduced. In certain cases falling under the pre-January 1996 rules, the authority is unable to restrict the claimant's eligible rent, or a rent increase. This applies, for example, where the claimant falls into a 'protected' category, e.g. the claimant is 60 or over and there is no suitable alternative accommodation available. In such cases, subsidy at the rate of 60% is payable on any rent allowance equal to or less than the amount by which the eligible rent exceeds the rent officer's determination.

Specific grant for administration costs

23.55 Authorities are partially reimbursed their administrative expenditure via a cash limited specific grant. Since 2003-04, DWP has had the sole responsibility for distribution of this funding.

23.56 Since 2004-05 additional grant has been awarded for the increased administrative costs associated with the tax credit and pension credit schemes. From 2006-07 the authority's administration cost subsidy also incorporates sums previously allocated for the setting up and operation of the Verification Framework, the WIBs scheme and the Sanctions and Prosecution Reward scheme.

23.57 The specific amounts awarded to each authority for 2005-06 are set out in Appendix A of S7/2004 and for 2006-07 in Appendix 2 of S2/2006. These circulars also explain the factors that determined each authority's share of the total amounts available to the DWP to assist with administration costs (i.e. the distribution methodology). DWP allocates administration subsidy among authorities on the basis of assumed workload rather than actual expenditure.

23.58 This administration cost subsidy fails to take account of 'quality of service' objectives such as the percentage of claims processed within the 14-day time period and error rates. As well as penalising inefficient authorities, a unit cost subsidy penalises those authorities that have sought to administer HB in a positive manner, for example by providing home visits to maximise take-up or by making their offices more accessible.

DWP funding for setting up and operating the Verification Framework

23.59 Prior to the 2006-07 financial year an authority could claim DWP monies for setting up and operating the Verification Framework. The *HB/CTB Security Manual* (June 2005), Appendix 3 sets out the additional subsidy payable per authority in 2005-06. From 2006-07 equivalent sums are distributed to authorities through a single administration cost subsidy.

Sanctions and prosecutions rewards scheme

23.60 Prior to 2006-07 rewards were available to the authority under the sanction and prosecution rewards scheme (*HB/CTB Security Manual* (June 2005), Appendix 19), i.e.

- £1,200 – for each administration penalty/formal caution issued and accepted;
- £1,200 – where information is laid with a court and the court issues a summons; and
- £2,000 – for a successful prosecution where the defendant has been found guilty.

23.61 From 2006-07 sums equivalent to those previously allocated through the sanctions and prosecutions rewards scheme are distributed to authorities through a single administration cost subsidy. The DWP Management Information System Guide 2006-07 indicates that information that was previously required for claiming WIBs is still required for DWP statistical returns.

Weekly incorrect benefit (WIBs)

23.62 Under the revised SAFE scheme that applied from April 2004-06 authorities were rewarded for identifying specific categories of overpayments (e.g. claimant error/fraud) found by authority initiative (including any attempt to contact the claimant such as under the VF review module). Rewards were not available for the actioning of changes of circumstances reported, unprompted, by claimants or Jobcentre Plus or the Pension Service. However, where an overpayment is identified by a claimant report made within 28 days of a contact made by the authority to that claimant, the overpayment was eligible for a reward. Overpayments categorised as authority error/technical were not eligible for a reward.

23.63 From 2006-07 sums equivalent to those previously allocated through the WIBs scheme are distributed to authorities through the single administration cost subsidy. The DWP Management Information System Guide 2006-07 indicates that information that was previously required for claiming WIBs is still required for DWP statistical returns.

Performance standard fund

23.64 The DWP £200 million Performance Standards Fund provides resources to help authorities improve their administration of HB/CTB. The life of the fund has been extended until March 2007 (S1/2006 para. 1). HB/CTB circular S6/2004 sets out detailed guidance on applying for the funding.

23.65 The Performance Standard Fund superseded The Help Fund that was set up in 2001 to provide support to authority initiatives for improving core administration of benefit.

Appendix 1: Main and recent regulations, orders and rules

Here we list the main statutory instruments for England, Wales and Scotland (also known as regulations and orders) that contain the detailed rules of the HB and CTB schemes, followed by the main statutory rules and orders in council governing the HB scheme in Northern Ireland.

MAIN REGULATIONS AND ORDERS: ENGLAND, WALES AND SCOTLAND

SI 2006/213	The Housing Benefit Regulations 2006
SI 2006/214	The Housing Benefit (Persons who have attained the qualifying age for state pension credit) Regulations 2006
SI 2006/215	The Council Tax Benefit Regulations 2006
SI 2006/216	The Council Tax Benefit (Persons who have attained the qualifying age for state pension credit) Regulations 2006
SI 2006/217	The Housing Benefit and Council Tax Benefit (Consequential Provisions) Regulations 2006
SI 2001/1002	The Housing Benefit and Council Tax Benefit (Decisions and Appeals) Regulations
SI 2001/1167	The Discretionary Financial Assistance Regulations
SI 1998/562	The Income-related Benefits (Subsidy to Authorities) Order
SI 1997/1984	The Rent Officers (Housing Benefit Functions) Order
SI 1997/1995	The Rent Officers (Housing Benefit Functions) (Scotland) Order
SI 1996/677	The Housing Benefit (Permitted Totals) Order
SI 1996/678	The Council Tax Benefit (Permitted Total) Order

The first five in the above list are the consolidating regulations which govern HB and CTB from 6th March 2006.

RECENT REGULATIONS AND ORDERS: ENGLAND, WALES AND SCOTLAND

The following is the full list of amendments made (or otherwise relevant) to the consolidating regulations (see above).

SI 2005/2465	The Social Security (Miscellaneous Amendments) (No. 2) Regulations 2005
SI 2005/2502	The Housing Benefit and Council Tax Benefit (Miscellaneous Amendments) (No. 3) Regulations 2005
SI 2005/2677	The Social Security (Deferral of Retirement Pensions, Shared Additional Pension and Gradated Retirement Benefit) (Miscellaneous Provisions) Regulations 2005 *(This amendment was done only to the pre-consolidation regulations but it is expected that it will be carried forward to the consolidating regulations.)*
SI 2005/2904	The Housing Benefit and Council Tax Benefit (General) Amendment Regulations 2005
SI 2005/3205	The State Pension Credit (Amendment) Regulations 2005
SI 2005/3238	The National Council for Education and Training for Wales (Transfer of Functions to the National Assembly for Wales and Abolition) Order 2005
SI 2005/3360	The Social Security (Hospital In-Patients) Regulations 2005
SI 2006/54	The Income-related Benefits (Subsidy to Authorities) Amendment Order 2006
SI 2006/559	The Income-related Benefits (Subsidy to Authorities) Amendment (No. 2) Order 2006
SI 2006/588	The Social Security (Miscellaneous Amendments) Regulations 2006
SI 2006/644	The Housing Benefit (Amendment) Regulations 2006
SI 2006/645	The Social Security Benefits Up-rating Order 2006
SI 2006/718	The Social Security (Young Persons) Amendment Regulations 2006
SI 2006/1026	The Social Security (Persons from Abroad) Amendment Regulations 2006

MAIN REGULATIONS: NORTHERN IRELAND

	The Housing Benefit Regulations (Northern Ireland) 2006
	The Housing Benefit (Persons who have attained the qualifying age for state pension credit) Regulations (Northern Ireland) 2006
	The Housing Benefit and Council Tax Benefit (Consequential Provisions) Regulations (Northern Ireland) 2006
SR 2001 No. 213	The Housing Benefit (Decisions and Appeals) Regulations (Northern Ireland)
SR 2001 No. 216	The Discretionary Financial Assistance Regulations (Northern Ireland)

The first three in the above list are the consolidating regulations which will govern HB and are expected to come into force during July 2006 (reference number not available at time of going to press).

At the point they come into force the consolidating regulations will incorporate any other changes made to the 1987 Regulations that have been made between that date and the 1 April 2006.

Appendix 2: Table of cases cited in guide

The following table lists all cases cited in the guide in the order they appear. Where possible the table indicates where a free on-line case transcript can be accessed. Where none is available both free and on-line the table provides a reference for a recognised published law report.

Social Security Commissioners' decisions cited in this guide are not included in this table. For further details on the status of Commissioners' decisions, see paras. 1.51-52 and 19.65-68. Hard copies of reported Commissioners' decisions (i.e. those prefixed by 'R') are available from Print Solutions, Room B0202, Benton Park Road, Longbenton, Newcastle upon Tyne, NE98 1YX (Tel: 0191 225 5422, Fax: 0191 225 7179). Reported decisions from 1991 are available on-line at *www.dwp.gov.uk/advisers/index.asp#commdecs.* All unreported Commissioners' decisions from 2002 and selected decisions from 2001 are available on-line at *www.osscsc.gov.uk/decisions/decisions.htm.* Earlier unreported decisions in print are available from the Office of the Social Security Commissioners (para. 19.95). For Northern Ireland Commissioners' decisions see paragraph 1.52.

Para	**Case** *Neutral Citation/European Case Reference* *Full online transcript*	**Date** *Published report*	**Court**
1.61	**R v Maidstone BC ex p Bunce**	**23/06/94** *27 HLR 375*	**QBD**
2.34	**R v Poole BC HBRB ex p Ross**	**05/05/95** *28 HLR 351*	**QBD**
2.44	**R v Sheffield C C HBRB ex p Smith**	**08/12/94** *28 HLR 36*	**QBD**
2.44	**R v Sutton BC HBRB ex p Partridge**	**04/11/94** *28 HLR 315*	**QBD**
2.44	**R v Poole BC HBRB ex p Ross**	*See 2.34 above*	
2.44	**Campbell v South Northamptonshire DC** *[2004] EWCA Civ 409* *www.bailii.org/ew/cases/EWCA/Civ/2004/409.html*	**07/04/04**	**CA**
2.48	**R v Solihull MBC HBRB ex p Simpson**	**03/12/93** *26 HLR 370*	**QBD**

Para	Case *Neutral Citation/European Case Reference* *Full online transcript*	Date *Published*	Court *report*
2.48	**R v Sutton LBC ex p Keegan**	**15/05/92** *27 HLR 92*	**QBD**
2.51	**R v Manchester CC ex p Baragrove Properties**	**15/03/91** *23 HLR 337*	**QBD**
2.54	**R (Painter) v Carmarthenshire CC HBRB** *[2001] EWHC Admin 308* *www.bailii.org/ew/cases/EWHC/Admin/2001/308.html*	**04/05/01**	**HC (Admin)**
2.56	**Secretary of State for Social Security v Tucker** *[2001] EWCA Civ 1646* *www.bailii.org/ew/cases/EWHC/CW/2001/1646.html*	**08/11/01**	**CA**
2.67	**The Governors of Peabody Donation Fund v Higgins**	**20/06/83** *[1983] 1 WLR 1091*	**CA**
3.3	**Secretary of State for Work and Pensions v Miah** *[2003] EWCA Civ 1111* *www.bailii.org/ew/cases/EWCA/Civ/2003/1111.html*	**25/07/03**	**CA**
3.25	**Secretary of State for Work and Pensions v Miah**	*See 3.3 above*	
3.32	**Secretary of State for Work and Pensions v Selby District Council** *[2006] EWCA Civ 271* *www.bailii.org/ew/cases/EWCA/Civ/2006/271.html*	**13/02/06**	**CA**
3.35	**R v Penwith DC HBRB ex p Burt**	**26/02/90** *22 HLR 292*	**QBD**
4.19	**Crake and Butterworth v Supplementary Benefit Commission**	**21/07/80** *[1982] 1 All ER 498*	**QBD**
4.22	**R v Penwith DC ex p Menear**	**11/10/91** *24 HLR 115*	**QBD**
4.35	**R v Swale BC HBRB ex p Marchant** *www.casetrack.com Subscriber site Case reference: QBCOF 1999/0071/C*	**9/11/99** *32 HLR 856*	**CA**

Para	Case	Date	Court
	Neutral Citation/European Case Reference *Full online transcript*	*Published report*	
4.35	**Hockenjos v Secretary of State for Social Security (No. 2)** *[2004] EWCA Civ 1749* *www.bailii.org/ew/cases/EWCA/Civ/2004/1749.html*	**21/12/04**	**CA**
4.45	**Kadhim v Brent LBC HBRB** *[2000] EWCA Civ 344* *www.bailii.org/ew/cases/EWCA/Civ/2000/344.html*	**20/12/00**	**CA**
5.18	**R v Liverpool CC ex p Johnson (No 2)**	**31/10/94** *[1995] COD 200*	**QBD**
5.21	**R v Penwith DC ex p Menear**	*See 4.15 above*	
5.22	**R v Winston** *[1998] EWCA Crim 2256* *www.bailii.org/ew/cases/EWCA/Crim/1998/2256.html*	**07/07/98**	**CA**
6.18	**R (Saadat and Others) v The Rent Service** *[2001] EWCA Civ 1559* *www.bailii.org/ew/cases/EWCA/Civ/2001/1559.html*	**26/10/01**	**CA**
6.26	**R v Swale BC HBRB ex p Marchant**	*See 4.35 above*	
6.26	**Hockenjos v Secretary of State**	*See 4.35 above*	
6.40	**R (Cumpsty) v The Rent Service** *[2002] EWHC 2526 Admin* *www.casetrack.com Subscriber site Case reference: CO/1892/2002*	**08/11/02**	**HC (Admin)**
10.6	**R (Naghshbandi) v Camden LBC HBRB** *[2002] EWCA Civ 1038* *www.bailii.org/ew/cases/EWCA/Civ/2002/1038.html*	**19/07/02**	**CA**
10.24	**Burton v Camden LBC**	**17/12/97** *30 HLR 991*	**CA**
10.49	**R (Laali) v Westminster CC HBRB** *www.casetrack.com Subscriber site Case reference: CO/1845/2000*	**08/12/00**	**QBD**
10.54	**R v Swale BC HBRB ex p Marchant**	*See 4.35 above*	
10.56	**R v Beverley DC HBRB ex p Hare**	**21/02/95** *27 HLR 637*	**QBD**

Para	Case *Neutral Citation/European Case Reference* *Full online transcript*	Date *Published report*	Court
10.56	**Malcolm v Tweedale HBRB**	**06/08/91** *1994 SLT 1212*	**CS**
10.57	**Malcolm v Tweedale HBRB**	*See 10.56 above*	
10.60	**R v East Devon DC HBRB ex p Gibson**	**10/03/93** *25 HLR 487*	**CA**
10.61	**R v Sefton MBC ex p Cunningham**	**22/05/91** *23 HLR 534*	**QBD**
10.62	**R v Westminster CC HBRB ex p Mehanne** *[2001] UKHL 11* *www.publications.parliament.uk/pa/ld200001/ldjudgmt/jd010308/mehann-1.htm*	**08/03/01** *33 HLR 46*	**HL**
10.62	**R v Beverley DC HBRB ex p Hare**	*See 10.56 above*	
10.62	**R v Brent LBC ex p Connery**	**20/10/89** *22 HLR 40*	**QBD**
10.64	**R v Brent LBC ex p Connery**	*See 10.62 above*	
13.20	**Hourigan v Secretary of State for Work and Pensions** *[2002] EWCA Civ 1890* *www.bailii.org/ew/cases/EWCA/Civ/2002/1890.html*	**19/12/02**	**CA**
13.115	**R v Doncaster MBC & Another ex p Boulton**	**11/12/92** *25 HLR 195*	**QBD**
13.126	**Morrell v Secretary of State for Work and Pensions** *[2003] EWCA Civ 526* *www.bailii.org/ew/cases/EWCA/Civ/2003/526.html*	**11/04/03**	**CA**
16.6	**R v Liverpool CC ex p Johnson (No 1)**	**23/06/94** *unreported*	**QBD**
16.17	**R v Haringey LBC ex p Ayub**	**13/04/92** *25 HLR 566*	**QBD**
16.31	**R v Haringey LBC ex p Ayub**	*See 16.17 above*	
16.40	**Bessa Plus PLC v Lancaster** *[1997] EWCA Civ 1260* *www.bailii.org/ew/cases/EWCA/Civ/1997/1260.html*	**17/03/97**	**CA**

Para	Case *Neutral Citation/European Case Reference* *Full online transcript*	Date *Published report*	Court
18.10	**R (Steele) v Secretary of State for Work and Pensions** *[2005] EWCA Civ 1824* *www.bailii.org/ew/cases/EWCA/Civ/2005/1824.html*	**16/12/05**	**CA**
18.11	**R v Cambridge CC HBRB ex p Sier** *[2001] EWCA Civ 1523* *www.bailii.org/ew/cases/EWCA/Civ/2001/1523.html*	**08/10/01**	**CA**
18.12	**R v Liverpool CC ex p Griffiths**	**14/03/90** *22 HLR 312*	**QBD**
18.15	**Adan v Hounslow LBC** *[2004] EWCA Civ 101* *www.bailii.org/ew/cases/EWCA/Civ/2004/101.html*	**19/02/04**	**CA**
18.35	**Warwick DC v Freeman**	**31/10/94** *27 HLR 616*	**CA**
18.40	**Secretary of State for Work and Pensions v Chiltern DC and Warden Housing Association** *[2003] EWCA Civ 508* *www.bailii.org/ew/cases/EWCA/Civ/2003/508.html*	**26/03/03**	**CA**
18.61	**R v Haringey ex p Ayub**	*See 16.17 above*	
18.88	**R v Thanet DC ex p Warren Court Hotels Ltd** *www.casetrack.com Subscriber site Case reference CO/523/1999*	**06/04/00** *33 HLR 32*	**QBD**
18.88	**Warwick DC v Freeman**	*See 18.30 above*	
18.89	**Haringey LBC v Awaritefe** *[1999] EWCA Civ 1491* *www.bailii.org/ew/cases/EWCA/Civ/1999/1491.html*	**26/05/99**	**CA**
18.90	**Waveney DC v Jones** *www.casetrack.com Subscriber site Case reference CCRTF 1998/1488/B2*	**01/12/99** *33 HLR 3*	**CA**
18.90	**Norwich CC v Stringer** *www.casetrack.com Subscriber site Case reference FC2 99/7400/B2*	**03/05/00** *33 HLR 15*	**CA**

Para	Case	Date	Court
	Neutral Citation/European Case Reference *Full online transcript*	*Published report*	
19.19	**Beltekian v Westminster CC**	**08/12/04**	**CA**
	[2004] EWCA Civ 1784 *www.bailii.org/ew/cases/EWCA/Civ/2004/1784.html*		
19.20	**Secretary of State for Work and Pensions v Chiltern DC**	*See 18.40 above*	
19.28	**R v Lambeth ex p Crookes**	**11/02/97** *29 HLR 28*	**QBD**
20.20	**R (Begum) v Social Security Commissioner**	**06/11/03**	**QBD**
	[2003] EWHC 3380 (Admin) *www.bailii.org/ew/cases/EWHC/Admin/2003/3380.html*		
20.20	**Secretary of State for Work and Pensions v Ahmed**	**19/04/05**	**CA**
	[2005] EWCA Civ 535 *www.bailii.org/ew/cases/EWCA/Civ/2001/309.html*		
20.25	**Szoma (FC) v Secretary of State for Work and Pensions**	**27/10/05**	**HL**
	[2005] UKHL 64 *www.publications.parliament.uk/pa/ld200506/ldjudgmt/jd051027/szoma-1.htm*		
20.38	**Levin v Staatsscretaris van Justitie**	**27/10/05**	**ECJ**
	53/81 *http://europa.eu.int/smartapi/cgi/sga_doc?smartapi!celexapi!prod!CELEXnumdoc&lg=EN&numdoc=61981J0053&model=guichett*		
20.38	**Raulin v Minister van Ondervijsen Wentenschappen**	**27/10/05**	**ECJ**
	C-357/89 *http://europa.eu.int/smartapi/cgi/sga_doc?smartapi!celexapi!prod!CELEXnumdoc&lg=EN&numdoc=61989J0357&model=guichett*		
20.65	**Re J (A Minor) (Abduction)**	**17/05/90** *[1990] 2 AC 562*	**HL**

Para	Case	Date	Court
	Neutral Citation/European Case Reference *Full online transcript*	*Published report*	
20.62	**Angenjeux v Hakenberg**	**12/07/73**	**ECJ**
	13/73 *http://europa.eu.int/smartapi/cgi/sga_doc?smartapi!celexapi!prod!CELEXnumdoc&lg=EN&numdoc=61973J0013&model=guichett*		
20.62	**Di Paolo v Office National de L'Emploi**	**17/02/77**	**ECJ**
	76/76 *http://europa.eu.int/smartapi/cgi/sga_doc?smartapi!celexapi!prod!CELEXnumdoc&lg=EN&numdoc=61976J0076&model=guichett*		
20.78	**Nessa v Chief Adjudication Officer**	**21/10/99**	**HL**
	www.publications.parliament.uk/pa/ld199899/ldjudgmt/jd991021/nessa.htm		
20.78	**Swaddling v Chief Adjudication Officer**	**25/02/99**	**ECJ**
	C-90/97 *http://europa.eu.int/smartapi/cgi/sga_doc?smartapi!celexapi!prod!CELEXnumdoc&lg=EN&numdoc=61997J0090&model=guichett*		
21.8	**O'Connor v Chief Adjudication Officer**	**03/03/99**	**CA**
	[1999] EWCA 884 *www.bailii.org/ew/cases/EWCA/Civ/1999/884.html*		
23.27	**R v Brent LBC ex p Connery**	*See 10.62 above*	
23.49	**R (Isle of Angelsey County Council) v Secretary of State for Work and Pensions**	**30/10/03**	**QBD**
	[2003] EWHC 2518 Admin *www.bailii.org/ew/cases/EWHC/Admin/2003/2518.html*		
23.49	**R (Lambeth LBC) v Secretary of State for Work and Pensions**	**20/04/05**	**QBD**
	[2005] EWHC 637 (Admin) *www.bailii.org/ew/cases/EWHC/Admin/2005/637.html*		

Abbreviations used in this appendix

AC	Appeal Cases, published by The Incorporated Council of Law Reporting for England and Wales, London
All ER	All England Law Reports, published by Butterworths
BC	Borough Council
CA	Court of Appeal for England and Wales
CC	City Council
COD	Crown Office Digest, published by Sweet & Maxwell
CS	Court of Session, Scotland
DC	District Council
ECJ	European Court of Justice
EWCA Civ	Court of Appeal Civil Division for England & Wales (neutral citation)
EWCA Crim	Court of Appeal Criminal Division for England & Wales (neutral citation)
EWHC Admin	High Court for England & Wales, Administrative Court (neutral citation)
HBRB	Housing Benefit Review Board
HC (Admin)	High Court for England and Wales, Administrative Court
HL	House of Lords
HLR	Housing Law Reports, published by Sweet & Maxwell
LBC	London Borough Council
MBC	Metropolitan Borough Council
QBD	High Court (England & Wales) Queens Bench Division
SLT	Scots Law Times, published by W. Green, Edinburgh
UKHL	House of Lords, UK case (neutral citation)
WLR	Weekly Law Reports, published by The Incorporated Council of Law Reporting for England and Wales, London

Appendix 3: Relevant HB and CTB circulars

This appendix lists:

- all DWP circulars in the 'A' (adjudication and operations) series which remain current following the issue of amendment 7 to the DWP's Housing Benefit and Council Tax Benefit Guidance Manual, the list being extrapolated from circular HB/CTB A21/2005; and
- all DWP circulars in the 'S' (subsidy) series since the beginning of 2005.

Circulars in the 'G' (general), 'U' (urgent) and 'F' (fraud) series are not listed here (but see para. 1.60).

ADJUDICATION AND OPERATION CIRCULARS

HB/CTB A27/2003 (September 2003, revised October 2003)
Employment Retention and Advancement (ERA) Scheme

HB/CTB A30/2003 (October 2003)
1 Return to Work Credit: Introduction in pilot areas from 27 October 2003 and 5 April 2004
2 Addendum to HB/CTB Guidance Manual Amendment 2

HB/CTB A9/2004 (February 2004)
1 Disregard of Lone Parent Work Search Premium and Lone Parent In Work Credit
2 Current HB/CTB A Circulars list

HB/CTB A10/2004 (February 2004)
Families given extended leave to remain in UK, granted exceptional leave outside Immigration Rules, as a result of Home Secretary's announcement of 24 October 2003

HB/CTB A13/2004 (March 2004)
1 Uprating 2004 – Frequently Asked Questions
2 The Pension Service Partnership Fund

HB/CTB A33/2004 (November 2004)
Take-up of Council Tax Benefit: DWP activities to raise awareness of Council Tax Benefit

HB/CTB A3/2005 (February 2005)
Change to HBMS Data Specification

HB/CTB A4/2005 (February 2005)
Take-up of Council Tax Benefit: Scan identifying customers receiving Pension Credit when there is no evidence of a live CTB (or HB) claim

HB/CTB A6/2005 (February 2005)
2005 HB/CTB Performance Standards

HB/CTB A9/2005 (April 2005)
Social Security, Child Support & Tax Credit (Miscellaneous Amendments) Regulations 2005 No 357

HB/CTB A10/2005 (April 2005)
1 2005 HB/CTB Performance Standards – clarifications
2 Issue of the 2005 HB/CTB MIS guide

HB/CTB A11/2005 (May 2005)
2005 HB/CTB Performance Standards self-assessment

HB/CTB A13/2005 (August 2005)
[1] Regulation changes - rent-free weeks
[2] Student loans and grants 2005-2006
[3] National Savings Certificates: valuation 1 July 2005

HB/CTB A14/2005 (August 2005)
HB/CTB Performance Standards Fund

HB/CTB A15/2005 (September 2005)
Miscellaneous Amendment Regulations

HB/CTB A16/2005 (September 2005)
Civil Partnerships - Impact on HB/CTB. The Civil Partnership (Pensions, Social Security and Child Support) (Consequential, etc. Provisions) Order 2005

HB/CTB A17/2005 (September 2005)
1 Submission of self-assessments against the 2005 HB/CTB Performance Standards
2 Amendments to the 2005 HB/CTB Performance Standards
3 Work Search Premium for Working Tax Credit Partners

HB/CTB A18/2005 (October 2005)
The Housing Benefit and Council Tax Benefit (Miscellaneous Amendments) (No. 3) Regulations 2005, Statutory Instrument Number 21005/2502

HB/CTB A19/2005 (October 2005)
Deferral of State Pension - the treatment of lump sum payments in HB/CTB

HB/CTB A20/2005 (October 2005)

The Social Security (Care Homes and Independent Hospitals) Regulations 2005, Statutory Instrument Number 2005/2687

HB/CTB A21/2005 (November 2005)

[1] The Housing Benefit and Council Tax Benefit (Miscellaneous Amendments) (No. 4) Regulations 2005

[2] Current HB/CTB circulars list

HB/CTB A22/2005 (December 2005)

Important new information to HCTB1(PCA) [Peter: sic]

HB/CTB A23/2005 (December 2005)

1 HB/CTB (Miscellaneous Amendments) (No. 5) Regulations 2005 (SI 2005/3294)

2 Payments from the Financial Assistance Scheme: The effects on HB/CTB

3 London Bombings Relief Charitable Fund

HB/CTB A24/2005 (December 2005) (Revised December 2005)

2006 Uprating

HB/CTB A25/2005 (December 2005)

CH/3801/2004 and staying cases

HB/CTB A1/2006 (January 2006)

Housing Benefit Matching Service (HBMS) Data Take on and Processing Schedule (DTOPS) 28

HB/CTB A2/2006 (January 2006)

Further guidance about HB/CTB suspension, termination and date of claim

HB/CTB A3/2006 (February 2006)

[1] Proposed changes to the 2005 HB/CTB Performance Standards

[2] Proposed Comprehensive Performance Assessment (CPA) methodology for single tier councils

[3] Revisions to the HB/CTB Security Manual

HB/CTB A4/2006 (February 2006)

The Housing Benefit and Council Tax Benefit (General) Amendments Regulations 2005, Statutory Instrument Number 2005/2904

HB/CTB A5/2006 (March 2006)

Changes to the HB and CTB Regulations (both for working age and pension age claimants) as a result of Social Security (Miscellaneous Amendments) Regulations 2006, SI 2006/588

HB/CTB A6/2006 (March 2006)

[1] Transfer of responsibility for the Appeals Service from the Department for Work and Pensions to the Department for Constitutional Affairs

[2] Financial support for 16/19 year olds. The Social Security (Young Persons) Amendment Regulations 2006. SI 2006/718

HB/CTB A7/2006 (March 2006)

[1] Changes to the 2005 HB/CTB Performance Standards from April 2006

[2] Annual requirements for interventions and visits for 2006/07

[3] Comprehensive Performance Assessment (CPA) methodology for single tier councils in 2006

SUBSIDY CIRCULARS

HB/CTB S1/2005 (January 2005)

Housing Benefit non-HRA thresholds and caps for 2005/06

HB/CTB S2/2005

HB/CTB subsidy arrangements 2005/06: Details of the benefit subsidy arrangments and the specific grant for administration costs

HB/CTB S3/2005

Withdrawal of Verification Framework (VF) set-up funding from April 2006

HB/CTB S4/2005 (Revised) (December 2005)

Details of the Department of Work and Pensions (DWP) specific grants for Local Authorities' (LAs) administration costs in 2006/07

HB/CTB S5/2005 (December 2005)

Non Housing Revenue Account (HRA) rent rebate subsidy thresholds and caps 2006/07

HB/CTB S1/2005 (January 2006)

[1] DWP strategy for allocating the remaining Performance Standards Fund

[2] Important information on the roll-out of national products

HB/CTB S2/2006 (March 2006)

HB/CTB subsidy arrangements 2006/07: Details of the benefit subsidy arrangements and the specific grant for administration costs. Details of the distribution of the government contribution and overall Discretionary Housing Payments for 2006/07

Appendix 4: HB and CTB rates and allowances (from April 2006)

Personal Allowances

SINGLE CLAIMANT	
aged under 25	£45.50
aged 25+ but under 60	£57.45
aged 60+ but under 65	£114.05
aged 65+	£131.95
LONE PARENT	
aged under 18 (HB only)	£45.50
aged 18+ but under 60	£57.45
aged 60+ but under 65	£114.05
aged 65+	£131.95
COUPLE	
both aged under 18 (HB only)	£68.65
at least one aged 18+ but both under 60	£90.10
at least one aged 60+ but both under 65	£174.05
at least one aged 65+	£197.65
CHILD/YOUNG PERSON ADDITION	£45.58

Premiums

1. 'ANY AGE PREMIUMS'

(premiums that do not depend on claimant's or partner's age)

Family premium	baby rate (at least one child under 1)	£26.75
	normal rate *(protected lone parent rates: see para.12.9)*	£16.25
Disabled child premium	each dependent child	£45.08
Enhanced disability premium	each dependent child	£18.13
Severe disability premium	single rate	£46.75
	double rate	£93.50
Carer premium	claimant or partner or each	£26.35

2. 'UNDER 60 PREMIUMS'

(premiums that apply only if claimant and any partner are under 60)

Disability premium	single claimant/lone parent	£24.50
	couple (one/both qualifying)	£34.95
Enhanced disability premium	single claimant/lone parent	£11.95
	couple (one/both qualifying)	£17.25
Bereavement premium	single claimant	£26.80*

* until 10.4.06 when bereavement premium ceases to apply.

Earned income disregards

STANDARD DISREGARD (HIGHEST ONE ONLY)

Lone parent	£25.00
Certain people who are: disabled, carers or in select occupations	£20.00
Couple	£10.00
All others (single)	£ 5.00

ADDITIONAL 16/30 HOUR WORK DISREGARD

Where conditions are met (para. 14.30)	£14.90

ADDITIONAL CHILDCARE DISREGARD (HIGHEST ONE ONLY)

Qualifying childcare charges for 1 child (actual costs up to)	£175.00
Qualifying childcare charges for 2 or more children (actual costs up to)	£300.00

Non–dependant deductions in HB

AGE 18 OR OVER AND WORKING AT LEAST 16 HOURS

Gross income	
£338.00 or more	£47.75
£271.00 - £337.99	£43.50
£204.00 - £270.99	£38.20
£157.00 - £203.99	£23.35
£106.00 - £156.99	£17.00
Under £106.00	£7.40

OTHERS NOT IN WORK OR WORKING UNDER 16 HOURS

On pension credit or under 25 on JSA(IB) or IS	£0.00
Most others	£7.40

Non–dependant deductions in main CTB

AGE 18 OR OVER AND WORKING AT LEAST 16 HOURS

Gross income	
£338.00 or more	£6.95
£271.00 - £337.99	£5.80
£157.00 - £270.99	£4.60
Under £157.00	£2.30

ALL OTHERS NOT IN WORK OR WORKING UNDER 16 HOURS

On pension credit, JSA(IB) or IS	£0.00
Most others	£2.30

Non–dependant deductions in NI rates

AGE 18 OR OVER AND WORKING AT LEAST 16 HOURS

Gross income

£338.00 or more	£6.95
£271.00 - £337.99	£5.80
£157.00 - £270.99	£4.60
Under £157.00	£2.30

ALL OTHERS NOT IN WORK OR WORKING UNDER 16 HOURS

On pension credit, JSA(IB) or IS	£0.00
Most others	£2.30

Second adult rebate

CIRCUMSTANCES	AMOUNT OF REBATE
General	
All second adults on JSA(IB) or IS or pension credit	25% of council tax
Second adults gross income under £157.00	15% of council tax
Second adults gross income £157.00 - £203.99	7.5% of council tax
Second adults gross income £204.00 or more	Nil
Student only	100% of council tax

Meals deductions (HB)

FULL BOARD

Each person aged 16+	£20.50
Each child under 16	£10.35

HALF BOARD

Each person aged 16+	£13.65
Each child under 16	£6.85

BREAKFAST ONLY

Each person (inc. children)	£2.50

Fuel charge deductions (HB)

PEOPLE OCCUPYING MORE THAN ONE ROOM

All fuel	£15.70
Heating	£11.95
Hot water	£1.40
Lighting	£0.95
Cooking	£1.40

PEOPLE OCCUPYING ONE ROOM ONLY

All fuel except cooking	£7.15
Cooking	£1.40

Appendix 5: Selected benefit rates (from April 2006)

ATTENDANCE ALLOWANCE

higher rate	£62.25
lower rate	£41.65

BEREAVEMENT ALLOWANCE/WIDOW'S PENSION

standard rate	£84.25

CHILD BENEFIT

only or older/oldest child (general rate)	£17.45
only or older/oldest child (protected lone parent rate)	£17.55
each other child (couple or lone parent)	£11.70

CARER'S ALLOWANCE

Claimant	£46.95

DISABILITY LIVING ALLOWANCE

Care component	
highest rate	£62.25
middle rate	£41.65
lowest rate	£16.50
Mobility component	
higher rate	£43.45
lower rate	£16.50

GUARDIAN'S ALLOWANCE	£12.50

INCAPACITY BENEFIT

Short-term lower rate (under pension age)	£59.20
Short-term higher rate (under pension age)	£70.05
Long-term rate	£78.50
Spouse or adult dependant (where appropriate)	£46.95
increase for age higher rate (under 35)	£16.50
increase for age lower rate (35-44)	£8.25

INDUSTRIAL DISABLEMENT PENSION

20% disabled	£25.42
For each further 10% disability up to 100%	£12.71
100% disabled	£127.10

JOBSEEKER'S ALLOWANCE (CONTRIBUTION-BASED)

Aged under 18	£34.60
Aged 18 to 24	£45.50
Aged 25 or more	£57.45

MATERNITY ALLOWANCE	£108.85

RETIREMENT PENSION BASIC RATE

single person	£84.25
spouse or adult dependant	£50.50

For details of other benefit rates from April 2006 (including means-tested benefits, tax credits and war pensions) see Circular A24/2005.

Appendix 6: Categories of people for non-dependant deduction and second adult rebate purposes

There are many categories of people relevant for non-dependant deductions in HB, for non-dependant deductions in main CTB, and for second adult rebate. The categories are not always the same for these three purposes.

This appendix defines all the categories relevant for these purposes, and answers the following questions for each category:

- Is there a non-dependant deduction for them in HB (including, in Northern Ireland, HB in respect of rates) and main CTB (paras. 7.17, 7.22)?
- Are they 'disregarded persons' for second adult rebate purposes?

The second question is relevant because a 'disregarded person' cannot be a second adult (para. 8.8); and because the rules about whether couples and joint occupiers can qualify for second adult rebate refer to 'disregarded persons' (paras. 8.17-18). It is also relevant to the rules about council tax discounts (para. 9.16).

People may fall into more than one category. If a particular category (e.g. category 1) indicates that a non-dependant deduction applies (or that they are not 'disregarded persons'), this is over-ridden if they fall into another category (e.g. category 13) where no non-dependant deduction applies (or where they are 'disregarded persons').

The category numbers have no significance except to aid cross-referencing.

1. (a) PEOPLE ON JSA(IB) OR INCOME SUPPORT (b) PEOPLE ON PENSION CREDIT

HB	(a): No non-dependant deduction if aged under 25. (b): No non-dependant deduction.
Main CTB	(a) and (b): No non-dependant deduction.
Second adult rebate	Not 'disregarded persons'.

Group (a) includes people receiving JSA(IB) or income support while on government training schemes, and people who would get JSA(IB) except that they are currently subject to a sanction.

2. PEOPLE UNDER 18

HB and main CTB	No non-dependant deduction.
Second adult rebate	'Disregarded persons' (because they do not count as 'residents').

This means anyone under 18 whether a member of the claimant's family or not.

3. PEOPLE UNDER 20 FOR WHOM CHILD BENEFIT IS PAYABLE

HB and main CTB	No non-dependant deduction.
Second adult rebate	'Disregarded persons'.

This means anyone under 20 for whom someone receives or could receive child benefit – e.g. at school and shortly after leaving school (see also category 4).

4. EDUCATION LEAVERS UNDER 20

HB	A non-dependant deduction applies unless they fall within categories 2 or 3.
Main CTB	No non-dependant deduction.
Second adult rebate	'Disregarded persons'.

This only applies from 1st May to 31st October inclusive each year. It means anyone who leaves the type of education described in category 5 or 6 within that period. It lasts until that person reaches 20 or until 31st October, whichever comes first.

5. STUDENTS UNDER 20 AT SCHOOL OR COLLEGE

HB and main CTB	Whether there is a non-dependant deduction depends on whether they fall within category 2, 3 or 10.
Second adult rebate	'Disregarded persons'.

The full definition is not given here. Its main elements are that the person:

- is under 20; and
- is studying up to (but not above) A level, ONC, OND or equivalent; and
- is on a course of at least three months' duration; and
- is normally required to study at least 12 hours per week in term times; and
- does not fall within categories 6 to 8.

6. FULL-TIME STUDENTS IN FURTHER OR HIGHER EDUCATION

HB and main CTB	Whether there is a non-dependant deduction depends on whether they fall within category 10.
Second adult rebate	'Disregarded persons'.

The full definition is not given here. Its main elements are that the person:

- is attending a course of further or higher education (e.g. university); and
- is on a course of at least one academic or calendar year's duration; and
- is normally required to study at least 21 hours per week for at least 24 weeks per year.

7. FOREIGN LANGUAGE ASSISTANTS

HB and main CTB	Whether there is a non-dependant deduction depends on whether they fall within category 10.
Second adult rebate	'Disregarded persons'.

They must be registered with the Central Bureau for Educational Visits and Exchanges.

8. STUDENTS ON NURSING AND RELATED COURSES

HB and main CTB	Whether there is a non-dependant deduction depends on whether they fall within category 10.
Second adult rebate	'Disregarded persons'.

This means anyone studying for a first inclusion in Parts 1 to 6 or 8 of the nursing register.

9. STUDENT NURSES STUDYING FOR THEIR FIRST NURSING REGISTRATION

HB and main CTB	Whether there is a non-dependant deduction depends on whether they fall within category 10.
Second adult rebate	'Disregarded persons'.

This means anyone studying for a first inclusion in Parts 1 to 6 or 8 of the nursing register.

10. FULL-TIME STUDENTS

HB	No non-dependant deduction except if claimant and any partner are under 65, and then only during any period the student takes up remunerative work (16 hours per week or more) in a summer vacation.
Main CTB	No non-dependant deduction.
Second adult rebate	'Disregarded persons'.

A student at a further education college counts as 'full-time' if he or she is normally expected to undertake more than 16 guided learning hours per week. All students on sandwich courses count as 'full-time'. Otherwise 'full-time' is not defined.

11. WORK BASED TRAINING ALLOWANCE TRAINEES

HB and main CTB	No non-dependant deduction.
Second adult rebate	'Disregarded persons' only if under 25.

This means people in receipt of a Work Based Training Allowance as a trainee.

12. APPRENTICES ON NCVQ/SVEC COURSES

HB	A non-dependant deduction applies.
Main CTB	No non-dependant deduction.
Second adult rebate	'Disregarded persons'.

This means someone who:

- is in employment; and
- is studying for a qualification accredited by the National Council for Vocational Qualifications (England and Wales) or Scottish Vocational Education Council (Scotland); and
- receives a reduced rate of pay because of being an apprentice; and
- receives gross pay which does not exceed £160 per week.

13. PEOPLE WHO ARE 'SEVERELY MENTALLY IMPAIRED'

HB	A non-dependant deduction applies.
Main CTB	No non-dependant deduction.
Second adult rebate	'Disregarded persons'.

This means someone who has 'a severe impairment of intelligence and social functioning (however caused) which appears to be permanent'; and has a medical certificate confirming this; and is receiving one or more of the following (or would do so apart from the fact that he or she has reached pension age):

- the highest or middle rate of the care component of disability living allowance (DLA), or
- attendance allowance, constant attendance allowance or certain equivalent additions to industrial injuries and war pensions, or
- incapacity benefit (IB), or severe disablement allowance (SDA), or
- income support or JSA(IB) (or his or her partner is) – but only if it includes a disability premium awarded because of the person's incapacity for work.

14. CARERS OF PEOPLE RECEIVING CERTAIN BENEFITS

HB	A non-dependant deduction applies unless they fall within category 17.
Main CTB	No non-dependant deduction.
Second adult rebate	'Disregarded persons'.

This applies to someone if:

- he or she is providing care or support for at least 35 hours a week; and
- he or she resides with the person receiving the care or support; and
- that person is not a child of his or hers under 18, nor his or her partner; and
- that person is entitled to the highest rate of the care component of disability living allowance, or a higher rate attendance allowance, or certain equivalent additions to industrial injuries and war pensions.

15. CARERS INTRODUCED BY AN OFFICIAL OR CHARITABLE BODY

HB	A non-dependant deduction applies unless they fall within category 17.
Main CTB	No non-dependant deduction.
Second adult rebate	'Disregarded persons'.

This means someone who:

- is engaged or employed to provide care or support for at least 24 hours a week for no more than £36 per week; and
- is resident (for the better performance of this work) in premises provided by or on behalf of the person receiving the care or support; and
- is employed by that person; and
- was introduced to that person by a local authority, government department or charitable body.

16. CARERS RESIDENT IN OFFICIAL OR CHARITABLE PREMISES

HB	A non-dependant deduction applies unless they fall within category 17.
Main CTB	No non-dependant deduction.
Second adult rebate	'Disregarded persons'.

This means someone who:

- is engaged or employed to provide care or support for at least 24 hours a week for no more than £36 per week; and
- is resident (for the better performance of this work) in premises provided by or on behalf of a local authority, government department or charitable body, on whose behalf the care or support is provided.

17. CARERS FOR WHOM THE CLAIMANT OR PARTNER IS CHARGED

HB and main CTB	No non-dependant deduction.
Second adult rebate	'Disregarded persons' only if they fall within categories 14 to 16.

This means carers caring for the claimant or partner, who are provided by a charitable or voluntary body which charges the claimant or partner for this.

18. PEOPLE IN PRISON OR OTHER FORMS OF DETENTION

HB	No non-dependant deduction.
Main CTB	No non-dependant deduction unless detained only for non-payment of a fine or (in England and Wales) council tax.
Second adult rebate	'Disregarded persons' unless detained only for non-payment of a fine or (in England and Wales) council tax.

The full definition is not given here, but this includes people in almost any kind of detention.

19. PEOPLE WHO HAVE BEEN IN AN NHS HOSPITAL FOR MORE THAN 52 WEEKS

HB and main CTB	No non-dependant deduction.
Second adult rebate	'Disregarded persons' only if they fall within category 20.

This means someone who is in hospital and has been for more than 52 weeks – but only in the case of NHS hospitals (including NHS Trust hospitals) and not for wholly private patients. Two or more stays in hospital are added together if the break between them is four weeks or less.

20. PEOPLE ACTUALLY RESIDENT ELSEWHERE

HB and main CTB	No non-dependant deduction.
Second adult rebate	'Disregarded persons' (because they are not 'residents').

A person is 'resident' in his or her 'sole or main residence'. It does not matter what type of accommodation this is: it could be an ordinary home, a hospital, a care home, a hostel, or any other type of accommodation. This category could apply to a visitor or to a student returning just for the holidays.

21. PEOPLE NORMALLY RESIDENT ELSEWHERE

HB and main CTB	No non-dependant deduction.
Second adult rebate	Not 'disregarded persons' unless they fall within category 20.

The concept is not defined. In practice, it is very difficult to distinguish it from category 20.

22. RESIDENTS IN HOSPITALS, CARE HOMES AND CERTAIN HOSTELS

'Disregarded persons'.

Although a claim for HB is possible in some of these types of accommodation (and in rare cases a claim for CTB might be possible), it is unlikely that any claimant would have a non-dependant/second adult. This category is included because it affects council tax discounts in such accommodation. It applies to any of the following:

- patients with sole or main residence in an NHS hospital, military hospital, residential care home, nursing home or mental nursing home;
- people with sole or main residence in non-self-contained accommodation which provides them with personal care for old age, disablement, or past or present alcohol or drug dependence or mental disorder;
- people with sole or main residence in non-self-contained accommodation which provides licences (not tenancies) for people of no fixed abode and no settled way of life;
- people with sole or main residence in a bail hostel or probation hostel.

23. MEMBERS OF RELIGIOUS COMMUNITIES

HB	A non-dependant deduction applies.
Main CTB	No non-dependant deduction.
Second adult rebate	'Disregarded persons'.

This means someone who:

- is a member of a religious community whose principal occupation is prayer, contemplation, education, the relief of suffering, or any combination of those; and
- has no income (other than an occupational pension) or capital; and
- is dependent on the community for his or her material needs.

24. (a) MEMBERS OF CERTAIN INTERNATIONAL BODIES OR OF VISITING FORCES, (b) THEIR NON-BRITISH SPOUSES OR CIVIL PARTNERS, AND (c) CERTAIN NON-BRITISH SPOUSES OR CIVIL PARTNERS OF STUDENTS

HB	A non-dependant deduction applies.
Main CTB	No non-dependant deduction.
Second adult rebate	'Disregarded persons'.

The full definitions are not given here. Group (a) includes members of certain international headquarters and defence organisations and certain visiting forces (and in some cases their dependents). For groups (b) and (c), in broad terms, the spouse or civil partner must be prevented from working or claiming. For group (c), 'student' means someone in category 4, 5 or 6.

25. ANYONE ELSE

HB and main CTB	A non-dependant deduction applies.
Second adult rebate	Not 'disregarded persons'.

This means anyone who does not fall into any of the previous categories.

Appendix 7: Third party payments of IS etc to a landlord

Qualifying conditions for third party payments of IS etc to the landlord

The power to make direct payments is discretionary even if all the qualifying conditions are met. The qualifying conditions are:

- the tenant or their partner must be in receipt of a 'qualifying benefit'; and
- be in receipt of HB (or in the case of a hostel resident have claimed HB); and
- they must be resident in the property for which the third party payments are to be made;

  and either:

  - (regardless of whether they have rent arrears or not) they live in a hostel (para. 6.10) for which the overall charge includes payment for one or more of the following services: water; a service charge for fuel; meals; laundry or cleaning (other than communal areas) and the DWP determines that third party payments should be made; or
  - they have rent arrears and meet one of the rent arrears conditions.

Qualifying benefits for third party direct payments

The qualifying benefits from which deductions can be made are:

- income support;
- state pension credit (savings credit or guarantee credit or both);
- income-based jobseeker's allowance;
- contribution-based jobseekers' allowance if income-based jobseeker's allowance is not being paid solely because contribution-based jobseeker's allowance is in payment and the amount of income-based jobseekers' allowance that would otherwise have been payable is the same as the amount of contribution based jobseeker's allowance which is being paid.

In addition, in the case where any of the first three qualifying benefits are in payment, deductions can also be made from any contribution-based jobseekers' allowance, incapacity benefit, retirement pension or severe disablement allowance that they also receive.

What are the rent arrears conditions?

There must be 'rent arrears' of at least four times the gross weekly rent and either:

- the rent arrears have accrued or persisted over a period of at least eight weeks and the landlord requests that deductions are made; or
- the rent arrears have accrued or persisted over a period of less than eight weeks but in the opinion of the DWP it is in the overriding interests of the family that payments should be made.

In calculating the four weeks' arrears and any period over which those arrears have persisted or accrued, any arrears which have arisen due to the tenant's failure to pay a non-dependant charge must be ignored.

What counts as rent and rent arrears?

For these rules 'rent' and 'rent arrears' includes:

- any charge which is covered by HB;
- any water charges or service charges payable with the rent which are ineligible for HB;
- fuel charges included in the rent provided the charge does not vary more than twice a year;
- any other inclusive charge paid with the rent, whether or not it is eligible for HB, except any unpaid non-dependant charge.

Rate of payment

In the case of third party payments for a hostel, the amount of the third party payment will be the same as whatever amount of the charge is ineligible for HB for water, fuel, etc.

In the case of third party payments for rent arrears the rate of payment will, subject to any maximum amount, be:

- £2.90 per week (the standard amount), plus, if it applies,
- the weekly charge for any fuel or water charged as part of the rent, provided that the qualifying benefit is at least equal to that charge.

When all of the rent arrears have been cleared, weekly payment of the amount for fuel or water can continue if it is in the 'interests of the family'.

Maximum deductions for rent arrears cases

In the case of third party payments for rent arrears, the rate of deduction from any qualifying benefit will be subject to the following rules:

- There must be at least 10 pence of any qualifying benefit(s) remaining after any deduction.
- If the standard amount together with any ongoing fuel/water exceeds 25% of their qualifying benefit applicable amount then the deduction cannot be made without the claimant's consent.
- If there are standard deductions for several items such as rent, fuel, water, council tax, child maintenance and fines, the total cannot exceed £8.70.
- If there are deductions for various debts such that the total would reduce the qualifying benefit to less than 10p, then they are paid in the following order of priority:
  - 1st rent arrears;
  - 2nd fuel;
  - 3rd water;
  - 4th council tax;
  - 5th unpaid fines.

Source:
The Social Security (Claims and Payments) Regulations 1987 No. 1968, schedule 9, paragraphs 1, 4A, 5, 8 & 9. See also GM D1.570-689.

Index

References in the index are to paragraph numbers (not page numbers), except that 'A' refers to appendices, 'T' refers to tables in the text and 'Ch' refers to a chapter.

D

S

T

U